Pro T-SQL Programmer's Guide

4th Edition

Miguel Cebollero

Jay Natarajan

Michael Coles

Apress®

Pro T-SQL Programmer's Guide

ISBN-13 (pbk): 978-1-4842-0146-6

ISBN-13 (electronic): 978-1-4842-0145-9

Managing Director: Welmoed Spahr
Lead Editor: Jonathan Gennick
Technical Reviewer: Edgar Lanting
Editorial Board: Steve Anglin, Gary Cornell, Louise Corrigan, Jim DeWolf, Jonathan Gennick,
    Robert Hutchinson, Michelle Lowman, James Markham, Matthew Moodie, Jeff Olson,
    Jeffrey Pepper, Douglas Pundick, Ben Renow-Clarke, Gwenan Spearing, Matt Wade, Steve Weiss
Coordinating Editor: Jill Balzano
Copy Editor: Tiffany Taylor
Compositor: SPi Global
Indexer: SPi Global
Artist: SPi Global
Cover Designer: Anna Ishchenko

Distributed to the book trade worldwide by Springer Science+Business Media New York, 233 Spring Street, 6th Floor, New York, NY 10013. Phone 1-800-SPRINGER, fax (201) 348-4505, e-mail orders-ny@springer-sbm.com, or visit www.springeronline.com.

For information on translations, please e-mail rights@apress.com, or visit www.apress.com.

Apress and friends of ED books may be purchased in bulk for academic, corporate, or promotional use. eBook versions and licenses are also available for most titles. For more information, reference our Special Bulk Sales–eBook Licensing web page at www.apress.com/bulk-sales.

Any source code or other supplementary materials referenced by the author in this text is available to readers at at www.apress.com/9781430245964. For detailed information about how to locate your book's source code, go to www.apress.com/source-code/.

Contents at a Glance

About the Authors..xxiii

About the Technical Reviewer..xxv

Acknowledgments xxvii

Introduction xxix

■Chapter 1: Foundations of T-SQL 1

■Chapter 2: Tools of the Trade 19

■Chapter 3: Procedural Code 47

■Chapter 4: User-Defined Functions 79

■Chapter 5: Stored Procedures 111

■Chapter 6: In-Memory Programming..153

■Chapter 7: Triggers 177

■Chapter 8: Encryption...207

■Chapter 9: Common Table Expressions and Windowing Functions 233

■Chapter 10: Data Types and Advanced Data Types...269

■Chapter 11: Full-Text Search 317

■Chapter 12: XML...347

■Chapter 13: XQuery and XPath 387

■Chapter 14: Catalog Views and Dynamic aent Views 433

■Chapter 15: .NET Client Programming 461

■Chapter 16: CLR Integration Programming...511

■**Chapter 17: Data Services** **559**

■**Chapter 18: Error Handling and Dynamic SQL** **589**

■**Chapter 19: Performance Tuning** **613**

■**Appendix A: Exercise Answers** **653**

■**Appendix B: XQuery Data Types** **663**

■**Appendix C: Glossary** **669**

■**Appendix D: SQLCMD Quick Reference** **683**

Index **693**

Contents

About the Authors...xxiii

About the Technical Reviewer...xxv

Acknowledgments xxvii

Introduction xxix

■Chapter 1: Foundations of T-SQL 1

A Short History of T-SQL..1

Imperative vs. Declarative Languages 1

SQL Basics 3

    Statements 3

    Databases...5

    Transaction Logs...5

    Schemas...6

    Tables 7

    Views 8

    Indexes 9

    Stored Procedures 10

    User-Defined Functions 10

    SQL CLR Assemblies...10

Elements of Style 10

    Whitespace...11

    Naming Conventions...12

    One Entry, One Exit 13

Defensive Coding 17

The SELECT * Statement 17

Variable Initialization 17

Summary 18

■Chapter 2: Tools of the Trade 19

SQL Server Management Studio 19

IntelliSense 20

Code Snippets 21

Keyboard Shortcut Schemes 23

T-SQL Debugging 24

SSMS Editing Options 25

Context-Sensitive Help 26

Graphical Query Execution Plans 28

Project-Management Features 30

The Object Explorer 32

The SQLCMD Utility 34

SQL Server Data Tools 36

SQL Profiler 37

Extended Events 39

SQL Server Integration Services 41

The Bulk Copy Program 42

SQL Server 2014 Books Online 43

The AdventureWorks Sample Database 44

Summary 45

■Chapter 3: Procedural Code 47

Three-Valued Logic 47

Control-of-Flow Statements 49

The BEGIN and END Keywords 49

The IF...ELSE Statement 50

The WHILE, BREAK, and CONTINUE Statements 52

The GOTO Statement...54

The WAITFOR Statement..55

The RETURN Statement..56

The CASE Expression 56

The Simple CASE Expression...56

The Searched CASE Expression...58

CASE and Pivot Tables 59

The IIF Statement 65

CHOOSE 66

COALESCE and NULLIF...67

Cursors 68

Summary..77

■Chapter 4: User-Defined Functions 79

Scalar Functions..79

Recursion in Scalar User-Defined Functions 82

Procedural Code in User-Defined Functions 84

Multistatement Table-Valued Functions 94

Inline Table-Valued Functions..104

Restrictions on User-Defined Functions 107

Nondeterministic Functions..107

State of the Database 109

Summary...109

■Chapter 5: Stored Procedures 111

Introducing Stored Procedures...111

Metadata Discovery..112

Natively Compiled Stored Procedures...113

Managing Stored Procedures...117

Stored Procedures Best Practices..117

Stored Procedure Example..120

Recursion in Stored Procedures 126

Table-Valued Parameters 136

Temporary Stored Procedures 139

Recompilation and Caching 139

Stored Procedure Statistics 139

Parameter Sniffing 142

Recompilation 146

Summary 150

■Chapter 6: In-Memory Programming 153

The Drivers for In-Memory Technology 153

Hardware Trends 153

Getting Started with In-Memory Objects 155

Step 1: Add a New Memory-Optimized Data FILEGROUP 156

Step 2: Add a New Memory-Optimized Container 157

Step 3: Create Your New Memory-Optimized Table 159

Limitations on Memory-Optimized Tables 165

In-Memory OLTP Table Indexes 165

Hash Indexes 166

Range Indexes 170

Natively Compiled Stored Procedures 173

■Chapter 7: Triggers 177

DML Triggers 177

Multiple Triggers 178

When to Use DML Triggers 179

Inserted and Deleted Virtual Tables 181

Auditing with DML Triggers 182

Using Change Data Capture Instead 182

Sharing Data with Triggers 188

Nested and Recursive Triggers 189

The UPDATE( ) and COLUMNS_UPDATED( ) Functions 190

Triggers on Views 194

DDL Triggers 197

    DDL Event Types and Event Groups 197

Logon Triggers 202

Summary 204

■ **Chapter 8: Encryption** **207**

The Encryption Hierarchy 207

Service Master Keys 208

Database Master Keys 210

Certificates 211

Limitations of Asymmetric Encryption 213

Asymmetric Keys 216

    Asymmetric Key "Backups" 220

Symmetric Keys 220

    Temporary Symmetric Keys 221

Salt and Authenticators 227

Encryption Without Keys 228

    Hashing Data 228

Extensible Key Management 229

Transparent Data Encryption 230

Summary 232

■ **Chapter 9: Common Table Expressions and Windowing Functions** **233**

Common Table Expressions 233

    Multiple Common Table Expressions 235

    CTE Readability Benefits 236

Recursive Common Table Expressions 238

Windowing Functions 243

    ROW_NUMBER Function 243

    Query Paging with OFFSET/FETCH 244

The RANK and DENSE_RANK Functions 247

The NTILE Function 252

Aggregate Functions, Analytic Functions, and the OVER Clause 254

Analytic Function Examples 259

    CUME_DIST and PERCENT_RANK 259

    PERCENTILE_CONT and PERCENTILE_DISC 262

    LAG and LEAD 263

    FIRST_VALUE and LAST_VALUE 265

Summary 267

■Chapter 10: Data Types and Advanced Data Types 269

Basic Data Types 269

    Characters 269

    The Max Data Types 270

    Numerics 272

    Date and Time Data Types 274

    UTC and Military Time 278

    Date and Time Functions 278

    Time Zones and Offsets 282

The Uniqueidentifier Data Type 282

The Hierarchyid Data Type 284

    Representing Hierarchical Data 284

    Hierarchyid Example 285

    Hierarchyid Methods 290

Spatial Data Types 291

    Hemisphere and Orientation 296

    Michigan and the Great lakes 297

FILESTREAM Support 300

    Enabling FILESTREAM Support 301

    Creating FILESTREAM Filegroups 302

    FILESTREAM-Enabling Tables 303

Accessing FILESTREAM Data 304

FileTable Support 305

Filetable Functions 309

Triggers on Filetables 313

Summary 314

■ Chapter 11: Full-Text Search 317

FTS Architecture 317

Creating Full-Text Catalogs and Indexes 318

Creating Full-Text Catalogs 319

Creating Full-Text Indexes 321

Full-Text Querying 327

The FREETEXT Predicate 327

FTS Performance Optimization 329

The CONTAINS Predicate 330

The FREETEXTTABLE and CONTAINSTABLE Functions 334

Thesauruses and Stoplists 337

Stored Procedures and Dynamic Management Views and Functions 341

Statistical Semantics 342

Summary 344

■ Chapter 12: XML 347

Legacy XML 347

OPENXML 347

OPENXML Result Formats 351

FOR XML Clause 355

FOR XML RAW 355

FOR XML AUTO 357

FOR XML EXPLICIT 358

FOR XML PATH 360

The xml Data Type 362

Untyped xml 363

Typed xml 364

The xml Data Type Methods 366

The query Method 366

The value Method... 368

The exist Method.. 369

The nodes Method 370

The modify Method 371

XML Indexes 373

XSL Transformations 378

SQL CLR Security Settings 382

Summary.. 384

■Chapter 13: XQuery and XPath 387

XPath and FOR XML PATH... 387

XPath Attributes... 389

Columns without Names and Wildcards... 389

Element Grouping 390

The data Function.. 391

Node Tests and Functions.. 392

XPath and NULL... 393

The WITH XMLNAMESPACES Clause... 394

Node Tests 395

XQuery and the xml Data Type.. 396

Expressions and Sequences... 396

The query Method.. 398

Location Paths... 399

Node Tests 400

Namespaces.. 402

Axis Specifiers... 404

Dynamic XML Construction... 406

XQuery Comments... 409

Data Types 410

Predicates... 410

Value Comparison Operators 411

General Comparison Operators... 412

Xquery Date Format... 413

Node Comparisons 414

Conditional Expressions (if...then...else).. 416

Arithmetic Expressions.. 416

Integer Division in XQuery 417

XQuery Functions 417

Constructors and Casting 420

FLWOR Expressions 421

The for and return Keywords.. 422

The where Keyword.. 425

The order by Keywords... 425

The let Keyword... 426

UTF-16 Support 427

Summary.. 430

■Chapter 14: Catalog Views and Dynamic aent Views 433

Catalog Views.. 433

Table and Column Metadata 434

Querying Permissions.. 435

Dynamic Management Views and Functions... 438

Index Metadata.. 438

Session Information... 443

Connection Information 445

Currently Executing SQL.. 445

Memory-Optimized System Views... 447

Most Expensive Queries 448

Tempdb Space... 450

Server Resources 453

Unused Indexes 455

Wait Stats 456

INFORMATION_SCHEMA Views.. 457

Summary... 460

■Chapter 15: .NET Client Programming 461

ADO.NET 461

The .NET SQL Client... 462

Connected Data Access.. 463

Disconnected Datasets... 467

Parameterized Queries... 469

Nonquery, Scalar, and XML Querying 474

SqlBulkCopy 477

Multiple Active Result Sets... 483

LINQ to SQL 488

Using the Designer... 489

Querying with LINQ to SQL... 491

Basic LINQ to SQL Querying 491

Deferred Query Execution 498

From LINQ to Entity Framework 500

Querying Entities.. 504

Summary... 509

■Chapter 16: CLR Integration Programming.. 511

The Old Way... 511

The CLR Integration Way 512

CLR Integration Assemblies.. 513

User-Defined Functions.. 518

Stored Procedures.. 527

User-Defined Aggregates 531

Creating a Simple UDA 532

Creating an Advanced UDA 536

CLR Integration User-Defined Types 542

Triggers 551

Summary 556

■Chapter 17: Data Services 559

SQL Server 2014 Express LocalDB 559

Asynchronous Programming with ADO.NET 4.5 564

ODBC for Linux 565

JDBC 570

Service-Oriented Architecture and WCF Data Services 573

Creating a WCF Data Service 575

Defining the Data Source 576

Creating the Data Service 577

Creating a WCF Data Service Consumer 581

Summary 587

■Chapter 18: Error Handling and Dynamic SQL 589

Error Handling 589

Legacy Error Handling 589

The RAISERROR Statement 591

Try...Catch Exception Handling 592

TRY_PARSE, TRY_CONVERT, and TRY_CAST 594

Throw Statement 597

Debugging Tools 598

PRINT Statement Debugging 598

Trace Flags 599

SSMS Integrated Debugger 599

Visual Studio T-SQL Debugger 600

Dynamic SQL 606

The EXECUTE Statement 606

SQL Injection and Dynamic SQL 606

Troubleshooting Dynamic SQL 609

The sp_executesql Stored Procedure 609

Dynamic SQL and Scope 610

Client-Side Parameterization 611

Summary 611

■Chapter 19: Performance Tuning 613

SQL Server Storage 613

Files and Filegroups 613

Space Allocation 614

Partitions 619

Data Compression 620

Sparse Columns 625

Indexes 630

Heaps 630

Clustered Indexes 631

Nonclustered Indexes 633

Filtered Indexes 636

Optimizing Queries 636

Reading Query Plans 637

Methodology 640

Waits 642

Extended Events 645

Summary 650

■Appendix A: Exercise Answers 653

Chapter 1 653

Chapter 2 653

Chapter 3 654

Chapter 4 655

Chapter 5 656

Chapter 6 656

Chapter 7 657

Chapter 8 657

Chapter 9 657

Chapter 10 658

Chapter 11 658

Chapter 12 659

Chapter 13 659

Chapter 14 660

Chapter 15 660

Chapter 16 660

Chapter 17 661

Chapter 18 661

Chapter 19 662

■Appendix B: XQuery Data Types 663

■Appendix C: Glossary 669

ACID 669

adjacency list model 669

ADO.NET Data Services 669

anchor query 669

application programming interface (API) 669

assembly 669

asymmetric encryption 669

atomic, list, and union data types 670

axis 670

Bulk Copy Program (BCP) 670

catalog view 670

certificate 670

check constraint 670

closed-world assumption (CWA) 670

clustered index 670

comment 671

computed constructor 671

content expression 671

context item expression 671

context node 671

database encryption key 671

database master key 671

data domain 671

data page 672

datum 672

empty sequence 672

entity data model (EDM) 672

Extended Events (XEvents) 672

extensible key management (EKM) 672

extent 672

Extract, Transform, Load (ETL) 672

facet 672

filter expression 673

FLWOR expression 673

foreign key constraint 673

full-text catalog 673

full-text index 673

full-text search (FTS) 673

Functions and Operators (F&O) 673

general comparison 673

Geography Markup Language (GML) 673

grouping set 674

hash 674

heap 674

heterogeneous sequence 674

homogenous sequence 674

indirect recursion 674

inflectional forms 674

initialization vector (IV) 674

Language Integrated Query (LINQ) 674

location path 675

logon trigger 675

materialized path model 675

Multiple Active Result Sets (MARS) 675

nested sets model 675

node 675

node comparison 676

node test 676

nonclustered index 676

object-relational mapping (O/RM) 676

open-world assumption (OWA) 676

optional occurrence indicator 676

parameterization 676

path expression 676

predicate 677

predicate truth value 677

primary expression 677

query plan 677

recompilation 677

recursion 677

row constructor 677

scalar function 677

searched CASE expression.. 678

sequence.. 678

server certificate 678

service master key (SMK) 678

shredding 678

simple CASE expression... 678

SOAP... 678

spatial data... 678

spatial index 679

SQL Server Data Tools 679

SQL injection 679

step 679

table type 679

three-valued logic (3VL) 679

transparent data encryption (TDE) 679

untyped XML 679

user-defined aggregate (UDA)... 679

user-defined type (UDT)... 680

value comparison 680

well-formed XML... 680

well-known text (WKT) 680

windowing functions 680

World Wide Web Consortium (W3C).. 680

XML 680

XML schema 680

XPath 680

XQuery 681

XQuery/XPath Data Model (XDM) 681

XSL 681

XSLT 681

■**Appendix D: SQLCMD Quick Reference** **683**

Command-Line Options 683

Scripting Variables 688

Commands 689

Index **693**

About the Authors

Miguel Cebollero is father to two beautiful children (Ava and Alex), husband to wife Sandy, and a database professional with more than 16 years of experience in the SQL Server and other database platforms. He has held positions in management, database administration, development, architecting, and BI development for Fortune 500 corporations in the software, reverse logistics, telecommunications, insurance, legal, professional sports and banking industries.

Miguel is a regular speaker at local user groups, regional SQL Saturday events, and the national Professional Association for SQL Server Users (PASS) Summit conference on various database topics. He has been an avid volunteer, chapter leader, and contributor to PASS since 2000 and a contributor to the insurance industry standards organization ACORD. He is a life-long learner with a BS from the University of Tampa and an MSc from the University of North Carolina Greensboro. Biking, the beach, reading, and time with family fulfill his life outside of work.

Jay Natarajan has more than 15 years of experience in the SQL Server space. Her skills lie in both the design and implementation arenas; she has architected and deployed complex solutions for enterprise customers. She joined Microsoft Consulting Services in 2008. She holds a bachelor's degree in mechanical engineering from the University of Madras. Jay currently lives in Atlanta with her husband, Chad, and their son, Satya.

Michael Coles has more than a decade's worth of experience designing and administering SQL Server databases. He is a prolific writer of articles on all aspects of SQL Server, particularly on the expert use of T-SQL, and he holds MCDBA and MCP certifications. He graduated magna cum laude with a bachelor's degree in information technology from American Intercontinental University in Georgia. A member of the United States Army Reserve, he was activated for two years following 9/11.

About the Technical Reviewer

Edgar Lanting is a certified Oracle and Microsoft SQL Server database engineer and is currently working at the file-transfer company WeTransfer (`www.wetransfer.com`), where he is responsible for all things related to databases. He has worked in IT for over 19 years; he started as a system administrator and made the change to DBA more than 15 years ago. He's currently living in a small Dutch village with his wife and two dogs.

Acknowledgments

I would like to thank my wife for her support during the weekends and nights when she took care of the bedtime routine with the kids so that I could finish this book. My family has been the biggest driver of why I want to become better every day in my career. I would like to thank Louis Davidson for introducing me to the Apress team and his publisher, Jonathan Gennick. I am grateful for this opportunity as a first-time writer. Many thanks to the SQL professionals in my community who gave me words of encouragement on this journey.

—Miguel E. Cebollero

Introduction

In the mid-1990s, when Microsoft parted ways with Sybase in their conjoint development of SQL Server, it was an entirely different product. When SQL Server 6.5 was released in 1996, it was starting to gain credibility as an enterprise-class database server. It still had rough management tools, only core functionalities, and some limitations that are forgotten today, like fixed-size devices and the inability to drop table columns. It functioned as a rudimentary database server: storing and retrieving data for client applications. There was already plenty for anyone new to the relational database world to learn. Newcomers had to understand many concepts, such as foreign keys, stored procedures, triggers, and the dedicated language, T-SQL (which could be a baffling experience—writing SELECT queries sometimes involves a lot of head-scratching). Even when developers mastered all that, they still had to keep up with the additions Microsoft made to the database engine with each new version. Some of the changes were not for the faint of heart, like .NET database modules, support for XML and the XQuery language, and a full implementation of symmetric and asymmetric encryption. These additions are today core components of SQL Server.

Because a relational database management server (RDBMS) like SQL Server is one of the most important elements of the IT environment, you need to make the best of it, which implies a good understanding of its more advanced features. We have designed this book with the goal of helping T-SQL developers get the absolute most out of the development features and functionality in SQL Server 2014. We cover all of what's needed to master T-SQL development, from using management and development tools to performance tuning. We hope you enjoy the book and that it helps you to become a pro SQL Server 2014 developer.

Whom This Book Is For

This book is intended for SQL Server developers who need to port code from prior versions of SQL Server, and those who want to get the most out of database development on the 2014 release. You should have a working knowledge of SQL, preferably T-SQL on SQL Server 2005 or later, because most of the examples in this book are written in T-SQL. The book covers some of the basics of T-SQL, including introductory concepts like data domain and three-valued logic, but this isn't a beginner's book. We don't discuss database design, database architecture, normalization, and the most basic SQL constructs in any detail. Apress offers a beginner's guide to T-SQL 2012 that covers more basic SQL constructs.

We focus here on advanced SQL Server 2014 functionalities, and so we assume you have a basic understanding of SQL statements like INSERT and SELECT. A working knowledge of C# and the .NET Framework is also useful (but not required), because two chapters are dedicated to .NET client programming and .NET database integration.

Some examples in the book are written in C#. When C# sample code is provided, it's explained in detail, so an in-depth knowledge of the .NET Framework class library isn't required.

How This Book Is Structured

This book was written to address the needs of four types of readers:

- SQL developers who are coming from other platforms to SQL Server 2014
- SQL developers who are moving from prior versions of SQL Server to SQL Server 2014
- SQL developers who have a working knowledge of basic T-SQL programming and want to learn about advanced features
- Database administrators and non-developers who need a working knowledge of T-SQL functionality to effectively support SQL Server 2014 instances

For all types of readers, this book is designed to act as a tutorial that describes and demonstrates T-SQL features with working examples, and as a reference for quickly locating details about specific features. The following sections provide a chapter-by-chapter overview.

Chapter 1

Chapter 1 starts this book by putting SQL Server 2014's implementation of T-SQL in context, including a short history, a discussion of the basics, and an overview of T-SQL coding best practices.

Chapter 2

Chapter 2 gives an overview of the tools that are packaged with SQL Server and available to SQL Server developers. Tools discussed include SQL Server Management Studio (SSMS), SQLCMD, SQL Server Data Tools (SSDT), and SQL Profiler, among others.

Chapter 3

Chapter 3 introduces T-SQL procedural code, including control-of-flow statements like IF...THEN and WHILE. This chapter also discusses CASE expressions and CASE-derived functions, and provides an in-depth discussion of SQL three-valued logic.

Chapter 4

Chapter 4 discusses the various types of T-SQL user-defined functions available to encapsulate T-SQL logic on the server. We talk about all forms of T-SQL–based user-defined functions, including scalar user-defined functions, inline table-valued functions, and multistatement table-valued functions.

Chapter 5

Chapter 5 covers stored procedures, which allow you to create server-side T-SQL subroutines. In addition to describing how to create and execute stored procedures on SQL Server, we also address an issue that is thorny for some: why you might want to use stored procedures.

Chapter 6

Chapter 6 covers the latest features available in SQL Server 2014: In-Memory OLTP tables. The In-Memory features provide the capability to dramatically increase the database performance of an OLTP or data-warehouse instance. With the new features also come some limitations.

Chapter 7

Chapter 7 introduces all three types of SQL Server triggers: classic DML triggers, which fire in response to DML statements; DDL triggers, which fire in response to server and database DDL events; and logon triggers, which fire in response to server LOGON events.

Chapter 8

Chapter 8 discusses SQL Server encryption, including the column-level encryption functionality introduced in SQL Server 2005 and the newer transparent database encryption (TDE) and extensible key management (EKM) functionality, both introduced in SQL Server 2008.

Chapter 9

Chapter 9 dives into the details of common table expressions (CTEs) and windowing functions in SQL Server 2014, which feature some improvements to the OVER clause to achieve row-level running and sliding aggregations.

Chapter 10

Chapter 10 discusses T-SQL data types: first some important things to know about basic data types, such as how to handle date and time in your code, and then advanced data types and features, such as the hierarchyid complex type and FILESTREAM and filetable functionality.

Chapter 11

Chapter 11 covers the full-text search (FTS) feature and advancements made since SQL Server 2008, including greater integration with the SQL Server query engine and greater transparency by way of FTS-specific data-management views and functions.

Chapter 12

Chapter 12 provides an in-depth discussion of SQL Server 2014 XML functionality, which carries forward and improve on the new features introduced in SQL Server 2005. We cover several XML-related topics in this chapter, including the xml data type and its built-in methods, the FOR XML clause, and XML indexes.

Chapter 13

Chapter 13 discusses XQuery and XPath support in SQL Server 2014, including improvements on the XQuery support introduced in SQL Server 2005, such as support for the xml data type in XML DML insert statements and the let clause in FLWOR expressions.

Chapter 14

Chapter 14 introduces SQL Server catalog views, which are the preferred tools for retrieving database and database object metadata. This chapter also discusses dynamic-management views and functions, which provide access to server and database state information.

Chapter 15

Chapter 15 covers SQL CLR Integration functionality in SQL Server 2014. In this chapter, we discuss and provide examples of SQL CLR stored procedures, user-defined functions, user-defined types, and user-defined aggregates.

Chapter 16

Chapter 16 focuses on client-side support for SQL Server, including ADO.NET-based connectivity and the newest Microsoft object-relational mapping (ORM) technology, Entity Framework 4.

Chapter 17

Chapter 17 discusses SQL Server connectivity using middle-tier technologies. Because native HTTP endpoints have been deprecated since SQL Server 2008, we discuss them as items that may need to be supported in existing databases but shouldn't be used for new development. We focus instead on possible replacement technologies, such as ADO.NET data services and IIS/.NET web services.

Chapter 18

Chapter 18 discusses improvements to server-side error handling made possible with the TRY...CATCH block. We also discuss various methods for debugging code, including using the Visual Studio T-SQL debugger. This chapter wraps up with a discussion of dynamic SQL and SQL injection, including the causes of SQL injection and methods you can use to protect your code against this type of attack.

Chapter 19

Chapter 19 provides an overview of performance-tuning SQL Server code. This chapter discusses SQL Server storage, indexing mechanisms, and query plans. We end the chapter with a discussion of a proven methodology for troubleshooting T-SQL performance issues.

Appendix A

Appendix A provides the answers to the exercise questions included at the end of each chapter.

Appendix B

Appendix B is designed as a quick reference to the XQuery Data Model (XDM) type system.

Appendix C

Appendix C provides a quick reference glossary to several terms, many of which may be new to those using SQL Server for the first time.

Appendix D

Appendix D is a quick reference to the SQLCMD command-line tool, which allows you to execute ad hoc T-SQL statements and batches interactively, or run script files.

Conventions

To help make reading this book a more enjoyable experience, and to help you get as much out of it as possible, we've used the following standardized formatting conventions throughout.

C# code is shown in code font. Note that C# code is case sensitive. Here's an example:

```
while (i < 10)
```

T-SQL source code is also shown in code font, with keywords capitalized. Note that we've lowercased the data types in the T-SQL code to help improve readability. Here's an example:

```
DECLARE @x xml;
```

XML code is shown in code font with attribute and element content in bold for readability.

Some code samples and results have been reformatted in the book for easier reading. XML ignores whitespace, so the significant content of the XML has not been altered. Here's an example:

```
<book publisher = "Apress">Pro SQL Server 2014 XML</book>:
```

■ **Note** Notes, tips, and warnings are displayed like this, in a special font with solid bars placed over and under the content.

SIDEBARS

Sidebars include additional information relevant to the current discussion and other interesting facts. Sidebars are shown on a gray background.

Prerequisites

This book requires an installation of SQL Server 2014 to run the T-SQL sample code provided. Note that the code in this book has been specifically designed to take advantage of SQL Server 2014 features, and some of the code samples won't run on prior versions of SQL Server. The code samples presented in the book are designed to be run against the AdventureWorks 2014 and SQL Server 2014 In-Memory OLTP sample databases, available from the CodePlex web site at `www.codeplex.com/MSFTDBProdSamples`. The database name used in the samples is not AdventureWorks2014, but AdventureWorks or 2014 In-Memory, for the sake of simplicity.

If you're interested in compiling and deploying the .NET code samples (the client code and SQL CLR examples) presented in the book, we highly recommend an installation of Visual Studio 2010 or a later version. Although you can compile and deploy .NET code from the command line, we've provided instructions for doing so through the Visual Studio Integrated Development Environment (IDE). We find that the IDE provides a much more enjoyable experience.

Some examples, such as the ADO.NET Data Services examples in Chapter 16, require an installation of Internet Information Server(IIS) as well. Other code samples presented in the book may have specific requirements, such as the Entity Framework 4 samples, which require the .NET Framework 3.5. We've added notes to code samples that have additional requirements like these.

Apress Web Site

Visit this book's apress.com web page at `www.apress.com/9781484201466` for the complete sample code download for this book. It's compressed in a zip file and structured so that each subdirectory contains all the sample code for its corresponding chapter.

We and the Apress team have made every effort to ensure that this book is free from errors and defects. Unfortunately, thex occasional error does slip past us, despite our best efforts. In the event that you find an error in the book, please let us know! You can submit errors to Apress by visiting `www.apress.com/9781484201466` and filling out the form on the Errata tab.

CHAPTER 1

Foundations of T-SQL

SQL Server 2014 is the latest release of Microsoft's enterprise-class database management system (DBMS). As the name implies, a DBMS is a tool designed to manage, secure, and provide access to data stored in structured collections in databases. Transact-SQL (T-SQL) is the language that SQL Server speaks. T-SQL provides query and data-manipulation functionality, data definition and management capabilities, and security administration tools to SQL Server developers and administrators. To communicate effectively with SQL Server, you must have a solid understanding of the language. In this chapter, you begin exploring T-SQL on SQL Server 2014.

A Short History of T-SQL

The history of Structured Query Language (SQL), and its direct descendant Transact-SQL (T-SQL), begins with a man. Specifically, it all began in 1970 when Dr. E. F. Codd published his influential paper "A Relational Model of Data for Large Shared Data Banks" in the *Communications of the Association for Computing Machinery* (ACM). In his seminal paper, Dr. Codd introduced the definitive standard for relational databases. IBM went on to create the first relational database management system, known as System R. It subsequently introduced the Structured English Query Language (SEQUEL, as it was known at the time) to interact with this early database to store, modify, and retrieve data. The name of this early query language was later changed from SEQUEL to the now-common SQL due to a trademark issue.

Fast-forward to 1986, when the American National Standards Institute (ANSI) officially approved the first SQL standard, commonly known as the ANSI SQL-86 standard. The original versions of Microsoft SQL Server shared a common code base with the Sybase SQL Server product. This changed with the release of SQL Server 7.0, when Microsoft partially rewrote the code base. Microsoft has since introduced several iterations of SQL Server, including SQL Server 2000, SQL Server 2005, SQL Server 2008, SQL 2008 R2, SQL 2012, and now SQL Server 2014. This book focuses on SQL Server 2014, which further extends the capabilities of T-SQL beyond what was possible in previous releases.

Imperative vs. Declarative Languages

SQL is different from many common programming languages such as C# and Visual Basic because it's a *declarative language*. In contrast, languages such as C++, Visual Basic, C#, and even assembler language are *imperative languages*. The imperative language model requires the user to determine what the end result should be and tell the computer step by step how to achieve that result. It's analogous to asking a cab driver to drive you to the airport and then giving the driver turn-by-turn directions to get there. Declarative languages, on the other hand, allow you to frame your instructions to the computer in terms of the end result. In this model, you allow the computer to determine the best route to achieve your objective, analogous to telling the cab driver to take you to the airport and trusting them to know the best route. The declarative model makes a lot of sense when you consider that SQL Server is privy to a lot of "inside information." Just like the cab driver who knows the shortcuts, traffic conditions, and other factors that affect your trip, SQL Server inherently knows several methods to optimize your queries and data-manipulation operations.

Consider Listing 1-1, which is a simple C# code snippet that reads in a flat file of names and displays them on the screen.

Listing 1-1. C# Snippet to Read a Flat File

```
StreamReader sr = new StreamReader("c:\\Person_Person.txt");
string FirstName = null;
while ((FirstName = sr.ReadLine()) != null) {
Console.WriteLine(s); } sr.Dispose();
```

The example performs the following functions in an orderly fashion:

1. The code explicitly opens the storage for input (in this example, a flat file is used as a "database").

2. It reads in each record (one record per line), explicitly checking for the end of the file.

3. As it reads the data, the code returns each record for display using `Console.Writeline()`.

4. Finally, it closes and disposes of the connection to the data file.

Consider what happens when you want to add a name to or delete a name from the flat-file "database." In those cases, you must extend the previous example and add custom routines to explicitly reorganize all the data in the file so that it maintains proper ordering. If you want the names to be listed and retrieved in alphabetical (or any other) order, you must write your own sort routines as well. Any type of additional processing on the data requires that you implement separate procedural routines.

The SQL equivalent of the C# code in Listing 1-1 might look something like Listing 1-2.

Listing 1-2. SQL Query to Retrieve Names from a Table

```
SELECT FirstName FROM Person.Person;
```

■ **Tip** Unless otherwise specified, you can run all the T-SQL samples in this book in the AdventureWorks 2014 or SQL 2014 In-Memory sample database using SQL Server Management Studio or SQLCMD.

To sort your data, you can simply add an `ORDER BY` clause to the `SELECT` query in Listing 1-2. With properly designed and indexed tables, SQL Server can automatically reorganize and index your data for efficient retrieval after you insert, update, or delete rows.

T-SQL includes extensions that allow you to use procedural syntax. In fact, you could rewrite the previous example as a cursor to closely mimic the C# sample code. These extensions should be used with care, however, because trying to force the imperative model on T-SQL effectively overrides SQL Server's built-in optimizations. More often than not, this hurts performance and makes simple projects a lot more complex than they need to be.

One of the great assets of SQL Server is that you can invoke its power, in its native language, from nearly any other programming language. For example, in .NET you can connect to SQL Server and issue SQL queries and T-SQL statements to it via the `System.Data.SqlClient` namespace, which is discussed further in Chapter 16. This gives you the opportunity to combine SQL's declarative syntax with the strict control of an imperative language.

SQL Basics

Before you learn about developments in T-SQL, or on any SQL-based platform for that matter, let's make sure we're speaking the same language. Fortunately, SQL can be described accurately using well-defined and time-tested concepts and terminology. Let's begin the discussion of the components of SQL by looking at *statements*.

Statements

To begin with, in SQL you use statements to communicate your requirements to the DBMS. A statement is composed of several parts, as shown in Figure 1-1.

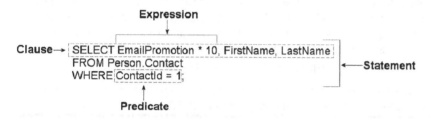

Figure 1-1. *Components of a SQL statement*

As you can see in the figure, SQL statements are composed of one or more *clauses,* some of which may be optional depending on the statement. In the SELECT statement shown, there are three clauses: the SELECT clause, which defines the columns to be returned by the query; the FROM clause, which indicates the source table for the query; and the WHERE clause, which is used to limit the results. Each clause represents a primitive operation in the relational algebra. For instance, in the example, the SELECT clause represents a relational *projection* operation, the FROM clause indicates the *relation,* and the WHERE clause performs a *restriction* operation.

■ **Note**   The *relational model* of databases is the model formulated by Dr. E. F. Codd. In the relational model, what are known in SQL as *tables* are referred to as *relations*; hence the name. *Relational calculus* and *relational algebra* define the basis of query languages for the relational model in mathematical terms.

ORDER OF EXECUTION

Understanding the logical order in which SQL clauses are applied within a statement or query is important when setting your expectations about results. Although vendors are free to physically perform whatever operations, in any order, that they choose to fulfill a query request, the results must be the same as if the operations were applied in a standards-defined order.

The WHERE clause in the example contains a *predicate,* which is a logical expression that evaluates to one of SQL's three possible logical results: true, false, or unknown. In this case, the WHERE clause and the predicate limit the results to only rows in which ContactId equals 1.

The SELECT clause includes an expression that is calculated during statement execution. In the example, the expression EmailPromotion * 10 is used. This expression is calculated for every row of the result set.

SQL THREE-VALUED LOGIC

SQL institutes a logic system that may seem foreign to developers coming from other languages like C++ or Visual Basic (or most other programming languages, for that matter). Most modern computer languages use simple two-valued logic: a Boolean result is either true or false. SQL supports the concept of NULL, which is a placeholder for a missing or unknown value. This results in a more complex three-valued logic (3VL).

Let's look at a quick example to demonstrate. If I asked you, "Is x less than 10?" your first response might be along the lines of, "How much is x?" If I refused to tell you what value x stood for, you would have no idea whether x was less than, equal to, or greater than 10; so the answer to the question is neither true nor false—it's the third truth value, *unknown.* Now replace x with NULL, and you have the essence of SQL 3VL. NULL in SQL is just like a variable in an equation when you don't know the variable's value.

No matter what type of comparison you perform with a missing value, or which other values you compare the missing value to, the result is always unknown. The discussion of SQL 3VL continues in Chapter 3.

The core of SQL is defined by statements that perform five major functions: querying data stored in tables, manipulating data stored in tables, managing the structure of tables, controlling access to tables, and managing transactions. These subsets of SQL are defined following:

- *Querying*: The SELECT query statement is complex. It has more optional clauses and vendor-specific tweaks than any other statement. SELECT is concerned simply with retrieving data stored in the database.

- *Data Manipulation Language (DML)*: DML is considered a sublanguage of SQL. It's concerned with manipulating data stored in the database. DML consists of four commonly used statements: INSERT, UPDATE, DELETE, and MERGE. DML also encompasses cursor-related statements. These statements allow you to manipulate the contents of tables and persist the changes to the database.

- *Data Definition Language (DDL)*: DDL is another sublanguage of SQL. The primary purpose of DDL is to create, modify, and remove tables and other objects from the database. DDL consists of variations of the CREATE, ALTER, and DROP statements.

- *Data Control Language (DCL)*: DCL is yet another SQL sublanguage. DCL's goal is to allow you to restrict access to tables and database objects. It's composed of various GRANT and REVOKE statements that allow or deny users access to database objects.

- *Transactional Control Language (TCL)*: TCL is the SQL sublanguage that is concerned with initiating and committing or rolling back *transactions.* A transaction is basically an atomic unit of work performed by the server. TCL comprises the BEGIN TRANSACTION, COMMIT, and ROLLBACK statements.

Databases

A SQL Server *instance*—an individual installation of SQL Server with its own ports, logins, and databases—can manage multiple *system databases* and *user databases*. SQL Server has five system databases, as follows:

- resource: The resource database is a read-only system database that contains all system objects. You don't see the resource database in the SQL Server Management Studio (SSMS) Object Explorer window, but the system objects persisted in the resource database logically appear in every database on the server.

- master: The master database is a server-wide repository for configuration and status information. It maintains instance-wide metadata about SQL Server as well as information about all databases installed on the current instance. It's wise to avoid modifying or even accessing the master database directly in most cases. An entire server can be brought to its knees if the master database is corrupted. If you need to access the server configuration and status information, use catalog views instead.

- model: The model database is used as the template from which newly created databases are essentially cloned. Normally, you won't want to change this database in production settings unless you have a very specific purpose in mind and are extremely knowledgeable about the potential implications of changing the model database.

- msdb: The msdb database stores system settings and configuration information for various support services, such as SQL Agent and Database Mail. Normally, you use the supplied stored procedures and views to modify and access this data, rather than modifying it directly.

- tempdb: The tempdb database is the main working area for SQL Server. When SQL Server needs to store intermediate results of queries, for instance, they're written to tempdb. Also, when you create temporary tables, they're actually created in tempdb. The tempdb database is reconstructed from scratch every time you restart SQL Server.

Microsoft recommends that you use the system-provided stored procedures and catalog views to modify system objects and system metadata, and let SQL Server manage the system databases. You should avoid modifying the contents and structure of the system databases directly through ad hoc T-SQL. Only modify the system objects and metadata by executing the system stored procedures and functions.

User databases are created by database administrators (DBAs) and developers on the server. These types of databases are so called because they contain user data. The AdventureWorks2014 sample database is one example of a user database.

Transaction Logs

Every SQL Server database has its own associated transaction log. The transaction log provides recoverability in the event of failure and ensures the atomicity of transactions. The transaction log accumulates all changes to the database so that database integrity can be maintained in the event of an error or other problem. Because of this arrangement, all SQL Server databases consist of at least two files: a database file with an .mdf extension and a transaction log with an .ldf extension.

THE ADVENTUREWORKS2014 CID TEST

SQL folks, and IT professionals in general, love their acronyms. A common acronym in the SQL world is ACID, which stands for "atomicity, consistency, isolation, durability." These four words form a set of properties that database systems should implement to guarantee reliability of data storage, processing, and manipulation:

- *Atomicity*: All data changes should be transactional in nature. That is, data changes should follow an all-or-nothing pattern. The classic example is a double-entry bookkeeping system in which every debit has an associated credit. Recording a debit-and-credit double entry in the database is considered one *transaction*, or a single unit of work. You can't record a debit without recording its associated credit, and vice versa. Atomicity ensures that either the entire transaction is performed or none of it is.

- *Consistency*: Only data that is consistent with the rules set up in the database is stored. Data types and constraints can help enforce consistency in the database. For instance, you can't insert the name Meghan in an `integer` column. Consistency also applies when dealing with data updates. If two users update the same row of a table at the same time, an inconsistency could occur if one update is only partially complete when the second update begins. The concept of isolation, described in the following bullet point, is designed to deal with this situation.

- *Isolation*: Multiple simultaneous updates to the same data should not interfere with one another. SQL Server includes several locking mechanisms and isolation levels to ensure that two users can't modify the exact same data at the exact same time, which could put the data in an inconsistent state. Isolation also prevents you from even reading uncommitted data by default.

- *Durability*: Data that passes all the previous tests is committed to the database. The concept of durability ensures that committed data isn't lost. The transaction log and data backup and recovery features help to ensure durability.

The transaction log is one of the main tools SQL Server uses to enforce the ACID concept when storing and manipulating data.

Schemas

SQL Server 2014 supports database *schemas*, which are logical groupings by the owner of database objects. The AdventureWorks2014 sample database, for instance, contains several schemas, such as HumanResources, Person, and Production. These schemas are used to group tables, stored procedures, views, and user-defined functions (UDFs) for management and security purposes.

■ **Tip** When you create new database objects, like tables, and don't specify a schema, they're automatically created in the default schema. The default schema is normally dbo, but DBAs may assign different default schemas to different users. Because of this, it's always best to specify the schema name explicitly when creating database objects.

Tables

SQL Server supports several types of objects that can be created in a database. SQL stores and manages data in its primary data structures: tables. A table consists of rows and columns, with data stored at the intersections of these rows and columns. As an example, the AdventureWorks HumanResources.Department table is shown in Figure 1-2. In SQL Server 2014, you now have the option of creating a table *In-Memory*. This feature allows all the table data to be stored in memory and can be accessed with extremely low latency.

	DepartmentID	Name	GroupName	ModifiedDate
1	1	Engineering	Research and Development	2002-06-01 00:00:00.000
2	2	Tool Design	Research and Development	2002-06-01 00:00:00.000
3	3	Sales	Sales and Marketing	2002-06-01 00:00:00.000
4	4	Marketing	Sales and Marketing	2002-06-01 00:00:00.000
5	5	Purchasing	Inventory Management	2002-06-01 00:00:00.000
6	6	Research and Development	Research and Development	2002-06-01 00:00:00.000
7	7	Production	Manufacturing	2002-06-01 00:00:00.000
8	8	Production Control	Manufacturing	2002-06-01 00:00:00.000
9	9	Human Resources	Executive General and Administration	2002-06-01 00:00:00.000
10	10	Finance	Executive General and Administration	2002-06-01 00:00:00.000
11	11	Information Services	Executive General and Administration	2002-06-01 00:00:00.000
12	12	Document Control	Quality Assurance	2002-06-01 00:00:00.000
13	13	Quality Assurance	Quality Assurance	2002-06-01 00:00:00.000
14	14	Facilities and Maintenance	Executive General and Administration	2002-06-01 00:00:00.000
15	15	Shipping and Receiving	Inventory Management	2002-06-01 00:00:00.000
16	16	Executive	Executive General and Administration	2002-06-01 00:00:00.000

Figure 1-2. `HumanResources.Department` table

In the table, each row is associated with columns and each column has certain restrictions placed on its content. These restrictions form the *data domain*. The data domain defines all the values a column can contain. At the lowest level, the data domain is based on the data type of the column. For instance, a smallint column can contain any integer values between -32,768 and +32,767.

The data domain of a column can be further constrained through the use of check constraints, triggers, and foreign key constraints. *Check constraints* provide a means of automatically checking that the value of a column is within a certain range or equal to a certain value whenever a row is inserted or updated. *Triggers* can provide functionality similar to that of check constraints. *Foreign key constraints* allow you to declare a relationship between the columns of one table and the columns of another table. You can use foreign key constraints to restrict the data domain of a column to include only those values that appear in a designated column of another table.

RESTRICTING THE DATA DOMAIN: A COMPARISON

This section has given a brief overview of three methods of constraining the data domain for a column. Each method restricts the values that can be contained in the column. Here's a quick comparison of the three methods:

- Foreign key constraints allow SQL Server to perform an automatic check against another table to ensure that the values in a given column exist in the referenced table. If the value you're trying to update or insert in a table doesn't exist in the referenced table, an error is raised and any changes are rolled back. The foreign key constraint provides a flexible means of altering the data domain, because adding values to or removing them from the referenced table automatically changes the data domain for the referencing table. Also, foreign key constraints offer an additional feature known as cascading *declarative referential integrity (DRI)*, which automatically updates or deletes rows from a referencing table if an associated row is removed from the referenced table.

- Check constraints provide a simple, efficient, and effective tool for ensuring that the values being inserted or updated in a column(s) are within a given range or a member of a given set of values. Check constraints, however, aren't as flexible as foreign key constraints and triggers because the data domain is normally defined using hard-coded constant values or logical expressions.

- Triggers are stored procedures attached to insert, update, or delete events on a table or view. Triggers can be set on DML or DDL events. Both DML and DDL triggers provide a flexible solution for constraining data, but they may require more maintenance than the other options because they're essentially a specialized form of stored procedure. Unless they're extremely well designed, triggers have the potential to be much less efficient than other methods of constraining data. Generally triggers are avoided in modern databases in favor of more efficient methods of constraining data. The exception to this is when you're trying to enforce a foreign key constraint across databases, because SQL Server doesn't support cross-database foreign key constraints.

Which method you use to constrain the data domain of your column(s) needs to be determined by your project-specific requirements on a case-by-case basis.

Views

A *view* is like a virtual table—the data it exposes isn't stored in the view object itself. Views are composed of SQL queries that reference tables and other views, but they're referenced just like tables in queries. Views serve two major purposes in SQL Server: they can be used to hide the complexity of queries, and they can be used as a security device to limit the rows and columns of a table that a user can query. Views are *expanded*, meaning their logic is incorporated into the execution plan for queries when you use them in queries and DML statements. SQL Server may not be able to use indexes on the base tables when the view is expanded, resulting in less-than-optimal performance when querying views in some situations.

To overcome the query performance issues with views, SQL Server also has the ability to create a special type of view known as an *indexed* view. An indexed view is a view that SQL Server persists to the database like a table. When you create an indexed view, SQL Server allocates storage for it and allows you to query it like any other table. There are, however, restrictions on inserting into, updating, and deleting from an indexed view. For instance, you can't perform data modifications on an indexed view if more than one of the view's base tables will be affected. You also can't perform data modifications on an indexed view if the view contains aggregate functions or a DISTINCT clause.

You can also create indexes on an indexed view to improve query performance. The downside to an indexed view is increased overhead when you modify data in the view's base tables, because the view must be updated as well.

Indexes

Indexes are SQL Server's mechanisms for optimizing access to data. SQL Server 2014 supports several types of indexes, including the following:

- *Clustered index*: A clustered index is limited to one per table. This type of index defines the ordering of the rows in the table. A clustered index is physically implemented using a b-tree structure with the data stored in the leaf levels of the tree. Clustered indexes order the data in a table in much the same way that a phone book is ordered by last name. A table with a clustered index is referred to as a *clustered table,* whereas a table with no clustered index is referred to as a *heap.*

- *Nonclustered index*: A nonclustered index is also a b-tree index managed by SQL Server. In a nonclustered index, *index rows* are included in the leaf levels of the b-tree. Because of this, nonclustered indexes have no effect on the ordering of rows in a table. The index rows in the leaf levels of a nonclustered index consist of the following:

  - A nonclustered key value

  - A row locator, which is the clustered index key on a table with a clustered index, or a SQL-generated row ID for a heap

  - Nonkey columns, which are added via the INCLUDE clause of the CREATE INDEX statement

- *Columnstore index*: A columnstore index is a special index used for very large tables (>100 million rows) and is mostly applicable to large data-warehouse implementations. A columnstore index creates an index on the column as opposed to the row and allows for efficient and extremely fast retrieval of large data sets. Prior to SQL Server 2014, tables with columnstore indexes were required to be read-only. In SQL Server 2014, columnstore indexes are now updateable. This feature is discussed further in Chapter 6.

- *XML index*: SQL Server supports special indexes designed to help efficiently query XML data. See Chapter 11 for more information.

- *Spatial index*: A spatial index is an interesting new indexing structure to support efficient querying of the new geometry and geography data types. See Chapter 2 for more information.

- *Full-text index*: A full-text index (FTI) is a special index designed to efficiently perform full-text searches of data and documents.

- *Memory-optimized index*: SQL Server 2014 introduced In-Memory tables that bring with them new index types. These types of indexes only exist in memory and must be created with the initial table creation. These index types are covered at length in Chapter 6:

  - *Nonclustered hash index*: This type of index is most efficient in scenarios where the query will return values for a specific value criteria. For example, `SELECT *`
    `FROM <Table> WHERE <Column> = @<ColumnValue>`.

  - *Memory-optimized nonclustered index*: This type of index supports the same functions as a hash index, in addition to seek operations and sort ordering.

You can also include nonkey columns in your nonclustered indexes with the `INCLUDE` clause of the `CREATE INDEX` statement. The included columns give you the ability to work around SQL Server's index size limitations.

Stored Procedures

SQL Server supports the installation of server-side T-SQL code modules via *stored procedures (SPs)*. It's very common to use SPs as a sort of intermediate layer or custom server-side *application programming interface (API)* that sits between user applications and tables in the database. Stored procedures that are specifically designed to perform queries and DML statements against the tables in a database are commonly referred to as *CRUD (create, read, update, delete)* procedures.

User-Defined Functions

User-defined functions (UDFs) can perform queries and calculations, and return either scalar values or tabular result sets. UDFs have certain restrictions placed on them. For instance, they can't use certain nondeterministic system functions, nor can they perform DML or DDL statements, so they can't make modifications to the database structure or content. They can't perform dynamic SQL queries or change the state of the database (cause side effects).

SQL CLR Assemblies

SQL Server 2014 supports access to Microsoft .NET functionality via the SQL Common Language Runtime (SQL CLR). To access this functionality, you must register compiled .NET SQL CLR assemblies with the server. The assembly exposes its functionality through class methods, which can be accessed via SQL CLR functions, procedures, triggers, user-defined types, and user-defined aggregates. SQL CLR assemblies replace the deprecated SQL Server extended stored procedure (XP) functionality available in prior releases.

■ **Tip** Avoid using extended stored procedures (XPs) on SQL Server 2014. The same functionality provided by XPs can be provided by SQL CLR code. The SQL CLR model is more robust and secure than the XP model. Also keep in mind that the XP library is deprecated, and XP functionality may be completely removed in a future version of SQL Server.

Elements of Style

Now that you've had a broad overview of the basics of SQL Server, let's look at some recommended development tips to help with code maintenance. Selecting a particular style and using it consistently helps immensely with both debugging and future maintenance. The following sections contain some general recommendations to make your T-SQL code easy to read, debug, and maintain.

Whitespace

SQL Server ignores extra whitespace between keywords and identifiers in SQL queries and statements. A single statement or query may include extra spaces and tab characters and can even extend across several lines. You can use this knowledge to great advantage. Consider Listing 1-3, which is adapted from the HumanResources.vEmployee view in the AdventureWorks2014 database.

Listing 1-3. The HumanResources.vEmployee View from the AdventureWorks2014 Database

```
SELECT e.BusinessEntityID, p.Title, p.FirstName, p.MiddleName, p.LastName, p.Suffix,
e.JobTitle, pp.PhoneNumber, pnt.Name AS PhoneNumberType, ea.EmailAddress,
p.EmailPromotion, a.AddressLine1, a.AddressLine2, a.City, sp.Name AS StateProvinceName,
a.PostalCode, cr.Name AS CountryRegionName, p.AdditionalContactInfo
FROM HumanResources.Employee AS e INNER JOIN Person.Person AS p ON p.BusinessEntityID =
e.BusinessEntityID INNER JOIN Person.BusinessEntityAddress AS bea ON bea.BusinessEntityID
= e.BusinessEntityID INNER JOIN Person.Address AS a ON a.AddressID = bea.AddressID INNER
JOIN Person.StateProvince AS sp ON sp.StateProvinceID = a.StateProvinceID INNER JOIN Person.
CountryRegion AS cr ON cr.CountryRegionCode = sp.CountryRegionCode LEFT OUTER JOIN Person.
PersonPhone AS pp ON pp.BusinessEntityID = p.BusinessEntityID LEFT OUTER JOIN Person.
PhoneNumberType AS pnt ON pp.PhoneNumberTypeID = pnt.PhoneNumberTypeID LEFT OUTER JOIN
Person.EmailAddress AS ea ON p.BusinessEntityID = ea.BusinessEntityID
```

This query will run and return the correct result, but it's very hard to read. You can use whitespace and table aliases to generate a version that is much easier on the eyes, as demonstrated in Listing 1-4.

Listing 1-4. The HumanResources.vEmployee View Reformatted for Readability

```
SELECT
  e.BusinessEntityID,
  p.Title,
  p.FirstName,
  p.MiddleName,
  p.LastName,
  p.Suffix,
  e.JobTitle,
  pp.PhoneNumber,
  pnt.Name AS PhoneNumberType,
  ea.EmailAddress,
  p.EmailPromotion,
  a.AddressLine1,
  a.AddressLine2,
  a.City,
  sp.Name AS StateProvinceName,
  a.PostalCode,
  cr.Name AS CountryRegionName,
  p.AdditionalContactInfo
FROM HumanResources.Employee AS e INNER JOIN Person.Person AS p
  ON p.BusinessEntityID = e.BusinessEntityID
INNER JOIN Person.BusinessEntityAddress AS bea
  ON bea.BusinessEntityID = e.BusinessEntityID
INNER JOIN Person.Address AS a
```

```
  ON a.AddressID = bea.AddressID
INNER JOIN Person.StateProvince AS sp
  ON sp.StateProvinceID = a.StateProvinceID
INNER JOIN Person.CountryRegion AS cr
  ON cr.CountryRegionCode = sp.CountryRegionCode
LEFT OUTER JOIN Person.PersonPhone AS pp
  ON pp.BusinessEntityID = p.BusinessEntityID
LEFT OUTER JOIN Person.PhoneNumberType AS pnt
  ON pp.PhoneNumberTypeID = pnt.PhoneNumberTypeID
LEFT OUTER JOIN Person.EmailAddress AS ea
  ON p.BusinessEntityID = ea.BusinessEntityID;
```

Notice that the ON keywords are indented, associating them visually with the INNER JOIN operators directly before them in the listing. The column names on the lines directly after the SELECT keyword are also indented, associating them visually with SELECT. This particular style is useful in helping visually break up a query into sections. The personal style you decide on may differ from this one, but once you've decided on a standard indentation style, be sure to apply it consistently throughout your code.

Code that is easy to read is easier to debug and maintain. The code in Listing 1-4 uses table aliases, plenty of whitespace, and the semicolon (;) terminator to mark the end of SELECT statements, to make the code more readable. (It's a good idea to get into the habit of using the terminating semicolon in your SQL queries—it's required in some instances.)

■ **Tip** Semicolons are required terminators for some statements in SQL Server 2014. Instead of trying to remember all the special cases where they are or aren't required, it's a good idea to use the semicolon statement terminator throughout your T-SQL code. You'll notice the use of semicolon terminators in all the examples in this book.

Naming Conventions

SQL Server allows you to name your database objects (tables, views, procedures, and so on) using just about any combination of up to 128 characters (116 characters for local temporary table names), as long as you enclose them in single quotes (' ') or brackets ([ ]). Just because you *can,* however, doesn't necessarily mean you *should.* Many of the allowed characters are hard to differentiate from other similar-looking characters, and some may not port well to other platforms. The following suggestions will help you avoid potential problems:

- Use alphabetic characters (A–Z, a–z, and Unicode Standard 3.2 letters) for the first character of your identifiers. The obvious exceptions are SQL Server variable names that start with the at (@) sign, temporary tables and procedures that start with the number sign (#), and global temporary tables and procedures that begin with a double number sign (##).

- Many built-in T-SQL functions and system variables have names that begin with a double at sign (@@), such as @@ERROR and @@IDENTITY. To avoid confusion and possible conflicts, don't use a leading double at sign to name your identifiers.

- Restrict the remaining characters in your identifiers to alphabetic characters (A–Z, a–z, and Unicode Standard 3.2 letters), numeric digits (0–9), and the underscore character (_). The dollar sign ($) character, although allowed, isn't advisable.

- Avoid embedded spaces, punctuation marks (other than the underscore character), and other special characters in your identifiers.

- Avoid using SQL Server 2014 reserved keywords as identifiers. You can find the list here: http://msdn.microsoft.com/en-us/library/ms189822.aspx.

- Limit the length of your identifiers. Thirty-two characters or less is a reasonable limit while not being overly restrictive. Much more than that becomes cumbersome to type and can hurt your code readability.

Finally, to make your code more readable, select a capitalization style for your identifiers and code, and use it consistently. My preference is to fully capitalize T-SQL keywords and use mixed-case and underscore characters to visually break up identifiers into easily readable words. Using all capital characters or inconsistently applying mixed case to code and identifiers can make your code illegible and hard to maintain. Consider the example query in Listing 1-5.

Listing 1-5. All-Capital SELECT Query

```
SELECT P.BUSINESSENTITYID, P.FIRSTNAME, P.LASTNAME, S.SALESYTD
FROM PERSON.PERSON P INNER JOIN SALES.SALESPERSON SP
ON P.BUSINESSENTITYID = SP.BUSINESSENTITYID;
```

The all-capital version is difficult to read. It's hard to tell the SQL keywords from the column and table names at a glance. Compound words for column and table names aren't easily identified. Basically, your eyes have to work a lot harder to read this query than they should, which makes otherwise simple maintenance tasks more difficult. Reformatting the code and identifiers makes this query much easier on the eyes, as Listing 1-6 demonstrates.

Listing 1-6. Reformatted, Easy-on-the-Eyes Query

```
SELECT
    p.BusinessEntityID,
    p.FirstName,
    p.LastName,
    sp.SalesYTD
FROM Person.Person p INNER JOIN Sales.SalesPerson sp
    ON p.BusinessEntityID = sp.BusinessEntityID;
```

The use of all capitals for the keywords in the second version makes them stand out from the mixed-case table and column names. Likewise, the mixed-case column and table names make the compound word names easy to recognize. The net effect is that the code is easier to read, which makes it easier to debug and maintain. Consistent use of good formatting habits helps keep trivial changes trivial and makes complex changes easier.

One Entry, One Exit

When writing SPs and UDFs, it's good programming practice to use the "one entry, one exit" rule. SPs and UDFs should have a single entry point and a single exit point (RETURN statement).

The SP in Listing 1-7 is a simple procedure with one entry point and several exit points. It retrieves the ContactTypeID number from the AdventureWorks2014 Person.ContactType table for the ContactType name passed into it. If no ContactType exists with the name passed in, a new one is created, and the newly created ContactTypeID is passed back.

Listing 1-7. Stored Procedure Example with One Entry and Multiple Exits

```
CREATE PROCEDURE dbo.GetOrAdd_ContactType
(
    @Name NVARCHAR(50),
    @ContactTypeID INT OUTPUT
)
AS
    DECLARE @Err_Code AS INT;

    SELECT @Err_Code = 0;

    SELECT @ContactTypeID = ContactTypeID
    FROM Person.ContactType
    WHERE [Name] = @Name;

    IF @ContactTypeID IS NOT NULL
    RETURN;     -- Exit 1: if the ContactType exists

    INSERT
    INTO Person.ContactType ([Name], ModifiedDate)
    SELECT @Name, CURRENT_TIMESTAMP;

    SELECT @Err_Code = 'error';
    IF @Err_Code <> 0
        RETURN @Err_Code;  -- Exit 2: if there is an error on INSERT

    SELECT @ContactTypeID = SCOPE_IDENTITY();

    RETURN @Err_Code;       -- Exit 3: after successful INSERT
GO
```

This code has one entry point but three possible exit points. Figure 1-3 shows a simple flowchart for the paths this code can take.

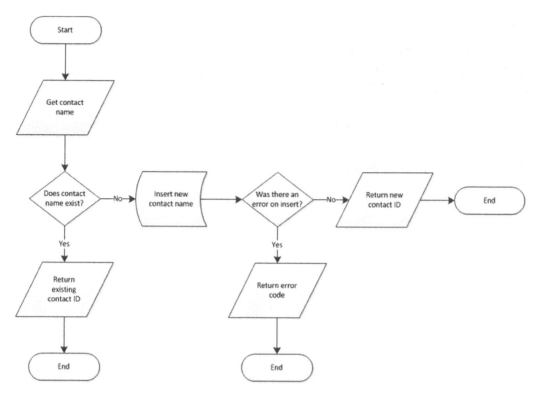

Figure 1-3. *Flowchart for an example with one entry and multiple exits*

As you can imagine, maintaining code such as that in Listing 1-7 becomes more difficult because the flow of the code has so many possible exit points, each of which must be accounted for when you make modifications to the SP. Listing 1-8 updates Listing 1-7 to give it a single entry point and a single exit point, making the logic easier to follow.

Listing 1-8. Stored Procedure with One Entry and One Exit

```
CREATE  PROCEDURE  dbo.GetOrAdd_ContactType
(
    @Name NVARCHAR(50),
    @ContactTypeID INT OUTPUT
)
AS
    DECLARE @Err_Code AS INT;
    SELECT @Err_Code = 0;

    SELECT @ContactTypeID = ContactTypeID
    FROM Person.ContactType
    WHERE [Name] = @Name;

    IF  @ContactTypeID  IS  NULL
    BEGIN
```

```
INSERT
INTO  Person.ContactType ([Name],  ModifiedDate)
SELECT  @Name,  CURRENT_TIMESTAMP;
SELECT @Err_Code = @@error;
IF  @Err_Code = 0     --  If  there's an error, skip next
SELECT  @ContactTypeID  =  SCOPE_IDENTITY();
END
RETURN @Err_Code;    -- Single exit point
GO
```

Figure 1-4 shows the modified flowchart for this new version of the SP.

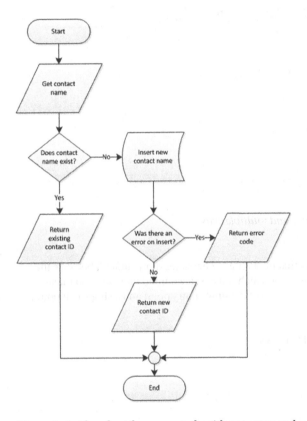

Figure 1-4. *Flowchart for an example with one entry and one exit*

The one entry and one exit model makes the logic easier to follow, which in turn makes the code easier to manage. This rule also applies to looping structures, which you implement via the WHILE statement in T-SQL. Avoid using the WHILE loop's CONTINUE and BREAK statements and the GOTO statement; these statements lead to old-fashioned, difficult-to-maintain spaghetti code.

Defensive Coding

Defensive coding involves anticipating problems before they occur and mitigating them through good coding practices. The first and foremost lesson of defensive coding is to always check user input. Once you open your system to users, expect them to do everything in their power to try to break your system. For instance, if you ask users to enter a number between 1 and 10, expect that they'll ignore your directions and key in ; DROP TABLE dbo.syscomments; -- at the first available opportunity. Defensive coding practices dictate that you should check and scrub external inputs. Don't blindly trust anything that comes from an external source.

Another aspect of defensive coding is a clear delineation between exceptions and run-of-the-mill issues. The key is that exceptions are, well, exceptional in nature. Ideally, exceptions should be caused by errors that you can't account for or couldn't reasonably anticipate, like a lost network connection or physical corruption of your application or data storage. Errors that can be reasonably expected, like data-entry errors, should be captured before they're raised to the level of exceptions. Keep in mind that exceptions are often resource-intensive, expensive operations. If you can avoid an exception by anticipating a particular problem, your application will benefit in both performance and control. SQL Server 2012 introduced a valuable new error-handling feature called THROW. The TRY/CATCH/THROW statements are discussed in more detail in Chapter 18.

The SELECT * Statement

Consider the SELECT * style of querying. In a SELECT clause, the asterisk (*) is a shorthand way of specifying that all columns in a table should be returned. Although SELECT * is a handy tool for ad hoc querying of tables during development and debugging, you normally shouldn't use it in a production system. One reason to avoid this method of querying is to minimize the amount of data retrieved with each call. SELECT * retrieves all columns, regardless of whether they're needed by the higher-level applications. For queries that return a large number of rows, even one or two extraneous columns can waste a lot of resources.

If the underlying table or view is altered, columns may be added to or removed from the returned result set. This can cause errors that are hard to locate and fix. By specifying the column names, your front-end application can be assured that only the required columns are returned by a query and that errors caused by missing columns will be easier to locate.

As with most things, there are always exceptions—for example, if you're using the FOR XML AUTO clause to generate XML based on the structure and content of your relational data. In this case, SELECT * can be quite useful, because you're relying on FOR XML to automatically generate the node names based on the table and column names in the source tables.

■ **Tip**   SELECT * should be avoided, but if you do need to use it, always try to limit the data set being returned. One way of doing so is to make full use of the T-SQL TOP command and restrict the number of records returned. In practice, though, you should never write SELECT * in your code—even for small tables. Small tables today could be large tables tomorrow.

Variable Initialization

When you create SPs, UDFs, or any script that uses T-SQL user variables, you should initialize those variables before the first use. Unlike some other programming languages that guarantee that newly declared variables will be initialized to 0 or an empty string (depending on their data types), T-SQL guarantees only that newly declared variables will be initialized to NULL. Consider the code snippet shown in Listing 1-9.

Listing 1-9. Sample Code Using an Uninitialized Variable

```
DECLARE @i INT; SELECT @i = @i + 5; SELECT @i;
```

The result is NULL, which is a shock if you were expecting 5. Expecting SQL Server to initialize numeric variables to 0 (like @i in the previous example) or an empty string will result in bugs that can be extremely difficult to locate in your T-SQL code. To avoid these problems, always explicitly initialize your variables after declaration, as demonstrated in Listing 1-10.

Listing 1-10. Sample Code Using an Initialized Variable

```
DECLARE @i INT = 0; -- Changed this statement to initialize @i to 0
SELECT @i = @i + 5;
SELECT @i;
```

Summary

This chapter has served as an introduction to T-SQL, including a brief history of SQL and a discussion of the declarative programming style. The chapter started with a discussion of ISO SQL standard compatibility in SQL Server 2014 and the differences between imperative and declarative languages, of which SQL is the latter. You also saw many of the basic components of SQL, including databases, tables, views, SPs, and other common database objects. Finally, I provided my personal recommendations for writing SQL code that is easy to debug and maintain. I subscribe to the "eat your own dog food" theory, and throughout this book I faithfully follow the best practice recommendations that I've asked you to consider.

The next chapter provides an overview of the new and improved tools available out of the box for developers. Specifically, Chapter 2 discusses the SQLCMD text-based SQL client (originally a replacement for osql), SSMS, SQL Server 2014 Books Online (BOL), and some of the other available tools that make writing, editing, testing, and debugging easier and faster than ever.

EXERCISES

1. Describe the difference between an imperative language and a declarative language.

2. What does the acronym *ACID* stand for?

3. SQL Server 2014 supports seven different types of indexes. Two of these indexes are newly introduced in SQL 2014. What are they?

4. Name two of the restrictions on any type of SQL Server UDF.

5. [True/False] In SQL Server, newly declared variables are always assigned the default value 0 for numeric data types and an empty string for character data types.

CHAPTER 2

■ ■ ■

Tools of the Trade

SQL Server 2014 comes with a wide selection of tools and utilities to make development easier and more productive for developers. This chapter introduces some of the most important tools for SQL Server developers, including SQL Server Management Studio (SSMS) and the SQLCMD utility, SQL Server Data Tool add-ins to Microsoft Visual Studio, SQL Profiler, Database Tuning Advisor, Extended Events, and SQL Server 2014 Books Online (BOL). You're also introduced to supporting tools like SQL Server Integration Services (SSIS), the Bulk Copy Program (BCP), and the AdventureWorks 2014 sample database, which you use in examples throughout the book.

SQL Server Management Studio

Back in the heyday of SQL Server 2000, it was common for developers to fire up the Enterprise Manager (EM) and Query Editor GUI database tools in rapid succession every time they sat down to write code. Historically, developer and DBA roles in the DBMS have been highly separated, and with good reason. DBAs have historically brought hardware and software administration and tuning skills, database design optimization experience, and healthy doses of skepticism and security to the table. On the other hand, developers have focused on coding skills, problem solving, system optimization, and debugging. This separation of powers works very well in production systems, but in development environments developers are often responsible for their own database design and management. Sometimes developers are put in charge of their own development server local security.

SQL Server 2000 EM was originally designed as a DBA tool, providing access to the graphical user interface (GUI) administration interface, including security administration, database object creation and management, and server management functionality. Query Editor was designed as a developer tool, the primary GUI tool for creating, testing, and tuning queries.

SQL Server 2014 continues the tradition begun with SQL Server 2005 by combining the functionality of both these GUI tools into a single GUI interface known as SQL Server Management Studio (SSMS). This makes perfect sense in supporting real-world SQL Server development, where the roles of DBA and developer are often intermingled in development environments.

Many SQL Server developers prefer the GUI administration and development tools to the text-based query tool SQLCMD to build their databases, and on this front SSMS doesn't disappoint. SSMS offers several features that make development and administration easier, including the following:

- Integrated, functional Object Explorer, which provides the ability to easily view all the objects in the server and manage them in a tree structure. The added filter functionality helps users narrow down the objects they want to work with.

- Color coding of scripts, making editing and debugging easier.

- Enhanced keyboard shortcuts that make searching faster and easier. Additionally, users can map predefined keyboard shortcuts to stored procedures that are used most often.

- Two keyboard shortcut schemes: keyboard shortcuts from SQL Server 2008 R2 and Microsoft Visual Studio 2010 compatibility.

- Usability enhancements such as the ability to zoom text in the Query Editor by holding the Ctrl key and scrolling to zoom in and out. Users can drag and drop tabs, and there is true multimonitor support.

- Breakpoint validation, which prevents users from setting breakpoints at invalid locations.

- T-SQL code snippets, which are templates that can be used as starting points to build T-SQL statement in scripts and batches.

- T-SQL Debugger Watch and Quick Watch windows, which support watching T-SQL expressions.

- Graphical query execution plans. These are the bread and butter of the query-optimization process. They greatly simplify the process of optimizing complex queries, quickly exposing potential bottlenecks in your code.

- Project-management and code-version control integration, including integration with Team Foundation Server (TFS) and Visual SourceSafe version control systems.

- SQLCMD mode, which allows you to execute SQL scripts using SQLCMD. You can take advantage of SQLCMD's additional script capabilities, like scripting variables and support for the AlwaysON feature.

SSMS also includes database and server management features, but this discussion is limited to some of the most important developer-specific features.

IntelliSense

IntelliSense is a feature that was introduced in SQL Server 2008. When coding, you often need to look up language elements such as functions, table names, and column names to complete your code. This feature allows the SQL Editor to automatically prompt for the completion of the syntax you input, based on partial words. To enable IntelliSense, go to Tools ➤ Options ➤ Text Editor ➤ Transact-SQL ➤ IntelliSense. Figure 2-1 demonstrates how the IntelliSense feature suggests language elements based on the first letter entered.

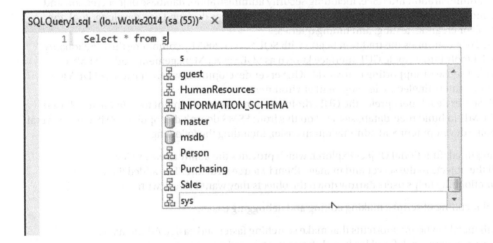

Figure 2-1. Using IntelliSense to complete a Select statement

Code Snippets

Code snippets aren't a new concept to the programming world. Visual Studio developers are very familiar with this feature; and because SSMS is built on the Visual Studio 2010 shell, SQL inherits this functionality as well. During the development cycle, developers often use a set of T-SQL statements multiple times throughout the code being worked on. It's much more efficient to access a block of code that contains common code elements such as `create stored procedure` and `create function`, to help you build on top of the code block. *Code snippets* are building blocks of code that you can use as a starting point when building T-SQL scripts. This feature can help you be more productivity while increasing reusability and standardization by enabling the development team to use existing templates or to create and customize a new template.

Code snippets help provide a better T-SQL code-editing experience. In addition, a snippet is an XML template that can be used to guarantee consistency across the development team. These snippets fall into three categories:

- *Expansion snippets* list the common outline of T-SQL commands such as `Select`, `Insert`, and `Create Table`.

- *Surround snippets* include constructs such as `while`, `if else`, and `begin end` statements.

- *Custom snippets* allow custom templates that can be invoked via the snippet menu. You can create a custom snippet and add it to the server by importing the snippet using the Code Snippet Manager. Once you add a custom snippet, the Custom Snippets category appears in the Code Snippet Manager.

To access the code snippets, select the Code Snippets Manager from the Tools menu. Figure 2-2 shows the Code Snippet Manager interface, which you can use to add, remove, or import code snippets.

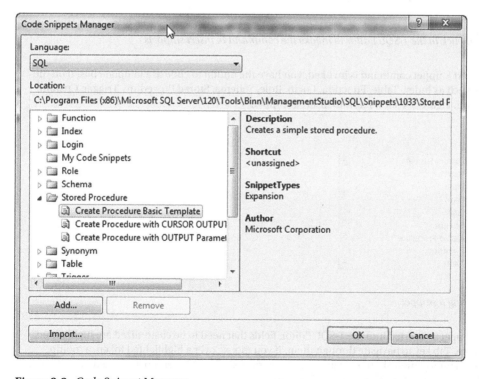

Figure 2-2. *Code Snippet Manager*

To insert a code snippet in the T-SQL Editor, right-click and select Insert Snippet or press Ctrl K+X. Figure 2-3 demonstrates how to invoke the Insert Snippet and Surround With commands.

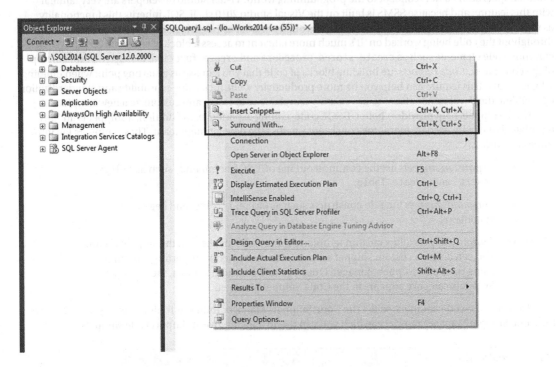

Figure 2-3. *Right-click in the T-SQL Editor to invoke the command to insert snippets*

Once the Insert Snippet command is invoked, you have the option to choose a template based on the SQL object type, such as Index, Table, Function, Login, Role, Schema, Stored Procedure, Trigger, Custom Snippets, and so on. Figure 2-4 shows how to insert a snippet.

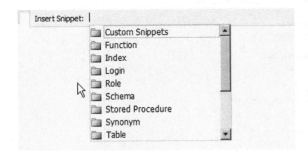

Figure 2-4. *Inserting a snippet*

When the snippet is inserted into the T-SQL Editor, fields that need to be customized are highlighted, and you can use the Tab key to navigate through them. If you mouse over a highlighted token, a tooltip provides additional information about it. Figure 2-5 shows the CREATE TABLE snippet invoked in the T-SQL Editor along with the tooltip that lists the field's description.

```
CREATE TABLE dbo.Sample Table
(
    column_1 int
    column_2 int NULL
);
```

Name of the table

Figure 2-5. Adding a CREATE TABLE snippet, with the tooltip displayed

Keyboard Shortcut Schemes

If you ask an SQL user and a Visual Studio user, "What is the shortcut key to execute queries?" you're bound to receive two different answers: Ctrl+E for SQL users and Ctrl+Shift+E for Visual Studio users. Because application developers are primarily Visual Studio users, it's prudent to have an option that lets users pick the keyboard shortcut scheme that's familiar based on the tool they have been using. Another advantage of defining and standardizing the keyboard shortcut scheme at the team level is that doing so helps team members avoid executing wrong actions in the team environment.

SQL Server 2014 offers two keyboard shortcut schemes: the default, the SQL Server 2014 shortcut scheme (the default) and the Visual Studio 2010 shortcut scheme. The SSMS interface hasn't been updated in SQL 2014. Functionality and color schemes operate the same as in SQL Server 2012. To change the keyboard shortcut settings, choose Tools ➤ Options ➤ Environment ➤ Keyboard. Figure 2-6 shows the option to change the keyboard mapping scheme.

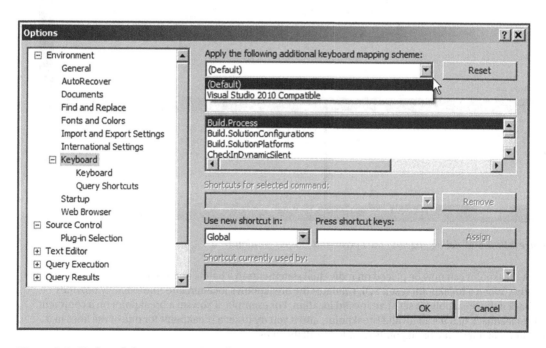

Figure 2-6. Keyboard shortcut mapping scheme

T-SQL Debugging

SQL Server 2012 introduced enhancements to T-SQL debugging by providing the ability to set conditional breakpoints, meaning a breakpoint is invoked only if a certain expression is evaluated. T-SQL debugging also extends support for expression evaluation in Watch and Quick Watch windows. You can also specify a *hit count*, meaning you can specify how many times a breakpoint can be hit before it's invoked. Breakpoints can also be exported from one session to the other. The Watch and Quick Watch windows support T-SQL expressions as well. Figure 2-7 shows the Debugging screen with the Output and Locals windows.

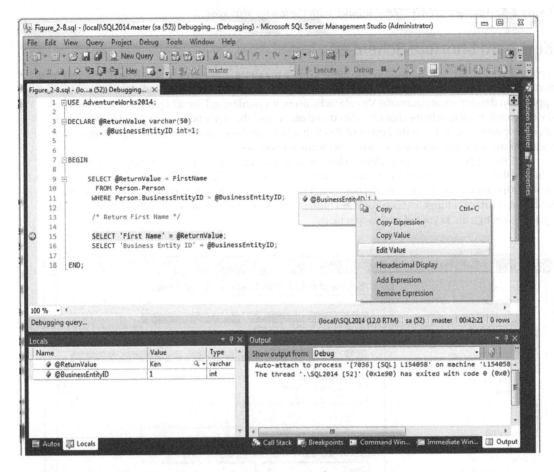

Figure 2-7. *T-SQL debugging with the Locals and Output windows*

A breakpoint can now be placed on individual statements in a batch, and breakpoints are context-sensitive. When a breakpoint is set, SQL validates the breakpoint's location and immediately provides feedback if the breakpoint is set at an invalid location. For example, if you set a breakpoint on a comment, you get feedback that it's an invalid breakpoint; and if you try to set a breakpoint for one of the lines in a multiline statement, the breakpoints is added to all the lines.

A DataTip is another debugging enhancement that was added in SQL Server 2012 to help you track variables and expressions in the scope of execution while debugging by providing ability to "pin" a DataTip to keep it visible (even when the debug session is restarted). When the debugger is in break mode, if you mouse over a T-SQL expression that is being evaluated, you can see the current value of that expression. Figure 2-8 shows a breakpoint and DataTip.

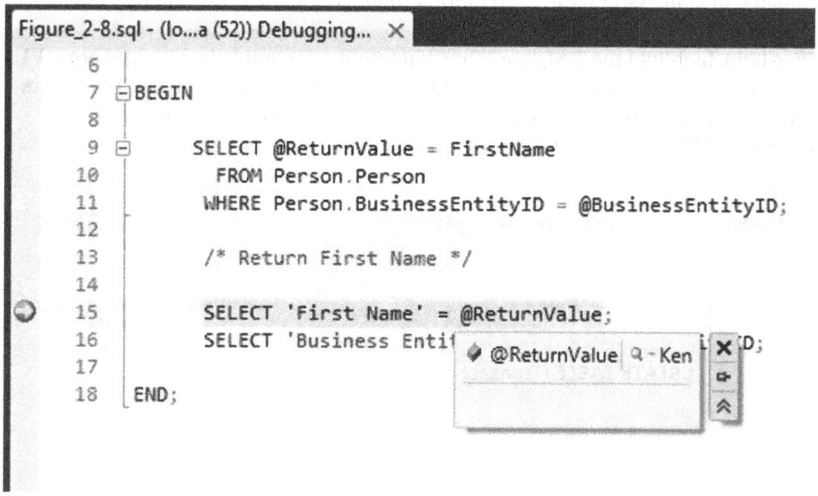

Figure 2-8. *A breakpoints and a DataTip*

■ **Note** The user login must be part of the sysadmin role on the SQL Server instance in order to use T-SQL debugging capabilities when using SSMS. With SQL Server Data Tools (SSDT), developers now have the option of debugging without being part of the sysadmin role, using their localdb instance of the schema.

SSMS Editing Options

SSMS incorporates and improves on many of the developer features found in Query Editor. You can change the editing options discussed in this section via the Tools ä Options.

SSMS includes fully customizable script color coding. The default font has been changed to the monotype font Consolas, and the background color is now blue to match Visual Studio 2012. You can customize the foreground and background colors, font face, size, and style for elements of T-SQL, XML, XSLT, and MDX scripts. Likewise, you can customize just about any feedback that SSMS generates, to suit your personal taste.

You can set other editing options, such as word wrap, line-number display, indentation, and tabs for different file types based on their associated file extensions. SSMS lets you configure your own keyboard shortcuts to execute common T-SQL statements or SPs.

By default, SSMS displays queries using a tabbed window environment. If you prefer the classic multiple-document interface (MDI) window style, you can switch the environment layout accordingly. You can also change the query result output style from the default grid output to text or file output.

Context-Sensitive Help

Starting with SQL Server 2012, the product documentation is hosted online (MSDN/TechNet) to ensure that the content is kept up to date. If you want to access the product documentation from your local computer, you have to download the help catalogs and set up the Help Viewer. To configure the documentation, go to the Help menu and select Manage Help Settings. Doing so launches the Help Library Manager. Scroll down to the SQL Server 2014 section, and click Add Next for the documentation you want to download. If the documentation is already available in your system, the Help Library Manager updates the catalog's index with the SQL Server documentation.

To access context-sensitive help, highlight the T-SQL or other statement you want help with and press F1. You can add help pages to your Help Favorites or go directly to MSDN. If pressing F1 doesn't work, remember to download the documentation locally and choose to use local help. Figure 2-9 shows the result of calling context-sensitive help for the CREATE TABLE statement.

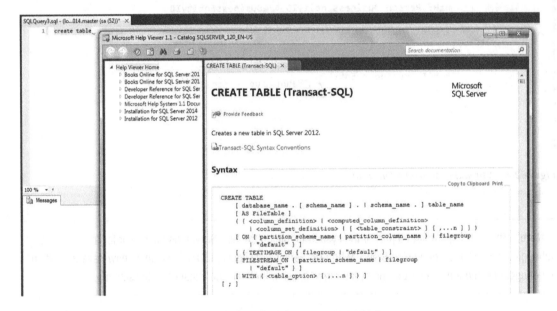

Figure 2-9. *Using SSMS context-sensitive help to find the **CREATE TABLE** statement*

SSMS has several options that allow you to control help functionality and presentation. You can, for example, use the SSMS Integrated Help Viewer, shown in Figure 2-9, or you can use the External Online Help Viewer. The Settings window in the Help Viewer allows you to set a preference to use online or offline help; it's shown in Figure 2-10.

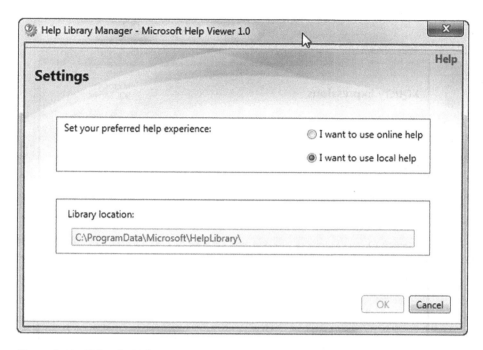

Figure 2-10. Using the Help Viewer Settings window to personalize SSMS help

Help Search rounds out this discussion of the help functionality in SSMS. The Help Search function automatically searches several online providers of SQL Server–related information for answers to your questions. Searches aren't restricted to SQL Server keywords or statements; you can search for anything, and the Help Search function scours registered web sites and communities for relevant answers. Figure 2-11 shows the result of using Help Search to find XQuery content and articles.

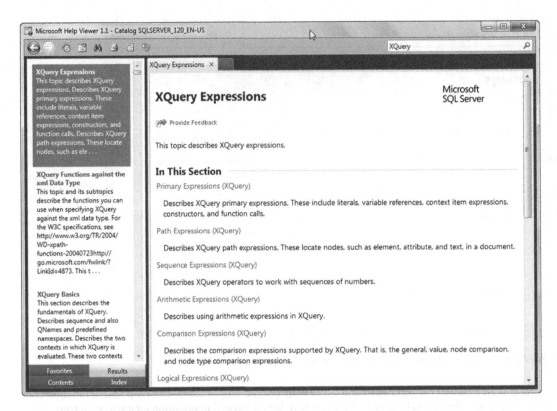

Figure 2-11. *Using Help Search to find help on XQuery*

Graphical Query Execution Plans

SSMS offers graphical query execution plans similar to the plans available in Query Editor. A graphical query execution plan is an excellent tool for aiding and optimizing query performance. SSMS allows you to view two types of graphical query execution plans: estimated and actual. An estimated query execution plan is SQL Server's cost-based performance estimate of a query. The actual execution plan is virtually identical to the estimated execution plan, except that it shows additional information such as actual row counts, number of rebinds, and number of rewinds when the query is run. Sometimes the actual execution plan differs from the estimated execution plan; this may be due to changes in indexes or statistics, parallelism, or, in some cases, a query using temporary tables or DDL statements. These options are available via the Query menu. Figure 2-12 shows an estimated query execution plan in SSMS.

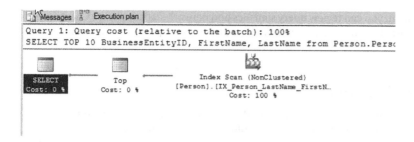

Figure 2-12. Estimated query execution plan for a simple query

In addition, you can right-click the Execution Plan window and choose to save the XML version of the graphical query plan to a file. SSMS can open these XML query plan files (with the extension `.sqlplan`) and automatically show you the graphical version. In addition, the Properties window of the SQL Server 2014 query plan contains details regarding the `MemoryGrantInfo`, `OptimizerHardwareDependentProperties`, and warnings about data that can affect plans. Figure 2-13 shows a sample Properties window for a query plan. You also have an option to view the execution plan in XML format by right-clicking the Execution Plan window and choosing Show Execution Plan XML.

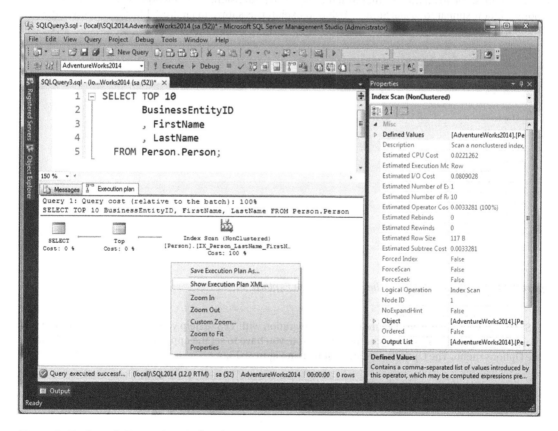

Figure 2-13. Sample Properties window for a simple query

Along with the execution plan, you can review query statistics and network statistics in the Client Statistics tab. This is extremely useful for remotely troubleshooting performance problems with slow-running queries.

Project-Management Features

SQL Server 2014 SSMS supports project-management features that will be familiar to Visual Studio developers using solution-based development. These types of solutions, referred to as SQL Server Management Studio database projects, are a deprecated feature in SQL Server 2014. There is no migration path for these types of solutions/projects, and they won't be supported in future releases of SQL Server. The replacement for this type of functionality is SQL Server Data Tools (SSDT) using Visual Studio database projects. The two products have completely different project types that can't be managed or opened in the other product.

This section explains how to use SSMS projects types, but the recommendation is that you start developing any new projects in SSDT. There is a section discussing SSDT at the end of this chapter.

SSMS lets you create solutions that consist of projects, which contain T-SQL scripts, XML files, connection information, and other files. By default, projects and solutions are saved in your My Documents\ SQL Server Management Studio\Projects directory. Solution files have the extension .ssmssln, and project files are saved in an XML format with the .smssproj extension. SSMS incorporates a Solution Explorer window similar to Visual Studio's Solution Explorer, as shown in Figure 2-14. You can access the Solution Explorer through the View menu.

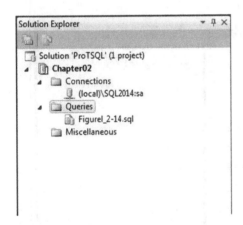

Figure 2-14. *Viewing a solution in the SSMS Solution Explorer*

SSMS can take advantage of source-control integration with TFS to help you manage versioning and deployment. To use SSMS's source-control integration, you have to set the appropriate source-control option in the Options menu. The Options window is shown in Figure 2-15.

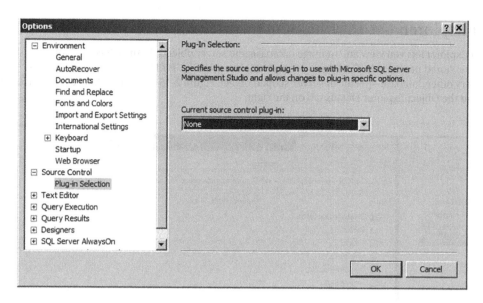

Figure 2-15. *Viewing the source-control options*

■ **Note**   To use SSMS with TFS, you need to download and install the appropriate Microsoft Source Code Control Interface (MSSCCI) provider from Microsoft. Go to www.microsoft.com/, search for "MSSCCI", and download the Visual Studio Team System 2010, 2012, or 2013 version of the MSSCCI provider, depending on which version you're already using.

After you create a solution and add projects, connections, and SQL scripts, you can add your solution to TFS by right-clicking the solution in the Solution Explorer and selecting Add Solution to Source Control.

To check out items from source control, open a local copy and choose Check Out for Edit. You can find options for checking out items from source control on the File ➤ Source Control menu. After checking out a solution from TFS, SSMS shows you the pending check-ins, letting you add comments to or check in individual files or projects.

The Object Explorer

The SSMS Object Explorer lets you view and manage database and server objects. In the Object Explorer, you can view tables, stored procedures (SPs), user-defined functions (UDFs), HTTP endpoints, users, logins, and just about every other database-specific or server-scoped object. Figure 2-16 shows the Object Explorer in the left pane and the Object Explorer Details tab on the right.

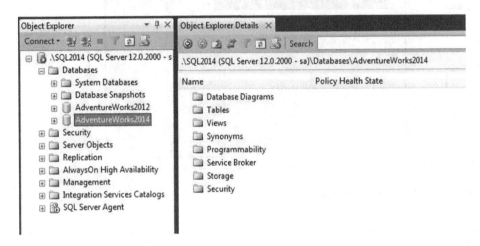

Figure 2-16. *Viewing the Object Explorer and the Object Explorer Details tab*

Most objects in the Object Explorer and the Object Explorer Details tab have object-specific pop-up context menus. Right-clicking any given object brings up the menu. Figure 2-17 shows an example pop-up context menu for database tables.

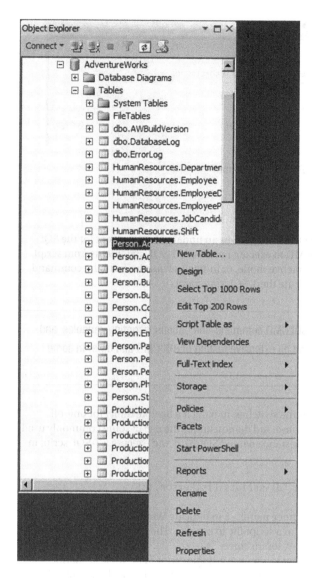

Figure 2-17. *Object Explorer database table pop-up context menusss*

Object Explorer in SQL Server 2014 allows developers to filter specific types of objects from all the database objects. To filter objects, type text with optional wildcard characters in the Object Explorer Details window, and press Enter. Optionally, you can filter objects using the Filter icon on the Object Explorer Details toolbar. Figure 2-18 shows an example of filtering objects named "Person".

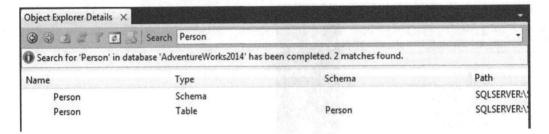

Figure 2-18. *Object Explorer with database objects filtered on "Person"*

The SQLCMD Utility

The SQLCMD utility was originally introduced in SQL Server 2005 as an updated replacement for the SQL 2000 `osql` command-line utility. You can use SQLCMD to execute batches of T-SQL statements from script files, individual queries or batches of queries in interactive mode, or individual queries from the command line. This utility uses SQL Server Native Client to execute the T-SQL statements.

■ **Note**   Appendix D provides a quick reference to SQLCMD command-line options, scripting variables, and commands. The descriptions in the appendix are based on extensive testing of SQLCMD and differ in some areas from the descriptions given in BOL.

SQLCMD supports a wide variety of command-line switches, making it a flexible utility for one-off batch or scheduled script execution. The following command demonstrates the use of some commonly used command-line options to connect to an SQL Server instance named SQL2014 and execute a T-SQL script in the AdventureWorks2014 database:

```
sqlcmd -S SQL2014 -E -d AdventureWorks2014 -i "d:\scripts\ListPerson.sql"
```

The options include -S to specify the server\instance name, -E to indicate Windows authentication, -d to set the database name, and -i to specify the name of a script file to execute. The command-line switches are all case sensitive, so -v is a different option from -V, for instance.

SQLCMD allows you to use scripting variables that let you use a single script in multiple scenarios. Scripting variables provide a mechanism for customizing the behavior of T-SQL scripts without modifying the scripts' content. You can reference scripting variables that were previously set with the -v command-line switch, with the SQLCMD :setvar command (discussed in the next section), or via Windows environment variables. You can also use any of the predefined SQLCMD scripting variables from within your script. The format to access any of these types of scripting variables from within your script is the same: $(variable_name). SQLCMD replaces your scripting variables with their respective values during script execution. Listing 2-1 shows some examples of scripting variables in action.

Listing 2-1. Using Scripting Variables in an SQLCMD Script

```
-- Windows environment variable
SELECT '$(PATH)';
-- SQLCMD scripting variable
SELECT '$(SQLCMDSERVER)';
-- Command-line scripting variable -v COLVAR= "Name" switch
SELECT $(COLVAR)
FROM Sys.Tables;
```

Because scripting variables are replaced in a script wholesale, some organizations may consider their use a security risk due to the possibility of SQL injection-style attacks. For this reason, you may choose to turn off this feature by using the -x command-line option, which disables variable substitution.

An example of an SQLCMD scripting variable is the predefined SOLCMDINI, which specifies the SQLCMD startup script. The startup script is run every time SQLCMD is run. It's useful for setting scripting variables with the :setvar command, setting initial T-SQL options such as QUOTED_IDENTIFIER and ANSI_PADDING, and performing any necessary database tasks before other scripts are run.

In addition to T-SQL statements, SQLCMD recognizes several commands specific to the application. SQLCMD commands allow you to perform tasks like listing servers and scripting variables, connecting to a server, and setting scripting variables, among others. Except for the batch terminator GO, all SQLCMD commands begin with a colon (:).

SQLCMD can also be run interactively. To start an interactive mode session, run SQLCMD with any of the previous options that don't exit immediately on completion.

■ **Note**   SQLCMD options such as -o, -i, -z, and -? exit immediately on completion. You can't start an interactive SQLCMD session if you specify any of these command-line options.

During an interactive SQLCMD session, you can run T-SQL queries and commands from the SQLCMD prompt. The interactive screen looks similar to Figure 2-19.

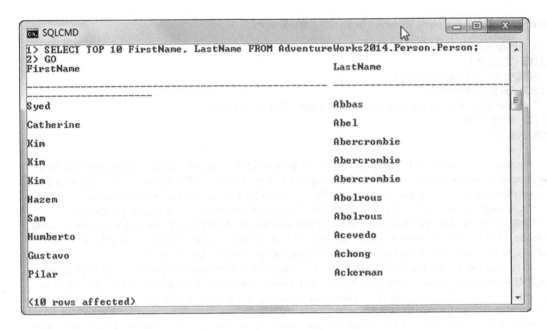

Figure 2-19. Sample query run from the SQLCMD interactive prompt

The SQLCMD prompt indicates the current line number of the batch (1>, 2>, and so on). You can enter T-SQL statements or SQLCMD commands at the prompt. T-SQL statements are stored in the statement cache as they're entered; SQLCMD commands are executed immediately. Once you have entered a complete batch of T-SQL statements, use the GO batch terminator to process all the statements in the cache.

SQLCMD has support for the new AlwaysOn feature. You can use the switch –K to specify the listener name.

There has been a behavior change for SQLCMD for XML as well. In SQL 2008, text data that contained a single quote was always replaced with an apostrophe. This behavior change has been addressed in SQL Server 2012. Additionally, legacy datetime values with no fractional seconds donot return three decimal digits; however, other datetime data types aren't affected.

SQL Server Data Tools

SQL Server 2014 ships with a new developer toolset named SQL Server Data Tools that serves as a replacement for Business Intelligence Development Studio (BIDS). In the highly competitive business world, the top three challenges today's developers face are collaboration, targeting different database platforms with the same codebase, and code stability. SSDT is designed to help with these challenges. It provides a tool that enables you to add validations at design time and not at runtime. A common pitfall for developers is that errors are discovered at runtime which aren't apparent and don't surface at design time, and SSDT serves to eliminate this issue.

You can code, build, debug, package, and deploy code without leaving the tool. After importing or creating a new database project, you can alter the project properties to target a specific database version. The underlying compiler uses the database version rules engine and compiles the project based on the database edition features. For example, if you're developing code for SQL Azure, the tool knows that you can't use sequence objects. This type of built-in intelligence in the tool is key to faster effective development so you don't discover issues at runtime, which would require rearchitecting the application.

This type of feature is also helpful when you're upgrading from an older version of SQL to a newer version. The compiler tells you if the older code will generate errors in the newer version of SQL.

SSDT can be used for connected development and disconnected development in case of a team project. Figure 2-20 shows the New Project window, which is based on the familiar SSMS Object Explorer.

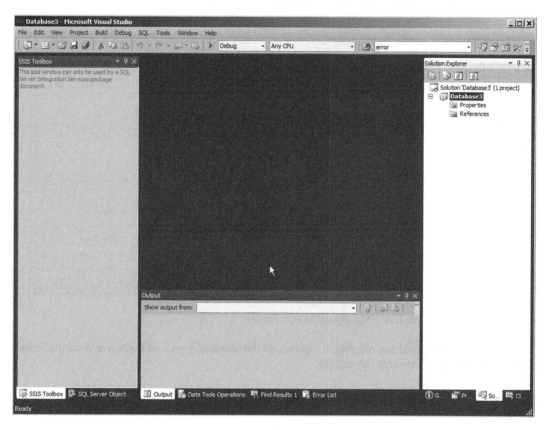

Figure 2-20. *SSDT New Project window*

You can create objects and buffer object editing, and T-SQL IntelliSense is also used. Once you finalize development, you can choose the platform to deploy to, and the project is deployed with a single click.

SQL Profiler

SQL Profiler is the primary tool for analyzing SQL Server performance. If you have a performance problem but aren't sure where the bottleneck lies, SQL Profiler can help you rapidly narrow down the suspects. It works by capturing events that occur on the server and logging them to a trace file or table. The classes of events that can be captured are exhaustive, covering a wide range of server-side events including T-SQL and SP preparation and execution, security events, transaction activity, locks, and database resizing.

When you create a new trace, SQL Profiler allows you to select all the events you wish to audit. Normally, you narrow this list as much as possible for both performance and manageability reasons. Figure 2-21 is a sample trace that captures T-SQL–specific events on the server.

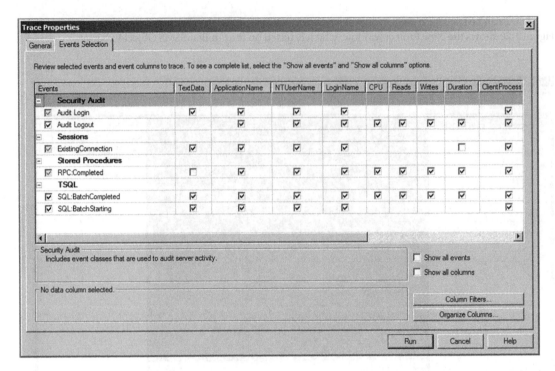

Figure 2-21. *Preparing to capture T-SQL events in SQL Profiler*

Once a trace is configured and running, it captures all the specified events on the server. A sample trace run using T-SQL events is shown in Figure 2-22.

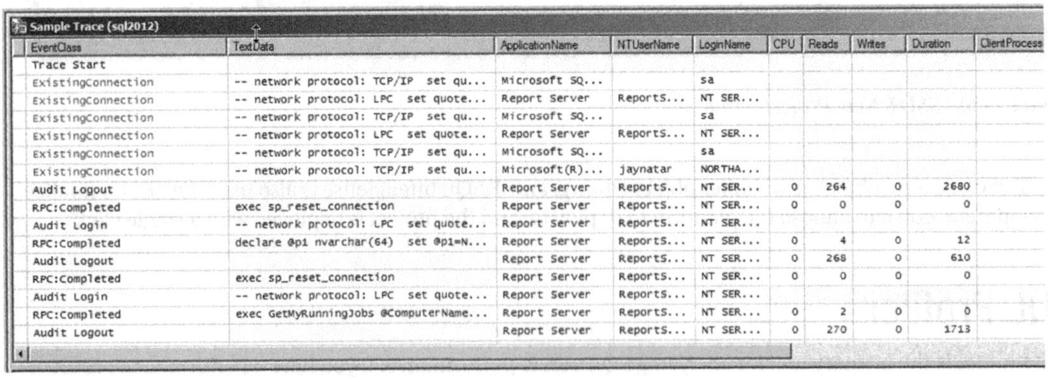

Figure 2-22. *Running a trace of T-SQL events*

As you can see in the example, even a simple trace that captures a relatively small number of events can easily become overwhelming, particularly if run against an SQL Server instance with several simultaneous user connections. SQL Profiler offers the Column Filter option, which lets you eliminate results from a trace. Using filters, you can narrow the results to include only actions performed by specific applications or users, or activities relevant only to a particular database. Figure 2-23 shows the Edit Filter window where you select trace filters.

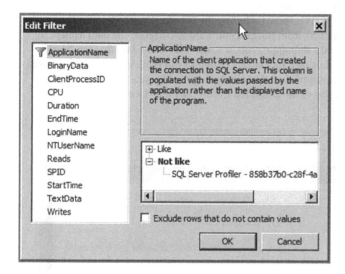

Figure 2-23. *Editing filters in SQL Profiler*

SQL Profiler offers several additional options, including trace replay and the ability to save trace results to either a file or a database table. SQL Profiler is vital to troubleshooting SQL Server performance and security issues.

SQL Server 2014 lists SQL Profiler for trace capture and trace replay as deprecated; they won't be supported in future versions of SQL Server. However, for analysis services workloads, both trace capture and trace replay will be supported. The replacement feature for the deprecated functionality is Extended Events.

Extended Events

These days it's common to have many complex systems with hundreds of cores that support applications with a scale-out model with a set of SQL Servers. The SQL Servers that support the complex applications use various features such as compression to reduce storage costs, high availability, and disaster-recovery features. For such a complex system, performance monitoring is vital: Extended Events is designed to handle these complex situations and diagnose issues in these systems without adding a performance penalty.

The Extended Events (XEvents) diagnostic tools was introduced in SQL 2008, and it received a makeover in SQL Server 2012 with a new GUI interface to aid ease of use. It's a lightweight, asynchronous eventing system that can retrieve information based on events triggered in the SQL engine. You can use XEventsto track both high-level issues such as query execution or blocking in the server, and low-level issues that are very close to the SQL Server code, such as how long it took for the spinlocks to back off. XEvents can be used to collect additional data about any event and perform predefined actions such as taking a memory dump when events happen; for example, you may be working with an application whose developer requests that you take a memory dump when a specific query executes.

Results from XEvents can be written to various targets, including the Windows trace file. If you have an application that is gathering diagnostic information from IIS, and you want to correlate the data from SQL Server, writing to the Windows trace file will make debugging much easier. The event data that has been written to the Windows trace file can be viewed using a tool such as Xperf or tracerpt. As with any diagnostic tool, the data that is collected can be saved to multiple locations including the file system, tables, and windows logging simultaneously. Figure 2-24 shows the Extended Events user interface.

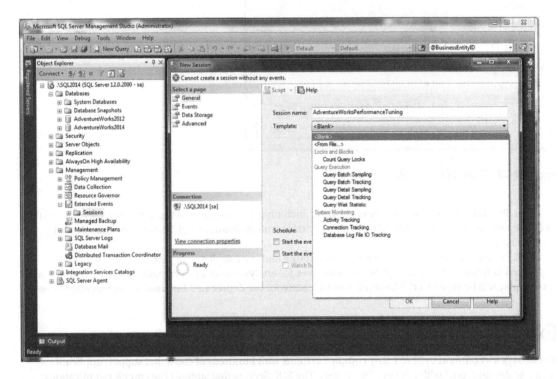

Figure 2-24. *Extended Events new session*

XEvents has been implemented by the SQL Engine, merge replication, analysis services, and reporting services in SQL Server 2014. In some of the components, such as analysis services, it's targeted information and not a complete implementation.

The XEvents UI is integrated with Management Studio: the tree has a separate node called Extended Events. You can create a new session by right-clicking the Extended Events node and selecting the session. XEvents sessions can be based on predefined templates, or you can create a session by choosing specific events.

XEvents offers a rich diagnostic framework that is highly scalable and offers the capability to collect little or large amounts of data in order to troubleshoot a given performance issue. Another reason to start using XEvents is that SQL Profiler has been marked for deprecation. Extended Events is discussed in detail in Chapter 19.

SQL Server Integration Services

SSIS was introduced in SQL Server 2005 as the replacement for SQL Server 7.0 and 2000 Data Transformation Services (DTS). SSIS provides an enterprise-class Extract Transform Load (ETL) tool that allows you to design simple or complex packages to extract data from multiple sources and integrate them into your SQL Server databases. It also provides rich BI integration and extensibility. In addition to data transformations, SSIS provides SQL Server-specific tasks that allow you to perform database-administration and -management functions like updating statistics and rebuilding indexes.

SSIS divides the ETL process into three major parts: control flow, data flow, and event handlers. The control flow provides structure to SSIS packages and controls execution via tasks, containers, and precedence constraints. The data flow imports data from various sources, transforms it, and stores it in specified destinations. The data flow, from the perspective of the control flow, is just another task. However, the data flow is important enough to require its own detailed design surface in a package. Event handlers allow you to perform actions in response to predefined events during the ETL process. Figure 2-25 shows a simple SSIS data flow that imports data from a table into a flat file.

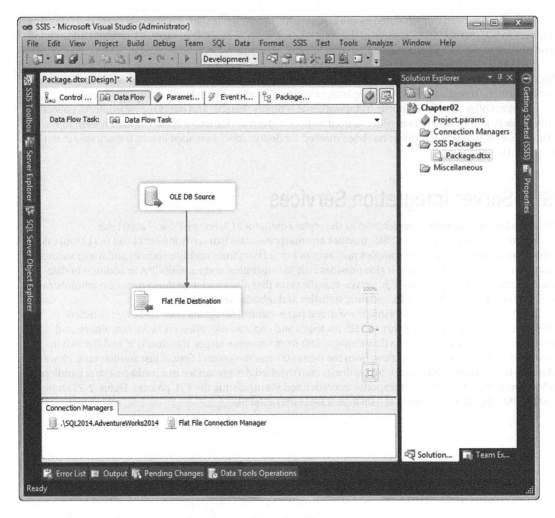

Figure 2-25. *Data flow to import data from a table to flat file*

SSIS is a far more advanced ETL tool than DTS, and it provides significant improvements in features, functionality, and raw power over the old DTS tools.

The Bulk Copy Program

Although it isn't as flashy or feature-rich as SSIS, BCP is small and fast, and it can perform simple imports with no hassle. BCP is handy for generating format files for BCP and other bulk-import tools, for one-off imports where a full-blown SSIS package would be overkill, for exporting data from database tables to files, and for backward compatibility when you don't have the resources to devote to immediately upgrading old BCP-based ETL processes.

Figure 2-26 shows a simple command-line call to BCP to create a BCP format file and a listing of the format file. The format files generated by BCP can be used by BCP, SSIS, and the T-SQL BULK INSERT statement.

```
Administrator: C:\WINDOWS\system32\cmd.exe

c:\>bcp adventureworks2014.person.person format null -S .\SQL2014 -T -fperson.fm
t -c

c:\>copy person.fmt con
11.0
13
1        SQLCHAR           0      12       "\t"     1      BusinessEntityID
                          ""
2        SQLCHAR           0      4        "\t"     2      PersonType
                  SQL_Latin1_General_CP1_CI_AS
3        SQLCHAR           0      1        "\t"     3      NameStyle
                          ""
4        SQLCHAR           0      16       "\t"     4      Title
                  SQL_Latin1_General_CP1_CI_AS
5        SQLCHAR           0      100      "\t"     5      FirstName
                  SQL_Latin1_General_CP1_CI_AS
6        SQLCHAR           0      100      "\t"     6      MiddleName
                  SQL_Latin1_General_CP1_CI_AS
7        SQLCHAR           0      100      "\t"     7      LastName
                  SQL_Latin1_General_CP1_CI_AS
8        SQLCHAR           0      20       "\t"     8      Suffix
                  SQL_Latin1_General_CP1_CI_AS
9        SQLCHAR           0      12       "\t"     9      EmailPromotion
                          ""
10       SQLCHAR           0      0        "\t"     10     AdditionalContactInfo
                          ""
11       SQLCHAR           0      0        "\t"     11     Demographics
                          ""
12       SQLCHAR           0      37       "\t"     12     rowguid
                          ""
13       SQLCHAR           0      24       "\r\n"   13     ModifiedDate
                          ""
        1 file(s) copied.
```

Figure 2-26. *Generating a format file with BCP*

SQL Server 2014 Books Online

Books Online (BOL) is the primary reference for SQL Server programming and administration. SQL Server 2014 introduces the Help Viewer piece from the VS2010 shell and doesn't include BOL along with the default setup. During the SQL installation, you have the option to choose the documentation feature, which in turn installs the Help Viewer.

You also have the option to install the BOL from an online resource. You can access a locally installed copy of BOL, or you can access it over the Web at Microsoft's web site. The help documentation can be found at www.microsoft.com/download/en/details.aspx?id=347. Figure 2-27 shows a search of a local copy of BOL.

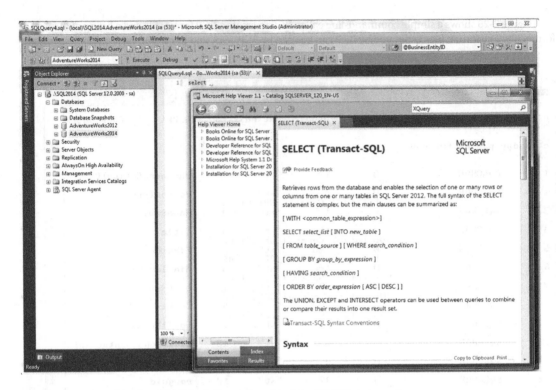

Figure 2-27. *Searching local BOL for information about the SELECT statement*

You can get updates for BOL at www.microsoft.com/sql/default.mspx. The online version of SQL Server 2012 BOL is available at http://msdn.microsoft.com/en-us/library/ms130214.aspx. Also keep in mind that you can search online and local versions of BOL, as well as several other SQL resources, via the Help Search function discussed previously in this chapter.

■ **Tip**   Microsoft now offers an additional option for obtaining the most up-to-date version of BOL. You can download the latest BOL updates from the Microsoft Update site, at http://update.microsoft.com/ microsoftupdate. Microsoft has announced plans to refresh BOL with updated content more often and to integrate SQL Server developer and DBA feedback into BOL more quickly.

The AdventureWorks Sample Database

SQL Server 2014 has two main sample databases: the AdventureWorks2014 OLTP and SQL Server 2014 RTM In-Memory OLTP databases. This book refers to the AdventureWorks2014 OLTP database for most examples. Microsoft now releases SQL Server sample databases through its CodePlex web site. You can download the AdventureWorks databases and associated sample code from www.codeplex.com/MSFTDBProdSamples.

■ **Note** It's highly recommended that you download the SQL Server AdventureWorks2014 OLTP database so that you can run the sample code in this book as you go through each chapter.

Summary

SQL Server 2014 includes the tools you've come to expect with any SQL Server release. This chapter has provided an overview of several tools that will be important to you as an SQL Server 2014 developer. The tools discussed include the following:

- SSMS, the primary GUI for SQL Server development and administration
- SQLCMD, SSMS's text-based counterpart
- SSDT, an integrated tool for developers
- SQL Profiler, which supplies event-capture and server-side tracing capabilities for analyzing SQL Server performance and auditing security
- Extended Events, a lightweight, asynchronous, event-based troubleshooting tool
- SSIS, the primary ETL tool for SQL Server 2014
- BCP, a command line–based bulk import tool
- BOL, the first place to look when you're trying to locate information about all things SQL Server
- AdventureWorks, the freely available Microsoft-supplied sample database

These topics could easily fill a book by themselves (and many, in fact, have). The following chapters review the SQL Server 2014 features in detail.

EXERCISES

1. SSDT is an SQL development tool. What tools did SSDT replace?

2. [Choose all that apply] SQL Server 2014 SSMS provides which of the following features?

   a. Ability to add code snippets and customize them

   b. An integrated Object Explorer for viewing and managing the server, databases, and database objects

   c. IntelliSense, which suggests table, object, and function names as you type SQL statements

   d. Customizable keyboard mapping scheme for Visual Studio users

3. SSIS is considered what type of tool?

4. [True/False] SQLCMD can use command-line options, environment variables, and SQLCMD :setvar commands to set scripting variables.

5. [Choose one] BCP can be used to perform which of the following tasks?

   a. Generating format files for use with SSIS

   b. Importing data into tables without format files

   c. Exporting data from a table to a file

   d. All of the above

6. What is one feature that Extended Events offers that SQL Profiler doesn't?

7. What are the target platforms that can be deployed using SSDT?

CHAPTER 3

■ ■ ■

Procedural Code

T-SQL has always included support for procedural programming in the form of control-of-flow statements and cursors. One thing that throws developers from other languages off their guard when migrating to SQL is the peculiar three-valued logic (3VL) we enjoy. Chapter 1 introduced you to SQL 3VL, and this chapter expands further on this topic. SQL 3VL is different from most other programming languages' simple two-valued Boolean logic. This chapter also discusses T-SQL control-of-flow constructs, which allow you to change the normally sequential order of statement execution. Control-of-flow statements let you branch your code logic with statements like IF...ELSE..., perform loops with statements like WHILE, and perform unconditional jumps with the GOTO statement. You're also introduced to CASE expressions and CASE-derived functions that return values based on given comparison criteria in an expression. Finally, we finish the chapter by explaining a topic closely tied to procedural code: SQL cursors.

■ **Note**   Technically the T-SQL TRY...CATCH and the newer TRY_PARSE and TRY_CONVERT are control-of-flow constructs. But these are specifically used for error handling and are discussed in Chapter 18, which describes error handling and dynamic SQL.

Three-Valued Logic

SQL Server 2014, like all ANSI-compatible SQL DBMS products, implements a peculiar form of logic known as 3VL. 3VL is necessary because SQL introduces the concept of NULL to serve as a placeholder for values that aren't known at the time they're stored in the database. The concept of NULL introduces an unknown logical result into SQL's ternary logic system. Let's begin looking at SQL 3VL with a simple set of propositions:

- Consider the proposition "1 is less than 3." The result is logically true because the value of the number 1 is less than the value of the number 3.

- The proposition "5 is equal to 6" is logically false because the value of the number 5 isn't equal to the value of the number 6.

- The proposition "X is greater than 10" presents a bit of a problem. The variable X is an algebraic placeholder for an actual value. Unfortunately, we haven't told you what value X stands for at this time. Because you don't know what the value of X is, you can't say the statement is true or false; instead you can say the result is unknown. SQL NULL represents an unknown value in the database in much the same way that the variable X represents an unknown value in this proposition, and comparisons with NULL produce the same unknown logical result in SQL.

Because NULL represents unknown values in the database, comparing anything with NULL (even other NULLs) produces an unknown logical result. Figure 3-1 is a quick reference for SQL Server 3VL, where p and q represent 3VL result values.

p	q	p AND q	p OR q
TRUE	TRUE	TRUE	TRUE
TRUE	FALSE	FALSE	TRUE
TRUE	UNKNOWN	UNKNOWN	TRUE
FALSE	TRUE	FALSE	TRUE
FALSE	FALSE	FALSE	FALSE
FALSE	UNKNOWN	FALSE	UNKNOWN
UNKNOWN	TRUE	UNKNOWN	TRUE
UNKNOWN	FALSE	FALSE	UNKNOWN
UNKNOWN	UNKNOWN	UNKNOWN	UNKNOWN

p	NOT p
TRUE	FALSE
FALSE	TRUE

Figure 3-1. SQL 3VL quick reference chart

As mentioned previously, the unknown logic values shown in the chart are the result of comparisons with NULL. The following predicates, for example, all evaluate to an unknown result:

```
@x = NULL
FirstName <> NULL
PhoneNumber > NULL
```

If you used one of these as the predicate in a WHERE clause of a SELECT statement, the statement would return no rows—SELECT with a WHERE clause returns only rows where the WHERE clause predicate evaluates to true; it discards rows for which the WHERE clause is false or unknown. Similarly, the INSERT, UPDATE, and DELETE statements with a WHERE clause only affect rows for which the WHERE clause evaluates to true.

SQL Server provides a proprietary mechanism, the SET ANSI_NULLS OFF option, to allow direct equality comparisons with NULL using the = and <> operators. The only ISO-compliant way to test for NULL is with the IS NULL and IS NOT NULL comparison predicates. We highly recommend that you stick with the ISO-compliant IS NULL and IS NOT NULL predicates for a few reasons:

- Many SQL Server features like computed columns, indexed views, and XML indexes require SET ANSI_NULLS ON at creation time.

- Mixing and matching SET ANSI_NULLS settings in your database can confuse other developers who have to maintain your code. Using ISO-compliant NULL-handling consistently eliminates confusion.

- SET ANSI_NULLS OFF allows direct equality comparisons with NULL, returning true if you compare a column or variable to NULL. It doesn't return true if you compare NULLs contained in two columns, though, which can be confusing.

- To top it all off, Microsoft has deprecated the SET ANSI_NULLS OFF setting. It will be removed in a future version of SQL Server, so it's a good idea to start future-proofing your code now.

IT'S A CLOSED WORLD, AFTER ALL

The *closed-world assumption* (CWA) is an assumption in logic that the world is "black and white," "true or false," or "ones and zeros." When applied to databases, the CWA basically states that all data stored in the database is true; everything else is false. The CWA presumes that only knowledge of the world that is complete can be stored in a database.

NULL introduces an open-world assumption (OWA) to the mix. It allows you to store information in the database that may or may not be true. This means an SQL database can store incomplete knowledge of the world—a direct violation of the CWA. Many relational management (RM) theorists see this as an inconsistency in the SQL DBMS model. This argument fills many an RM textbook and academic blog, including web sites like Hugh Darwen's and C. J. Date's *The Third Manifesto* (www.thethirdmanifesto.com), so we won't go deeply into the details here. Just realize that many RM experts dislike SQL NULL. As an SQL practitioner in the real world, however, you may discover that NULL is often the best option available to accomplish many tasks.

Control-of-Flow Statements

T-SQL implements procedural language control-of-flow statements, including such constructs as BEGIN...END, IF...ELSE, WHILE, and GOTO. T-SQL's control-of-flow statements provide a framework for developing rich server-side procedural code. Procedural code in T-SQL does come with some caveats, though, which we discuss in this section.

The BEGIN and END Keywords

T-SQL uses the keywords BEGIN and END to group multiple statements together in a statement block. The BEGIN and END keywords don't alter execution order of the statements they contain, nor do they define an atomic transaction, limit scope, or perform any function other than defining a simple grouping of T-SQL statements.

Unlike other languages, such as C++ and C#, which use braces ({ }) to group statements in logical blocks, T-SQL's BEGIN and END keywords don't define or limit scope. The following sample C# code, for instance, won't even compile:

```
{
int j = 10; } Console.WriteLine (j);
```

C# programmers will automatically recognize that the variable j in the previous code is defined inside braces, limiting its scope and making it accessible only inside the braces. T-SQL's roughly equivalent code, however, doesn't limit scope in this manner:

```
BEGIN
    DECLARE @j int = 10;
END
PRINT @j;
```

The previous T-SQL code executes with no problem, as long as the DECLARE statement is encountered before the variable is referenced in the PRINT statement. The scope of variables in T-SQL is defined in terms of command batches and database object definitions (such as SPs, UDFs, and triggers). Declaring two or more variables with the same name in one batch or SP results in errors.

■ **Caution** T-SQL's BEGIN and END keywords create a statement block but don't define a scope. Variables declared in a BEGIN...END block aren't limited in scope just to that block, but are scoped to the whole batch, SP, or UDF in which they're defined.

BEGIN...END is useful for creating statement blocks where you want to execute multiple statements based on the results of other control-of-flow statements like IF...ELSE and WHILE. BEGIN...END can also have another added benefit if you're using SSMS 2014 or a good third-party SQL editor like ApexSQL Edit (www.apexsql.com). BEGIN...END can alert the GUI that a section of code is collapsible. Figure 3-2 shows more than one region of code that is collapsible. This can speed up development and ease debugging, especially if you're writing complex T-SQL scripts.

```
SQLQuery1.sql - (lo...Works2014 (sa (51))*  ×
 1 ⊟BEGIN -- region 1
 2 |
 3 | DECLARE @x INT = 0, @y INT = 2;
 4 |
 5 ⊟IF @x = 1
 6 ⊟ BEGIN -- region 2
 7 |     SELECT @x;
 8 |
 9 ⊟    IF @y = 2
10 |
11 ⊟        SELECT LastName
12 |               , FirstName
13 |           FROM Person.Person;
14 |
15 | END; -- endregion 2
16 |
17 ⌊END; -- endregion 1
```

Figure 3-2. BEGIN...END statement blocks marked collapsible in SSMS

■ **Tip** Although it's not required, we like to wrap the body of CREATE PROCEDURE statements with BEGIN...END. This clearly delineates the body of the stored procedure. This is purely a coding style preference and has no affect on the stored procedure performance or function.

The IF...ELSE Statement

Like many procedural languages, T-SQL implements conditional execution of code using the simplest of procedural statements: the IF...ELSE construct. The IF statement is followed by a logical predicate. If the predicate evaluates to true, the single SQL statement or statement block wrapped in BEGIN...END is executed. If the predicate evaluates to either false or unknown, SQL Server falls through to the ELSE statement and executes the single statement or statement block following ELSE.

■ **Tip**   A *predicate* in SQL is an expression that evaluates to one of the logical results true, false, or unknown. Predicates are used in IF...ELSE statements, WHERE clauses, and anywhere that a logical result is needed.

The example in Listing 3-1 performs up to three comparisons to determine whether a variable is equal to a specified value. The second ELSE statement executes if and only if the tests for both true and false conditions fail.

Listing 3-1. Simple IF...ELSE Example

```
DECLARE @i int = NULL;
IF @i = 10
    PRINT 'TRUE.';
ELSE IF NOT (@i = 10)
    PRINT 'FALSE.';
ELSE
    PRINT 'UNKNOWN.';
```

Because the variable @i is NULL in the example, SQL Server reports that the result is unknown. If you assign the value 10 to the variable @i, SQL Server will report that the result is true; all other values will report false.

To create a statement block containing multiple T-SQL statements after either the IF statement or the ELSE statement, simply wrap your statements with the T-SQL BEGIN and END keywords discussed in the previous section. The example in Listing 3-2 is an IF...ELSE statement with statement blocks. The example uses IF...ELSE to check the value of the variable @direction. If @direction is ASCENDING, a message is printed, and the top ten names, in order of last name, are selected from the Person.Contact table. If @direction is DESCENDING, a different message is printed, and the bottom ten names are selected from the Person.Contact table. Any other value results in a message that @direction was not recognized. The results of Listing 3-2 are shown in Figure 3-3.

Listing 3-2. IF...ELSE with Statement Blocks

```
DECLARE @direction NVARCHAR(20) = N'DESCENDING';

IF @direction = N'ASCENDING'
BEGIN
        PRINT 'Start at the top!';

        SELECT TOP (10)
        LastName,
        FirstName,
        MiddleName
        FROM Person.Person
        ORDER BY LastName ASC;
END
ELSE   IF @direction = N'DESCENDING'
BEGIN
        PRINT 'Start at the bottom!';

        SELECT TOP (10)
        LastName,
```

51

```
        FirstName,
        MiddleName
        FROM Person.Person
        ORDER BY LastName DESC;
ENDs
ELSE

        PRINT '@direction  was not recognized!';
```

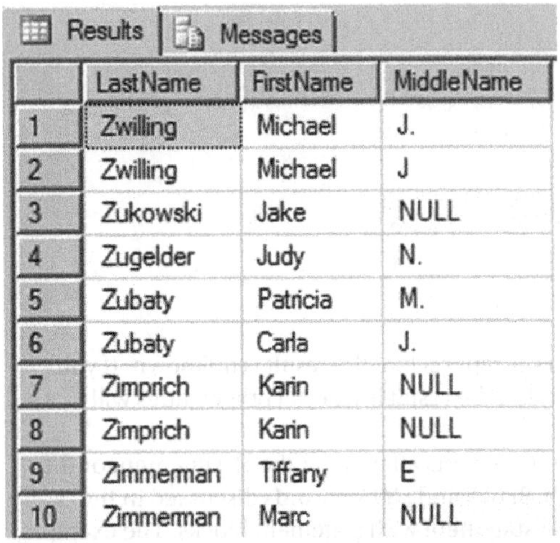

	LastName	FirstName	MiddleName
1	Zwilling	Michael	J.
2	Zwilling	Michael	J
3	Zukowski	Jake	NULL
4	Zugelder	Judy	N.
5	Zubaty	Patricia	M.
6	Zubaty	Carla	J.
7	Zimprich	Karin	NULL
8	Zimprich	Karin	NULL
9	Zimmerman	Tiffany	E
10	Zimmerman	Marc	NULL

Figure 3-3. The last ten contact names in the AdventureWorks database

The WHILE, BREAK, and CONTINUE Statements

Looping is a standard feature of procedural languages, and T-SQL provides looping support through the WHILE statement and its associated BREAK and CONTINUE statements. The WHILE loop is immediately followed by a predicate; WHILE executes a given SQL statement or statement block bounded by the BEGIN and END keywords as long as the associated predicate evaluates to true. If the predicate evaluates to false or unknown, the code in the WHILE loop doesn't execute and control passes to the next statement after the WHILE loop. The WHILE loop in Listing 3-3 is a very simple example that counts from 1 to 10. The result is shown in Figure 3-4.

Listing 3-3. WHILE Statement Example

```
DECLARE @i int = 1;
WHILE @i <= 10
BEGIN
   PRINT @i;
   SET @i = @i + 1;
END
```

Figure 3-4. Counting from 1 to 10 with WHILE

■ **Tip**   Be sure to update your counter or other flag in the WHILE loop. The WHILE statement will keep looping until its predicate evaluates to false or unknown. A simple coding mistake can create a nasty infinite loop.

T-SQL also includes two additional keywords that can be used with the WHILE statement: BREAK and CONTINUE. The CONTINUE keyword forces the WHILE loop to immediately jump to the start of the code block, as in the modified example in Listing 3-4.

Listing 3-4. WHILE...CONTINUE Example

```
DECLARE @i int = 1;
WHILE @i <= 10
BEGIN
    PRINT @i;
    SET @i = @i + 1;

CONTINUE; -- Force the WHILE loop to restart

PRINT 'The CONTINUE keyword ensures that this will never be printed.';

END
```

The BREAK keyword, on the other hand, forces the WHILE loop to terminate immediately. In Listing 3-5, BREAK forces the WHILE loop to exit during the first iteration so that the numbers 2 through 10 are never printed.

Listing 3-5. WHILE...BREAK Example

```
DECLARE @i int = 1;
WHILE @i <= 10
BEGIN
    PRINT @i;
    SET @i  = @i  + 1;

    BREAK; -- Force the WHILE loop to terminate

    PRINT 'The BREAK keyword ensures that this will never be printed.';
END
```

■ **Tip** BREAK and CONTINUE should be avoided in most cases. It's not uncommon to see a WHILE 1 = 1 statement with a BREAK in the body of the loop. This can always be rewritten, usually very easily, to remove the BREAK statement. Most of the time, the BREAK and CONTINUE keywords introduce additional complexity to your logic and cause more problems than they solve.

The GOTO Statement

Despite Edsger W. Dijkstra's best efforts at warning developers (see Dijkstra's 1968 letter, "Go To Statement Considered Harmful"),[1] T-SQL still has a GOTO statement. The GOTO statement transfers control of your program to a specified label unconditionally. Labels are defined by placing the label identifier on a line followed by a colon (:), as shown in Listing 3-6. This simple example executes its step 1 and uses GOTO to dive straight into step 3, skipping step 2. The results are shown in Figure 3-5.

Listing 3-6. Simple GOTO Example

```
PRINT 'Step 1 Begin.';
GOTO Step3_Label;

PRINT 'Step 2 will not be printed.';

Step3_Label:
PRINT 'Step 3 End.';
```

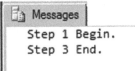

```
Step 1 Begin.
Step 3 End.
```

Figure 3-5. *The GOTO statement transfers control unconditionally*

The GOTO statement is best avoided, because it can quickly degenerate your programs into unstructured spaghetti code. When you have to write procedural code, you're much better off using structured programming constructs like IF...ELSE and WHILE statements.

---

[1] A Case against the GO TO Statement by: Edsger W Dijkstra; Technology University Eindhoven, The Netherlands http://www.cs.utexas.edu/users/EWD/transcriptions/EWD02xx/EWD215.html

The WAITFOR Statement

The WAITFOR statement suspends execution of a transaction, SP, or T-SQL command batch until a specified time is reached, a time interval has elapsed, or a message is received from Service Broker.

■ **Note** Service Broker is an SQL Server messaging system. We don't detail Service Broker in this book, but you can find out more about it in *Pro SQL Server 2008 Service Broker*, by Klaus Aschenbrenner (Apress, 2008).

The WAITFOR statement has a DELAY option that tells SQL Server to suspend code execution until one of the following criteria is met or a specified time interval has elapsed. The time interval is specified as a valid time string in the format hh:mm:ss. The time interval can't contain a date portion; it must only include the time, and it can be up to 24 hours. Listing 3-7 is an example of the WAITFOR statement with the DELAY option, which blocks execution of the batch for 3 seconds.

WAITFOR CAVEATS

There are some caveats associated with the WAITFOR statement. In some situations, WAITFOR can cause longer delays than the interval you specify. SQL Server also assigns each WAITFOR statement its own thread, and if SQL Server begins experiencing thread starvation, it can randomly stop WAITFOR threads to free up thread resources. If you need to delay execution for an exact amount of time, you can guarantee more consistent results by suspending execution through an external application like SQL Server Integration Services (SSIS).

In addition to its DELAY and TIME options, you can use WAITFOR with the RECEIVE and GET CONVERSATION GROUP options with Service Broker–enabled applications. When you use WAITFOR with RECEIVE, the statement waits for receipt of one or more messages from a specified queue.

When you use WAITFOR with the GET CONVERSATION GROUP option, it waits for a conversation group identifier of a message. GET CONVERSATION GROUP allows you to retrieve information about a message and lock the conversation group for the conversation containing the message, all before retrieving the message itself.

Listing 3-7. WAITFOR Example

```
PRINT 'Step 1 complete. ';
GO

DECLARE @time_to_pass nvarchar(8);
SELECT @time_to_pass = N'00:00:03';
WAITFOR DELAY @time_to_pass;
PRINT 'Step 2 completed three seconds later. ';
```

You can also use the TIME option with the WAITFOR statement. If you use the TIME option, SQL Server waits until the appointed time before allowing execution to continue. Datetime variables are allowed, but the date portion is ignored when the TIME option is used.

The RETURN Statement

The RETURN statement exits unconditionally from an SP or command batch. When you use RETURN, you can optionally specify an integer expression as a return value. The RETURN statement returns a given integer expression to the calling routine or batch. If you don't specify an integer expression to return, a value of 0 is returned by default. RETURN isn't normally used to return calculated results, except for UDFs, which offer more RETURN options (as detailed in Chapter 4). For SPs and command batches, the RETURN statement is used almost exclusively to return a success indicator, a failure indicator, or an error code.

WHAT NUMBER, SUCCESS?

All system SPs return 0 to indicate success, or a nonzero value to indicate failure (unless otherwise documented in BOL). It's considered bad form to use the RETURN statement to return anything other than an integer status code from a script or SP.

UDFs, on the other hand, have their own rules. UDFs have a flexible variation of the RETURN statement, which exits the body of the UDF. In fact, a UDF requires the RETURN statement be used to return scalar or tabular results to the caller. You see UDFs again in detail in Chapter 4.

▓ **Note** There are a couple of methods in T-SQL to redirect logic flow based on errors. These include the TRY...CATCH statement and the THROW statement. Both statements are discussed in detail in Chapter 18.

The CASE Expression

The T-SQL CASE function is SQL Server's implementation of the ISO SQL CASE expression. Whereas the previously discussed T-SQL control-of-flow statements allow for conditional execution of SQL statements or statement blocks, the CASE expression allows for set-based conditional processing in a single query. CASE provides two syntaxes, simple and searched, which are discussed in this section.

The Simple CASE Expression

The simple CASE expression returns a result expression based on the value of a given input expression. The simple CASE expression compares the input expression to a series of expressions following WHEN keywords. Once a match is encountered, CASE returns a corresponding result expression following the keyword THEN. If no match is found, the expression following the keyword ELSE is returned. NULL is returned if no ELSE keyword is supplied.

Consider the example in Listing 3-8, which uses a simple CASE expression to count all the AdventureWorks customers on the West Coast (arbitrarily defined as the states of California, Washington, and Oregon). The query also uses a common table expression (CTE, discussed more thoroughly in Chapter 9). The results are shown in Figure 3-6.

Listing 3-8. Counting West Coast Customers with a Simple CASE Expression

```
WITH  EmployeesByRegion(Region)
AS
(
    SELECT
        CASE sp.StateProvinceCode
        WHEN 'CA' THEN 'West Coast'
        WHEN 'WA' THEN 'West Coast'
        WHEN 'OR' THEN 'West Coast'
        ELSE 'Elsewhere'
        END
    FROM  HumanResources.Employee e
    INNER JOIN Person.Person p
        ON e.BusinessEntityID = p.BusinessEntityID
        INNER JOIN Person.BusinessEntityAddress bea
            ON bea.BusinessEntityID = e.BusinessEntityID
        INNER JOIN Person.Address a
            ON a.AddressID = bea.AddressID
        INNER JOIN Person.StateProvince sp
            ON sp.StateProvinceID = a.StateProvinceID
    WHERE sp.CountryRegionCode = 'US'
)
SELECT  COUNT(Region) AS  NumOfEmployees,  Region
FROM    EmployeesByRegion
GROUP  BY  Region;
```

	NumOfEmployees	Region
1	6	Elsewhere
2	278	West Coast

Figure 3-6. *Results of the West Coast Customer Count*

The CASE expression in the subquery compares the StateProvinceCode value to each of the state codes following the WHEN keywords, returning the name West Coast when StateProvinceCode is equal to CA, WA, or OR. For any other StateProvinceCode in the United States, it returns a value of Elsewhere:

```
SELECT CASE sp.StateProvinceCode
        WHEN 'CA' THEN 'West Coast'
        WHEN 'WA' THEN 'West Coast'
        WHEN 'OR' THEN 'West Coast'
        ELSE 'Elsewhere'
    END
```

The remainder of the example counts the number of rows returned by the query, grouped by Region.

A SIMPLE CASE OF NULL

The simple CASE expression performs basic equality comparisons between the input expression and the expressions following the WHEN keywords. This means you can't use the simple CASE expression to check for NULLs. Recall from the "Three-Valued Logic" section of this chapter that a NULL, when compared to anything, returns unknown. The simple CASE expression only returns the expression following the THEN keyword when the comparison returns true. This means if you ever try to use NULL in a WHEN expression, the corresponding THEN expression won't be returned. If you need to check for NULL in a CASE expression, use a searched CASE expression with the IS NULL or IS NOT NULL comparison operators.

The Searched CASE Expression

The searched CASE expression provides a mechanism for performing more complex comparisons. The searched CASE evaluates a series of predicates following WHEN keywords until it encounters one that evaluates to true. At that point, it returns the corresponding result expression following the THEN keyword. If none of the predicates evaluates to true, the result following the ELSE keyword is returned. If none of the predicates evaluates to true and ELSE isn't supplied, the searched CASE expression returns NULL.

Predicates in the searched CASE expression can take advantage of any valid SQL comparison operators (such as <, >, =, LIKE, and IN). The simple CASE expression from Listing 3-8 can be easily expanded to cover multiple geographic regions using the searched CASE expression and the IN logical operator, as shown in Listing 3-9. This example uses a searched CASE expression to group states into West Coast, Pacific, and New England regions. The results are shown in Figure 3-7.

Listing 3-9. Counting Employees by Region with a Searched CASE Expression

```
WITH  EmployeesByRegion(Region)
AS
(
    SELECT
        CASE WHEN sp.StateProvinceCode IN ('CA', 'WA', 'OR') THEN 'West Coast'
        WHEN sp.StateProvinceCode IN ('HI', 'AK') THEN 'Pacific'
        WHEN sp.StateProvinceCode IN ('CT', 'MA', 'ME', 'NH', 'RI', 'VT')
        THEN 'New England'
        ELSE 'Elsewhere'
        END
    FROM  HumanResources.Employee e
    INNER JOIN Person.Person p
        ON e.BusinessEntityID = p.BusinessEntityID
        INNER JOIN Person.BusinessEntityAddress bea
            ON bea.BusinessEntityID = e.BusinessEntityID
        INNER JOIN Person.Address a
            ON a.AddressID = bea.AddressID
        INNER JOIN Person.StateProvince sp
            ON sp.StateProvinceID = a.StateProvinceID
    WHERE sp.CountryRegionCode = 'US'
)
SELECT  COUNT(Region) AS NumOfCustomers,  Region
FROM    EmployeesByRegion
GROUP   BY  Region;
```

	NumOfCustomers	Region
1	5	Elsewhere
2	1	New England
3	278	West Coast

Figure 3-7. *Results of the regional customer count*

The searched CASE expression in the example uses the IN operator to return the geographic area that StateProvinceCode is in: California, Washington, and Oregon all return West Coast; and Connecticut, Massachusetts, Maine, New Hampshire, Rhode Island, and Vermont all return New England. If the StateProvinceCode doesn't fit in one of these regions, the searched CASE expression returns Elsewhere:

```
SELECT
    CASE WHEN sp.StateProvinceCode IN ('CA', 'WA', 'OR') THEN 'West Coast'
        WHEN sp.StateProvinceCode IN ('HI', 'AK') THEN 'Pacific'
        WHEN sp.StateProvinceCode IN ('CT', 'MA', 'ME', 'NH', 'RI', 'VT')
        THEN 'New England'
        ELSE 'Elsewhere'
    END
```

The balance of the sample code in Listing 3-9 counts the rows returned, grouped by Region. The CASE expression, either simple or searched, can be used in SELECT, UPDATE, INSERT, MERGE, and DELETE statements.

A CASE BY ANY OTHER NAME

Many programming and query languages offer expressions that are analogous to the SQL CASE expression. C++ and C#, for instance, offer the ?: operator, which fulfills the same function as a searched CASE expression. XQuery has its own flavor of if...then...else expression that is also equivalent to the SQL searched CASE.

C# and Visual Basic supply the switch and Select statements, respectively, which are semi-analogous to SQL's simple CASE expression. The main difference, of course, is that SQL's CASE expression returns a scalar value, whereas the C# and Visual Basic statements actually control program flow, allowing you to execute statements based on an expression's value. The similarities and differences between SQL expressions and statements and similar constructs in other languages provide a great starting point for learning the nitty-gritty details of T-SQL.

CASE and Pivot Tables

Many times, business reporting requirements dictate that a result should be returned in pivot table format. *Pivot table format* simply means the labels for columns and/or rows are generated from the data contained in rows. Microsoft Access and Excel users have long had the ability to generate pivot tables on their data, and SQL Server 2014 supports the PIVOT and UNPIVOT operators introduced in SQL Server 2005. Back in the days of SQL Server 2000 and before, however, CASE expressions were the only method of generating pivot table-type queries. And even though SQL Server 2014 provides the PIVOT and UNPIVOT operators, truly dynamic pivot tables still require using CASE expressions and dynamic SQL. The static pivot table query shown in Listing 3-10 returns a pivot table-formatted result with the total number of orders for each AdventureWorks sales region in the United States. The results are shown in Figure 3-8.

Listing 3-10. CASE-Style Pivot Table

```
SELECT
    t.CountryRegionCode,
    SUM
    (
        CASE WHEN t.Name = 'Northwest' THEN 1
        ELSE    0
        END
    ) AS      Northwest,
    SUM
    (
        CASE WHEN t.Name = 'Northeast' THEN 1
        ELSE    0
        END
    ) AS      Northeast,
    SUM
    (
        CASE WHEN t.Name = 'Southwest' THEN 1
        ELSE    0
        END
    ) AS      Southwest,
    SUM
    (
        CASE WHEN t.Name = 'Southeast' THEN 1
        ELSE    0
        END
    ) AS      Southeast,
    SUM
    (
        CASE WHEN t.Name = 'Central' THEN 1
        ELSE    0
        END
    ) AS  Central
FROM  Sales.SalesOrderHeader soh
INNER  JOIN  Sales.SalesTerritory  t
    ON  soh.TerritoryID = t.TerritoryID
WHERE  t.CountryRegionCode  =  'US'
GROUP  BY  t.CountryRegionCode;
```

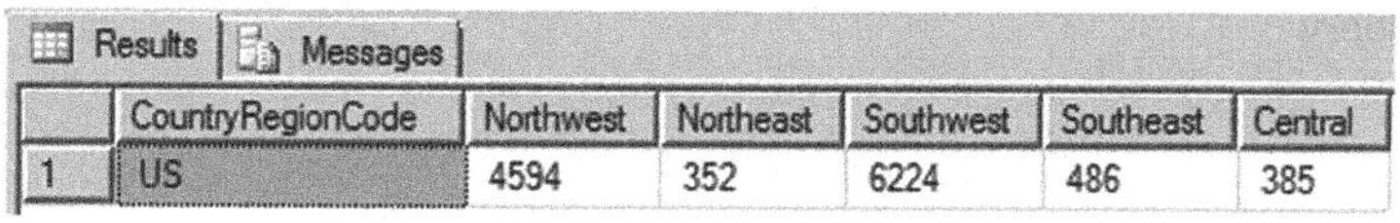

	CountryRegionCode	Northwest	Northeast	Southwest	Southeast	Central
1	US	4594	352	6224	486	385

Figure 3-8. *Number of sales by region in pivot table format*

This type of static pivot table can also be used with the SQL Server 2014 `PIVOT` operator. The sample code in Listing 3-11 uses the `PIVOT` operator to generate the same result as the `CASE` expressions in Listing 3-10.

Listing 3-11. `PIVOT` Operator Pivot Table

```
SELECT
    CountryRegionCode,
    Northwest,
    Northeast,
    Southwest,
    Southeast,
    Central
FROM
(
    SELECT
        t.CountryRegionCode,
        t.Name
    FROM  Sales.SalesOrderHeader  soh
    INNER JOIN Sales.SalesTerritory t
        ON  soh.TerritoryID  =  t.TerritoryID
    WHERE t.CountryRegionCode = 'US'
) p
PIVOT
(
    COUNT (Name)
    FOR  Name
    IN
    (
        Northwest,
        Northeast,
        Southwest,
        Southeast,
        Central
    )
) AS  pvt;
```

On occasion, you may need to run a pivot table–style report where you don't know the column names in advance. This is a dynamic pivot table script that uses a temporary table and dynamic SQL to generate a pivot table, without specifying the column names in advance. Listing 3-12 demonstrates one method of generating dynamic pivot tables in T-SQL. The results are shown in Figure 3-9.

Listing 3-12. Dynamic Pivot Table Query

```
-- Declare variables
DECLARE @sql nvarchar(4000);

DECLARE @temp_pivot table
 (
  TerritoryID int NOT NULL PRIMARY KEY,
  CountryRegion nvarchar(20) NOT NULL,
  CountryRegionCode nvarchar(3) NOT NULL
 );

-- Get column names from source table rows
INSERT INTO @temp_pivot
 (
  TerritoryID,
  CountryRegion,
  CountryRegionCode
 )
 SELECT
  TerritoryID,
  Name,
  CountryRegionCode
  FROM Sales.SalesTerritory
  GROUP BY
     TerritoryID,
     Name,
     CountryRegionCode;

-- Generate dynamic SQL query
SET @sql = N'SELECT' +
    SUBSTRING(
       (
         SELECT N', SUM(CASE WHEN t.TerritoryID = ' +
           CAST(TerritoryID AS NVARCHAR(3)) +
         N' THEN 1 ELSE 0 END) AS ' + QUOTENAME(CountryRegion) AS "*"
         FROM @temp_pivot
         FOR XML PATH('')
    ), 2, 4000) +
    N' FROM Sales.SalesOrderHeader soh ' +
       N' INNER JOIN Sales.SalesTerritory t ' +
       N' ON soh.TerritoryID = t.TerritoryID; ' ;

-- Print and execute dynamic SQL
PRINT @sql;

EXEC (@sql);
```

	Northwest	Northeast	Central	Southwest	Southeast	Canada	France	Germany	Australia	United Kingdom
1	4594	352	385	6224	486	4067	2672	2623	6843	3219

Figure 3-9. *Dynamic pivot table result*

The script in Listing 3-12 first declares an nvarchar variable that holds the dynamically generated SQL script and a table variable that holds all the column names, which are retrieved from the row values in the source table:

```
-- Declare variables
DECLARE @sql nvarchar(4000);

DECLARE @temp_pivot table
 (
  TerritoryID int NOT NULL PRIMARY KEY,
  CountryRegion nvarchar(20) NOT NULL,
  CountryRegionCode nvarchar(3) NOT NULL
 );
```

Next, the script grabs a list of distinct territory-specific values from the table and stores them in the @temp_pivot table variable. These values from the table become column names in the pivot table result:

```
-- Get column names from source table rows
INSERT INTO @temp_pivot
 (
  TerritoryID,
  CountryRegion,
  CountryRegionCode
 )
 SELECT
  TerritoryID,
  Name,
  CountryRegionCode
  FROM Sales.SalesTerritory
  GROUP BY
     TerritoryID,
     Name,
     CountryRegionCode;
```

The script then uses FOR XML PATH to efficiently generate the dynamic SQL SELECT query that contains CASE expressions and column names generated dynamically based on the values in the @temppivot table variable. This SELECT query creates the dynamic pivot table result:

```
-- Generate dynamic SQL query
SET @sql = N'SELECT' +
    SUBSTRING(
        (
          SELECT N', SUM(CASE WHEN t.TerritoryID = ' +
            CAST(TerritoryID AS NVARCHAR(3)) +
```

```
         N' THEN 1 ELSE 0 END) AS ' + QUOTENAME(CountryRegion) AS "*"
         FROM @temp_pivot
         FOR XML PATH('')
     ), 2, 4000) +
     N' FROM Sales.SalesOrderHeader soh ' +
         N' INNER JOIN Sales.SalesTerritory t ' +
         N' ON soh.TerritoryID = t.TerritoryID; ' ;
```

Finally, the dynamic pivot table query is printed out and executed with the T-SQL PRINT and EXEC statements:

```
-- Print and execute dynamic SQL
PRINT @sql;

EXEC (@sql);
```

Listing 3-13 shows the dynamic SQL pivot table query generated by the code in Listing 3-12.

Listing 3-13. Autogenerated Dynamic SQL Pivot Table Query

```
SELECT SUM
(
    CASE  WHEN  t.TerritoryID  =  1  THEN 1
        ELSE 0
    END
) AS   [Northwest],
SUM
(
    CASE  WHEN  t.TerritoryID  =  2  THEN 1
        ELSE 0
    END
) AS   [Northeast],
SUM
(
    CASE  WHEN  t.TerritoryID  =  3  THEN 1
        ELSE 0
    END
) AS  [Central],
SUM
(
    CASE  WHEN  t.TerritoryID  =  4  THEN 1
        ELSE 0
    END
) AS   [Southwest],
SUM
(
    CASE  WHEN  t.TerritoryID  =  5  THEN 1
        ELSE 0
    END
) AS   [Southeast],
```

```
SUM
(
    CASE  WHEN  t.TerritoryID  =  6  THEN 1
        ELSE 0
    END
) AS  [Canada],
SUM
(
    CASE  WHEN  t.TerritoryID  =  7  THEN 1
        ELSE 0
    END
) AS  [France],
SUM
(
    CASE  WHEN  t.TerritoryID  =  8  THEN 1
        ELSE 0
    END
) AS  [Germany],
SUM
(
    CASE  WHEN  t.TerritoryID  =  9  THEN 1
        ELSE 0
    END
) AS  [Australia],
SUM
(
    CASE  WHEN  t.TerritoryID  =  10  THEN 1
        ELSE 0
    END
) AS  [United Kingdom]
FROM  Sales.SalesOrderHeader soh
INNER JOIN  Sales.SalesTerritory  t
    ON  soh.TerritoryID = t.TerritoryID;
```

■ **Caution** Any time you use dynamic SQL, make sure you take precautions against SQL injection—that is, malicious SQL code being inserted into your SQL statements. This example uses the QUOTENAME function to quote the column names being dynamically generated, to help avoid SQL injection problems. Chapter 18 covers dynamic SQL and SQL injection in greater detail.

The IIF Statement

SQL Server 2012 simplified the standard CASE statement by introducing the concept of an IIF statement. You get the same results as you would using the CASE statement but with much less code. Those familiar with Microsoft .NET will be glad to see that the same functionality is now part of T-SQL.

The syntax is simple. The command takes a Boolean expression, a value for when the expression equates to true, and a value for when the expression equates to false. Listing 3-14 show two examples: one uses variables, and the other uses table columns. The output for both statements is shown in Figure 3-10.

Listing 3-14. Examples Using the IIF statement

```
--Example 1. IIF Statement Using Variables

DECLARE @valueA int = 85
DECLARE @valueB int = 45

SELECT IIF (@valueA < @valueB, 'True', 'False') AS Result

--Example 2. IIF Statement Using Table Column

SELECT IIF (Name in ('Alberta', 'British Columbia'), 'Canada', Name)
FROM [Person].[StateProvince]
```

Figure 3-10. *Partial output of IIF statements*

CHOOSE

Another logical function introduced in SQL Server 2012 is the CHOOSE function. The CHOOSE function allows you to select a member of an array based on an integer index value. Simply put, CHOOSE lets you select a member from a list. The member you select can be based on either a static index value or a computed value. The syntax for the CHOOSE function is as follows:

```
CHOOSE ( index, val_1, val_2 [, val_n ] )
```

If the index value isn't an integer (let's say it's a decimal), then SQL converts it to an integer. If the index value is out of range for the index, then the function returns NULL. Listing 3-15 shows a simple example, and Figure 3-11 shows the output. The example uses the integer value of PhoneNumberTypeID to determine the type of phone. In this case, the phone type is defined in the table, so a CHOOSE function wouldn't be necessary; but in other cases, the value may not be defined.

Listing 3-15. Example Using the CHOOSE Statement

```
SELECT p.FirstName,
       pp.PhoneNumber,
       CHOOSE(pp.PhoneNumberTypeID, 'Cell', 'Home', 'Work') 'Phone Type'
FROM Person.Person p
JOIN Person.PersonPhone pp
ON p.BusinessEntityID = pp.BusinessEntityID
```

	FirstName	PhoneNumber	Phone Type
1	Syed	926-555-0182	Work
2	Catherine	747-555-0171	Cell
3	Kim	334-555-0137	Work
4	Kim	919-555-0100	Work
5	Kim	208-555-0114	Cell
6	Hazem	869-555-0125	Work
7	Sam	567-555-0100	Work
8	Humberto	599-555-0127	Cell
9	Gustavo	398-555-0132	Cell
10	Pilar	1 (11) 500 555-0132	Cell
11	Pilar	577-555-0185	Work
12	Aaron	417-555-0154	Cell
13	Adam	129-555-0195	Home
14	Alex	346-555-0124	Cell
15	Alexandra	629-555-0159	Home

Figure 3-11. Partial output of the CHOOSE statement

COALESCE and NULLIF

The COALESCE function takes a list of expressions as arguments and returns the first non-NULL value from the list. COALESCE is defined by ISO as shorthand for the following equivalent searched CASE expression:

```
CASE
WHEN (expression1 IS NOT NULL) THEN expression1 WHEN (expression2 IS NOT NULL) THEN expression2
[ ... " ] END
```

The following COALESCE function returns the value of MiddleName when MiddleName is not NULL, and the string No Middle Name when MiddleName is NULL:

```
COALESCE (MiddleName, 'No Middle Name')
```

The NULLIF function accepts exactly two arguments. NULLIF returns NULL if the two expressions are equal, and it returns the value of the first expression if the two expressions aren't equal. NULLIF is defined by the ISO standard as equivalent to the following searched CASE expression:

```
CASE WHEN expression1 = expression2 THEN NULL
ELSE expression1
END
```

NULLIF is often used in conjunction with COALESCE. Consider Listing 3-16, which combines COALESCE with NULLIF to return the string "This is NULL or A" if the variable @s is set to the character value *A* or NULL.

Listing 3-16. Using COALESCE with NULLIF

```
DECLARE @s varchar(10);
SELECT @s = 'A';
SELECT COALESCE(NULLIF(@s, 'A'), 'This is NULL or A');
```

T-SQL has long had alternate functionality similar to COALESCE. Specifically, the ISNULL function accepts two parameters and returns NULL if they're equal.

COALESCE OR ISNULL?

The T-SQL functions COALESCE and ISNULL perform similar functions, but which one should you use? COALESCE is more flexible than ISNULL and is compliant with the ISO standard to boot. This means it's also the more portable option among ISO-compliant systems. COALESCE also implicitly converts the result to the data type with the highest precedence from the list of expressions. ISNULL implicitly converts the result to the data type of the first expression. Finally, COALESCE is a bit less confusing than ISNULL, especially considering that there's already a comparison operator called IS NULL. In general, we recommend using the COALESCE function instead of ISNULL.

Cursors

The word *cursor* comes from the Latin word for runner, and that is exactly what a T-SQL cursor does: it "runs" through a result set, returning one row at a time. Many T-SQL programming experts rail against the use of cursors for a variety of reasons—the chief among these include the following:

- Cursors use a lot of overhead, often much more than an equivalent set-based approach.

- Cursors override SQL Server's built-in query optimizations, often making them much slower than an equivalent set-based solution.

Because cursors are procedural in nature, they're often the slowest way to manipulate data in T-SQL. Rather than spend the balance of the chapter ranting against cursor use, however, we'd like to introduce T-SQL cursor functionality and play devil's advocate to point out some areas where cursors provide an adequate solution.

The first such area where we can recommend the use of cursors is in scripts or procedures that perform administrative tasks. In administrative tasks, the following items often hold true:

- Unlike normal data queries and data manipulations that are performed dozens, hundreds, or potentially thousands of times per day, administrative tasks are often performed on a one-off basis or on a regular schedule like once per day.

- Administrative tasks often require calling an SP or executing a procedural code block once for each row when the tasks are based on a table of entries.

- Administrative tasks generally don't need to query or manipulate massive amounts of data to perform their jobs.

- The order of the steps in which administrative tasks are performed and the order of the database objects they touch are often important.

The sample SP in Listing 3-17 is an example of an administrative task performed with a T-SQL cursor. The sample uses a cursor to loop through all indexes on all user tables in the current database. It then creates dynamic SQL statements to rebuild every index whose fragmentation level is above a user-specified threshold. The results are shown in Figure 3-12. Be aware that your results may return different values for each row.

Listing 3-17. Sample Administrative Task Performed with a Cursor

```
CREATE PROCEDURE dbo.RebuildIndexes
(    @ShowOrRebuild nvarchar(10) = N'show'
   , @MaxFrag decimal(20, 2) = 20.0
)
AS
SET NOCOUNT ON;

BEGIN

-- Declare variables
DECLARE
   @Schema nvarchar(128), @Table nvarchar(128)
  , @Index nvarchar(128), @Sql nvarchar(4000)
  , @DatabaseId int, @SchemaId int
  , @TableId int, @IndexId int;

-- Create the index list table
DECLARE @IndexList TABLE
(    DatabaseName nvarchar(128) NOT NULL
   , DatabaseId int NOT NULL
   , SchemaName nvarchar(128) NOT NULL
   , SchemaId int NOT NULL
   , TableName nvarchar(128) NOT NULL
   , TableId int NOT NULL
   , IndexName nvarchar(128)
```

```
    , IndexId int NOT NULL
    , Fragmentation decimal(20, 2)
    , PRIMARY KEY (DatabaseId, SchemaId, TableId, IndexId)
);

-- Populate index list table
INSERT INTO @IndexList
(    DatabaseName, DatabaseId
    , SchemaName, SchemaId
    , TableName, TableId
    , IndexName, IndexId
    , Fragmentation
)
 SELECT db_name(), db_id()
        , s.Name, s.schema_id
        , t.Name, t.object_id
        , i.Name, i.index_id
        , MAX(ip.avg_fragmentation_in_percent)
   FROM sys.tables t
  INNER JOIN sys.schemas s ON
        t.schema_id = s.schema_id
  INNER JOIN sys.indexes i ON
        t.object_id = i.object_id
  INNER JOIN sys.dm_db_index_physical_stats (db_id(), NULL, NULL, NULL, NULL) ip ON
        ip.object_id = t.object_id AND ip.index_id = i.index_id
  WHERE ip.database_id = db_id()
  GROUP BY
        s.Name
        , s.schema_id
        , t.Name
        , t.object_id
        , i.Name
        , i.index_id;

-- If user specified rebuild, use a cursor to loop through all indexes
-- rebuild them
IF @ShowOrRebuild = N'rebuild'
BEGIN

-- Declare a cursor to create the dynamic SQL statements
DECLARE Index_Cursor CURSOR FAST_FORWARD
    FOR SELECT SchemaName, TableName, IndexName
          FROM @IndexList
         WHERE Fragmentation > @MaxFrag
         ORDER BY Fragmentation DESC, TableName ASC, IndexName ASC;

-- Open the cursor for reading
OPEN Index_Cursor;
-- Loop through all the tables in the database
FETCH NEXT FROM Index_Cursor
          INTO @Schema, @Table, @Index;
```

```
WHILE @@FETCH_STATUS = 0
BEGIN -- Create ALTER INDEX statement to rebuild index
    SET @Sql = N'ALTER INDEX ' +
        QUOTENAME(RTRIM(@Index)) + N' ON ' + QUOTENAME(RTRIM(@Table)) + N'.' +
        QUOTENAME(RTRIM(@Table)) + N' REBUILD WITH (ONLINE = OFF); ';

    PRINT @Sql;

    -- Execute dynamic SQL
    EXEC (@Sql);

    -- Get the next index
    FETCH NEXT FROM Index_Cursor
    INTO @Schema, @Table, @Index;
END

-- Close and deallocate the cursor.
CLOSE Index_Cursor;
DEALLOCATE Index_Cursor;
END

-- Show results, including old fragmentation and new fragmentation
-- after index rebuild
 SELECT il.DatabaseName
        , il.SchemaName
        , il.TableName
        , il.IndexName
        , il.Fragmentation AS FragmentationStart
        , MAX(   CAST(ip.avg_fragmentation_in_percent AS DECIMAL(20, 2))
            ) AS FragmentationEnd
   FROM @IndexList il
   INNER JOIN sys.dm_db_index_physical_stats(@DatabaseId, NULL, NULL, NULL, NULL) ip ON
        DatabaseId = ip.database_id AND
        TableId = ip.object_id AND
        IndexId = ip.index_id
  GROUP BY
        il.DatabaseName
        , il.SchemaName
        , il.TableName
        , il.IndexName
        , il.Fragmentation
  ORDER BY
        Fragmentation DESC
        , TableName ASC
        , IndexName ASC;
  RETURN;
END
GO

-- Execute index rebuild stored procedure
EXEC dbo.RebuildIndexes N'rebuild', 30;
```

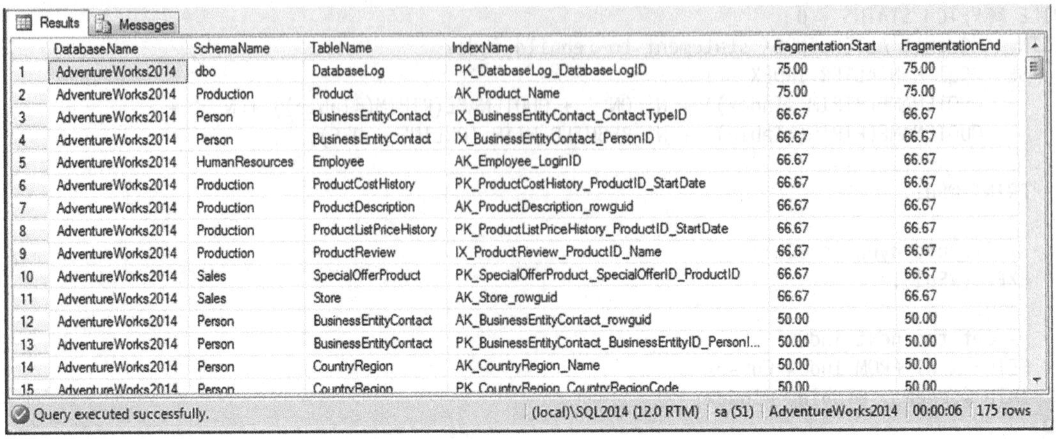

Results | Messages

	DatabaseName	SchemaName	TableName	IndexName	FragmentationStart	FragmentationEnd
1	AdventureWorks2014	dbo	DatabaseLog	PK_DatabaseLog_DatabaseLogID	75.00	75.00
2	AdventureWorks2014	Production	Product	AK_Product_Name	75.00	75.00
3	AdventureWorks2014	Person	BusinessEntityContact	IX_BusinessEntityContact_ContactTypeID	66.67	66.67
4	AdventureWorks2014	Person	BusinessEntityContact	IX_BusinessEntityContact_PersonID	66.67	66.67
5	AdventureWorks2014	HumanResources	Employee	AK_Employee_LoginID	66.67	66.67
6	AdventureWorks2014	Production	ProductCostHistory	PK_ProductCostHistory_ProductID_StartDate	66.67	66.67
7	AdventureWorks2014	Production	ProductDescription	AK_ProductDescription_rowguid	66.67	66.67
8	AdventureWorks2014	Production	ProductListPriceHistory	PK_ProductListPriceHistory_ProductID_StartDate	66.67	66.67
9	AdventureWorks2014	Production	ProductReview	IX_ProductReview_ProductID_Name	66.67	66.67
10	AdventureWorks2014	Sales	SpecialOfferProduct	PK_SpecialOfferProduct_SpecialOfferID_ProductID	66.67	66.67
11	AdventureWorks2014	Sales	Store	AK_Store_rowguid	66.67	66.67
12	AdventureWorks2014	Person	BusinessEntityContact	AK_BusinessEntityContact_rowguid	50.00	50.00
13	AdventureWorks2014	Person	BusinessEntityContact	PK_BusinessEntityContact_BusinessEntityID_PersonI...	50.00	50.00
14	AdventureWorks2014	Person	CountryRegion	AK_CountryRegion_Name	50.00	50.00
15	AdventureWorks2014	Person	CountryRegion	PK_CountryRegion_CountryRegionCode	50.00	50.00

Query executed successfully. | (local)\SQL2014 (12.0 RTM) | sa (51) | AdventureWorks2014 | 00:00:06 | 175 rows

***Figure 3-12.** The results of a cursor-based index rebuild in the AdventureWorks database*

The dbo.RebuildIndexes procedure shown in Listing 3-17 populates a table variable with the information necessary to identify all indexes on all tables in the current database. It also uses the sys.dm_db_indexphysical_stats catalog function to retrieve initial index fragmentation information:

```
--Populate index list table

INSERT INTO @IndexList
(
DatabaseName,
DatabaseId,
SchemaName,
SchemaId,
TableName,
TableId,
IndexName,
IndexId,
Fragmentation
)
SELECT
  db_name(),
db_id(),
s.Name,
s.schema_id,
t.Name,
t.object_id,
i.Name,
i.index_id,
MAX(ip.avg_fragmentation_in_percent)
FROM sys.tables t
INNER JOIN sys.schemas s
  ON t.schema_id = s.schema_id
INNER JOIN sys.indexes i
  ON t.object_id = i.object_id
```

```
INNER JOIN sys.dm_db_index_physical_stats (db_id(), NULL, NULL,NULL, NULL) ip
ON ip.object_id = t.object_id
   AND ip.index_id = i.index_id
WHERE ip.database_id = db_id()
 GROUP BY
   s.Name,
   s.schema_id,
   t.Name,
   t.object_id,
   i.Name,
   i.index_id;
```

If you specify a rebuild action when you call the procedure, it creates a cursor to loop through the rows of the @IndexList table, but only for indexes with a fragmentation percentage higher than the level you specified when calling the procedure:

```
-- Declare a cursor to create the dynamic SOL statements
DECLARE Index_Cursor CURSOR FAST_FORWARD
FOR
SELECT
  SchemaName,
  TableName,
  IndexName FROM @IndexList
WHERE Fragmentation > @MaxFrag
ORDER BY
  Fragmentation DESC,
  TableName ASC,
  IndexName ASC;
```

The procedure then loops through all the indexes in the @IndexList table, creating an ALTER INDEX statement to rebuild each index. Each ALTER INDEX statement is created as dynamic SQL to be printed and executed using the SQL PRINT and EXEC statements:

```
-- Open the cursor for reading
OPEN Index_Cursor;

-- Loop through all the tables in the database
FETCH NEXT FROM Index_Cursor
INTO @Schema,@Table, @Index;

WHILE @@FETCH_STATUS = 0
BEGIN
 -- Create ALTER INDEX statement to rebuild index
SET @Sql =N'ALTER INDEX ' +
 QUOTENAME(RTRIM(@Index)) + N' ON ' + QUOTENAME(l@Schema) + N'.' +
 QUOTENAME(RTRIM(@Table)) + N' REBUILD WITH (ONLINE = OFF); ';

PRINT @Sql;

-- Execute dynamic SQL
EXEC (@Sql);
```

```
-- Get the next index
FETCH NEXT FROM Index_Cursor
INTO @Schema, @Table, @lndex;
END

-- Close and deallocate the cursor.
CLOSE Index_Cursor;
DEALLOCATE Index_Cursor;
```

The dynamic SQL statements generated by the procedure look similar to the following:

```
ALTER INDEX [IX_PurchaseOrderHeader_EmployeeID]
ON [Purchasing].[PurchaseOrderHeader] REBUILD WITH (ONLINE = OFF);
```

The balance of the code simply displays the results, including the new fragmentation percentage after the indexes are rebuilt.

NO DBCC?

Notice in the example code in Listing 3-17 that we specifically avoided using database console commands (DBCCs) like DBCC DBREINDEX and DBCC SHOWCONTIG to manage index fragmentation and rebuild the indexes in the database. There is a very good reason for this: these DBCC statements, and many others, are deprecated. Microsoft is planning to do away with many common DBCC statements in favor of catalog views and enhanced T-SQL statement syntax. The DBCC DBREINDEX statement, for instance, is being replaced by the ALTER INDEX REBUILD syntax, and DBCC SHOWCONTIG is being replaced by the sys.dm_db_index_physical_stats catalog function. Keep this in mind when porting code from legacy systems and creating new code.

Another situation where we advise developers to use cursors is when the solution required is a one-off task, a set-based solution would be very complex, and time is short. Examples include creating complex running sum-type calculations and performing complex data-scrubbing routines on a very limited timeframe. We don't using a cursor as a permanent production application solution without exploring all available set-based options. Remember that whenever you use a cursor, you override SQL Server's automatic optimizations—and the SQL Server query engine has much better and more current information to optimize operations than you have access to at any given point in time. Also keep in mind that tasks you consider extremely complex today will become much easier as SQL's set-based processing becomes second nature to you.

CURSORS, CURSORS EVERYWHERE

Although cursors commonly get a lot of bad press from SQL gurus, there is nothing inherently evil about them. They're just another tool in the toolkit and should be viewed as such. What *is* wrong is the ways in which developers abuse them. Generally speaking, as much as 90% of the time, cursors absolutely are not the best tool for the job when you're writing T-SQL code. Unfortunately, many SQL newbies find set-based logic difficult to grasp at first. Cursors provide a comfort zone for procedural developers because they lend themselves to procedural design patterns.

One of the worst design patterns you can adopt is the "cursors, cursors everywhere" design pattern. Believe it or not, there are developers who have been writing SQL code for years and have never bothered learning about SQL's set-based processing. These developers tend to approach every SQL problem as if it were a C# or Visual Basic problem, and their code tends to reflect it with "cursors, cursors everywhere." Replacing cursor-based code with WHILE loops doesn't solve the problem. Simulating the behavior of cursors with WHILE loops doesn't fix the design flaw inherent in the cursor-based solution: row-by-row processing of data. WHILE loops may, under some circumstances, perform comparably to cursors; and in some situations even a cursor will outperform a WHILE loop.

Another horrible design pattern results from what are actually best practices in other procedural languages. Code reuse isn't SQL's strong point. Many programmers coming from object-oriented languages that promote heavy code reuse tend to write layers and layers of SPs that call one another. These SPs often have cursors, and cursors within cursors, to feed each layer of procedures. Although it does promote code reuse, this design pattern causes severe performance degradation. A commonly used term for this type of design pattern, popularized by SQL professional Jeff Moden, is "row-by-agonizing-row" (RBAR) processing. This design pattern is high on our top-ten list of ways to abuse SQL Server and will cause you far more problems than it ever solves. SQL Server 2014 offers a feature, the table-valued parameter, that may help increase manageability and performance of the layered SP design methodology. Chapter 5 discusses table-valued parameters.

SQL Server supports syntax for both ISO standard cursors and T-SQL extended syntax cursors. The ISO standard supports the following cursor options:

- The INSENSITIVE option makes a temporary copy of the cursor result set and uses that copy to fulfill cursor requests. This means changes to the underlying tables aren't reflected when you request rows from the cursor.

- The SCROLL option allows you to use all cursor fetch options to position the cursor on any row in the cursor result set. The cursor fetch options include FIRST, LAST, NEXT, PRIOR, ABSOLUTE, and RELATIVE. If the SCROLL option isn't specified, only the NEXT cursor fetch option is allowed.

- The READ ONLY option in the cursor FOR clause prevents updates to the underlying data through the cursor. In a non-read only cursor, you can update the underlying data with the WHERE CURRENT OF clause in the UPDATE and DELETE statements.

- The UPDATE OF option allows you to specify a list of updatable columns in the cursor's result set. You can specify UPDATE without the OF keyword and its associated column list to allow updates to all columns.

The T-SQL extended syntax provides many more options than the ISO syntax. In addition to supporting read-only cursors, the UPDATE OF option, the SCROLL option, and insensitive cursors (using the STATIC keyword), T-SQL extended syntax cursors support the following options:

- Cursors that are local to the current batch, procedure, or trigger in which they're created via the LOCAL keyword. Cursors that are global to the connection in which they're created can be defined using the GLOBAL keyword.

- The FORWARDONLY option, which is the opposite of the SCROLL option, allowing you to only fetch rows from the cursor using the NEXT option.

- The KEYSET option, which specifies that the number and order of rows is fixed at the time the cursor is created. Trying to fetch rows that are subsequently deleted doesn't succeed, and a @@FETCH_STATUS value of -2 is returned.

- The DYNAMIC option, which specifies a cursor that reflects all data changes made to the rows in its underlying result set. This type of cursor is one of the slowest, because every change to the underlying data must be reflected whenever you scroll to a new row of the result set.

- The FAST_FORWARD option, which specifies a performance-optimized combination forward-only/read-only cursor.

- The SCROLLLOCKS option, which locks underlying data rows as they're read to ensure that data modifications will succeed. The SCROLLLOCKS option is mutually exclusive with the FAST_FORWARD and STATIC options.

- The OPTIMISTIC option, which uses timestamps to determine if a row has changed since the cursor was loaded. If a row has changed, the OPTIMISTIC option doesn't allow the current cursor to update the same row. The OPTIMISTIC option is incompatible with the FAST_FORWARD option.

- The TYPEWARNING option, which sends a warning if a cursor will be automatically converted from the requested type to another type. This can happen, for instance, if SQL Server needs to convert a forward-only cursor to a static cursor.

■ **Note** If you don't specify a cursor as LOCAL or GLOBAL, cursors that are created default to the setting defined by the default to local cursor database setting.

CURSOR COMPARISONS

Cursors come in several flavors, and you could spend a lot of time just trying to figure out which one you need to perform a given task. Most of the time, you need forward-only/read-only cursors. These cursors are efficient because they move in only one direction and don't need to perform updates on the underlying data. Maximizing cursor efficiency by choosing the right type of cursor for the job is a quick-win strategy that you should keep in mind when you have to resort to a cursor.

Summary

This chapter introduced SQL 3VL, which consists of three logical result values: true, false, and unknown. This is a key concept to understanding SQL development in general, but it can be a foreign idea to developers coming from backgrounds in other programming languages. If you're not yet familiar with the 3VL chart, we highly recommend revisiting Figure 3-1. This chart summarizes the logic that governs SQL 3VL.

This chapter also introduced T-SQL's control-of-flow statement offerings, which allow you to branch conditionally and unconditionally, loop, handle exceptions, and force delays in your code. We also covered the two flavors of CASE expression and some of the more advanced uses of CASE, including dynamic pivot table queries and CASE-based functions like COALESCE and NULLIF.

Finally, we discussed the redheaded stepchild of SQL development, the cursor. Although cursors commonly get a bad rep, there's nothing inherently bad about them; the problem is with how people use them. The discussion of cursors focused on some common scenarios where they might be considered the best tool for the job, including administrative and complex one-off tasks. Finally, we presented the options available for ISO-compliant cursors and T-SQL extended syntax cursors, both of which are supported by SQL Server 2014.

The next chapter begins to discuss T-SQL programmability features, starting with an in-depth look at T-SQL UDFs in all their various forms.

EXERCISES

1. [True/False] SQL 3VL supports the logical result values true, false, and unknown.

2. [Choose one] SQL NULL represents which of the following?

   a. An unknown or missing value

   b. The number 0

   c. An empty (zero-length) string

   d. All of the above

3. [True/False] The BEGIN and END keywords delimit a statement block and limit the scope of variables declared in that statement block, like curly braces ({ }) in C#.

4. [Fill in the blank] The ____keyword forces a WHILE loop to terminate immediately.

5. [True/False] The TRY...CATCH block can catch every possible SQL Server error.

6. [Fill in the blanks] SQL CASE expressions come in two forms, ___ and ___.

7. [Choose all that apply] T-SQL supports which of the following cursor options?

   a. Read-only cursors

   b. Forward-only cursors

   c. Backward-only cursors

   d. Write-only cursors

8. Modify the code in Listing 3-10 to generate a pivot table result set that returns the total dollar amount (TotalDue) of orders by region, instead of the count of orders by region.

Summary

This chapter introduces SQL, which consists of three logical result values: true, false, and unknown. This is a key concept to understanding SQL development in general, but it can be a foreign idea to developers coming from backgrounds in other programming languages. If you come to familiar yet the 3VL concept is highly recognize in relating figure 3-1. This chapter covers the logic that governs SQL 3VL.

This chapter also introduced T-SQL's control-of-flow statements offerings, which allow you to branch conditionally and unconditionally, loop, handle exceptions, and force delays in your code. We also covered the two flavors of CASE expression and some of the more advanced uses of CASE, including the dynamic pivot table queries and CASE-based functions like COALESCE and NULLIF.

Finally, we discussed the efficiency and speed lid of SQL development, the cursor. Although cursors consistently get a bad rap, there's nothing inherently bad about them, the problem is with how people use or misuse them. The discussion of cursors focuses on common scenarios where they might be considered the best tool for the job, including administrative and complex one-off tasks. Finally, we presented the options available for the complex cursors and T-SQL extended cursor resources, both of which are supported by the SQL Server 2014.

The next chapter begins to discuss T-SQL programmability features, starting with an in-depth look at SQL UDFs in all their various forms.

---

1. The three SQL 3VL result values are true, false, and unknown.

2. [Choose one] SQL can return the result which of the following:

   a. An unknown or missing value

   b. The number 0

   c. An alphabetic identity string

   d. All of the above

3. [Fill in the blank] A T-SQL BEGIN-END statement block bounds the scope within a declared in that statement block, becomes only inside of that job.

4. [Fill in the blank] The ___ keyword forces a code delay for a specific time entry.

5. [True/False] Properly written T-SQL work can alleviate many possible SQL Server error.

6. [Fill in the blank] SQL CASE expressions come in two forms ___ and ___.

7. [Choose one] true/false T-SQL supports which of the following cursor options.

   a. Read-only cursors

   b. Forward-only cursors

   c. Backward-only cursors

   d. Write-only cursors

8. Modify the cursor in Listing 3-10 to generate a pivot table result set that returns the total dollar amount of orders by region, instead of the count of orders by region.

CHAPTER 4

■ ■ ■

User-Defined Functions

Each new version of SQL Server features improvements to T-SQL that make development easier. SQL Server 2000 introduced (among other things) the concept of user-defined functions (UDFs). Like functions in other programming languages, T-SQL UDFs provide a convenient way for developers to define routines that accept parameters, perform actions based on those parameters, and return data to the caller. T-SQL functions come in three flavors: inline table-valued functions (TVFs), multistatement TVFs, and scalar functions. SQL Server 2014 also supports the ability to create CLR integration UDFs, which are discussed in Chapter 15.

Scalar Functions

Basically, a scalar UDF is a function that accepts zero or more parameters and returns a single scalar value as the result. You're probably already familiar with scalar functions in mathematics, and with T-SQL's built-in scalar functions (such as ABS and SUBSTRING). The CREATE FUNCTION statement allows you to create custom scalar functions that behave like the built-in scalar functions.

To demonstrate scalar UDFs, let's a trip back in time to high school geometry class. In accordance with the rules passed down from Euclid, this UDF accepts a circle's radius and returns the area of the circle using the formula area = $\pi \times r^2$. Listing 4-1 demonstrates this simple scalar UDF.

Listing 4-1. Simple Scalar UDF

```
CREATE FUNCTION dbo.CalculateCircleArea (@Radius float =1.0)
RETURNS float
WITH RETURNS NULL ON NULL INPUT
AS
BEGIN
   RETURN PI() * POWER(@Radius, 2);
END;
```

The first line of the CREATE FUNCTION statement defines the schema and name of the function using a standard SQL Server two-part name (dbo.CalculateCircleArea) and a single required parameter, the radius of the circle (@Radius). The @Radius parameter is defined as a T-SQL float type. The parameter is assigned a default value of 1.0 by the = 1.0 after the parameter declaration:

```
CREATE FUNCTION dbo.CalculateCircleArea (@Radius float =1.0)
```

The next line contains the RETURNS keyword, which specifies the data type of the result that will be returned by the UDF. In this instance, the RETURNS keyword indicates that the UDF will return a float result:

```
RETURNS float
```

The third line contains additional options following the WITH keyword. The example uses the RETURNS NULL ON NULL INPUT function option for a performance improvement. The RETURNS NULL ON NULL INPUT option is a performance-enhancing option that automatically returns NULL if any of the parameters passed in are NULL. The performance enhancement occurs because SQL Server won't execute the body of the function if a NULL is passed in and this option is specified:

```
WITH RETURNS NULL ON NULL INPUT
```

The AS keyword indicates the start of the function body which must be enclosed in the T-SQL BEGIN and END keywords. The sample function in Listing 4-1 is very simple, consisting of a single RETURN statement that immediately returns the value of the circle area calculation. The RETURN statement must be the last statement before the END keyword in every scalar UDF:

```
RETURN PI() * POWER(@radius, 2);
```

You can test this simple UDF with a few SELECT statements like the following. The results are shown in Figure 4-1:

```
SELECT dbo.CalculateCircleArea(10);
SELECT dbo.CalculateCircleArea(NULL);
SELECT dbo.CalculateCircleArea(2.5);
```

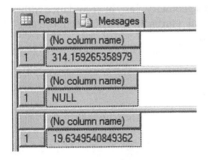

Figure 4-1. *The results of the sample circle area calculations*

UDF PARAMETERS

UDF parameters operate similarly to, but slightly differently from, stored procedure (SP) parameters. It's important to be aware of the differences. For instance, if you create a UDF that accepts no parameters, you still need to include empty parentheses after the function name—both when creating and when invoking the function. Some built-in functions, like the PI() function used in Listing 4-1, which represents the value of the constant π (3.14159265358979), don't take parameters. Notice that when the function is called in the UDF, it's still called with empty parentheses.

When SPs are assigned default values, you can simply leave the parameter off your parameter list completely when calling the procedure. This isn't an option with UDFs. To use a UDF default value, you must use the `DEFAULT` keyword when calling the UDF. To use the default value for the `@radius` parameter of the example `dbo.CalculateCircleArea` UDF, you call the UDF like this:

```
SELECT dbo.CalculateCircleArea (DEFAULT);
```

Finally, SPs have no equivalent to the `RETURNS NULL ON NULL INPUT` option. You can simulate this functionality to some extent by checking your parameters for `NULL` immediately on entering the SP, though. SPs are discussed in greater detail in Chapter 5.

UDFs provide several creation-time options that allow you to improve performance and security, including the following:

- The `ENCRYPTION` option can be used to store your UDF in the database in obfuscated format. Note that this isn't true encryption, but rather an easily circumvented obfuscation of your code. See the "UDF 'Encryption'" sidebar for more information.

- The `SCHEMABINDING` option indicates that your UDF will be bound to database objects referenced in the body of the function. With `SCHEMABINDING` turned on, attempts to change or drop referenced tables and other database objects result in an error. This helps to prevent inadvertent changes to tables and other database objects that can break your UDF. Additionally, the SQL Server Database Engine team has published information indicating that `SCHEMABINDING` can improve the performance of UDFs, even if they don't reference other database objects (`http://blogs.msdn.com/b/sqlprogrammability/archive/2006/05/12/596424.aspx`).

- The `CALLED ON NULL INPUT` option is the opposite of `RETURNS NULL ON NULL INPUT`. When `CALLED ON NULL INPUT` is specified, SQL Server executes the body of the function even if one or more parameters are `NULL`. `CALLED ON NULL INPUT` is a default option for all scalar-valued functions.

- The `EXECUTE AS` option manages caller security on UDFs. You can specify that the UDF be executed as any of the following:

  - `CALLER` indicates that the UDF should run under the security context of the user calling the function. This is the default.

  - `SELF` indicates that the UDF should run under the security context of the user who created (or altered) the function.

  - `OWNER` indicates that the UDF should run under the security context of the owner of the UDF (or the owner of the schema containing the UDF).

  - Finally, you can specify that the UDF should run under the security context of a specific user by specifying a username.

UDF "ENCRYPTION"

Using the ENCRYPTION option on UDFs performs a simple obfuscation of your code. It actually does little more than "keep honest people honest," and in reality it tends to be more trouble than it's worth. Many developers and DBAs have spent precious time scouring the Internet for tools to decrypt their database objects because they were convinced the scripts in their source control database were out of sync with the production database. Keep in mind that those same decryption tools are available to anyone with an Internet connection and a browser. If you write commercial database scripts or perform database consulting services, your best (and really only) protection against curious DBAs and developers reverse-engineering and modifying your code is a well-written contract. Keep this in mind when deciding whether to "encrypt" your database objects.

Recursion in Scalar User-Defined Functions

Now that you've learned the basics, let's hang out in math class for a few more minutes to talk about recursion. Like most procedural programming languages that allow function definitions, T-SQL allows recursion in UDFs. There's hardly a better way to demonstrate recursion than the most basic recursive algorithm around: the factorial function.

For those who put factorials out of their minds immediately after graduation, here's a brief rundown of what they are. A factorial is the product of all natural (or counting) numbers less than or equal to n, where $n > 0$. Factorials are represented in mathematics with the bang notation: $n!$. As an example, $5! = 1 \times 2 \times 3 \times 4 \times 5 = 120$. The simple scalar dbo.CalculateFactorial UDF in Listing 4-2 calculates a factorial recursively for an integer parameter passed into it.

Listing 4-2. Recursive Scalar UDF

```
CREATE FUNCTION dbo.CalculateFactorial (@n int = 1)
RETURNS decimal(38, 0)
WITH  RETURNS NULL ON NULL INPUT
AS
BEGIN
        RETURN
        (CASE
            WHEN @n <= 0 THEN NULL
            WHEN @n > 1 THEN CAST(@n AS float) * dbo.CalculateFactorial (@n - 1)
            WHEN @n = 1 THEN 1
        END);
END;
```

The first few lines are similar to Listing 4-1. The function accepts a single int parameter and returns a scalar decimal value. The RETURNS NULL ON NULL INPUT option returns NULL immediately if NULL is passed in:

```
CREATE FUNCTION dbo.CalculateFactorial (@n int = 1)
RETURNS decimal(38, 0)
WITH RETURNS NULL ON NULL INPUT
```

You return a decimal result in this example because of the limitations of the int and bigint types. Specifically, the int type overflows at 13! and bigint bombs out at 21!. In order to put the UDF through its paces, you have to allow it to return results up to 32!, as discussed later in this section. As in Listing 4-1, the body of this UDF is a single RETURN statement, this time with a searched CASE expression:

```
RETURN (CASE
WHEN @n <= 0 THEN NULL
WHEN @n > 1 THEN CAST(@n AS float) * dbo.CalculateFactorial (@n - 1)
WHEN @n = 1 THEN 1 END);
```

The CASE expression checks the value of the UDF parameter, @n. If @n is 0 or negative, dbo. CalculateFactorial returns NULL because the result is undefined. If @n is greater than 1, dbo. CalculateFactorial returns @n * dbo.CalculateFactorial(@n - 1), the recursive part of the UDF. This ensures that the UDF will continue calling itself recursively, multiplying the current value of @n by (@n-1)!.

Finally, when @n reaches 1, the UDF returns 1. This is the part of dbo.CalculateFactorial that stops the recursion. Without the check for @n = 1, you could theoretically end up in an infinite recursive loop. In practice, however, SQL Server saves you from yourself by limiting you to a maximum of 32 levels of recursion. Demonstrating the 32-level limit on recursion is why it was important for the UDF to return results up to 32!. Following are some examples of dbo.CalculateFactorial calls with various parameters, and their results:

```
SELECT dbo.CalculateFactorial(NULL); -- Returns NULL
SELECT dbo.CalculateFactorial(-1);   -- Returns NULL
SELECT dbo.CalculateFactorial(0);    -- Returns NULL
SELECT dbo.CalculateFactorial(5);    -- Returns 120
SELECT dbo.CalculateFactorial(32);   -- Returns 263130836933693520000000000000000000
```

As you can see, the dbo.CalculateFactorial function easily handles the 32 levels of recursion required to calculate 32!. If you try to go beyond that limit, you get an error message. Executing the following code, which attempts 33 levels of recursion, doesn't work:

```
SELECT dbo.CalculateFactorial(33);
```

This causes SQL Server to grumble loudly with an error message similar to the following:

```
Msg 217, Level 16, State 1, Line 1
Maximum stored procedure, function, trigger, or view nesting level exceeded (limit 32).
```

MORE THAN ONE WAY TO SKIN A CAT

The 32-level recursion limit is a hard limit; that is, you can't programmatically change it through server or database settings. This really isn't as bad a limitation as you might think. Very rarely do you actually need to recursively call a UDF more than 32 times, and doing so could result in a severe performance penalty. There's generally more than one way to get the job done. You can work around the 32-level recursion limitation in the dbo.CalculateFactorial function by rewriting it with a WHILE loop or using a recursive common table expression (CTE), as shown here:

```
CREATE FUNCTION dbo.CalculateFactorial (@n int = 1)
RETURNS float
WITH RETURNS NULL ON NULL INPUT
```

```
AS
BEGIN
    DECLARE @result float;
    SET @result = NULL;

IF @n > 0
BEGIN
    SET @result = 1.0;

WITH Numbers (num)
AS (
    SELECT 1
    UNION ALL
    SELECT num + 1
    FROM Numbers
    WHERE num < @n
    )
    SELECT @result = @result * num
    FROM Numbers;
 END;
 RETURN @result;
END;
```

This rewrite of the `dbo.CalculateFactorial` function averts the recursive function call limit by eliminating the recursive function calls. Instead, it pushes the recursion back into the body of the function through the use of a recursive common table expression (CTE). By default, SQL Server allows up to 100 levels of recursion in a CTE (you can override this with the MAXRECURSION option), greatly expanding your factorial calculation power. With this function, you can easily find out that 33! is 8.68331761881189E+36, or even that 100! is 9.33262154439441E+157. The important idea to take away from this discussion is that although recursive function calls have hard limits on them, you can often work around those limitations using other T-SQL functionality.

Also keep in mind that although you used factorial calculation as a simple example of recursion, this method is considered naive, and there are several more-efficient methods of calculating factorials.

Procedural Code in User-Defined Functions

So far, you've seen simple functions that demonstrate the basic points of scalar UDFs. But in all likelihood, unless you're implementing business logic for a swimming pool installation company, you aren't likely to need to spend much time calculating the area of a circle in T-SQL.

A common problem that you have a much greater chance of running into is name-based searching. T-SQL offers tools for exact matching, partial matching, and even limited pattern matching via the LIKE predicate. T-SQL even offers built-in phonetic matching (sound-alike matching) through the built-in SOUNDEX function.

Heavy-duty approximate matching usually requires a more advanced tool, like a better phonetic matching algorithm. Let's use one of these algorithms, the New York State Identification and Intelligence System (NYSIIS) algorithm, to demonstrate procedural code in UDFs.

THE SOUNDEX ALGORITHM

The NYSIIS algorithm is an improvement on the Soundex phonetic encoding algorithm, itself nearly 90 years old. The NYSIIS algorithm converts groups of one, two, or three alphabetic characters (known as *n-grams*) in names to a phonetic ("sounds like") approximation. This makes it easier to search for names that have similar pronunciations but different spellings, such as Smythe and Smith. As mentioned in this section, SQL Server provides a built-in SOUNDEX function, but Soundex provides very poor accuracy and usually results in many false hits. NYSIIS and other modern algorithms provide much better results than Soundex.

To demonstrate procedural code in UDFs, you can implement a UDF that phonetically encodes names using NYSIIS encoding rules. The rules for NYSIIS phonetic encoding are relatively simple, with the majority of the rules requiring simple n-gram substitutions. The following is a complete list of NYSIIS encoding rules:

1. Remove all non-alphabetic characters from the name.

2. The first characters of the name are encoded according to the n-gram substitutions shown in the Start of Name table in Figure 4-2. In Figure 4-2, the n-grams shown to the left of the arrows are replaced with the n-grams to the right of the arrows during the encoding process.

NYSIIS Phonetic Encoding Rules

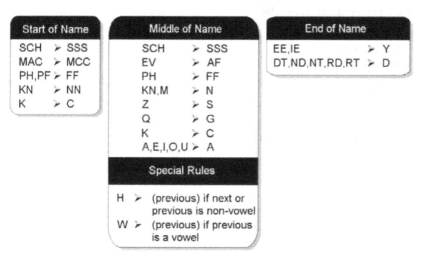

Figure 4-2. NYSIIS phonetic encoding rules / character substitutions

3. The last characters of the name are encoded according to the n-gram substitutions shown in the End of Name table in Figure 4-2.

4. The first character of the encoded value is set to the first character of the name.

5. After the first and last n-grams are encoded, all remaining characters in the name are encoded according to the n-gram substitutions shown in the Middle of Name table in Figure 4-2.

6. All side-by-side duplicate characters in the encoded name are reduced to a single character. This means that *AA* is reduced to *A* and *SS* is reduced to *S*.

7. If the last character of the encoded name is *S*, it's removed.

8. If the last characters of the encoded name are *AY*, they're replaced with *Y*.

9. If the last character of the encoded name is *A*, it's removed.

10. The result is truncated to a maximum length of six characters.

You could use some fairly large CASE expressions to implement these rules, but let's go with a more flexible option: using a replacement table. This table will contain the majority of the replacement rules in three columns,
as described here:

- Location: This column tells the UDF whether the rule should be applied to the start, end, or middle of the name.

- NGram: This column is the n-gram, or sequence of characters, that will be encoded. These n-grams correspond to the left side of the arrows in Figure 4-2.

- Replacement: This column represents the replacement value for the corresponding n-gram on the same row. These character sequences correspond to the right side of the arrows in Figure 4-2.

Listing 4-3 is a CREATE TABLE statement that builds the NYSIIS phonetic encoding replacement rules table.

Listing 4-3. Creating the NYSIIS Replacement Rules Table

```
-- Create the NYSIIS replacement rules table
CREATE TABLE dbo.NYSIIS_Replacements
  (Location nvarchar(10) NOT NULL,
   NGram nvarchar(10) NOT NULL,
   Replacement nvarchar(10) NOT NULL,
   PRIMARY KEY (Location, NGram));
```

Listing 4-4 is a single INSERT statement that uses row constructors to populate all the NYSIIS replacement rules, as shown in Figure 4-2.

Listing 4-4. INSERT Statement to Populate the NYSIIS Replacement Rules Table

```
INSERT INTO NYSIIS_Replacements (Location, NGram, Replacement)
  VALUES(N'End', N'DT', N'DD'),
(N'End', N'EE', N'YY'),
(N'End', N'IE', N'YY'),
(N'End', N'ND', N'DD'),
(N'End', N'NT', N'DD'),
(N'End', N'RD', N'DD'),
(N'End', N'RT', N'DD'),
(N'Mid', N'A', N'A'),
(N'Mid', N'E', N'A'),
(N'Mid', N'T', N'A'),
(N'Mid', N'K', N'C'),
(N'Mid', N'M', N'N'),
(N'Mid', N'O', N'A'),
(N'Mid', N'Q', N'G'),
```

```
      (N'Mid', N'U', N'A'),
      (N'Mid', N'Z', N'S'),
      (N'Mid', N'AW', N'AA'),
      (N'Mid', N'EV', N'AF'),
      (N'Mid', N'EW', N'AA'),
      (N'Mid', N'lW', N'AA'),
      (N'Mid', N'KN', N'NN'),
      (N'Mid', N'OW', N'AA'),
      (N'Mid', N'PH', N'FF'),
      (N'Mid', N'UW', N'AA'),
      (N'Mid', N'SCH', N'SSS'),
      (N'Start', N'K', N'C'),
      (N'Start', N'KN', N'NN'),
      (N'Start', N'PF', N'FF'),
      (N'Start', N'PH', N'FF'),
      (N'Start', N'MAC', N'MCC'),
      (N'Start', N'SCH', N'SSS');
GO
```

Listing 4-5 is the UDF that encodes a string using NYSIIS. This UDF demonstrates the complexity of the control-of-flow logic that can be implemented in a scalar UDF.

Listing 4-5. Function to Encode Strings Using NYSIIS

```
CREATE FUNCTION dbo.EncodeNYSIIS
(
    @String nvarchar(100)
)
RETURNS nvarchar(6)
WITH RETURNS NULL ON NULL INPUT
AS
BEGIN
  DECLARE @Result nvarchar(100);
  SET @Result = UPPER(@String);

-- Step 1: Remove All Nonalphabetic Characters
WITH Numbers (Num)
AS
(
  SELECT 1

UNION ALL

SELECT Num + 1
FROM Numbers
WHERE Num < LEN(@Result)
)
SELECT @Result = STUFF
(
  @Result,
  Num,
  1,
```

```
 CASE WHEN SUBSTRING(@Result, Num, 1) >= N'A'
      AND SUBSTRING(@Result, Num, 1) <= N'Z'
      THEN SUBSTRING(@Result, Num, 1)
      ELSE N'.'
 END )
FROM Numbers;

SET @Result = REPLACE(@Result, N'.', N'');

-- Step 2: Replace the Start N-gram
SELECT TOP (1) @Result = STUFF
(
  @Result,
  1,
  LEN(NGram),
  Replacement
)
FROM dbo.NYSIIS_Replacements
WHERE Location = N'Start'
  AND SUBSTRING(@Result, 1, LEN(NGram)) = NGram
ORDER BY LEN(NGram) DESC;

-- Step 3: Replace the End N-gram
SELECT TOP (1) @Result = STUFF
 (
   @Result,
   LEN(@Result) - LEN(NGram) + 1,
   LEN(NGram),
   Replacement
 )
FROM dbo.NYSIIS_Replacements
WHERE Location = N'End'
  AND SUBSTRING(@Result, LEN(@Result) - LEN(NGram) + 1, LEN(NGram)) = NGram
ORDER BY LEN(NGram) DESC;

-- Step 4: Save the First Letter of the Name
DECLARE @FirstLetter nchar(1);
SET @FirstLetter = SUBSTRING(@Result, 1, 1);

-- Step 5: Replace All Middle N-grams
DECLARE @Replacement nvarchar(10);
DECLARE @i int;
SET @i = 1;
WHILE @i <= LEN(@Result)
BEGIN
    SET @Replacement = NULL;

-- Grab the middle-of-name replacement n-gram
SELECT TOP (1) @Replacement = Replacement
FROM dbo.NYSIIS_Replacements
```

```
WHERE Location = N'Mid'
    AND SUBSTRING(@Result, @i, LEN(NGram)) = NGram
ORDER BY LEN(NGram) DESC;

SET @Replacement = COALESCE(@Replacement, SUBSTRING(@Result, @i, 1));

-- If we found a replacement, apply it
  SET @Result = STUFF(@Result, @i, LEN(@Replacement), @Replacement)

-- Move on to the next n-gram
  SET @i = @i + COALESCE(LEN(@Replacement), 1);
END;

-- Replace the first character with the first letter we saved at the start
SET @Result = STUFF(@Result, 1, 1, @FirstLetter);

-- Here we apply our special rules for the 'H' character. Special handling for 'W'
-- characters is taken care of in the replacement rules table
WITH Numbers (Num)
AS
(
  SELECT 2 -- Don't bother with the first character

  UNION ALL

  SELECT Num + 1
  FROM Numbers
  WHERE Num < LEN(@Result)
)
SELECT @Result = STUFF
  (
  @Result,
  Num,
  1,
  CASE SUBSTRING(@Result, Num, 1)
    WHEN N'H' THEN
      CASE WHEN SUBSTRING(@Result, Num + 1, 1)
          NOT IN (N'A', N'E', N'I', N'O', N'U')
        OR SUBSTRING(@Result, Num - 1, 1)
          NOT IN (N'A', N'E', N'I', N'O', N'U')
        THEN SUBSTRING(@Result, Num - 1, 1)
      ELSE N'H'
  END
 ELSE SUBSTRING(@Result, Num, 1)
END
)
FROM Numbers;

-- Step 6: Reduce All Side-by-side Duplicate Characters
-- First replace the first letter of any sequence of two side-by-side
-- duplicate letters with a period
```

```
WITH Numbers (Num)
AS
(
   SELECT 1

   UNION ALL

   SELECT Num + 1
   FROM Numbers
   WHERE Num < LEN(@Result)
)
SELECT @Result = STUFF
   (
   @Result,
   Num,
   1,
   CASE SUBSTRING(@Result, Num, 1)
      WHEN SUBSTRING(@Result, Num + 1, 1) THEN N'.'
      ELSE SUBSTRING(@Result, Num, 1)
   END
   )
FROM Numbers;

-- Next replace all periods '.' with an empty string ''
SET @Result = REPLACE(@Result, N'.', N'');

-- Step 7: Remove Trailing 'S' Characters
WHILE RIGHT(@Result, 1) = N'S' AND LEN(@Result) > 1
   SET @Result = STUFF(@Result, LEN(@Result), 1, N'');

-- Step 8: Remove Trailing 'A' Characters
WHILE RIGHT(@Result, 1) = N'A' AND LEN(@Result) > 1
   SET @Result = STUFF(@Result, LEN(@Result), 1, N'');

-- Step 9: Replace Trailing 'AY' Characters with 'Y'
IF RIGHT(@Result, 2) = 'AY'
   SET @Result = STUFF(@Result, LEN(@Result) - 1, 1, N'');

-- Step 10: Truncate Result to 6 Characters
RETURN COALESCE(SUBSTRING(@Result, 1, 6), '');
END;
GO
```

The NYSIISReplacements table rules reflect most of the NYSIIS rules described by Robert L. Taft in his famous paper "Name Search Techniques."[1] The start and end n-grams are replaced, and then the remaining n-gram rules are applied in a WHILE loop. The special rules for the letter *H* are applied, side-by-side duplicates are removed, special handling of certain trailing characters is performed, and the first six characters of the result are returned.

---

[1]Robert L. Taft, "Name Search Techniques," Special Report (Albany, NY: Bureau of Systems Development, 1970).

NUMBERS TABLES

This example uses recursive CTEs to dynamically generate virtual numbers tables in a couple of places. A *numbers table* is simply a table of numbers counting up to a specified maximum. The following recursive CTE generates a small numbers table (the numbers 1 through 100):

```
WITH Numbers (Num)
AS
(
    SELECT 1
    UNION ALL
    SELECT Num + 1
    FROM Numbers
    WHERE Num < 100
)

SELECT Num FROM Numbers;
```

Listing 4-5 used the number of characters in the name to limit the recursion of the CTEs. This speeds up the UDF overall. You can get even more performance gains by creating a permanent numbers table in your database with a clustered index/primary key on it, instead of using CTEs. A numbers table is always handy to have around, doesn't cost you very much to build or maintain, doesn't take up much storage space, and is extremely useful for converting loops and cursors to set-based code. A numbers table is by far one of the handiest and simplest tools you can add to your T-SQL toolkit.

As an example, you can use the query in Listing 4-6 to phonetically encode the last names of all contacts in the AdventureWorks database using NYSIIS. Partial results are shown in Figure 4-3.

Listing 4-6. Using NYSIIS to Phonetically Encode All AdventureWorks Contacts

```
SELECT LastName,
    dbo.EncodeNYSIIS(LastName) AS NYSIIS
FROM Person.Person
GROUP BY LastName;
```

	LastName	NYSIIS
1	Abbas	AB
2	Abel	ABAL
3	Abercrombie	ABARCR
4	Abolrous	ABALR
5	Acevedo	ACAFAD
6	Achong	ACANG
7	Ackerman	ACARNA
8	Adams	ADAN
9	Adina	ADIN
10	Agbonile	AGBANI
11	Agcaoili	AGCAIL
12	Aguilar	AGAILA
13	Ahlering	ALARIN
14	Ajenstat	AJANS
15	Akers	ACAR
16	Alameda	ALANAD
17	Alan	ALAN
18	Alberts	ALBAR

Figure 4-3. *Partial results of NYSIIS encoding AdventureWorks contacts*

Using the dbo.EncodeNYSIIS UDF is relatively simple. Listing 4-7 is a simple example of using the new UDF in the WHERE clause to retrieve all AdventureWorks contacts whose last name is phonetically similar to the name Liu. The results are shown in Figure 4-4.

Listing 4-7. Retrieving All Contact Phonetic Matches for Liu

```
SELECT
  BusinessEntityID,
  LastName,
  FirstName,
  MiddleName,
  dbo.EncodeNYSIIS(LastName) AS NYSIIS
FROM Person.Person
WHERE dbo.EncodeNYSIIS(LastName) = dbo.EncodeNYSIIS(N' Liu');
```

	BusinessEntityID	LastName	FirstName	MiddleName	NYSIIS
1	5520	Li	Aaron	NULL	LI
2	5264	Li	Adam	NULL	LI
3	5792	Li	Aimee	NULL	LI
4	17301	Li	Alan	M	LI
5	12470	Li	Alejandro	A	LI
6	11941	Li	Alisha	W	LI
7	4341	Li	Alvin	NULL	LI
8	20702	Li	Amy	J	LI
9	9768	Li	Arturo	NULL	LI
10	6279	Li	Austin	B	LI
11	5909	Li	Autumn	P	LI
12	11538	Li	Barbara	NULL	LI
13	6739	Li	Benjamin	H	LI
14	6938	Li	Brandon	NULL	LI
15	17989	Li	Brent	P	LI
16	5575	Li	Caleb	NULL	LI
17	6331	Li	Cameron	NULL	LI
18	4831	Li	Cara	NULL	LI

Figure 4-4. Partial listing of AdventureWorks contacts with names phonetically similar to Liu

The example in Listing 4-7 is the naive method of using a UDF. The query engine must apply the UDF to every single row of the source table. In this case, the dbo.EncodeNYSIIS function is applied to the nearly 20,000 last names in the Person.Contact table, resulting in an inefficient query plan and excessive I/O. A more efficient method is to perform the NYSIIS encodings ahead of time—to pre-encode the names. The pre-encoding method is demonstrated in Listing 4-8.

Listing 4-8. Pre-encoding AdventureWorks Contact Names with NYSIIS

```
CREATE TABLE Person.ContactNYSIIS
(
    BusinessEntityID int NOT NULL,
    NYSIIS nvarchar(6) NOT NULL,
    PRIMARY KEY(NYSIIS, BusinessEntityID)
);
GO

INSERT INTO Person.ContactNYSIIS
(
    BusinessEntityID,
    NYSIIS
)
```

```
SELECT
    BusinessEntityID,
    dbo.EncodeNYSIIS(LastName)
FROM Person.Person;
GO
```

Once you have pre-encoded the data, queries are much more efficient. The query shown in Listing 4-9 uses the table created in Listing 4-8 to return the same results as Listing 4-7—just much more efficiently, because this version doesn't need to encode every row of data for comparison in the WHERE clause at query time.

Listing 4-9. Efficient NYSIIS Query Using Pre-encoded Data

```
SELECT
    cn.BusinessEntityID,
    c.LastName,
    c.FirstName,
    c.MiddleName,
    cn.NYSIIS
FROM Person.ContactNYSIIS cn
INNER JOIN Person.Person c
    ON cn.BusinessEntityID = c.BusinessEntityID
WHERE cn.NYSIIS = dbo.EncodeNYSIIS(N'Liu');
```

To keep the efficiency of the dbo.EncodeNYSIIS UDF-based searches optimized, I highly recommend pre-encoding your search data. This is especially true in production environments where performance is critical. NYSIIS (and phonetic matching in general) is an extremely useful tool for approximate name-based searches in a variety of applications, such as customer service, business reporting, and law enforcement.

Multistatement Table-Valued Functions

Multistatement TVFs are similar in style to scalar UDFs, but instead of returning a single scalar value, they return their result as a table data type. The declaration is very similar to that of a scalar UDF, with a few important differences:

- The return type following the RETURNS keyword is actually a table variable declaration, with its structure declared immediately following the table variable name.

- The RETURNS NULL ON NULL INPUT and CALLED ON NULL INPUT function options aren't valid in a multistatement TVF definition.

- The RETURN statement in the body of the multistatement TVF has no values or variables following it.

Inside the body of the multistatement TVF, you can use the SQL Data Manipulation Language (DML) statements INSERT, UPDATE, MERGE, and DELETE to create and manipulate the return results in the table variable that will be returned as the result.

For the example of a multistatement TVF, let's create another business application function: a product pull list for AdventureWorks. This TVF matches the AdventureWorks sales orders stored in the Sales.SalesOrderDetail table against the product inventory in the Production.ProductInventory table. It effectively creates a list for AdventureWorks employees, telling them exactly which inventory bin to go to when they need to fill an order. Some business rules need to be defined before you write this multistatement TVF:

- In some cases, the number of ordered items may be more than are available in one bin. In that case, the pull list will instruct the employee to grab the product from multiple bins.

- Any partial fills from a bin will be reported on the list.

- Any substitution work (for example, substituting a different-colored item of the same model) will be handled by a separate business process and won't be allowed on this list.

- No zero fills (ordered items for which there is no matching product in inventory) will be reported back on the list.

For purposes of this example, let's say there are three customers: Jill, Mike, and Dave. Each of these three customers places an order for exactly five of item number 783, the black Mountain-200 42-inch mountain bike. Let's also say that AdventureWorks has six of this particular inventory item in bin 1, shelf A, location 7, and another three of this particular item in bin 2, shelf B, location 10. Your business rules will create a pull list like the following:

- *Jill's order*: Pull five of item 783 from bin 1, shelf A, location 7; mark the order as a complete fill.

- *Mike's order*: Pull one of item 783 from bin 1, shelf A, location 7; mark the order as a partial fill.

- *Mike's order*: Pull three of item 783 from bin 2, shelf B, location 10; mark the order as a partial fill.

In this example, there are only 9 of the ordered items in inventory, but 15 total items have been ordered (3 customers multiplied by 5 items each). Because of this, Dave's order is zero-filled—no items are pulled from inventory to fill his order. Figure 4-5 is designed to help you visualize the sample inventory/order fill scenario.

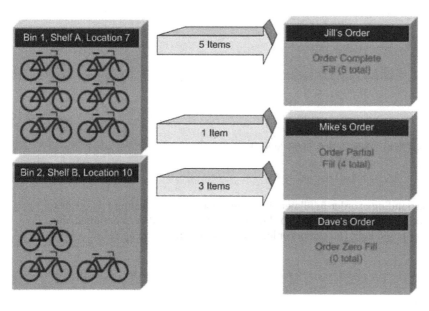

Figure 4-5. *Filling orders from inventory*

Because the inventory is out of item 783 at this point (there were nine items in inventory and all nine were used to fill Jill's and Mike's orders), Dave's order is not even listed on the pull list report. This function doesn't concern itself with product substitutions—for example, completing Mike's and Dave's orders with a comparable product such as item ID number 780 (the silver Mountain-200 42-inch mountain bike), if there happens to be some in stock. The business rule for substitutions states that a separate process handles this aspect of order fulfillment.

Many developers may see this problem as an opportunity to flex their cursor-based coding muscles. If you look at the problem from a procedural point of view, it essentially calls for performing nested loops through AdventureWorks' customer orders and inventory to match them up. However, this code doesn't require procedural code, and the task can be completed in a set-based fashion using a numbers table, as described in the previous section. A numbers table with numbers from 0 to 30,000 is adequate for this task; the code to create it is shown in Listing 4-10.

Listing 4-10. Creating a Numbers Table

```
USE [AdventureWorks2014]
GO

IF EXISTS (SELECT * FROM sys.objects
          WHERE object_id = OBJECT_ID(N'[dbo].[Numbers]')
            AND type in (N'U'))
DROP TABLE [dbo].[Numbers];

-- Create a numbers table to allow the product pull list to be
-- created using set-based logic
CREATE TABLE dbo.Numbers (Num int NOT NULL PRIMARY KEY);
GO
-- Fill the numbers table with numbers from 0 to 30,000
WITH NumCTE (Num)
AS
(
SELECT 0

UNION ALL

SELECT Num + 1
FROM NumCTE
WHERE Num < 30000
)

INSERT INTO dbo.Numbers (Num) SELECT Num FROM NumCTE
OPTION (MAXRECURSION 0);
GO
```

So, with a better understanding of order-fulfillment logic and business rules, Listing 4-11 creates a multistatement TVF to return the product pull list according to the rules provided. As mentioned, this multistatement TVF uses set-based logic (no cursors or loops) to retrieve the product pull list.

LOOK MA, NO CURSORS!

Many programming problems in business present a procedural loop-based solution on first glance. This applies to problems that you must solve in T-SQL as well. If you look at business problems with a set-based mindset, you often find a set-based solution. In the product pull list example, the loop-based process of comparing every row of inventory to the order-detail rows is immediately apparent.

However, if you think of the inventory items and order-detail items as two sets, then the problem becomes a set-based problem. In this case, the solution is a variation of the classic computer science/mathematics bin-packing problem. In the bin-packing problem, you're given a set of bins (in this case, orders) in which to place a finite set of items (inventory items in this example). The natural bounds provided are the number of each item in inventory and the number of each item on each order-detail line.

By solving this as a set-based problem in T-SQL, you allow SQL Server to optimize the performance of your code based on the most current information available. As mentioned in Chapter 3, when you use cursors and loops, you take away SQL Server's performance-optimization options, and you assume the responsibility for performance optimization. You can use set-based logic instead of cursors and loops to solve this particular problem. In reality, solving this problem with a set-based solution took only about 30 minutes of my time. A cursor or loop-based solution would have taken just as long or longer, and it wouldn't have been nearly as efficient.

Listing 4-11. Creating a Product Pull List

```
CREATE FUNCTION dbo.GetProductPullList()
RETURNS @result table
(
    SalesOrderID int NOT NULL,
    ProductID int NOT NULL,
    LocationID smallint NOT NULL,
    Shelf nvarchar(10) NOT NULL,
    Bin tinyint NOT NULL,
    QuantityInBin smallint NOT NULL,
    QuantityOnOrder smallint NOT NULL,
    QuantityToPull smallint NOT NULL,
    PartialFillFlag nchar(1) NOT NULL,
    PRIMARY KEY (SalesOrderID, ProductID, LocationID, Shelf, Bin)
)
AS
BEGIN
    INSERT INTO @result
    (
        SalesOrderID,
        ProductID,
        LocationID,
        Shelf,
        Bin,
        QuantityInBin,
        QuantityOnOrder,
        QuantityToPull,
        PartialFillFlag
    )
```

```
SELECT
    Order_Details.SalesOrderID,
    Order_Details.ProductID,
    Inventory_Details.LocationID,
    Inventory_Details.Shelf,
    Inventory_Details.Bin,
    Inventory_Details.Quantity,
    Order_Details.OrderQty,
    COUNT(*) AS PullQty,
    CASE WHEN COUNT(*) < Order_Details.OrderQty
    THEN N'Y'
    ELSE N'N'
    END AS PartialFillFlag
FROM
(
    SELECT ROW_NUMBER() OVER
    (
    PARTITION BY p.ProductID
    ORDER BY p.ProductID,
    p.LocationID,
    p.Shelf,
    p.Bin
    ) AS Num,
    p.ProductID,
    p.LocationID,
    p.Shelf,
    p.Bin,
    p.Quantity
    FROM Production.ProductInventory p
    INNER JOIN dbo.Numbers n
    ON n.Num BETWEEN 1 AND Quantity
) Inventory_Details
INNER JOIN
(
    SELECT ROW_NUMBER() OVER
    (
    PARTITION BY o.ProductID
    ORDER BY o.ProductID,
    o.SalesOrderID
    ) AS Num,
    o.ProductID,
    o.SalesOrderID,
    o.OrderQty
    FROM Sales.SalesOrderDetail o
    INNER JOIN dbo.Numbers n
    ON n.Num BETWEEN 1 AND o.OrderQty
) Order_Details
ON Inventory_Details.ProductID = Order_Details.ProductID
    AND Inventory_Details.Num = Order_Details.Num
```

```
    GROUP BY
        Order_Details.SalesOrderID,
        Order_Details.ProductID,
        Inventory_Details.LocationID,
        Inventory_Details.Shelf,
        Inventory_Details.Bin,
        Inventory_Details.Quantity,
        Order_Details.OrderQty;
    RETURN;
END;
GO
```

Retrieving the product pull list involves a simple SELECT query like the following. Partial results are shown in Figure 4-6:

```
SELECT
    SalesOrderID,
    ProductID,
    LocationID,
    Shelf,
    Bin,
    QuantityInBin,
    QuantityOnOrder,
    QuantityToPull,
    PartialFillFlag
FROM dbo.GetProductPullList();
```

	SalesOrderID	ProductID	LocationID	Shelf	Bin	QuantityInBin	QuantityOnOrder	QuantityToPull	PartialFillFlag
1	43659	709	7	N/A	0	180	6	6	N
2	43659	711	7	N/A	0	216	4	4	N
3	43659	712	7	N/A	0	288	2	2	N
4	43659	714	7	N/A	0	180	3	3	N
5	43659	716	7	N/A	0	252	1	1	N
6	43659	771	7	N/A	0	49	1	1	N
7	43659	772	7	N/A	0	88	1	1	N
8	43659	773	7	N/A	0	83	2	2	N
9	43659	774	7	N/A	0	62	1	1	N
10	43659	776	7	N/A	0	78	1	1	N
11	43659	777	7	N/A	0	49	3	3	N
12	43659	778	7	N/A	0	88	1	1	N
13	43660	758	7	N/A	0	116	1	1	N
14	43660	762	7	N/A	0	75	1	1	N
15	43661	708	7	N/A	0	324	5	5	N

Figure 4-6. *AdventureWorks product pull list (partial)*

One interesting aspect of the multistatement TVF is the CREATE FUNCTION keyword and its RETURNS clause, which define the name of the procedure, parameters passed in (if any), and the resulting set table structure:

```
CREATE FUNCTION dbo.GetProductPullList()
RETURNS @result table
(
    SalesOrderIlD int NOT NULL,
    ProductID int NOT NULL,
    LocationID smallint NOT NULL,
    Shelf nvarchar(10) NOT NULL,
    Bin tinyint NOT NULL,
    QuantityInBin smallint NOT NULL,
    QuantityOnOrder smallint NOT NULL,
    QuantityToPull smallint NOT NULL,
    PartialFillFlag nchar(1) NOT NULL,
PRIMARY KEY (SalesOrderID, ProductID, LocationID, Shelf, Bin)
)
```

Notice that you define a primary key on the table result. This also serves as the clustered index for the result set. Due to limitations in table variables, you can't explicitly specify other indexes on the result set.

The body of the function begins with the INSERT INTO and SELECT clauses that follow:

```
INSERT INTO @result
(
    SalesOrderID,
    ProductID,
    LocationID,
    Shelf,
    Bin,
    QuantitylnBin,
    QuantityOnOrder,
    QuantityToPull,
    PartialFillFlag
)
SELECT
    Order_Details.SalesOrderID,
    Order_Details.ProductID,
    Inventory_Details.LocationID,
    Inventory_Details.Shelf,
    Inventory_Details.Bin,
    Inventory_Details.Quantity,
    Order_Details.OrderQty,
    COUNT(*) AS PullQty,
    CASE WHEN COUNT(*) < Order_Details.OrderQty
        THEN N'Y'
        ELSE N'N'
END AS PartialFillFlag
```

These clauses establish population of the @result table variable. The most important point to notice here is that the return results of this multistatement TVF are created by manipulating the contents of the @result table variable. When the function ends, the @result table variable is returned to the caller.

Some other important facts about this portion of the multistatement TVF are that the COUNT(*) AS PullQty aggregate function returns the total number of each item to pull from a given bin to fill a specific order-detail row, and the CASE expression returns Y when an order-detail item is partially filled from a single bin and N when an order-detail item is completely filled from a single bin.

The source for the SELECT query is composed of two subqueries joined together. The first subquery, aliased as InventoryDetails, is shown next. This subquery returns a single row for every item in inventory with information identifying the precise location where the inventory item can be found:

```
(
    SELECT ROW_NUMBER() OVER
        (
        PARTITION BY p.ProductID
        ORDER BY p.ProductID,
        p.LocationID,
        p.Shelf,
        p.Bin
        ) AS Num,
        p.ProductID,
        p.LocationID,
        p.Shelf,
        p.Bin,
        p.Quantity
    FROM Production.ProductInventory p
    INNER JOIN dbo.Numbers n
        ON n.Num BETWEEN 1 AND Quantity
) Inventory_Details
```

Consider the previous example with the customers Jill, Mike, and Dave. If there are nine black Mountain-200 42-inch mountain bikes in inventory, this query returns nine rows, one for each instance of the item in inventory, and each with a unique row number counting from 1.

The InventoryDetails subquery is inner-joined to a second subquery, identified as Order_Details:

```
(
    SELECT ROW_NUMBER() OVER
        (
        PARTITION BY o.ProductID
        ORDER BY o.ProductID,
        o.SalesOrderID
        ) AS Num,
        o.ProductID,
        o.SalesOrderID,
        o.OrderQty
    FROM Sales.SalesOrderDetail o
    INNER JOIN dbo.Numbers n
        ON n.Num BETWEEN 1 AND o.OrderQty
) Order_Details
```

This subquery breaks up quantities of items in all order details into individual rows. Again, in the example of Jill, Mike, and Dave, this query breaks each of the order details into five rows, one for each item of each order detail. The rows are assigned unique numbers for each product. So in the example, the rows for each black Mountain-200 42-inch mountain bike that the three customers ordered are numbered individually from 1 to 15.

The rows of both subqueries are joined based on their ProductID numbers and the unique row numbers assigned to each row of each subquery. This effectively assigns one item from inventory to fill exactly one item in each order. Figure 4-7 is a visualization of the process described here, where the inventory items and order-detail items are split into separate rows and the two rowsets are joined together.

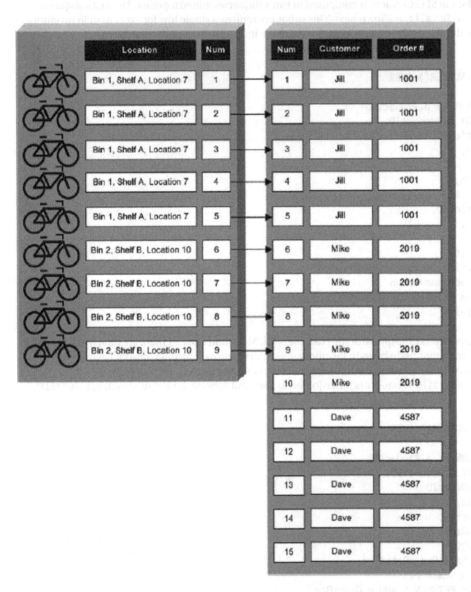

Figure 4-7. *Splitting and joining individual inventory and order-detail items*

The SELECT statement also requires a GROUP BY to aggregate the total number of items to be pulled from each bin to fill each order detail, as opposed to returning the raw inventory-to-order detail items on a one-to-one basis:

```
GROUP BY
  Order_Details.SalesOrderID,
  Order_Details.ProductID,
  Inventory_Details.LocationID,
  Inventory_Details.Shelf,
  Inventory_Details.Bin,
  Inventory_Details.Quantity,
  Order_Details.OrderQty;
```

Finally, the RETURN statement returns the @result table back to the caller as the multistatement TVF result. Notice that the RETURN statement in a multistatement TVF isn't followed by an expression or variable as it is in a scalar UDF:

```
RETURN;
```

The table returned by a TVF can be used just like a table in a WHERE clause or a JOIN clause of an SQL SELECT query. Listing 4-12 is a sample query that joins the example TVF to the Production.Product table to get the product names and colors for each product listed in the pull list. Figure 4-8 shows the output of the product pull list joined to the Production.Product table.

Listing 4-12. Retrieving a Product Pull List with Product Names

```
SELECT
  p.Name AS ProductName,
  p.ProductNumber,
  p.Color,
  ppl.SalesOrderID,
  ppl.ProductID,
  ppl.LocationID,
  ppl.Shelf,
  ppl.Bin,
  ppl.QuantityInBin,
  ppl.QuantityOnOrder,
  ppl.QuantityToPull,
  ppl.PartialFillFlag
FROM Production.Product p
INNER JOIN dbo.GetProductPullList() ppl
  ON p.ProductID = ppl.ProductID;
```

	ProductName	ProductNumber	Color	SalesOrderID	ProductID	LocationID	Shelf	Bin	QuantityInBin	QuantityOnOrder	QuantityToPull	PartialFillFlag
1	Mountain Bike Socks, M	SO-B909-M	White	43659	709	7	N/A	0	180	6	6	N
2	Sport-100 Helmet, Blue	HL-U509-B	Blue	43659	711	7	N/A	0	216	4	4	N
3	AWC Logo Cap	CA-1098	Multi	43659	712	7	N/A	0	288	2	2	N
4	Long-Sleeve Logo Jersey, M	LJ-0192-M	Multi	43659	714	7	N/A	0	180	3	3	N
5	Long-Sleeve Logo Jersey, XL	LJ-0192-X	Multi	43659	716	7	N/A	0	252	1	1	N
6	Mountain-100 Silver, 38	BK-M82S-38	Silver	43659	771	7	N/A	0	49	1	1	N
7	Mountain-100 Silver, 42	BK-M82S-42	Silver	43659	772	7	N/A	0	88	1	1	N
8	Mountain-100 Silver, 44	BK-M82S-44	Silver	43659	773	7	N/A	0	83	2	2	N
9	Mountain-100 Silver, 48	BK-M82S-48	Silver	43659	774	7	N/A	0	62	1	1	N
10	Mountain-100 Black, 42	BK-M82B-42	Black	43659	776	7	N/A	0	78	1	1	N
11	Mountain-100 Black, 44	BK-M82B-44	Black	43659	777	7	N/A	0	49	3	3	N
12	Mountain-100 Black, 48	BK-M82B-48	Black	43659	778	7	N/A	0	88	1	1	N
13	Road-450 Red, 52	BK-R68R-52	Red	43660	758	7	N/A	0	116	1	1	N
14	Road-650 Red, 44	BK-R50R-44	Red	43660	762	7	N/A	0	75	1	1	N
15	Sport-100 Helmet, Black	HL-U509	Black	43661	708	7	N/A	0	324	5	5	N
16	Sport-100 Helmet, Blue	HL-U509-B	Blue	43661	711	7	N/A	0	216	2	2	N
17	AWC Logo Cap	CA-1098	Multi	43661	712	7	N/A	0	288	4	4	N
18	Long-Sleeve Logo Jersey, L	LJ-0192-L	Multi	43661	715	7	N/A	0	216	4	4	N
19	Long-Sleeve Logo Jersey, XL	LJ-0192-X	Multi	43661	716	7	N/A	0	252	2	2	N
20	HL Mountain Frame - Black,...	FR-M94B-38	Black	43661	747	10	N/A	0	121	2	2	N
21	Mountain-100 Silver, 44	BK-M82S-44	Silver	43661	773	7	N/A	0	83	2	2	N

Figure 4-8. *Joining the product pull list to the* `Production.Product` *table*

Inline Table-Valued Functions

If scalar UDFs and multistatement TVFs aren't enough to get you excited about T-SQL's UDF capabilities, here comes a third form of UDF: the inline TVF. Inline TVFs are similar to multistatement TVFs in that they return a tabular rowset result.

However, whereas a multistatement TVF can contain multiple SQL statements and control-of-flow statements in the function body, the inline function consists of only a single SELECT query. The inline TVF is literally "inlined" by SQL Server (expanded by the query optimizer as part of the SELECT statement that contains it), much like a view. In fact, because of this behavior, inline TVFs are sometimes referred to as *parameterized views.*

The inline TVF declaration must simply state that the result is a table via the RETURNS clause. The body of the inline TVF consists of an SQL query after a RETURN statement. Because the inline TVF returns the result of a single SELECT query, you don't need to bother with declaring a table variable or defining the return-table structure. The structure of the result is implied by the SELECT query that makes up the body of the function.

The sample inline TVF performs a function commonly implemented by developers in T-SQL using control-of-flow statements. Many times, a developer determines that a function or SP requires that a large or variable number of parameters be passed in to accomplish a particular goal. The ideal situation would be to pass an array as a parameter. T-SQL doesn't provide an array data type per se, but you can split a comma-delimited list of strings into a table to simulate an array. This gives you the flexibility of an array that you can use in SQL joins.

■ **Tip** SQL Server 2012 forward allows table-valued parameters, which are covered in Chapter 5 in the discussion of SPs. Because table-valued parameters have special requirements, they may not be optimal in all situations.

Although you could do this using a multistatement TVF and control-of-flow statement such as a WHILE loop, you get better performance if you let SQL Server do the heavy lifting with a set-based solution. The sample function accepts a comma-delimited varchar(max) string and returns a table with two columns, Num and Element, which are described here:

- The Num column contains a unique number for each element of the array, counting from 1 to the number of elements in the comma-delimited string.

- The Element column contains the substrings extracted from the comma-delimited list.

Listing 4-13 is the full code listing for the comma-separated string-splitting function. This function accepts a single parameter, which is a comma-delimited string like Ronnie,Bobbie,Ricky,Mike. The output is a table-like rowset with each comma-delimited item returned on its own row. To avoid looping and procedural constructs (which aren't allowed in an inline TVF), you use the same Numbers table created previously in Listing 4-10.

Listing 4-13. Comma-Separated String-Splitting Function

```
CREATE FUNCTION dbo.GetCommaSplit (@String nvarchar(max))
RETURNS table
AS
RETURN
(
    WITH Splitter (Num, String)
    AS
    (
        SELECT Num, SUBSTRING(@String,
        Num,
        CASE CHARINDEX(N',', @String, Num)
        WHEN O THEN  LEN(@String) - Num + 1
        ELSE CHARINDEX(N',', @String, Num) - Num
        END
        ) AS String
    FROM dbo.Numbers
    WHERE Num <= LEN(@String)
        AND (SUBSTRING(@String, Num - 1, 1) = N',' OR Num = 0)
    )
    SELECT
        ROW_NUMBER() OVER (ORDER BY Num) AS Num,
        RTRIM(LTRIM(String)) AS Element
    FROM Splitter
    WHERE String <> ''
);
GO
```

The inline TVF name and parameters are defined at the beginning of the CREATE FUNCTION statement. The RETURNS table clause specifies that the function returns a table. Notice that the structure of the table isn't defined as it is with a multistatement TVF:

```
CREATE FUNCTION dbo.GetCommaSplit (@String varchar(max)) RETURNS table
```

The body of the inline TVF consists of a single RETURN statement followed by a SELECT query. This example uses a CTE called Splitter to perform the actual splitting of the comma-delimited list. The query of the CTE returns each substring from the comma-delimited list. CASE expressions are required to handle two special cases, as follows:

- The first item in the list, because it isn't preceded by a comma

- The last item in the list, because it isn't followed by a comma

```
WITH Splitter (Num, String)
AS
(
  SELECT Num, SUBSTRING(@String,
    Num,
    CASE CHARINDEX(N',', @String, Num)
      WHEN 0 THEN LEN(@String) - Num + 1
      ELSE CHARINDEX(N',', @String, Num) - Num
    END
  ) AS String
  FROM dbo.Numbers
  WHERE Num <= LEN(@String)
    AND (SUBSTRING(@String, Num - 1, 1) = N',' OR Num = 0)
)
```

Finally, the query selects each ROWNUMBER and Element from the CTE as the result to return to the caller. Extra space characters are stripped from the beginning and end of each string returned, and empty strings are ignored:

```
SELECT
  ROW_NUMBER() OVER (ORDER BY Num) AS Num,
  LTRIM(RTRIM(String)) AS Element
FROM Splitter
WHERE String <> ''
```

You can use this inline TVF to split up the Jackson family, as shown in Listing 4-14. The results are shown in Figure 4-9.

	Num	Element
1	1	Michael
2	2	Tito
3	3	Jermaine
4	4	Marlon
5	5	Rebbie
6	6	Jackie
7	7	Janet
8	8	La Toya
9	9	Randy

Figure 4-9. Splitting up the Jacksons

Listing 4-14. Splitting Up the Jacksons

```
SELECT Num, Element
FROM dbo.GetCommaSplit ('Michael,Tito,Jermaine,Marlon,Rebbie,Jackie,Janet,La Toya,Randy');
```

You can use this technique to pull descriptions for a specific set of AdventureWorks products. A usage like this is good for front-end web page displays or business reports where end users can select multiple items for which they want data returned. Listing 4-15 retrieves product information for a comma-delimited list of AdventureWorks product numbers. The results are shown in Figure 4-10.

Listing 4-15. Using the FnCommaSplit Function

```
SELECT n.Num,
    p.Name,
    p.ProductNumber,
    p.Color,
    p.Size,
    p.SizeUnitMeasureCode,
    p.StandardCost,
    p.ListPrice
FROM Production.Product p
INNER JOIN dbo.GetCommaSplit('FR-R38R-52,FR-M94S-52,FR-M94B-44,BK-M68B-38') n
    ON p.ProductNumber = n.Element;
```

	Num	Name	ProductNumber	Color	Size	SizeUnitMeasureCode	StandardCost	ListPrice
1	4	Mountain-200 Black, 38	BK-M68B-38	Black	38	CM	1251.9813	2294.99
2	3	HL Mountain Frame - Black, 44	FR-M94B-44	Black	44	CM	699.0928	1349.60
3	2	HL Mountain Frame - Silver, 48	FR-M94S-52	Silver	48	CM	706.811	1364.50
4	1	LL Road Frame - Red, 52	FR-R38R-52	Red	52	CM	187.1571	337.22

Figure 4-10. *Using a comma-delimited list to retrieve product information*

Restrictions on User-Defined Functions

T-SQL imposes some restrictions on UDFs. This section discusses these restrictions and some of the reasoning behind them.

Nondeterministic Functions

T-SQL prohibits the use of nondeterministic functions in UDFs. A *deterministic* function is one that returns the same value every time when passed a given set of parameters (or no parameters). A nondeterministic function can return different results with the same set of parameters passed to it. An example of a deterministic function is ABS, the mathematical absolute value function. Every time and no matter how many times you call ABS(-10), the result is always 10. This is the basic idea behind determinism.

On the flip side, there are functions that don't return the same value despite the fact that you pass in the same parameters, or no parameters. Built-in functions such as RAND (without a seed value) and NEWID are nondeterministic because they return a different result every time they're called. One hack that people sometimes use to try to circumvent this restriction is creating a view that invokes the nondeterministic function and selecting from that view inside their UDFs. Although this may work to some extent, it isn't recommended: it could fail to produce the desired results or cause a significant performance hit, because SQL can't cache or effectively index the results of nondeterministic functions. Also, if you create a computed column that tries to reference your UDF, the nondeterministic functions you're trying to access via your view can produce unpredictable results. If you need to use nondeterministic functions in your application logic, SPs are probably the better alternative. Chapter 5 discusses SPs.

NONDETERMINISTIC FUNCTIONS IN A UDF

In previous versions of SQL, there were several restrictions on the use of nondeterministic system functions in UDFs. In SQL Server 2012, these restrictions were somewhat relaxed. You can use the nondeterministic system functions listed in the following table in your UDFs. One thing these system functions have in common is that they don't cause side effects or change the database state when you use them:

@@CONNECTIONS	@@PACK_RECEIVED	@@TOTAL_WRITE
@@CPU_BUSY	@@PACK_SENT	CURRENT_TIMESTAMP
@@DBTS	@@PACKET_ERRORS	GET_TRANSMISSION_STATUS
@@IDLE	@@TIMETICKS	GETDATE
@@IO_BUSY	@@TOTAL_ERRORS	GETUTCDATE
@@MAX_CONNECTIONS	@@TOTAL_READ	

If you want to build an index on a view or computed column that uses a UDF, your UDF has to be deterministic. The requirements to make a UDF deterministic include the following:

- The UDF must be declared using the WITH SCHEMABINDING option. When a UDF is schema-bound, no changes are allowed to any tables or objects on which it's dependent without dropping the UDF first.

- Any functions you refer to in your UDF must also be deterministic. This means if you use a nondeterministic system function—such as GETDATE—in your UDF, it's marked nondeterministic.

- You can't invoke extended stored procedures (XPs) in the function. This shouldn't be a problem, because XPs are deprecated and will be removed from future versions of SQL Server.

If your UDF meets all these criteria, you can check to see if SQL Server has marked it deterministic via the OBJECTPROPERTY function, with a query like the following:

```
SELECT OBJECTPROPERTY (OBDECT_ID('dbo.GetCommaSplit'), 'IsDeterministic');
```

The OBJECTPROPERTY function returns 0 if your UDF is nondeterministic and 1 if it's deterministic.

State of the Database

One of the restrictions on UDFs is that they aren't allowed to change the state of the database or cause other side effects. This prohibition on side effects in UDFs means you can't even execute PRINT statements from within a UDF. It also means that although you can query database tables and resources, you can't execute INSERT, UPDATE, MERGE, or DELETE statements against database tables. Some other restrictions include the following:

- You can't create temporary tables within a UDF. You can, however, create and modify table variables in the body of a UDF.

- You can't execute CREATE, ALTER, or DROP on database tables from within a UDF.

- Dynamic SQL isn't allowed within a UDF, although XPs and SQLCLR functions can be called.

- A TVF can return only a single table/result set. If you need to return more than one table/result set, you may be better served by an SP.

MORE ON SIDE EFFECTS

Although XPs and SQL CLR functions can be called from a UDF, Microsoft warns against depending on results returned by XPs and SQL CLR functions that cause side effects. If your XP or SQL CLR function modifies tables, alters the database schema, accesses the file system, changes system settings, or utilizes non-deterministic resources external to the database, you may get unpredictable results from your UDF. If you need to change database state or rely on side effects in your server-side code, consider using an SQL CLR function or a regular SP instead of a UDF.

The prohibition on UDF side effects extends to the SQL Server display and error systems. This means you can't use the T-SQL PRINT or RAISERROR statement in a UDF. The PRINT and RAISERROR statements are useful in debugging stored procedures and T-SQL code batches but are unavailable for use in UDFs. One workaround that I often use is to temporarily move the body of the UDF code to an SP while testing. This gives you the ability to use PRINT and RAISERROR while testing and debugging code in development environments.

Variables and table variables created in UDFs have a well-defined scope and can't be accessed outside of the UDF. Even if you have a recursive UDF, you can't access the variables and table variables that were previously declared and assigned values by the calling function. If you need values that were generated by a UDF, you must pass them in as parameters to another UDF call or return them to the caller in the UDF result.

Summary

This chapter discussed the three types of T-SQL UDFs and provided working examples of the different types. Scalar UDFs are analogous to mathematical functions that accept zero or more parameters and return a single scalar value for a result. You can use the standard SQL statements, as well as control-of-flow statements, in a scalar UDF. Multistatement TVFs allow control-of-flow statements as well but return a table-style result set to the caller. You can use the result set returned by a multistatement TVF in WHERE and JOIN clauses. Finally, inline TVFs also return table-style result sets to the caller; however, the body consists of a single SELECT query, much like an SQL view. In fact, inline TVFs are sometimes referred to as parameterized views.

The type of UDF that you need to accomplish a given task depends on the problem you're trying to solve. For instance, if you need to calculate a single scalar value, a scalar UDF will do the job. On the other hand, if you need to perform complex calculations or manipulations and return a table, a multistatement TVF might be the correct choice.

You also learned about recursion in UDFs, including the 32-level recursion limit. Although 32 levels of recursion is the hard limit, for all practical purposes you should rarely—if ever—hit this limit. If you do need recursion beyond 32 levels, you can replace recursive function calls with CTEs and other T-SQL constructs.

Finally, the chapter talked about determinism and side effects in UDFs. Specifically, your UDFs should not cause side effects, and specific criteria must be met in order for SQL Server to mark your UDFs as deterministic. Determinism is an important aspect of UDFs if you plan to use them in indexed views or computed columns.

The next chapter looks at SPs—another tool that allows procedural T-SQL code to be consolidated into server-side units.

EXERCISES

1. [Fill in the blank] SQL Server supports three types of T-SQL UDFs: _____, _____, and _____.

2. [True/False] The RETURNS NULL ON NULL INPUT option is a performance-enhancing option available for use with scalar UDFs.

3. [True/False] The ENCRYPTION option provides a secure option that prevents anyone from reverse-engineering your source code.

4. [Choose all that apply] You aren't allowed to do which of the following in a multistatement TVF?

   a. Execute a PRINT statement

   b. Call RAISERROR to generate an exception

   c. Declare a table variable

   d. Create a temporary table

5. The algebraic formula for converting Fahrenheit measurements to the Celsius scale is:
   $C = (F - 32.0) \times (5/9)$, where F is the measurement in degrees Fahrenheit and C is the measurement in degrees Celsius.

Write a deterministic scalar UDF that converts a measurement in degrees Fahrenheit to degrees Celsius. The UDF should accept a single float parameter and return a float result. You can use the OBJECTPROPERTY function to ensure that the UDF is deterministic.

CHAPTER 5

■ ■ ■

Stored Procedures

Stored procedures (SPs) have been a part of T-SQL from the beginning. SPs provide a means for creating server-side subroutines written in T-SQL. SQL Server 2014 introduces the ability to natively compile an SP that accesses memory-optimized tables. The efficiencies gained with natively compiled SPs are an absolute game-changer in how you consider architecting an OLTP database solution.

This chapter begins with a discussion of what SPs are and why you might want to use them, and it continues with a discussion of SP creation and usage, including examples. Natively compiled SPs are introduced in this chapter, but the complete picture of how they work with in-memory tables is covered in more detail in Chapter 6.

Introducing Stored Procedures

SPs are saved collections of one or more T-SQL statements stored on the server as code units. They're analogous to procedures or subroutines in procedural languages like Visual Basic and C#. And just like procedures in procedural languages, SPs give you the ability to effectively extend the language of SQL Server by letting you add named custom subroutines to your databases.

An SP declaration begins with the CREATE PROCEDURE keywords followed by the name of the SP. Microsoft recommends against naming the SP with the prefix sp_. This prefix is used by SQL Server to name system SPs and isn't recommended for user SPs in databases other than the master database. The name can specify a schema name and procedure name, or just a procedure name. If you don't specify a schema name when creating an SP, SQL Server creates it in the default schema for your login. It's a best practice to always specify the schema name so your SPs are always created in the proper schema, rather than leaving it up to SQL Server. SQL Server allows you to drop groups of procedures with the same name with a single DROP PROCEDURE statement.

■ **Warning**   You can also define a stored procedure with the group number option during SP creation. The group number option is deprecated and will be removed from future versions of SQL Server. Don't use this option in new development, and start planning to update code that uses it.

SPs, like the T-SQL user-defined functions (UDFs) discussed in Chapter 4, can accept parameter values from and return them to the caller. The parameters are specified in a comma-separated list following the procedure name in the CREATE PROCEDURE statement. Unlike with UDFs, when you call an SP, you can specify the parameters in any order; and you can omit them altogether if you assigned a default value at creation time. You can also specify OUTPUT parameters, which return values from the procedure. All this makes SP parameters far more flexible than those of UDFs.

111

Each parameter is declared as a specific type and can also be declared as OUTPUT or with the VARYING keyword (for cursor parameters only). When calling SPs, you have two choices: you can specify parameters by position or by name. If you specify an unnamed parameter list, the values are assigned based on position. If you specify named parameters in the format @parameter = value, they can be in any order. If your parameter specifies a default value in its declaration, you don't have to pass in a value for that parameter. Unlike UDFs, SPs don't require the DEFAULT keyword as a placeholder to specify default values. Leaving out a parameter when you call the SP applies the default value to that parameter.

Unlike UDFs, which can return results only via the RETURN statement, SPs can communicate with the caller in a variety of ways:

- The SP's RETURN statement can return an int value to the caller. Unlike UDFs, SPs don't require a RETURN statement. If the RETURN statement is left out of the SP, 0 is returned by default if no errors were raised during execution.

- SPs don't have the same restrictions on database side effects and determinism as do UDFs. SPs can read, write, delete, and update permanent tables. In this way, the caller and SP can communicate information to one another through the use of permanent tables.

- When a temporary table is created in an SP, that temporary table is available to any SPs called by that SP. There are two types of temporary tables: local and global. The scope of a local temporary table is the current session, and the scope of a global temporary table is all sessions. A local temporary table is prefixed with #, and a global temporary table is prefixed with ##. As an example, if dbo.MyProc1 creates a local temporary table named #Temp and then calls dbo.MyProc2, dbo.MyProc2 can access #Temp as well. If dbo.MyProc2 then calls dbo.MyProc3, dbo.MyProc3 can also access the same #Temp temporary table. Global temporary tables are accessible by all users and all connections after they're created. This provides a useful method of passing an entire table of temporary results from one SP to another for further processing.

- Output parameters provide the primary method of retrieving scalar results from an SP. Parameters are specified as output parameters with the OUTPUT keyword.

- To return table-type results from an SP, the SP can return one or more result sets. Result sets are like virtual tables that can be accessed by the caller. Unlike with views, updates to these result sets by applications don't change the underlying tables used to generate them. Also, unlike table-valued function (TVFs) and inline functions that return a single table only, SPs can return multiple result sets with a single call.

SP RETURN STATEMENTS

Because the SP RETURN statement can't return tables, character data, decimal numbers, and so on, it's normally used only to return an int status or error code. This is a good convention to follow, because most developers who use your SPs will expect it. The normal practice, followed by most of SQL Server's system SPs, is to return a value of 0 to indicate success and a nonzero value or an error code to indicate an error or a failure.

Metadata Discovery

SQL Server 2012 introduced two new stored procedures and supporting Dynamic Management Views (DMVs) to provide new capabilities for determining metadata associated with code batches or SPs. This set of capabilities replaces the SET FMTONLY option, which is being deprecated.

Often it's necessary to determine the format of a result set without actually executing the query. There are also scenarios in which you have to ensure that the column and parameter metadata from query execution is compatible with or identical to the format you specified before executing the query. For example, if you want to generate dynamic screens based on a SELECT statement, you need to make sure there are no metadata errors after query execution, so in turn you need to determine whether the parameter metadata is compatible before and after query execution. This functionality introduces metadata discovery capabilities for result sets and parameters using the SPs sp_describe_first_result_set and sp_describe_ undeclared_parameters and the DMVs dm_exec_describe_first_result_set and dm_exec_describe_ first_result_set_for_object.

The SP sp_describe_first_result_set analyzes all possible first result sets and returns the metadata information for the first result set that is executed from the input T-SQL batch. If the SP returns multiple result sets, this procedure only returns the first result set. If SQL Server is unable to determine the metadata for the first query, then an error is raised. This procedure takes three parameters: @tsql passes the T-SQL batch, @params passes the parameters for the T-SQL batch, and @browse_information_mode determines whether additional browse information for each result set is returned.

Alternatively, you can use the DMV sys.dm_exec_describe_first_result_set to query against; this DMV returns the same details as the SP sp_describe_first_result_set. You can use the DMV sys.dm_exec_describe_first_result_set_for_object to analyze objects such as SPs or triggers in the database and return the metadata for the first possible result set and the errors associated with them. Let's say you want to analyze all the objects in the database and use the information for documentation purposes. Instead of analyzing the objects one by one, you can use the DMV sys.dm_exec_describe_first_result_ set_for_object with a query similar to following:

```
SELECT p.name, p.schema_id, x.* FROM sys.procedures p CROSS APPLY sys.dm_exec_describe_
first_result_set_for_object(p.object_id,0) x
```

The SP sp_describe_undeclared_parameters analyzes the T-SQL batch and returns the suggestion for the best parameter datatype based on least number of conversions. This feature is very useful when you have complicated calculations or expressions and you're trying to figure out the best datatype for the undeclared parameter value.

Natively Compiled Stored Procedures

Natively compiled stored procedures are new in SQL Server 2014 and can provide massive performance gains. These SPs are similar to traditional T-SQL compiled SPs in the way you call them and how they function. Natively compiled SPs are compiled into native C machine code, which is stored as a DLL in machine code. This allows the CPU to run the code without the need to interpret the code at runtime, providing for some extreme performance gains. By contrast, traditional T-SQL SPs are interpretive; they're compiled and then executed every time the SP is called. Natively compiled SPs have several limitations and can only access memory-optimized tables. (Memory-optimized tables are discussed in Chapter 6.) As of SQL Server 2014 RTM, creating a natively compiled SP has several limitations and requires a very specific syntax.

Listing 5-1 is a simple example of a traditional T-SQL interpreted SP in the Person schema that accepts an AdventureWorks employee's ID and returns the employee's full name and e-mail address via output parameters. The following section contrasts a new natively compiled SP using the same memory-optimized table objects in Listing 5-1.

▨ **Note** The SP in the example, Person.GetEmployee, accepts a business entity ID number as an input parameter and returns the corresponding employee's e-mail address and full name as output parameters. If the business entity ID number passed in is valid, the SP returns 0 as a return value; otherwise 1 is returned.

Listing 5-1. Creating a Traditional T-SQL SP That Retrieves an Employee's Name and E-mail

```
CREATE PROCEDURE Person.GetEmployee
(
    @BusinessEntityID  int  =  NULL
  , @Email_Address nvarchar(50) OUTPUT
  , @Full_Name nvarchar(100) OUTPUT
)
AS

BEGIN

    -- Retrieve email address and full name from HumanResources.Employee table
    SELECT @Email_Address = ea.EmailAddress,
        @Full_Name = p.FirstName + ' ' + COALESCE(p.MiddleName,'') + ' ' + p.LastName
    FROM  HumanResources.Employee  e
    INNER JOIN Person.Person p
        ON  e.BusinessEntityID  =  p.BusinessEntityID
    INNER JOIN Person.EmailAddress ea
        ON  p.BusinessEntityID  =  ea.BusinessEntityID
    WHERE e.BusinessEntityID = @BusinessEntityID;

    --  Return a code of 1 when no match is found, 0 for success
    RETURN (
        CASE
        WHEN  @Email_Address  IS  NULL  THEN  1
        ELSE 0
        END
    );
END;
GO
```

To contrast the differences, see Listing 5-2. I break down the differences line by line following this listing.

■ **Note**   The code in Listing 5-2 will not execute correctly on a test machine until all the in-memory tables have been created. Chapter 6 discusses all the code samples, with an explanation of how to set up the in-memory tables.

Listing 5-2. Natively Compiled SP Person.GetEmployee_inmem

```
CREATE PROCEDURE Person.GetEmployee_inmem
(
    @BusinessEntityID  int  =  NULL
  , @Email_Address nvarchar(50) OUTPUT
  , @Full_Name nvarchar(100) OUTPUT
)

/*** New InMemory Syntax ***/
WITH NATIVE_COMPILATION, SCHEMABINDING, EXECUTE AS OWNER
AS
```

```
/*** New InMemory Syntax ***/
BEGIN ATOMIC WITH
  (TRANSACTION ISOLATION LEVEL = SNAPSHOT,
   LANGUAGE = N'us_english')

/*** New Variable to handle ReturnCode Logic ***/
DECLARE @ReturnCode bit = 0;

    -- Retrieve email address and full name from HumanResources.Employee table
    SELECT @Email_Address = ea.EmailAddress,
           @Full_Name = p.FirstName + ' ' + ISNULL(p.MiddleName,'') + ' ' + p.LastName
     /*** New Code to handle ReturnCode Logic ***/
           , @ReturnCode = ISNULL( LEN(ea.EmailAddress,1) )
      FROM HumanResources.Employee_inmem  e
    INNER JOIN Person.Person_inmem p ON
           e.BusinessEntityID  =  p.BusinessEntityID
    INNER JOIN Person.EmailAddress_inmem ea ON
           p.BusinessEntityID  =  ea.BusinessEntityID
     WHERE e.BusinessEntityID = @BusinessEntityID;

    --  Return a code of 1 when no match is found, 0 for success
    RETURN ( @ReturnCode )
END;
GO
```

There should several obvious differences when you look at the SPs in Listing 5-1 and 5-2. Following is an outline of the differences and how to create a natively compiled SP:

1. The tables accessed in Listing 5-2 reference in-memory tables only. The new tables are identified with the _inmem suffix. It's an absolute requirement to access memory-optimized tables from a natively compiled SP. Chapter 6 goes over how to create in-memory tables, in addition to several of the limitations and requirements for these types of tables.

2. The first difference from a traditional T-SQL SP is in line 9:

    a. The WITH option is required with the indicator NATIVE_COMPILATION to show that it's a natively compiled SP.

    b. SCHEMABINDING must be specified so it's bound to the schema of the objects it references. The tables referenced in the SP can't be dropped without first dropping the SP itself.

    c. The EXECUTE AS execution context must be specified as EXECUTE AS OWNER, EXECUTE AS USER, or EXECUTE AS SELF. The default behavior of a T-SQL SP is EXECUTE AS CALLER, which isn't supported in a natively compiled SP.

3. The second line with a difference is line 13. BEGIN ATOMIC must be specified so the execution is guaranteed to be atomic. There are two required options for the atomic blocks:

   a. TRANSACTION ISOLATION LEVEL must be specified

   b. LANGUAGE must be specified.

4. Line 33 is completely different from the original version of the code (see Figure 5-1), for a very important reason. Natively compiled SPs don't support the CASE statement. This limitation forced me to accommodate for the logic in a different manner. In the SELECT clause (line 24 in Listing 5-2), I check the column for ISNULL and set the variable @ReturnCode so that the valid value is returned.

```
Person_GetEmployee...orks2014 (sa (52))*  ✕

        --  Return a code of 1 when no match is found, 0 for success
☐    RETURN (
                CASE
                WHEN  @Email_Address  IS  NULL  THEN  1
                ELSE 0
                END
            );
   END;
   GO
100 %   ▾  ◂
```

```
        --  Return a code of 1 when no match is found, 0 for success
     RETURN ( @ReturnCode )
   END;
     GO
100 %   ▾  ◂
```

Figure 5-1. Differences in the RETURN code blocks between the original T-SQL SP and the natively compiled SP

Natively compiled SPs have a significant number of limitations. They're so numerous that it's best to reference the Microsoft MSDN for the latest limitations and workarounds at http://msdn.microsoft.com/en-us/library/dn246937.aspx.

One thing to keep in mind: this is the first version of this type of functionality. Each time a SP is compiled into native machine code, it's translating all the T-SQL into C. The limitations arise from the challenges involved in doing this accurately. Microsoft has promised to continue investing in additional capabilities in the next version of the in-memory features. Even with their limitations, the enhanced performance gains of using these features are too compelling to not begin using them now.

Managing Stored Procedures

T-SQL provides two statements that allow you to modify and delete SPs: ALTER PROCEDURE and DROP PROCEDURE, respectively. ALTER PROCEDURE lets you modify the code for an SP without first dropping it. The syntax is the same as for the CREATE PROCEDURE statement, except that the keywords ALTER PROCEDURE are used in place of CREATE PROCEDURE. ALTER PROCEDURE, like CREATE PROCEDURE, must always be the first statement in a batch. Using the CREATE, DROP, and ALTER PROCEDURE statements forces SQL Server to generate a new query plan. The advantage of ALTER over CREATE or DROP is that ALTER preserves the permissions for the object, whereas CREATE and DROP reset the permissions. If you're using a natively compiled SP, the ALTER PROCEDURE code isn't allowed. The only way to alter a natively compiled SP is to drop the procedure and re-create it.

To delete a procedure from your database, use the DROP PROCEDURE statement. Listing 5-3 shows how to drop the procedure created in Listing 5-1.

Listing 5-3. Dropping the Person.GetEmployee SP

```
DROP PROCEDURE Person.GetEmployee;
```

You can specify multiple SPs in a single DROP PROCEDURE statement by putting the SP names in a comma-separated list. Note that you can't specify the database or server name when dropping an SP, and you must be in the database containing the SP in order to drop it. Additionally, as with other database objects, you can grant or deny EXECUTE permissions on an SP through the GRANT and DENY statements.

Stored Procedures Best Practices

Stored procedures enable you to store batches of Transact-SQL or Managed Common Language Runtime (CLR) code centrally on the server. SPs can be very efficient; here are some best practices that can aid development and avoid common pitfalls that can hurt performance:

- Use the SET NOCOUNT ON statement after the AS keyword, as the first statement in the body of the procedure, when you have multiple statements in your SP. This turns off the DONE_IN_PROC messages that SQL Server sends back to the client after each statement in the SP is executed. This also reduces the processing performed by SQL Server and the size of the response sent across the network.

- Use schema names when creating or referencing the SP and the database objects in the procedure. This helps SQL Server find the objects more quickly and thus reduces compile lock, which results in less processing time.

- Don't use the SP_ and sys** prefixes to name user-created database objects. They're reserved for Microsoft and have different behaviors.

- Avoid using scalar functions in SELECT statements that return many rows of data. Because the scalar function must be applied to every row, the resulting behavior is like row-based processing and degrades performance.

- Avoid using SELECT *, and select only the columns you need. This reduces processing in the database server as well as network traffic.

- Use parameters when calling SPs to increase performance. In your SPs, explicitly create parameters with type, size, and precision to avoid type conversions.

- Use explicit transactions by using BEGIN/END TRANSACTION, and keep transactions as short as possible. The longer the transaction, the more chances you have for locking or blocking, and in some cases deadlocking, as well. Keep transactions short to reduce blocking and locking.

- Use the T-SQL TRY...CATCH feature for error handling in procedures. TRY...CATCH can encapsulate an entire block of T-SQL statements. If you're using TRY...CATCH with loops, place it outside the loop for better performance. This not only creates less performance overhead, but also makes error reporting more accurate with significantly less programming.

- Use NULL or NOT NULL for each column in a temporary table. The ANSI_DFLT_ON and ANSI_DFLT_OFF options control the way the database engine assigns the NULL or NOT NULL attribute to columns when these attributes aren't specified in a CREATE TABLE or ALTER TABLE statement. If a connection executes a procedure with different settings for these options than the connection that created the procedure, the columns of the table created for the second connection can have different nullability and exhibit different behavior. If NULL or NOT NULL is explicitly stated for each column, the temporary tables are created by using the same nullability for all connections that execute the procedure.

- Use the UNION ALL operator instead of the UNION or OR operator, unless there is a specific need for distinct values. UNION filters and removes the duplicate records, whereas the UNION ALL operator requires less processing overhead because duplicates aren't filtered out of the result set.

WHY STORED PROCEDURES?

Debates have raged through the years over the utility of SQL Server SPs. Traditional SPs in SQL Server 2014 offer the same execution plan caching and reuse, but the luster of this benefit has faded somewhat. Query optimization, query caching, and reuse of query execution plans for parameterized queries have been in a state of constant improvement since SQL Server 2000. Query optimization has been improved even more in SQL Server 2014. SPs still offer the performance benefit of not having to send large and complex queries over the network, but the primary benefit of query execution plan caching and reuse isn't as enticing as it once was.

So why use SPs? Apart from the performance benefit, which isn't as big a factor in these days of highly efficient parameterized queries, SPs offer code modularization and security. Creating code modules helps reduce redundant code, eliminating potential maintenance nightmares caused by duplicate code stored in multiple locations. By using SPs, you can deny users the ability to perform direct queries against tables, but still allow them to use SPs to retrieve the relevant data from those tables. SPs also offer the advantage of centralized administration of portions of your database code. Finally, SPs can return multiple result sets with a single procedure call, such as the sp_help system SP demonstrated here (the results are shown in Figure 5-2):

```
EXECUTE dbo.sp_help;
```

	Name	Ow...	Object_type	
1	AWBuildVersion	dbo	user table	
2	DatabaseLog	dbo	user table	
3	ErrorLog	dbo	user table	
4	Numbers	dbo	user table	
5	NYSIIS_Replacements	dbo	user table	
6	GetProductPullList	dbo	table function	
7	ufnGetContactInformation	dbo	table function	

	User_type	Storage_ty...	Len...	Pr...	Scale	Nulla...	Default_na...	Rule_na...	Collation
1	AccountNumber	nvarchar	30	15	NULL	yes	none	none	SQL_Latin1_Ge
2	Flag	bit	1	1	NULL	no	none	none	NULL
3	Name	nvarchar	100	50	NULL	yes	none	none	SQL_Latin1_Ge
4	NameStyle	bit	1	1	NULL	no	none	none	NULL
5	OrderNumber	nvarchar	50	25	NULL	yes	none	none	SQL_Latin1_Ge
6	Phone	nvarchar	50	25	NULL	yes	none	none	SQL_Latin1_Ge

Figure 5-2. *Results of the dbo.sp_help SP call*

Using SPs, you can effectively build an application programming interface (API) for your database. You can also minimize and almost prevent SQL injection by using SPs with input parameters to filter and validate all the inputs. Creation and adherence to such an API can help ensure consistent access across applications and make development easier for front-end and client-side developers who need to access your database. Some third-party applications, such as certain ETL programs and database drivers, also require SPs.

Using natively compiled SPs will change the way SPs are thought of in the architecture of an application. Because they're compiled into machine language, there will be instances that placing business logic directly in the database layer will perform better than other architectures.

What are the arguments against SPs? One major issue tends to be that they tightly couple your code to the DBMS. A code base that is tightly integrated with SQL Server 2014 will be more difficult to port to another RDBMS (such as Oracle, DB2, or MySQL) in the future. A loosely coupled application, on the other hand, is much easier to port to different SQL DBMSs.

Portability, in turn, has its own problems. Truly portable code can result in databases and applications that are slow and inefficient. To get true portability out of any RDBMS system, you have to take great care to code everything in *plain vanilla* SQL, meaning a lot of the platform-specific performance-enhancing functionality offered by SQL Server is off-limits.

I'm not going to dive too deeply into a discussion of the pluses and minuses of SPs. In the end, the balance between portability and performance needs to be determined by your business requirements and corporate IT policies on a per-project basis. Just keep these competing factors in mind when making that decision.

Stored Procedure Example

A common application of SPs is to create a layer of abstraction for various data query, aggregation, and manipulation functionality. The example SP in Listing 5-4 performs the common business reporting task of calculating a running total. The results are shown in Figure 5-3.

Listing 5-4. Procedure to Calculate and Retrieve a Running Total for Sales

```
CREATE PROCEDURE Sales.GetSalesRunningTotal (@Year int)
AS
BEGIN
WITH RunningTotalCTE
AS

    (
        SELECT soh.SalesOrderNumber,
        soh.OrderDate,
        soh.TotalDue,
        (
        SELECT  SUM(soh1.TotalDue)
        FROM   Sales.SalesOrderHeader  soh1
        WHERE  soh1.SalesOrderNumber  <=  soh.SalesOrderNumber
        ) AS  RunningTotal,
        SUM(soh.TotalDue) OVER () AS GrandTotal
        FROM Sales.SalesOrderHeader soh
        WHERE DATEPART(year, soh.OrderDate) = @Year
        GROUP BY soh.SalesOrderNumber,
        soh.OrderDate,
        soh.TotalDue
    )
    SELECT rt.SalesOrderNumber,
        rt.OrderDate,
        rt.TotalDue,
        rt.RunningTotal,
        (rt.RunningTotal / rt.GrandTotal) * 100 AS PercentTotal
    FROM  RunningTotalCTE  rt
    ORDER BY rt.SalesOrderNumber;
    RETURN 0;
END;
GO

EXEC  Sales.GetSalesRunningTotal @Year = 2014;
GO
```

	SalesOrderNumber	OrderDate	TotalDue	RunningTotal	PercentTotal
1	SO63363	2014-01-01 00:00:00.000	30.1444	100797317.9446	449.59
2	SO63364	2014-01-01 00:00:00.000	33.0727	100797351.0173	449.59
3	SO63365	2014-01-01 00:00:00.000	5.514	100797356.5313	449.59
4	SO63366	2014-01-01 00:00:00.000	69.5929	100797426.1242	449.59
5	SO63367	2014-01-01 00:00:00.000	2738.5657	100800164.6899	449.60
6	SO63368	2014-01-01 00:00:00.000	937.5594	100801102.2493	449.61
7	SO63369	2014-01-01 00:00:00.000	2596.7279	100803698.9772	449.62
8	SO63370	2014-01-01 00:00:00.000	2596.7279	100806295.7051	449.63
9	SO63371	2014-01-01 00:00:00.000	2538.4944	100808834.1995	449.64
10	SO63372	2014-01-01 00:00:00.000	2602.264	100811436.4635	449.65
11	SO63373	2014-01-01 00:00:00.000	2.5305	100811438.994	449.65
12	SO63374	2014-01-01 00:00:00.000	40.0784	100811479.0724	449.65
13	SO63375	2014-01-01 00:00:00.000	40.0784	100811519.1508	449.66
14	SO63376	2014-01-01 00:00:00.000	16.5529	100811535.7037	449.66
15	SO63377	2014-01-01 00:00:00.000	136.9979	100811672.7016	449.66
16	SO63378	2014-01-01 00:00:00.000	76.2119	100811748.9135	449.66
17	SO63379	2014-01-01 00:00:00.000	104.4004	100811853.3139	449.66
18	SO63380	2014-01-01 00:00:00.000	87.2729	100811940.5868	449.66

Figure 5-3. *Partial results of the running total calculation for the year 2014*

The SP in Listing 5-4 accepts a single int parameter indicating the year for which the calculation should be performed:

```
CREATE PROCEDURE Sales.GetSalesRunningTotal (@Year int)
```

The SP uses a common table expression (CTE) to return the relevant data for the year specified, including calculations for the running total via a simple scalar subquery and the grand total via a SUM calculation with an OVER clause:

```
WITH RunningTotalCTE
AS
(
    SELECT soh.SalesOrderNumber,
        soh.OrderDate,
        soh.TotalDue,
        (
        SELECT  SUM(soh1.TotalDue)
        FROM  Sales.SalesOrderHeader  soh1
        WHERE  soh1.SalesOrderNumber  <=  soh.SalesOrderNumber
        )  AS  RunningTotal,
        SUM(soh.TotalDue) OVER () AS GrandTotal
    FROM Sales.SalesOrderHeader soh
    WHERE DATEPART(year, soh.OrderDate) = @Year
    GROUP BY soh.SalesOrderNumber,
        soh.OrderDate,
        soh.TotalDue
)
```

The result set is returned by the CTE's outer SELECT query, and the SP finishes with a RETURN statement that sends a return code of 0 back to the caller:

```
SELECT rt.SalesOrderNumber,
rt.OrderDate,
rt.TotalDue,
rt.RunningTotal,
(rt.RunningTotal / rt.GrandTotal) * 100 AS PercentTotal FROM RunningTotalCTE rt ORDER BY
rt.SalesOrderNumber; RETURN 0;
```

RUNNING SUMS

The *running sum*, or running total, is a very commonly used business reporting tool. A running sum calculates totals as of certain points in time (usually dollar amounts, and often calculated over days, months, quarters, or years—but not always). In Listing 5-4, the running sum is calculated per order, for each day over the course of a given year.

The running sum generated in the sample gives you a total sales amount as of the date and time when each order is placed. When the first order is placed, the running sum is equal to the amount of that order. When the second order is placed, the running sum is equal to the amount of the first order plus the amount of the second order, and so on. Another closely related and often used calculation is the *running average,* which represents a calculated point-in-time average as opposed to a point-in-time sum.

As an interesting aside, the ISO SQL standard allows you to use the OVER clause with aggregate functions like SUM and AVG. The ISO SQL standard allows the ORDER BY clause to be used with the aggregate function OVER clause, making for extremely efficient and compact running sum calculations. Unfortunately, SQL Server 2012 doesn't support this particular option, so you still have to resort to subqueries and other less efficient methods of performing these calculations for now.

For the next example, assume that AdventureWorks management has decided to add a database-driven feature to its web site. The feature they want is a "recommended products list" that will appear when customers add products to their online shopping carts. Of course, the first step to implementing any solution is to clearly define the requirements. The details of the requirements-gathering process are beyond the scope of this book, so you work under the assumption that the AdventureWorks business analysts have done their due diligence and reported back the following business rules for this particular function:

- The recommended products list should include additional items on orders that contain the product selected by the customer. As an example, if the product selected by the customer is product ID 773 (the silver Mountain-100 44-inch bike), then items previously bought by other customers in conjunction with this bike—like product ID 712 (the AWC logo cap)—should be recommended.

- Products that are in the same category as the product the customer selected should not be recommended. As an example, if a customer has added a bicycle to an order, other bicycles should not be recommended.

- The recommended product list should never contain more than ten items.

- The default product ID should be 776, the black Mountain-100 42-inch bike.

- The recommended products should be listed in descending order of the total quantity that has been ordered. In other words, the best-selling items will be listed in the recommendations list first.

Listing 5-5 shows the SP that implements all these business rules to return a list of recommended products based on a given product ID.

Listing 5-5. Recommended Product List SP

```
CREATE PROCEDURE Production.GetProductRecommendations (@ProductID int = 776)
AS
BEGIN
WITH RecommendedProducts
(
ProductID,
ProductSubCategoryID,
TotalQtyOrdered,
TotalDollarsOrdered
)
AS
(
SELECT
od2.ProductID,
p1.ProductSubCategoryID,
SUM(od2.OrderQty) AS TotalQtyOrdered,
SUM(od2.UnitPrice * od2.OrderQty) AS TotalDollarsOrdered
FROM Sales.SalesOrderDetail od1
INNER JOIN Sales.SalesOrderDetail od2
ON od1.SalesOrderID = od2.SalesOrderID
INNER JOIN Production.Product p1
ON od2.ProductID = p1.ProductID
WHERE od1.ProductID = @ProductID
AND od2.ProductID <> @ProductID
GROUP BY
od2.ProductID,
p1.ProductSubcategoryID
)
SELECT TOP(10) ROW_NUMBER() OVER
(
ORDER BY rp.TotalQtyOrdered DESC
) AS Rank,
rp.TotalQtyOrdered,
rp.ProductID,
rp.TotalDollarsOrdered,
p.[Name]
FROM RecommendedProducts rp
INNER JOIN Production.Product p
ON rp.ProductID = p.ProductID
```

```
WHERE rp.ProductSubcategoryID <>
(
SELECT ProductSubcategoryID
FROM Production.Product
WHERE ProductID = @ProductID
)
ORDER BY TotalQtyOrdered DESC;
END;
GO
```

The SP begins with a declaration that accepts a single parameter, @ProductID. The default @ProductID is set to 776, per the AdventureWorks management team's rules:

```
CREATE PROCEDURE Production.GetProductRecommendations (@ProductID int = 776)
```

Next, the CTE that will return the TotalQtyOrdered, ProductID, TotalDollarsOrdered, and ProductSubCategoryID for each product is defined:

```
WITH RecommendedProducts (
ProductID,
ProductSubCategorylD,
TotalQtyOrdered,
TotalDollarsOrdered )
```

In the body of the CTE, the Sales.SalesOrderDetail table is joined to itself based on SalesOrderlD. A join to the Production.Product table is also included to get each product's SubcategorylD. The point of the self-join is to grab the total quantity ordered (OrderQty) and the total dollars ordered (UnitPrice * OrderQty) for each product.

The query is designed to include only orders that contain the product passed in via @ProductID in the WHERE clause, and it also eliminates results for @ProductID itself from the final results. All the results are grouped by ProductID and ProductSubcategorylD:

```
(
SELECT
od2.ProductID,
p1.ProductSubCategoryID,
SUM(od2.OrderQty) AS TotalQtyOrdered,
SUM(od2.UnitPrice * od2.OrderQty) AS TotalDollarsOrdered
FROM Sales.SalesOrderDetail od1
INNER JOIN Sales.SalesOrderDetail od2
ON od1.SalesOrderID = od2.SalesOrderID
INNER JOIN Production.Product p1
ON od2.ProductID = p1.ProductID
WHERE od1.ProductID = @ProductID
AND od2.ProductID <> @ProductID
GROUP BY
od2.ProductID,
p1.ProductSubcategoryID
)
```

The final part of the CTE excludes products that are in the same category as the item passed in by @ProductID. It then limits the results to the top ten and numbers the results from highest to lowest by TotalQtyOrdered. It also joins on the Production.Product table to get each product's name:

```
SELECT TOP(10) ROW_NUMBER() OVER (
ORDER BY rp.TotalQtyOrdered DESC ) AS Rank,
rp.TotalQtyOrdered,
rp.ProductID,
rp.TotalDollarsOrdered,
p.[Name]

FROM RecommendedProducts rp INNER JOIN Production.Product p
ON rp.ProductID = p.ProductID WHERE rp.ProductSubcategoryID <> (
SELECT ProductSubcategoryID FROM Production.Product WHERE ProductID = @ProductID ) ORDER BY
TotalQtyOrdered DESC;
```

Figure 5-4 shows the result set of a recommended product list for people who bought a silver Mountain-100 44-inch bike (ProductID = 773), as shown in Listing 5-6.

	Rank	TotalQtyOrde...	ProductID	TotalDollarsOrde...	Name
1	1	878	709	4881.72	Mountain Bike Socks, M
2	2	340	715	9762.4748	Long-Sleeve Logo Jersey, L
3	3	297	712	1538.3157	AWC Logo Cap
4	4	235	711	4743.8275	Sport-100 Helmet, Blue
5	5	201	708	4057.4865	Sport-100 Helmet, Black
6	6	177	707	3573.0105	Sport-100 Helmet, Red
7	7	156	716	4499.1024	Long-Sleeve Logo Jersey, XL
8	8	150	714	4326.06	Long-Sleeve Logo Jersey, M
9	9	148	748	108944.0452	HL Mountain Frame - Silver, 38
10	10	145	741	118711.50	HL Mountain Frame - Silver, 48

Figure 5-4. *Recommended product list for ProductID 773*

Listing 5-6. Getting a Recommended Product List

```
EXECUTE Production..GetProductRecommendations 773;
```

Implementing this business logic in an SP provides a layer of abstraction that makes it easier to use from front-end applications. Front-end application programmers don't need to worry about the details of which tables need to be accessed, how they need to be joined, and so on. All your application developers need to know to utilize this logic from the front end is that they need to pass the SP a ProductID number parameter, and it will return the relevant information in a well-defined result set.

The same procedure promotes code reuse, and if you have business logic implemented with complex code in an SP, the code doesn't have to be written multiple times; instead you can simply call the SP to access the code. Also, if you need to change the business logic, it can be done one time, in one place. Consider what happens if the AdventureWorks management decides to make suggestions based on total dollars' worth of a product ordered instead of the total quantity ordered. You can change the ORDER BY clause from this

```
ORDER BY TotalQtyOrdered DESC;
```

to the following:

```
ORDER BY TotalDollarsOrdered DESC;
```

This simple change in the procedure does the trick. No additional changes to front-end code or logic are required, and no recompilation and redeployment of code to web server farms is needed, because the interface to the SP remains the same.

Recursion in Stored Procedures

Like UDFs, SPs can call themselves recursively. There is an SQL Server–imposed limit of 32 levels of recursion. To demonstrate recursion, let's solve a very old puzzle.

The Towers of Hanoi puzzle consists of three pegs and a specified number of discs of varying sizes that slide onto the pegs. The puzzle begins with the discs stacked on top of one another, from smallest to largest, all on one peg. The Towers of Hanoi puzzle's starting position is shown in Figure 5-5.

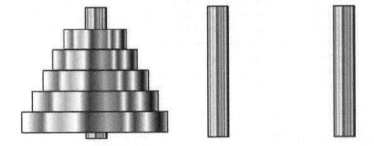

Figure 5-5. *The Towers of Hanoi puzzle's starting position*

The object of the puzzle is to move all the discs from the first tower to the third tower. The trick is that you can only move one disc at a time, and no larger disc may be stacked on top of a smaller disc at any time. You can temporarily place discs on the middle tower as necessary, and you can stack any smaller disc on top of a larger disc on any tower. The Towers of Hanoi puzzle is often used as an exercise in computer science courses to demonstrate recursion in procedural languages. This makes it a perfect candidate for a T-SQL solution to demonstrate SP recursion.

The T-SQL implementation of the Towers of Hanoi puzzle uses five discs and displays each move as the computer makes it. The complete solution is shown in Listing 5-7.

Listing 5-7. The Towers of Hanoi Puzzle

```
--  This stored procedure displays all the discs in the appropriate
--  towers.
CREATE  PROCEDURE  dbo.ShowTowers
AS
BEGIN

    -- Each disc is displayed like this "===3===" where the number is the disc
    -- and the width of the === signs on either side indicates the width of the
    -- disc.
-- These CTEs are designed for displaying the discs in proper order on each
-- tower.
WITH FiveNumbers(Num) -- Recursive CTE generates table with numbers 1...5
AS
(
    SELECT 1

    UNION ALL

    SELECT Num + 1
    FROM FiveNumbers
    WHERE Num < 5
),
GetTowerA (Disc)                -- The discs for Tower A
AS
(
    SELECT COALESCE(a.Disc, -1) AS Disc
    FROM FiveNumbers f
    LEFT JOIN #TowerA a
    ON  f.Num =         a.Disc
),
GetTowerB (Disc)                -- The discs for Tower B
AS
(
    SELECT COALESCE(b.Disc, -1) AS Disc
    FROM FiveNumbers f
    LEFT JOIN #TowerB b
    ON  f.Num =         b.Disc
),
GetTowerC (Disc)                -- The discs for Tower C
AS
(
    SELECT COALESCE(c.Disc, -1) AS Disc
    FROM FiveNumbers f
    LEFT JOIN #TowerC c
    ON  f.Num =         c.Disc
)
```

127

```sql
-- This SELECT query generates the text representation for all three towers
-- and all five discs. FULL OUTER JOIN is used to represent the towers in a
--  side-by-side format.
SELECT CASE a.Disc
        WHEN 5 THEN '  =====5===== '
        WHEN 4 THEN '   ====4==== '
        WHEN  3  THEN   '===3===      '
        WHEN  2  THEN   ' ==2==     '
        WHEN  1  THEN   ' =1=     '
        ELSE '  |  '
        END  AS Tower_A,
        CASE b.Disc
        WHEN 5 THEN '  =====5===== '
        WHEN 4 THEN '   ====4==== '
        WHEN  3  THEN  ' ===3===      '
        WHEN  2  THEN  ' ==2==     '
        WHEN  1  THEN  '  =1=      '
        ELSE '  |  '
        END  AS Tower_B,
        CASE c.Disc
        WHEN 5 THEN '  =====5===== '
        WHEN 4 THEN '   ====4==== '
        WHEN  3  THEN  ' ===3===      '
        WHEN  2  THEN  '  ==2==      '
        WHEN  1  THEN  '   =1=       '
        ELSE '  |  '
        END AS Tower_C
    FROM (
        SELECT ROW_NUMBER() OVER(ORDER BY Disc) AS Num,
        COALESCE(Disc, -1) AS Disc
        FROM GetTowerA
    ) a
    FULL  OUTER  JOIN (
        SELECT ROW_NUMBER() OVER(ORDER BY Disc) AS Num,
        COALESCE(Disc,  -1)  AS  Disc
        FROM GetTowerB
    ) b
        ON  a.Num  =  b.Num
    FULL  OUTER  JOIN   (
        SELECT ROW_NUMBER() OVER(ORDER BY Disc) AS Num,
        COALESCE(Disc, -1) AS Disc
        FROM GetTowerC
    ) c
        ON  b.Num  =  c.Num
    ORDER BY a.Num;
END;
GO
```

```
-- This SP moves a single disc from the specified source tower to the
-- specified destination tower.
CREATE  PROCEDURE  dbo.MoveOneDisc  (@Source  nchar(1),
    @Dest nchar(1))
AS
BEGIN
    -- @SmallestDisc is the smallest disc on the source tower
    DECLARE @SmallestDisc int = 0;
-- IF ... ELSE conditional statement gets the smallest disc from the
-- correct source tower
IF  @Source = N'A'
BEGIN
    -- This  gets  the  smallest  disc  from  Tower    A
    SELECT @SmallestDisc = MIN(Disc)
    FROM #TowerA;

    -- Then  delete  it  from  Tower    A
    DELETE FROM #TowerA
    WHERE Disc = @SmallestDisc;
END
ELSE  IF  @Source  =    N'B'
BEGIN
    -- This  gets  the  smallest  disc  from  Tower    B
    SELECT @SmallestDisc = MIN(Disc)
    FROM #TowerB;

    -- Then  delete  it  from  Tower    B
    DELETE FROM #TowerB
    WHERE Disc = @SmallestDisc;
END
ELSE  IF  @Source  =      N'C'
BEGIN
    -- This  gets  the  smallest  disc  from  Tower    C
    SELECT @SmallestDisc = MIN(Disc)
    FROM #TowerC;

    -- Then  delete  it  from  Tower    C
    DELETE FROM #TowerC
    WHERE Disc = @SmallestDisc;
END

-- Show the disc move performed
SELECT N'Moving Disc (' + CAST(COALESCE(@SmallestDisc, 0) AS nchar(1)) +
    N') from Tower ' + @Source + N' to Tower ' + @Dest + ':' AS Description;
```

```
-- Perform the move - INSERT the disc from the source tower into the
-- destination tower
IF  @Dest = N'A'
    INSERT INTO #TowerA (Disc) VALUES (@SmallestDisc);
ELSE IF @Dest = N'B'
    INSERT INTO #TowerB (Disc) VALUES (@SmallestDisc);
ELSE IF @Dest = N'C'
    INSERT INTO #TowerC (Disc) VALUES (@SmallestDisc);
    -- Show the towers
    EXECUTE dbo.ShowTowers;
END;
GO


-- This SP moves multiple discs recursively
CREATE  PROCEDURE  dbo.MoveDiscs  (@DiscNum  int,
    @MoveNum int OUTPUT,
    @Source nchar(1) = N'A',
    @Dest nchar(1) = N'C',
    @Aux nchar(1) = N'B'
)
AS
BEGIN
    -- If the number of discs to move is 0, the solution has been found
    IF  @DiscNum = 0
        PRINT N'Done';
    ELSE
    BEGIN
        -- If the number of discs to move is 1, go ahead and move it
        IF @DiscNum = 1
        BEGIN

        -- Increase the move counter by 1
        SELECT @MoveNum += 1;

        -- And finally move one disc from source to destination
        EXEC dbo.MoveOneDisc @Source, @Dest;
        END
        ELSE
        BEGIN
        -- Determine number of discs to move from source to auxiliary tower
        DECLARE @n int = @DiscNum - 1;

        -- Move (@DiscNum - 1) discs from source to auxiliary tower
        EXEC dbo.MoveDiscs @n, @MoveNum     OUTPUT, @Source, @Aux, @Dest;

        -- Move 1 disc from source to final destination tower
        EXEC dbo.MoveDiscs 1, @MoveNum OUTPUT, @Source, @Dest, @Aux;
```

```
        -- Move (@DiscNum - 1) discs from auxiliary to final destination tower
        EXEC dbo.MoveDiscs @n, @MoveNum    OUTPUT, @Aux, @Dest, @Source;
        END;
    END;
END;
GO
-- This SP creates the three towers and populates Tower A with 5 discs
CREATE PROCEDURE        dbo.SolveTowers
AS
BEGIN
    -- SET NOCOUNT ON to eliminate system messages that will clutter up
    -- the Message display
    SET NOCOUNT ON;

    --   Create the three towers: Tower A, Tower B, and Tower C
    CREATE TABLE #TowerA (Disc int PRIMARY KEY NOT NULL);
    CREATE TABLE #TowerB (Disc int PRIMARY KEY NOT NULL);
    CREATE TABLE #TowerC (Disc int PRIMARY KEY NOT NULL);

    -- Populate Tower A with all five discs
    INSERT INTO #TowerA (Disc)
    VALUES (1), (2), (3), (4), (5);

    -- Initialize the move number to 0
    DECLARE @MoveNum int = 0;

    -- Show the initial state of the towers
    EXECUTE dbo.ShowTowers;

    -- Solve the puzzle. Notice you don't need to specify the parameters
    -- with defaults
    EXECUTE dbo.MoveDiscs 5, @MoveNum OUTPUT;

    -- How many moves did it take?
    PRINT N'Solved in ' + CAST (@MoveNum AS nvarchar(10)) + N' moves.';

    -- Drop the temp tables to clean up - always a good idea.
    DROP TABLE #TowerC;
    DROP TABLE #TowerB;
    DROP TABLE #TowerA;

    -- SET NOCOUNT OFF before we exit
    SET NOCOUNT        OFF;
END;
GO
```

To solve the puzzle, just run the following statement:

```
-- Solve the puzzle
EXECUTE dbo.SolveTowers;
```

Figure 5-6 is a screenshot of the processing as the discs are moved from tower to tower.

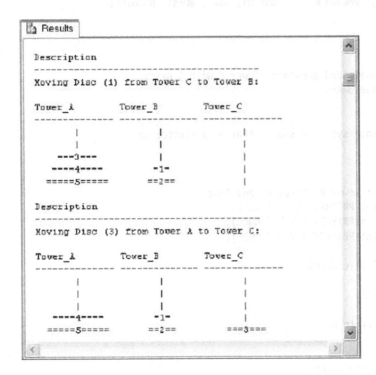

Figure 5-6. *Discs are moved from tower to tower.*

■ **Note**   The results of Listing 5-7 are best viewed in Results to Text mode. You can put SSMS in Results to Text mode by pressing Ctrl+T while in the Query Editor window. To switch to Results to Grid mode, press Ctrl+D.

The main procedure you call to solve the puzzle is dbo.SolveTowers. This SP creates three temporary tables named #TowerA, #TowerB, and #TowerC. It then populates #TowerA with five discs and initializes the current move number to 0:

```
-- Create the three towers: Tower A, Tower B, and Tower C
CREATE TABLE #TowerA (Disc int PRIMARY KEY NOT NULL);
CREATE TABLE #TowerB (Disc int PRIMARY KEY NOT NULL);
CREATE TABLE #TowerC (Disc int PRIMARY KEY NOT NULL);

-- Populate Tower A with all five discs
INSERT INTO #TowerA (Disc)
VALUES (1), (2), (3), (4), (5);

-- Initialize the move number to 0
DECLARE @MoveNum INT = 0;
```

Because this SP is the entry point for the entire puzzle-solving program, it displays the start position of the towers and calls dbo.MoveDiscs to get the ball rolling:

```
-- Show the initial state of the towers
EXECUTE dbo.ShowTowers;
-- Solve the puzzle. Notice you don't need to specify the parameters
-- with defaults
EXECUTE dbo.MoveDiscs 5, @MoveNum OUTPUT;
```

When the puzzle is finally solved, control returns back from dbo.MoveDiscs to dbo.SolveTowers, which displays the number of steps it took to complete the puzzle and performs some cleanup work, like dropping the temporary tables:

```
-- How many moves did it take?
PRINT N'Solved in ' + CAST (@MoveNum AS nvarchar(10)) + N' moves.';
-- Drop the temp tables to clean up - always a good idea.
DROP TABLE #TowerC;
DROP TABLE #TowerB;
DROP TABLE #TowerA;
-- SET NOCOUNT OFF before we exit
SET NOCOUNT OFF;
```

■ **Tip** When an SP that created local temporary tables is no longer in scope, the local temporary tables are automatically dropped. Because temporary tables are created in the tempdb system database, it's a good idea to get in the habit of explicitly dropping temporary tables. By explicitly dropping temporary tables, you can guarantee that they exist only as long as they're needed, which can help minimize contention in the tempdb database.

The procedure responsible for moving discs from tower to tower recursively is dbo.MoveDiscs. This procedure accepts several parameters, including the number of discs to move (@DiscNum); the number of the current move (@MoveNum); and the names of the source, destination, and auxiliary/intermediate towers. This procedure uses T-SQL procedural IF statements to determine which types of moves are required—single-disc moves, recursive multiple-disc moves, or no more moves (when the solution is found). If the solution has been found, the message Done is displayed, and control is subsequently passed back to the calling procedure, dbo.SolveTowers:

```
-- If the number of discs to move is 0, the solution has been found
IF @DiscNum = 0
   PRINT N'Done';
ELSE
RETURN 0;
```

If there is only one disc to move, the move counter is incremented and dbo.MoveOneDisc is called to perform the move:

```
-- If the number of discs to move is 1, go ahead and move it
IF @DiscNum = 1
BEGIN
```

```
-- Increase the move counter by 1
SELECT @MoveNum += 1;

-- And finally move one disc from source to destination
EXEC dbo.MoveOneDisc @Source, @Dest;
END
```

Finally, if there is more than one disc move required, dbo.MoveDiscs calls itself recursively until there are either one or zero discs left to move:

```
ELSE
BEGIN
-- Determine number of discs to move from source to auxiliary tower
DECLARE @n INT = @DiscNum - 1;

-- Move (@DiscNum - 1) discs from source to auxiliary tower
EXEC dbo.MoveDiscs @n, @MoveNum OUTPUT, @Source, @Aux, @Dest;

-- Move 1 disc from source to final destination tower
EXEC dbo.MoveDiscs 1, @MoveNum OUTPUT, @Source, @Dest, @Aux;

-- Move (@DiscNum - 1) discs from auxiliary to final destination tower
EXEC dbo.MoveDiscs @n, @MoveNum OUTPUT, @Aux, @Dest, @Source;
END;
```

The basis of the Towers of Hanoi puzzle is the movement of a single disc at a time from tower to tower, so the most basic procedure, dbo.MoveOneDisc, simply moves a disc from the specified source tower to the specified destination tower. Given source and destination towers as inputs, this procedure first determines the smallest (or top) disc on the source and moves it to the destination table using simple SELECT queries. The smallest disc is then deleted from the source table:

```
-- @SmallestDisc is the smallest disc on the source tower
DECLARE @SmallestDisc int = 0;
-- IF ... ELSE conditional statement gets the smallest disc from the
-- correct source tower
IF @Source = N'A'
BEGIN
-- This gets the smallest disc from Tower A
SELECT @SmallestDisc = MIN(Disc)
FROM #TowerA;

-- Then delete it from Tower A
DELETE FROM #TowerA
WHERE Disc = @SmallestDisc;
END
```

Once the smallest disc of the source table is determined, dbo.MoveOneDisc displays the move it's about to perform and then performs the INSERT to place the disc in the destination tower. Finally, it calls the dbo.ShowTowers procedure to show the current state of the towers and discs:

```
-- Show the disc move performed
SELECT N'Moving Disc
        (' + CAST(COALESCE(@SmallestDisc, 0) AS nchar(1)) + N')
 FROM Tower ' + @Source + N' to Tower '
        + @Dest + ':' AS Description;

-- Perform the move - INSERT the disc from the source tower into the
-- destination tower
IF @Dest = N'A'
INSERT INTO #TowerA (Disc) VALUES (@SmallestDisc);
ELSE IF @Dest = N'B'
INSERT INTO #TowerB (Disc) VALUES (@SmallestDisc);
ELSE IF @Dest = N'C
INSERT INTO #TowerC (Disc) VALUES (@SmallestDisc);
-- Show the towers
EXECUTE dbo.ShowTowers;
```

The dbo.ShowTowers procedure doesn't affect processing; it's included as a convenience to output a reasonable representation of the towers and discs they contain at any given point during processing.

This implementation of a solver for the Towers of Hanoi puzzle demonstrates several aspects of SPs introduced in this chapter, including the following:

- SPs can call themselves recursively. This is demonstrated with the dbo.MoveDiscs procedure, which calls itself until the puzzle is solved.

- When default values are assigned to parameters in an SP declaration, you don't have to specify values for them when you call the procedure. This concept is demonstrated in the dbo.SolveTowers procedure, which calls the dbo.MoveDiscs procedure.

- The scope of temporary tables created in an SP includes the procedure in which they're created, as well as any SPs it calls and any SPs they in turn call. This is demonstrated in dbo.SolveTowers, which creates three temporary tables and then calls other procedures that access those same temporary tables. The procedures called by dbo.SolveTowers and those called by those procedures (and so on) can also access these same temporary tables.

- The dbo.MoveDiscs SP demonstrates output parameters. This procedure uses an output parameter to update the count of the total number of moves performed after each move.

Table-Valued Parameters

Beginning with SQL Server 2008, you can pass table-valued parameters to SPs and UDFs. Prior to SQL Server 2008, the primary methods of passing multiple rows of data to an SP included the following:

- Converting multiple rows to an intermediate format like comma-delimited or XML. If you use this method, you have to parse out the parameter into a temporary table, table variable, or subquery to extract the rows from the intermediate format. These conversions to and from intermediate format can be costly, especially when large amounts of data are involved.

- Placing rows in a permanent or temporary table and calling the procedure. This method eliminates conversions to and from the intermediate format, but it isn't without problems of its own. Managing multiple sets of input rows from multiple simultaneous users can introduce a lot of overhead and additional conversion code that must be managed.

- Passing lots and lots of parameters to the SP. SQL Server SPs can accept up to 2,100 parameters. Conceivably, you could pass several rows of data using thousands of parameters and ignore those parameters you don't need. One big drawback to this method, however, is that it results in complex code that can be extremely difficult to manage.

- Calling procedures multiple times with a single row of data each time. This method is probably the simplest, resulting in code that is very easy to create and manage. The downside to this method is that querying and manipulating potentially tens of thousands of rows of data or more, one row at a time, can result in a big performance penalty.

A table-valued parameter allows you to pass rows of data to your T-SQL statement or SPs and UDFs in tabular format. To create a table-valued parameter, you must first create a *table type* that defines your table structure, as shown in Listing 5-8.

Listing 5-8. Creating a Table Type

```
CREATE TYPE HumanResources.LastNameTableType
AS TABLE (LastName nvarchar(50) NOT NULL PRIMARY KEY);
GO
```

The CREATE TYPE statement in Listing 5-8 creates a simple table type that represents a table with a single column named LastName, which also serves as the primary key for the table. To use table-valued parameters, you must declare your SP with parameters of the table type. The SP in Listing 5-9 accepts a single table-valued parameter of the HumanResources.LastNameTableType type from Listing 5-8. It then uses the rows in the table-valued parameter in an inner join to restrict the rows returned by the SP.

Listing 5-9. Simple Procedure Accepting a Table-Valued Parameter

```
CREATE  PROCEDURE  HumanResources.GetEmployees
    (@LastNameTable HumanResources.LastNameTableType READONLY)
AS
BEGIN
    SELECT
        p.LastName,
        p.FirstName,
        p.MiddleName,
```

```
        e.NationalIDNumber,
        e.Gender,
        e.HireDate
    FROM  HumanResources.Employee  e
    INNER JOIN Person.Person p
        ON  e.BusinessEntityID  =  p.BusinessEntityID
    INNER JOIN @LastNameTable lnt
        ON p.LastName = lnt.LastName
    ORDER BY
        p.LastName,
        p.FirstName,
        p.MiddleName;
END;
GO
```

The CREATE PROCEDURE statement in Listing 5-9 declares a single table-valued parameter, @LastNameTable, of the HumanResources.LastNameTableType created in Listing 5-8:

```
CREATE PROCEDURE HumanResources.GetEmployees
(@LastNameTable HumanResources.LastNameTableType READONLY)
```

The table-valued parameter is declared READONLY, which is mandatory. Although you can query and join to the rows in a table-valued parameter just like a table variable, you can't manipulate the rows in table-valued parameters with INSERT, UPDATE, DELETE, or MERGE statements.

The HumanResources.GetEmployees procedure performs a simple query to retrieve the names, national ID number, gender, and hire date for all employees whose last names match any of the last names passed into the SP via the @LastNameTable table-valued parameter. As you can see in Listing 5-9, the SELECT query performs an inner join against the table-valued parameter to restrict the rows returned:

```
SELECT
    p.LastName,
    p.FirstName,
    p.MiddleName,
    e.NationalIDNumber,
    e.Gender,
    e.HireDate
FROM HumanResources.Employee e
INNER JOIN Person.Person p
    ON e.BusinessEntityID = p.BusinessEntityID
INNER JOIN @LastNameTable lnt
    ON p.LastName = lnt.LastName
ORDER BY
    p.LastName,
    p.FirstName,
    p.MiddleName;
```

To call a procedure with a table-valued parameter, like the HumanResources.GetEmployees SP in Listing 5-9, you need to declare a variable of the same type as the table-valued parameter. Then you populate the variable with rows of data and pass the variable as a parameter to the procedure. Listing 5-10 demonstrates how to call the HumanResources.GetEmployees SP with a table-valued parameter. The results are shown in Figure 5-7.

Listing 5-10. Calling a Procedure with a Table-valued Parameter

```
DECLARE @LastNameList HumanResources.LastNameTableType;
INSERT INTO @LastNameList
(LastName)
VALUES
(N'Walters'),
(N'Anderson'),
(N'Chen'),
(N'Rettig'),
(N'Lugo'),
(N'Zwilling'),
(N'Johnson');

EXECUTE HumanResources.GetEmployees @LastNameList;
```

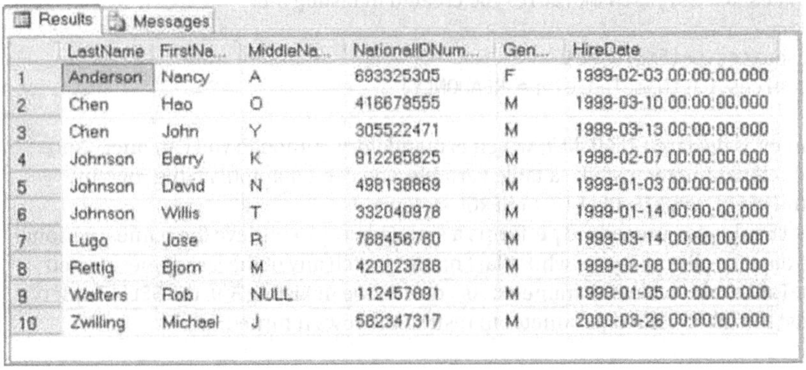

	LastName	FirstNa...	MiddleNa...	NationalIDNum...	Gen...	HireDate
1	Anderson	Nancy	A	693325305	F	1999-02-03 00:00:00.000
2	Chen	Hao	O	416678555	M	1999-03-10 00:00:00.000
3	Chen	John	Y	305522471	M	1999-03-13 00:00:00.000
4	Johnson	Barry	K	912265825	M	1998-02-07 00:00:00.000
5	Johnson	David	N	498138869	M	1999-01-03 00:00:00.000
6	Johnson	Willis	T	332040978	M	1999-01-14 00:00:00.000
7	Lugo	Jose	R	788456780	M	1999-03-14 00:00:00.000
8	Rettig	Bjorn	M	420023788	M	1999-02-08 00:00:00.000
9	Walters	Rob	NULL	112457891	M	1998-01-05 00:00:00.000
10	Zwilling	Michael	J	582347317	M	2000-03-26 00:00:00.000

Figure 5-7. *Employees returned by the SP call in Listing 5-10*

In addition to being read-only, the following additional restrictions apply to table-valued parameters:

- As with table variables, you can't use a table-valued parameter as the target of an INSERT EXEC or SELECT INTO assignment statement.

- Table-valued parameters are scoped just like other parameters and local variables declared in a procedure or function. They aren't visible outside of the procedure in which they're declared.

- SQL Server doesn't maintain column-level statistics for table-valued parameters, which can affect performance if you're passing large numbers of rows of data via table-valued parameters.

You can also pass table-valued parameters to SPs from ADO.NET clients, as discussed in Chapter 16.

Temporary Stored Procedures

In addition to normal SPs, T-SQL provides what are known as *temporary SPs*. Temporary SPs are created just like any other SPs; the only difference is that the name must begin with a number sign (#) for a local temporary SP and two number signs (##) for a global temporary SP. A third possibility is to create a temporary SP in the tempdb database. The scope of anything created in the tempdb database is until the instance is restarted, because tempdb is re-created each time an instance is restarted. It isn't possible to create a temporary natively compiled SP. Temporary SPs are only used in traditional T-SQL interpretive SPs.

Whereas a normal SP remains in the database and schema it was created in until it's explicitly dropped via the DROP PROCEDURE statement, temporary SPs are dropped automatically. A local temporary SP is visible only to the current session and is dropped when the current session ends. A global temporary SP is visible to all connections and is automatically dropped when the last session using it ends.

Normally you won't use temporary SPs; they're usually used for specialized solutions, like database drivers. Open Database Connectivity (ODBC) drivers, for instance, use temporary SPs to implement SQL Server connectivity functions. Temporary SPs are useful when you want the advantages of using SPs, such as execution plan reuse and improved error handling, with the advantages of ad hoc code. However, temporary SPs bring some other effects, as well. They're often not destroyed until the connection is closed or explicitly dropped. This may cause the procedures to fill up tempdb over time and cause queries to fail. Creating temporary SPs in a transaction may also cause blocking problems, because the SP creation causes data-page locking in several system tables for the transaction duration.

Recompilation and Caching

SQL Server has several features that work behind the scenes to optimize SP performance. The first time you execute an SP, SQL Server compiles it into a query plan, which it then caches. This compilation process invokes a certain amount of overhead, which can be substantial for procedures that are complex or that are run very often. SQL Server uses a complex caching mechanism to store and reuse query plans on subsequent calls to the same SP, in an effort to minimize the impact of SP compilation overhead. This section talks about managing query-plan recompilation and cached query-plan reuse.

Stored Procedure Statistics

SQL Server 2014 provides DMVs and *dynamic management functions (DMFs)* to expose SP query-plan usage and caching information that can be useful for performance tuning and general troubleshooting. Listing 5-11 is a procedure that retrieves and displays several relevant SP statistics from a few different DMVs and DMFs.

Listing 5-11. Procedure to Retrieve SP Statistics with DMVs and DMFs

```
CREATE  PROCEDURE dbo.GetProcStats  (@order  varchar(100)  =  'use')
AS
BEGIN
    WITH GetQueryStats
    (
        plan_handle,
        total_elapsed_time,
        total_logical_reads,
        total_logical_writes,
        total_physical_reads
    )
```

```
AS
(
    SELECT
    qs.plan_handle,
    SUM(qs.total_elapsed_time) AS total_elapsed_time,
    SUM(qs.total_logical_reads) AS total_logical_reads,
    SUM(qs.total_logical_writes) AS total_logical_writes,
    SUM(qs.total_physical_reads) AS total_physical_reads
    FROM sys.dm_exec_query_stats qs
    GROUP BY qs.plan_handle
)
SELECT
    DB_NAME(st.dbid) AS database_name,
    OBJECT_SCHEMA_NAME(st.objectid, st.dbid) AS schema_name,
    OBJECT_NAME(st.objectid, st.dbid) AS proc_name,
    SUM(cp.usecounts) AS use_counts,
    SUM(cp.size_in_bytes) AS size_in_bytes,
    SUM(qs.total_elapsed_time) AS total_elapsed_time,
    CAST
    (
    SUM(qs.total_elapsed_time) AS decimal(38, 4)
    ) / SUM(cp.usecounts) AS avg_elapsed_time_per_use,
    SUM(qs.total_logical_reads) AS total_logical_reads,
    CAST
    (
    SUM(qs.total_logical_reads) AS decimal(38, 4)
    ) / SUM(cp.usecounts) AS avg_logical_reads_per_use,
    SUM(qs.total_logical_writes) AS total_logical_writes,
    CAST
    (
    SUM(qs.total_logical_writes) AS decimal(38, 4)
    ) / SUM(cp.usecounts) AS avg_logical_writes_per_use,
    SUM(qs.total_physical_reads) AS total_physical_reads,
    CAST
    (
    SUM(qs.total_physical_reads) AS decimal(38, 4)
    ) / SUM(cp.usecounts) AS avg_physical_reads_per_use,
    st.text
FROM sys.dm_exec_cached_plans cp
CROSS APPLY sys.dm_exec_sql_text(cp.plan_handle) st
INNER JOIN GetQueryStats qs
    ON cp.plan_handle = qs.plan_handle
INNER JOIN sys.procedures p
    ON st.objectid = p.object_id
    WHERE p.type IN ('P', 'PC')
    GROUP BY st.dbid, st.objectid, st.text
    ORDER BY
    CASE @order
    WHEN 'name' THEN OBJECT_NAME(st.objectid)
    WHEN 'size' THEN SUM(cp.size_in_bytes)
    WHEN 'read' THEN SUM(qs.total_logical_reads)
```

```
            WHEN  'write'  THEN  SUM(qs.total_logical_writes)
            ELSE  SUM(cp.usecounts)
            END DESC;
END;
GO
```

This procedure uses the sys.dm_exec_cached_plans and sys.dm_exec_query_stats DMVs in conjunction with the sys.dmexecsqltext DMF to retrieve relevant SP execution information. The sys. procedures catalog view is used to limit the results to only SPs (type P). Aggregation is required on most of the statistics because the DMVs and DMFs can return multiple rows, each representing individual statements in SPs. The dbo.GetProcStats procedure accepts a single parameter that determines how the result rows are sorted. Setting the @order parameter to size sorts the results in descending order by the sizeinbytes column, whereas read sorts in descending order by the totallogicalreads column. Other possible values include name and write—all other values sort by the default usecounts column in descending order.

■ **Tip**   This SP uses a few useful system functions: DB_NAME accepts the ID of a database and returns the database name, OBDECT_SCHEMA_NAME accepts the ID of an object and a database ID and returns the name of the schema in which the object resides, and OBJECT_NAME accepts the object ID and returns the name of the object itself. These are handy functions, and you can retrieve the same information via SQL Server's catalog views.

Listing 5-12 demonstrates how to call this SP. Sample results are shown in Figure 5-8.

Listing 5-12. Retrieving SP Statistics

```
EXEC dbo.GetProcStats @order = 'use';
GO
```

	database_name	schema_name	proc_name	use_counts	size_in_bytes	total_elapsed_time	avg_elapsed_time_per_use	total_logic
1	AdventureWorks	Sales	GetSalesRunningTotal	2	147456	18967722	9483861.000000	954353
2	AdventureWorks	Production	GetProductRecommendations	1	90112	135876	135876.000000	2647
3	AdventureWorks	HumanResources	GetEmployees	1	73728	42842	42842.000000	582

Figure 5-8. *Partial results of calling the GetProcStats procedure*

SQL Server DMVs and DMFs can be used this way to answer several questions about your SPs, including the following:

- Which SPs are executed the most?
- Which SPs take the longest to execute?
- Which SPs perform the most logical reads and writes?

The answers to these types of questions can help you quickly locate performance bottlenecks and focus your performance-tuning efforts where they're most needed. Chapter 20 discusses performance tuning in detail.

Parameter Sniffing

SQL Server uses a method known as *parameter sniffing* to further optimize SP calls. During compilation or recompilation of an SP, SQL Server captures the parameters used and passes the values along to the optimizer. The optimizer then generates and caches a query plan optimized for those parameters. This can actually cause problems in some cases—for example, when your SP can return wildly varying numbers of rows based on the parameters passed in. Listing 5-13 shows a simple SP that retrieves all products from the Production.Product table with a Name like the @Prefix parameter passed into the SP.

Listing 5-13. Simple Procedure to Demonstrate Parameter Sniffing

```
CREATE  PROCEDURE  Production.GetProductsByName
    @Prefix NVARCHAR(100)
AS
BEGIN
    SELECT
        p.Name,
        p.ProductID
    FROM  Production.Product  p
    WHERE p.Name LIKE @Prefix;
END;
GO
```

Calling this SP with the @Prefix parameter set to % results in a query plan optimized to return 504 rows of data with a nonclustered index scan, as shown in Figure 5-9.

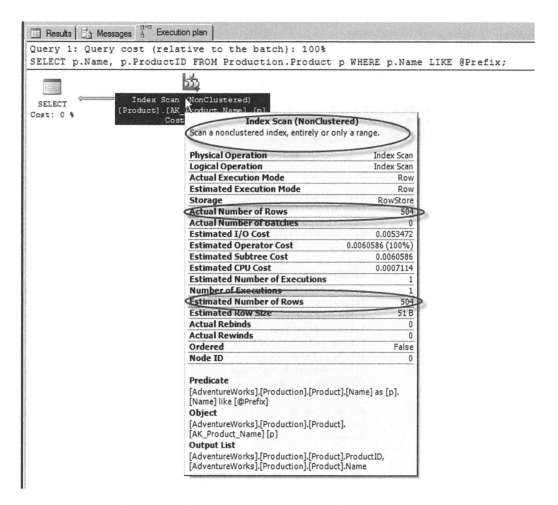

Figure 5-9. *Query plan optimized to return 504 rows*

If you run the Production.GetProductsByName procedure a second time with the @Prefix parameter set to M%, the query plan shows that the plan is still optimized to return 504 estimated rows, although only 102 rows are returned by the SP. Figure 5-10 shows the query plan for the second procedure call.

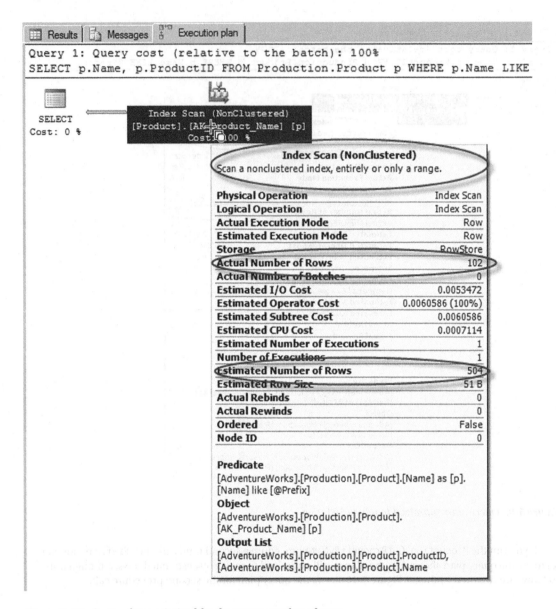

Figure 5-10. *Query plan optimized for the wrong number of rows*

In cases where you expect widely varying numbers of rows to be returned by your SPs, you can override parameter sniffing on a per-procedure basis. Overriding parameter sniffing is simple—just declare a local variable in your SP, assign the parameter value to the variable, and use the variable in place of the parameter in your query. When you override parameter sniffing, SQL Server uses the source table data-distribution statistics to estimate the number of rows to return. The theory is that the estimate will be better for a wider variety of possible parameter values. In this case, the estimate will still be considerably off for the extreme case of the 504 rows returned in this example, but it will be much closer and will therefore generate better query plans for other possible parameter values. Listing 5-14 alters the SP in Listing 5-13 to override parameter sniffing. Figure 5-11 shows the results of calling the updated SP with a @Prefix parameter of M%.

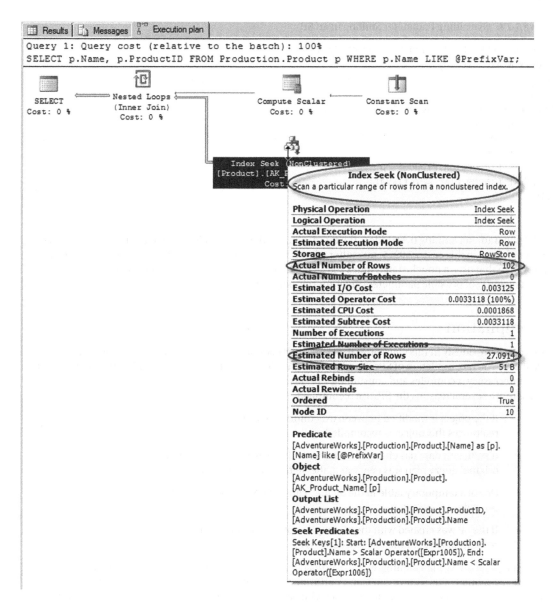

Figure 5-11. *Results of the SP with parameter sniffing overridden*

Listing 5-14. Overriding Parameter Sniffing in an SP

```
ALTER PROCEDURE Production.GetProductsByName
@Prefix NVARCHAR(100)
AS
BEGIN
DECLARE @PrefixVar NVARCHAR(100) = @Prefix;
    SELECT
        p.Name,
        p.ProductID
    FROM  Production.Product  p
    WHERE p.Name LIKE @PrefixVar;
END;
GO
```

With parameter sniffing overridden, the query plan for the SP in Listing 5-14 uses the same estimated number of rows, in this case 27.0914, no matter what value you pass in the @Prefix parameter. This results in a query plan that uses a nonclustered index seek—not an index scan—which is a much better query plan for the vast majority of possible parameter values for this particular SP.

Recompilation

As discussed previously in this chapter, SQL Server optimizes performance by caching compiled query plans while it can. The recompilation of SPs is performed on individual statements in SPs rather than entire SPs to avoid unnecessary recompiles and consuming CPU resources.

There are several reasons the SPs are recompiled:

- If the object is modified between executions, each statement in the SP that references this object is recompiled.

- If sufficient data has changed in the table that is being referenced by the SP since the original query plan was generated, the SP recompiles the plan.

- Use of a temporary table in the SP may cause the SP to be recompiled every time the procedure is executed.

- If the SP was created with the recompile option, this may cause the SP to be recompiled every time the procedure is executed.

Caching the query plan eliminates the overhead associated with recompiling your query on subsequent runs, but occasionally this feature can cause performance to suffer. When you expect your SP to return widely varying numbers of rows in the result set with each call, the cached query-execution plan is only optimized for the first call. It isn't optimized for subsequent executions. In cases like this, you may decide to force recompilation with each call. Consider Listing 5-15, which is an SP that returns order header information for a given salesperson.

Listing 5-15. SP to Retrieve Orders by Salesperson

```
CREATE  PROCEDURE  Sales.GetSalesBySalesPerson  (@SalesPersonId  int)
AS
BEGIN
    SELECT
        soh.SalesOrderID,
        soh.OrderDate,
        soh.TotalDue
    FROM  Sales.SalesOrderHeader  soh
    WHERE soh.SalesPersonID = @SalesPersonId;
END;
GO
```

There happens to be a nonclustered index on the SalesPersonID column of the Sales.SalesOrderHeader table, which you might expect to be considered by the optimizer. However, when this SP is executed with the EXECUTE statement in Listing 5-16, the optimizer ignores the nonclustered index and instead performs a clustered index scan, as shown in Figure 5-12.

Listing 5-16. Retrieving Sales for Salesperson 277

```
EXECUTE Sales.GetSalesBySalesPerson 277;
```

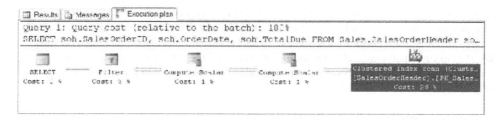

Figure 5-12. *The SP ignores the nonclustered index*

The SP ignores the nonclustered index on the SalesPersonID column because 473 matching rows are returned by the query in the procedure. SQL Server uses a measure called *selectivity,* the ratio of qualifying rows to the total number of rows in the table, as a factor in determining which index, if any, to use. In Listing 5-16, the parameter value 277 represents low selectivity, meaning a large number of rows are returned relative to the number of rows in the table. SQL Server favors indexes for highly selective queries, to the point of completely ignoring indexes when the query has low selectivity.

If you subsequently call the SP with the @SalesPersonId parameter set to 285, which represents a highly selective value (only 16 rows are returned), query-plan caching forces the same clustered index scan, even though it's suboptimal for a highly selective query. Fortunately, SQL Server provides options that allow you to force recompilation at the SP level or the statement level. You can force a recompilation in an SP call by adding the WITH RECOMPILE option to the EXECUTE statement, as shown in Listing 5-17.

Listing 5-17. Executing an SP with Recompilation

```
EXECUTE Sales.GetSalesBySalesPerson 285 WITH RECOMPILE;
```

The WITH RECOMPILE option of the EXECUTE statement forces a recompilation of the SP when you execute it. This option is useful if your data has significantly changed since the last SP recompilation or if the parameter value you're passing to the procedure represents an atypical value. The query plan for this SP call with the highly selective value 285 is shown in Figure 5-13.

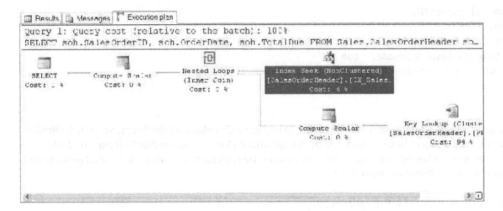

Figure 5-13. SP query plan optimized for a highly selective parameter value

You can also use the sp_recompile system SP to force an SP to recompile the next time it's run.

If you expect that the values submitted to your SP will vary a lot, and that the "one execution plan for all parameters" model will cause poor performance, you can specify statement-level recompilation by adding OPTION (RECOMPILE) to your statements. The statement-level recompilation also considers the values of local variables during the recompilation process. Listing 5-18 alters the SP created in Listing 5-16 to add statement-level recompilation to the SELECT query.

Listing 5-18. Adding Statement-Level Recompilation to the SP

```
ALTER  PROCEDURE  Sales.GetSalesBySalesPerson  (@SalesPersonId  int)
AS
BEGIN
    SELECT
        soh.SalesOrderID,
        soh.OrderDate,
        soh.TotalDue
    FROM  Sales.SalesOrderHeader  soh
    WHERE soh.SalesPersonID = @SalesPersonId
    OPTION (RECOMPILE);
END;
GO
```

As an alternative, you can specify procedure-level recompilation by adding the WITH RECOMPILE option to your CREATE PROCEDURE statement. This option is useful if you don't want SQL Server to cache the query plan for the SP. With this option in place, SQL Server recompiles the entire SP every time you run it. This can be useful for procedures containing several statements that need to be recompiled often. Keep in mind, however, that this option is less efficient than a statement-level recompile because the entire SP needs to be recompiled. Because it's less efficient than statement-level recompilation, this option should be used with care.

To expand on the "Stored Procedure Statistics" section of this chapter, SQL Server 2014 provides details about the last time the SP or the statements were recompiled with DMVs. This can help you identify the most-recompiled SPs and allow you to focus on resolving the recompilation issues. Listing 5-19 is a procedure that returns the SPs that have been recompiled.

Listing 5-19. SP to Return a List of Stored Procedures That Have Been Recompiled

```
CREATE  PROCEDURE  dbo.GetRecompiledProcs
AS
BEGIN
    SELECT
        sql_text.text,
        stats.sql_handle,
        stats.plan_generation_num,
        stats.creation_time,
        stats.execution_count,
        sql_text.dbid,
        sql_text.objectid
    FROM sys.dm_exec_query_stats stats
        Cross apply sys.dm_exec_sql_text(sql_handle) as sql_text
    WHERE stats.plan_generation_num > 1
        and sql_text.objectid is not null --Filter adhoc queries
    ORDER BY stats.plan_generation_num desc
END;
GO
```

This procedure uses the sys.dm_exec_query_stats DMV with the sys.dm_exec_sql_text DMF to retrieve relevant SP execution information. The query returns only the SPs that have been recompiled by filtering plan_generation_num, and the ad hoc queries are filtered out by removing object_ids with null values.

Listing 5-20 demonstrates how to call this SP, and partial results are shown in Figure 5-14.

Listing 5-20. Retrieving SP Statistics

```
EXEC dbo.GetRecompiledProcs;
GO
```

	text	sql_handle	plan_generation_num
1	CREATE PROCEDURE [dbo].[CleanBrokenSnapshots] @...	0x03000500C80EF6438BD82A012DA0000001000000000000...	8
2	CREATE PROCEDURE [dbo].[CleanBrokenSnapshots] @...	0x03000500C80EF6438BD82A012DA0000001000000000000...	7
3	CREATE PROCEDURE [dbo].[CleanBrokenSnapshots] @...	0x03000500C80EF6438BD82A012DA0000001000000000000...	6
4	CREATE PROCEDURE [dbo].[CleanBrokenSnapshots] @...	0x03000500C80EF6438BD82A012DA0000001000000000000...	5
5	CREATE PROCEDURE [dbo].[CleanBrokenSnapshots] @...	0x03000500C80EF6438BD82A012DA0000001000000000000...	4
6	CREATE PROCEDURE [dbo].[CleanBrokenSnapshots] @...	0x03000500C80EF6438BD82A012DA0000001000000000000...	3
7	CREATE PROCEDURE [dbo].[CleanBrokenSnapshots] @...	0x03000500C80EF6438BD82A012DA0000001000000000000...	2

Figure 5-14. *Partial results for the SP dbo.GetRecompiledProcs*

Summary

SPs are powerful tools for SQL Server development. They provide a flexible method of extending the power of SQL Server by allowing you to create custom server-side subroutines. Although some of the performance advantages provided by SPs in older releases of SQL Server aren't as pronounced in SQL Server 2014, the ability to modularize server-side code, administer your T-SQL code base in a single location, provide additional security, and ease front-end programming development still make SPs useful development tools in any T-SQL developer's toolkit. With the newly added functionality of compiling SPs into machine code, the manner in which you have traditionally architected a solution should come into question. Pulling your business logic into your database may make sense in some use cases, but as with any decision in software, it always depends.

This chapter introduced key aspects of SP development: creating natively compiled SPs; management; passing scalar parameters to SPs; and retrieving result sets, output parameters, and return values from SPs. You also saw some advanced topics, including the use of temporary tables to pass tabular data between SPs, writing recursive SPs, and SQL Server 2014's table-valued parameters.

Finally, the chapter ended with a discussion of SP optimizations, including SP caching, accessing SP cache statistics through DMVs and DMFs, parameter sniffing, and recompilation options, including statement-level and procedure-level recompilation.

The examples provided in this chapter are designed to demonstrate several aspects of SP functionality in SQL Server 2014. The next chapter goes into the newly available In-Memory OLTP features available in SQL Server 2014.

EXERCISES

1. [True/False] The SP RETURN statement can return a scalar value of any data type.

2. The recursion level for SPs is 32 levels, as demonstrated by the following code sample, which errors out after reaching the maximum depth of recursion:

```
CREATE PROCEDURE dbo.FirstProc (@i int)
AS
BEGIN
PRINT @i;
SET @i += 1;
EXEC dbo.FirstProc @i; END; GO
EXEC dbo.FirstProc 1;
```

   Write a second procedure and modify this one to prove that the recursion limit applies to two SPs that call each other recursively.

3. [Choose one] Table-valued parameters must be declared with which of the following modifiers:

   - READWRITE

   - WRITEONLY

   - RECOMPILE

   - READONLY

4. When creating a natively compiled stored procedure, which of the following options are required? [Choose all that apply]

   a. SCHEMABINDING

   b. WITH NATIVE_COMPILATION

   c. EXECUTE AS

   d. BEGIN ATOMIC

CHAPTER 6

■ ■ ■

In-Memory Programming

SQL Server 2014 introduces new In-Memory features that are a game-changer in how you consider the data and physical architecture of database solutions. The manner in which data is accessed, the indexes used for in-memory tables, and the methods used for concurrency make this a significant new feature of the database software in SQL Server 2014. In-Memory OLTP is a performance enhancement that allows you to store data in memory using a completely new architecture. In addition to storing data in memory, database objects are compiled into a native DLL in the database.

This release of SQL Server has made investments in three different In-Memory technologies: In-Memory OLTP, In-Memory data warehousing (DW), and the SSD Buffer Pool Extension. This chapter covers the In-Memory OLTP programming features; In-Memory DW and the Buffer Pool Extension aren't applicable to the subject matter in this book.

In-Memory solutions provide a significant performance enhancement targeted at OLTP workloads. In-Memory OLTP specifically targets the high concurrency, processing, and retrieval contention typical in OLTP transactional workloads. These are the first versions of such features for SQL Server, and therefore they have numerous limitations, which are discussed in this chapter. Regardless of the limitations, some use cases see as much as a 30x performance improvement. Such performance improvements make In-Memory OLTP compelling for use in your environment.

In-Memory OLTP is available in existing SQL Server 2014 installations; no specialized software is required. Additionally, the use of commodity hardware is a benefit of SQL Server's implementation of this feature over other vendors that may require expensive hardware or specialized versions of their software.

The Drivers for In-Memory Technology

Hardware trends, larger datasets, and the speed at which OLTP data needs to become available are all major drivers for the development of in-memory technology. This technology has been in the works for the past several years, as Microsoft has sought to address these technological trends.

Hardware Trends

CPU, memory, disk speeds, and network connections have continually increased in speed and capacity since the invention of computers. However, we're at the point that traditional approaches to making computers run faster are changing due to the economics of the cost of memory versus the speed of CPU processing. In 1965, Gordon E Moore "made the observation that, over the history of computing hardware, the number of transistors in a dense integrated circuit doubles approximately every two years."[1] Since then, this statement has been known as Moore's Law. Figure 6-1 shows a graph of the increase in the number of transistors on a single circuit.

---

[1] "Moore's Law," http://en.wikipedia.org/wiki/Moore's_law.

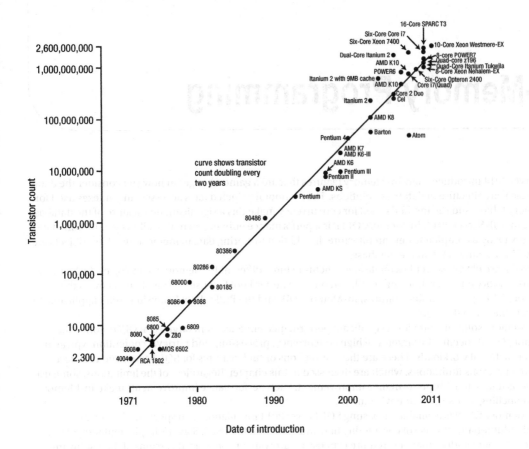

Figure 6-1. *Moore's Law transistor counts*

Manufacturers of memory, pixels on a screen, network bandwidth, CPU architecture, and so on have all used Moore's Law as a guide for long-term planning. It's hard to believe, but today, increasing the amount of power to a transistor, for faster CPU clock speed, no longer makes economic sense. As the amount of power being sent to a transistor is increased, the transistor heats up to the point that the physical components begin to melt and malfunction. We've essentially hit a practical limitation on the clock speed for an individual chip, because it isn't possible to effectively control the temperature of a CPU. The best way to continue to increase the power of a CPU with the same clock speed is via additional cores per socket.

In parallel to the limitations of CPUs, the cost of memory has continued to decline significantly over time. It's common for servers and commodity hardware to come equipped with more memory than multimillion-dollar servers had available 20 years ago. Table 6-1 shows the historical price of 1 gigabyte of memory.

Table 6-1. Price of RAM over time[2]

Historic RAM Prices	
Year	Average Cost per Gigabyte
1980	$6,635,520.00
1985	$ 901,120.00
1990	$ 108,544.00
1995	$ 31,641.60
2000	$ 1,149.95
2005	$ 189.44
2010	$ 12.50
2014	$ 9.34

In order to make effective use of additional cores and the increase in memory available with modern hardware, software has to be written to take advantage of these hardware trends. The SQL Server 2014 In-Memory features are the result of these trends and customer demand for additional capacity on OLTP databases.

Getting Started with In-Memory Objects

SQL Server 2014 In-Memory features are offered in Enterprise, Developer, and Evaluation (64-bit only) Editions of the software. These features were previously available only to corporations that had a very large budget to spend on specialized software and hardware. Given the way Microsoft has deployed these features in existing editions, you may be able to use them an existing installation of your OLTP database system.

The in-memory objects require a FILESTREAM data file (container) to be created using a memory-optimized data filegroup. From here on, this chapter uses the term *container* rather than *data file*; it's more appropriate because a data file is created on disk at the time data is written to the new memory-optimized tables. Several checkpoint files are created in the memory-optimized data filegroup for the purposes of keeping track of changes to data in the FILESTREAM container file. The data for memory-optimized tables is stored in a combination of the transaction log and checkpoint files until a background thread called an *offline checkpoint* appends the information to data and delta files. In the event of a server crash or availability group failover, all durable table data is recovered from a combination of the data, delta, transaction log, and checkpoint files. All nondurable tables are re-created, because the schema is durable, but the data is lost. The differences between durable and non-durable tables, advantages, disadvantages, and some use cases are explained further in the section "Step 3," later in this chapter.

You can alter any existing database or new database to accommodate in-memory data files (containers) by adding the new data and filegroup structures. Several considerations should be taken into account prior to doing so. The following sections cover the steps listed in the code format and SQL Server Management Studio to create these structures.

---

[2]"Average Historic Price of RAM," Statistic Brain, www.statisticbrain.com/average-historic-price-of-ram.

Step 1: Add a New Memory-Optimized Data FILEGROUP

Typically, before you can begin to using FILESTREAM in SQL Server, you must enable FILESTREAM on the instance of the SQL Server Database Engine. With memory-optimized filegroups, you don't need to enable FILESTREAM because the mapping to it's handled by the In-Memory OLTP engine.

The memory-optimized data filegroup should be created on a solid state drive (SSD) or fast serial attached SCSI (SAS) drive. Memory-optimized tables have different access patterns than traditional disk-based tables and require the faster disk subsystems to fully realize the speed benefit of this filegroup. Listing 6-1, adds a new memory-optimized filegroup to our existing AdventureWorks2014 database. This syntax can be used against any existing 2014 database on the proper SQL Server edition of the software.

Listing 6-1. Adding a New Filegroup

```
IF NOT EXISTS
  (SELECT * FROM AdventureWorks2014.sys.data_spaces WHERE TYPE = 'FX')
ALTER DATABASE AdventureWorks2014
  ADD FILEGROUP [AdventureWorks2014_mem] CONTAINS MEMORY_OPTIMIZED_DATA
GO
```

This adds an empty memory-optimized data filegroup to which you'll add containers in the next step. The key words in the syntax are CONTAINS MEMORY_OPTIMIZED_DATA, to create as a memory-optimized data filegroup. You can create multiple containers but only one memory-optimized data filegroup. Adding additional memory-optimized data filegroups results in the following error:

```
Msg 10797, Level 15, State 2, Line 2
Only one MEMORY_OPTIMIZED_DATA filegroup is allowed per database.
```

In Listing 6-1, we added a new memory-optimized filegroup using T-SQL code. In the following example, we will do the same using SQL Server Management Studio. Following are the steps to accomplish adding the filegroup via Management Studio (see Figure 6-2):

1. Right-click the database to which you want to add the new filegroup, and select Properties.

2. Select the Filegroups option, and type in the name of the memory-optimized data filegroup you wish to add.

3. Click the Add Filegroup button.

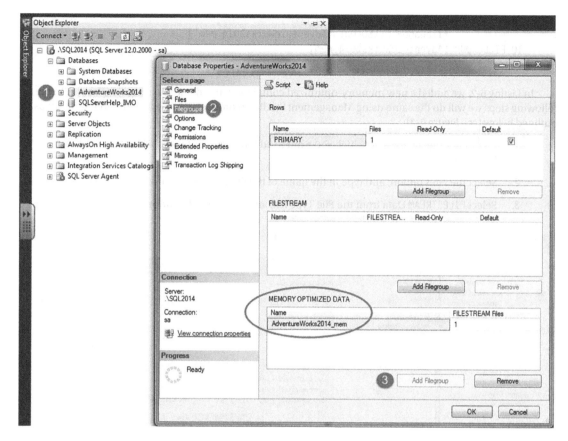

Figure 6-2. *Adding a new memory-optimized data filegroup*

■ **Note** Memory-optimized data filegroups can only be removed by dropping the database. Therefore, you should careful consider the decision to move forward with this architecture.

Step 2: Add a New Memory-Optimized Container

In step-2 we will add a new memory-optimized container. Listing 6-2 shows an example of how this is accomplished using T-SQL code. This code can be used against any database that has a memory-optimized filegroup.

Listing 6-2. Adding a New Container to the Database

```
IF NOT EXISTS
  ( SELECT * FROM AdventureWorks2014.sys.data_spaces ds
         JOIN AdventureWorks2014.sys.database_files df ON
             ds.data_space_id=df.data_space_id
       WHERE ds.type='FX'    )
  ALTER DATABASE AdventureWorks2014
```

```
    ADD FILE (name=' AdventureWorks2014_mem',
                filename='C:\SQLData\AdventureWorks2014_mem')
    TO FILEGROUP [AdventureWorks2014_mem]
GO
```

In Listing 6-2, we added a new memory-optimized container to our database using T-SQL code. In the following steps we will do the same using Management Studio. In order to accomplish this, follow the steps outlined below (see Figure 6-3):

1. Right-click the database to which you want to add the new container, and select Properties.

2. Select the Files option, and type in the name of the file you wish to add.

3. Select FILESTREAM Data from the File Type list, and click the Add button.

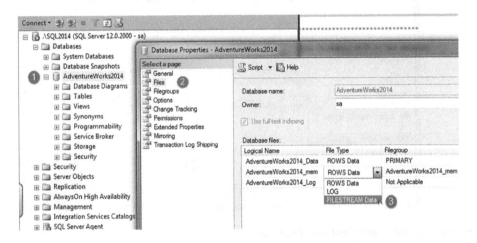

Figure 6-3. *Adding a new filestream container file to a memory-optimized filegroup*

It is a best practice to adjust the Autogrowth / Maxsize of a fiegroup; this option is to the right of the "Filegroup" column in Figure 6-4. For a memory-optimized filegroup, you will not be able to adjust this option when creating the fielgroup through Management Studio. This filegroup lives in memory; therefore, the previous practice of altering this option no longer applies. Leave the Autogrowth / Maxsize option set to Unlimited. It's a limitation of the current version that you can't specify a MAXSIZE for the specific container you're creating.

You now have a container in the memory-optimized data filegroup that you previously added to the database. Durable tables save their data to disk in the containers you just defined; therefore, it's recommended that you create multiple containers across multiple disks, if they're available to you. SSDs won't necessarily help performance, because data is accessed in a sequential manner and not in a random-access pattern. The only requirement is that you have performant disks so the data can be accessed efficiently from disk. Multiple disks allow SQL Server to recover data in parallel in the event of a system crash or availability group failover. Your in-memory tables won't become available until SQL Server has recovered the data into memory.

■ **Note**   Data and delta file pairs can't be moved to other containers in the memory-optimized filegroup.

Step 3: Create Your New Memory-Optimized Table

Step 1 and Step 2 laid out the foundation necessary to add memory-optimized objects. Listing 6-3 creates a table that in memory. The result is a compiled table with data that resides in memory.

Listing 6-3. Creating a New Memory-Optimized Table

```
USE AdventureWorks2014;
GO

CREATE SCHEMA [MOD] AUTHORIZATION [dbo];
GO

CREATE TABLE [MOD].[Address]
  (
        AddressID INT NOT NULL IDENTITY(1,1)
      , AddressLine1 NVARCHAR(120) COLLATE Latin1_General_100_BIN2 NOT NULL
      , AddressLine2 NVARCHAR(120) NULL
      , City NVARCHAR(60) COLLATE Latin1_General_100_BIN2 NOT NULL
      , StateProvinceID INT NOT NULL
      , PostalCode NVARCHAR(30) COLLATE Latin1_General_100_BIN2 NOT NULL
      , rowguid UNIQUEIDENTIFIER NOT NULL
                    INDEX [AK_MODAddress_rowguid] NONCLUSTERED
                    CONSTRAINT [DF_MODAddress_rowguid] DEFAULT (NEWID())
      , ModifiedDate DATETIME NOT NULL
            INDEX [IX_MODAddress_ModifiedDate] NONCLUSTERED
                    CONSTRAINT [DF_MODAddress_ModifiedDate] DEFAULT (GETDATE())

      , INDEX [IX_MODAddress_AddressLine1_ City_StateProvinceID_PostalCode]
          NONCLUSTERED
      ( [AddressLine1] ASC, [StateProvinceID] ASC, [PostalCode] ASC )

        , INDEX [IX_MODAddress_City]
        ( [City] DESC )

      , INDEX [IX_MODAddress_StateProvinceID]
          NONCLUSTERED
      ( [StateProvinceID] ASC)

      , CONSTRAINT PK_MODAddress_Address_ID
              PRIMARY KEY NONCLUSTERED HASH
      ( [AddressID]) WITH (BUCKET_COUNT=30000)

) WITH(MEMORY_OPTIMIZED=ON, DURABILITY=SCHEMA_AND_DATA);
GO
```

■ **Note**   You don't need to specify a filegroup when you create an in-memory table. You're limited to a single memory-optimized filegroup; therefore, SQL Server knows the filegroup to which to add this table.

The sample table used for this memory-optimized table example is similar to the AdventureWorks2014. Person.Address table, with several differences:

- The hint at the end of the CREATE TABLE statement is extremely important:

  WITH(MEMORY_OPTIMIZED=ON, DURABILITY=SCHEMA_AND_DATA);

  The option MEMORY_OPTIMIZED=ON tells SQL Server that this is a memory-optimized table.

- The DURABILITY=SCHEMA_AND_DATA option defines whether this table will be durable (data recoverable) or non-durable (schema-only recovery) after a server restart. If the durability option isn't specified, it defaults to SCHEMA_AND_DATA.

- PRIMARY KEY is NONCLUSTERED, because data isn't physically sorted:

  , CONSTRAINT PK_MODAddress_Address_ID
          PRIMARY KEY NONCLUSTERED HASH
  ([AddressID]) WITH (BUCKET_COUNT=30000)

  The NONCLUSTERED hint is required on a PRIMARY KEY constraint, because SQL Server attempts to create it as a CLUSTERED index by default. Because CLUSTERED indexes aren't allowed, not specifying the index type results in an error. Additionally, you can't add a sort hint on the column being used in this index, because HASH indexes can't be defined in a specific sort order.

- All character string data that is used in an index must use BIN2 collation:

  COLLATE Latin1_General_100_BIN2

  Notice that the MOD.Address table purposely doesn't declare BIN2 collation for the AddressLine2 column, because it isn't used in an index. Figure 6-8 shows the effect that BIN2 collation has on data in different collation types.

- If you compare the MOD.Address table to Person.Address, you see that the column SpatialLocation is missing. In-memory tables don't support LOB objects. The SpatialLocation column in Person.Address is defined as a GEOGRAPHY data type, which isn't supported for memory-optimized tables. If you were converting this data type to be used in a memory-optimized table, you would potentially need to make coding changes to accommodate the lack of the data type.

- The index type HASH with the hint WITH (BUCKET_COUNT=30000) is new. This is discussed further in the "In-Memory OLTP Table Indexes" section of this chapter.

Listing 6-3 added a memory-optimized table using T-SQL. We will now add add a memory-optimized table using Management Studio. Right-click the Tables folder, and select New ➤ Memory-Optimized Table (see Figure 6-4). A new query window opens with the In-Memory Table Creation template script available.

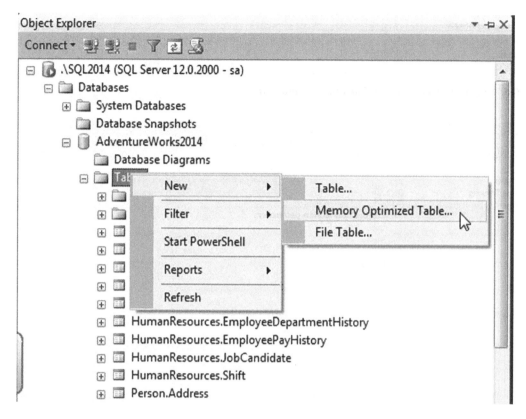

Figure 6-4. Creating a new memory-optimized table

You now have a very basic working database and table and can begin using the In-Memory features. You can access the table and different index properties using a system view (see Listing 6-4 and Figure 6-5) or Management Studio (see Figure 6-6).

Listing 6-4. Selecting Table Properties from a System View

```
SELECT t.name as 'Table Name'
    , t.object_id
      , t.schema_id
    , filestream_data_space_id
    , is_memory_optimized
    , durability
    , durability_desc
  FROM sys.tables t
 WHERE type='U'
   AND t.schema_id = SCHEMA_ID(N'MOD');
```

	Table Name	schema_id	object_id	filestream_data_space_id	is_memory_optimized	durability	durability_desc
1	Address	10	1367675920	NULL	1	0	SCHEMA_AND_DATA

Figure 6-5. *System view showing* MOD.Address *table properties*

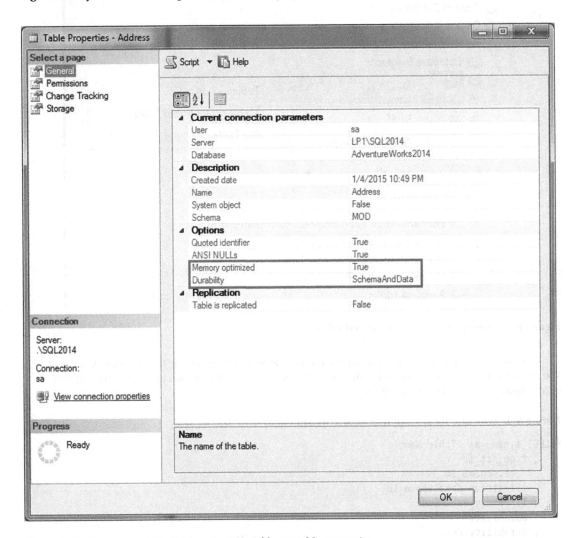

Figure 6-6. *Management Studio showing* MOD.Address *table properties*

Now that you've configured your database and created a new table, let's look at an example of the data in this table and some specific issues you may encounter. First you must load the data in the newly created memory-optimized table [MOD].[Address], as shown in Listing 6-5.

Listing 6-5. Inserting Data into the Newly Created Table

```
SET IDENTITY_INSERT [MOD].[Address] ON;

 INSERT INTO [MOD].[Address]
 (    AddressID, AddressLine1, AddressLine2
      , City, StateProvinceID, PostalCode
    --, SpatialLocation
    , rowguid, ModifiedDate  )

 SELECT AddressID, AddressLine1, AddressLine2
     , City, StateProvinceID, PostalCode
    --, SpatialLocation
    , rowguid, ModifiedDate
    FROM [Person].[Address];

 SET IDENTITY_INSERT [MOD].[Address] OFF;

 UPDATE STATISTICS [MOD].[Address] WITH FULLSCAN, NORECOMPUTE;
 GO
```

■ **Note**   In-memory tables don't support statistics auto-updates. In Listing 6-5, you manually update the statistics after inserting new data.

Because `AddressLine1` is being used in an index on the table, you have to declare the column with a BIN2 collation. The limitation with this collation is that all uppercase `AddressLine1` values are sorted before lowercase string values (*Z* sorts before *a*). In addition, string comparisons of BIN2 columns don't give correct results. A lowercase value doesn't equal an uppercase value when selecting data (*A* != *a*). Listing 6-6 gives an example query of the string-comparison scenario.

Listing 6-6. Selecting Data from the `AddressLine1` Column

```
SELECT AddressID, AddressLine1, RowGuid
   FROM [MOD].[Address]
  WHERE AddressID IN (804, 831)
    AND AddressLine1 LIKE '%plaza'
```

This query correctly results in only one record. However, you would expect two records to be returned, using disk-based tables. Pay careful attention in this area when you're considering moving your disk-based tables to memory-optimized tables. Figure 6-7 displays the result of the query.

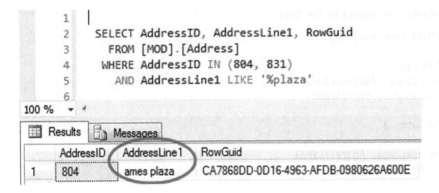

```
1
2    SELECT AddressID, AddressLine1, RowGuid
3      FROM [MOD].[Address]
4     WHERE AddressID IN (804, 831)
5       AND AddressLine1 LIKE '%plaza'
6
```

100 % ▾ ◂

	AddressID	AddressLine1	RowGuid
1	804	ames plaza	CA7868DD-0D16-4963-AFDB-0980626A600E

Figure 6-7. *AddressLine1 results with no collation*

When the collation for the column is altered with a hint (Listing 6-7), the query correctly returns two records (Figure 6-8).

Listing 6-7. Selecting Data from the AddressLine1 Column with Collation

```
SELECT AddressID, AddressLine1, RowGuid
  FROM [MOD].[Address]
 WHERE AddressID IN (804, 831)
   AND AddressLine1 COLLATE SQL_Latin1_General_CP1_CI_AS LIKE '%plaza';
```

```
1
2    SELECT AddressID, AddressLine1, RowGuid
3      FROM [MOD].[Address]
4     WHERE AddressID IN (804, 831)
5       AND AddressLine1 COLLATE SQL_Latin1_General_CP1_CI_AS LIKE '%plaza';
6
```

100 % ▾ ◂

	AddressID	AddressLine1	RowGuid
1	804	ames plaza	CA7868DD-0D16-4963-AFDB-0980626A600E
2	831	Amity Plaza	9B0D186C-61E0-453B-9F37-7A8E03194F6B

Figure 6-8. *AddressLine1 results with collation*

In order to ensure proper results and behavior, you need to specify the collation for all string type columns, with BIN2 collation for comparison and sort operations.

Limitations on Memory-Optimized Tables

When you create a table, you need to take several limitations into account. Following are some of the more common restrictions that you may encounter:

- None of the LOB data types can be used to declare a column (XML, CLR, spatial data types, or any of the MAX data types).

- All the row lengths in a table are limited to 8,060 bytes. This limit is enforced at the time the table is initially created. Disk-based tables allow you to create tables that could potentially exceed 8,060 bytes per row.

- All in-memory tables must have at least one index defined. No heap tables are allowed.

- No DDL/DML triggers are allowed.

- No schema changes are allowed (ALTER TABLE). To change the schema of the table, you would need to drop and re-create the table.

- Partitioning or compressing a memory-optimized table isn't allowed.

- When you use an IDENTITY column property, it must be initialized to start at 1 and increment by 1.

- If you're creating a durable table, you must define a primary key constraint.

■ **Note**   For a comprehensive and up-to-date list of limitations, visit
http://msdn.microsoft.com/en-us/library/dn246937.aspx.

In-Memory OLTP Table Indexes

Indexes are used to more efficiently access data stored in tables. Both in-memory tables and disk-based tables benefit from indexes; however, In-Memory OLTP table indexes have some significant differences from their disk-based counterparts. Two types of indexes differ from those of disk-based tables: nonclustered hashes and nonclustered range indexes. These indexes are both contained in memory and are optimized for memory-optimized tables. The differences between in-memory and disk-based table indexes are outlined in Table 6-2.

Table 6-2. Comparison of in-memory and disk-based indexes

In-Memory Table	Disk-Based Table
Must have at least one index	No indexes required
Clustered Index not allowed; Only hash or range non-clustered indexes allowed.	Clustered Index usually recommended
Indexes added only at table creation	Indexes can be added to the table after table creation
No auto update statistics	Auto update statistics allowed
In-memory table indexes only exist in memory	Indexes persist on disk and the transaction log
Indexes are created during table creation or database startup	Indexes are persisted to disk; therefore, they are not rebuilt and can be read from disk
Indexes are covering, since the index contains a memory pointer to the actual row of the data	Indexes are not covering by default.
There is a limitation of 8 indexes per table	1 Clustered Index+999 NonClustered=1000 Indexes or 249 XML Indexes

■ **Note**   Durable memory-optimized tables require a primary key. By default, a primary key attempts to create a clustered index, which will generate an error for a memory-optimized table. You must specifically indicate NONCLUSTERED as the index type.

The need for at least one index stems from the architecture of an in-memory table. The table uses index pointers as the only method of linking rows in memory into a table. This is also why clustered indexes aren't needed on memory-optimized tables; the data isn't specifically ordered or arranged in any manner.

A new feature of SQL Server 2014 is that you can create indexes inline with the table create statement. Earlier, notice that Listing 6-3 creates an inline nonclustered index with table create:

```
, rowguid UNIQUEIDENTIFIER NOT NULL
            INDEX [AK_MODAddress_rowguid] NONCLUSTERED
            CONSTRAINT [DF_MODAddress_rowguid] DEFAULT (NEWID())
```

Inline index creation is new to SQL Server 2014 but not unique to memory-optimized tables. It's also valid for disk-based tables.

Both hash and range indexes are allowed on the same column. This can be a good strategy when the use cases vary for how the data is accessed.

Hash Indexes

A *hash index* is an efficient mechanism that accepts input values into a hashing function and maps to a hash bucket. The *hash bucket* is an array that contains pointers to efficiently return a row of data. The collection of pointers in the hash bucket is the hash index. When created, this index exists entirely in memory.

Hash indexes are best used for single-item lookups, a WHERE clause with an =, or equality joins. They can't be used for range lookups such as LIKE operations or between queries. The optimizer won't give you an error, but it isn't an efficient way of accessing the data. When creating the hash index, you must decide at table-creation time how many buckets to assign for the index. It's recommended that it should be created at 1.5 to 2 times larger than the existing unique key counts in your table. This is an important assessment, because the bucket count can't be extended by re-creating the index and the table. The performance of the point lookups doesn't degrade if you have a bucket count that is larger than necessary. However, performance will suffer if the bucket count is too small. Listing 6-3 used a hash bucket count of 30,000, because the number of unique rows in the table is slightly less than 20,000. Here's the code that defines the constraint with the bucket count:

```
, CONSTRAINT PK_MODAddress_Address_ID PRIMARY KEY NONCLUSTERED HASH
(    [AddressID] ASC ) WITH (BUCKET_COUNT=30000)
```

If your use case requires it, you can create a composite index on a hash index. There are some limitations to be aware of if you decide to use a composite index. The hash index will be used only if the point-lookup search is done on both columns in the index. If both columns aren't used in the search, the result is an index scan or a scan of all the hash buckets. This occurs because the hash function converts the values from both columns into a hash values. Therefore, in a composite hash index, the value of one column never equates to the hash value of two columns:

```
HASH(<Column1>) <> HASH(<Column1>, <Column2>)
```

Let's compare the affect of a hash index on a memory-optimized table versus a disk-based table clustered index.

■ **Warning**   This applies to the code in Listing 6-8 and several other examples. Do not attempt to run the DBCC commands on a production system, because they can severely affect the performance of your entire instance.

Listing 6-8 includes some DBCC commands to flush all cache pages and make sure the comparisons start in a repeatable state with nothing in memory. It's highly recommended that these types of commands be run only in a non-production environment that won't affect anyone else on the instance.

Listing 6-8. Point Lookup on a Hash Index vs. Disk-Based Clustered Index

```
CHECKPOINT
GO
DBCC DROPCLEANBUFFERS
GO
DBCC FREEPROCCACHE
GO

SET STATISTICS IO ON;

SELECT * FROM Person.Address WHERE AddressId = 26007;
SELECT * FROM MOD.Address WHERE AddressId = 26007;
```

This first example simply looks at what happens when you compare performance when doing a simple point lookup for a specific value. Both the disk-based table (Person.Address) and the memory-optimized table (MOD.Address) have a clustered and hash index on the AddressID column. The result of running the entire batch is as shown in Figure 6-9 in the Messages tab.

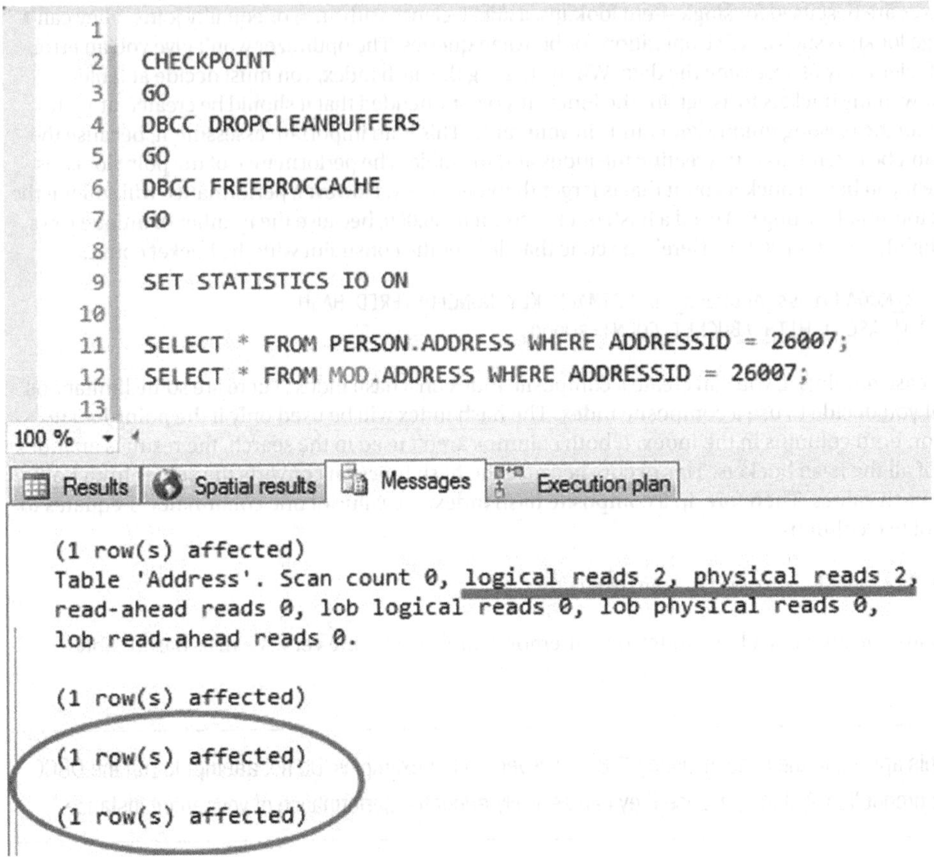

```
1
2    CHECKPOINT
3    GO
4    DBCC DROPCLEANBUFFERS
5    GO
6    DBCC FREEPROCCACHE
7    GO
8
9    SET STATISTICS IO ON
10
11   SELECT * FROM PERSON.ADDRESS WHERE ADDRESSID = 26007;
12   SELECT * FROM MOD.ADDRESS WHERE ADDRESSID = 26007;
13
```

100 % ▼ ◂

☰ Results | 🌐 Spatial results | 🔢 Messages | 🔢 Execution plan

```
(1 row(s) affected)
Table 'Address'. Scan count 0, logical reads 2, physical reads 2,
read-ahead reads 0, lob logical reads 0, lob physical reads 0,
lob read-ahead reads 0.

(1 row(s) affected)

(1 row(s) affected)

(1 row(s) affected)
```

Figure 6-9. *Hash index vs. clustered index IO statistics*

There are two piece of information worth noting. The first batch to run was the disk-based table, which resulted in two logical reads and two physical reads. The second batch was the memory-optimized table, which didn't register any logical or physical IO reads because this table's data and indexes are completely held in memory.

Figure 6-10 clearly shows that the disk-based table took 99% of the entire batch execution time; the memory-optimized table took 1% of the time relative to the entire batch. Both query plans are exactly the same; however, this illustrates the significant difference that a memory-optimized table can make to the simplest of queries.

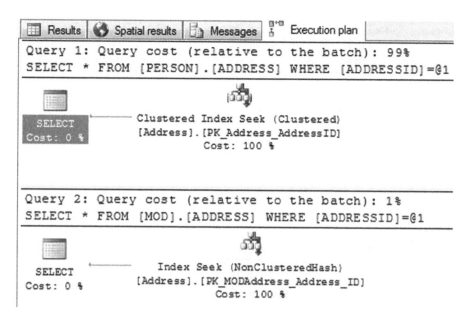

Figure 6-10. *Hash index vs. clustered index point lookup execution plan*

Hovering over the Index Seek operator in the execution plan shows a couple of differences. The first is that the Storage category now differentiates between the disk-based table as RowStore and the memory-optimized table as MemoryOptimized. There is also a significant difference between the estimated row size of the two tables.

Next let's experiment with running a range lookup against the disk-based table and the memory-optimized table. Listing 6-9 does a simple range lookup against the primary key of the table to demonstrate some of the difference in performance (see Figure 6-11).

Listing 6-9. Range Lookup Using a Hash Index

```
SELECT * FROM PERSON.ADDRESS WHERE ADDRESSID BETWEEN 100 AND 26007;
SELECT * FROM MOD.ADDRESS WHERE ADDRESSID BETWEEN 100 AND 26007;
```

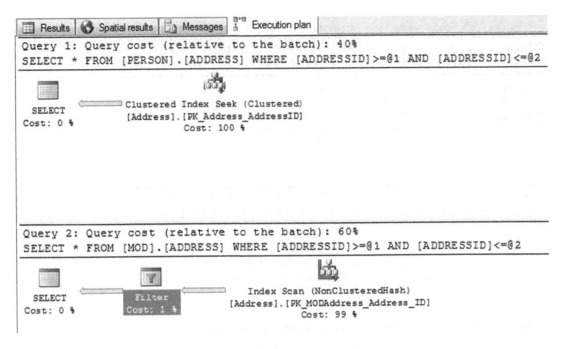

Figure 6-11. *Hash index vs. clustered index range lookup execution plan*

This example clearly displays that a memory-optimized table hash index isn't necessarily quicker than a disk-based clustered index for all use cases. The memory-optimized table had to perform an index scan and then filter the results for the specific criteria you're looking to get back. The disk-based table clustered index seek is still more efficient for this particular use case. The moral of the story is that it always depends. You should always run through several use cases and determine the best method of accessing your data.

Range Indexes

A range index might best be defined as a memory-optimized nonclustered index. When created, this index exists entirely in memory. The memory-optimized nonclustered index works similarly to a disk-based nonclustered index, but it has some significant architectural differences. The architecture for range indexes is based on a new data structure called a *Bw-tree*.[3] The Bw-tree architecture is a latch-free architecture that can take advantage of modern processor caches and multicore chips.

Memory-optimized nonclustered indexes are best used for range-type queries such as (<,>,IN), (All sales orders between dates), and so on. These indexes also work with point lookups but aren't as optimized for those types of lookups as a hash index. Memory-optimized nonclustered indexes should also be considered over hash indexes when you're migrating a disk-based table that has a considerable number of duplicate values in a column. The size of the index grows with the size of the data, similar to B-tree disk-based table structures.

---

[3]Justin J. Levandoski, David B. Lomet, and Sudipta Sengupta, "The Bw-Tree: A B-tree for New Hardware Platforms," Microsoft Research, April 8, 2013, http://research.microsoft.com/apps/pubs/default.aspx?id=178758.

When you're using memory-optimized nonclustered indexes, a handful of limitations and differences from disk-based nonclustered indexes are worth mentioning. Listing 6-3 created the nonclustered index on the City column. Below is an excerpt from the listing, that displays the creation of the nonclustered index.

```
INDEX [IX_MODAddress_City]
( [City] DESC)
```

- All the columns that are part of an index must be defined as NOT NULL.

- If the column is defined as a string data type, it must be defined using a BIN2 collation.

- The NONCLUSTERED hint is optional unless the column is the primary key for the table, because SQL Server will try to define a primary key constraint as clustered.

- The sort-order hint on a column in a range index is especially important for a memory-optimized table. SQL Server can't perform a seek on the index if the order in which the records are accessed is different from the order in which the index was originally defined, which would result in an index scan.

Following are a couple of examples that demonstrate the comparison of a disk-based nonclustered index and a memory-optimized nonclustered index (range index). The two queries in Listing 6-10 select all columns from the Address disk-based table and the memory-optimized table using a single-point lookup of the date. The result of the queries is displayed in Figure 6-12.

Listing 6-10. Single-Point Lookup Using a Range Index

```
CHECKPOINT
GO
DBCC DROPCLEANBUFFERS
GO
DBCC FREEPROCCACHE
GO

SET STATISTICS IO ON

SELECT * FROM [Person].[Address] WHERE ModifiedDate = '2013-12-21';
SELECT * FROM [MOD].[Address] WHERE ModifiedDate = '2013-12-21';
```

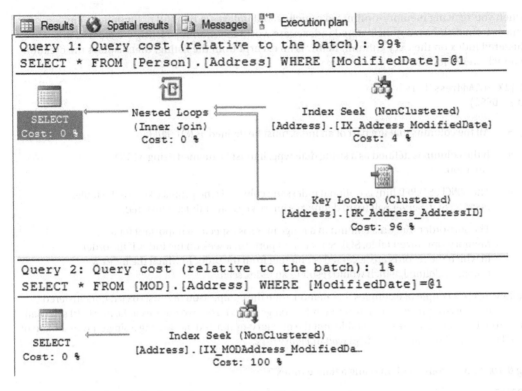

Figure 6-12. Single-point lookup using a nonclustered index comparison

This example displays a significant difference between Query 1 (disk-based table) and Query 2 (memory-optimized index). Both queries use an index seek to get to the row in the table, but the disk-based table has to do an additional key-lookup operation on the clustered index. Because the query is asking for all the columns of data in the row, the disk-based nonclustered index must obtain the pointer to the data through the clustered index. The memory-optimized index doesn't have the added cost of the key lookup, because all the indexes are covering and, therefore, the index already has a pointer to the additional columns of data.

Next, Listing 6-11 does a range lookup on the disk-based table nonclustered index and a range lookup on the memory-optimized nonclustered index. The difference between the two queries is displayed in Figure 6-13.

Listing 6-11. Range Lookup Using a Range Index

```
CHECKPOINT
GO
DBCC DROPCLEANBUFFERS
GO
DBCC FREEPROCCACHE
GO

SET STATISTICS IO ON
```

```
SELECT * FROM [Person].[Address] WHERE ModifiedDate
            BETWEEN '2013-12-01' AND '2013-12-21';
SELECT * FROM [MOD].[Address] WHERE ModifiedDate
            BETWEEN '2013-12-01' AND '2013-12-21';
```

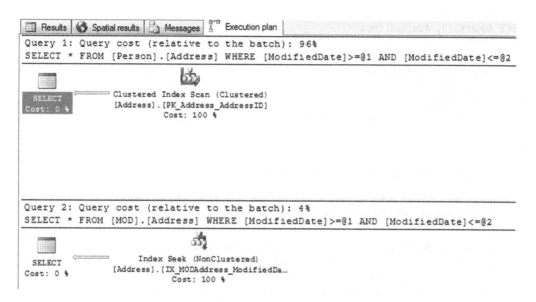

Figure 6-13. Range Lookup Comparison

The results are as expected. The memory-optimized nonclustered index performs significantly better than the disk-based nonclustered index when performing a range query using a range index.

Natively Compiled Stored Procedures

Natively compile stored procedures are similar in purpose to disk-based stored procedures, with the major difference that a natively compiled stored procedure is compiled into C and then into machine language stored as a DLL. The DLL allows SQL Server to access the stored-procedure code more quickly, to take advantage of parallel processing and significant improvements in execution. There are several limitations, but if used correctly, natively compiled stored procedures can yield a 2x or more increase in performance.

To get started, let's examine the outline of a natively compiled stored procedure in Listing 6-12 in detail.

Listing 6-12. Natively Compiled Stored Procedure Example

```
1 CREATE PROCEDURE selAddressModifiedDate
2 (    @BeginModifiedDate DATETIME
3    , @EndmodifiedDate DATETIME )
4  WITH
5    NATIVE_COMPILATION
6    , SCHEMABINDING
7    , EXECUTE AS OWNER
8  AS
```

```
9  BEGIN ATOMIC
10 WITH
11 ( TRANSACTION ISOLATION LEVEL = SNAPSHOT
12     LANGUAGE = N'us_english')
13
14 -- T-SQL Logic Here
15 SELECT AddressID, AddressLine1
16        , AddressLine2, City
17        , StateProvinceID, PostalCode
18        , rowguid, ModifiedDate
19   FROM [MOD].[Address]
20  WHERE ModifiedDate
21        BETWEEN @BeginModifiedDate AND @EndmodifiedDate;
22
23 END;
```

The requirements to create a natively compiled stored procedure are as follows:

- Line 5, NATIVE COMPILATION: This option tells SQL Server that the procedure is to be compiled into a DLL. If you add this option, you must also specify the SCHEMABINDING, EXECUTE AS, and BEGIN ATOMIC options.

- Line 6, SCHEMABINDING: This option binds the stored procedure to the schema of the objects it references. At the time the stored procedure is compiled, the schema and of the objects it references are compiled into the DLL. When the procedure is executed, it doesn't have to check to see whether the columns of the objects it references have been altered. This offers the fastest and shortest method of executing a stored procedure. If any of the underlying objects it references are altered, you're first forced to drop and recompile the stored procedure with any changes to the underlying objects it references.

- Line 7, EXECUTE AS OWNER: The default execution context for a stored procedure is EXECUTE AS CALLER. Natively compiled stored procedures don't support this caller context and must be specified as one of the options EXECUTE AS OWNER, SELF, or USER. This is required so that SQL Server doesn't have to check execution rights for the user every time they attempt to execute the stored procedure. The execution rights are hardcoded and compiled into the DLL to optimize the speed of execution.

- Line 9, BEGIN ATOMIC: Natively compiled stored procedures have the requirement that the body must consist of exactly one atomic block. The atomic block is part of the ANSI SQL standard that specifies that either the entire stored procedure succeeds or the entire stored procedure logic fails and rolls back as a whole. At the time the stored procedure is called, if an existing transaction is open, the stored procedure joins the transaction and commits. If no transaction is open, then the stored procedure creates its own transaction and commits.

- Lines 11 and 12, TRANSACTION ISOLATION: All the session settings are fixed at the time the stored procedure is created. This is done to optimize the stored procedure's performance at execution time.

Those are the main options in a natively compiled stored procedure that are unique to its syntax, versus a disk-based stored procedure. There are a significant number of limitations when creating a natively compiled stored procedure. Some of the more common limitations are listed next:

- Objects must be called using two-part names (schema.table).

- Temporary tables from tempdb can't be used and should be replaced with table variables or nondurable memory-optimized tables.

- A natively compiled stored procedure can't be accessed from a distributed transaction.

- The stored procedure can't access disk-based tables, only memory-optimized tables.

- The stored procedure can't use any of the ranking functions.

- DISTINCT in a query isn't supported.

- EXISTS or IN are not supported functions.

- Common table expressions (CTEs) are not supported constructs.

- Subqueries aren't available.

■ **Note** For a comprehensive list of limitations, visit http://msdn.microsoft.com/en-us/library/dn246937.aspx.

Execution plans for queries in the procedure are optimized when the procedure is compiled. This happens only when the procedure is created and when the server restarts, not when statistics are updated. Therefore, the tables need to contain a representative set of data, and statistics need to be up-to-date before the procedures are created. (Natively compiled stored procedures are recompiled if the database is taken offline and brought back online.)

EXERCISES

1. Which editions of SQL Server support the new In-Memory features?

   a. Developer Edition

   b. Enterprise Edition

   c. Business Intelligence Edition

   d. All of the above

2. When defining a string type column in an in-memory table, you must always use a BIN2 collation.

   [True / False]

3. You want to define the best index type for a date column in your table. Which index type might be best suited for this column, if it is being used for reporting purposes using a range of values?

    a. Hash index

    b. Clustered index

    c. Range index

    d. A and B

4. When creating a memory-optimized table, if you do not specify the durability option for the table, it will default to SCHEMA_AND_DATA.

    [True / False]

5. Memory-optimized tables always require a primary key constraint.

    [True / False]

6. Natively compiled stored procedures allow for which of the following execution contexts?

    a. EXECUTE AS OWNER

    b. EXECUTE AS SELF

    c. EXECUTE AS USER

    d. A and B

    e. A, B, and C

CHAPTER 7

■ ■ ■

Triggers

SQL Server provides triggers as a means of executing T-SQL code in response to database object, database, and server events. SQL Server 2014 implements three types of triggers: classic T-SQL Data Manipulation Language (DML) triggers, which fire in response to INSERT, UPDATE, and DELETE events against tables; Data Definition Language (DDL) triggers, which fire in response to CREATE, ALTER, and DROP statements; and logon triggers, which fire in response to LOGON events. DDL triggers can also fire in response to some system SPs that perform DDL-like operations.

Triggers are a form of specialized SP, closely tied to your data and database objects. In the past, DML triggers were used to enforce various aspects of business logic, such as foreign key and other constraints on data, and other more complex business logic. Cascading declarative referential integrity (DRI) and robust check constraints in T-SQL have supplanted DML triggers in many areas, but they're still useful in their own right. This chapter discusses how triggers work, how to use them, and when they're most appropriate. You also learn about DDL triggers and explore their use.

As discussed in Chapter 6, one of the limitations of in-memory tables is that triggers aren't available. This chapter of the book still applies to all disk-based tables.

DML Triggers

DML triggers are composed of T-SQL code that is executed (fired) in response to an INSERT, an UPDATE, a DELETE, or a MERGE statement on a table or view. DML triggers are created via the CREATE TRIGGER statement, which allows you to specify the following details about the trigger:

- The name of the trigger, which is the identifier you can use to manage the trigger. You can specify a two-part name for a trigger (schema and trigger name), but the schema must be the same as the schema for the table on which the trigger executes.

- The table or view on which the trigger executes.

- The triggering events, which can be any combination of INSERT, UPDATE, and DELETE. The triggering events indicate the type of events that the trigger fires in response to.

- The AFTER/FOR and INSTEAD OF indicators, which determine whether the trigger is fired after the triggering statement completes or the trigger overrides the firing statement.

- Additional options like the ENCRYPTION and EXECUTE AS clauses, which allow you to obfuscate the trigger source code and specify the context under which the trigger executes, respectively.

■ **Note**   DML triggers have some restrictions on their creation that you should keep in mind. DML triggers can't be defined on temporary tables, they can't be declared on table variables, and they can't be defined on in-memory tables. Finally, only INSTEAD OF triggers can be used on views.

In addition to the CREATE TRIGGER statement, SQL Server provides an ALTER TRIGGER statement to modify the definition of a trigger, a DROP TRIGGER statement to remove an existing trigger from the database, and DISABLE TRIGGER and ENABLE TRIGGER statements to disable and enable a trigger, respectively. Listing 7-1 shows how to disable and enable a specific trigger named HumanResources.EmployeeUpdateTrigger or all triggers on an object, namely, the HumanResources.Employee table. It also contains an example of how to query the sys.triggers catalog view to return all the disabled triggers in the current database.

Listing 7-1. Disabling and Enabling Triggers

```
DISABLE TRIGGER HumanResources.EmployeeUpdateTrigger
ON HumanResources.Employee;

SELECT
    name,
    OBJECT_SCHEMA_NAME(parent_id) + '.' + OBJECT_NAME(parent_id) as Parent
FROM sys.triggers
WHERE is_disabled = 1;

ENABLE TRIGGER HumanResources.EmployeeUpdateTrigger
ON HumanResources.Employee;

-- disabling and enabling all triggers on the object
DISABLE TRIGGER ALL ON HumanResources.Employee;
ENABLE TRIGGER ALL ON HumanResources.Employee;
```

Disabling triggers can greatly improve performance when you apply a batch of modifications on a table. Just make sure the rules enforced by the trigger(s) are checked another way: for instance, manually after the batch. Also don't forget to re-enable the trigger at the end of the process.

Multiple Triggers

You can create multiple triggers on the same objects. They will fire in no specific order. If you really need to, you can specify that a trigger should be fired first or last, by using the sp_settriggerorder system stored procedure. For example:

```
EXEC sp_settriggerorder @triggername = 'MyTrigger', @order = 'first', @stmttype = 'UPDATE';
```

That sets the MyTrigger trigger to fire first on UPDATE actions. However, in our opinion, this shouldn't be used, because it adds unnecessary complexity in the database. If you need to manage precedence between trigger actions, it's best to consolidate what you need to do in the same trigger.

When to Use DML Triggers

Way back in the day, using triggers was the best (and in some cases only) way to perform a variety of tasks, such as ensuring cascading DRI, validating data before storing it in tables, auditing changes, and enforcing complex business logic. Newer releases of SQL Server have added functionality that more closely integrates many of these functions into the core database engine. For instance, in most cases, you can use SQL Server's built-in cascading DRI to ensure referential integrity and check constraints for simple validations during insert and update operations. DML triggers are still a good choice when simple auditing tasks or validations with complex business logic are required.

■ **Note** DRI isn't enforced across databases. This means you can't reference a table in a different database in a DRI/foreign-key constraint. Because they can reference objects such as tables and views in other databases, triggers are still a good option when this type of referential-integrity enforcement is necessary.

Listing 7-2 shows a very simple trigger created on the HumanResources.Employee table of the AdventureWorks database. The HumanResources.EmployeeUpdateTrigger trigger updates the ModifiedDate column of the HumanResources.Employee table with the current date and time whenever a row is updated.

Listing 7-2. HumanResources.EmployeeUpdateTrigger Code

```
CREATE TRIGGER HumanResources.EmployeeUpdateTrigger
ON HumanResources.Employee
AFTER UPDATE
NOT FOR REPLICATION
AS
BEGIN
    -- stop if no row was affected
    IF @@ROWCOUNT = 0 RETURN
    -- Turn off "rows affected" messages
    SET NOCOUNT ON;

    -- Make sure at least one row was affected
    -- Update ModifiedDate for all affected rows
    UPDATE HumanResources.Employee
    SET ModifiedDate = GETDATE()
    WHERE EXISTS
      (
        SELECT 1
        FROM inserted i
        WHERE i.BusinessEntityID = HumanResources.Employee.BusinessEntityID
      );
END;
```

The first part of the CREATE TRIGGER statement defines the name of the trigger and specifies that it will be created on the HumanResources.Employee table. The definition also specifies that the trigger will fire after rows are updated, and the NOT FOR REPLICATION keywords prevent replication events from firing the trigger:

```
CREATE TRIGGER HumanResources.EmployeeUpdateTrigger
ON HumanResources.Employee
AFTER UPDATE
NOT FOR REPLICATION
```

The body of the trigger starts by checking the number of rows affected by the UPDATE with the @@ROWCOUNT system function. This is an optimization that skips the body of the trigger if no rows were affected.

Whenever any trigger is fired, it's implicitly wrapped in the same transaction as the DML statement that fired it. This has big performance and concurrency implications. It means that whatever your trigger does, it should do as quickly and efficiently as possible. The T-SQL statements in a trigger body can potentially create locks in your database, a situation that you want to minimize. It's not unheard of for inefficient triggers to cause blocking problems. You should also minimize the amount of work done inside the trigger and optimize the operations it has to perform. It also means a ROLLBACK TRANSACTION statement in the trigger will roll back DML statements executed in the trigger, as well as the original DML statement that fired the trigger (and all explicit transactions in which the statement is run).

Checking @@ROWCOUNT at the start of the trigger helps ensure that your triggers are efficient. If @@ROWCOUNT is 0, it means no rows were affected by the original DML statement that fired the trigger. Then the trigger has no work to do, and you can skip the rest:

```
-- stop if no row was affected
IF @@ROWCOUNT = 0 RETURN
```

■ **Caution** Checking @@ROWCOUNT must be done at the very first line. Any previous action in the trigger, even SET commands, could change the @@ROWCOUNT value.

Next, the trigger turns off the rows affected messages via the SET NOCOUNT ON statement:

```
-- Turn off "rows affected" messages
SET NOCOUNT ON;
```

■ **Note** Using SET NOCOUNT ON isn't strictly required in triggers, but it prevents superfluous rows affected messages from being generated by the trigger. Some older database drivers—and even some more recent ones, such as certain Java Database Connectivity (JDBC) drivers—can get confused by these extra messages, so it's not a bad idea to disable them in the body of your triggers. Any SET statement can be used in the body of a trigger. The statement remains in effect while the trigger executes and reverts to its former setting when the trigger completes.

The IF statement contains an UPDATE statement that sets the ModifiedDate column to the current date and time when rows in the table are updated. An important concept of trigger programming is to be sure you account for multiple row updates. It's not safe to assume that a DML statement will update only a single row of your table, because triggers in SQL Server are set-oriented and fire only once for a statement. There is no such thing as a per-row trigger in SQL Server. In this trigger, the UPDATE statement uses the EXISTS predicate in the

WHERE clause to ensure that ModifiedDate is updated for every row that was affected. It accomplishes this by using the inserted virtual table, described in the "inserted and deleted Virtual Tables" section below.

```
-- Update ModifiedDate for all affected rows
UPDATE HumanResources.Employee
SET ModifiedDate = GETDATE()
WHERE EXISTS
(
    SELECT 1
    FROM inserted i
    WHERE i.BusinessEntityID = HumanResources.Employee.BusinessEntityID
);
```

Inserted and Deleted Virtual Tables

A DML trigger needs to know which rows were affected by the DML statement that fired it. The inserted and deleted virtual tables fulfill this need. When a trigger fires, SQL Server populates the inserted and deleted virtual tables and makes them available within the body of the trigger. These two virtual tables have the same structure as the affected table and contain the data from all affected rows.

The inserted table contains all rows inserted into the destination table by an INSERT statement. The deleted table contains all rows deleted from the destination table by a DELETE statement. For UPDATE statements, the rows are treated as a DELETE followed by an INSERT, so the pre-UPDATE-affected rows are stored in the deleted table, and the post-UPDATE-affected rows are stored in the inserted table.

The virtual tables are read-only and can't be modified directly. The example in Listing 7-2 uses the inserted virtual table to determine which rows were affected by the UPDATE statement that fired the trigger. The trigger updates the ModifiedDate column for every row in the HumanResources.Employee table with a matching row in the inserted table. You use the inserted and deleted virtual tables in other example code in this section.

Testing the trigger is as simple as using SELECT and UPDATE. The example in Listing 7-3 changes the marital status of employees with BusinessEntityID numbers 1 and 2 to M (for "married").

Listing 7-3. Testing HumanResources.EmployeeUpdateTrigger

```
UPDATE HumanResources.Employee
SET MaritalStatus = 'M'
WHERE BusinessEntityID IN (1, 2);

SELECT BusinessEntityID, NationalIDNumber, MaritalStatus, ModifiedDate
FROM HumanResources.Employee
WHERE BusinessEntityID IN (1, 2);
```

The results, shown in Figure 7-1, demonstrate that the UPDATE statement fired the trigger and properly updated ModifiedDate for the two specified rows.

	BusinessEntityID	NationalIDNumber	MaritalStatus	ModifiedDate
1	1	295847284	M	2012-04-22 13:49:42.447
2	2	245797967	M	2012-04-22 13:49:42.447

Figure 7-1. *Updated marital status for two employees*

■ **Caution** If the RECURSIVE_TRIGGERS database option is turned on in the AdventureWorks database, HumanResources.EmployeeUpdateTrigger will error out with a message that the "nesting limit has been exceeded." This is caused by the trigger recursively firing itself after the UPDATE statement in the trigger is executed. Use ALTER DATABASE AdventureWorks SET RECURSIVE_TRIGGERS OFF to turn off recursive triggers and ALTER DATABASE AdventureWorks SET RECURSIVE_TRIGGERS ON to turn the option back on. The default is OFF. Recursive triggers are covered later in this chapter.

Auditing with DML Triggers

Another common use for DML triggers is auditing DML actions against tables. The primary purpose of DML auditing is to maintain a record of changes to the data in your database. This may be required for a number of reasons, including regulatory compliance or to fulfill contractual obligations.

Using Change Data Capture Instead

Since SQL Server 2008, you can use the feature known as Change Data Capture (CDC), which provides built-in auditing functionality. The CDC functionality provides another option for logging DML actions against tables. Although CDC functionality is beyond the scope of this book, we recommend looking into this option before deciding which method to use when you need DML logging functionality; it may be a more elegant and efficient way to audit data changes. One of the drawbacks with triggers is the performance impact they have on DML operations, especially because they're part of the DML transaction. CDC is much faster because it acts as a separate process that tracks the database-transaction log for modifications applied to the audited tables and writes changes to internal change tables, using the same technology as transaction replication. Moreover, CDC can automatically prune the audit tables to keep their size manageable. Note that CDC is available only in Enterprise Edition.

The first step to implementing DML auditing is to create a table to store your audit information. Listing 7-4 creates just such a table.

Listing 7-4. DML Audit Logging Table

```
CREATE TABLE dbo.DmlActionLog (
    EntryNum int IDENTITY(1, 1) PRIMARY KEY NOT NULL,
    SchemaName sysname NOT NULL,
    TableName sysname NOT NULL,
    ActionType nvarchar(10) NOT NULL,
    ActionXml xml NOT NULL,
    LoginName sysname NOT NULL,
    ApplicationName sysname NOT NULL,
    HostName sysname NOT NULL,
    ActionDateTime datetime2(0) NOT NULL DEFAULT (SYSDATETIME())
);
GO
```

The dbo.DmlActionLog table in Listing 7-4 stores information for each DML action performed against a table, including the name of the schema and table against which the DML action was performed, the type of DML action performed, XML-formatted snapshots of the before and after states of the rows affected, and additional information to identify who performed the DML action and when the action was performed. Once the audit logging table is created, it's time to create a trigger to log DML actions. This is shown in Listing 7-5.

Listing 7-5. DML Audit Logging Trigger

```
CREATE TRIGGER HumanResources.DepartmentChangeAudit
ON HumanResources.Department
AFTER INSERT, UPDATE, DELETE
NOT FOR REPLICATION
AS
BEGIN
    -- stop if no row was affected
    IF @@ROWCOUNT = 0 RETURN

    -- Turn off "rows affected" messages
    SET NOCOUNT ON;

    DECLARE @ActionType nvarchar(10), @ActionXml xml;

    -- Get count of inserted rows
    DECLARE @inserted_count int = (
        SELECT COUNT(*)
        FROM inserted
    );
    -- Get count of deleted rows
    DECLARE @deleted_count int = (
        SELECT COUNT(*)
        FROM deleted
    );

    -- Determine the type of DML action that fired the trigger
    SET @ActionType = CASE
        WHEN (@inserted_count > 0) AND (@deleted_count = 0) THEN N'insert'
        WHEN (@inserted_count = 0) AND (@deleted_count > 0) THEN N'delete'
        ELSE N'update'
    END;

    -- Use FOR XML AUTO to retrieve before and after snapshots of the changed
    -- data  in  XML  format
    SELECT @ActionXml = COALESCE
    (
        (
            SELECT  *
            FROM  deleted
            FOR  XML  AUTO
        ), N'<deleted/>'
    )  +  COALESCE
```

```
(
    (
        SELECT *
        FROM inserted
        FOR XML AUTO
    ), N'<inserted/>'
);

-- Insert a row for the logged action in the audit logging table
INSERT INTO dbo.DmlActionLog
(
    SchemaName,
    TableName,
    ActionType,
    ActionXml,
    LoginName,
    ApplicationName,
    HostName
)
SELECT
    OBJECT_SCHEMA_NAME(@@PROCID, DB_ID()),
    OBJECT_NAME(t.parent_id, DB_ID()),
    @ActionType,
    @ActionXml,
    SUSER_SNAME(),
    APP_NAME(),
    HOST_NAME()
FROM sys.triggers t
WHERE t.object_id = @@PROCID;
END;
GO
```

The trigger in Listing 7-5 is created on the HumanResources.Department table, although it's written in such a way that the body of the trigger contains no code specific to the table it's created on. This means you can easily modify the trigger to work as-is on most tables.

The HumanResources.DepartmentChangeAudit trigger definition begins with the CREATE TRIGGER statement, which names the trigger and creates it on the HumanResources.Department table. It also specifies that the trigger should fire after INSERT, UPDATE, and DELETE statements are performed against the table. Finally, the NOT FOR REPLICATION clause specifies that replication events won't cause the trigger to fire:

```
CREATE TRIGGER HumanResources.DepartmentChangeAudit
ON HumanResources.Department
AFTER INSERT, UPDATE, DELETE
NOT FOR REPLICATION
```

The trigger body begins by checking the number of rows affected by the DML statement with the @@ROWCOUNT function. The trigger skips the remainder of the statements in the body if no rows were affected:

```
-- stop if no row was affected
IF @@ROWCOUNT = 0 RETURN
```

The main body of the trigger begins with an initialization that turns off extraneous rows affected messages, declares local variables, and gets the count of rows inserted and deleted by the DML statement from the inserted and deleted virtual tables:

```
-- Turn off "rows affected" messages
SET NOCOUNT ON;

DECLARE @ActionType nvarchar(10), @ActionXml xml;

-- Get count of inserted rows
DECLARE @inserted_count int = (
    SELECT COUNT(*)
    FROM inserted
);
-- Get count of deleted rows
DECLARE @deleted_count int = (
    SELECT COUNT(*)
    FROM deleted
);
```

Because the trigger is logging the type of DML action that caused it to fire (an INSERT, a DELETE, or an UPDATE action), it must determine the type programmatically. This can be done by applying the following simple rules to the counts of rows from the inserted and deleted virtual tables:

1. If at least one row was inserted but no rows were deleted, the DML action was an insert.

2. If at least one row was deleted but no rows were inserted, the DML action was a delete.

3. If at least one row was deleted and at least one row was inserted, the DML action was an update.

These rules are applied in the form of a CASE expression, as shown in the following:

```
-- Determine the type of DML action that fired the trigger
SET @ActionType = CASE
    WHEN (@inserted_count > 0) AND (@deleted_count = 0) THEN N'insert'
    WHEN (@inserted_count = 0) AND (@deleted_count > 0) THEN N'delete'
    ELSE N'update'
END;
```

The next step in the trigger uses the SELECT statement's FOR XML AUTO clause to generate XML-formatted before and after snapshots of the affected rows. FOR XML AUTO is useful because it automatically uses the source table name as the XML element name—in this case, inserted or deleted. The FOR XML AUTO clause automatically uses the names of the columns in the table as XML attributes for each element. Because the inserted and deleted virtual tables have the same column names as this affected table, you don't have to hard-code column names into the trigger. In the resulting XML, the <deleted> elements represent the before snapshot and the <inserted> elements represent the after snapshot of the affected rows:

```
-- Use FOR XML AUTO to retrieve before and after snapshots of the changed
--    data  in  XML  format
SELECT @ActionXml = COALESCE
(
```

```
    (
        SELECT *
        FROM deleted
        FOR XML AUTO
    ), N'<deleted/>'
) + COALESCE
(
    (
        SELECT *
        FROM inserted
        FOR XML AUTO
    ), N'<inserted/>'
);
```

■ **Tip** The DML audit logging trigger was created to be flexible so you can use it with minimal changes on most tables. However, there are some circumstances where it may require the use of additional options or more extensive changes to work with a given table. As an example, if your table contains a varbinary column, you have to use the FOR XML clause's BINARY BASE64 directive (FOR XML, BINARY BASE64).

The final step in the trigger inserts a row representing the logged action into the dbo.DmlActionLog table. Several SQL Server metadata functions—like @@PROCID, OBJECT_SCHEMA_NAME(), and OBJECT_NAME(), as well as the sys.triggers catalog view—are used in the INSERT statement to dynamically identify the current trigger procedure ID, and the schema and table name information. Also, functions like SUSER_SNAME(), APP_NAME(), and HOST_NAME() allow you to retrieve useful audit information on the execution context. Again, this means almost nothing needs to be hard-coded into the trigger, making it easier to use the trigger on multiple tables with minimal changes:

```
-- Insert a row for the logged action in the audit logging table
INSERT INTO dbo.DmlActionLog
(
    SchemaName,
    TableName,
    ActionType,
    ActionXml,
    LoginName,
    ApplicationName,
    HostName
)
SELECT
    OBJECT_SCHEMA_NAME(@@PROCID, DB_ID()),
    OBJECT_NAME(t.parent_id, DB_ID()),
    @ActionType,
    @ActionXml,
    SUSER_SNAME(),
    APP_NAME(),
    HOST_NAME()
FROM sys.triggers t
WHERE t.object_id = @@PROCID;
```

■ **Tip** SQL Server includes several metadata functions, catalog views, and dynamic management views and functions that are useful for dynamically retrieving information about databases, database objects, and the current state of the server. More of these useful T-SQL functions and views are described as they're encountered in later chapters.

You can easily verify the trigger with a few simple DML statements. Listing 7-6 changes the name of the AdventureWorks Information Services department to Information Technology, and then inserts and deletes a Customer Service department. The results are shown in Figure 7-2.

Listing 7-6. Testing the DML Audit Logging Trigger

```
UPDATE HumanResources.Department SET Name = N'Information Technology'
WHERE DepartmentId = 11;

INSERT INTO HumanResources.Department
(
    Name,
    GroupName
)
VALUES
(
    N'Customer Service',
    N'Sales and Marketing'
);

DELETE
FROM HumanResources.Department
WHERE Name = N'Customer Service';

SELECT
    EntryNum,
    SchemaName,
    TableName,
    ActionType,
    ActionXml,
    LoginName,
    ApplicationName,
    HostName,
    ActionDateTime
FROM dbo.DmlActionLog;
```

	EntryNum	SchemaName	TableName	ActionType	ActionXml	LoginName	ApplicationName
1	1	HumanResources	Department	update	<deleted DepartmentID="11"...	SQL2012\Administrator	Microsoft SQL Server
2	2	HumanResources	Department	insert	<deleted /><inserted Departm...	SQL2012\Administrator	Microsoft SQL Server
3	3	HumanResources	Department	delete	<deleted DepartmentID="17"...	SQL2012\Administrator	Microsoft SQL Server

Figure 7-2. Audit logging results

The FOR XML AUTO-generated ActionXml column data deserves a closer look. As mentioned earlier in this section, the FOR XML AUTO clause automatically generates element and attribute names based on the source table and source column names. The UPDATE statement in Listing 7-6 generates the ActionXml entry shown in Figure 7-3. Note that the XML has been formatted for easier reading, but the content hasn't changed.

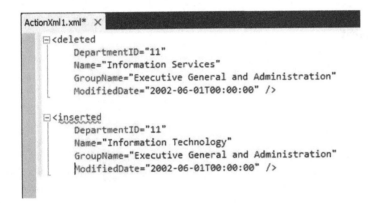

Figure 7-3. The ActionXml entry generated by the UPDATE statement

Sharing Data with Triggers

A commonly asked question is, "How do you pass parameters to triggers?" The short answer is, you can't. Because they're automatically fired in response to events, SQL Server triggers provide no means to pass parameters. If you need to pass additional data to a trigger, you do have a couple of options available, however. The first option is to create a table, which the trigger can then access via SELECT queries. The advantage of this method is that the amount of data a trigger can access is effectively unlimited. A disadvantage is the additional overhead required to query the table within the trigger.

Another option, if you have small amounts of data to share with your triggers, is to use the CONTEXT_INFO function. You can assign up to 128 bytes of varbinary data to the CONTEXT_INFO for the current session through the SET CONTEXT_INFO statement. This statement accepts only a variable or constant value—no other expressions are allowed. After you've set the CONTEXT_INFO for your session, you can access it in your trigger via the CONTEXT_INFO() function. The disadvantage of this method is the small amount of data you can store in CONTEXT_INFO. Keep these methods in mind, because you may one day find that you need to pass information into a trigger from a batch or SP.

Nested and Recursive Triggers

SQL Server supports triggers firing other triggers through the concept of nested triggers. A nested trigger is simply a trigger that is fired by the action of another trigger, on the same or a different table. Triggers can be nested up to 32 levels deep. We advise against nesting triggers deeply, however, because the additional levels of nesting affect performance. If you do have triggers nested deeply, you may want to reconsider your trigger design. Nested triggers are turned on by default, but you can turn them off with the sp_configure statement, as shown in Listing 7-7.

Listing 7-7. Turning Off Nested Triggers

```
EXEC sp_configure 'nested triggers', 0;
RECONFIGURE;
GO
```

Set the nested triggers option to 1 to turn nested triggers back on. This option affects only AFTER triggers. INSTEAD OF triggers can be nested and will execute regardless of the setting. Triggers can also be called recursively. There are two types of trigger recursion:

- Direct recursion: Occurs when a trigger performs an action that causes it to recursively fire itself.

- Indirect recursion: Occurs when a trigger fires another trigger (which can fire another trigger, and so on), which eventually fires the first trigger.

Direct and indirect recursion of triggers applies only to triggers of the same type. As an example, an INSTEAD OF trigger that causes another INSTEAD OF trigger to fire is direct recursion. Even if a different type of trigger is fired between the first and second firing of the same trigger, it's still considered direct recursion. For example, if one or more AFTER triggers are fired between the first and second firings of the same INSTEAD OF trigger, it's still considered direct recursion. Indirect recursion occurs when a trigger of the same type is called between firings of the same trigger.

You can use the ALTER DATABASE statement's SET RECURSIVE_TRIGGERS option to turn direct recursion of AFTER triggers on and off, as shown in Listing 7-8. Turning off direct recursion of INSTEAD OF triggers requires that you also set the nested triggers option to 0, as shown previously in Listing 7-7.

Listing 7-8. Turning Off Recursive AFTER Triggers

```
ALTER DATABASE AdventureWorks SET RECURSIVE_TRIGGERS OFF;
```

Actions taken with an INSTEAD OF trigger don't cause it to fire again. Instead, the INSTEAD OF trigger performs constraint checks and fires any AFTER triggers. As an example, if an INSTEAD OF UPDATE trigger on a table is fired, and during the course of its execution it performs an UPDATE statement against the table, the UPDATE doesn't fire the INSTEAD OF trigger again. Instead, the UPDATE statement initiates constraint-check operations and fires AFTER triggers on the table.

■ **Caution**   Nested and recursive triggers should be used with care, because nesting and recursion that are too deep will cause your triggers to throw exceptions. You can use the TRIGGER_NESTLEVEL() function to determine the current level of recursion from within a trigger.

The UPDATE() and COLUMNS_UPDATED() Functions

Triggers can take advantage of two system functions, UPDATE() and COLUMNS_UPDATED(), to tell you which columns are affected by the INSERT or UPDATE statement that fires the trigger in the first place. UPDATE() takes the name of a column as a parameter and returns true if the column is updated or inserted, and false otherwise. COLUMNS_UPDATED() returns a bit pattern indicating which columns are affected by the INSERT or UPDATE statement.

In the case of an UPDATE, affected means the column is present in the statement, not that the value of the column effectively changed. There is only one way to know if the value of a column really changed: by comparing the content of the deleted and inserted virtual tables. You can adapt the following query example to do that with your trigger:

```
SELECT i.ProductId, d.Color as OldColor, i.Color as NewColor
FROM deleted as d
JOIN inserted as i ON d.ProductId = i.ProductId
    AND COALESCE(d.Color, '') <> COALESCE(i.Color, '');
```

This fragment is designed to be part of a trigger that could be created on the Production.Product table. The JOIN condition associates lines from the deleted and inserted tables on the primary key column and adds a non-equi join condition (joining on difference rather than on equivalence) on the Color column, to keep only rows where the Color value was changed. The COALESCE() function allows you to take into account the possibility of a NULL being present in the previous or new value.

Getting back to the UPDATE() and COLUMNS_UPDATED() functions, the example trigger in Listing 7-9 demonstrates the use of triggers to enforce business rules. In this example, the trigger uses the UPDATE function to determine whether Size or SizeUnitMeasureCode has been affected by an INSERT or UPDATE statement. If either of these columns is affected by an INSERT or UPDATE statement, the trigger checks whether a recognized SizeUnitMeasureCode was used. If so, the trigger converts Size to centimeters. The trigger recognizes several SizeUnitMeasureCode values, including centimeters (CM), millimeters (MM), and inches (IN).

Listing 7-9. Trigger to Enforce Standard Sizes

```
CREATE TRIGGER Production.ProductEnforceStandardSizes
ON Production.Product
AFTER INSERT, UPDATE
NOT FOR REPLICATION
AS
BEGIN
    -- Make sure at least one row was affected and either the Size or
    -- SizeUnitMeasureCode column was changed
    IF (@@ROWCOUNT > 0) AND (UPDATE(SizeUnitMeasureCode) OR UPDATE(Size))
    BEGIN
        -- Eliminate "rows affected" messages
        SET NOCOUNT ON;
        -- Only accept recognized units of measure or NULL
        IF EXISTS
        (
            SELECT 1
            FROM inserted
            WHERE NOT
                ( SizeUnitMeasureCode IN (N'M', N'DM', N'CM', N'MM', N'IN')
                    OR SizeUnitMeasureCode IS NULL
                )
        )
```

```
        BEGIN
            -- If the unit of measure wasn't recognized raise an error and roll back
            -- the transaction
            RAISERROR ('Invalid Size Unit Measure Code.', 10, 127);
            ROLLBACK TRANSACTION;
        END
        ELSE
        BEGIN
            -- If the unit of measure is a recognized unit of measure then set the
            -- SizeUnitMeasureCode to centimeters and perform the Size conversion
            UPDATE Production.Product
            SET SizeUnitMeasureCode = CASE
                    WHEN Production.Product.SizeUnitMeasureCode IS NULL THEN NULL ELSE N'CM' END,
                Size = CAST (
                    CAST ( CAST(i.Size AS float) *
                        CASE i.SizeUnitMeasureCode
                            WHEN N'M' THEN 100.0
                            WHEN N'DM' THEN 10.0
                            WHEN N'CM' THEN 1.0
                            WHEN N'MM' THEN 0.10
                            WHEN N'IN' THEN 2.54
                        END
                    AS int
                    ) AS nvarchar(5)
                )
            FROM inserted i
            WHERE Production.Product.ProductID = i.ProductID
            AND i.SizeUnitMeasureCode IS NOT NULL;
        END;
    END;
END;
GO
```

The first part of the trigger definition gives the trigger its name, Production.ProductEnforceStandardSizes, and creates it on the Production.Product table. It's specified as an AFTER INSERT, UPDATE trigger and is declared as NOT FOR REPLICATION:

```
CREATE TRIGGER Production.ProductEnforceStandardSizes
ON Production.Product
AFTER INSERT, UPDATE
NOT FOR REPLICATION
```

The code in the body of the trigger immediately checks @@ROWCOUNT to make sure at least one row was affected by the DML statement that fired the trigger, and uses the UPDATE function to ensure that the Size and SizeUnitMeasureCode columns were affected by the DML statement:

```
IF (@@ROWCOUNT > 0)
AND (UPDATE(SizeUnitMeasureCode) OR UPDATE(Size)) BEGIN
• • •
END;
```

Once the trigger has verified that at least one row was affected and the appropriate columns were modified, the trigger sets NOCOUNT ON to prevent the rows affected messages from being generated by the trigger. The IF EXISTS statement checks to make sure valid unit-of-measure codes are used. If not, the trigger raises an error and rolls back the transaction:

```
-- Eliminate "rows affected" messages
SET NOCOUNT ON;
-- Only accept recognized units of measure or NULL
IF EXISTS
(
    SELECT 1
    FROM inserted
    WHERE NOT
        ( SizeUnitMeasureCode IN (N'M', N'DM', N'CM', N'MM', N'IN')
            OR SizeUnitMeasureCode IS NULL
        )
)
BEGIN
    -- If the unit of measure wasn't recognized raise an error and roll back
    -- the transaction
    RAISERROR ('Invalid Size Unit Measure Code.', 10, 127);
    ROLLBACK TRANSACTION;
END
```

■ **Tip** The ROLLBACK TRANSACTION statement in the trigger rolls back the transaction and prevents further triggers from being fired by the current trigger. Two error messages are received by the client: the one raised by RAISERROR(), and the error 3609 or 3616, warning that the transaction ended in the trigger.

If the unit-of-measure validation is passed, SizeUnitMeasureCode is set to centimeters and Size is converted to centimeters for each inserted or updated row:

```
BEGIN
    -- If the unit of measure is a recognized unit of measure then set the
    -- SizeUnitMeasureCode to centimeters and perform the Size conversion
    UPDATE Production.Product
        SET SizeUnitMeasureCode = CASE
            WHEN Production.Product.SizeUnitMeasureCode IS NULL THEN NULL ELSE N'CM' END,
            Size = CAST (
                CAST ( CAST(i.Size AS float) *
                    CASE i.SizeUnitMeasureCode
                        WHEN N'M' THEN 100.0
                        WHEN N'DM' THEN 10.0
                        WHEN N'CM' THEN 1.0
                        WHEN N'MM' THEN 0.10
                        WHEN N'IN' THEN 2.54
                    END
```

```
            AS int
        ) AS nvarchar(5)
    )
FROM inserted i
WHERE Production.Product.ProductID = i.ProductID
AND i.SizeUnitMeasureCode IS NOT NULL;
END;
```

This trigger enforces simple business logic by ensuring that standard-size codes are used when updating the Production.Product table and converting the Size values to centimeters. To test the trigger, you can perform updates of existing rows in the Production.Product table. Listing 7-10 updates the sizes of the products with ProductID 680 and 780 to 600 millimeters and 22.85 inches, respectively. The results, with the Size values automatically converted to centimeters, are shown in Figure 7-4.

Listing 7-10. Testing the Trigger by Adding a New Product

```
UPDATE  Production.Product
SET Size = N'600',
    SizeUnitMeasureCode = N'MM'
WHERE  ProductId  =  680;

UPDATE  Production.Product
SET Size = N'22.85',
    SizeUnitMeasureCode = N'IN'
WHERE  ProductId  =  706;

SELECT  ProductID,
    Name,
    ProductNumber,
    Size,
    SizeUnitMeasureCode
FROM  Production.Product
WHERE  ProductID  IN  (680,  706);
```

	ProductID	Name	ProductNumber	Size	SizeUnitMeasureCode
1	680	HL Road Frame - Black, 58	FR-R92B-58	60	CM
2	706	HL Road Frame - Red, 58	FR-R92R-58	58	CM

Figure 7-4. *Results of the Production.ProductEnforceStandardSizes trigger test*

Whereas the UPDATE() function accepts a column name and returns true if the column is affected, the COLUMNS_UPDATED() function accepts no parameters and returns a varbinary value with a single bit representing each column. You can use the bitwise AND operator (&) and a bit mask to test which columns are affected. The bits are set from left to right, based on the ColumnID number of the columns from the sys.columns catalog view or the COLUMNPROPERTY() function.

■ **Caution**   The position of COLUMNS_UPDATED() is not the same as the ORDINAL_POSITION value found in the INFORMATION_SCHEMA.COLUMNS catalog view. Rely on the sys.columns.ColumnID value instead.

To create a bit mask, you must use 20 (1) to represent the first column, 21 (2) to represent the second column, and so on. Because COLUMNS_UPDATED() returns a varbinary result, the column indicator bits can be spread out over several bytes. To test columns beyond the first eight, like the Size and SizeUnitMeasureCode columns in the example code (columns 11 and 12), you can use the SUBSTRING function to return the second byte of COLUMNS_UPDATED() and test the appropriate bits with a bit mask of 12 (12 = 22 + 23). The example trigger in Listing 7-9 can be modified to use the COLUMNS_UPDATED() function, as shown here:

```
IF (@@ROWCOUNT > 0) AND (SUBSTRING(COLUMNS_UPDATED(), 2, 1) & 12 <> 0x00)
```

The COLUMNS_UPDATED() function won't return correct results if the ColumnID values of the table are changed. If the table is dropped and re-created with columns in a different order, you need to change the triggers that use COLUMNS_UPDATED() to reflect the changes. There may be specialized instances in which you can take advantage of the COLUMNS_UPDATED() functionality, but in general we advise against using COLUMNS_UPDATED(): instead, use the UPDATE() function to determine which columns were affected by the DML statement that fired your trigger.

Triggers on Views

Although you can't create AFTER triggers on views, SQL Server does allow you to create INSTEAD OF triggers on your views. A trigger can be useful for updating views that are otherwise non-updatable, such as views with multiple base tables or views that contain aggregate functions. INSTEAD OF triggers on views also give you fine-grained control, because you can control which columns of the view are updatable through the trigger. The AdventureWorks database comes with a view named Sales.vSalesPerson, which is formed by joining 11 separate tables together. The INSTEAD OF trigger in Listing 7-11 allows you to update specific columns of two of the base tables used in the view by executing UPDATE statements directly against the view.

Listing 7-11. INSTEAD OF Trigger on a View

```
CREATE TRIGGER Sales.vIndividualCustomerUpdate
ON Sales.vIndividualCustomer
INSTEAD OF UPDATE
NOT FOR REPLICATION
AS
BEGIN
    -- First make sure at least one row was affected
    IF @@ROWCOUNT = 0 RETURN
    -- Turn off "rows affected" messages
```

```
SET NOCOUNT ON;
-- Initialize a flag to indicate update success
DECLARE @UpdateSuccessful bit = 0;

-- Check for updatable columns in the first table
IF UPDATE(FirstName) OR UPDATE(MiddleName) OR UPDATE(LastName)
BEGIN
    -- Update columns in the base table
    UPDATE Person.Person
    SET FirstName = i.FirstName,
        MiddleName = i.MiddleName,
        LastName = i.LastName
    FROM inserted i
    WHERE i.BusinessEntityID = Person.Person.BusinessEntityID;

    -- Set flag to indicate success
    SET @UpdateSuccessful = 1;
END;
-- If updatable columns from the second table were specified, update those
-- columns in the base table
IF UPDATE(EmailAddress)
BEGIN
    -- Update columns in the base table
    UPDATE Person.EmailAddress
    SET EmailAddress = i.EmailAddress
    FROM inserted i
    WHERE i.BusinessEntityID = Person.EmailAddress.BusinessEntityID;

    -- Set flag to indicate success
    SET @UpdateSuccessful = 1;
END;
-- If the update was not successful, raise an error and roll back the
-- transaction
IF @UpdateSuccessful = 0
    RAISERROR('Must specify updatable columns.', 10, 127);
END;
GO
```

The trigger in Listing 7-11 is created as an INSTEAD OF UPDATE trigger on the Sales.
vIndividualCustomer view, as shown here:

```
CREATE TRIGGER Sales.vIndividualCustomerUpdate
ON Sales.vIndividualCustomer
INSTEAD OF UPDATE
NOT FOR REPLICATION
```

As with the previous examples in this chapter, this trigger begins by checking @@ROWCOUNT to ensure that at least one row was updated:

```
-- First make sure at least one row was affected
IF @@ROWCOUNT = 0 RETURN;
```

Once the trigger verifies that one or more rows were affected by the DML statement that fired the trigger, it turns off the rows affected messages and initializes a flag to indicate success or failure of the update operation:

```
-- Turn off "rows affected" messages
SET NOCOUNT ON;
-- Initialize a flag to indicate update success
DECLARE @UpdateSuccessful bit = 0;
```

The trigger then checks to see whether the columns designated as updatable were affected by the UPDATE statement. If the proper columns were affected by the UPDATE statement, the trigger performs updates on the appropriate base tables for the view. For purposes of this demonstration, the columns that are updatable by the trigger are the FirstName, MiddleName, and LastName columns from the Person.Person table, and the EmailAddress column from the Person.EmailAddress column:

```
-- Check for updatable columns in the first table
IF UPDATE(FirstName) OR UPDATE(MiddleName) OR UPDATE(LastName)
BEGIN
    -- Update columns in the base table
    UPDATE Person.Person
    SET FirstName = i.FirstName,
        MiddleName = i.MiddleName,
        LastName = i.LastName
    FROM inserted i
    WHERE i.BusinessEntityID = Person.Person.BusinessEntityID;

    -- Set flag to indicate success
    SET @UpdateSuccessful = 1;
END;

-- If updatable columns from the second table were specified, update those
-- columns in the base table
IF UPDATE(EmailAddress) BEGIN
    -- Update columns in the base table
    UPDATE Person.EmailAddress
    SET EmailAddress = i.EmailAddress
    FROM inserted i
    WHERE i.BusinessEntityID = Person.EmailAddress.BusinessEntityID;

    -- Set flag to indicate success
    SET @UpdateSuccessful = 1;
END;
```

Finally, if no updatable columns were specified by the UPDATE statement that fired the trigger, an error is raised and the transaction is rolled back:

```
-- If the update was not successful, raise an error and roll back the
-- transaction
IF @UpdateSuccessful = 1
    RAISERROR('Must specify updatable columns.', 10, 127);
```

Listing 7-12 demonstrates a simple UPDATE against the Sales.vIndividualCustomer view with the INSTEAD OF trigger from Listing 7-11 created on it. The result is shown in Figure 7-5.

Listing 7-12. Updating a View Using an INSTEAD OF Trigger

```
UPDATE Sales.vIndividualCustomer
SET FirstName = N'Dave',
    MiddleName = N'Robert',
    EmailAddress = N'dave.robinett@adventure-works.com'
WHERE BusinessEntityID = 1699;

SELECT BusinessEntityID, FirstName, MiddleName, LastName, EmailAddress
FROM Sales.vIndividualCustomer
WHERE BusinessEntityID = 1699;
```

	BusinessEntityID	FirstName	MiddleName	LastName	EmailAddress
1	1699	Dave	Robert	Robinett	dave.robinett@adventure-works.com

Figure 7-5. *Result of the INSTEAD OF trigger view update*

DDL Triggers

Since SQL Server 2005, T-SQL programmers have had the ability to create DDL triggers that fire when DDL events occur in a database or on the server. This section discusses DDL triggers, the events that fire them, and their purpose. The format of the CREATE TRIGGER statement for DDL triggers is only slightly different from the DML trigger syntax, with the major difference being that you must specify the scope for the trigger: either ALL SERVER or DATABASE. The DATABASE scope causes the DDL trigger to fire if an event of a specified event type or event group occurs in the database in which the trigger was created. ALL SERVER scope causes the DDL trigger to fire if an event of the specified event type or event group occurs anywhere on the current server.

DDL triggers can only be specified as FOR or AFTER (there's no INSTEAD OF-type DDL trigger). The event types that can fire a DDL trigger are largely of the form CREATE, ALTER, DROP, GRANT, DENY, or REVOKE. Some system SPs that perform DDL functions also fire DDL triggers. The ALTER TRIGGER, DROP TRIGGER, DISABLE TRIGGER, and ENABLE TRIGGER statements work for DDL triggers just as they do for DML triggers.

DDL triggers are useful when you want to prevent changes to your database, perform actions in response to a change in the database, or audit changes to the database. Which DDL statements can fire a DDL trigger depends on the scope of the trigger.

DDL Event Types and Event Groups

DDL triggers can fire in response to a wide variety of event types and event groups, scoped at either the database or server level. The events that fire DDL triggers are largely DDL statements like CREATE and DROP, and Data Control Language (DCL) statements like GRANT and DENY. Event groups form a hierarchical structure of DDL events in logical groupings, like DDL_FUNCTION_EVENTS and DDL_PROCEDURE_EVENTS. Event groups allow you to fire triggers in response to a wide range of DDL events.

BOL has complete listings of all available DDL trigger event types and event groups, so they aren't reproduced fully here. Just keep in mind that you can fire triggers in response to most T-SQL DDL and DCL statements. You can also query the sys.trigger_event_types catalog view to retrieve available DDL events.

With DDL triggers, you can specify either an event type or an event group, the latter of which can encompass multiple events or other event groups. If you specify an event group, any events included in that group, or in the subgroups of that group, will fire the DDL trigger.

■ **Note**   Creating a DDL trigger with ALL SERVER scope requires CONTROL SERVER permission on the server. Creating a DDL trigger with DATABASE scope requires ALTER ANY DATABASE DDL TRIGGER permissions.

Once the DDL trigger fires, you can access metadata about the event that fired the trigger with the EVENTDATA() function. EVENTDATA() returns information such as the time, connection, object name, and type of event that fired the trigger. The results are returned as a SQL Server xml data type instance. Listing 7-13 shows a sample of the type of data returned by the EVENTDATA function.

Listing 7-13. EVENTDATA() Function Example Data

```
<EVENT_INSTANCE>
 <EventType>CREATE_TABLE</EventType>
 <PostTime>2012-04-21T17:08:28.527</PostTime>
 <SPID>115</SPID>
 <ServerName>SQL2012</ServerName>
 <LoginName>SQL2012\Rudi</LoginName>
 <UserName>dbo</UserName>
 <DatabaseName>AdventureWorks</DatabaseName>
 <SchemaName>dbo</SchemaName>
 <ObjectName>MyTable</ObjectName>
 <ObjectType>TABLE</ObjectType>
 <TSQLCommand>
 <SetOptions ANSI_NULLS="ON"ANSI_NULL_DEFAULT="ON"ANSI_PADDING="ON"QUOTED_IDENTIFIER="ON"EN
   CRYPTED="FALSE" />
 <CommandText>CREATE TABLE dbo.MyTable (i int);</CommandText>
 </TSQLCommand>
</EVENT_INSTANCE>
```

You can use the xml data type's value() method to retrieve specific nodes from the result. The example DDL trigger in Listing 7-14 creates a DDL trigger that fires in response to the CREATE TABLE statement in the AdventureWorks database. It logs the event data to a table named dbo.DdlActionLog.

Listing 7-14. CREATE TABLE DDL Trigger Example

```
-- Create a table to log DDL CREATE TABLE actions
CREATE TABLE dbo.DdlActionLog
(
    EntryId int NOT NULL IDENTITY(1, 1) PRIMARY KEY,
    EventType nvarchar(200) NOT NULL,
    PostTime datetime NOT NULL,
    LoginName sysname NOT NULL,
    UserName sysname NOT NULL,
```

```
    ServerName sysname NOT NULL,
    SchemaName sysname NOT NULL,
    DatabaseName sysname NOT NULL,
    ObjectName sysname NOT NULL,
    ObjectType sysname NOT NULL,
    CommandText nvarchar(max) NOT NULL
);
GO


CREATE TRIGGER AuditCreateTable
ON DATABASE
FOR CREATE_TABLE
AS
BEGIN
    -- Assign the XML event data to an xml variable
    DECLARE @eventdata xml = EVENTDATA();

    -- Shred the XML event data and insert a row in the log table
    INSERT INTO dbo.DdlActionLog
    (
        EventType,
        PostTime,
        LoginName,
        UserName,
        ServerName,
        SchemaName,
        DatabaseName,
        ObjectName,
        ObjectType,
        CommandText
    )
    SELECT
        EventNode.value(N'EventType[1]', N'nvarchar(200)'),
        EventNode.value(N'PostTime[1]', N'datetime'),
        EventNode.value(N'LoginName[1]', N'sysname'),
        EventNode.value(N'UserName[1]', N'sysname'),
        EventNode.value(N'ServerName[1]', N'sysname'),
        EventNode.value(N'SchemaName[1]', N'sysname'),
        EventNode.value(N'DatabaseName[1]', N'sysname'),
        EventNode.value(N'ObjectName[1]', N'sysname'),
        EventNode.value(N'ObjectType[1]', N'sysname'),
        EventNode.value(N'(TSQLCommand/CommandText)[1]', 'nvarchar(max)')
    FROM @eventdata.nodes('/EVENT_INSTANCE') EventTable(EventNode);
END;
GO
```

The first part of the example in Listing 7-14 creates a simple table to store the event-specific data generated by events that fire the DDL trigger:

```
-- Create a table to log DDL CREATE TABLE actions
CREATE TABLE dbo.DdlActionLog
(
    EntryId int NOT NULL IDENTITY(1, 1) PRIMARY KEY,
    EventType nvarchar(200) NOT NULL,
    PostTime datetime NOT NULL,
    LoginName sysname NOT NULL,
    UserName sysname NOT NULL,
    ServerName sysname NOT NULL,
    SchemaName sysname NOT NULL,
    DatabaseName sysname NOT NULL,
    ObjectName sysname NOT NULL,
    ObjectType sysname NOT NULL,
    CommandText nvarchar(max) NOT NULL
);
GO
```

The DDL trigger definition begins with the name, the scope (DATABASE), and the DDL action that fires the trigger. In this example, the action that fires the trigger is the CREATE TABLE event. Notice that unlike DML triggers, DDL triggers don't belong to schemas and don't have schemas specified in their names:

```
CREATE TRIGGER AuditCreateTable
ON DATABASE
FOR CREATE_TABLE
```

The body of the trigger begins by declaring an xml variable, @eventdata. This variable holds the results of the EVENTDATA() function for further processing later in the trigger:

```
-- Assign the XML event data to an xml variable
DECLARE @eventdata xml = EVENTDATA();
```

Next, the trigger uses the nodes() and value() methods of the @eventdata xml variable to shred the event data, which is then inserted into the dbo.DdlActionLog table in relational form:

```
-- Shred the XML event data and insert a row in the log table
INSERT INTO dbo.DdlActionLog
(
    EventType,
    PostTime,
    LoginName,
    UserName,
    ServerName,
    SchemaName,
    DatabaseName,
    ObjectName,
    ObjectType,
    CommandText
)
```

```
SELECT
    EventNode.value(N'EventType[1]', N'nvarchar(200)'),
    EventNode.value(N'PostTime[1]', N'datetime'),
    EventNode.value(N'LoginName[1]', N'sysname'),
    EventNode.value(N'UserName[1]', N'sysname'),
    EventNode.value(N'ServerName[1]', N'sysname'),
    EventNode.value(N'SchemaName[1]', N'sysname'),
    EventNode.value(N'DatabaseName[1]', N'sysname'),
    EventNode.value(N'ObjectName[1]', N'sysname'),
    EventNode.value(N'ObjectType[1]', N'sysname'),
    EventNode.value(N'(TSQLCommand/CommandText)[1]', 'nvarchar(max)')
FROM @eventdata.nodes('/EVENT_INSTANCE') EventTable(EventNode);
```

Listing 7-15 demonstrates the DDL trigger by performing a CREATE TABLE statement. Partial results are shown in Figure 7-6.

Listing 7-15. Testing the DDL Trigger with a CREATE TABLE Statement

```
CREATE TABLE dbo.MyTable (i int);
GO

SELECT
    EntryId,
    EventType,
    UserName,
    ObjectName,
    CommandText
FROM DdlActionLog;
```

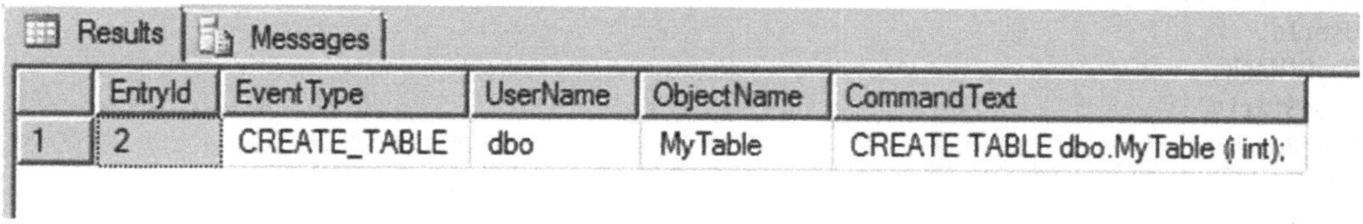

	EntryId	EventType	UserName	ObjectName	CommandText
1	2	CREATE_TABLE	dbo	MyTable	CREATE TABLE dbo.MyTable (i int);

Figure 7-6. DDL audit logging results

Dropping a DDL trigger is as simple as executing the DROP TRIGGER statement, as shown in Listing 7-16. Notice that the ON DATABASE clause is required in this instance. The reason is that the DDL trigger exists outside the schemas of the database, so you must tell SQL Server whether the trigger exists at the database or server scope.

Listing 7-16. Dropping a DDL Trigger

```
DROP TRIGGER AuditCreateTable
ON DATABASE;
```

Logon Triggers

SQL Server offers yet another type of trigger: the logon trigger. Logon triggers were first made available in SQL Server 2005 SP 2. These triggers fire in response to an SQL Server LOGON event—after authentication succeeds, but before the user session is established. You can perform tasks ranging from simple LOGON event auditing to more advanced tasks like restricting the number of simultaneous sessions for a login or denying users the ability to create sessions at certain times.

The code example for this section uses logon triggers to deny a given user the ability to log in to SQL Server during a specified time period (for example, during a resource-intensive nightly batch process). Listing 7-17 begins by creating a sample login and a table that holds a logon-denial schedule. The first entry in this table will be used to deny the example login the ability to log in to SQL Server between the hours of 9:00 and 11:00 p.m. on Saturday nights.

Listing 7-17. Creating a Test Login and Logon-Denial Schedule

```
CREATE LOGIN PublicUser WITH PASSWORD = 'p@$$w0rd';
GO

USE Master;

CREATE TABLE dbo.DenyLogonSchedule (
    UserId sysname NOT NULL,
    DayOfWeek tinyint NOT NULL,
    TimeStart time NOT NULL,
    TimeEnd time NOT NULL,
    PRIMARY KEY (UserId, DayOfWeek, TimeStart, TimeEnd)
);
GO

INSERT INTO dbo.DenyLogonSchedule (
    UserId,
    DayOfWeek,
    TimeStart,
    TimeEnd
) VALUES (
    'PublicUser',
    7,
    '21:00:00',
    '23:00:00'
);
```

The logon trigger that uses this table to deny logons on a schedule is shown in Listing 7-18.

Listing 7-18. Example Logon Trigger

```
USE Master;

CREATE TRIGGER DenyLogons
ON ALL SERVER
WITH EXECUTE AS 'sa'
FOR LOGON
AS
BEGIN
```

```
    IF EXISTS ( SELECT 1
        FROM Master .dbo.DenyLogonSchedule
        WHERE UserId = ORIGINAL_LOGIN()
        AND DayOfWeek = DATEPART(WeekDay, GETDATE())
        AND CAST(GETDATE() AS TIME) BETWEEN TimeStart AND TimeEnd
    ) BEGIN
        ROLLBACK TRANSACTION;
    END;
END;
```

■ **Caution**   If your logon trigger errors out, you can't log on into SQL Server normally. You can still connect using the Dedicated Administrator Connection (DAC), which bypasses logon triggers. Make sure the table dbo.DenyLogonSchedule exists and that your logon trigger works properly before putting it in production.

The CREATE TRIGGER statement begins much like the other trigger examples you've used to this point, by specifying the name and scope (ALL SERVER). The WITH EXECUTE clause is used to specify that the logon trigger should run under the sa security context, and the FOR LOGON clause indicates that this is actually a logon trigger:

```
CREATE TRIGGER DenyLogons
ON ALL SERVER
WITH EXECUTE AS 'sa'
FOR LOGON
```

The trigger body is fairly simple. It checks for the existence of an entry in the AdventureWorks.dbo. DenyLogonSchedule table, indicating that the current user (retrieved with the ORIGINAL_LOGIN() function) is denied login based on the current date and time. If there is an entry indicating that the login should be denied, then the ROLLBACK TRANSACTION statement is executed, denying the login:

```
IF EXISTS ( SELECT 1
    FROM AdventureWorks.dbo.DenyLogonSchedule
    WHERE UserId = ORIGINAL_LOGIN()
    AND DayOfWeek = DATEPART(WeekDay, GETDATE())
    AND CAST(GETDATE() AS TIME) BETWEEN TimeStart AND TimeEnd
) BEGIN
    ROLLBACK TRANSACTION;
END;
```

Notice that the three-part name of the table is used in this statement, because the user attempting to log in may be connecting to a different default database. Attempting to log in to SQL Server using the PublicUser account on Saturday night between the hours indicated results in an error message like the one shown in Figure 7-7.

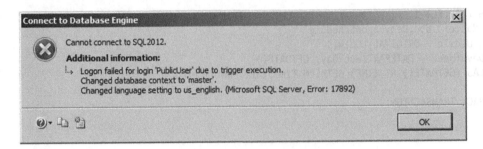

Figure 7-7. A logon trigger denying a login

■ **Tip**   Logon triggers are useful for auditing and restricting logins, but because they only fire after a successful authentication, they can't be used to log unsuccessful login attempts.

The logon trigger also makes logon information available in XML format in the trigger via the EVENTDATA() function. An example of the logon information generated by the LOGON event is shown in Listing 7-19.

Listing 7-19. Example Event Data Generated by a LOGON Event

```
<EVENT_INSTANCE>
  <EventType>LOGON</EventType>
  <PostTime>2012-04-21T23:18:33.357</PostTime>
  <SPID>110</SPID>
  <ServerName>SQL2012</ServerName>
  <LoginName>PublicUser</LoginName>
  <LoginType>SQL Login</LoginType>
  <SID>zgPcN6UCBE2j/HYTugOi4A==</SID>
  <ClientHost>&lt;local machine&gt;</ClientHost>
  <IsPooled>0</IsPooled>
</EVENT_INSTANCE>
```

■ **Note**   Logon triggers to deny access to logins based on day of week, time of day, and number of sessions per login are available in the Common Criteria compliance package for SQL Server. You can download them on the SQL Server Common Criteria Certifications website: http://msdn.microsoft.com/en-us/library/bb326650.aspx.

Summary

This chapter discussed triggers, including traditional DML triggers, DDL triggers, and logon triggers. As you've seen, triggers are useful tools for a variety of purposes.

DML triggers are the original form of trigger. Much of the functionality that DML triggers were used for in the past, such as enforcing referential integrity, has been supplanted by newer and more efficient T-SQL functionality over the years, like cascading DRI. DML triggers are useful for auditing DML statements and for enforcing complex business rules and logic in the database. They can also be used to implement updating for views that normally aren't updatable.

This chapter discussed the `inserted` and `deleted` virtual tables, which hold copies of the rows being affected by a DML statement. You also saw the `UPDATE()` and `COLUMNS_UPDATED()` functions in DML triggers, which identify the columns affected by the DML statement that fired a trigger. Finally, you learned about the differences between `AFTER` and `INSTEAD OF` triggers along with nested triggers and trigger recursion.

DDL triggers can be used to audit and restrict database object and server changes. DDL triggers can help provide protection against accidental or malicious changes to, or destruction of, database objects. This chapter discussed the `EVENTDATA()` function and how you can use it to audit DDL actions in a database or on the server.

Logon triggers can likewise be used to audit successful logins and restrict logins for various reasons. The next chapter discusses the native encryption functionality available in SQL Server 2014.

EXERCISES

1. [True/False] The `EVENTDATA()` function returns information about DDL events within DDL triggers.

2. [True/False] In a DML trigger, the `inserted` and `deleted` virtual tables are both populated with rows during an `UPDATE` event.

3. [True/False] DML triggers are available on in-memory tables and disk-based tables.

4. [Choose all that apply] Which of the following types of triggers does SQL Server 2014 support?

    *   Logon triggers

    *   TCL triggers

    *   DDL triggers

    *   Hierarchy triggers

    *   DML triggers

5. [Fill in the blank] The _____ statement prevents triggers from generating extraneous `rows affected` messages.

6. [Choose one] The `COLUMNS_UPDATED()` function returns data in which of the following formats?

    *   A `varbinary` string with bits set to represent affected columns

    *   A comma-delimited `varchar` string with a column ID number for each affected column

    *   A table consisting of column ID numbers for each affected column

    *   A table consisting of all rows that were inserted by the DML operation

7. [True/False] `@@ROWCOUNT`, when used at the beginning of a DML trigger, reflects the number of rows affected by the DML statement that fired the trigger.

8. [True/False] You can create recursive `AFTER` triggers on views.

CHAPTER 8

■ ■ ■

Encryption

SQL Server 2014 supports built-in column-and database-level encryption functionality directly through T-SQL. Column-level encryption allows you to encrypt the data in your database at the column level. Back in the days of SQL Server 2000 (and before), you had to turn to third-party tools or write your own extended stored procedures (XPs) to encrypt sensitive data. Even with these tools in place, subpar implementation of various aspects of the system, such as encryption key management, could leave many systems in a vulnerable state.

SQL Server 2014's encryption model takes advantage of the Windows CryptoAPI to secure your data. With built-in encryption key management and facilities to handle encryption, decryption, and one-way hashing through T-SQL statements, SQL Server 2014 provides useful tools for efficient and secure data encryption. SQL Server 2014 also supports two encryption options: transparent data encryption (TDE) for supporting encryption of an entire database; and extensible key management (EKM), which allows you to use third-party hardware-based encryption key management and encryption acceleration.

This chapter discusses SQL Server 2014's built-in column-level encryption and decryption functionality, key management capabilities, one-way hashing functions, and TDE and EKM functionality.

The Encryption Hierarchy

SQL Server 2014 offers a layered approach to encryption key management by allowing several levels of key-encrypting keys between the top-level master key and the lowest-level data-encrypting keys. SQL Server also allows for encryption by certificates, symmetric keys, and asymmetric keys. The SQL Server 2014 encryption model is hierarchical, as shown in Figure 8-1.

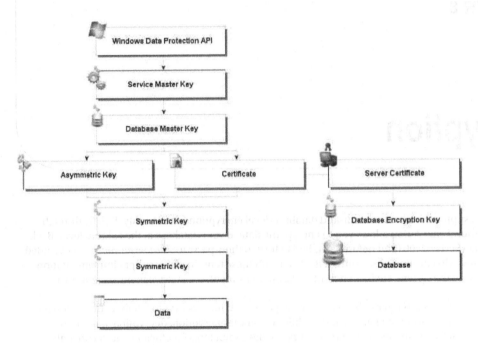

Figure 8-1. *SQL Server 2014 encryption hierarchy*

At the top of the SQL Server 2014 encryption hierarchy is the Windows Data Protection API (DPAPI), which is used to protect the granddaddy of all SQL Server 2014 encryption keys: the service master key (SMK). The SMK is automatically generated by SQL Server the first time it's needed to encrypt another key. There is only one SMK per SQL Server instance, and it directly or indirectly secures all keys in the SQL Server encryption key hierarchy on the server.

Although each SQL Server instance has only a single SMK, each database can have a database master key (DMK). The DMK is encrypted by the SMK and is used to encrypt lower-level keys and certificates.

At the bottom of the SQL Server 2014 key hierarchy are the certificates, symmetric keys, and asymmetric keys used to encrypt data.

SQL Server 2014 also introduces the concept of the *server certificate*, which is a certificate created in the master database for the purpose of protecting database encryption keys. Database encryption keys are symmetric encryption keys created to encrypt entire databases via TDE.

Service Master Keys

As mentioned in the previous section, the SMK is automatically generated by SQL Server the first time it's needed. Because the SMK is generated automatically and managed by SQL Server, there are only a couple of administrative tasks you need to perform for this key: backing it up and restoring it on a server as necessary. You also need access to the directory where the backup file is located. For example, in Listing 8-1, you want to create a folder named CH08 on your C drive. Listing 8-1 demonstrates the BACKUP and RESTORE SERVICE MASTER KEY statements.

Listing 8-1. BACKUP and RESTORE SMK Examples

```
-- Back up the SMK to a file
BACKUP SERVICE MASTER KEY TO FILE = 'c:\CH08\SQL2012.SMK'
ENCRYPTION BY PASSWORD = 'p@$$w0rd';

-- Restore the SMK from a file
RESTORE SERVICE MASTER KEY FROM FILE = 'c:\CH08\SQL2012.SMK'
DECRYPTION BY PASSWORD = 'p@$$w0rd';
```

The BACKUP SERVICE MASTER KEY statement allows you to back up your SMK to a file. The SMK is encrypted in the file, so the ENCRYPTION BY PASSWORD clause of this statement is mandatory.

The RESTORE SERVICE MASTER KEY statement restores the SMK from a previously created backup file. The DECRYPTION BY PASSWORD clause must specify the same password used to encrypt the file when you created the backup. Backing up and restoring an SMK requires CONTROL SERVER permissions. In the previous scenario, SQL Server is intelligent enough to know that the backup SMK and the SMK in the restore are the same, so it doesn't need to go through an unnecessary decryption and encryption process. The data is encrypted again only if the SMK you're trying to restore is different from the SMK you backed up.

The RESTORE SERVICE MASTER KEY statement can include the optional keyword FORCE to force the SMK to restore even if there is a data decryption failure. If you have to use the FORCE keyword, you can expect to lose data, so use this option with care and only as a last resort.

■ **Tip** After installing SQL Server 2014, you should immediately back up your SMK and store a copy of it in a secure offsite location. If your SMK becomes corrupted or is otherwise compromised, you could lose access to all of your encrypted data if you don't have a backup of the SMK.

In addition to BACKUP and RESTORE statements, SQL Server provides the ALTER SERVICE MASTER KEY statement to allow you to change the SMK for an instance of SQL Server. When SQL Server generates the SMK, it uses the credentials of the SQL Server service account to encrypt the SMK. If you change the SQL Server service account, you can use ALTER SERVICE MASTER KEY to update it using the current service account credentials. Alternatively, you can advise SQL Server to secure the SMK using the local machine key, which is managed by the operating system. You can also use ALTER SERVICE MASTER KEY to regenerate the SMK completely.

As with the RESTORE SERVICE MASTER KEY statement, the ALTER SERVICE MASTER KEY statement allows use of the FORCE keyword. Normally, if there is a decryption error during the process of altering the SMK, SQL Server stops the process with an error message. When FORCE is used, the SMK is regenerated even at the risk of data loss. Just like the RESTORE statement, the FORCE option should be used with care, and only as a last resort.

■ **Tip** When you regenerate the SMK, all keys that are encrypted by it must be decrypted and re-encrypted. This operation can be resource intensive and should be scheduled during off-peak time periods.

Database Master Keys

Each database can have a single DMK, which is used to encrypt certificate private keys and asymmetric key-pair private keys in the current database. The DMK is created with the CREATE MASTER KEY statement, as shown in Listing 8-2.

Listing 8-2. Creating a Master Key

```
USE AdventureWorks2014;
GO
CREATE MASTER KEY
ENCRYPTION BY PASSWORD = 'p@$$w0rd' ;
```

The CREATE MASTER KEY statement creates the DMK and uses the Advanced Encryption Standard (AES) to encrypt it with the supplied password. If the password you supply doesn't meet Windows' password-complexity requirements, SQL Server will complain with an error message like the following:

```
Msg 15118, Level 16, State 1, Line 1
Password validation failed. The password does not meet Windows
policy requirements because it is not complex enough.
```

■ **Note** Versions of SQL prior to SQL 2012 used Triple Data Encryption Standard (3DES) for encrypting SMKs and DMKs. SQL Server 2012 and later use the more advanced AES encryption. If you upgrade SQL Server from a previous version, you need to also upgrade your encryption keys. This can be accomplished by using either ALTER SERVICE MASTER KEY or ALTER MASTER KEY and the REGENERATE clause.

SQL Server 2014 automatically uses the SMK to encrypt a copy of the DMK. When this feature is used, SQL Server can decrypt your DMK when necessary without the need to first open the master key. When this feature isn't in use, you must issue the OPEN MASTER KEY statement and supply the same password initially used to encrypt the DMK whenever you need to use it. The potential downside to encrypting your DMK with the SMK is that any member of the sysadmin server role can decrypt the DMK. You can use the ALTER MASTER KEY statement to change the method SQL Server uses to decrypt the DMK. Listing 8-3 shows how to turn off encryption by SMK for a DMK.

Listing 8-3. Turning Off DMK Encryption by the SMK

```
ALTER MASTER KEY
    DROP ENCRYPTION BY SERVICE MASTER KEY;
```

When the DMK is regenerated, all the keys it protects are decrypted and re-encrypted with the new DMK. The FORCE keyword is used to force SQL Server to regenerate the DMK even if there are decryption errors. As with the SMK, the FORCE keyword should be used only as a last resort. You can expect to lose data if you have to use FORCE.

You can also back up and restore a DMK with the BACKUP MASTER KEY and RESTORE MASTER KEY statements. The BACKUP MASTER KEY statement is similar in operation to the BACKUP SERVICE MASTER KEY statement. When you back up the DMK, you must specify the password that SQL Server will use to encrypt the DMK in the output file. When you restore the DMK, you must specify the same password in the DECRYPTION BY PASSWORD clause to decrypt the DMK in the output file. In addition, you must specify an encryption password that SQL Server will use to encrypt the password in the ENCRYPTION BY PASSWORD clause. Listing 8-4 demonstrates backing up and restoring a DMK.

Listing 8-4. Backing Up and Restoring a DMK

```
USE AdventureWorks2014;
GO

OPEN MASTER KEY DECRYPTION BY PASSWORD = 'p@$$w0rd' ;

BACKUP MASTER KEY
    TO FILE = 'c:\CH08\AdventureWorks2014.DMK'
    ENCRYPTION BY PASSWORD = 'p@$$w0rd';

-- Restore DMK from backup
RESTORE MASTER KEY
    FROM FILE = 'c:\CH08\AdventureWorks2014.DMK'
    DECRYPTION BY PASSWORD = 'p@$$w0rd'
    ENCRYPTION BY PASSWORD = '3rt=d4uy';

CLOSE MASTER KEY;
```

The FORCE keyword is available for use with the RESTORE MASTER KEY statement. But as with other statements, it should only be used as a last resort, because it could result in unrecoverable encrypted data.

The DROP MASTER KEY statement can be used to remove a DMK from the database. DROP MASTER KEY doesn't remove a DMK if it's currently being used to encrypt other keys in the database. If you want to drop a DMK that is protecting other keys in the database, the protected keys must first be altered to remove their encryption by the DMK.

■ **Tip**   Always make backups of your DMKs immediately on creation and store them in a secure location.

If you choose to disable automatic key management with the ALTER MASTER KEY statement, you need to use the OPEN MASTER KEY and CLOSE MASTER KEY statements every time you wish to perform encryption and decryption in a database.

OPEN MASTER KEY requires you to supply the same password used to encrypt the DMK in the DECRYPTION BY PASSWORD clause. This password is used to decrypt the DMK, a required step when you're encrypting and decrypting data. When you're finished using the DMK, issue the CLOSE MASTER KEY statement. If your DMK is encrypted by the SMK, you don't need to use the OPEN MASTER KEY and CLOSE MASTER KEY statements; SQL Server handles that task for you automatically.

Certificates

Certificates are asymmetric encryption key pairs with additional metadata, such as subject and expiration date, in the X.509 certificate format. *Asymmetric encryption* is a method of encrypting data using two separate but mathematically related keys. SQL Server 2014 uses the standard public key/private key encryption methodology. You can think of a certificate as a wrapper for an asymmetric encryption public key/private key pair. The CREATE CERTIFICATE statement can be used to either install an existing certificate or create a new certificate on SQL Server. Listing 8-5 shows how to create a new certificate on SQL Server.

Listing 8-5. Creating a Certificate on SQL Server

```
CREATE CERTIFICATE TestCertificate
  ENCRYPTION BY PASSWORD = 'p@$$wOrd'
  WITH SUBJECT = 'AdventureWorks2014 Test Certificate',
  EXPIRY_DATE = '2026-10-31';
```

The CREATE CERTIFICATE statement includes several options. The only mandatory things are the SQL Server identifier for the certificate immediately following the CREATE CERTIFICATE statement (in this case TestCertificate) and the WITH SUBJECT clause, which sets the certificate subject name. If the ENCRYPTION BY PASSWORD clause isn't used when you create a certificate, the certificate's private key is encrypted by the DMK. Additional options available to the CREATE CERTIFICATE statement include START_DATE and EXPIRY_DATE, which set the start and expiration dates for the certificate; and the ACTIVE FOR BEGIN DIALOG clause, which makes the certificate available for use by Service Broker dialogs.

■ **Tip** If START_DATE isn't specified, the current date is used. If EXPIRY_DATE is omitted, the expiration date is set to one year after the start date.

You can also use the CREATE CERTIFICATE statement to load an existing certificate in a variety of ways, including the following:

- You can use the FROM ASSEMBLY clause to load an existing certificate from a signed assembly already loaded in the database.

- You can use the EXECUTABLE FILE clause to create a certificate from a signed DLL file.

- You can use the FILE clause to create a certificate from an existing Distinguished Encoding Rules (DER) X.509 certificate file.

- You can also use the WITH PRIVATE KEY clause with the FILE or EXECUTABLE FILE option to specify a separate file containing the certificate's private key. When you specify the WITH PRIVATE KEY clause, you can specify the optional DECRYPTION BY PASSWORD and ENCRYPTION BY PASSWORD clauses to specify the password that will be used to decrypt the private key if it's encrypted in the source file, and to secure the private key once it's loaded.

■ **Note** SQL Server generates private keys that are 1,024 bits in length. If you import a private key from an external source, it must be a multiple of 64 bits, between 384 and 3,456 bits in length.

After creating a certificate—as with DMKs and SMKs—you should immediately make a backup and store it in a secure location. Listing 8-6 demonstrates how to make a backup of a certificate.

Listing 8-6. Backing Up a Certificate

```
BACKUP CERTIFICATE TestCertificate
  TO FILE = 'c:\CH08\TestCertificate.CER'
  WITH PRIVATE KEY
  (
    FILE = 'c:\CH08\TestCertificate.PVK',
    ENCRYPTION BY PASSWORD = ' 7&rtOxp2',
    DECRYPTION BY PASSWORD = 'p@$$wOrd'
  );
```

The `BACKUP CERTIFICATE` statement in Listing 8-6 backs up the TestCertificate certificate to the c:\TestCertificate.CER file and the certificate's private key to the c:\TestCertificate.PVK file. The `DECRYPTION BY PASSWORD` clause specifies the password to use to decrypt the certificate, and `ENCRYPTION BY PASSWORD` gives SQL Server the password to use when encrypting the private key in the file. There is no `RESTORE` statement for certificates; instead, the `CREATE CERTIFICATE` statement has all the options necessary to restore a certificate from a backup file by simply creating from an existing certificate using the `FROM FILE` clause. T-SQL also provides an `ALTER CERTIFICATE` statement that allows you to make changes to an existing certificate.

You can use certificates to encrypt and decrypt data directly with the certificate encryption and decryption functions, `EncryptByCert` and `DecryptByCert`. The `EncryptByCert` function encrypts a given clear text message with a specified certificate. The function accepts an `int` certificate ID and a plain text value to encrypt. The `int` certificate ID can be retrieved by passing the certificate name to the `CertID` function. Listing 8-7 demonstrates this function. `EncryptByCert` returns a `varbinary` value up to a maximum of 432 bytes in length (the length of the result depends on the length of the key). The following section, "Limitations of Asymmetric Encryption," describes some of the limitations of asymmetric encryption on SQL Server, including encryption by certificate.

Limitations of Asymmetric Encryption

Asymmetric encryption has certain limitations that should be noted before you attempt to encrypt data directly with certificates or asymmetric keys. The `EncryptByCert` function can accept a `char`, `varchar`, `binary`, `nchar`, `nvarchar`, or `varbinary` constant, column name, or variable as clear text to encrypt. Asymmetric encryption, including encryption by certificate, on SQL Server returns a `varbinary` result, but it won't return a result longer than 432 bytes. As mentioned, the maximum length of the result depends on the length of the encryption key used. As an example, with the default private key length of 1,024 bits, you can encrypt a `varchar` plain text message with a maximum length of 117 characters and an `nvarchar` plain text message with a maximum length of 58 characters. The result in either case is a `varbinary` result of 128 bytes.

Microsoft recommends that you avoid using asymmetric encryption to encrypt data directly because of the size limitations, and for performance reasons. Symmetric encryption algorithms use shorter keys but operate more quickly than asymmetric encryption algorithms. The SQL Server 2014 encryption key hierarchy provides the best of both worlds, with the long key lengths of asymmetric keys protecting the shorter, more efficient symmetric keys. To maximize performance, Microsoft recommends using symmetric encryption to encrypt data and asymmetric encryption to encrypt symmetric keys.

The `DecryptByCert` function decrypts text previously encrypted by `EncryptByCert`. The `DecryptByCert` function accepts an `int` certificate ID, an encrypted `varbinary` cipher text message, and an optional certificate password that must match the one used when the certificate was created (if one was specified at creation time). If no certificate password is specified, the DMK is used to decrypt it. Listing 8-7 demonstrates encryption and decryption by certificate for short plain text. The results are shown in Figure 8-2. If you get an error during the `CREATE MASTER KEY` and `CREATE CERTIFICATE` commands, be sure to run the final `DROP` statements prior to creating the objects.

Listing 8-7. Example Encryption and Decryption by Certificate

```
--      Create a DMK
CREATE  MASTER  KEY
    ENCRYPTION BY PASSWORD = 'P@55w0rd';

-- Create a certificate
CREATE  CERTIFICATE  TestCertificate
    WITH  SUBJECT  =  N'AdventureWorks  Test  Certificate',
    EXPIRY_DATE = '2026-10-31';

-- Create the plain text data to encrypt
DECLARE @plaintext nvarchar(58) =
    N'This is a test string to encrypt';
SELECT  'Plain  text  =  ',  @plaintext;

-- Encrypt the plain text by certificate
DECLARE @ciphertext varbinary(128) =
    EncryptByCert(Cert_ID('TestCertificate'), @plaintext);
SELECT 'Cipher text = ', @ciphertext;

-- Decrypt the cipher text by certificate
DECLARE @decryptedtext nvarchar(58) =
    DecryptByCert(Cert_ID('TestCertificate'), @ciphertext);
SELECT  'Decrypted  text  =  ',  @decryptedtext;

-- Drop the test certificate
DROP  CERTIFICATE TestCertificate;

--      Drop the DMK
DROP  MASTER KEY;
```

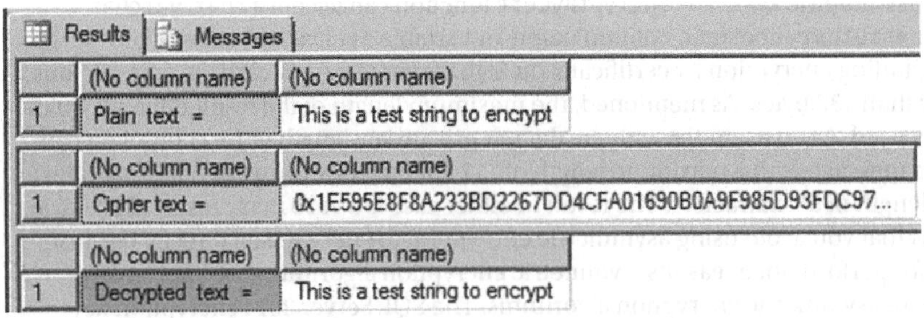

Figure 8-2. *Result of encrypting and decrypting by certificate*

Listing 8-7 first creates a DMK and a test certificate using the CREATE MASTER KEY and CREATE CERTIFICATE statements presented previously in this chapter. It then generates an nvarchar plain text message to encrypt:

```
-- Create a DMK
CREATE MASTER KEY ENCRYPTION BY PASSWORD = 'P@55w0rd';

-- Create a certificate
CREATE CERTIFICATE TestCertificate
WITH SUBJECT = N'AdventureWorks Test Certificate',
EXPIRY_DATE = '2026-10-31';

-- Create the plain text data to encrypt
DECLARE @plaintext nvarchar(58) =
N'This is a test string to encrypt';
SELECT 'Plain text = ', @plaintext;
```

The example uses the EncryptByCert function to encrypt the plain text message. The CertID function is used to retrieve the int certificate ID for TestCertificate:

```
-- Encrypt the plain text by certificate
DECLARE @ciphertext varbinary(128) =
EncryptByCert(Cert_ID('TestCertificate'), @plaintext);
SELECT 'Cipher text = ', @ciphertext;
```

The DecryptByCert function is then used to decrypt the cipher text. Again, the CertID function is used to retrieve the TestCertificate certificate ID:

```
-- Decrypt the cipher text by certificate
DECLARE @decryptedtext nvarchar(58) =
DecryptByCert(Cert_ID('TestCertificate'), @ciphertext);
SELECT 'Decrypted text = ', @decryptedtext;
```

The balance of the code performs some cleanup, dropping the certificate and DMK:

```
-- Drop the test certificate
DROP CERTIFICATE TestCertificate;
-- Drop the DMK
DROP MASTER KEY;
```

You can also use a certificate to generate a signature for a plain text message. SignByCert accepts a certificate ID, a plain text message, and an optional certificate password. The result is a varbinary string, up to a length of 432 characters (again, the length of the result is determined by the length of the encryption key). When SignByCert is used, the slightest change in the plain text message—even a single character—will result in a completely different signature being generated for the message. This allows you to easily detect whether your plain text has been tampered with. Listing 8-8 uses the SignByCert function to create a signature for a plain text message. The results are shown in Figure 8-3.

Listing 8-8. Signing a Message with the SignByCert Function

```
-- Create a DMK
CREATE MASTER KEY ENCRYPTION BY PASSWORD = 'P@55w0rd';
-- Create a certificate
CREATE CERTIFICATE TestCertificate
WITH SUBJECT = 'AdventureWorks Test Certificate',
EXPIRY_DATE = '2026-10-31';
-- Create message
DECLARE @message nvarchar(4000) = N'Four score and seven years ago our fathers brought forth
on this continent a new nation, conceived in Liberty, and dedicated to the proposition that
all men are created equal.
Now we are engaged in a great civil war, testing whether that nation, or any nation, so
conceived and so dedicated, can long endure. We are met on a great battle-field of that
war. We have come to dedicate a portion of that field, as a final resting place for those
who here gave their lives that that nation might live. It is altogether fitting and proper
that we should do this. ';
-- Sign the message by certificate
SELECT SignByCert(Cert_ID(N'TestCertificate'), @message);
-- Drop the certificate
DROP CERTIFICATE TestCertificate;
-- Drop the DMK DROP MASTER KEY;
```

Figure 8-3. *Signature generated by SignByCert (partial)*

Asymmetric Keys

Asymmetric keys are actually composed of a key pair: a public key, which is publicly accessible, and a private key, which is kept secret. The mathematical relationship between the public and private keys allows for encryption and decryption without revealing the private key. T-SQL includes statements for creating and managing asymmetric keys.

The CREATE ASYMMETRIC KEY statement allows you to generate an asymmetric key pair or install an existing key pair on the server, in much the same manner as when creating a certificate. Encryption-key length is often used as an indicator of relative encryption strength, and when you create an asymmetric key on SQL Server, you can specify an RSA key length, as shown in Table 8-1.

Table 8-1. *Asymmetric Key Algorithms and Limits*

Algorithm	Key Length	Plain Text	Cipher Text	Signature Length
RSA_512	512 bits	53 bytes	64 bytes	64 bytes
RSA_1024	1,024 bits	117 bytes	128 bytes	128 bytes
RSA_2048	2,048 bits	245 bytes	256 bytes	256 bytes

Listing 8-9 creates an asymmetric key pair on SQL Server 2014.

Listing 8-9. Creating an Asymmetric Key Pair

```
CREATE ASYMMETRIC KEY TempAsymmetricKey WITH ALGORITHM = RSA_1024;
```

You can alter an existing asymmetric key with the ALTER ASYMMETRIC KEY statement. ALTER ASYMMETRIC KEY offers the following options for managing your asymmetric keys:

- You can use the REMOVE PRIVATE KEY clause to remove the private key from the asymmetric public key/private key pair.

- You can use the WITH PRIVATE KEY clause to change the method used to protect the private key.

- You can change the asymmetric key protection method from DMK encryption to password encryption with the ENCRYPTION BY PASSWORD option.

- You can switch from password protection for your asymmetric key to DMK protection with the DECRYPTION BY PASSWORD clause.

- You can specify both the ENCRYPTION BY PASSWORD and DECRYPTION BY PASSWORD clauses together to change the password used to encrypt the private key.

- The DROP ASYMMETRIC KEY statement removes an asymmetric key from the database.

The EncryptByAsymKey and DecryptByAsymKey functions allow you to encrypt and decrypt data with an asymmetric key in the same way as EncryptByCert and DecryptByCert.

The EncryptByAsymKey function accepts an int asymmetric key ID and plain text to encrypt. The AsymKeyID function can be used to retrieve an asymmetric key ID by name. DecryptByAsymKey accepts an asymmetric key ID, encrypted cipher text to decrypt, and an optional password to decrypt the asymmetric key. If the password is specified, it must be the same password used to encrypt the asymmetric key at creation time.

■ **Tip** The limitations for asymmetric key encryption and decryption on SQL Server are the same as those for certificate encryption and decryption.

Listing 8-10 demonstrates the use of asymmetric key encryption and decryption functions. Be sure to drop any master keys prior to running the code. The results are shown in Figure 8-4.

Listing 8-10. Encrypting and Decrypting with Asymmetric Keys

```
-- Create DMK
CREATE MASTER KEY
ENCRYPTION BY PASSWORD = 'P@55w0rd';

-- Create asymmetric key
CREATE ASYMMETRIC KEY TestAsymmetricKey WITH ALGORITHM = RSA_512;

--Assign a credit card number to encrypt
DECLARE @CreditCard nvarchar(26) = N'9000 1234 5678 9012';
SELECT @CreditCard;
```

```
--Encrypt the credit card number
DECLARE @EncryptedCreditCard varbinary(64) =
  EncryptByAsymKey(AsymKey_ID(N'TestAsymmetricKey'), @CreditCard);
  SELECT @EncryptedCreditCard;

--Decrypt the encrypted credit card number
DECLARE @DecryptedCreditCard nvarchar(26) =
  DecryptByAsymKey(AsymKey_ID(N'TestAsymmetricKey'), @EncryptedCreditCard);
SELECT @DecryptedCreditCard;

-- Drop asymmetric key
DROP ASYMMETRIC KEY TestAsymmetricKey;

--Drop DMK
DROP MASTER KEY;
```

Figure 8-4. Asymmetric key encryption results

This example first creates a DMK and an RSA asymmetric key with a 512-bit private key length. Then it creates plain text representing a simple credit card number:

```
-- Create DMK
CREATE MASTER KEY ENCRYPTION BY PASSWORD = 'P@55w0rd';

-- Create asymmetric key
CREATE ASYMMETRIC KEY TestAsymmetricKey WITH ALGORITHM = RSA_512;

--Assign a credit card number to encrypt
DECLARE @CreditCard nvarchar(26) = N'9000 1234 5678 9012';
SELECT @CreditCard;
```

■ **Note** You have the option to create an asymmetric key without a corresponding database master key. If you decide to do this, you must have a password assigned to the asymmetric key; otherwise, a password is optional.

218

The example then encrypts the credit card number with the EncryptByAsymKey function and decrypts it with the DecryptByAsymKey function. Both functions use the AsymKeyID function to retrieve the asymmetric key ID:

```
-- Encrypt the credit card number
DECLARE @EncryptedCreditCard varbinary(64) =
EncryptByAsymKey(AsymKey_ID(N'TestAsymmetricKey'), @CreditCard);
SELECT @EncryptedCreditCard;

-- Decrypt the encrypted credit card number
DECLARE @DecryptedCreditCard nvarchar(26) =
DecryptByAsymKey(AsymKey_ID(N'TestAsymmetricKey'), @EncryptedCreditCard);
SELECT @DecryptedCreditCard;
```

The code finishes up with a little housekeeping, namely dropping the asymmetric key and the DMK created for the example:

```
-- Drop asymmetric key
DROP ASYMMETRIC KEY TestAsymmetricKey;
-- Drop DMK
DROP MASTER KEY;
```

Like certificates, asymmetric keys offer a function to generate digital signatures for plain text. The SignByAsymKey function accepts a string up to 8,000 bytes in length and returns a varbinary signature for the string. The length of the signature is dependent on the key length, as previously shown in Table 8-1. Listing 8-11 is a simple example of the SignByAsymKey function in action. The results are shown in Figure 8-5.

Listing 8-11. Signing a Message by Asymmetric Key

```
-- Create DMK
CREATE MASTER KEY
ENCRYPTION BY PASSWORD = 'P@55w0rd';

-- Create asymmetric key
CREATE ASYMMETRIC KEY TestAsymmetricKey WITH ALGORITHM = RSA_512;

-- Create message
DECLARE @message nvarchar(4000) = N'Alas, poor Yorick!';
SELECT @message;

-- Sign message by asymmetric key
SELECT SignByAsymKey(AsymKey_ID(N'TestAsymmetricKey'), @message);

-- Drop asymmetric key
DROP ASYMMETRIC KEY TestAsymmetricKey;

-- Drop DMK
DROP MASTER KEY;
```

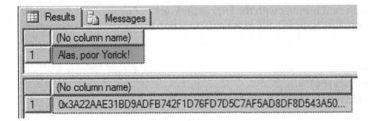

Figure 8-5. Signing a message with an asymmetric key

Asymmetric Key "Backups"

SQL Server provides no BACKUP or RESTORE statement for asymmetric keys. For physical backups of your asymmetric keys, you should install the asymmetric keys from an external source like an assembly, an executable file, a strong-name file, or a hardware security module (HSM). You can make backups of the source files containing your asymmetric keys. As an alternative, you can use certificates instead of asymmetric keys. Keep these options in mind when you're planning to take advantage of SQL Server 2014 encryption.

Symmetric Keys

Symmetric keys are at the bottom of the SQL Server encryption key hierarchy. *Symmetric encryption* algorithms use trivially related keys to both encrypt and decrypt your data. *Trivially related* simply means the algorithm can use either the same key for both encryption and decryption, or two keys that are mathematically related via a simple transformation to derive one key from the other. Symmetric keys on SQL Server 2014 are specifically designed to support SQL Server's symmetric encryption functionality. The algorithms provided by SQL Server 2014 use a single key for both encryption and decryption. In the SQL Server 2014 encryption model, symmetric keys are encrypted by certificates or asymmetric keys, and they can be used in turn to encrypt other symmetric keys or raw data. The CREATE SYMMETRIC KEY statement allows you to generate symmetric keys, as shown in Listing 8-12.

Listing 8-12. Creating a Symmetric Key

```
CREATE SYMMETRIC KEY TestSymmetricKey WITH ALGORITHM = AES_128 ENCRYPTION BY PASSWORD =
'p@55w0rd';
```

The options specified in the CREATE SYMMETRIC KEY statement in Listing 8-12 specify that the symmetric key is created with the name TestSymmetricKey, it's protected by the password p@55w0rd, and it uses AES with a 127-bit key (AES128) to encrypt data.

When creating a symmetric key, you can specify any of several encryption algorithms, including the following:

- AES128, AES192, and AES256 specify the AES block-encryption algorithm with a symmetric key length of 128, 192, or 256 bits and a block size of 128 bits.

- DES specifies the DES block-encryption algorithm, which has a symmetric key length of 56 bits and a block size of 64 bits.

- DESX specifies the DES-X block-encryption algorithm, which was introduced as a successor to the DES algorithm. DES-X also has a symmetric key length of 56 bits (although because the algorithm includes security augmentations, the effective key length is calculated at around 118 bits) and a block size of 64 bits.

- RC2 specifies the RC2 block-encryption algorithm, which has a key size of 128 bits and a block size of 64 bits.

- RC4 and RC4_128 specify the RC4 stream-encryption algorithm, which has a key length of 40 or 128 bits. RC4 and RC4_128 aren't recommended, because they don't generate random initialization vectors to further obfuscate the cipher text.

The CREATE SYMMETRIC KEY statement provides additional options that allow you to specify options for symmetric key creation, including the following:

- You can specify a KEYSOURCE to designate a passphrase to be used as key material from which the symmetric key is derived. If you don't specify a KEY SOURCE, SQL Server generates the symmetric key from random key material.

- The ENCRYPTION BY clause specifies the method used to encrypt this symmetric key in the database. You can specify encryption by a certificate, a password, an asymmetric key, another symmetric key, or HSM.

- The PROVIDER_KEY_NAME and CREATION_DISPOSITION clauses allow you to use your symmetric key with EKM security.

- The IDENTITYVALUE clause specifies an identity phrase that is used to generate a GUID to "tag" data encrypted with the key.

■ **Caution**   When a symmetric key is encrypted with a password instead of the public key of the database master key, the 3DES encryption algorithm is used. Because of this, keys that are created with a strong encryption algorithm, such as AES, are themselves secured by a weaker algorithm.

Temporary Symmetric Keys

You can create temporary symmetric keys by prefixing the symmetric key name with a number sign (#). A temporary symmetric key exists only during the current session and is automatically removed when the current session ends. Temporary symmetric keys aren't accessible to any sessions outside of the session they're created in. When referencing a temporary symmetric key, the number sign (#) prefix must be used. You can use the same WITH clause options described in this section to specify how the symmetric key should be created. To be honest, we don't see much use for temporary symmetric keys at this point, although we don't want to discount them totally. After all, someone may find a use for them in the future.

SQL Server also provides the ALTER SYMMETRIC KEY and DROP SYMMETRIC KEY statements for symmetric key management. The ALTER statement allows you to add or remove encryption methods on a symmetric key. As an example, if you created a symmetric key and encrypted it by password but later wished to change it to encryption by certificate, you would issue two ALTER SYMMETRIC KEY statements—the first ALTER statement would specify the ADD ENCRYPTION BY CERTIFICATE clause, and the second would specify DROP ENCRYPTION BY PASSWORD, as shown in Listing 8-13. Again, you may need to drop the certificate and key prior to running the code.

Listing 8-13. Changing the Symmetric Key Encryption Method

```
-- Create certificate to protect symmetric key
CREATE CERTIFICATE TestCertificate
  WITH SUBJECT = 'AdventureWorks Test Certificate',
  EXPIRY_DATE = '2026-10-31';

CREATE SYMMETRIC KEY TestSymmetricKey WITH ALGORITHM = AES_128 ENCRYPTION BY
PASSWORD = 'p@55w0rd';

OPEN SYMMETRIC KEY TestSymmetricKey
  DECRYPTION BY PASSWORD = 'p@55w0rd';

ALTER SYMMETRIC KEY TestSymmetricKey
  ADD ENCRYPTION BY CERTIFICATE TestCertificate;

ALTER SYMMETRIC KEY TestSymmetricKey
  DROP ENCRYPTION BY PASSWORD = 'p@55w0rd';

CLOSE SYMMETRIC KEY TestSymmetricKey;

-- Drop the symmetric key
DROP SYMMETRIC KEY TestSymmetricKey;

-- Drop the certificate
DROP CERTIFICATE TestCertificate;
```

■ **Note** Before you alter a symmetric key, you must first open it with the OPEN SYMMETRIC KEY statement.

The DROP SYMMETRIC KEY statement allows you to remove a symmetric key from the database.

Once you create a symmetric key, you can encrypt and decrypt data with the EncryptByKey and DecryptByKey functions. Listing 8-14 creates a symmetric key and encrypts 100 names with it. Partial results are shown in Figure 8-6.

Listing 8-14. Encrypting Data with a Symmetric Key

```
-- Create a temporary table to hold results
CREATE TABLE #TempNames
(
   BusinessEntityID int PRIMARY KEY,
   FirstName       nvarchar(50),
   MiddleName      nvarchar(50),
   LastName        nvarchar(50),
   EncFirstName     varbinary(200),
   EncMiddleName    varbinary(200),
   EncLastName      varbinary(200)
);
```

```
-- Create DMK
CREATE MASTER KEY
  ENCRYPTION BY PASSWORD = 'Test_P@sswOrd';

-- Create certificate to protect symmetric key
CREATE CERTIFICATE TestCertificate
  WITH SUBJECT = 'AdventureWorks Test Certificate',
  EXPIRY_DATE = '2026-10-31';

-- Create symmetric key to encrypt data
CREATE SYMMETRIC KEY TestSymmetricKey
  WITH ALGORITHM = AES_128
  ENCRYPTION BY CERTIFICATE TestCertificate;

-- Open symmetric key
OPEN SYMMETRIC KEY TestSymmetricKey
  DECRYPTION BY CERTIFICATE TestCertificate;

-- Populate temp table with 100 encrypted names from the Person.Person table
INSERT
INTO #TempNames
(
BusinessEntityID,
EncFirstName,
EncMiddleName,
EncLastName
)
SELECT TOP(100) BusinessEntityID,
  EncryptByKey(Key_GUID(N'TestSymmetricKey'), FirstName),
  EncryptByKey(Key_GUID(N'TestSymmetricKey'), MiddleName),
  EncryptByKey(Key_GUID(N'TestSymmetricKey'), LastName)
FROM Person.Person
ORDER BY BusinessEntityID;

-- Update the temp table with decrypted names
UPDATE #TempNames
SET FirstName = DecryptByKey(EncFirstName),
  MiddleName = DecryptByKey(EncMiddleName),
  LastName = DecryptByKey(EncLastName);

-- Show the results
SELECT BusinessEntityID,
  FirstName,
  MiddleName,
  LastName,
  EncFirstName,
  EncMiddleName,
  EncLastName
FROM #TempNames;
```

```
-- Close the symmetric key
CLOSE SYMMETRIC KEY TestSymmetricKey;

-- Drop the symmetric key
DROP SYMMETRIC KEY TestSymmetricKey;

-- Drop the certificate
DROP CERTIFICATE TestCertificate;

--Drop the DMK
DROP MASTER KEY;

--Drop the temp table
DROP TABLE #TempNames;
```

	Busi...	FirstName	MiddleName	LastName	EncFirstName	EncMiddleName	EncLastName
1	1	Ken	J	Sánchez	0x00524377DAF38C468528F0E5D...	0x00524377DAF38C468528F0...	0x00524377DAF38C468528F0E5D521E79701...
2	2	Terri	Lee	Duffy	0x00524377DAF38C468528F0E5D...	0x00524377DAF38C468528F0...	0x00524377DAF38C468528F0E5D521E79701...
3	3	Roberto	NULL	Tamburello	0x00524377DAF38C468528F0E5D...	NULL	0x00524377DAF38C468528F0E5D521E79701...
4	4	Rob	NULL	Walters	0x00524377DAF38C468528F0E5D...	NULL	0x00524377DAF38C468528F0E5D521E79701...
5	5	Gail	A	Erickson	0x00524377DAF38C468528F0E5D...	0x00524377DAF38C468528F0...	0x00524377DAF38C468528F0E5D521E79701...
6	6	Jossef	H	Goldberg	0x00524377DAF38C468528F0E5D...	0x00524377DAF38C468528F0...	0x00524377DAF38C468528F0E5D521E79701...
7	7	Dylan	A	Miller	0x00524377DAF38C468528F0E5D...	0x00524377DAF38C468528F0...	0x00524377DAF38C468528F0E5D521E79701...
8	8	Diane	L	Margheim	0x00524377DAF38C468528F0E5D...	0x00524377DAF38C468528F0...	0x00524377DAF38C468528F0E5D521E79701...
9	9	Gigi	N	Matthew	0x00524377DAF38C468528F0E5D...	0x00524377DAF38C468528F0...	0x00524377DAF38C468528F0E5D521E79701...
10	10	Michael	NULL	Raheem	0x00524377DAF38C468528F0E5D...	NULL	0x00524377DAF38C468528F0E5D521E79701...
11	11	Ovidiu	V	Cracium	0x00524377DAF38C468528F0E5D...	0x00524377DAF38C468528F0...	0x00524377DAF38C468528F0E5D521E79701...
12	12	Thierry	B	D'Hers	0x00524377DAF38C468528F0E5D...	0x00524377DAF38C468528F0...	0x00524377DAF38C468528F0E5D521E79701...
13	13	Janice	M	Galvin	0x00524377DAF38C468528F0E5D...	0x00524377DAF38C468528F0...	0x00524377DAF38C468528F0E5D521E79701...

Figure 8-6. *Symmetric key encryption results (partial)*

Listing 8-14 first creates a temporary table to hold the encryption and decryption results:

```
-- Create a temporary table to hold results
CREATE TABLE #TempNames
(
BusinessEntityID  int PRIMARY KEY,
FirstName               nvarchar(50),
MiddleName              nvarchar(50),
LastName                nvarchar(50),
EncFirstName            varbinary(200),
EncMiddleName           varbinary(200),
EncLastName             varbinary(200)
);
```

Then a DMK is created to protect the certificate that will be created next. The certificate that's created is then used to encrypt the symmetric key:

```
-- Create DMK
CREATE MASTER KEY
  ENCRYPTION BY PASSWORD = 'Test_P@ssw0rd';
```

```
-- Create certificate to protect symmetric key
CREATE CERTIFICATE TestCertificate
  WITH SUBJECT = 'AdventureWorks Test Certificate',
  EXPIRY_DATE = '2026-10-31';

-- Create symmetric key to encrypt data
CREATE SYMMETRIC KEY TestSymmetricKey
  WITH ALGORITHM = AES_128
  ENCRYPTION BY CERTIFICATE TestCertificate;
```

In order to encrypt data with the symmetric key, the example must first execute the OPEN SYMMETRIC KEY statement to open the symmetric key. The DECRYPTION BY clause specifies the method to use to decrypt the symmetric key for use. In this example, the key is protected by certificate, so DECRYPTION BY CERTIFICATE is used. You can specify decryption by certificate, asymmetric key, symmetric key, or password. If the DMK was used to encrypt the certificate or asymmetric key, leave off the WITH PASSWORD clause:

```
-- Open symmetric key
OPEN SYMMETRIC KEY TestSymmetricKey
  DECRYPTION BY CERTIFICATE TestCertificate;
```

The next step is to use the EncryptByKey function to encrypt the data. In this example, the FirstName, MiddleName, and LastName for 100 rows from the Person.Person table are encrypted with EncryptByKey. The EncryptByKey function accepts a clear text char, varchar, binary, varbinary, nchar, or nvarchar constant, column, or T-SQL variable with a maximum length of 8,000 bytes. The result returned is the encrypted data in varbinary format with a maximum length of 8,000 bytes. In addition to clear text, EncryptByKey accepts a GUID identifying the symmetric key with which you wish to encrypt the clear text. The KeyGUID function returns a symmetric key's GUID by name:

```
-- Populate temp table with 100 encrypted names from the Person.Person table
INSERT
INTO #TempNames
(
    BusinessEntityID,
EncFirstName,
EncMiddleName,
EncLastName
)

SELECT TOP(100) BusinessEntityID,
   EncryptByKey(Key_GUID(N'TestSymmetricKey'), FirstName),
   EncryptByKey(Key_GUID(N'TestSymmetricKey'), MiddleName),
   EncryptByKey(Key_GUID(N'TestSymmetricKey'), LastName)
FROM Person.Person
ORDER BY BusinessEntityID;
```

The example code then uses the DecryptByKey function to decrypt the previously encrypted cipher text in the temporary table. SQL Server stores the GUID of the symmetric key used to encrypt the data with the encrypted data, so you don't need to supply the symmetric key GUID to DecryptByKey. In the example code, the varbinary encrypted cipher text is all that's passed to the EncryptByKey function:

```
-- Update the temp table with decrypted names
UPDATE #TempNames
SET FirstName = DecryptByKey(EncFirstName),
    MiddleName = DecryptByKey(EncMiddleName),
    LastName = DecryptByKey(EncLastName);
```

Finally, the results are shown and the symmetric key is closed with the CLOSE SYMMETRIC KEY statement:

```
-- Show the results
SELECT BusinessEntityID,
 FirstName,
 MiddleName,
 LastName,
 EncFirstName,
 EncMiddleName,
 EncLastName
FROM #TempNames;

-- Close the symmetric key
CLOSE SYMMETRIC KEY TestSymmetricKey;
```

The balance of the code drops the symmetric key, the certificate, the master key, and the temporary table:

```
-- Drop the symmetric key
DROP SYMMETRIC KEY TestSymmetricKey;

-- Drop the certificate
DROP CERTIFICATE TestCertificate;

-- Drop the DMK
DROP MASTER KEY;

-- Drop the temp table
DROP TABLE #TempNames;
```

■ **Note**   You can close a single symmetric key by name or use the CLOSE ALL SYMMETRIC KEYS statement to close all open symmetric keys. Opening and closing symmetric keys affects only the current session on the server. All open symmetric keys available to the current session are automatically closed when the current session ends.

Salt and Authenticators

The initialization vector (IV), or *salt*, is an important aspect of encryption security. The IV is a block of bits that further obfuscates the result of an encryption. The idea is that the IV helps prevent the same data from generating the same cipher text if it's encrypted more than once by the same key and algorithm. SQL Server doesn't allow you to specify an IV when encrypting data with a symmetric key, however. Instead, SQL Server generates a random IV automatically when you encrypt data with block ciphers like AES and DES. The obfuscation provided by the IV helps eliminate patterns from your encrypted data patterns that cryptanalysts can use to their advantage when attempting to hack your encrypted data. The downside to SQL Server's randomly generated IVs is that they make indexing an encrypted column a true exercise in futility.

In addition to random IV generation, SQL Server's EncryptByKey and DecryptByKey functions provide another tool to help eliminate patterns in encrypted data. Both functions provide two options parameters: an add_authenticator flag and an authenticator value. If the add_authenticator flag is set to 1, SQL Server derives an authenticator from the authenticator value passed in. The authenticator is then used to obfuscate your encrypted data further, preventing patterns that can reveal information to hackers through correlation analysis attacks. If you supply an authenticator value during encryption, the same authenticator value must be supplied during decryption.

When SQL Server encrypts your data with a symmetric key, it automatically adds metadata to the encrypted result, as well as padding, making the encrypted result larger (sometimes significantly larger) than the unencrypted plain text. The format for the encrypted result with metadata follows the following format:

- The first 16 bytes of the encrypted result represent the GUID of the symmetric key used to encrypt the data.

- The next 4 bytes represent a version number, currently hard-coded as 0x01000000.

- The next 8 bytes for DES encryption (16 bytes for AES encryption) represent the randomly generated IV.

- If an authenticator was used, the next 8 bytes contain header information with an additional 20-byte SHA1 hash of the authenticator, making the header information 28 bytes in length.

- The last part of the encrypted data is the actual padded data. For DES algorithms, the length of this encrypted data is a multiple of 8 bytes. For AES algorithms, the length is a multiple of 16 bytes.

In addition to DecryptByKey, SQL Server 2014 provides DecryptByKeyAutoCert and DecryptByKeyAutoAsymKey functions. Both functions combine the functionality of the OPEN SYMMETRIC KEY statement with the DecryptByKey function, meaning you don't need to issue an OPEN SYMMETRIC KEY to decrypt your cipher text. The DecryptByKeyAutoAsymKey function automatically opens an asymmetric key protecting a symmetric key, whereas DecryptByKeyAutoCert automatically opens a certificate protecting a symmetric key. If a password is used to encrypt your asymmetric key or certificate, that same password must be passed to these functions. If the asymmetric key is encrypted with the DMK, you pass NULL as the password. You can also specify an authenticator with these functions if one was used during encryption. Decryption of data in bulk using these functions may cause a pretty severe performance penalty over using the OPEN SYMMETRIC KEY statement and the DecryptByKey function.

Encryption Without Keys

SQL Server 2014 provides additional functions for encryption and decryption without keys and for *one-way hashing*, which is the concept of inputting a value into a function to get a hash value but not being able to use the hash value to reproduce the input. These functions are named EncryptByPassPhrase, DecryptByPassPhrase, and HashBytes, respectively.

The EncryptByPassPhrase function accepts a passphrase and clear text to encrypt. The passphrase is simply a plain text phrase from which SQL Server can derive an encryption key. The idea behind the passphrase is that users are more likely to remember a simple phrase than a complex encryption key. The function derives a temporary encryption key from the passphrase and uses it to encrypt the plain text. You can also pass an optional authenticator value to EncryptByPassPhrase if you wish. EncryptByPassPhrase always uses the 3DES algorithm to encrypt the clear text passed in.

DecryptByPassPhrase decrypts cipher text that was previously encrypted with EncryptByPassPhrase. To decrypt using this function, you must supply the same passphrase and authenticator options that you used when encrypting the clear text.

Hashing Data

The HashBytes function performs a one-way hash on the data passed to it and returns the hash value generated. HashBytes accepts two parameters: a hash algorithm name and the data to hash. The return value is a fixed-length varbinary hash value, which is analogous to a fingerprint for any given data. Table 8-2 lists the SQL Server-supported hash algorithms.

Table 8-2. *SQL Server-Supported Hash Algorithms*

Algorithm	Hash Length
MD2, MD4, MD5	128 bits (16 bytes)
SHA, SHA1	160 bits (20 bytes)

■ **Caution**   For highly secure applications, the MD2, MD4, and MD5 series of hashes should be avoided. Cryptanalysts have produced meaningful hash collisions with these algorithms over the past few years that have revealed vulnerabilities to hacker attacks. A *hash collision* is a string of bytes that produces a hash value that is identical to another string of bytes. A *meaningful* hash collision is one that can be produced with meaningful (or apparently meaningful) strings of bytes. Generating a hash collision by modifying the content of a certificate would be an example of a meaningful, and dangerous, hash collision.

Listing 8-15 demonstrates the EncryptByPassPhrase, DecryptByPassPhrase, and HashBytes functions. The results are shown in Figure 8-7.

Listing 8-15. Encryption and Decryption by Passphrase and Byte Hashing

```
DECLARE @cleartext nvarchar(256);
DECLARE @encrypted varbinary(512);
DECLARE @decrypted nvarchar(256);

SELECT @cleartext = N'To be, or not to be: that is the question: ' +
    N'Whether ''tis nobler in the mind to suffer ' +
    N'The slings and arrows of outrageous fortune, ' +
    N'Or to take arms against a sea of troubles';

SELECT @encrypted = EncryptByPassPhrase(N'Shakespeare''s Donkey', @cleartext);

SELECT @decrypted = CAST
(
    DecryptByPassPhrase(N'Shakespeare''s Donkey', @encrypted)
        AS  nvarchar(128)
);

SELECT @cleartext AS ClearText;
SELECT @encrypted AS Encrypted;
SELECT @decrypted AS Decrypted;
SELECT HashBytes ('SHA1', @ClearText) AS Hashed;
```

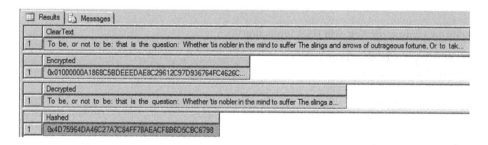

Figure 8-7. Results of encryption by passphrase and hashing

Extensible Key Management

SQL Server 2014 contains a feature added in SQL 2008 known as EKM, which allows you to encrypt your SQL Server asymmetric keys (and symmetric keys) with keys generated and stored on a third-party HSM. To use EKM, you must first turn on the EKM provider enabled option with spconfigure, as shown in Listing 8-16.

■ **Note**   EKM is available only on the Enterprise, Developer, and Evaluation editions of SQL Server 2014, and it requires third-party HSM and supporting software.

Listing 8-16. Enabling EKM Providers

```
sp_configure 'show advanced', 1;
GO
RECONFIGURE;
GO
sp_configure 'EKM provider enabled', 1;
GO
RECONFIGURE;
GO
```

Once you've enabled EKM providers and have an HSM available, you must register a cryptographic provider with SQL Server. The cryptographic provider references a vendor-supplied DLL file installed on the server. Listing 8-17 gives an example of registering a cryptographic provider with SQL Server.

Listing 8-17. Registering a Cryptographic Provider

```
CREATE CRYPTOGRAPHIC PROVIDER Eagle_EKM_Provider
FROM FILE = 'c:\Program Files\Eagle_EKM\SQLEKM.DLL';
 GO
```

After your EKM provider is registered with SQL Server, creating an asymmetric key that is encrypted by an existing key on the HSM is simply a matter of specifying the EKM provider, the `CREATIONDISPOSITION` option, and the name of the key on the EKM device via the `PROVIDER_KEY_NAME` option. Listing 8-18 gives an example.

Listing 8-18. Creating an Asymmetric Key with HSM Protection

```
CREATE ASYMMETRIC KEY AsymKeyEKMProtected
  FROM PROVIDER Eagle_EKM_Provider
  WITH PROVIDER_KEY_NAME = 'EKM_Key_1',
    CREATION_DISPOSITION = OPEN_EXISTING;
GO
```

EKM is designed to support enterprise-level encryption key management by providing additional encryption key security. It provides this additional security by physically separating the encryption keys from the data they encrypt. In addition to external storage of encryption keys, HSM vendors can also provide hardware-based bulk encryption and decryption functionality and external support for additional encryption options beyond what is supported natively by SQL Server 2014. Some of the additional options provided by HSM vendors include key aging and key rotation functionality.

Transparent Data Encryption

Up to this point, we've talked about the column-level encryption functionality available in SQL Server 2014. These functions are specifically designed to encrypt data stored in the columns of your database tables. SQL Server 2014 provides a method of encryption, TDE, which allows you to encrypt your entire database at once.

TDE automatically encrypts every page in your database and decrypts pages as required when you access them. This feature allows you to secure an entire database without worrying about all those little details that pop up when encrypting at the column level. TDE doesn't require extra storage space, and it lets the query optimizer generate far more efficient query plans than it can when you search on encrypted columns. As an added bonus, TDE is easy to implement and allows you to secure the data in your databases with no changes to middle-tier or front-end code.

The first step to implement TDE in your database is to create a server certificate (see Listing 8-19). A *server certificate* is a certificate created in the master database for the purpose of encrypting databases with TDE.

Listing 8-19. Creating a Server Certificate

```
CREATE CERTIFICATE ServerCert
  WITH SUBJECT = 'Server Certificate for TDE',
  EXPIRY_DATE = '2022-12-31';
GO
```

■ **Tip** Remember to back up your server certificate immediately after you create it!

Once you've created a server certificate, you can create a database encryption key in the database to be encrypted (see Listing 8-20). The database encryption key is created with the CREATE DATABASE ENCRYPTION KEY statement. Using this statement, you can create a key using one of the four different algorithms listed in Table 8-3.

Listing 8-20. Creating as Database Encryption Key and Securing the Database

```
USE AdventureWorks2014;
GO

CREATE DATABASE ENCRYPTION KEY
  WITH ALGORITHM = AES_128
  ENCRYPTION BY SERVER CERTIFICATE ServerCert;
GO

ALTER DATABASE AdventureWorks2014
SET ENCRYPTION ON;

GO
```

Table 8-3. *Database Encryption Key Algorithms*

Algorithm	Description
AES_128	AES, 127-bit key
AES_192	AES, 192-bit key
AES_256	AES, 256-bit key
TRIPLE_DES_3KEY	Three-key 3DES, ~112-bit effective key

The obvious question at this point is, because TDE is so simple and secure, why not use it all the time? Well, the simplicity and security of TDE come at a cost. When you encrypt a database with TDE, SQL Server also encrypts the database log file and the tempdb database. This is done to prevent leaked data that a hacker with the right tools might be able to access. Because tempdb is encrypted, the performance of every database on the same server takes a hit. Also, SQL Server incurs additional CPU overhead because it has to decrypt noncached data pages that are accessed by queries.

Summary

Back in the days of SQL Server 2000, database encryption functionality could be achieved only through third-party tools or by creating your own encryption and decryption functions. SQL Server 2014 continues the tradition of T-SQL column-level encryption and decryption functionality introduced in SQL Server 2005. The tight integration of Windows DPAPI encryption functionality with native T-SQL statements and functions makes database encryption easier and more secure than ever.

SQL Server 2012 introduced new functionality, including TDE for quickly and easily encrypting entire databases transparently, and EKM for providing access to third-party HSMs to implement enterprise-level security solutions and bulk encryption functionality.

This chapter discussed the SQL Server hierarchical encryption model, which defines the relationship between SMKs, DMKs, certificates, asymmetric keys, and symmetric keys. SQL Server provides a variety of T-SQL statements to create and manage encryption keys and certificates, which you saw demonstrated in code examples throughout the chapter. SQL Server also provides several functions for generating one-way hashes, generating data signatures, and encrypting data by certificate, asymmetric key, symmetric key, and passphrase.

The next chapter covers the topics of SQL windowing functions and common table expressions (CTEs).

EXERCISES

1. [True/False] Symmetric keys can be used to encrypt other symmetric keys or data.

2. [Choose all that apply] SQL Server provides native support for which of the following built-in encryption algorithms?

   a. DES

   b. AES

   c. Loki

   d. Blowfish

   e. RC4

3. [True/False] SQL Server 2014 T-SQL includes a BACKUP ASYMMETRIC KEY statement.

4. [Fill in the blank] You must set the _____ option to turn on EKM for your server.

5. [True/False] TDE automatically encrypts the tempdb, model, and master databases.

6. [True/False] SQL Server automatically generates random initialization vectors when you use symmetric encryption.

■ ■ ■

CHAPTER 9

Common Table Expressions and Windowing Functions

SQL Server 2014 continues support for the extremely useful common table expression (CTE), first introduced in SQL Server 2005. CTEs can simplify your queries to make them more readable and maintainable. SQL Server also supports self-referential CTEs, which make for very powerful recursive queries.

In addition, SQL Server supports windowing functions, which allow you to partition your results and apply numbering and ranking values to the rows in the result-set partitions. This chapter begins with a discussion of the power and benefits of CTEs and finishes with a discussion of SQL Server windowing functions.

Common Table Expressions

CTEs are a powerful addition to SQL Server. A CTE is more like temporary table that generates a named result set that exists only during the life of a single query or DML statement or until explicitly dropped. A CTE is built in the same code line as the SELECT statement or the DML statement that uses it, whereas creating and using a temporary table is usually a two-step process. CTEs offer several benefits over derived tables and views, including the following:

- CTEs are transient, existing only for the life of a single query or DML statement. This means you don't have create them as permanent database objects like views.

- A single CTE can be referenced multiple times by name in a single query or DML statement, making your code more manageable. Derived tables have to be rewritten in their entirety every place they're referenced.

- CTEs can be used to enable grouping by columns that are derived from a scalar subset or a function that isn't deterministic.

- CTEs can be self-referencing, providing a powerful recursion mechanism.

- Queries referencing a CTE can be used to define a cursor.

CTEs can range in complexity from extremely simple to highly elaborate constructs. All CTEs begin with the WITH keyword followed by the name of the CTE and a list of the columns it returns. This is followed by the AS keyword and the body of the CTE, which is the associated query or DML statement with a semicolon as a terminator for a multistatement batch. Listing 9-1 is a very simple example of a CTE designed to show the basic syntax.

Listing 9-1. Simple CTE

```
WITH GetNamesCTE ( BusinessEntityID, FirstName,
                            MiddleName, LastName )
AS
(
  SELECT
        BusinessEntityID, FirstName, MiddleName, LastName
    FROM Person.Person
)
  SELECT
        BusinessEntityID,
        FirstName,
        MiddleName,
        LastName
  FROM GetNamesCTE;
```

In Listing 9-1, the CTE is defined with the name GetNamesCTE and returns columns named BusinessEntityID, FirstName, MiddleName, and LastName. The CTE body consists of a simple SELECT statement from the AdventureWorks 2014 Person.Person table. The CTE has an associated SELECT statement immediately following it. The SELECT statement references the CTE in its FROM clause.

WITH OVERLOADED

The WITH keyword is overloaded in SQL Server, meaning it's used in many different ways for many different purposes in T-SQL. It's used to specify additional options in DDL CREATE statements, to add table hints to queries and DML statements, and to declare XML namespaces when used in the WITH XMLNAMESPACES clause, just to name a few. Now it's also used as the keyword that indicates the beginning of a CTE definition. Because of this, whenever a CTE isn't the first statement in a batch, the statement preceding it must end with a semicolon. This is one reason we strongly recommend using the statement-terminating semicolon throughout your code.

Simple CTEs have some restrictions on their definition and declaration:

- A CTE must be followed by single INSERT, DELETE, UPDATE, or SELECT statement.

- All columns returned by a CTE must have a unique name. If all the columns returned by the query in the CTE body have unique names, you can leave the column list out of the CTE declaration.

- A CTE can reference other previously defined CTEs in the same WITH clause, but it can't reference CTEs defined after the current CTE (known as a *forward reference*).

- You can't use the following keywords, clauses, and options in a CTE: COMPUTE, COMPUTE BY, FOR BROWSE, INTO, and OPTION (query hint). Also, you can't use ORDER BY unless you specify the TOP clause.

- Multiple CTEs can be defined in a nonrecursive CTE. All the definitions must be combined with one of these set operators: UNION ALL, UNION, INTERSECT, or EXCEPT.

- As mentioned in the "WITH Overloaded" sidebar, when a CTE is not the first statement in a batch, the preceding statement must end with a semicolon statement terminator.

Keep these restrictions in mind when you create CTEs.

Multiple Common Table Expressions

You can define multiple CTEs for a single query or DML statement by separating your CTE definitions with commas. The main reason for doing this is to simplify your code to make it easier to read and manage. CTEs provide a means of visually splitting your code into smaller functional blocks, making it easier to develop and debug. The query in Listing 9-2 includes multiple CTEs, with the second CTE referencing the first. The results are shown in Figure 9-1.

Listing 9-2. Multiple CTEs

```
WITH GetNamesCTE ( BusinessEntityID, FirstName,
                                    MiddleName,LastName )
AS (
SELECT
        BusinessEntityID, FirstName,
        MiddleName, LastName
  FROM Person.Person ),

GetContactCTE ( BusinessEntityID, FirstName,
                MiddleName, LastName,
                Email, HomePhoneNumber
)
AS (
        SELECT gn.BusinessEntityID, gn.FirstName
               , gn.MiddleName, gn.LastName
               , ea.EmailAddress, pp.PhoneNumber
               FROM GetNamesCTE gn
         LEFT JOIN Person.EmailAddress ea
             ON gn.BusinessEntityID = ea.BusinessEntityID
         LEFT JOIN Person.PersonPhone pp
             ON gn.BusinessEntityID = pp.BusinessEntityID
                 AND pp.PhoneNumberTypeID = 2 )
SELECT BusinessEntityID, FirstName
       , MiddleName, LastName
       , Email, HomePhoneNumber
  FROM GetContactCTE;
```

	BusinessEntityID	FirstName	MiddleName	LastName	Email	HomePhoneNumber
135	7458	Ana	R	Alexander	ana17@adventure-works.com	1 (11) 500 555-0181
136	7678	Angela	NULL	Alexander	angela21@adventure-works.com	NULL
137	7161	Angelica	NULL	Alexander	angelica18@adventure-works.com	214-555-0150
138	3683	Anna	NULL	Alexander	anna44@adventure-works.com	150-555-0156
139	13220	Antonio	NULL	Alexander	antonio19@adventure-works.com	NULL
140	7719	Arianna	NULL	Alexander	arianna17@adventure-works.com	140-555-0167
141	12597	Ashley	J	Alexander	ashley46@adventure-works.com	NULL
142	6266	Austin	NULL	Alexander	austin15@adventure-works.com	1 (11) 500 555-0140
143	6726	Benjamin	A	Alexander	benjamin20@adventure-works.com	240-555-0151
144	6919	Brandon	NULL	Alexander	brandon16@adventure-works.com	780-555-0152
145	19276	Brianna	NULL	Alexander	brianna64@adventure-works.com	242-555-0137
146	7210	Brittany	NULL	Alexander	brittany17@adventure-works.com	804-555-0125
147	5561	Caleb	NULL	Alexander	caleb15@adventure-works.com	670-555-0141
148	6315	Cameron	NULL	Alexander	cameron14@adventure-works.com	399-555-0196
149	6800	Caroline	NULL	Alexander	caroline20@adventure-works.com	NULL

Figure 9-1. *Partial results of a query with multiple CTEs*

CTE Readability Benefits

You can use CTEs to make your queries more readable than equivalent query designs that use nested subqueries. To demonstrate, the following query uses nested subqueries to return the same result as the CTE-based query in Listing 9-2:

```
SELECT
    gn.BusinessEntityID,
    gn.FirstName,
    gn.MiddleName,
    gn.LastName,
    gn.EmailAddress,
    gn.HomePhoneNumber
FROM
(
    SELECT
    p.BusinessEntityID,
    p.FirstName,
    p.MiddleName,
    p.LastName,
    ea.EmailAddress,
    ea.HomePhoneNumber

    FROM Person.Person p
    LEFT JOIN
    (
    SELECT
    ea.BusinessEntityID,
    ea.EmailAddress,
```

```
pp.HomePhoneNumber
FROM Person.EmailAddress ea
LEFT JOIN
(
SELECT
pp.BusinessEntityID,
pp.PhoneNumber  AS  HomePhoneNumber,
pp.PhoneNumberTypeID
FROM  Person.PersonPhone  pp
)  pp
ON  ea.BusinessEntityID  =  pp.BusinessEntityID
AND pp.PhoneNumberTypeID = 2
)  ea
ON  p.BusinessEntityID  =  ea.BusinessEntityID
)  gn
```

The CTE-based version of this query, as shown in Listing 9-2, simplifies the code, encapsulates the query logic, and is much easier to read and understand than the nested subquery version, which makes it easier to debug and maintain in the long term.

The example in Listing 9-2 contains two CTEs named GetNamesCTE and GetContactCTE. GetNamesCTE is borrowed from Listing 9-1; it retrieves the names from the Person.Person table:

```
WITH GetNamesCTE ( BusinessEntityID, FirstName, MiddleName, LastName )
AS
(
  SELECT
       BusinessEntityID, FirstName,
       MiddleName, LastName
    FROM Person.Person
)
```

The second CTE, GetContactCTE, joins the results of GetNamesCTE to the Person.EmailAddress and Person.PersonPhone tables:

```
GetContactCTE
(
   BusinessEntityID, FirstName, MiddleName, LastName, Email, HomePhoneNumber
)
AS (
       SELECT gn. BusinessEntityID, gn.FirstName
             , gn.MiddleName, gn.LastName
             , ea.EmailAddress, pp.PhoneNumber
           FROM GetNamesCTE gn
       LEFT JOIN Person.EmailAddress ea
               ON gn. BusinessEntityID = ea. BusinessEntityID
     LEFT JOIN Person.PersonPhone pp
           ON gn. BusinessEntityID = pp. BusinessEntityID
                   AND pp.PhoneNumberTypeID = 2 )
```

Notice that the WITH keyword is used only once at the beginning of the entire statement. The second CTE declaration is separated from the first by a comma and doesn't accept the WITH keyword. Finally, notice how simple and readable the SELECT query associated with the CTEs becomes when the joins are moved into CTEs:

```
SELECT
        BusinessEntityID,
        FirstName,
        MiddleName,
        LastName,
        EmailAddress,
        HomePhoneNumber
   FROM GetContactCTE;
```

■ **Tip**   You can reference a CTE from within the body of another CTE, from the associated query or DML statement. Both types of CTE references are shown in Listing 9-2—GetNamesCTE is referenced by GetContactCTE, and GetContactCTE is referenced in the query associated with the CTEs.

Recursive Common Table Expressions

A *recursive CTE* is one where the initial CTE is executed repeatedly to return a subset of the data until the complete result set is returned. A CTE can reference itself in the body of the CTE, which is a powerful feature for querying hierarchical data stored in the adjacency list model. Recursive CTEs are similar to nonrecursive CTEs, except that the body of the CTE consists of multiple sets of queries that generate result sets with multiple rows unioned together with the UNION ALL set operator. At least one of the queries in the body of the recursive CTE must not reference the CTE; this query is known as the *anchor query*. Recursive CTEs also contain one or more recursive queries that reference the CTE. These recursive queries are unioned together with the anchor query (or queries) in the body of the CTE. Recursive CTEs require a top-level UNION ALL operator to union the recursive and nonrecursive queries together. Multiple anchor queries may be unioned together with INTERSECT, EXCEPT, and UNION operators, and multiple recursive queries can be unioned together with UNION ALL. The recursion stops when no rows are returned from the previous query. Listing 9-3 is a simple recursive CTE that retrieves a result set consisting of the numbers 1 through 10.

Listing 9-3. Simple Recursive CTE

```
WITH Numbers (n)
AS (
SELECT 1 AS n
   UNION ALL
SELECT n + 1
   FROM Numbers
WHERE n < 10 )

SELECT n FROM Numbers;
```

The CTE in Listing 9-3 begins with a declaration that defines the CTE name and the column returned:

```
WITH Numbers (n)
```

The CTE body contains a single anchor query that returns a single row with the number 1 in the n column:

```
SELECT 1 AS n
```

The anchor query is unioned together with the recursive query using the UNION ALL set operator. The recursive query contains a self-reference to the Numbers CTE, adding 1 to the n column with each recursive reference. The WHERE clause limits the result set to the first ten numbers:

```
SELECT n + 1 FROM Numbers WHERE n < 10
```

Recursive CTEs have a maximum recursion level of 100 by default. This means the recursive query in the CTE body can only call itself 100 times. You can use the MAXRECURSION option to increase the maximum recursion level of CTEs on an individual basis. Listing 9-4 modifies the CTE in Listing 9-3 to return the numbers 1 to 1,000. The modified query uses the MAXRECURSION option to increase the maximum recursion level. Without the MAXRECURSION option, this CTE would error out after the first 100 levels of recursion.

Listing 9-4. Recursive CTE with the MAXRECURSION Option

```
WITH Numbers (n)
AS (
SELECT 0 AS n
  UNION ALL
SELECT n + 1
  FROM Numbers
WHERE n < 1000 )
SELECT n
  FROM Numbers OPTION (MAXRECURSION 1000);
```

The MAXRECURSION value specified must be between 0 and 32,767. SQL Server throws an exception if the MAXRECURSION limit is surpassed. A MAXRECURSION value of 0 indicates that no limit should be placed on recursion for the CTE. Be careful with this option—if you don't properly limit the results in the query with a WHERE clause, you can easily end up in an infinite loop.

■ **Tip**   Creating a permanent table of counting numbers can be more efficient than using a recursive CTE to generate numbers, particularly if you plan to execute the CTEs that generate numbers often.

Recursive CTEs are useful for querying data stored in a hierarchical adjacency list format. The adjacency list provides a model for storing hierarchical data in relational databases. In the adjacency list model, each row of the table contains a pointer to its parent in the hierarchy. The Production. BillOfMaterials table in the AdventureWorks database is a practical example of the adjacency list model. This table contains two important columns, ComponentID and ProductAssemblyID, that reflect the hierarchical structure. ComponentID is a unique number identifying every component that AdventureWorks uses to manufacture its products. ProductAssemblyID is a parent component created from one or more AdventureWorks product components. Figure 9-2 shows the relationship between components and product assemblies in the AdventureWorks database.

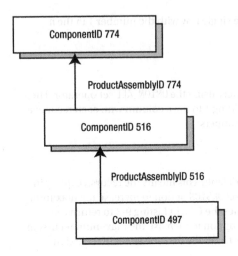

Figure 9-2. *Component/product assembly relationship*

The recursive CTE shown in Listing 9-5 retrieves the complete AdventureWorks hierarchical bill of materials (BOM) for a specified component. The component used in the example is the AdventureWorks silver Mountain-100 48-inch bike, `ComponentID` 774. Partial results are shown in Figure 9-3.

Listing 9-5. Recursive BOM CTE

```
DECLARE @ComponentID int = 774;

WITH  BillOfMaterialsCTE
(
    BillOfMaterialsID,
    ProductAssemblyID,
    ComponentID,
    Quantity,
    Level
)
AS
(
SELECT
        bom.BillOfMaterialsID,
        bom.ProductAssemblyID,
        bom.ComponentID,
        bom.PerAssemblyQty AS  Quantity,
        0  AS  Level
    FROM Production.BillOfMaterials bom
WHERE bom.ComponentID = @ComponentID

        UNION ALL
```

```
SELECT
        bom.BillOfMaterialsID,
        bom.ProductAssemblyID,
        bom.ComponentID,
        bom.PerAssemblyQty,
        Level + 1
   FROM Production.BillOfMaterials bom
  INNER JOIN BillOfMaterialsCTE bomcte
                ON  bom.ProductAssemblyID  =  bomcte.ComponentID
WHERE bom.EndDate IS NULL
)
SELECT
        bomcte.ProductAssemblyID,
        p.ProductID,
        p.ProductNumber,
        p.Name,
        p.Color,
        bomcte.Quantity,
        bomcte.Level
   FROM  BillOfMaterialsCTE bomcte
  INNER  JOIN  Production.Product  p
        ON bomcte.ComponentID = p.ProductID
ORDER BY bomcte.Level;
```

	ProductAssemblyID	ProductID	ProductNumber	Name	Color	Quantity	Level
1	NULL	774	BK-M82S-48	Mountain-100 Silver, 48	Silver	1.00	0
2	774	516	SA-M687	HL Mountain Seat Assembly	NULL	1.00	1
3	774	741	FR-M94S-52	HL Mountain Frame - Silver, 48	Silver	1.00	1
4	774	807	HS-3479	HL Headset	NULL	1.00	1
5	774	810	HB-M918	HL Mountain Handlebars	NULL	1.00	1
6	774	817	FW-M928	HL Mountain Front Wheel	Black	1.00	1
7	774	825	RW-M928	HL Mountain Rear Wheel	Black	1.00	1
8	774	894	RD-2308	Rear Derailleur	Silver	1.00	1
9	774	907	RB-9231	Rear Brakes	Silver	1.00	1
10	774	937	PD-M562	HL Mountain Pedal	Silver/Black	1.00	1
11	774	945	FD-2342	Front Derailleur	Silver	1.00	1
12	774	948	FB-9873	Front Brakes	Silver	1.00	1
13	774	951	CS-9183	HL Crankset	Black	1.00	1
14	774	952	CH-0234	Chain	Silver	1.00	1
15	774	996	BB-9108	HL Bottom Bracket	NULL	1.00	1
16	996	3	BE-2349	BB Ball Bearing	NULL	10.00	2
17	996	526	SH-9312	HL Shell	NULL	1.00	2

Figure 9-3. Partial results of the recursive BOM CTE

241

Like the previous CTE examples, Listing 9-3 begins with the CTE name and column list declaration:

```
WITH BillOfMaterialsCTE
(
    BillOfMaterialsID, ProductAssemblyID, Components, Quantity, Level
)
```

The anchor query simply retrieves the row from the table where the ComponentID matches the specified ID. This is the top-level component in the BOM, set to 774 in this case. Notice that the CTE can reference T-SQL variables like @ComponentID in the example:

```
SELECT
        bom.BillOfMaterialsID,
        bom.ProductAssemblyID,
        bom.Components,
        bom.PerAssemblyQty AS Quantity,
        0 AS Level
  FROM Production.BillOfMaterials bom
 WHERE bom.ComponentID = @ComponentID
```

The recursive query retrieves successive levels of the BOM from the CTE where the ProductAssemblyID of each row matches the ComponentID of the higher-level rows. That is to say, the recursive query of the CTE retrieves lower-level rows in the hierarchy that match the hierarchical relationship previously illustrated in Figure 9-2:

```
SELECT
        bom.BillOfMaterialsID,
        bom.ProductAssemblyID,
        bom.ComponentID,
        bom.PerAssemblyQty,
        Level + 1
  FROM Production.BillOfMaterials bom
 INNER JOIN BillOfMaterialsCTE bomcte
        ON bom.ProductAssemblyID = bomcte.ComponentID
 WHERE bom.EndDate IS NULL
```

The CTE has a SELECT statement associated with it that joins the results to the Production.Product table to retrieve product-specific information like the name and color of the component:

```
SELECT
        bomcte.ProductAssemblyID,
        p.ProductID,
        p.ProductNumber,
        p.Name,
        p.Color,
        bomcte.Quantity,
        bomcte.Level
  FROM BillOfMaterialsCTE bomcte
 INNER JOIN Production.Product p
        ON bomcte.ComponentID = p.ProductID;
```

The restrictions on simple CTEs described earlier in this chapter also apply to recursive CTEs. In addition, the following restrictions apply specifically to recursive CTEs:

- Recursive CTEs must have at least one anchor query and at least one recursive query specified in the body of the CTE. All anchor queries must appear before any recursive queries.

- All anchor queries must be unioned with a UNION, UNION ALL, INTERSECT, or EXCEPT set operator. When using multiple anchor queries and recursive queries, the last anchor query and the first recursive query must be unioned together with the UNION ALL operator. Additionally, all recursive queries must be unioned together with UNION ALL.

- The data types of all columns in the anchor queries and recursive queries must match.

- The from clause of the recursive member should refer to the CTE name only once.

- The recursive queries can't contain the following operators and keywords: GROUP BY, HAVING, LEFT JOIN, RIGHT JOIN, OUTER JOIN, and SELECT DISTINCT. Recursive queries also can't contain aggregate functions (like SUM and MAX), windowing functions, subqueries, or hints on the recursive CTE reference.

Windowing Functions

SQL Server 2014 supports windowing functions that partition results and can apply numbering, ranking, and aggregate functions to each partition. The key to windowing functions is the OVER clause, which allows you to define the partitions, and in some cases the ordering of rows in the partition, for your data. This section discusses SQL Server 2014 windowing functions and the numbering, ranking, and aggregate functions that support the OVER clause.

ROW_NUMBER Function

The ROW_NUMBER function takes the OVER clause with an ORDER BY clause and an optional PARTITION BY clause. Listing 9-6 retrieves names from the Person.Person table. The OVER clause is used to partition the rows by LastName and order the rows in each partition by LastName, FirstName, and MiddleName. The ROW_NUMBER function is used to assign a number to each row.

Listing 9-6. ROW_NUMBER with Partitioning

```
SELECT
    ROW_NUMBER() OVER
    (
        PARTITION BY
        LastName
        ORDER BY
        LastName,
        FirstName,
        MiddleName
    ) AS Number,
    LastName,
    FirstName,
    MiddleName
FROM Person.Person;
```

The partition created in Listing 9-6 acts as a window that slides over your result set (hence the name *windowing function*). The ORDER BY clause orders the rows of each partition by LastName, FirstName, and MiddleName. SQL Server applies the ROW_NUMBER function to each partition. The net result is that the ROW_NUMBER function numbers all rows in the result set, restarting the numbering at 1 every time it encounters a new LastName, as shown in Figure 9-4.

	Number	LastName	FirstName	MiddleName
1	1	Abbas	Syed	E
2	1	Abel	Catherine	R.
3	1	Abercrombie	Kim	NULL
4	2	Abercrombie	Kim	NULL
5	3	Abercrombie	Kim	B
6	1	Abolrous	Hazem	E
7	2	Abolrous	Sam	NULL
8	1	Acevedo	Humberto	NULL
9	1	Achong	Gustavo	NULL
10	1	Ackerman	Pilar	NULL
11	2	Ackerman	Pilar	G
12	1	Adams	Aaron	B
13	2	Adams	Adam	NULL
14	3	Adams	Alex	C
15	4	Adams	Alexandra	J

Figure 9-4. Using ROW_NUMBER to number rows in partitions

■ **Note** When PARTITION BY is used, it must appear before ORDER BY in the OVER clause.

The ROW_NUMBER function can also be used without the PARTITION BY clause, in which case the entire result set is treated as one partition. Treating the entire result set as a single partition can be useful in some cases, but it's more common to partition.

Query Paging with OFFSET/FETCH

SQL Server gives you various options for paging through result sets. The traditional way of paginating is to use the TOP operator to select the TOP n number of rows returned by the query. SQL Server 2005 introduced ROW_NUMBER, which you can use to achieve the same functionality in a slightly different manner. SQL Server 2012 introduced new keywords in the SELECT statement specifically in support of query pagination.

The OFFSET keyword provides support for much easier pagination. It essentially allows you to specify the row from which you want to start returning the data. FETCH then lets you return a specified number of rows in the result set. If you combine OFFSET and FETCH, along with the ORDER BY clause, you can return any part of the data you like from the result set, paging through the data as desired.

Listing 9-7 shows the approach to pagination using OFFSET and FETCH. The stored procedure uses the OFFSET and FETCH clauses to retrieve rows from the Person.Person table in the AdventureWorks database based on input parameter values specified in the procedure call. The procedure determines how the pagination is determined using the @RowsPerPage and @StartPageNum input parameters. @RowsPerPage determines how many rows per page should be included in the result set. @StartPageNum determines the page for which the result set should be returned. OFFSET specifies the number of rows to skip from the beginning of the possible query result. FETCH specifies the number of rows to return in each query page.

Listing 9-7. OFFSET/FETCH Example

```
CREATE  PROCEDURE  Person.GetContacts
    @StartPageNum int,
    @RowsPerPage int
AS
    SELECT
        LastName,
        FirstName,
        MiddleName
    FROM Person.Person
    ORDER BY
        LastName,
        FirstName,
        MiddleName
    OFFSET (@StartPageNum - 1) * @RowsPerPage ROWS
    FETCH NEXT @RowsPerPage ROWS ONLY;
GO
```

The example procedure call that uses the OFFSET/FETCH clause EXEC Person.GetContacts 16,10 passes an @RowsPerPage parameter value of 10 and an @StartPageNum parameter value of 16 to the procedure and returns the 10 rows for the 16th page, as shown in Figure 9-5. The OFFSET keyword in the SELECT statement skips the rows before the page number specified in @StartPageNum and @RowsPerPage. This example skips 150 rows and begins to return results at the 151st row. The FETCH keyword returns the number of rows specified by @RowsPerPage (10). The query plan is shown in Figure 9-6.

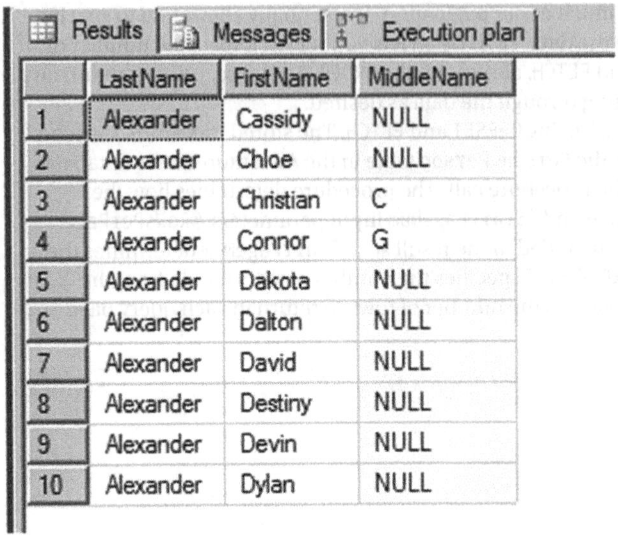

Figure 9-5. Using OFFSET and FETCH to implement client-side paging

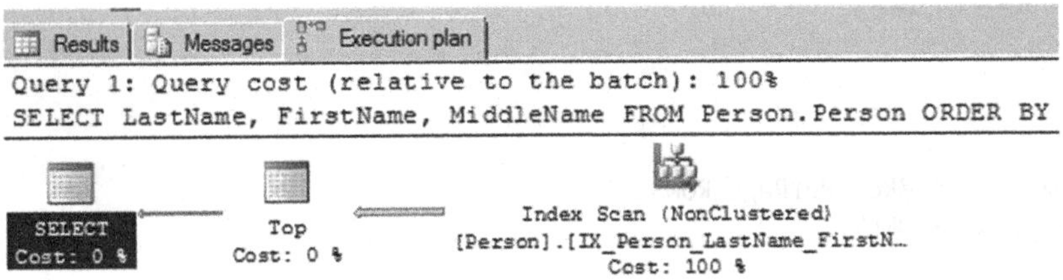

Figure 9-6. Query plan for the client-side paging implementation using OFFSET and FETCH

The query in Listing 9-7 is a much more readable and elegant solution for query pagination than using the Top clause or ROW_NUMBER function with CTEs. The only exception would be if you're using OFFSET/FETCH and want to retrieve ROW_NUMBER; in that case, you would have to add ROW_NUMBER to your query. Thus the OFFSET/FETCH clause provides a much cleaner way to implement ad hoc pagination.

There are some restrictions, though. Keep the following in mind when using OFFSET and FETCH:

- OFFSET and FETCH must be used with an ORDER BY clause.

- FETCH can't be used without OFFSET; however, OFFSET can be used without FETCH.

- The number of rows specified using the OFFSET clause must be greater than or equal to 0.

- The number of rows specified by the FETCH clause must be greater than or equal to 1.

- Queries that use OFFSET and FETCH can't use the TOP operator.

- The OFFSET/FETCH values must be constants, or they must be parameters that have integer values.

- OFFSET and FETCH aren't supported with the OVER clause.

- OFFSET and FETCH aren't supported with indexed views or the view's WITH CHECK OPTION.

In general, under SQL Server 2012 or later, the combination of OFFSET and FETCH provides for the cleanest approach to paginating through query results.

The RANK and DENSE_RANK Functions

The RANK and DENSE_RANK functions are SQL Server's ranking functions. They both assign a numeric rank value to each row in a partition; however, the difference lies in how ties are dealt with. For example:

- If you have three values 7, 7, and 9, then RANK assigns ranks as 1, 1, and 3. That's because the two 7s are tied for first place, whereas the 9 is third in the list. RANK doesn't respect the earlier tie when computing the rank for the value 9.

- But DENSE_RANK assigns ranks 1, 1, and 2. That's because DENSE_RANK lumps both 7s together in rank 1 and doesn't count them separately when computing the rank for the value 9.

There's no right or wrong way to rank your data, absent any business requirements. SQL Server provides two options, and you can choose the one that fits your business need.

Suppose you want to figure out AdventureWorks' best one-day sales dates for the calendar year 2012. This scenario can be phrased with a business question like, "What were the best one-day sales days in 2012?" RANK can easily give you that information, as shown in Listing 9-8. Partial results are shown in Figure 9-7.

Listing 9-8. Ranking AdventureWorks' Daily Sales Totals

```
WITH TotalSalesBySalesDate
(
    DailySales,
    OrderDate
)
AS
(
    SELECT
        SUM(soh.SubTotal) AS DailySales,
        soh.OrderDate
    FROM  Sales.SalesOrderHeader  soh
    WHERE soh.OrderDate >= '20120101'
        AND soh.OrderDate < '20130101'
    GROUP BY soh.OrderDate
)
SELECT
    RANK() OVER
    (
        ORDER BY
        DailySales  DESC
    ) AS  Ranking,
    DailySales,
    OrderDate
FROM  TotalSalesBySalesDate
ORDER  BY  Ranking;
```

	Ranking	DailySales	OrderDate
1	1	3617451.9232	2012-06-30 00:00:00.000
2	2	3064632.131	2012-09-30 00:00:00.000
3	3	2888213.6087	2012-07-31 00:00:00.000
4	4	2408187.2542	2012-05-30 00:00:00.000
5	5	2402984.3967	2012-12-31 00:00:00.000
6	6	2306297.6081	2012-03-30 00:00:00.000
7	7	2205251.3127	2012-10-30 00:00:00.000
8	8	1919379.3786	2012-01-01 00:00:00.000
9	9	1815297.7111	2012-08-30 00:00:00.000
10	10	1473667.5818	2012-01-29 00:00:00.000

Figure 9-7. *Ranking AdventureWorks' daily sales totals*

Listing 9-8 is a CTE that returns two columns: DailySales and OrderDate. DailySales is the sum of all sales grouped by OrderDate. The results are limited by the WHERE clause to include only sales in the 2012 sales year:

```
WITH  TotalSalesBySalesDate
(
    DailySales,
    OrderDate
)
AS
(
    SELECT
        SUM(soh.SubTotal) AS DailySales,
        soh.OrderDate
    FROM  Sales.SalesOrderHeader  soh
    WHERE soh.OrderDate >= '20120101'
        AND soh.OrderDate < '20130101'
    GROUP BY soh.OrderDate
)
```

The RANK function is used with the OVER clause to apply ranking values to the rows returned by the CTE in descending order (highest to lowest) by the DailySales column:

```
SELECT
RANK() OVER ( ORDER BY
DailySales DESC ) AS Ranking, DailySales, OrderDate

FROM TotalSalesBySalesDate ORDER BY Ranking;
```

Like the ROW_NUMBER function, RANK can accept the PARTITION BY clause in the OVER clause. Listing 9-9 builds on the previous example and uses the PARTITION BY clause to rank the daily sales for each month. This type of query can answer a business question like, "What were AdventureWorks' best one-day sales days for each month of 2012?" Partial results are shown in Figure 9-8.

Listing 9-9. Determining the Daily Sales Rankings, Partitioned by Month

```
WITH TotalSalesBySalesDatePartitioned
(
    DailySales,
    OrderMonth,
    OrderDate
)
AS
(
    SELECT
        SUM(soh.SubTotal) AS DailySales,
        DATENAME(MONTH, soh.OrderDate) AS OrderMonth,
        soh.OrderDate
    FROM  Sales.SalesOrderHeader  soh
    WHERE soh.OrderDate >= '20120101'
        AND soh.OrderDate < '20130101'
    GROUP BY soh.OrderDate
)
SELECT
    RANK() OVER
    (
        PARTITION BY
        OrderMonth
        ORDER BY
        DailySales  DESC
    ) AS  Ranking,
    DailySales,
    OrderMonth,
    OrderDate
FROM TotalSalesBySalesDatePartitioned
ORDER BY DATEPART(mm,OrderDate),
    Ranking;
```

	Ranking	DailySales	OrderMonth	OrderDate
1	1	1573991.4236	January	2013-01-28 00:00:00.000
2	2	30851.0645	January	2013-01-03 00:00:00.000
3	3	28936.5003	January	2013-01-24 00:00:00.000
4	4	24793.3784	January	2013-01-16 00:00:00.000
5	5	24439.5834	January	2013-01-17 00:00:00.000
6	6	22601.3742	January	2013-01-05 00:00:00.000
7	7	21481.0103	January	2013-01-21 00:00:00.000
8	8	20491.4012	January	2013-01-08 00:00:00.000
9	9	20359.7088	January	2013-01-12 00:00:00.000
10	10	20287.6502	January	2013-01-20 00:00:00.000

Figure 9-8. *Partial results of daily sales rankings, partitioned by month*

The query in Listing 9-9, like the example in Listing 9-8, begins with a CTE to calculate one-day sales totals for the year. The main differences between this CTE and the previous example are that Listing 9-9 returns an additional OrderMonth column and the results are limited to the year 2012. Here is that CTE:

```
WITH TotalSalesBySalesDatePartitioned
(
    DailySales,
    OrderMonth,
    OrderDate
)
AS
(
    SELECT
        SUM(soh.SubTotal) AS DailySales,
        DATENAME(MONTH, soh.OrderDate) AS OrderMonth,
        soh.OrderDate
    FROM  Sales.SalesOrderHeader  soh
    WHERE soh.OrderDate >= '20120101'
        AND soh.OrderDate < '20130101'
    GROUP BY soh.OrderDate
)
```

The SELECT query associated with the CTE uses the RANK function to assign rankings to the results. The PARTITION BY clause is used to partition the results by OrderMonth so that the rankings restart at 1 for each new month. For example:

```
SELECT
RANK() OVER
(
PARTITION BY OrderMonth

        ORDER BY
        DailySales  DESC
    )  AS  Ranking,
    DailySales,
    OrderMonth,
    OrderDate
FROM TotalSalesBySalesDatePartitioned
ORDER BY DATEPART(mm,OrderDate),
    Ranking;
```

When the RANK function encounters two equal DailySales amounts in the same partition, it assigns the same rank number to both and skips the next number in the ranking. As shown in Figure 9-9, the DailySales total for two days in October 2012 was $7479.3221, resulting in the RANK function assigning the two days a Ranking value of 25. The RANK function then skips Ranking value 26 and assigns the next row a Ranking of 27.

	Ranking	DailySales	OrderMonth	OrderDate
296	22	8761.1932	October	2012-10-16 00:00:00.000
297	23	8745.4303	October	2012-10-01 00:00:00.000
298	24	7712.5325	October	2012-10-04 00:00:00.000
299	25	7479.3221	October	2012-10-21 00:00:00.000
300	25	7479.3221	October	2012-10-08 00:00:00.000
301	27	7302.5178	October	2012-10-18 00:00:00.000
302	28	7036.8471	October	2012-10-06 00:00:00.000
303	28	7036.8471	October	2012-10-22 00:00:00.000
304	30	5297.7596	October	2012-10-14 00:00:00.000
305	31	2443.35	October	2012-10-03 00:00:00.000

Figure 9-9. *The RANK function skips a value in the case of a tie*

DENSE_RANK, like RANK, assigns duplicate values the same rank, but with one important difference: it doesn't skip the next ranking in the list. Listing 9-10 modifies Listing 9-9 to use the RANK and DENSE_RANK functions. As you can see in Figure 9-10, DENSE_RANK still assigns the same Ranking to both rows in the result, but it doesn't skip the next Ranking value, whereas RANK does.

Listing 9-10. Using DENSE_RANK to Rank the Best Daily Sales per Month

```
WITH TotalSalesBySalesDatePartitioned
(
    DailySales,
    OrderMonth,
    OrderDate
)
AS
(
    SELECT
        SUM(soh.SubTotal) AS DailySales,
        DATENAME(MONTH, soh.OrderDate) AS OrderMonth,
        soh.OrderDate
    FROM  Sales.SalesOrderHeader  soh
    WHERE soh.OrderDate >= '20120101'
        AND soh.OrderDate < '20130101'
    GROUP BY soh.OrderDate
)
SELECT
 RANK() OVER
    (
        PARTITION BY
        OrderMonth
        ORDER BY
        DailySales  DESC
    ) AS  Ranking,
```

```
    DENSE_RANK() OVER
    (
        PARTITION BY
        OrderMonth
        ORDER BY
        DailySales  DESC
    ) AS  Dense_Ranking,
    DailySales,
    OrderMonth,
    OrderDate
FROM TotalSalesBySalesDatePartitioned
ORDER BY DATEPART(mm,OrderDate),
    Ranking;
```

	Ranking	DailySales	OrderMonth	OrderDate
296	22	8761.1932	October	2012-10-16 00:00:00.000
297	23	8745.4303	October	2012-10-01 00:00:00.000
298	24	7712.5325	October	2012-10-04 00:00:00.000
299	25	7479.3221	October	2012-10-21 00:00:00.000
300	25	7479.3221	October	2012-10-08 00:00:00.000
301	27	7302.5178	October	2012-10-18 00:00:00.000
302	28	7036.8471	October	2012-10-06 00:00:00.000
303	28	7036.8471	October	2012-10-22 00:00:00.000
304	30	5297.7596	October	2012-10-14 00:00:00.000
305	31	2443.35	October	2012-10-03 00:00:00.000

Figure 9-10. DENSE_RANK *doesn't skip ranking values after a tie*

The NTILE Function

NTILE is another ranking function that fulfills a slightly different need. This function divides your result set into approximate n-tiles. An *n-tile* can be a quartile (1/4, or 25% slices), a quintile (1/5, or 20% slices), a percentile (1/100, or 1% slices), or just about any other fractional slice you can imagine. NTILE divides result sets into approximate n-tiles because the number of rows returned may not be evenly divisible into the required number of groups. A table with 27 rows, for instance, isn't evenly divisible into quartiles or quintiles. When you query a table with the NTILE function and the number of rows isn't evenly divisible by the specified number of groups, NTILE creates groups of two different sizes. The larger groups are all one row larger than the smaller groups, and the larger groups are numbered first. In the example of 27 rows divided into quintiles (1/5), the first two groups have 6 rows each, and the last three groups have 5 rows each.

Like the ROW_NUMBER function, you can include both PARTITION BY and ORDER BY in the OVER clause. NTILE requires an additional parameter that specifies how many groups it should divide your results into.

NTILE is useful for answering business questions like, "Which salespeople made up the top 4% of the sales force in July 2013?" and "What were their sales totals?" Listing 9-11 uses NTILE to divide the AdventureWorks salespeople into four groups, each one representing 4% of the total sales force. The ORDER BY clause is used to specify that rows are assigned to the groups in order of their total sales. The results are shown in Figure 9-11.

Listing 9-11. Using NTILE to Group and Rank Salespeople

```
WITH SalesTotalBySalesPerson
(
        SalesPersonID, SalesTotal
)
AS
(
SELECT
        soh.SalesPersonID,
        SUM(soh.SubTotal) AS SalesTotal
    FROM Sales.SalesOrderHeader soh
WHERE DATEPART(YEAR, soh.OrderDate) = 2013
AND DATEPART(MONTH, soh.OrderDate) = 2
GROUP BY soh.SalesPersonID
)
SELECT
        NTILE(4) OVER( ORDER BY st.SalesTotal DESC) AS Tile,
        p.LastName,
        p.FirstName,
        p.MiddleName,
        st.SalesPersonID,
        st.SalesTotal
    FROM SalesTotalBySalesPerson st
  INNER JOIN Person.Person p
        ON st.SalesPersonID = p.BusinessEntityID ;
```

	Tile	LastName	FirstName	MiddleName	SalesPersonID	SalesTotal
1	1	Pak	Jae	B	289	430730.8928
2	1	Carson	Jillian	NULL	277	400651.4944
3	1	Blythe	Michael	G	275	314936.4504
4	1	Reiter	Tsvi	Michael	279	172527.4835
5	2	Campbell	David	R	283	155124.1524
6	2	Mitchell	Linda	C	276	88379.2611
7	2	Ito	Shu	K	281	87934.131
8	2	Varkey Chudukatil	Ranjit	R	290	56935.0391
9	3	Ansman-Wolfe	Pamela	O	280	49152.4316
10	3	Saraiva	José	Edvaldo	282	47113.0052
11	3	Jiang	Stephen	Y	274	43254.2036
12	4	Mensa-Annan	Tete	A	284	9479.9522
13	4	Vargas	Garrett	R	278	8091.5083
14	4	Alberts	Amy	E	287	968.4284

Figure 9-11. *AdventureWorks salespeople grouped and ranked by NTILE*

The code begins with a simple CTE that returns the SalesPersonID and sum of the order SubTotal values from the Sales.SalesOrderHeader table. The CTE limits its results to the sales that occurred in the month of July in the year 2014. Here is the CTE:

```
WITH SalesTotalBySalesPerson (
        SalesPersonID,
        SalesTotal )
AS (
SELECT
        son.SalesPersonID,
        SUM(soh.SubTotal) AS SalesTotal
    FROM Sales.SalesOrderHeader soh
WHERE DATEPART(YEAR, soh.OrderDate) = 2014
        AND DATEPART(MONTH, soh.OrderDate) = 7
GROUP BY soh.SalesPersonID )
```

The SELECT query associated with this CTE uses NTILE(4) to group the AdventureWorks salespeople into four groups of approximately 4% each. The OVER clause specifies that the groups should be assigned based on SalesTotal in descending order. The entire SELECT query is as follows:

```
SELECT
        NTILE(4) OVER(ORDER BY st.SalesTotal DESC) AS Tile,
        p.LastName,
        p.FirstName,
        p.MiddleName,
        st.SalesPersonID,
        st.SalesTotal
    FROM SalesTotalBySalesPerson st
  INNER JOIN Person.Person p
        ON st.SalesPersonID = p.BusinessEntityID ;
```

Aggregate Functions, Analytic Functions, and the OVER Clause

As previously discussed, the numbering and ranking functions (ROW_NUMBER, RANK, and so on) all work with the OVER clause to define the order and partitioning of their input rows via the ORDER BY and PARTITION BY clauses. The OVER clause also provides windowing functionality to T-SQL aggregate functions such as SUM, COUNT, and SQL CLR user-defined aggregates.

Windowing functions can help with common business questions like those involving running totals and sliding averages. For instance, you can apply the OVER clause to the Purchasing.PurchaseOrderDetail table in the AdventureWorks database to retrieve the SUM of the dollar values of products ordered in the form of a running total. You can further restrict the result set in which you want to perform the aggregation by partitioning the result set by PurchaseOrderId, essentially generating the running total separately for each purchase order. An example query is shown in Listing 9-12. Partial results are shown in Figure 9-12.

Listing 9-12. Using the OVER Clause with SUM

```
SELECT
PurchaseOrderID,
ProductID,
OrderQty,
UnitPrice,
LineTotal,
SUM(LineTotal)
        OVER (PARTITION BY PurchaseOrderIDORDER BY ProductId
            RANGE BETWEEN UNBOUNDED PRECEDING
            AND CURRENT ROW)
        AS CumulativeOrderQty
    FROM Purchasing.PurchaseOrderDetail;
```

	PurchaseOrderID	ProductID	OrderQty	UnitPrice	LineTotal	CumulativeOrderOty
1	1	1	4	50.26	201.04	201.04
2	2	359	3	45.12	135.36	135.36
3	2	360	3	45.5805	136.7415	272.1015
4	3	530	550	16.086	8847.30	8847.30
5	4	4	3	57.0255	171.0765	171.0765
6	5	512	550	37.086	20397.30	20397.30
7	6	513	550	26.5965	14628.075	14628.075
8	7	317	550	27.0585	14882.175	14882.175
9	7	318	550	33.579	18468.45	33350.625
10	7	319	550	46.0635	25334.925	58685.55
11	8	403	3	47.4705	142.4115	142.4115
12	8	404	3	45.3705	136.1115	278.523
13	8	405	3	49.644	148.932	427.455
14	8	406	3	45.3705	136.1115	563.5665
15	8	407	3	43.2705	129.8115	693.378
16	9	422	3	47.523	142.569	142.569
17	9	423	3	45.423	136.269	278.838
18	9	424	3	49.6965	149.0895	427.9275
19	9	425	3	45.423	136.269	564.1965
20	9	426	3	43.323	129.969	694.1655
21	10	320	3	47.4705	142.4115	142.4115

Figure 9-12. Partial results from a query generating a running SUM

Notice the following new clause in Listing 9-12:

`RANGE BETWEEN UNBOUNDED PRECEDING AND CURRENT ROW`

This is known as a *framing clause*. In this case, it specifies that each sum includes all values from the first row in the partition through to the current row. A framing clause like this makes sense only when there is order to the rows, and that is the reason for the `ORDER BY ProductId` clause. The framing clause in combination with the `ORDER BY` clause generate the running sum that you see in Figure 9-12.

■ **Tip** Other framing clauses are possible. The `RANGE BETWEEN UNBOUNDED PRECEDING AND CURRENT ROW` in Listing 9-12 will be the default if no framing clause is specified. Keep that point in mind: it's common for query writers to be confounded by unexpected results because they don't know a default framing clause is being applied.

Let's look at an example to see how the default framing clause can affect the query results. For example, let's say you want to calculate and return the total sales amount by `PurchaseOrder` with each line item. Based on how the framing is defined, you can get very different results, because *total* can mean grand total or running total. Let's modify the query in Listing 9-12 and specify the framing clause `RANGE BETWEEN UNBOUNDED PRECEDING AND UNBOUNDED FOLLOWING` along with the default framing clause and review the results. The modified query is shown in Listing 9-13, and the results are shown in Figure 9-13.

Listing 9-13. Query Results Due to the Default Framing Specification

```
SELECT
PurchaseOrderID,
ProductID,
OrderQty,
UnitPrice,
LineTotal,
SUM(LineTotal)
         OVER (PARTITION BY PurchaseOrderID ORDER BY ProductId)
            AS TotalSalesDefaultFraming,
SUM(LineTotal)
         OVER (PARTITION BY PurchaseOrderID ORDER BY ProductId
               RANGE BETWEEN UNBOUNDED PRECEDING
               AND UNBOUNDED FOLLOWING)
         AS TotalSalesDefinedFraming
  FROM Purchasing.PurchaseOrderDetail
ORDER BY PurchaseOrderID;
```

	PurchaseOrderID	ProductID	OrderQty	Unit Price	Line Total	Total Sales Default Framing	Total Sales Defined Framing
1	1	1	4	50.26	201.04	201.04	201.04
2	2	359	3	45.12	135.36	135.36	272.1015
3	2	360	3	45.5805	136.7415	272.1015	272.1015
4	3	530	550	16.086	8847.30	8847.30	8847.30
5	4	4	3	57.0255	171.0765	171.0765	171.0765
6	5	512	550	37.086	20397.30	20397.30	20397.30
7	6	513	550	26.5965	14628.075	14628.075	14628.075
8	7	317	550	27.0585	14882.175	14882.175	58685.55
9	7	318	550	33.579	18468.45	33350.625	58685.55
10	7	319	550	46.0635	25334.925	58685.55	58685.55
11	8	403	3	47.4705	142.4115	142.4115	693.378
12	8	404	3	45.3705	136.1115	278.523	693.378
13	8	405	3	49.644	148.932	427.455	693.378
14	8	406	3	45.3705	136.1115	563.5665	693.378
15	8	407	3	43.2705	129.8115	693.378	693.378
16	9	422	3	47.523	142.569	142.569	694.1655
17	9	423	3	45.423	136.269	278.838	694.1655

Figure 9-13. *Partial results from the query with different windowing specifications*

In Figure 9-13, you can see that the total sales in the last two columns differ significantly. Column 6, TotalSalesDefaultFraming, lists total cumulative sales: because framing isn't specified for that column, the default framing RANGE BETWEEN UNBOUNDED PRECEDING AND CURRENT ROW is extended to the column, which means the aggregate is calculated only until the current row. But for column 7, TotalSalesDefinedFraming, the framing clause RANGE BETWEEN UNBOUNDED PRECEDING AND UNBOUNDED FOLLOWING is specified, meaning the framing is extended for all the rows in the partition and hence the total is calculated for sales across the entire PurchaseOrder. The objective is to calculate and return the total sales amount for the purchase order with each line item, so not specifying the framing clause yields a running total. This example shows that it's important to specify the proper framing clause to achieve the desired result set.

Now let's look at another example. Listing 9-14 modifies Listing 9-13: it again applies the OVER clause to the Purchasing.PurchaseOrderDetail table in the AdventureWorks database, but this time to retrieve the two-day average of the total dollar amount of products ordered. Results are sorted by DueDate. Notice the different framing clause in this query: ROWS BETWEEN 1 PRECEDING AND CURRENT ROW. Rows are sorted by date. For each row, the two-day average considers the current row and the row from the previous day. Partial results are shown in Figure 9-14.

Listing 9-14. Using the OVER Clause to Define Frame Sizes That Return a Two-Day Moving Average

```
SELECT
PurchaseOrderID,
ProductID,
Duedate,
LineTotal,
Avg(LineTotal)
        OVER (ORDER BY Duedate
              ROWS BETWEEN 1 PRECEDING AND CURRENT ROW) AS [2DayAvg]
  FROM Purchasing.PurchaseOrderDetail
ORDER BY Duedate;
```

257

	PurchaseOrderID	ProductID	Duedate	Line Total	2DayAvg
1	1	1	2011-04-30 00:00:00.000	201.04	201.04
2	2	359	2011-04-30 00:00:00.000	135.36	168.20
3	2	360	2011-04-30 00:00:00.000	136.7415	136.0507
4	3	530	2011-04-30 00:00:00.000	8847.30	4492.0207
5	4	4	2011-04-30 00:00:00.000	171.0765	4509.1882
6	5	512	2011-05-14 00:00:00.000	20397.30	10284.1882
7	6	513	2011-05-14 00:00:00.000	14628.075	17512.6875
8	7	317	2011-05-14 00:00:00.000	14882.175	14755.125
9	7	318	2011-05-14 00:00:00.000	18468.45	16675.3125
10	7	319	2011-05-14 00:00:00.000	25334.925	21901.6875
11	8	403	2011-05-14 00:00:00.000	142.4115	12738.6682
12	8	404	2011-05-14 00:00:00.000	136.1115	139.2615
13	8	405	2011-05-14 00:00:00.000	148.932	142.5217
14	8	406	2011-05-14 00:00:00.000	136.1115	142.5217

Figure 9-14. Partial results from a query returning a two-day moving average

Let's review one last scenario that calculates the running total of sales by ProductID to provide information to management about which products are selling quickly. Listing 9-15 modifies the query from Listing 9-14 further to define multiple windows by partitioning the result set by ProductID. You can see how the frame expands as the calculation is done in the frame. Once the ProductID changes, the frame is reset and the calculation is restarted. Figure 9-15 shows a partial result set.

Listing 9-15. Defining Frames from within the OVER Clause to Calculate a Running Total

```
SELECT
PurchaseOrderID,
ProductID,
OrderQty,
UnitPrice,
LineTotal,
SUM(LineTotal)
        OVER (PARTITION BY ProductId ORDER BY DueDateRANGE
            BETWEEN UNBOUNDED PRECEDING AND
            CURRENT ROW) AS  CumulativeTotal,
ROW_NUMBER()
        OVER (PARTITION BY ProductId ORDER BY DueDate ) AS  No
  FROM Purchasing.PurchaseOrderDetail
 ORDER BY ProductId, DueDate;
```

	PurchaseOrderID	ProductID	OrderQty	UnitPrice	LineTotal	CumulativeTotal	No
46	3536	1	3	50.2635	150.7905	6986.6125	46
47	3615	1	3	50.2635	150.7905	7137.403	47
48	3694	1	3	50.2635	150.7905	7288.1935	48
49	3773	1	3	50.2635	150.7905	7438.984	49
50	3852	1	3	50.2635	150.7905	7589.7745	50
51	3931	1	3	50.2635	150.7905	7740.565	51
52	79	2	3	41.916	125.748	125.748	1
53	158	2	3	41.916	125.748	251.496	2
54	237	2	3	41.916	125.748	377.244	3
55	316	2	3	41.916	125.748	502.992	4
56	395	2	3	41.916	125.748	628.74	5

Figure 9-15. *Partial results showing a running total by product ID*

You can also see in the query in Listing 9-15 that you aren't limited to using one aggregate function in the SELECT statement. You can specify multiple aggregate functions in the same query.

Framing can be defined by either ROWS or RANGE with a lower boundary and an upper boundary. If you define only the lower boundary, then the upper boundary is set to the current row. When you define the framing with ROWS, you can specify the boundary with a number or scalar expression that returns an integer. If you don't define the boundary for framing, then the default value of RANGE BETWEEN UNBOUNDED PRECEDING AND CURRENT ROW is assumed.

Analytic Function Examples

SQL Server 2012 introduced several helpful analytical functions. Some of the more useful of these are described in the subsections to follow. Some are statistics oriented; others are useful for reporting scenarios in which you need to access values across rows in a result set.

CUME_DIST and PERCENT_RANK

CUME_DIST and PERCENT_RANK are two analytical functions that were introduced in SQL Server 2012. Suppose you want to figure out how AdventureWorks' best, average, and worst salespeople perform in comparison to each other. You're especially interested in the data for a salesperson named Jillian Carson, who you know exists in the table by pre-querying the data. This scenario might be phrased with a business question like, "How does salesperson Jillian Carson rank when compared to the total sales of all the salespeople?" CUME_DIST can easily give you that information, as shown in Listing 9-16. The query results are shown in Figure 9-16.

Listing 9-16. Using the CUME_DIST Function

```
SELECT
    round(SUM(TotalDue),1) AS Sales,
    LastName,
    FirstName,
    SalesPersonId,
    CUME_DIST() OVER (ORDER BY round(SUM(TotalDue),1)) as CUME_DIST
FROM
    Sales.SalesOrderHeader soh
        JOIN Sales.vSalesPerson sp
        ON soh.SalesPersonID = sp.BusinessEntityID
GROUP BY SalesPersonID,LastName,FirstName;
```

	Sales	LastName	FirstName	SalesPersonId	CUME_DIST
1	195528.80	Abbas	Syed	285	0.0588235294117647
2	826417.50	Alberts	Amy	287	0.117647058823529
3	1235934.40	Jiang	Stephen	274	0.176470588235294
4	1606441.40	Tsoflias	Lynn	286	0.235294117647059
5	2062393.10	Valdez	Rachel	288	0.294117647058824
6	2608116.40	Mensa-Annan	Tete	284	0.352941176470588
7	3748246.10	Ansman-Wolfe	Pamela	280	0.411764705882353
8	4069422.20	Vargas	Garrett	278	0.470588235294118
9	4207894.60	Campbell	David	283	0.529411764705882
10	5087977.20	Varkey Chudukatil	Ranjit	290	0.588235294117647
11	6683536.70	Saraiva	José	282	0.647058823529412
12	7259567.90	Ito	Shu	281	0.705882352941177
13	8086073.70	Reiter	Tsvi	279	0.764705882352941
14	9585124.90	Pak	Jae	289	0.823529411764706
15	10475367.10	Blythe	Michael	275	0.882352941176471
16	11342385.90	Carson	Jillian	277	0.941176470588235
17	11695019.10	Mitchell	Linda	276	1

Figure 9-16. Results of the CUME_DIST calculation

The query in Listing 9-16 rounds the TotalDue for the Sales amount, to improve the query value's readability. Because CUME_DIST returns the position of the row, the column results are returned as a decimal percent. The results can be formatted to return as a percentage by multiplying by 100. The result in Figure 9-16 shows that 94.11% of the total salespeople have total sales less than or equal to Jillian Carson, as represented by the cumulative distribution value of 0.9411.

If you slightly rephrase the question as "In what percentile are the total sales of salesperson Jillian Carson?" PERCENT_RANK can provide the answer. Listing 9-17 is a modified version of Listing 9-16's query, now including a call to PERCENT_RANK. Partial results are shown in Figure 9-17.

Listing 9-17. Using the PERCENT_RANK Function

```
SELECT
        round(SUM(TotalDue),1) AS Sales,
        LastName,
        FirstName,
        SalesPersonId,
        CUME_DIST() OVER (ORDER BY round(SUM(TotalDue),1)) as CUME_DIST
        ,PERCENT_RANK() OVER (ORDER BY round(SUM(TotalDue),1)) as PERCENT_RANK
    FROM Sales.SalesOrderHeader soh
    JOIN Sales.vSalesPerson sp
        ON soh.SalesPersonID = sp.BusinessEntityID
GROUP BY SalesPersonID,LastName,FirstName;
```

	Sales	Last Name	First Name	SalesPersonId	CUME_DIST	PERCENT_RANK
1	195528.80	Abbas	Syed	285	0.0588235294117647	0
2	826417.50	Alberts	Amy	287	0.117647058823529	0.0625
3	1235934.40	Jiang	Stephen	274	0.176470588235294	0.125
4	1606441.40	Tsoflias	Lynn	286	0.235294117647059	0.1875
5	2062393.10	Valdez	Rachel	288	0.294117647058824	0.25
6	2608116.40	Mensa-Annan	Tete	284	0.352941176470588	0.3125
7	3748246.10	Ansman-Wolfe	Pamela	280	0.411764705882353	0.375
8	4069422.20	Vargas	Garrett	278	0.470588235294118	0.4375
9	4207894.60	Campbell	David	283	0.529411764705882	0.5
10	5087977.20	Varkey Chudukatil	Ranjit	290	0.588235294117647	0.5625
11	6683536.70	Saraiva	José	282	0.647058823529412	0.625
12	7259567.90	Ito	Shu	281	0.705882352941177	0.6875
13	8086073.70	Reiter	Tsvi	279	0.764705882352941	0.75
14	9585124.90	Pak	Jae	289	0.823529411764706	0.8125
15	10475367.10	Blythe	Michael	275	0.882352941176471	0.875
16	11342385.90	Carson	Jillian	277	0.941176470588235	0.9375
17	11695019.10	Mitchell	Linda	276	1	1

Figure 9-17. *Results of the CUME_DIST and PERCENT_RANK calculation for salespeople*

The PERCENT_RANK function returns the percentage of total sales from all sales in AdventureWorks. As you can see in the results, there are 17 unique values: the first value is 0, and the last value is 1. The other rows have values based on the number of rows less than 1. In this example, Jillian Carson is at the 93.75% percentile of overall sales in AdventureWorks, represented by a percent rank value of 0.9375.

___

■ **Note** You can apply the PARTITION BY clause to the CUME_DIST and PERCENT_RANK functions to define the window in which you apply those calculations.

___

PERCENTILE_CONT and PERCENTILE_DISC

PERCENTILE_CONT and PERCENTILE_DISC are new distribution functions that are essentially the inverse of the CUME_DIST and PERCENT_RANK functions. Suppose you want to figure out AdventureWorks' 40th percentile sales total for all the accounts. This can be phrased with the business question, "What is the 40th percentile for all sales for all accounts?" PERCENTILE_CONT and PERCENTILE_DISC require the WITHIN GROUP clause to specify the ordering and columns for the calculation. PERCENTILE_CONT interpolates over all the values in the window, so the result is a calculated value. PERCENTILE_DISC returns the value of the actual column. Both PERCENTILE_CONT and PERCENTILE_DISC require the percentile as an argument, given as a value in the range from 0.0 to 1.0. The example in Listing 9-18 calculates the sales total for the 40th percentile, partitioned by account number. The example uses PERCENTILE_CONT and PERCENTILE_DISC with the median value of 0.4 as the percentile to compute, meaning the 40th percentile value. The query results are shown in Figure 9-18.

Listing 9-18. Using PERCENTILE_CONT and PERCENTILE_DISC

```
SELECT
    round(SUM(TotalDue),1) AS Sales,
    LastName,
    FirstName,
    SalesPersonId,
    AccountNumber,
    PERCENTILE_CONT(0.4) WITHIN GROUP (ORDER BY round(SUM(TotalDue),1))
            OVER(PARTITION BY AccountNumber ) AS PERCENTILE_CONT,
    PERCENTILE_DISC(0.4) WITHIN GROUP(ORDER BY round(SUM(TotalDue),1))
        OVER(PARTITION BY AccountNumber ) AS PERCENTILE_DISC
FROM
    Sales.SalesOrderHeader soh
        JOIN Sales.vSalesPerson sp
        ON soh.SalesPersonID = sp.BusinessEntityID
GROUP BY AccountNumber,SalesPersonID,LastName,FirstName
```

	Sales	Last Name	First Name	SalesPersonId	Account Number	PERCENTILE_CONT	PERCENTILE_DISC
1	95924.00	Ansman-Wolfe	Pamela	280	10-4020-000001	95924	95924.00
2	28310.00	Campbell	David	283	10-4020-000002	28310	28310.00
3	176830.40	Carson	Jillian	277	10-4020-000003	198391.28	176830.40
4	230732.60	Blythe	Michael	275	10-4020-000003	198391.28	176830.40
5	222309.60	Carson	Jillian	277	10-4020-000004	308720.28	222309.60
6	438336.30	Blythe	Michael	275	10-4020-000004	308720.28	222309.60
7	97031.20	Ito	Shu	281	10-4020-000005	97031.2	97031.20
8	3023.30	Mitchell	Linda	276	10-4020-000006	3023.3	3023.30
9	3302.50	Jiang	Stephen	274	10-4020-000007	4166.78	3302.50
10	5463.20	Mitchell	Linda	276	10-4020-000007	4166.78	3302.50
11	25064.60	Reiter	Tsvi	279	10-4020-000008	25064.6	25064.60

Figure 9-18. *Results from the PERCENTILE_CONT and PERCENTILE_DISC functions*

You can see in Figure 9-18 that the PERCENTILE_CONT and PERCENTILE_DISC values differ based on the account number. For account number 10-4020-000003, regardless of the salesperson, PERCENTILE_CONT is 198391.28, which is an interpolated value and may not exist in the data set. PERCENTILE_DISC is 176830.40, which is the value from the actual column. For account 10-4020-000004, PERCENTILE_CONT is 308720.28 and PERCENTILE_DISC is 222309.60.

LAG and LEAD

LAG and LEAD are new offset functions that enable you to perform calculations based on a specified row that is before or after the current row. These functions provide a method to access more than one row at a time without having to create a self-join. LAG gives you access to the row preceding the current row, whereas LEAD lets you access the row after the current row.

LAG helps answer business questions such as, "For all active products that have not been discontinued, what are the current and previous production costs?" Listing 9-19 shows an example query that calculates the current production cost and the previous production cost for all active products using the LAG function. Partial results are shown in Figure 9-19.

Listing 9-19. Using the LAG Function

```
WITH ProductCostHistory AS
(SELECT
        ProductID,
        LAG(StandardCost)
            OVER (PARTITION BY ProductID ORDER BY ProductID) AS PreviousProductCost,
        StandardCost AS CurrentProductCost,
        Startdate,Enddate
FROM   Production.ProductCostHistory
)
SELECT
        ProductID,
        PreviousProductCost,
        CurrentProductCost,
        StartDate,
        EndDate
FROM ProductCostHistory
WHERE Enddate IS NULL
```

	ProductID	PreviousProductCost	CurrentProductCost	StartDate	EndDate
1	707	13.8782	13.0863	2013-05-30 00:00:00.000	NULL
2	708	13.8782	13.0863	2013-05-30 00:00:00.000	NULL
3	711	13.8782	13.0863	2013-05-30 00:00:00.000	NULL
4	712	5.2297	6.9223	2013-05-30 00:00:00.000	NULL
5	713	29.0807	38.4923	2013-05-30 00:00:00.000	NULL
6	714	29.0807	38.4923	2013-05-30 00:00:00.000	NULL
7	715	29.0807	38.4923	2013-05-30 00:00:00.000	NULL
8	716	29.0807	38.4923	2013-05-30 00:00:00.000	NULL
9	717	722.2568	868.6342	2013-05-30 00:00:00.000	NULL
10	718	722.2568	868.6342	2013-05-30 00:00:00.000	NULL
11	719	722.2568	868.6342	2013-05-30 00:00:00.000	NULL
12	720	722.2568	868.6342	2013-05-30 00:00:00.000	NULL
13	721	722.2568	868.6342	2013-05-30 00:00:00.000	NULL
14	722	170.1428	204.6251	2013-05-30 00:00:00.000	NULL

Figure 9-19. *Results of the production cost history comparison using the LAG function*

In this example, Listing 9-19 uses the LAG function in a CTE to calculate the difference between the current production cost and the previous product production cost by partitioning the data set by ProductID:

```
SELECT
        ProductID,
        LAG(StandardCost)
            OVER (PARTITION BY ProductID ORDER BY ProductID) AS PreviousProductCost,
        StandardCost AS CurrentProductCost,
        Startdate,Enddate
FROM  Production.ProductCostHistory
```

The SELECT query associated with the CTE returns the rows with the latest production cost from the dataset, with EndDate being NULL in the call:

```
SELECT
        ProductID,
        PreviousProductCost,
        CurrentProductCost,
        StartDate,
        EndDate
FROM ProductCostHistory
WHERE Enddate IS NULL
```

LEAD, which is the opposite of LAG, helps answer business questions such as, "How do each month's sales compare with sales from the following month for all AdventureWorks salespeople over the year 2007?" Listing 9-20 shows an example query that lists the next month's total sales relative to the current month's sales for year 2007 using the LEAD function. Partial results are shown in Figure 9-20.

Listing 9-20. Using the LEAD Function

```
SELECT
  LastName,
  SalesPersonID,
  Sum(SubTotal) CurrentMonthSales,
  DateNAME(Month,OrderDate) Month,
  DateName(Year,OrderDate) Year,
  LEAD(Sum(SubTotal),1)
            OVER (ORDER BY SalesPersonID, OrderDate) TotalSalesNextMonth
    FROM Sales.SalesOrderHeader soh
      JOIN Sales.vSalesPerson sp
        ON soh.SalesPersonID = sp.BusinessEntityID
WHERE DateName(Year,OrderDate)  = 2007
GROUP BY FirstName, LastName, SalesPersonID,OrderDate
ORDER BY SalesPersonID,OrderDate;
```

	LastName	SalesPersonID	CurrentMonthSales	Month	Year	TotalSalesNextMonth
162	Pak	289	388950.7724	October	2007	230046.2238
163	Pak	289	230046.2238	November	2007	509599.3448
164	Pak	289	509599.3448	December	2007	34516.2132
165	Varkey ...	290	34516.2132	January	2007	113442.2926
166	Varkey ...	290	113442.2926	February	2007	59856.0271
167	Varkey ...	290	59856.0271	March	2007	56935.0391
168	Varkey ...	290	56935.0391	April	2007	188133.5582
169	Varkey ...	290	188133.5582	May	2007	87056.0785
170	Varkey ...	290	87056.0785	June	2007	55465.4076
171	Varkey ...	290	55465.4076	July	2007	686874.3293
172	Varkey ...	290	686874.3293	August	2007	196850.7723
173	Varkey ...	290	196850.7723	September	2007	53834.4018
174	Varkey ...	290	53834.4018	October	2007	614268.4004
175	Varkey ...	290	614268.4004	November	2007	139467.2278
176	Varkey ...	290	139467.2278	December	2007	NULL

Figure 9-20. Results of comparing each employee's sales performance for year 2007 using the LEAD function

In Figure 9-20 you can see that the last row returns NULL for the next month's sales, because there is no LEAD for the last row.

FIRST_VALUE and LAST_VALUE

FIRST_VALUE and LAST_VALUE are offset functions that return the first and last values in the window defined using the OVER clause. FIRST_VALUE returns the first value in the window, and LAST_VALUE returns the last value in the window.

These functions help answer questions like, "What are the beginning and ending sales amounts for any given month for a given salesperson?" Listing 9-21 shows an example query that answers this question, and Figure 9-21 shows partial query results.

Listing 9-21. Using FIRST_VALUE and LAST_VALUE

```
SELECT DISTINCT
LastName,
SalesPersonID,
datename(year,OrderDate) OrderYear,
datename(month, OrderDate) OrderMonth,
FIRST_VALUE(SubTotal)
            OVER (PARTITION BY SalesPersonID, OrderDate ORDER BY  SalesPersonID )
              FirstSalesAmount,
        LAST_VALUE(SubTotal)
            OVER (PARTITION BY SalesPersonID, OrderDate ORDER BY  SalesPersonID)
              LastSalesAmount,
        OrderDate
  FROM Sales.SalesOrderHeader soh
    JOIN Sales.vSalesPerson sp
        ON soh.SalesPersonID = sp.BusinessEntityID
ORDER BY OrderDate;
```

	LastName	SalesPersonID	OrderYear	OrderMonth	FirstSalesAmount	LastSalesAmount	OrderDate
1	Blythe	275	2011	May	6122.082	20541.4072	2011-05-31 00:00:00.000
2	Mitchell	276	2011	May	419.4589	5056.4896	2011-05-31 00:00:00.000
3	Carson	277	2011	May	6107.082	33997.3702	2011-05-31 00:00:00.000
4	Vargas	278	2011	May	7793.1108	1316.0575	2011-05-31 00:00:00.000
5	Reiter	279	2011	May	5596.4705	13787.5434	2011-05-31 00:00:00.000
6	Ansman-Wolfe	280	2011	May	24432.6088	24432.6088	2011-05-31 00:00:00.000
7	Ito	281	2011	May	38510.8973	9799.9243	2011-05-31 00:00:00.000
8	Saraiva	282	2011	May	6124.182	35944.1562	2011-05-31 00:00:00.000
9	Campbell	283	2011	May	714.7043	42813.4333	2011-05-31 00:00:00.000
10	Jiang	274	2011	July	20544.7015	20544.7015	2011-07-01 00:00:00.000
11	Blythe	275	2011	July	4079.988	4049.988	2011-07-01 00:00:00.000
12	Mitchell	276	2011	July	11584.459	39450.7884	2011-07-01 00:00:00.000

Figure 9-21. Results showing the first and last sales amount

This example returns the first and last sales amounts for each salesperson by month and year. You can see in Figure 9-21 that in some cases, FirstSalesAmount and LastSalesAmount are the same, which means there was only one sale in those months. In months with more than one sale, the values for FirstSalesOrder and LastSalesOrder are listed.

Summary

CTEs are powerful SQL Server features that come in two varieties: recursive and nonrecursive. Nonrecursive CTEs allow you to write expressive T-SQL code that is easier to code, debug, and manage than complex queries that make extensive use of derived tables. Recursive CTEs simplify queries of hierarchical data and let you easily generate result sets consisting of sequential numbers, which are very useful in themselves.

SQL Server's support for windowing functions and the OVER clause makes it simple to calculate aggregates with window framing and ordering. SQL Server supports several windowing functions, including the following:

- ROW_NUMBER numbers the rows of a result set sequentially, beginning with 1.

- RANK and DENSE_RANK rank a result set, applying the same rank value in the case of a tie.

- NTILE groups a result set into a user-specified number of groups.

- CUME_DIST, PERCENTILE_CONT, PERCENT_RANK, and PERCENTILE_DISC provide analytical capabilities in T-SQL and enable cumulative distribution value calculations.

- LAG and LEAD provide access to the rows at a given offset value.

- FIRST_VALUE and LAST_VALUE return the first and last row for a given window defined by the partition subclause.

You can also use the OVER clause to apply windowing functionality to built-in aggregate functions and SQL CLR user-defined aggregates.

Both CTEs and windowing functions provide useful functionality and extend the syntax of T-SQL, allowing you to write more powerful code than ever in a simpler syntax than was possible without them.

EXERCISES

1. [True/false] When a CTE is not the first statement in a batch, the statement preceding it must end with a semicolon statement terminator.

2. [Choose all that apply] A recursive CTE requires which of the following?

   a. The WITH keyword

   b. An anchor query

   c. The EXPRESSION keyword

   d. A recursive query

3. [Fill in the blank] The MAXRECURSION option can accept a value between 0 and _____.

4. [Choose one] SQL Server supports which of the following windowing functions?

   a. ROW_NUMBER

   b. RANK

   c. DENSE_RANK

   d. NTILE

   e. All of the above

5. [True/false] You can use ORDER BY in the OVER clause when used with aggregate functions.

6. [True/false] When PARTITION BY and ORDER BY are both used in the OVER clause, PARTITION BY must appear first.

7. [Fill in the blank] The names of all columns returned by a CTE must be_____.

8. [Fill in the blank] The default framing clause is _____.

9. [True/False] If ORDER BY is not specified for functions that do not require an OVER clause, the window frame is defined for the entire partition.

10. [True/False] Checksum can be used with an OVER clause.

CHAPTER 10

■ ■ ■

Data Types and Advanced Data Types

Transact-SQL is a strongly-typed language. Columns and variables must have a valid data type, and the type is a constraint of the column. In this chapter, we will not cover all data types comprehensively. We will skip the obvious part and concentrate on specific information and on more complex and sophisticated data types that were introduced in SQL Server over time.

Basic Data Types

Basic data types like integer or varchar are pretty much self-explanatory. Some of these types have interesting and important-to-know properties or behavior, and even the most used, like varchar, are worth a look.

Characters

Many tools, like the Microsoft Access Upsizing Wizard, generate tables in SQL Server using some default choices. For all character strings, they create nvarchar columns by default. The n stands for UNICODE, the double-bytes representation of a character, with enough room to fit all worldwide language signs (also called logograms in liguistics), like traditional and simplified Chinese, Arabic, and Farsi. nvarchar must be used when the column has to store non-European languages, but as they induce an obvious overhead, you should avoid creating unneeded nvarchar or nchar columns.

The real size of the data in bytes is returned by the DATALENGTH( ) function, while the LEN( ) string function, designed to hide internal storage specifics from the T-SQL developer, will return the number of characters. We test the different values returned by these functions in Listing 10-1. The results are shown in Figure 10-1.

Listing 10-1. Unicode Handling

```
DECLARE
    @string VARCHAR(50) = 'hello earth',
    @nstring NVARCHAR(50) = 'hello earth';

SELECT
    DATALENGTH(@string) as DatalengthString,
    DATALENGTH(@nstring) as DatalengthNString,
    LEN(@string) as lenString,
    LEN(@nstring) as lenNString;
```

	DatalengthString	DatalengthNString	lenString	lenNString
1	11	22	11	11

Figure 10-1. *The Results of LEN() and DATALENGTH()*

You can see the the the nvarchar storage of our 'hello earth' is 22 bytes. Imagine a 100 million-row table: having such a column with an average of 11-character strings, the storage needed to accomodate the extra bytes would be 1.1 GB.

■ **Note**   To represent a T-SQL identifier, like a login name or a table name, you can use the special sysname type, which corresponds to nvarchar(128).

The Max Data Types

In the heady days of SQL Server 2000, large object (LOB) data storage and manipulation required use of the old style text, ntext, and image data types. These types have been deprecated and were replaced with easier-to-use types in SQL Server 2005, namely the varchar(max), nvarchar(max), and varbinary(max) types.

Like the older types, each of these new data types can hold over 2.1 billion bytes of character or binary data, but they handle data in a much more efficient way. The old text or image types required a dedicated type of allocation that created a b-tree structure for each value inserted, regardless of its size. This of course had a significant performance impact when retrieving the columns' content, because the storage engine had to follow pointers to this complex allocation structure for each and every row being read, even if its value was a few bytes long. The (n)varchar(max) or varbinary(max) are more clever types that are handled differently depending on the size of the value. The storage engine creates the LOB structure only if the data inserted cannot be kept in the 8 KB page.

Also, unlike the legacy LOB types, the max data types operate similarly to the standard varchar, nvarchar, and varbinary data types. Standard string manipulation functions such as LEN() and CHARINDEX(), which didn't work well with the older LOB data types, work as expected with the new max data types. The new data types also eliminate the need for awkward solutions involving the TEXTPTR, READTEXT, and WRITETEXT statements to manipulate LOB data.

■ **Note**   The varchar(max), nvarchar(max), and varbinary(max) data types are complete replacements for the SQL Server 2000 text, ntext, and image data types. The text, ntext, and image data types and their support functions will be removed in a future version of SQL Server. Because they are deprecated, Microsoft recommends you avoid these older data types for new development.

The new max data types support a .WRITE clause extension to the UPDATE statement to perform optimized minimally logged updates and appends to varchar(max), varbinary(max), and nvarchar(max) types. You can use the .WRITE clause by appending it to the end of the column name in your UPDATE statement. The example in Listing 10-2 compares performance of the .WRITE clause to a simple string concatenation when updating a column. The results of this simple comparison are shown in Figure 10-2.

Listing 10-2. Comparison of .WRITE Clause and String Append

```
-- Turn off messages that can affect performance
SET NOCOUNT ON;
-- Create and initially populate a test table
CREATE TABLE #test (
    Id int NOT NULL PRIMARY KEY,
    String varchar(max) NOT NULL
);

INSERT INTO #test (
    Id,
    String
) VALUES (
    1,
    ''
), (
    2,
    ''
);
-- Initialize variables and get start time
DECLARE @i int = 1;
DECLARE @quote varchar(50) = 'Four score and seven years ago...';
DECLARE @start_time datetime2(7) = SYSDATETIME();
-- Loop 2500 times and use .WRITE to append to a varchar(max) column
WHILE @i < 2500
BEGIN
    UPDATE #test
    SET string.WRITE(@quote, LEN(string), LEN(@quote))
    WHERE Id = 1;

    SET @i += 1;
END;

SELECT '.WRITE Clause', DATEDIFF(ms, @start_time, SYSDATETIME()), 'ms';

-- Reset variables and get new start time
SET @i   = 1;
SET @start_time = SYSDATETIME();

-- Loop 2500 times and use string append to a varchar(max) column
WHILE @i < 2500
BEGIN
    UPDATE #test
    SET string += @quote
    WHERE Id = 2;

    SET @i += 1;
END;
```

```
SELECT 'Append Method', DATEDIFF(ms, @start_time, SYSDATETIME()), 'ms';

SELECT
    Id,
    String,
    LEN(String)
FROM #test;

DROP TABLE #test;
```

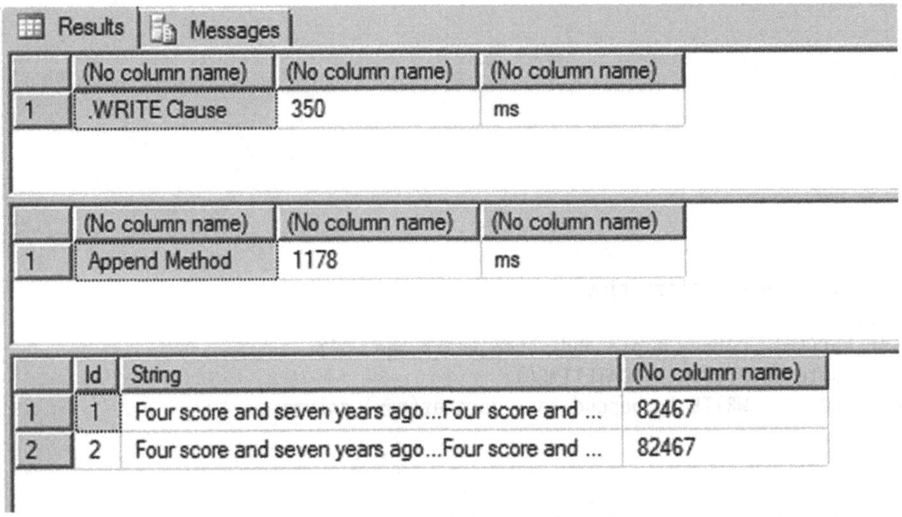

	(No column name)	(No column name)	(No column name)
1	.WRITE Clause	350	ms

	(No column name)	(No column name)	(No column name)
1	Append Method	1178	ms

	Id	String	(No column name)
1	1	Four score and seven years ago...Four score and ...	82467
2	2	Four score and seven years ago...Four score and ...	82467

Figure 10-2. Testing the .WRITE Clause against Simple String Concatenation

As you can see in this example, the .WRITE clause is appreciably more efficient than a simple string concatenation when updating a max data type column. Note that these times were achieved on one of our development machines, and your results may vary significantly depending on your specific configuration. You can expect the .WRITE method to perform more efficiently than simple string concatenation when updating max data type columns, however.

You should note the following about the .WRITE clause:

- The second .WRITE parameter, @offset, is a zero-based bigint and cannot be negative. The first character of the target string is at offset 0.

- If the @offset parameter is NULL, the expression is appended to the end of the target string. @length is ignored in this case.

- If the third parameter, @length, is NULL, SQL Server truncates anything past the end of the string expression (the first .WRITE parameter) after the target string is updated. The @length parameter is a bigint and cannot be negative.

Numerics

There are two types of numeric: exact and approximate. Integer and decimal are exact numbers. It is worth knowing that any exact numeric can be used as an auto-incremented IDENTITY column. Most of the time of course, a 32-bit int is chosen as an auto-incremented surrogate key.

■ **Note** We call surrogate key a technical, non-natural unique key, in other words a column storing values created inside the database, and having no meaning outside of it. Most of the time in SQL Server it is an IDENTITY (auto-incremented) number, of a `uniqueidentifier` (a Globally Unique Identifier, or GUID) that we will see later in this chapter.

Because there is no unsigned numeric in SQL Server, the range of values that can be generated by the IDENTITY property is from −2,147,483,648 to +2,147,483,647. Indeed, as the IDENTITY property takes a seed and an increment as parameters, nothing prevents you from declaring it as in Listing 10-3:

Listing 10-3. Use the Full Range of 32-bit Integer for IDENTITY Columns

```
CREATE TABLE dbo.bigtable (
    bigtableId int identity(-2147483648,1) NOT NULL
);

INSERT INTO dbo.bigtable DEFAULT VALUES;
INSERT INTO dbo.bigtable DEFAULT VALUES;

SELECT * FROM dbo.bigtable;
```

The seed parameter of the `bigtableId` column IDENTITY property is set as the lowest possible int value, instead of the most commonly seen IDENTITY(1,1) declaration. The results follow in Figure 10-3.

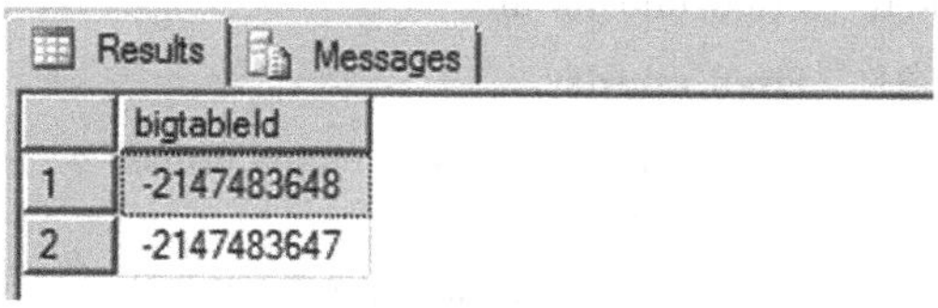

Figure 10-3. The First Two IDENTITY Values Inserted

This allows for twice the range of available values in your key and might save you from choosing a `bigint` (64-bit integer) to accommodate values for a table in which you expect to have more than 2 billion rows but less than 4 billion rows. Once again, on a 100-million row table, it will save about 400 MB, and probably much more than that because there are strong chances that the key value will be used in indexes and foreign keys.

■ **Note** Some are reluctant to use this tip because it creates keys with negative numbers. Theoretically, a surrogate key is precisely meaningless by nature and should not be seen by the end user. It is merely there to provide a unique value to identify and reference a row. Sometimes, when these surrogate keys are shown to users, they start to acquire a life of their own, a purpose. For example, people start to talk about customer 3425 instead of using her name—hence the difficulty with negative values.

We talked about exact numeric types. A word of caution about approximate type: do not use approximate numeric types for anything other than scientific purpose. A column defined as float or real stores floating-point values as defined by the IEEE Standard for Floating-Point Arithmetic (IEEE 754), and any result of an operation on float or real will be approximate. Think about the number pi: you always give a non-precise representation of pi, and you will never get the precise value of pi because you need to round or truncate it at some decimal. To store the precise decimal values that most of us manipulate in business applications—amounts, measurements, etc.— you need to use either money or decimal which are fixed data types.

The bit data type is mostly used to store Boolean values. It can be 0, 1, or NULL, and it consumes one byte of storage, but with an optimization: if you create up to 8-bit columns in your table, they will share the same byte. So bit columns take very little space. SQL Server recognizes also the string values 'TRUE' and 'FALSE' when they are applied to a bit, and they will be converted to 1 and 0, respectively.

Date and Time Data Types

The date and time types were enriched in SQL Server 2008 by the distinct date and time types, and the more precise datetime2 and datetimeoffset. Before that, only datetime and smalldatetime were available. Table 10-1 summarizes the differences between all SQL Server 2014 date and time data types before we delve more into details.

Table 10-1. *SQL Server 2012 Date and Time Data Type Comparison*

Data Type	Components	Range	Precision
datetime	Date and time	1753-01-01 to 9999-12-31	Fixed, three fractional second digits, 3.33 ms.
smalldatetime	Date and time	1900-01-01 to 2079-06-06	Fixed, one minute.
date	Date	0001-01-01 to 9999-12-31	Fixed, one day.
time	Time	00:00:00 to 23:59:59	User-defined, one to seven fractional second digits, 100 ns.
datetime2	Date and time	0001-01-01 to 9999-12-31	User-defined, one to seven fractional second digits, 100 ns.
datetimeoffset	Date, time, and offset	0001-01-01 9999-12-31	User-defined, one to seven fractional second digits, 100 ns, offset range of -14:00 to +14:00.

The date data type allows solving a very common problem we had until SQL server 2008. How can we express date without having to take time into account? Before date, it was tricky to do a straight comparison as shown in Listing 10-4.

Listing 10-4. Date Comparison

```
SELECT *
FROM Person.StateProvince
WHERE ModifiedDate = '2008-03-11';
```

Because the ModifiedDate column data type is datetime, SQL Server converts implictly the '2008-03-11' value to the full '2008-03-11 00:00:00.000' datetime representation before carrying out the comparison. If the ModifiedDate time part is not '00:00:00.000', no line will be returned, which is the case in our example. With datetime-like data types, we are forced to do things as shown in Listing 10-5.

Listing 10-5. Date Comparison Executed Correctly

```
SELECT *
FROM Person.StateProvince
WHERE ModifiedDate BETWEEN '2008-03-11' AND '2008-03-12';
-- or
SELECT *
FROM Person.StateProvince
WHERE CONVERT(CHAR(10), ModifiedDate, 126) = '2008-03-11';
```

But both tricks are unsatisfactory. The first one has a flaw: because the BETWEEN operator is inclusive, lines with ModifiedDate set at '2008-03-12 00:00:00.000' would be included. To be safe, we should have written the query as in Listing 10-6.

Listing 10-6. Correcting the Date Comparison

```
SELECT *
FROM Production.Product
WHERE ModifiedDate BETWEEN '2008-03-11' AND '2008-03-11 23:59:59.997';
-- or
SELECT *
FROM Person.StateProvince
WHERE ModifiedDate >= '2008-03-11' AND ModifiedDate < '2008-03-12';
```

The second example, in Listing 10-5, has a performance implication, because it makes the condition non-sargable.

■ **Note** We say that a predicate is sargable (from Search ARGument–able) when it can take advantage of an index seek. Here, no index on the ModifiedDate column can be used for a seek operation if its value is altered in the query, and thus does not match what was indexed in the first place.

So, the best choice we had was to enforce, maybe by trigger, that every value entered in the column had its time part stripped off or written with '00:00:00.000', but that time part was still taking up storage space for nothing. Now, the date type, costing 3 bytes, stores a date with one day accuracy.

Listing 10-7 shows a simple usage of the date data type, demonstrating that the DATEDIFF() function works with the date type just as it does with the datetime data type.

Listing 10-7. Sample Date Data Type Usage

```
-- August 19, 14 C.E.
DECLARE @d1 date = '0014-08-19';

-- February 26, 1983
DECLARE @d2 date = '1983-02-26';
SELECT @d1  AS Date1, @d2 AS Date2, DATEDIFF(YEAR, @d1,  @d2) AS YearsDifference;
```

The results of this simple example are shown in Figure 10-4.

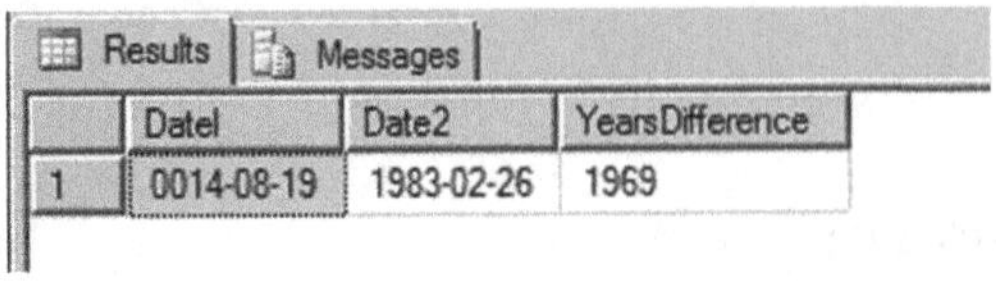

	Date1	Date2	YearsDifference
1	0014-08-19	1983-02-26	1969

Figure 10-4. *The Results of the Date Data Type Example*

In contrast to the date data type, the time data type lets you store time-only data. The range for the time data type is defined on a 24-hour clock, from 00:00:00.0000000 through 23:59:59.9999999, with a user-definable fractional second precision of up to seven digits. The default precision, if you don't specify one, is seven digits of fractional second precision. Listing 10-8 demonstrates the time data type in action.

Listing 10-8. Demonstrating Time Data Type Usage

```
-- 6:25:19.1 AM
DECLARE @start_time time(1) = '06:25:19.1'; -- 1 digit fractional precision
-- 6:25:19.1234567 PM
DECLARE @end_time time = '18:25:19.1234567'; -- default fractional precision
SELECT @start_time AS start_time, @end_time AS end_time,
DATEADD(HOUR, 6, @start_time) AS StartTimePlus, DATEDIFF(HOUR, @start_time, @end_time) AS
 EndStartDiff;
```

In Listing 10-8, two data type instances are created. The @start_time variable is explicitly declared with a fractional second precision of one digit. You can specify a fractional second precision of one to seven digits with 100-nanosecond (ns) accuracy; the fixed fractional precision of the classic datetime data type is three digits with 3.33-millisecond (ms) accuracy. The default fractional precision for the time data type, if no precision is specified, is seven digits. The @end_time variable in the listing is declared with the default precision. As with the date and datetime data types, the DATEDIFF() and DATEADD() functions also work with the time data type. The results of Listing 10-8 are shown in Figure 10-5.

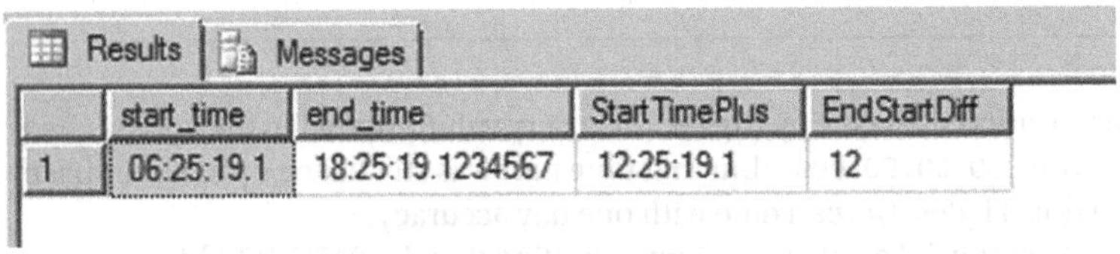

	start_time	end_time	StartTimePlus	EndStartDiff
1	06:25:19.1	18:25:19.1234567	12:25:19.1	12

Figure 10-5. *The Results of the Time Data Type Example*

The cleverly named datetime2 data type is an extension to the standard datetime data type. The datetime2 data type combines the benefits of the date and time data types, giving you the wider date range of the date data type and the greater fractional-second precision of the time data type. Listing 10-9 demonstrates simple declaration and usage of datetime2 variables.

Listing 10-9. Declaring and Querying Datetime2 Variables

```
DECLARE @start_dt2 datetime2 = '1972-07-06T07:13:28.8230234',
        @end_dt2   datetime2 = '2009-12-14T03:14:13.2349832';
SELECT @start_dt2 AS start_dt2, @end_dt2 AS end_dt2;
```

The results of Listing 10-9 are shown in Figure 10-6.

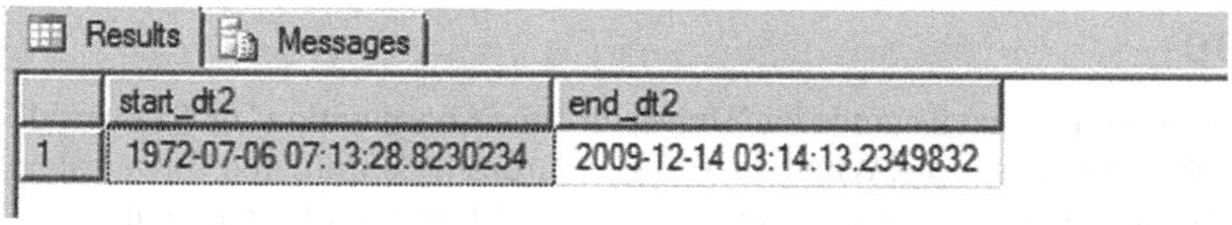

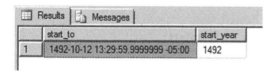

Figure 10-6. *Declaring and Selecting Datetime2 data Type Variables*

The datetimeoffset data type builds on datetime2 by adding the ability to store offsets relative to the International Telecommunication Union (ITU) standard for Coordinated Universal Time (UTC) with your date and time data. When creating a datetimeoffset instance, you can specify an offset that complies with the ISO 8601 standard, which is in turn based on UTC. Basically, the offset must be specified in the range -14:00 to +14:00. The Z offset identifier is shorthand for the offset designated "zulu," or +00:00. Listing 10-10 shows the datetimeoffset data type in action.

Listing 10-10. Datetimeoffset Data Type Sample

```
DECLARE @start_dto datetimeoffset = '1492-10-12T13:29:59.9999999-05:00';
SELECT @start_dto AS start_to, DATEPART(YEAR, @start_dto) AS start_year;
```

The results of Listing 10-10 are shown in Figure 10-7.

start_to	start_year
1492-10-12 13:29:59.9999999 -05:00	1492

Figure 10-7. *The Result of the Datetimeoffset Sample*

A sampling of possible offsets is shown in Table 10-2. Note that this list is not exhaustive, but demonstrates some common offsets.

Table 10-2. *Common Standard Time Zones*

Time Zone Offset	Name	Locations
–10:00	Hawaii-Aleutian Standard	Alaska (Aleutian Islands), Hawaii
–08:00	Pacific Standard	US West Coast; Los Angeles, CA
–05:00	Eastern Standard	US East Coast; New York, NY
–04:00	Atlantic Standard	Bermuda
+00:00	Coordinated Universal	Dublin, Lisbon, London
+01:00	Central European	Paris, Berlin, Madrid, Rome
+03:00	Baghdad	Kuwait, Riyadh
+06:00	Indian Standard	India
+09:00	Japan Standard	Japan

UTC and Military Time

Some people see the acronym UTC and think that it stands for "Universal Time Coordination" or "Universal Time Code." Unfortunately, the world is not so simple. When the ITU standardized Coordinated Universal Time, it was decided that it should have the same acronym in every language. Of course, international agreement could not be reached, with the English-speaking countries demanding the acronym CUT and French-speaking countries demanding that TUC (temps universel coordonné) be used. In the final compromise, the nonsensical UTC was adopted as the international standard.

You may notice that we use "military time," or the 24-hour clock, when representing time in the code samples throughout this book. There's a very good reason for that—the 24-hour clock is an ISO international standard. The ISO 8601 standard indicates that time should be represented in computers using the 24-hour clock to prevent ambiguity.

The 24-hour clock begins at 00:00:00, which is midnight or 12 am. Noon, or 12 pm, is represented as 12:00:00. One second before midnight is 23:59:59, or 11:59:59 pm. In order to convert the 24-hour clock to am/pm time, simply look at the hours. If the hours are less than 12, then the time is am. If the hours are equal to 12, you are in the noon hour, which is pm. If the hours are greater than 12, subtract 12 and add pm to your time.

So, with all these types at your disposal, which do you choose? As a rule, avoid datetime: it doesn't align with the SQL Standard, takes generally more space and has lower precision than the other types. It costs 8 bytes, ranges from 1753 through 9999, and rounds the time to 3 milliseconds. For example, let's try the code in Listing 10-11.

Listing 10-11. Demonstration of Datetime Rounding

```
SELECT CAST('2011-12-31T23:59:59.999' as datetime) as WhatTimeIsIt;
```

You can see the result in Figure 10-8.

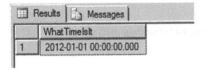

Figure 10-8. *The Results of the Datetime Rounding Sample*

The 999 milliseconds were rounded to the next value, and 998 would have been rounded to 997. For most usages this is not an issue, but datetime2 does not have this drawback, or at least you have control over it by defining the precision.

Date and Time Functions

One of the difficulties of T-SQL is the handling of dates in the code. Internally, the date and time data types are stored in a numeric representation, but of course, they have to be made human-readable in a string format. The format is important for input or output, but it has nothing to do with storage, and it is a common misconception to consider that a date is stored in a particular format. The output is managed by the client. For example, in SSMS, dates are always returned in the ODBC API ts (timestamp) format (yyyy-mm-dd hh:mm:ss....), regardless of the computer's regional settings. If you want to force a particular format in T-SQL, you will need to use a conversion function. The CONVERT() function is a legacy function that returns a formatted string from a date and time data type or vice-versa, while the FORMAT() function, introducedin

SQL Server 2012, uses the more common .NET format strings and an optional culture to return a formatted nvarchar value. We demonstrate usage of these two functions in Listing 10-12.

Listing 10-12. CONVERT() and FORMAT() Usage Sample

```
DECLARE @dt2 datetime2 = '2011-12-31T23:59:59';

SELECT FORMAT(@dt2, 'F', 'en-US') as with_format,
       CONVERT(varchar(50), @dt2, 109) as with_convert;
```

The results are shown in Figure 10-9.

	with_format	with_convert
1	Saturday, December 31, 2011 11:59:59 PM	Dec 31 2011 11:59:59.0000000PM

Figure 10-9. *The Results of the Datetime2 Formatting Sample*

Of course, data input must also be done using a string representation that can be understood by SQL Server as a date. This depends on the language settings of the session. Each session has a language environment that is the default language of the login, unless a SET LANGUAGE command changed it at some time. You can retrieve the language of the current session with one of the two ways shown in Listing 10-13.

Listing 10-13. How to Check the Current Language of the Session

```
SELECT language
FROM sys.dm_exec_sessions
WHERE session_id = @@SPID;
-- or
SELECT @@LANGUAGE;
```

Formatting your date strings for input with a language dependent format is risky, because anyone running the code under another language environment would get an error, as shown in Listing 10-14.

Listing 10-14. Language Dependent Date String Representations

```
DECLARE @lang sysname;

SET @lang = @@LANGUAGE

SELECT CAST('12/31/2012' as datetime2); --this works

SET LANGUAGE 'spanish';

SELECT
    CASE WHEN TRY_CAST('12/31/2012' as datetime2) IS NULL
    THEN 'Cast failed'
    ELSE 'Cast succeeded'
END AS Result;

SET LANGUAGE @lang;
```

The second CAST() attempt, using the TRY_CAST() to prevent an exception from being raised, will return 'Cast failed' because 'MM/dd/yyyy' is not recognized as a valid date format in Spanish. If we would have used CAST() instead of TRY_CAST(), we would have received a conversion error in the Spanish language, and the last SET LANGUAGE command wouldn't have been executed, due to the preceding exception.

You have two options to prevent this. First, you can use the SET DATEFORMAT instruction that sets the order of the month, day, and year date parts for interpreting date character strings, as shown in Listing 10-15.

Listing 10-15. Usage of SET DATEFORMAT

```
SET DATEFORMAT mdy;
SET LANGUAGE 'spanish';
SELECT CAST('12/31/2012' as datetime2); --this works now
```

Or you can decide—this is a better option—to stick with a language-neutral format that will be recognized regardless of what the language environment is. You can do that by making sure you always have your date strings formatted in an ISO 8601 standard variant. In ISO 8601, date and time values are organized from the most to the least significant, starting with the year. The two most common ones are yyyy-MM-ddTHH:mm:ss (note the T character to separate date and time) and yyyyMMdd HH:mm:ss. In a .NET client code, you could generate those formats with the .NET format strings, as shown in the pseudo-code examples of Listing 10-16.

Listing 10-16. Samples of ISO 8601 Date Formatting in .NET Pseudo-code

```
DateTime.Now.Format( "s" );
DateTime.Now.ToString ( "s", System.Globalization.CultureInfo.InvariantCulture );
```

The first line calls the Format() method of the the DateTime .NET type, and the second line uses the ToString() method of .NET objects, that can take a format string and a culture as parameters when applied to a DateTime.

With more complete and precise date and time data types comes also a wide range of built-in date- and time-related functions. You might already know the GETDATE() and CURRENT_TIMESTAMP functions. Since SQL Server 2008, you have had more functions for returning the current date and time of the server.

The SYSDATETIME() function returns the system date and time, as reported by the server's local operating system, as a datetime2 value without time offset information. The value returned by GETDATE(), CURRENT_TIMESTAMP and SYSDATETIME() is the date and time reported by Windows on the computer where your SQL Server instance is installed.

The SYSUTCDATETIME() function returns the system date and time information converted to UTC as a datetime2 value. As with the SYSDATETIME() function, the value returned does not contain additional time offset information.

The SYSDATETIMEOFFSET() function returns the system date and time as a datetimeoffset value, including the time offset information. Listing 10-17 uses these functions to display the current system date and time in various formats. The results are shown in Figure 10-10.

Listing 10-17. Using the Date and Time Functions

```
SELECT SYSDATETIME() AS [SYSDATETIME];
SELECT SYSUTCDATETIME() AS [SYSUTCDATETIME];
SELECT SYSDATETIMEOFFSET() AS [SYSDATETIMEOFFSET];
```

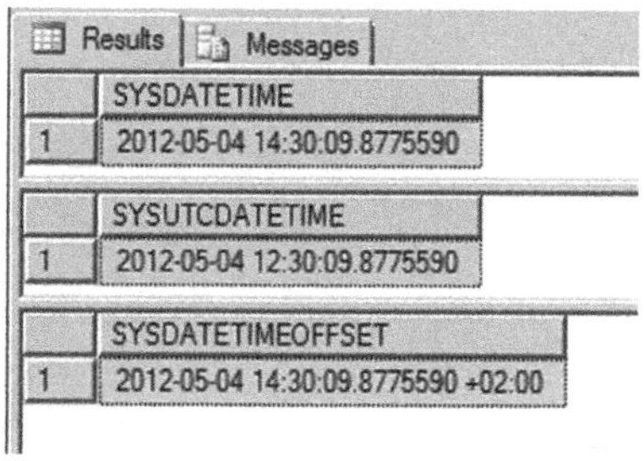

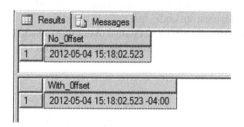

Figure 10-10. *The Current System Date and Time in a Variety of Formats*

The TODATETIMEOFFSET() function allows you to add time offset information to date and time data without time offset information. You can use TODATETIMEOFFSET to add time offset information to a date, time, datetime, datetime2, or datetimeoffset value. The result returned by the function is a datetimeoffset value with time offset information added. Listing 10-18 demonstrates by adding time offset information to a datetime value. The results are shown in Figure 10-11.

Listing 10-18. Adding an Offset to a Datetime Value

```
DECLARE @current datetime = CURRENT_TIMESTAMP;
SELECT @current AS [No_Offset];
SELECT TODATETIMEOFFSET(@current, '-04:00') AS [With_Offset];
```

Figure 10-11. *Converting a Datetime Value to a Datetimeoffset*

The SWITCHOFFSET() function adjusts a given datetimeoffset value to another given time offset. This is useful when you need to convert a date and time to another time offset. In Listing 10-19, we use the SWITCHOFFSET() function to convert a datetimeoffset value in Los Angeles to several other regional time offsets. The values are calculated for Daylight Saving Time. The results are shown in Figure 10-12.

Listing 10-19. Converting a Datetimeoffset to Several Time Offsets

```
DECLARE @current datetimeoffset = '2012-05-04 19:30:00 -07:00';
SELECT 'Los Angeles' AS [Location], @current AS [Current Time]
UNION ALL
SELECT 'New York', SWITCHOFFSET(@current, '-04:00')
UNION ALL
SELECT 'Bermuda', SWITCHOFFSET(@current, '-03:00')
UNION ALL
SELECT 'London', SWITCHOFFSET(@current, '+01:00');
```

	Location	Current Time
1	Los Angeles	2012-05-04 19:30:00.0000000 -07:00
2	New York	2012-05-04 22:30:00.0000000 -04:00
3	Bermuda	2012-05-04 23:30:00.0000000 -03:00
4	London	2012-05-05 03:30:00.0000000 +01:00

Figure 10-12. *Date and Time Information in Several Different Time Offsets*

■ **Tip** You can use the Z time offset in datetimeoffset literals as an abbreviation for UTC (+00:00 offset). You cannot, however, specify Z as the time offset parameter with the TODATETIMEOFFSET and SWITCHOFFSET functions.

Time Zones and Offsets

Time offsets are not the same thing as time zones. A time offset is relatively easy to calculate—it's simply a plus or minus offset in hours and minutes from the UTC offset (+00:00), as defined by the ISO 8601 standard. A time zone, however, is an identifier for a specific location or region and is defined by regional laws and regulations. Time zones can have very complex sets of rules that include such oddities as Daylight Saving Time (DST). SQL Server uses time offsets in calculations, not time zones. If you want to perform date and time calculations involving actual time zones, you will have to write custom code. Just keep in mind that time zone calculations are fairly involved, especially since calculations like DST can change over time. Case in point—the start and end dates for DST were changed to extend DST in the United States beginning in 2007.

The Uniqueidentifier Data Type

In Windows, you see a lot of GUIDs (Globally Unique IDentifiers) in the registry and as a way to provide code and modules (like COM objects) with unique identifiers. GUIDs are 16-byte values generally represented as 32-character hexadecimal strings, and can be stored in SQL Server in the uniqueidentifier data type. uniqueidentifier could be used to create unique keys across tables, servers or data centers. To create a new GUID and store it in a uniqueidentifier column, you use the NEWID() function, as demonstrated in Listing 10-20. The results are shown in Figure 10-13.

Listing 10-20. Using Uniqueidentifier

```
CREATE TABLE dbo.Document (
    DocumentId uniqueidentifier NOT NULL PRIMARY KEY DEFAULT (NEWID())
);

INSERT INTO dbo.Document DEFAULT VALUES;
INSERT INTO dbo.Document DEFAULT VALUES;
INSERT INTO dbo.Document DEFAULT VALUES;

SELECT * FROM dbo.Document;
```

	DocumentId
1	8BEAD517-5068-4CF7-B768-10322C13728A
2	9BDC122F-148A-42C2-9DA8-75718EEE8DE2
3	05A8D779-A15D-4CCE-A317-AFD6AABE990E

Figure 10-13. *Results Generated by the Newid() Function*

Each time the NEWID() function is called, it generates a new value using an algorithm based on a pseudo-random generator. The risk of two generated numbers being the same is statistically negligible: hence the global uniqueness it offers.

However, usage of uniqueidentifier columns should be carefully considered, because it bears significant consequences. We have already talked about the importance of data type size, and especially key size. Choosing a uniqueidentifier over an int as a primary key creates an overhead of 12 bytes per row that impacts the size of the table, of the primary key index, of all other indexes if the primary key is defined as clustered (as it is by default), and of all tables that have a foreign key associated to it, and finally on all indexes on these foreign keys. Needless to say, it could considerably increase the size of your database.

There is another problem with uniqueidentifier values, because of their inherent randomness. If your primary key is clustered, the physical order of the table depends upon the value of the key, and at each insert or update, SQL Server must place the new or modified lines at the right place, in the right data pages. GUID random values will cause page splits that will noticeably decrease performances and generate table fragmentation.

To address this last issue, SQL Server 2008 introduced the NEWSEQUENTIALID() function to use as a default constraint with an uniqueidentifier primary key. NEWSEQUENTIALID() generates sequential GUIDs in increasing order. Its usage is shown in Listing 10-21. Results are shown in Figure 10-14; notice that the GUID digits are displayed in groups in reverse order. In the results, the first byte of each GUID represents the sequentially increasing values generated by NEWSEQUENTIALID() with each row inserted.

Listing 10-21. Generating Sequential GUIDs

```
CREATE TABLE #TestSeqID (
    ID uniqueidentifier DEFAULT NEWSEQUENTIALID() PRIMARY KEY NOT NULL,
    Num int NOT NULL
);

INSERT INTO #TestSeqID (Num)
VALUES (1), (2), (3);

SELECT ID, Num
FROM #TestSeqID;

DROP TABLE #TestSeqID;
```

	ID	Num
1	4CDDEF6B-F395-E111-897E-080027D3B4E2	1
2	4DDDEF6B-F395-E111-897E-080027D3B4E2	2
3	4EDDEF6B-F395-E111-897E-080027D3B4E2	3

Figure 10-14. *Results Generated by the NEWSEQUENTIALID Function*

The Hierarchyid Data Type

The hierarchyid data type offers a new twist on an old model for representing hierarchical data in the database. This data type introduced in SQL Server 2008 offers built-in support for representing your hierarchical data using one of the simplest models available: materialized paths.

Representing Hierarchical Data

The representation of hierarchical data in relational databases has long been an area of interest for SQL developers. The most common model of representing hierarchical data with SQL Server is the adjacency list model. In this model, each row of a table maintains a reference to its parent row. The following illustration demonstrates how the adjacency list model works in an SQL table.

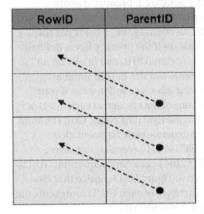

The AdventureWorks sample database makes use of the adjacency list model in its Production. BillOfMaterials table, where every component references its parent assembly.

The materialized path model requires that you store the actual hierarchical path from the root node to the current node. The hierarchical path is similar to a modern file system path, where each folder or directory represents a node in the path. The hierarchyid data type supports generation and indexing of materialized paths for hierarchical data modeling. The following illustration shows how the materialized path might look in SQL.

Path
/a
/a/b
/a/b/c
/a/b/d

It is a relatively simple matter to represent adjacency list model data using materialized paths, as you'll see later in this section in the discussion on converting AdventureWorks adjacency list data to the materialized path model using the hierarchyid data type.

Another model for representing hierarchical data is the nested sets model. In this model, every row in the table is considered a set that may contain or be contained by another set. Each row is assigned a pair of numbers defining the lower and upper bounds for the set. The following illustration shows a logical representation of the nested sets model, with the lower and upper bounds for each set shown to the set's left and right. Notice that the sets in the figure are contained within one another logically, in a structure from which this model derives its name.

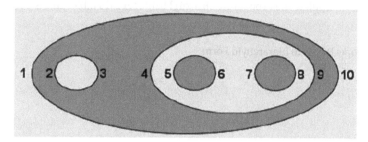

In this section, we'll use the AdventureWorks Production.BillOfMaterials table extensively to demonstrate the adjacency list model, the materialized path model, and the hierarchyid data type. Technically speaking, a bill of materials (BOM), or "parts explosion," is a directed acyclic graph. A directed acyclic graph is essentially a generalized tree structure in which some subtrees may be shared by different parts of the tree. Think of a cake recipe, represented as a tree, in which "sugar" can be used multiple times (once in the "cake mix" subtree, once in the "frosting" subtree, and so on). This book is not about graph theory, though, so we'll pass on the technical details and get to the BOM at hand. Although directed acyclic graph is the technical term for a true BOM, we'll be representing the AdventureWorks BOMs as materialized path hierarchies using the hierarchyid data type, so you'll see the term hierarchy used a lot in this section.

In order to understand the AdventureWorks BOM hierarchies, it's important to understand the relationship between product assemblies and components. Basically, a product assembly is composed of one or more components. An assembly can become a component for use in other assemblies, defining the recursive relationship. All components with a product assembly of NULL are top-level components, or "root nodes," of each hierarchy. If a hierarchyid data type column is declared a primary key, it can contain only a single hierarchyid root node.

The hierarchyid data type stores hierarchy information as an optimized materialized path, which is a very efficient way to store hierarchical information. We will go though a complete example of its use.

Hierarchyid Example

In this example, we will convert the AdventureWorks BOMs to materialized path form using the hierarchyid data type. The first step, shown in Listing 10-22, is to create the table that will contain the hierarchyid BOMs. To differentiate it from the Production.BillOfMaterials table, we have called this table Production.HierBillOfMaterials.

Listing 10-22. Creating the Hierarchyid Bill of Materials Table

```
CREATE TABLE Production.HierBillOfMaterials
(
    BomNode hierarchyid NOT NULL PRIMARY KEY NONCLUSTERED,
    ProductAssemblyID int NULL,
    ComponentID int NULL,
```

```
    UnitMeasureCode nchar(3) NULL,
    PerAssemblyQty decimal(8, 2) NULL,
    BomLevel AS BomNode.GetLevel()
);
```

The Production.HierBillOfMaterials table consists of the BomNode hierarchyid column, which will contain the hierarchical path information for each component. The ProductAssemblyID, ComponentID, UnitMeasureCode, and PerAssemblyQty are all pulled from the source tables. BomLevel is a calculated column that contains the current level of each BomNode. The next step is to convert the adjacency list BOMs to hierarchyid form, which will be used to populate the Production.HierBillOfMaterials table. This is demonstrated in Listing 10-23.

Listing 10-23. Converting AdventureWorks BOMs to hierarchyid Form

```
;WITH BomChildren
(
    ProductAssemblyID,
    ComponentID
)
AS
(
    SELECT
        b1.ProductAssemblyID,
        b1.ComponentID
    FROM  Production.BillOfMaterials b1
    GROUP BY
        b1.ProductAssemblyID,
        b1.ComponentID
),
BomPaths
(
    Path,
    ComponentID,
    ProductAssemblyID
)
AS
(
    SELECT
        hierarchyid::GetRoot() AS Path,
        NULL,
        NULL
    UNION ALL

    SELECT
        CAST
        ('/' + CAST (bc.ComponentId AS varchar(30)) + '/' AS hierarchyid) AS Path,
        bc.ComponentID,
        bc.ProductAssemblyID
    FROM BomChildren AS bc
    WHERE bc.ProductAssemblyID IS NULL
```

```
    UNION ALL

    SELECT
        CAST
        (bp.path.ToString()  +
            CAST(bc.ComponentID AS varchar(30)) + '/' AS hierarchyid) AS Path,
        bc.ComponentID,
        bc.ProductAssemblyID
    FROM BomChildren AS bc
    INNER JOIN BomPaths AS bp
        ON bc.ProductAssemblyID = bp.ComponentID
)
INSERT INTO Production.HierBillOfMaterials
(
    BomNode,
    ProductAssemblyID,
    ComponentID,
    UnitMeasureCode,
    PerAssemblyQty
)
SELECT
    bp.Path,
    bp.ProductAssemblyID,
    bp.ComponentID,
    bom.UnitMeasureCode,
    bom.PerAssemblyQty
FROM BomPaths AS bp
LEFT OUTER JOIN Production.BillOfMaterials bom
    ON  bp.ComponentID = bom.ComponentID
        AND COALESCE(bp.ProductAssemblyID, -1) = COALESCE(bom.ProductAssemblyID, -1)
WHERE bom.EndDate IS NULL
GROUP BY
    bp.path,
    bp.ProductAssemblyID,
    bp.ComponentID,
    bom.UnitMeasureCode,
    bom.PerAssemblyQty;
```

This statement is a little more complex than the average hierarchyid data example you'll probably run into, since most people currently out there are demonstrating conversion of the simple, single-hierarchy AdventureWorks organizational chart. The AdventureWorks Production.BillOfMaterials table actually contains several individual hierarchies.

We will go through the code step by step here to show you exactly what's going on in this statement. The first part of the statement is a common table expression (CTE) called BomChildren. It returns all ProductAssemblyIDs and ComponentIDs from the Production.BillOfMaterials table.

```
;WITH BomChildren
(
    ProductAssemblyID,
    ComponentID
)
```

```
AS
(
    SELECT
        b1.ProductAssemblyID,
        b1.ComponentID
    FROM Production.BillOfMaterials b1
    GROUP BY
        b1.ProductAssemblyID,
        b1.ComponentID
),
```

While the organizational chart represents a simple top-down hierarchy with a single root node, the BOM is actually composed of dozens of separate hierarchies with no single hierarchyid root node. BomPaths is a recursive CTE that returns the current hierarchyid, ComponentID, and ProductAssemblyID for each row.

```
BomPaths
(
    Path,
    ComponentID,
    ProductAssemblyID
)
```

The anchor query for the CTE is in two parts. The first part returns the root node for the entire hierarchy. In this case, the root just represents a logical grouping of all the BOM's top-level assemblies; it does not represent another product that can be created by mashing together every product in the AdventureWorks catalog.

```
SELECT
    hierarchyid::GetRoot(),
    NULL,
    NULL
```

The second part of the anchor query returns the hierarchyid path to the top-level assemblies. Each top-level assembly has its ComponentId appended to the root path, represented by a leading forward slash (/).

```
SELECT
    CAST
    ('/' + CAST (bc.ComponentId AS varchar(30)) + '/' AS hierarchyid) AS Path,
    bc.ComponentID,
    bc.ProductAssemblyID
FROM BomChildren AS bc
WHERE bc.ProductAssemblyID IS NULL
```

The recursive part of the CTE recursively appends forward slash-separated ComponentId values to the path to represent each component in any given assembly:

```
SELECT
    CAST
    (bp.path.ToString()  +
        CAST(bc.ComponentID AS varchar(30)) + '/' AS hierarchyid) AS Path,
    bc.ComponentID,
    bc.ProductAssemblyID
```

```
    FROM BomChildren AS bc
    INNER JOIN BomPaths AS bp
        ON bc.ProductAssemblyID = bp.ComponentID
)
```

The next part of the statement inserts the results of the recursive BomPaths CTE into the Production.HierBillOfMaterials table. The results of the recursive CTE are joined to the Production.BillOfMaterials table for a couple of reasons:

- to ensure that only components currently in use are put into the hierarchy by making sure that the EndDate is NULL for each component

- to retrieve the UnitMeasureCode and PerAssemblyQty columns for each component

We use a LEFT OUTER JOIN in this statement instead of an INNER JOIN because of the inclusion of the hierarchyid root node, which has no matching row in the Production.BillOfMaterials table. If you had opted not to include the hierarchyid root node, you could turn this join back into an INNER JOIN.

```
INSERT INTO Production.HierBillOfMaterials
(
    BomNode,
    ProductAssemblyID,
    ComponentID,
    UnitMeasureCode,
    PerAssemblyQty
)
SELECT
    bp.Path,
    bp.ProductAssemblyID,
    bp.ComponentID,
    bom.UnitMeasureCode,
    bom.PerAssemblyQty
FROM BomPaths AS bp
LEFT OUTER JOIN Production.BillOfMaterials bom
    ON  bp.ComponentID = bom.ComponentID
        AND COALESCE(bp.ProductAssemblyID, -1) = COALESCE(bom.ProductAssemblyID, -1)
WHERE bom.EndDate IS NULL
GROUP BY
    bp.path,
    bp.ProductAssemblyID,
    bp.ComponentID,
    bom.UnitMeasureCode,
    bom.PerAssemblyQty;
```

The simple query in Listing 10-24 shows the BOM after conversion to materialized path form with the hierarchyid data type, and ordered by the hierarchyid column to demonstrate that the hierarchy is reflected from the hierarchyid content itself. Partial results are shown in Figure 10-15.

Listing 10-24. Viewing the Hierarchyid BOMs

```
SELECT
    BomNode,
    BomNode.ToString(),
    ProductAssemblyID,
    ComponentID,
    UnitMeasureCode,
    PerAssemblyQty,
    BomLevel
FROM Production.HierBillOfMaterialsORDER BY BomNode;
```

	BomNode	(No column name)	ProductAssemblyID	ComponentID	UnitMeasureCode	PerAssemblyQty	BomLevel
1	0x	/	NULL	NULL	NULL	NULL	0
2	0xEA2EC0	/749/	NULL	749	EA	1.00	1
3	0xEA2EF999F0	/749/519/	749	519	EA	1.00	2
4	0xEA2EF999FE644C	/749/519/497/	519	497	EA	4.00	3
5	0xEA2EF999FE6844	/749/519/528/	519	528	EA	1.00	3
6	0xEA2EF999FE6854	/749/519/530/	519	530	EA	1.00	3
7	0xEA2EF999FEC84C	/749/519/913/	519	913	EA	1.00	3
8	0xEA2EFA3BB0	/749/717/	749	717	EA	1.00	2
9	0xEA2EFA3BBE2E64	/749/717/324/	717	324	EA	2.00	3
10	0xEA2EFA3BBE2E67989D	/749/717/324/486/	324	486	EA	1.00	4
11	0xEA2EFA3BBE2E6C	/749/717/325/	717	325	EA	2.00	3
12	0xEA2EFA3BBE2E74	/749/717/326/	717	326	EA	1.00	3

Figure 10-15. *Partial Results of the hierarchical BOM Conversion*

As you can see, the hierarchyid column, BomNode, represents the hierarchy as a compact path in a variable-length binary format. Converting the BomNode column to string format with the ToString() method results in a forward slash-separated path reminiscent of a file path. The BomLevel column uses the GetLevel() method to retrieve the level of each node in the hierarchy. The hierarchyid root node has a BomLevel of 0. The top-level assemblies are on level 1, and their children are on levels 2 and below.

Hierarchyid Methods

The hierarchyid data type includes several methods for querying and manipulating hierarchical data. The IsDescendantOf() method, for instance, can be used to retrieve all descendants of a given node. The example in Listing 10-25 retrieves the descendant nodes of product assembly 749. The results are shown in Figure 10-16.

Listing 10-25. Retrieving Descendant Nodes of Assembly 749

```
DECLARE @CurrentNode hierarchyid;

SELECT @CurrentNode = BomNode
FROM Production.HierBillOfMaterials
WHERE ProductAssemblyID = 749;
```

```
SELECT
    BomNode,
    BomNode.ToString(),
    ProductAssemblyID,
    ComponentID,
    UnitMeasureCode,
    PerAssemblyQty,
    BomLevel
FROM Production.HierBillOfMaterials
WHERE @CurrentNode.IsDescendantOf(BomNode) = 1;
```

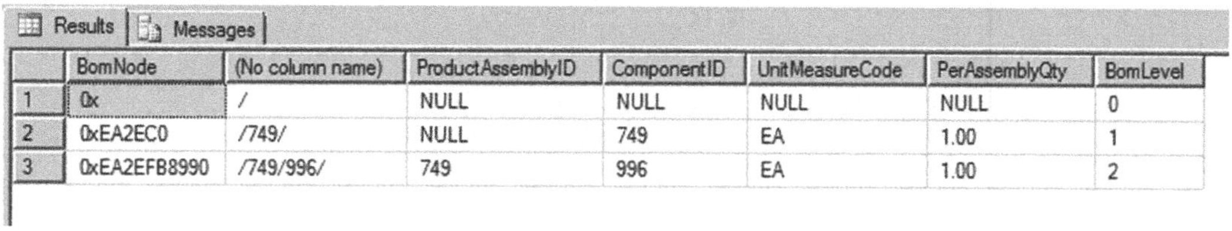

	BomNode	(No column name)	ProductAssemblyID	ComponentID	UnitMeasureCode	PerAssemblyQty	BomLevel
1	0x	/	NULL	NULL	NULL	NULL	0
2	0xEA2EC0	/749/	NULL	749	EA	1.00	1
3	0xEA2EFB8990	/749/996/	749	996	EA	1.00	2

Figure 10-16. *Descendant Nodes of Assembly 749*

Table 10-3 is a quick summary of the hierarchyid data type methods.

Table 10-3. *hierarchyid Data Type Methods*

Method	Description
GetAncestor(n)	Retrieves the nth ancestor of the hierarchyid node instance.
GetDescendant(n)	Retrieves the nth descendant of the hierarchyid node instance.
GetLevel()	Gets the level of the hierarchyid node instance in the hierarchy.
GetRoot()	Gets the hierarchyid instance root node; GetRoot() is a static method.
IsDescendantOf(node)	Returns 1 if a specified node is a descendant of the hierarchyid instance node.
Parse(string)	Converts the given canonical string, in forward slash-separated format, to a hierarchyid path.
GetReparentedValue(old_root, new_root)	Returns a node reparented from old_root to new_root.
ToString()	Converts a hierarchyid instance to a canonical forward slash-separated string representation.

Spatial Data Types

Since version 2008, SQL Server includes two data types for storing, querying, and manipulating spatial data. The geometry data type is designed to represent flat-earth, or Euclidean, spatial data per the Open Geospatial Consortium (OGC) standard. The geography data type supports round-earth, or ellipsoidal, spatial data. Figure 10-17 shows a simple two-dimensional flat geometry for a small area, with a point plotted at location (2, 1).

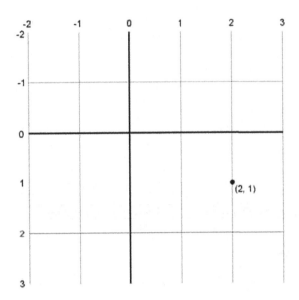

Figure 10-17. *Flat Spatial Representation*

The spatial data types store representations of spatial data using instance types. There are 12 instance types, all derived from the Geography Markup Language (GML) abstract Geometry type. Of those 12 instance types, only 7 are concrete types that can be instantiated; the other 5 serve as abstract base types from which other types derive. Figure 10-18 shows the spatial instance type hierarchy with the XML-based GML top-level elements.

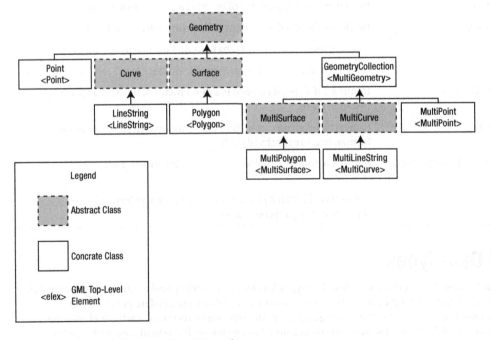

Figure 10-18. *Spatial Instance Type Hierarchy*

The available spatial instance types include the following:

- Point: This object represents a zero-dimensional object representing a single location. The Point requires, at a minimum, a two-dimensional (x, y) coordinate pair, but it may also have an elevation coordinate (z) and an additional user-defined measure. The Point object has no area or length.

- MultiPoint: This type represents a collection of multiple points. It has no area or length.

- LineString: This is a one-dimensional object representing one or more connected line segments. Each segment is defined by a start point and an endpoint, and all segments are connected in such a way that the endpoint of one line segment is the start point for the next line segment. The LineString has length, but no area.

- MultiLineString: This is a one-dimensional object composed of multiple LineString objects. The LineString objects in a MultiLineString do not necessarily have to be connected to one another. The MultiLineString has no area, but it has an associated length, which is the sum of the lengths of all LineString objects in the MultiLineString.

- Polygon: This is a two-dimensional object defined by a sequence of connected points. The Polygon object must have a single exterior bounding ring, which defines the interior region of the Polygon object. In addition, the Polygon may have interior bounding rings, which exclude portions of the area inside the interior bounding ring from the Polygon's area. Polygon objects have a length, which is the length of the exterior bounding ring, and an area, which is the area defined by the exterior bounding ring minus the areas defined by any interior bounding rings.

- MultiPolygon: This is a collection of Polygon objects. Like the Polygon, the MultiPolygon has both length and area.

- GeometryCollection: This is the base class for the "multi" types (e.g. MultiPoint, MultiLine, and MultiPolygon). This class can be instantiated and can contain a collection of any spatial objects.

You can populate spatial data using Well-Known Text (WKT) strings or GML-formatted data. WKT strings are passed into the geometry and geography data types' STGeomFromText() static method and related static methods. Spatial data types can be populated from GML-formatted data with the GeomFromGml() static method. Listing 10-26 shows how to populate a spatial data type with a Polygon instance via a WKT-formatted string. The coordinates in the WKT Polygon are the borders of the state of Wyoming, chosen for its simplicity. The result of the SELECT in the SSMS spatial data pane is shown in Figure 10-19.

Listing 10-26. Representing Wyoming as a Geometry Object

```
DECLARE @Wyoming geometry;
SET @Wyoming = geometry::STGeomFromText ('POLYGON (
( -104.053108 41.698246, -104.054993 41.564247,
-104.053505 41.388107, -104.051201 41.003227,
-104.933968 40.994305, -105.278259 40.996365,
-106.202896 41.000111, -106.328545 41.001316,
-106.864838 40.998489, -107.303436 41.000168,
-107.918037 41.00341, -109.047638 40.998474,
-110.001457 40.997646, -110.062477 40.99794,
```

```
-111.050285 40.996635, -111.050911 41.25848,
-111.050323 41.578648, -111.047951 41.996265,
-111.046028 42.503323, -111.048447 43.019962,
-111.04673 43.284813, -111.045998 43.515606,
-111.049629 43.982632, -111.050789 44.473396,
-111.050842 44.664562, -111.05265 44.995766,
-110.428894 44.992348, -110.392006 44.998688,
-109.994789 45.002853, -109.798653 44.99958,
-108.624573 44.997643, -108.258568 45.00016,
-107.893715 44.999813, -106.258644 44.996174,
-106.020576 44.997227, -105.084465 44.999832,
-105.04126 45.001091, -104.059349 44.997349,
-104.058975 44.574368, -104.060547 44.181843,
-104.059242 44.145844, -104.05899 43.852928,
-104.057426 43.503738, -104.05867 43.47916,
-104.05571 43.003094, -104.055725 42.614704,
-104.053009 41.999851, -104.053108 41.698246) )', 0);

SELECT @Wyoming as Wyoming;
```

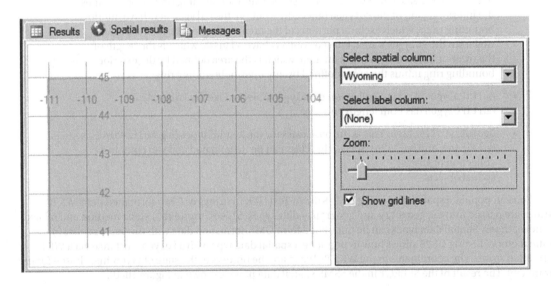

Figure 10-19. *The Wyoming Polygon*

Listing 10-26 demonstrates a couple of interesting items. The first point is that the coordinates are given in latitude-longitude order, not in (x, y).

(X, Y) OR (LATITUDE, LONGITUDE)?

Coordinates in spatial data are generally represented using (x, y) coordinate pairs. However, we often say "latitude-longitude" when we refer to coordinates. The problem is that latitude is the y axis, while longitude is the x axis. The Well-Known Text format we'll discuss later in this section represents spatial data using (x, y) coordinate pair ordering for the geometry and geography data types. But the GML syntax expresses coordinates the other way around, with latitude before longitude. You need to be aware of this difference when entering coordinates.

The second point is that the final coordinate pair, (-104.053108, 41.698246), is the same as the first coordinate pair. This is a requirement for Polygon objects.

You can populate a geography instance similarly using WKT or GML. Listing 10-27 populates a geography instance with the border coordinates for the state of Wyoming using GML. The result will be the same as shown previously in Figure 10-19.

Listing 10-27. Using GML to Represent Wyoming as a Geography Object

```
DECLARE @Wyoming geography;
SET @Wyoming = geography::GeomFromGml ('<Polygon
    xmlns="http://www.opengis.net/gml">
    <exterior>
        <LinearRing>
        <posList>
        41.698246  -104.053108  41.999851      -104.053009
        43.003094  -104.05571   43.503738      -104.057426
        44.145844  -104.059242  44.574368      -104.058975
        45.001091  -105.04126   44.997227      -106.020576
        44.999813  -107.893715  44.997643      -108.624573
        45.002853  -109.994789  44.992348      -110.428894
        44.664562  -111.050842  43.982632      -111.049629
        43.284813  -111.04673   42.503323      -111.046028
        41.578648  -111.050323  40.996635      -111.050285
        40.997646  -110.001457  41.00341       -107.918037
        40.998489  -106.864838  41.000111      -106.202896
        40.994305  -104.933968  41.388107      -104.053505
        41.698246  -104.053108
        </posList>
        </LinearRing>
    </exterior>
</Polygon>', 4269);
```

Like the geometry data type, the geography data type has some interesting features. The first thing to notice is that the coordinates are given in latitude-longitude order, because of the GML format. Another thing to notice is that in GML format, there are no comma separators between coordinate pairs. All coordinates are separated by whitespace characters. GML also requires you to declare the GML namespace http://www.opengis.net/gml.

The coordinate pairs in Listing 10-27 are also listed in reverse order from the geometry instance in Listing 10-26. This is required because the geography data type represents ellipsoidal spatial data. Ellipsoidal data in SQL Server has a couple of restrictions on it: an object must all fit in one hemisphere and it must be expressed with a counterclockwise orientation. These limitations do not apply to the geometry data type. These limitations are discussed further in the Hemisphere and Orientation sidebar in this section.

The final thing to notice is that when you create a geometry instance, you must specify a spatial reference identifier (SRID). The SRID used here is 4269, which is the GCS North American Datum 1983 (NAD 83). A datum is an associated ellipsoid model of Earth on which the coordinate data is based. We used SRID 4269 because the coordinates used in the example are borrowed from the US Census Bureau's TIGER/Line data, which is in turn based on NAD 83. As you can see, using the geography data type is slightly more involved than using the geometry data type, but it can provide more accurate results and additional functionality for Earth-based geographic information systems (GISs).

Hemisphere and Orientation

In SQL Server 2008, the geography data type required spatial objects to be contained in a single hemisphere—they couldn't cross the equator. That was mostly for performance reasons. Beginning in SQL Server 2012, you can create geography instances larger than a single hemisphere by using the new object type named FULLGLOBE.

You need also to specifiy the right ring orientation. So why is ring orientation so important, and what is the "right" ring orientation? To answer these questions, you have to ask yet another question: "What is the inside of a Polygon?" You might instinctively say that the inside of a Polygon is the smallest area enclosed by the coordinates you supply. But you could end up in a situation where your Polygon should be the larger area enclosed by your coordinates. If you created a border around the North Pole, for instance, is your Polygon the area within the border or is it the rest of the Earth minus the North Pole? Your answer to this question determines what the "inside" of the Polygon really is.

The next step is to tell SQL Server where the inside of the Polygon lies. SQL Server's geography instance makes you define your coordinates in counterclockwise order, so the inside of the Polygon is everything that falls on the left-hand side of the lines connecting the coordinates. In the following illustration, the image on the left side is an invalid orientation because the coordinates are defined in a clockwise order. The image on the right side is a valid orientation because its coordinates are defined in a counterclockwise order. If you follow the direction of the arrows on the image, you'll notice that the area on the left-hand side of the arrows is the area "inside" the Polygon. This eliminates any ambiguity from your Polygon definitions.

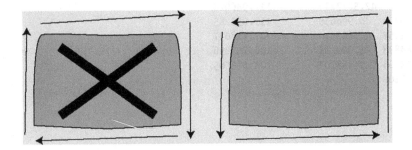

Keep these restrictions in mind if you decide to use the geography data type in addition to, or instead of, the geometry data type.

Polygon and MultiPolygon are two of the more interesting and complex spatial objects you can create. We like to use the state of Utah as a real-world example of a Polygon object for a couple of reasons. First, the exterior bounding ring for the state is very simple, composed of relatively straight lines. Second, the Great Salt Lake within the state can be used as a highly visible example of an interior bounding ring. Figure 10-20 shows the state of Utah.

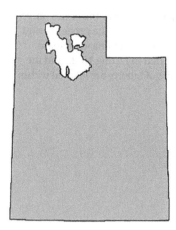

Figure 10-20. *The state of Utah with the Great*

The state of Michigan provides an excellent example of a MultiPolygon object. Michigan is composed of two distinct peninsulas, known as the Upper Peninsula and Lower Peninsula, respectively. The two peninsulas are separated by the Straits of Mackinac, which join Lake Michigan to Lake Huron. Figure 10-21 shows the Michigan `MultiPolygon`.

Figure 10-21. *Michigan as a MultiPolygon Salt Lake as an Interior Bounding Ring*

Michigan and the Great lakes

Michigan's two peninsulas are separated by the Straits of Mackinac, which is a five-mile-wide channel that joins two of the Great Lakes, Lake Michigan and Lake Huron. Although these two bodies of water are historically referred to as separate lakes, hydrologists consider them to be one contiguous body of water. Hydrology experts sometimes refer to the lakes as a single entity, Lake Michigan-Huron. On the other hand, it makes sense to consider the two lakes as separate from a political point of view, since Lake Michigan is wholly within the borders of the United States, while the border between the United States and Canada divides Lake Huron. For the purposes of this section, the most important fact is that the lakes separate Michigan into two peninsulas, making it a good example of a `MultiPolygon`.

Through the use of the spatial instance types, you can create spatial objects that cover the entire range from very simple to extremely complex. Once you've created spatial objects, you can use the geometry and geography data type methods on them or create spatial indexes on spatial data type columns to increase calculation efficiency. Listing 10-28 uses the geography data type instance created in Listing 10-22 and the STIntersects() method to report whether the town of Laramie and the Statue of Liberty are located within the borders of Wyoming. The results are shown in Figure 10-22.

Listing 10-28. Are the Statue of Liberty and Laramie in Wyoming?

```
DECLARE @Wyoming geography,
    @StatueOfLiberty geography,
    @Laramie geography;

SET @Wyoming = geography::GeomFromGml ('<Polygon
    xmlns="http://www.opengis.net/gml">
    <exterior>
        <LinearRing>
        <posList>
        41.698246  -104.053108  41.999851    -104.053009
        43.003094  -104.05571   43.503738    -104.057426
        44.145844  -104.059242  44.574368    -104.058975
        45.001091  -105.04126   44.997227    -106.020576
        44.999813  -107.893715  44.997643    -108.624573
        45.002853  -109.994789  44.992348    -110.428894
        44.664562  -111.050842  43.982632    -111.049629
        43.284813  -111.04673   42.503323    -111.046028
        41.578648  -111.050323  40.996635    -111.050285
        40.997646  -110.001457  41.00341     -107.918037
        40.998489  -106.864838  41.000111    -106.202896
        40.994305  -104.933968  41.388107    -104.053505
        41.698246  -104.053108
        </posList>
        </LinearRing>
    </exterior>
</Polygon>', 4269);

SET @StatueOfLiberty = geography::GeomFromGml('<Point
    xmlns="http://www.opengis.net/gml">
    <pos>
        40.689124 -74.044483
    </pos>
    </Point>', 4269);

SET @Laramie = geography::GeomFromGml('<Point
    xmlns="http://www.opengis.net/gml">
    <pos>
        41.312928 -105.587253
    </pos>
    </Point>', 4269);
```

```
SELECT 'Is the Statue of Liberty in Wyoming?',
    CASE @Wyoming.STIntersects(@StatueOfLiberty)
        WHEN O THEN 'No'
        ELSE 'Yes'
    END AS Answer
UNION
SELECT 'Is Laramie in Wyoming?',
    CASE @Wyoming.STIntersects(@Laramie)
        WHEN O THEN 'No'
        ELSE 'Yes'
    END;
```

	(No column name)	Answer
1	Is the Statue of Liberty in Wyoming?	No
2	Is Laramie in Wyoming?	Yes

Figure 10-22. *The Results of the STIntersection() Method Example*

SQL Server also allows you to create spatial indexes that optimize spatial data calculations. Spatial indexes are created by decomposing your spatial data into a b-tree-based grid hierarchy four levels deep. Each level represents a further subdivision of the cells above it in the hierarchy. Figure 10-23 shows a simple example of a decomposed spatial grid hierarchy.

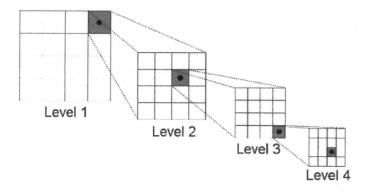

Figure 10-23. *Decomposing Space for Spatial Indexing*

The CREATE SPATIAL INDEX statement allows you to create spatial indexes on spatial data type columns. Listing 10-29 is an example of a CREATE SPATIAL INDEX statement.

Listing 10-29. Creating a Spatial Index

```
CREATE SPATIAL INDEX SIX_Location ON MyTable (SpatialColumn);
```

Spatial indexing is one of the biggest benefits of storing spatial data inside the database. As one astute developer pointed out, "Without spatial indexing, you may as well store your spatial data in flat files."

■ **Note** Pro Spatial with SQL Server 2012, by Alastair Aitchison (Apress, 2012), is a fully dedicated book about SQL Server Spatial, a feature much more complex that what we present here.

FILESTREAM Support

SQL Server is optimized for dealing with highly structured relational data, but SQL developers have long had to deal with heterogeneous unstructured data. The varbinary(max) LOB (Large Object) data type provides a useful method of storing arbitrary binary data directly in database tables; however, it still has some limitations, including
the following:

- There is a hard 2.1 GB limit on the size of binary data that can be stored in a varbinary(max) column, which can be an issue if the documents you need to store are larger.

- Storing and managing large varbinary(max) data in SQL Server can have a negative impact on performance, owing largely to the fact that the SQL Server engine must maintain proper locking and isolation levels to ensure data integrity in the database.

Many developers and administrators have come up with clever solutions to work around this problem. Most of these solutions are focused on storing LOB data as files in the file system and storing file paths pointing to those files in the database. This introduces additional complexities to the system since you must maintain the links between database entries and physical files in the file system. You also must manage LOB data stored in the file system using external tools, outside of the scope of database transactions. Finally, this type of solution can double the amount of work required to properly secure your data, since you must manage security in the database and separately in the file system.

SQL Server provides a third option: integrated FILESTREAM support. SQL Server can store FILESTREAM-enabled varbinary(max) data as files in the file system. SQL Server can manage the contents of the FILESTREAM containers on the file system for you and control access to the files, while the NT File System (NTFS) provides efficient file streaming and file system transaction support. This combination of SQL Server and NTFS functionality provides several advantages when dealing with LOB data, including increased efficiency, manageability, and concurrency. Microsoft provides some general guidelines for use of FILESTREAM over regular LOB data types, including the following:

- When the average size of your LOBs is greater than 1 MB

- When you have to store any LOBs that are larger than 2.1 GB

- When fast-read access is a priority

- When you want to access LOB data from middle-tier code

■ **Tip** For smaller and limited LOB data, storing the data directly in the database might make more sense than using FILESTREAM.

Enabling FILESTREAM Support

The first step to using FILESTREAM functionality in SQL Server is enabling it. You can enable FILESTREAM support through the SQL Server Configuration Manager. You can set FILESTREAM access in the SQL Server service Properties FILESTREAM page. Once you've enabled FILESTREAM support, you can set the level of access for the SQL Server instance with sp_configure and then restart the SQL Server service. Listing 10-30 enables FILESTREAM support on the SQL Server instance for the maximum allowable access.

Listing 10-30. Enabling FILESTREAM Support on the Server

```
EXEC sp_configure 'filestream access level', 2;
RECONFIGURE;
```

The configuration value defines the access level for FILESTREAM support. The levels supported are listed in Table 10-4.

Table 10-4. *FILESTREAM Access Levels*

Configuration Value	Description
0	Disabled (default)
1	Access via T-SQL only
2	Access via T-SQL and file system

You can use the query in Listing 10-31 to see the FILESTREAM configuration information at any time. Sample results from our local server are shown in Figure 10-24.

Listing 10-31. Viewing FILESTREAM Configuration Information

```
SELECT
    SERVERPROPERTY('ServerName') AS ServerName,
    SERVERPROPERTY('FilestreamSharename') AS ShareName,
    CASE SERVERPROPERTY('FilestreamEffectiveLevel')
        WHEN 0 THEN 'Disabled'
        WHEN 1 THEN 'T-SQL Access Only'
        WHEN 2 THEN 'Local T-SOL/File System Access Only'
        WHEN 3 THEN 'Local T-SOL/File System and Remote File System Access'
    END AS Effective_Level,
    CASE SERVERPROPERTY('FilestreamConfiguredLevel')
        WHEN 0 THEN 'Disabled'
        WHEN 1 THEN 'T-SQL Access Only'
        WHEN 2 THEN 'Local T-SOL/File System Access Only'
        WHEN 3 THEN 'Local T-SOL/File System and Remote File System Access'
    END AS Configured_Level;
```

	ServerName	ShareName	Effective_Level	Configured_Level
1	SQL2012	MSSQLSERVER	Local T-SOL/File System and Remote File System A...	Local T-SOL/File System and Remote File System A...

Figure 10-24. Viewing FILESTREAM Configuration Information

Creating FILESTREAM Filegroups

Once you've enabled FILESTREAM support on your SQL Server instance, you have to create an SQL Server filegroup with the CONTAINS FILESTREAM option. This filegroup is where SQL Server will store FILESTREAM LOB files. As AdventureWorks 2014 is shipped without a FILESTREAM filegroup, we need to add it manually. Listing 10-32 shows the final generated CREATE DATABASE statement as if we had created the database from scratch. The FILEGROUP clause of the statement that creates the FILESTREAM filegroup is shown in bold.

Listing 10-32. CREATE DATABASE for AdventureWorks Database

```
CREATE DATABASE [AdventureWorks]
 CONTAINMENT = NONE
 ON PRIMARY
( NAME = N'AdventureWorks2014_Data', FILENAME = N'C:\sqldata\MSSQL12.MSSQLSERVER\MSSQL\DATA\
AdventureWorks2014_Data.mdf', SIZE = 226304KB, MAXSIZE = UNLIMITED, FILEGROWTH = 16384KB ),
 FILEGROUP [FILESTREAM1] CONTAINS FILESTREAM  DEFAULT
( NAME = N'AdventureWordsFS', FILENAME = N'C:\sqldata\MSSQL12.MSSQLSERVER\MSSQL\DATA\
AdventureWordsFS', MAXSIZE = UNLIMITED)
 LOG ON
( NAME = N'AdventureWorks2014_Log', FILENAME = N'C:\sqldata\MSSQL12.MSSQLSERVER\MSSQL\DATA\
AdventureWorks2014_log.ldf', SIZE = 5696KB, MAXSIZE = UNLIMITED, FILEGROWTH = 10%);
```

To create this FILESTREAM filegroup on an already existing database, we used the ALTER DATABASE statement as shown in Listing 10-33.

Listing 10-33. Adding a FILESTREAM Filegroup to an Existing Database

```
ALTER DATABASE AdventureWorks
ADD FILEGROUP FILESTREAM1 CONTAINS FILESTREAM;
GO
ALTER DATABASE AdventureWorks
ADD FILE
(
NAME = N' AdventureWordsFS',
FILENAME = N' C:\sqldata\MSSQL12.MSSQLSERVER\MSSQL\DATA\AdventureWordsFS' )
TO FILEGROUP FILESTREAM1;
```

You can see that the file created is in fact not a file, but a directory where the files will be stored by SQL Server.

FILESTREAM-Enabling Tables

Once you've enabled FILESTREAM on the server instance and created a FILESTREAM filegroup, you're ready to create FILESTREAM-enabled tables. FILESTREAM storage is accessed by creating a varbinary(max) column in a table with the FILESTREAM attribute. The FILESTREAM-enabled table must also have a uniqueidentifier column with a ROWGUIDCOL attribute and a unique constraint on it. The Production.Document table in the AdventureWorks sample database is ready for FILESTREAM. In fact, its Document column was declared as a varbinary(max) with the FILESTREAM attribute in AdventureWorks 2008, but this dependency was removed in AdventureWorks 2012. Now, the Document column is still a varbinary(max), and the rowguid column is declared as a uniqueidentifier with the ROWGUIDCOL attribute. To convert it to a FILESTREAM-enabled table, we create a new table named Production.DocumentFS and import the lines from Production.Document into that new table. Let's see how it works in Listing 10-34. The Document and rowguid columns are shown in bold.

Listing 10-34. Production.Document FILESTREAM-Enabled Table

```
CREATE TABLE Production.DocumentFS (
    DocumentNode     hierarchyid NOT NULL PRIMARY KEY,
    DocumentLevel    AS (DocumentNode.GetLevel()),
    Title            nvarchar(50) NOT NULL,
    Owner            int NOT NULL,
    FolderFlag       bit NOT NULL,
    FileName         nvarchar(400) NOT NULL,
    FileExtension    nvarchar(8) NOT NULL,
    Revision         nchar(5) NOT NULL,
    ChangeNumber     int NOT NULL,
    Status           tinyint NOT NULL,
    DocumentSummary  nvarchar(max) NULL,
    Document         varbinary(max) FILESTREAM NULL,
    rowguid          uniqueidentifier ROWGUIDCOL NOT NULL UNIQUE,
    ModifiedDate     datetime NOT NULL
);
GO

INSERT INTO Production.DocumentFS
    (DocumentNode, Title, Owner, FolderFlag, FileName, FileExtension, Revision,
ChangeNumber, Status, DocumentSummary, Document, rowguid, ModifiedDate)
SELECT
    DocumentNode, Title, Owner, FolderFlag, FileName, FileExtension, Revision, ChangeNumber,
Status, DocumentSummary, Document, rowguid, ModifiedDate
FROM Production.Document;
```

When the table is created, we insert the content of Production.Document into it. Now, we can open Windows Explorer and go to the location of the FILESTREAM directory. The content of the directory is shown in Figure 10-25. The file names appear as a jumble of grouped digits that don't offer up much information about the LOB files' contents, because SQL Server manages the file names internally.

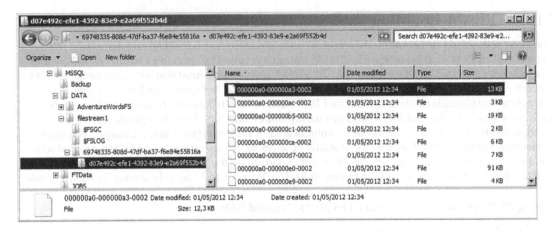

Figure 10-25. *LOB Files Stored in the FILESTREAM Filegroup*

■ **Caution** SQL Server also creates a file named `filestream.hdr`. This file is used by SQL Server to manage `FILESTREAM` data. Do not open or modify this file.

Accessing FILESTREAM Data

You can access and manipulate your `FILESTREAM`-enabled `varbinary(max)` columns using standard SQL Server `SELECT` queries and DML statements like `INSERT` and `DELETE`. Listing 10-35 demonstrates querying the `varbinary(max)` column of the `Production.DocumentFS` table. The results are shown in Figure 10-26.

Listing 10-35. Querying a FILESTREAM-Enabled Table

```
SELECT
    d.Title,
    d.Document.PathName() AS LOB_Path,
    d.Document AS LOB_Data
FROM Production.DocumentFS d
WHERE d.Document IS NOT NULL;
```

	Title	LOB_Path	LOB_Data
1	Introduction 1	\\SQL2012\MSSQLSERVER\v02-A60EC2F8-2B24-11DF-9CC...	0xD0CF11E0A1B11AE1000000000000000000000000000000...
2	Repair and Service Guidelines	\\SQL2012\MSSQLSERVER\v02-A60EC2F8-2B24-11DF-9CC...	0xD0CF11E0A1B11AE1000000000000000000000000000000...
3	Crank Arm and Tire Maintenance	\\SQL2012\MSSQLSERVER\v02-A60EC2F8-2B24-11DF-9CC...	0xD0CF11E0A1B11AE1000000000000000000000000000000...
4	Lubrication Maintenance	\\SQL2012\MSSQLSERVER\v02-A60EC2F8-2B24-11DF-9CC...	0xD0CF11E0A1B11AE1000000000000000000000000000000...
5	Front Reflector Bracket and Reflector Assembly 3	\\SQL2012\MSSQLSERVER\v02-A60EC2F8-2B24-11DF-9CC...	0xD0CF11E0A1B11AE1000000000000000000000000000000...
6	Front Reflector Bracket Installation	\\SQL2012\MSSQLSERVER\v02-A60EC2F8-2B24-11DF-9CC...	0xD0CF11E0A1B11AE1000000000000000000000000000000...
7	Installing Replacement Pedals	\\SQL2012\MSSQLSERVER\v02-A60EC2F8-2B24-11DF-9CC...	0xD0CF11E0A1B11AE1000000000000000000000000000000...
8	Seat Assembly	\\SQL2012\MSSQLSERVER\v02-A60EC2F8-2B24-11DF-9CC...	0xD0CF11E0A1B11AE1000000000000000000000000000000...
9	Training Wheels 2	\\SQL2012\MSSQLSERVER\v02-A60EC2F8-2B24-11DF-9CC...	0xD0CF11E0A1B11AE1000000000000000000000000000000...

Figure 10-26. *Results of Querying the FILESTREAM-enabled Table*

A property called PathName() is exposed on FILESTREAM-enabled varbinary(max) columns to retrieve the full path to the file containing the LOB data. The query in Listing 10-35 uses PathName() to retrieve the LOB path along with the LOB data. As you can see from this example, SQL Server abstracts away the NTFS interaction to a large degree, allowing you to query and manipulate FILESTREAM data as if it were relational data stored directly in the database.

■ **Tip**   In most cases, it's not a good idea to retrieve all LOB data from a FILESTREAM-enabled table in a single query as in this example. For large tables with large LOBs, this can cause severe performance problems and make client applications unresponsive. In this case, however, the LOB data being queried is actually very small in size, and there are few rows in the table.

SQL Server 2008, 2012 and 2014 provide support for the OpenSqlFilestream API for accessing and manipulating FILESTREAM data in client applications. A full description of the OpenSqlFilestream API is beyond the scope of this book, but Accelerated SQL Server 2008, by Rob Walters et al. (Apress, 2008), provides a description of the OpenSqlFilestream API with source code for a detailed client application.

FileTable Support

SQL Server 2012 improved greatly the FILESTREAM type by introducing filetables. As we have seen, to use FILESTREAM we need to manage the content only through SQL Server, by T-SQL or with the OpenSqlFilestream API. It is unfortunate, because we have access to a directory on our file system, which cannot be managed simply and publishes cryptic file names. In short, we have a great functionality that could be more flexible and user-friendly. Filetable brings that to the table. It makes the Windows filesystem namespace compatible with SQL Server tables. With it, you can create a table in SQL Server that merely reflects the content of a directory and its subdirectories, and you can manage its content at the file system level, out of SQL Server, with regular tools like the Windows Explorer, or by file I/O APIs in your client application. All changes made to the file system will be immediately reflected in the filetable. In fact, the file system as we see it in the share does not exist per se; it is a kind of mirage created by SQL Server. Files or directories will be internally handled by SQL Server and filestream objects, and if you try to access the real directory with Windows Explorer, it will be as jumbled as any other FILESTREAM directory.

To be able to use filetables, you first need to have activated the filestream support at the instance level as we have seen in the previous section. The filestream_access_level option needs to be set to 2 to accept file I/O streaming access. In addition, the FILESTREAM property of the database must be set to accept non-transacted access. We will see how to do that in our example. We have downloaded a zip package from the http://openclipart.org/ web site, containing the entire collection of free cliparts. It represents almost 27,000 image files at this time. We will add them in a filetable. First, in Listing 10-36, we create a dedicated database with a FILESTREAM filegroup that will store our filetable. The FILESTREAM filegroup creation is shown in bold.

Listing 10-36. Creating a Database with a FILESTREAM Filegroup

```
CREATE DATABASE cliparts
CONTAINMENT = NONE
ON PRIMARY
( NAME = N'cliparts', FILENAME = N'C:\sqldata\MSSQL12.MSSQLSERVER\MSSQL\DATA\cliparts.mdf',
SIZE = 5120KB, FILEGROWTH = 1024KB ),
FILEGROUP [filestreamFG1] CONTAINS FILESTREAM
( NAME = N'filestream1', FILENAME = N'C:\sqldata\MSSQL12.MSSQLSERVER\MSSQL\DATA\filestream1' )
```

```
LOG ON
( NAME = N'cliparts_log', FILENAME = N'C:\sqldata\MSSQL12.MSSQLSERVER\MSSQL\DATA\cliparts_
log.ldf', SIZE = 1024KB , FILEGROWTH = 10%);
GO

ALTER DATABASE [cliparts] SET FILESTREAM( NON_TRANSACTED_ACCESS = FULL,
DIRECTORY_NAME = N'cliparts' );
```

■ **Note**   As filetables are stored in a `FILESTREAM` filegroup, filetables are included in database backups, unless you perform filegroup backups and you exclude the `FILESTREAM` filegroup.

In the last line of Listing 10-36, we set the filestream option to `NON_TRANSACTED_ACCESS = FULL`, which will ensure that files will be writable from the share outside of SQL Server. We also specify the directory name `'cliparts'`. It will be shown as a sub-directory in the `FILESTREAM` share.

The path where a filetable will be found on the share depends on the directory set at the database level, plus a sub-directory set when the table is created. In Listing 10-37, we create the filetable and a directory by inserting a line in the filetable.

Listing 10-37. Creating the Filetable

```
USE [cliparts];
GO

CREATE TABLE dbo.OpenClipartsLibrary AS FILETABLE
WITH
    (
        FILETABLE_DIRECTORY = 'OpenClipartsLibrary'
    );
GO

INSERT INTO dbo.OpenClipartsLibrary (name,is_directory)
VALUES ('import_20120501',1);
```

To create a filetable, we simple create a table `AS FILETABLE`. We specify with the option `FILETABLE_ DIRECTORY = 'OpenClipartsLibrary'` in which directory in the share the content of the table will be found.

■ **Note**   The directory of a filetable can be changed later with an `ALTER TABLE`.

As you can see, the table structure is not part of the `CREATE TABLE` statement. A filetable schema is fixed. We describe the filetable columns in Table 10-5.

Table 10-5. *Filetable Structure*

Column	Type	Description
stream_id	uniqueindetifier	The unique id of the line, being a file (a FILESTREAM document) or a directory. There is a UNIQUE constraint on it.
file_stream	varbinary(max)	The FILESTREAM column containing the file. NULL if it is a directory.
name	nvarchar(255)	Contains the name of the file or directory.
path_locator	hierarchyid	The position of the file or directory in the directory's hierarchy. The primary key of the table.
parent_path_locator	hierarchyid	The path_locator of the parent (ie., the directory containing the file or directory). A calculated column.
file_type	nvarchar(255)	The type (extension) of the file. A calculated column. NULL if it is a directory.
cached_file_size	bigint	The size of the file in bytes. A calculated column. NULL if it is a directory.
creation_time	datetimeoffset(7)	The date and time of creation. It is set by default at the current date and time when the object is created.
last_write_time	datetimeoffset(7)	The date and time of the last modification of the file or directory. Can be set manually like creation_time.
last_access_time	datetimeoffset(7)	The date and time when the file was last accessed. Can be set manually like creation_time.
is_directory	bit	1 if it is a directory. Calculated.
is_offline	bit	1 if the extended NTFS attribute Offline is set on the file. That would mean that the file is not physically in the directory but stored remotely.
is_hidden	bit	1 if the file has the hidden attribute.
is_readonly	bit	1 if the file has the read-only attribute.
is_archive	bit	1 if the file has the archive bit set.
is_system	bit	1 if the file has the system attribute.
is_temporary	bit	1 if the file has the temporary attribute.

To retrieve the filetables in our database, we can query the `sys.filetables` catalog view. We also can find them in SSMS Object Explorer, in the Tables | FileTables node, as shown in Figure 10-27.

307

Figure 10-27. *Filetables in SSMS*

You can see the share itself in Windows Explorer by going to Network, choosing your server name and entering the share name you set in the SQL Server Configuration Manager. You can also right-click on the filetable in the SSMS Object Explorer—as we see in Figure 10-27—and click on "Explore FileTable Directory," which will open a Windows Explorer window directly on the filetable directory. You need to access it through the network share, and not directly through the local directory, because the local directory will only show you FILESTREAM GUID names, while the network share, managed by SQL Server, will show you a virtual directory hierarchy that looks like a regular hierarchy of directores and files. This is logical anyway, as clients are not supposed to access directly local server directories. For our example, we did that and copied the full unzipped cliparts directory and subdirectories. When the copy was finished, a COUNT(*) from dbo.OpenClipartsLibrary returned 27,890 lines.

To manage files and directories, you can do it by issuing T-SQL statements against the filetable, directly in the share with Windows tools, or programmatically with Windows I/O APIs. As an example of how to do it also by T-SQL, Listing 10-38 creates a new directory under the OpenClipartsLibrary root directory.

Listing 10-38. Inserting a Directory in the Filetable

```
INSERT INTO dbo.OpenClipartsLibrary (name, is_directory)
VALUES ('directory01',1);
```

Setting the is_directory column to 1 is all you have to do to create a directory. You can also modifiy the file or directory properties by Windows I/O APIs or by T-SQL queries against the table. In Listing 10-39, we insert a subdirectory or the newly created directory01 and set a creation date as different from the current date and time.

Listing 10-39. Inserting a Subdirectory

```
INSERT INTO dbo.OpenClipartsLibrary
    (name, is_directory, creation_time, path_locator)
SELECT
    'directory02',1, dateadd(year, -1, sysdatetime()), path_locator.GetDescendant(NULL, NULL)
FROM dbo.OpenClipartsLibrary
WHERE name = 'directory01'
AND is_directory = 1
AND parent_path_locator IS NULL;
```

The code in Listing 10-39 creates a directory named directory02 as a subdirectory of directory01 by setting the path_locator of the created directory with the GetDescendant() hierarchyId method of the directory01 path_locator column. GetDescendant(NULL, NULL) returns the least descendant node of the current hierarchyId value. To be sure that directory01 is the one we created at the root level, we check that its parent_path_locator is NULL. We also set manually the creation_date to be one year ago.

In Figure 10-28, we verify with Windows Explorer that the directory was effectively created. Once again, you need to do it through the network share.

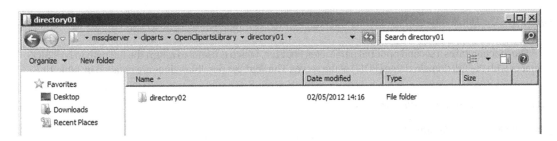

Figure 10-28. *The Newly Created Directory02 Directory*

■ **Note**   You cannot change a file to be a directory or vice versa. A check constraint on the filetable enforces that is_directory cannot be set to 1 when the file_stream column is not NULL.

Whenever you add, move or delete a file on the share, or by T-SQL statements against the filetable, it will be immediately reflected at both places. SQL Server intercepts all I/O operations on the share and converts them into DML actions on the filetable. File system rules like name limitations are enforced by constraints on the filetable, and trying to create invalid files or folders (with names containing / ? < > \ : * | ") in the filetable will result in a constraint violation.

There is however an important difference between managing the filetable content by T-SQL or at the Windows level. The DML statements against a filetable can be part of a transaction and rolled back, while creating, modifying, moving, or deleting files and folders by the means of the Windows I/O APIs cannot be part of a transaction. That's the reason why we enabled non_transacted_access support in our database. If you want to enable transactional modification of a file in a filetable outside of T-SQL context, you can use the OpenSqlFileStream API in your client code, which we discussed previously.

Filetable Functions

You can use dedicated functions, FILESTREAM related functions, and hierarchyid functions to manipulate files and folders in a filetable.

The FileTableRootPath() function returns the database share directory if called without argument, or the filetable share directory if called with the name of a filetable provided in a nvarchar argument, as shown in Listing 10-40. The results are shown in Figure 10-29.

Listing 10-40. Using FileTableRootPath()

```
USE cliparts;

SELECT FileTableRootPath();
SELECT FileTableRootPath('dbo.OpenClipartsLibrary');
```

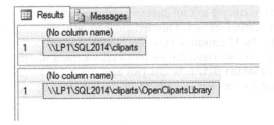

Figure 10-29. The Results of FileTableRootPath()

The function takes a second optional parameter, @option, which is useful to return the full path in NETBIOS format or with the full domain name (FDN) of the server. The @option possible values are detailed in Table 10-6.

Table 10-6. FileTableRootPath @options

@option value	Description
0	Returns the path in NETBIOS format; this is the default value. A NETBIOS computer name has a maximum of 16 characters in uppercase.
1	Returns the path without conversion.
2	Returns the path with the full domain name (FDN) of the machine.

To get the path of a specific file or folder in the filetable, the GetFileNamespacePath() function comes in handy. It is called as a method of the file_stream column, and takes two optional parameters, the first, @is_full_path, allows the path returned to be relative (0) or absolute (1). Calling GetFileNamespacePath(1) will produce full paths and saves you from concatenating the result of FileTableRootPath() with the relative path. The second option, @option, has the same values as the @option parameter of the FileTableRootPath() function. We demonstrate the usage of GetFileNamespacePath() in Listing 10-41.

Listing 10-41. Using GetFileNamespacePath(),

```
SELECT file_stream.GetFileNamespacePath(1) as path
FROM dbo.OpenClipartsLibrary
WHERE is_directory = 1
ORDER BY path_locator.GetLevel(), path;
```

The statement in Listing 10-41 returns all the directories of absolute paths ordered by their level in the directories' hierarchy and their name. The GetLevel() hierarchyid function applied to the path_locator column allows you to return the current level of the item in the file system relative to the filetable root.

As we can see, hierarchyid functions are interesting ways to move through the hierarchy. An example is given in Listing 10-42 that returns a directory and the name of its parent directory. A partial result is shown in Figure 10-30.

Listing 10-42. Using hierarchyid Functions

```
SELECT l1.name, l1.path_locator.GetLevel(), l2.name as parent_directory
FROM dbo.OpenClipartsLibrary l1
JOIN dbo.OpenClipartsLibrary l2 ON l1.path_locator.GetAncestor(1) = l2.path_locator
WHERE l1.is_directory = 1;
```

	name	Level	parent_directory
1	_Tyizael_	2	import_20120501
2	00lnkscape	2	import_20120501
3	1in9ui5t	2	import_20120501
4	43ad5web	2	import_20120501
5	a_sanyal59	2	import_20120501
6	aaha	2	import_20120501
7	zeratul	2	import_20120501
8	zerothis	2	import_20120501
9	zesarvictoria	2	import_20120501
10	zlatkodesign	2	import_20120501
11	Ztyx	2	import_20120501
12	yyycatch	2	import_20120501

Figure 10-30. *The Results of Using hierarchyid Functions*

By using the GetAncestor() hierarchyid function on the path_locator in the JOIN clause, we retrieve the parent path_locator and display its name. An easier way to do that is to use directly the parent_path_locator computed column that maintains a foreign key relationship with the path_locator column in the same table. The query in Listing 10-43 returns exactly the same result as the query in Listing 10-42.

Listing 10-43. Using Parent_path_locator Column

```
SELECT l1.name, l1.path_locator.GetLevel(), l2.name as parent_directory
FROM dbo.OpenClipartsLibrary l1
JOIN dbo.OpenClipartsLibrary l2 ON l1.parent_path_locator = l2.path_locator
WHERE l1.is_directory = 1;
```

Thanks to the recursive relationship between parent_path_locator and path_locator, we can travel down the directory's path with a recursive Common Table Expression (CTE), as follows in Listing 10-44.

Listing 10-44. Using a CTE to Travel Down the Directories' Hierarchy

```
;WITH mycte AS (
    SELECT name, path_locator.GetLevel() as Level, path_locator
    FROM dbo.OpenClipartsLibrary
    WHERE name = 'Yason'
    AND is_directory = 1

    UNION ALL

    SELECT l1.name, l1.path_locator.GetLevel() as Level, l1.path_locator
    FROM dbo.OpenClipartsLibrary l1
    JOIN mycte l2 ON l1.parent_path_locator = l2.path_locator
    WHERE l1.is_directory = 1
)
SELECT name, Level
FROM mycte
ORDER BY level, name;
```

Of course, as the path_locator column is a hierarchyid, we might as well express it as in Listing 10-45.

Listing 10-45. Using hierarchyid Functions to Travel Down the Directory's Hierarchy

```
SELECT l1.name, l1.path_locator.GetLevel() as Level
FROM dbo.OpenClipartsLibrary l1
JOIN dbo.OpenClipartsLibrary l2 ON l1.path_locator.IsDescendantOf(l2.path_locator) = 1 OR
l1.path_locator = l2.path_locator
WHERE l1.is_directory = 1
AND l2.is_directory = 1
AND l2.name = 'Yason'
ORDER BY level, name;
```

In Listing 10-45, we use the IsDescendantOf() function to retrieve all descendent directories of the directory named Yason. We have copied a few directories in Yason, and the queries in Listings 10-44 and 10-45 return exactly the same result shown in Figure 10-31.

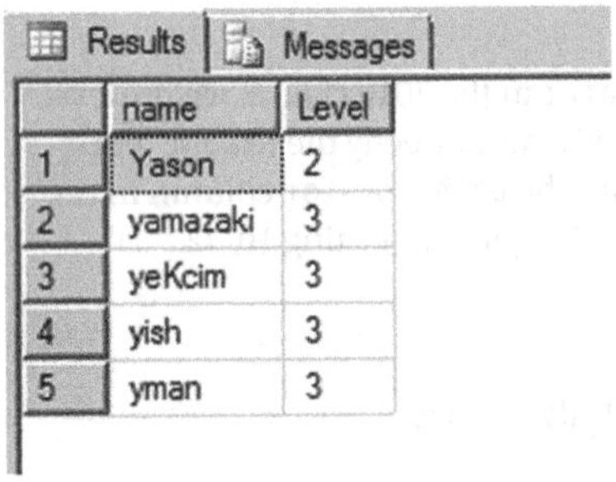

	name	Level
1	Yason	2
2	yamazaki	3
3	yeKcim	3
4	yish	3
5	yman	3

Figure 10-31. *The Results of the Queries in Listings 10-44 and 10-45*

Finally, the GetPathLocator() function returns a path_locator value for a file system full path. The example in Listing 10-46 retrieves the path_locator of the Yason directory, and uses it to find the matching line in the OpenClipartsLibrary table. The result is shown in Figure 10-32.

Listing 10-46. Using the GetPathLocator() function.

```
DECLARE @path_locator hierarchyid

SET @path_locator = GetPathLocator('\\Sql2012\mssqlserver\cliparts\OpenClipartsLibrary\
import_20120501\Yason');

SELECT *
FROM dbo.OpenClipartsLibrary
WHERE path_locator = @path_locator;
```

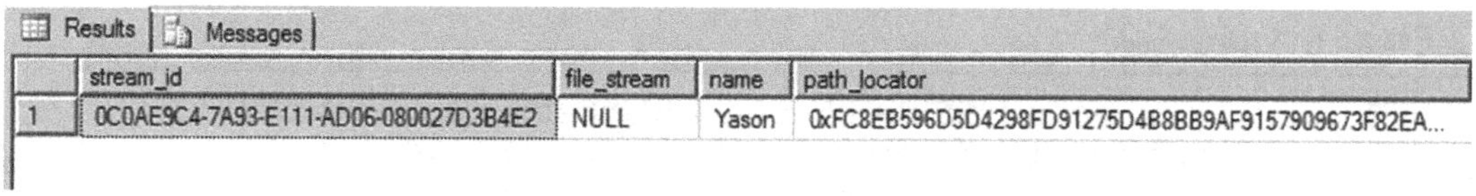

	stream_id	file_stream	name	path_locator
1	0C0AE9C4-7A93-E111-AD06-080027D3B4E2	NULL	Yason	0xFC8EB596D5D4298FD91275D4B8BB9AF9157909673F82EA...

Figure 10-32. The Line Found Using the GetPathLocator() Function

Triggers on Filetables

Filetables can have triggers like any other tables. Because making changes in the filetable share at the Windows level results in SQL Server calls behind the scene, a trigger will also receive these events.

■ **Note** But replication and related features (including transactional replication, merge replication, change data capture, and change tracking) are not supported with FileTables. You can see a FileTable Compatibility list with SQL Server features at this address: http://msdn.microsoft.com/en-us/library/gg492086.aspx.

We will demonstrate that with the audit table and the trigger created in Listing 10-47.

Listing 10-47. Creating an Audit Table and a Trigger on the OpenClipartsLibrary Table

```
CREATE TABLE dbo.cliparts_log (
    path nvarchar(4000) not null,
    deletion_date datetime2(0),
    deletion_user sysname,
    is_directory bit
)
GO

CREATE TRIGGER OpenClipartsLibrary_logTrigger
ON [dbo].[OpenClipartsLibrary]
AFTER DELETE
AS BEGIN
    IF @@ROWCOUNT = 0 RETURN;
    SET NOCOUNT ON;

    INSERT INTO dbo.cliparts_log (path, deletion_date, deletion_user, is_directory)
    SELECT name, SYSDATETIME(), SUSER_SNAME(),is_directory
    FROM deleted
END;
```

First, we create an audit table named cliparts_log. We want to keep track of file and directory deletions. We want to keep the date and time of deletion and name of the account that deleted the item. To record deletion into the table, we create a trigger named OpenClipartsLibrary_logTrigger that will fire for every DELETE statement against the OpenClipartsLibrary table.

To test it, we go to the filetable share with Windows Explorer and delete the \\Sql2014\mssqlserver\ cliparts\OpenClipartsLibrary\import_20140501\acspike directory. It contains two files. What gets written in the table is shown in Figure 10-33.

	path	deletion_date	deletion_user	is_directory
1	acspike_male_user_icon.png	2012-05-02 17:32:25	SQL2012\Administrator	0
2	acspike_male_user_icon.svg	2012-05-02 17:32:25	SQL2012\Administrator	0
3	acspike	2012-05-02 17:32:25	SQL2012\Administrator	1

Figure 10-33. The Content of the Cliparts_log Table after the Directory's Deletion

Summary

In this chapter, we first discussed some details to know about basic data types. Mastering how basic data types work allows you to understand the impact they have on the storage, and therefore on the performance, of your database. For instance, the nvarchar data type stores UNICODE values and consumes twice the space of the same varchar content. If used lightly, it can blow up the size of your database file. The varchar(max) and varbinary(max) types replace the legacy text and image data types. They allow an easy and more performant handling on Large Objects (LOB) inside the database. We then spent some time on the date and time data types. They have been improved in SQL Server 2008 with new types that are more precise and compact.

We also covered more advanced data types, like uniqueidentifier, which stored a 16-byte globally unique identifier, and hierarchyid, a .NET-based data type that can be used in a hierarchical table to represent a tree structure, as well as the spatial geometry and geography data types.

Finally, we explored the FILESTREAM type. With FILESTREAM, you can keep binary documents inside a database more efficiently. Through SQL Server, the document will be stored in the NTFS file system and can be retrieved directly with I/O APIs. Transactional coherence is maintained on the files as if they were inside the database file. The new filetable feature improves upon FILESTREAM by offering special database tables storing FILESTREAM documents and folder definitions that can be accessed simply on the filesystem with a network share managed by SQL Server.

EXERCISES

1. [True/False] Storing character strings with European language accents (é,à, ö, for instance) requires you to use a UNICODE encoding.

2. [Choose all that apply] Which of the following LOB data types are deprecated?

   a. image

   b. varchar(max)

   c. text

   d. ntext

   e. All of the above

3. [True/False] The new `date` data type stores time offset information.

4. What model does the `hierarchyid` data type use to represent hierarchical data in the database?

5. [Choose one] Which of the following is true of `Polygon` spatial objects when created in `geography` data type instances?

    f. They must have a clockwise orientation.

    g. They must have a counterclockwise orientation.

    h. Orientation does not matter.

    i. They cannot cross up to two hemispheres.

6. [Choose one] Which of the following functions adjusts a given `datetimeoffset` value to another specified time offset?

    j. TODATETIMEOFFSET

    k. SWITCHOFFSET

    l. CHANGEOFFSET

    m. CALCULATEOFFSET

7. [True/False] The `FILESTREAM` functionality in SQL Server 2014 uses NTFS to provide streaming LOB data support.

8. What is the name of the filetable column that allows you to retrieve the path of the file or directory on the filetable network share?

3. (True/False) The new date/time data type stores time offset information.

4. What model does the hierarchyid data type use to represent hierarchical data in the database?

5. (Choose one) Which of the following is true of polygon spatial objects when creating a geography data type instance?

    f. They must have a clockwise orientation.

    g. They must have a counterclockwise orientation.

    h. Orientation does not matter.

    i. They cannot cross up to two hemispheres.

6. (Yes/No) Which of the following functions returns a given date/time value to another specified date offset?

    TODATETIMEOFFSET

    SWITCHOFFSET

    SYSDATETIME

    CAST OR CONVERT TO

7. (True/False) The FILESTREAM functionality in SQL Server 2014 uses NTFS to provide streaming LOB data support.

8. What is the name of the filetable column that allows you to retrieve the path of the file or directory of the file in a FileTable object's share?

■ ■ ■

CHAPTER 11

Full-Text Search

Full-text search (FTS) is a powerful SQL Server feature allowing for advanced searches using multiple languages to find information in documents as well as document properties. FTS is tightly integrated with SQL Server 2014 and can be easily managed with SQL Server Management Studio (SSMS) and monitored with standard dynamic management views. FTS broadens the scope of what is thought of as a T-SQL search by providing meaningful results from sometimes seemingly unstructured textual data. SQL Server 2012 introduced statistical semantics which allow for searching on document meaning as opposed to simply searching content. Based on word distributions and other factors, statistical semantics allows you to find documents with similar contents.

FTS Architecture

As mentioned earlier, the FTS architecture is tightly integrated with the SQL Server database engine. In fact, FTS consists of two main components: the sqlserver process (sqlserver.exe) and the filter daemon host (fdhost.exe). The filter daemon is responsible for retrieving the text data from the tables and applying word breaks as well as determining the type of text is being retrieved. The filter daemon host applies different rules based on whether the document is a Word document, an Excel file, or even XML. Information is passed between the SQL Server process and the filter daemon host. Because the fdhost process has the responsibility to directly access and filter the data, the process requires a separate security account. This keeps the entire FTS process much more secure than in previous implementations.

The SQL Server process is primarily responsible for maintaining full-text indexes, controlling query optimization, and maintaining the stoplist and theasaures objects. A stoplist is a list of non-essentials words which should be ignored in most linguistic searches. A thesaurus is something you fill out in order to extend the reach of searches to find matches that FTS may not have been able to suggest on its own. Figure 11-1 shows how these architectural components are put to together.

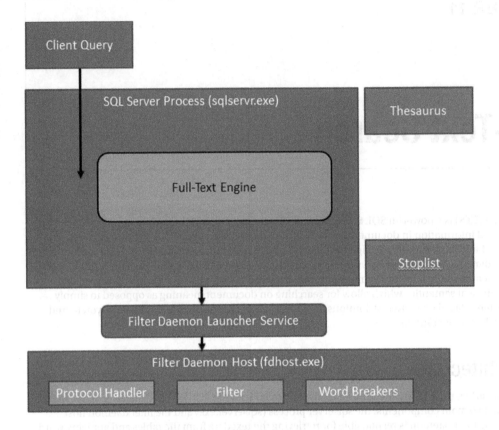

Figure 11-1. *FTS architecture (simplified)*

Here is a quick summary of some of the beneficial features of FTS:

- The full-text engine is hosted in the SQL Server process, eliminating much of the overhead associated with interservice communications.

- Integration with the SQL Server process to better predict query performance through the use of new query operators.

- Full-text indexes are maintained by the SQL Server process for better optimization.

- Ability to create customized stoplists of words to ignore during FTS, and the ability to create a thesaurus for more efficient and accurate searching.

- Dynamic management views and functions that provide greater transparency in understanding how FTS queries are processed and executed.

Creating Full-Text Catalogs and Indexes

The first step to take advantage of SQL Server FTS is to create full-text catalogs and full-text indexes. A full-text catalog can contain one or more full-text indexes, and each full-text index can only be assigned to one full-text catalog. You can create full-text catalogs and full-text indexes in SSMS using GUI (graphical user interface) wizards or T-SQL statements.

Creating Full-Text Catalogs

You can access the GUI full-text catalog wizard by right-clicking Full Text Catalogs in the SSMS Object Explorer. The New Full-Text Catalog option on the pop-up context menu starts the wizard (see Figure 11-2).

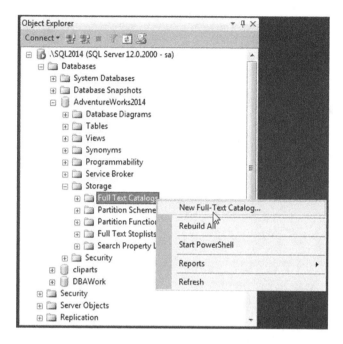

Figure 11-2. *New Full-Text Catalog Context Menu Option*

After selecting New Full-Text Catalog, SSMS presents the wizard's New Full-Text Catalog window. This window allows you to define the name of your full-text catalog, the full-text catalog's owner, an accent sensitivity setting, and whether or not this full-text catalog is designated as the default for a database. The New Full-Text Catalog window is shown in Figure 11-3.

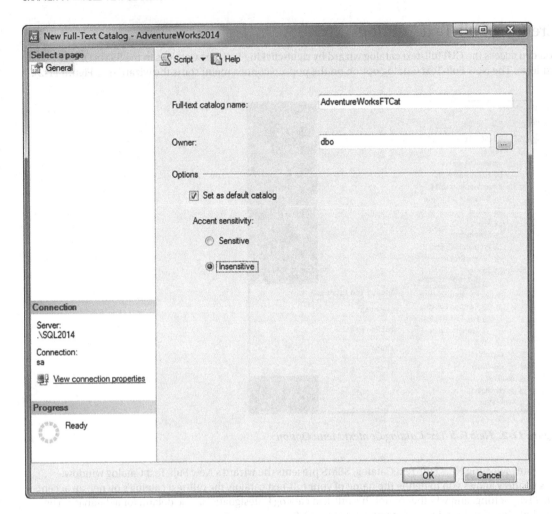

Figure 11-3. *New Full-Text Catalog Window*

For this sample full-text catalog, we chose the following options:

The full-text catalog is named AdventureWorksFTCat, and dbo is designated as the owner.

The first created full-text catalog is designated the default full-text catalog for the database. When a new full-text index is created you will have a choice to create it in the default catalog or in any additional non-default catalogs.

The accent sensitivity is set to Insensitive, meaning that words with accent marks are treated as equivalent to those without accent marks (e.g., for search purposes, resumé is the same as resume).

You can also create and manage full-text catalogs using T-SQL statements. Listing 11-1 shows how to create the same full-text catalog that we created previously in this section with the SSMS wizard.

Listing 11-1. Creating a Full-Text Catalog with T-SQL

```
CREATE FULLTEXT CATALOG AdventureWorksFTCat
  WITH ACCENT_SENSITIVITY = OFF
  AS DEFAULT
  AUTHORIZATION dbo;
```

Once you've created your full-text catalog, the next step is to build full-text indexes. We describe full-text index creation in the next section. Maximum performance full-text catalogs, particularly those you anticipate will become very large, should be created on filegroups that are located on their own physical drives. This is also useful for administrative functions such as performing filegroup backups and restores independent of data and log files.

Creating Full-Text Indexes

As with full-text catalogs, you have two options for creating full-text indexes—you can use the GUI wizard in SSMS, or you can use T-SQL statements. Once you've created a full-text catalog, as described in the previous section, it's time to define your full-text indexes. Begin by right-clicking a table; the example in Figure 11-4 uses the Production.ProductModel table, in the SSMS Object Explorer to pull up the table context menu. From the context menu, choose the Full-Text Index ➤ Define Full-Text Index option, shown in Figure 11-4.

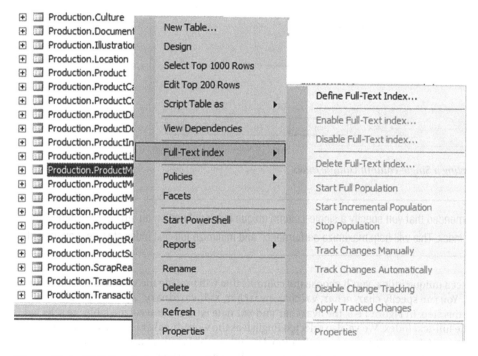

Figure 11-4. *"Full-Text Index" Context Menu*

The full-text index wizard shows a splash screen the first time you access it. You can choose to turn off the splash screen or just ignore it. On the next screen, shown in Figure 11-5, the wizard allows you to select a single-column unique index on the table. Every full-text index requires a single-column unique index that allows the full-text index to reference individual rows in the table. If you don't have a single-column unique index defined on the table you're trying to create a full-text index on, the wizard will display an error message as soon as you try to run it. In this example, we've chosen to use the table's integer primary key for the full-text index.

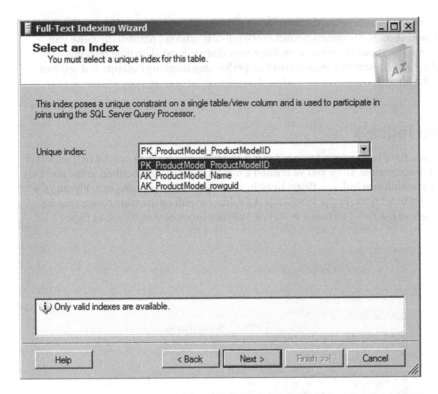

Figure 11-5. Selecting a Single-column Unique Index

■ **Tip** It's recommended that you specify a single-column unique index defined on an `integer` column when creating a full-text index. This will help maximize performance and minimize full-text index storage requirements.

After you select a unique index, you'll choose the columns that will provide the searchable content for the full-text index. You can specify char, nchar, varchar, nvarchar, xml, varbinary, varbinary(max), and image columns in this step. In Figure 11-6, the nvarchar and xml data type columns of the table are selected to participate in the full-text index. We've also selected English as the word-breaker language for each of these columns. The word-breaker language specification determines the language used for word-breaking and stemming. SQL Server 2014 currently recognizes over 50 different languages.

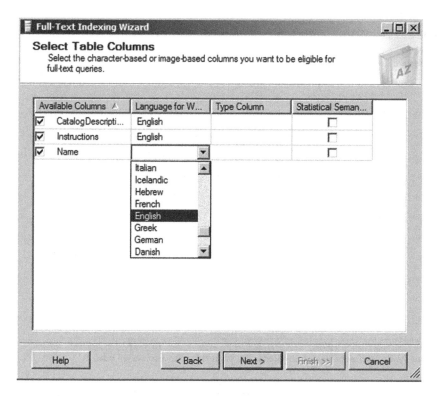

Figure 11-6. *Selecting Columns to Participate in Full-text Searches*

■ **Note** The type column is the name of a column indicating the document type (e.g., Microsoft Word, Excel, PowerPoint, Adobe PDF, and others) when you full-text index documents stored in `varbinary(max)` or `image` columns. Be aware that some document types require installation and configuration of additional IFilter components. More information about full-text and the new filetable feature is available on Microsoft TechNet at `http://social.technet.microsoft.com/wiki/contents/articles/9809.store-and-index-documents-in-sql-server-2012-an-end-to-end-walkthrough.aspx`.

After you've selected the columns that will participate in full-text searches against a table, you must select the change-tracking option. Change tracking determines whether SQL Server maintains a change log for the full-text indexed columns, and how the log is used to update the full-text index. Figure 11-7 shows the change-tracking options available through the wizard.

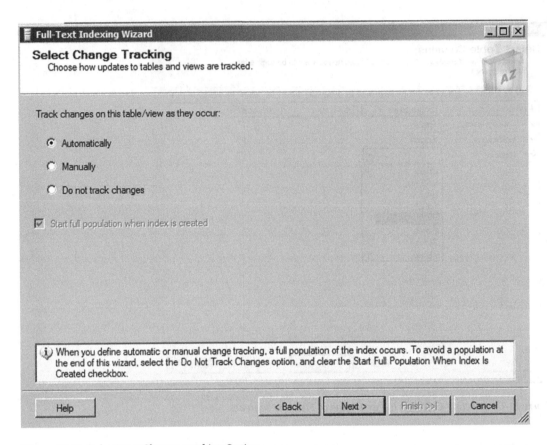

Figure 11-7. *Selecting a Change-tracking Option*

The change-tracking options available through the wizard include the following:

- Automatically: SQL Server updates the full-text index automatically when data is modified in the columns that participate in the full-text index. This is the default option.

- Manually: The change-tracking log is either used to update the full-text index via SQL Agent on a scheduled basis, or through manual intervention. This option is useful when automatic full-text index updates could slow down your server during business hours.

- Do not track changes: SQL Server does not track changes. Updating the full-text index requires you to issue an ALTER FULLTEXT INDEX statement with the START FULL or INCREMENTAL POPULATION clause to populate the entire full-text index.

■ **Tip** Keep in mind that automatic updates to the full-text index are not necessarily immediate updates. When automatic change tracking is specified, there may be some lag time between changes in the table data and updates to the full-text index.

The next step in the wizard allows you to assign your full-text index to a full-text catalog. You can choose a preexisting full-text catalog, like the AdventureWorksFTCat shown in Figure 11-8, or you can create a new full-text catalog. You can also choose a filegroup and full-text stoplist for the full-text index in this step.

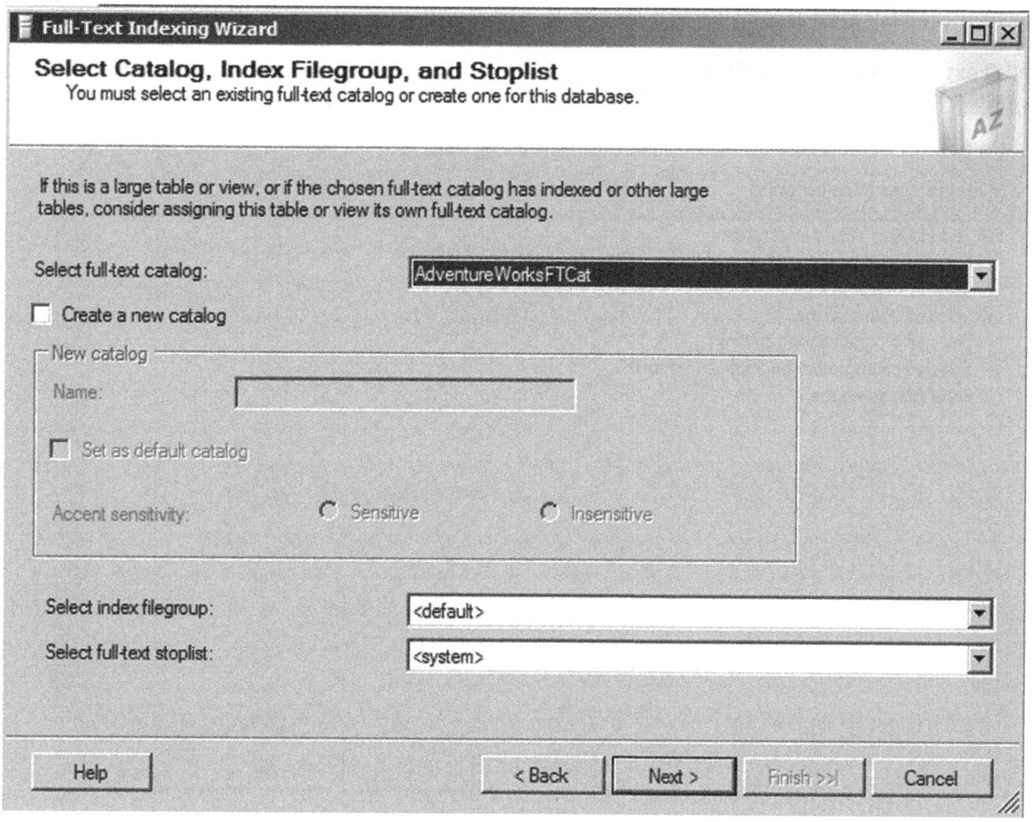

Figure 11-8. *Assigning a Full-text Index to a Catalog*

The final steps of the wizard allow you to create a full-text index population schedule and review your previous wizard selections. Since automatic population is used in the example, no schedule is necessary.

■ **Note**   It is possible you may receive an error on the population schedule screen when using SQL Server 2014 Express Advanced Services. This might be due to a bug in the application. You can ignore the error and continue. Express Advanced Services does support population schedules so you can avoid the error by manually creating the schedule and bypassing the GUI. It also may be possible to create the schedule through the GUI later by selecting the index properties. For more, go to http://connect.microsoft.com/SQLServer/feedback/ details/740181/management-studio-does-not-fully-manage-full-text-in-sql-server-express.

In the review window of the wizard, shown in Figure 11-9, you can look at the choices you've made in each step of the wizard and go back to previous steps to make changes if necessary. Once you click the Finish button, the full-text index is created in your database.

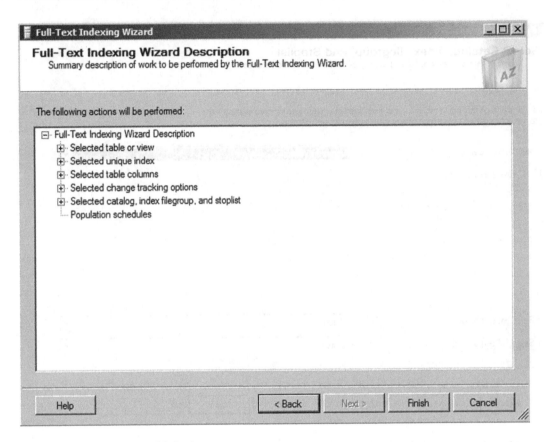

Figure 11-9. Review Wizard Selections

The SSMS full-text index wizard is very thorough, but you can also create and manage full-text indexes using T-SQL statements. Listing 11-2 shows the T-SQL statements required to create and enable a full-text index with the same options previously selected in the SSMS wizard example.

Listing 11-2. Creating a Full-Text Index with T-SQL Statements

```
CREATE FULLTEXT INDEX
ON Production.ProductModel
(
  CatalogDescription LANGUAGE English,
  Instructions LANGUAGE English,
  Name LANGUAGE English
  )
```

```
KEY INDEX PK_ProductModel_ProductModelID
ON
(
  AdventureWorksFTCat
)
WITH
(
CHANGE_TRACKING AUTO
);
GO

ALTER FULLTEXT INDEX
ON Production.ProductModel ENABLE;
GO
```

The CREATE FULLTEXT INDEX statement builds the full-text index on the Production.ProductModel table with the specified options. In this example, the CatalogDescription, Instructions, and Name columns are all participating in the full-text index. The LANGUAGE clause specifies that the English language word breaker will be used to index the columns. A word breaker is a naturally occurring break between words based on a language's lexicon. Setting the word breaker language to English helps FTS understand how the sentences are structured in order to better search on individual words. The KEY INDEX clause specifies the primary key of the table, PK_ProductModel_ProductModelID, as the single-column unique index for the table. Finally, the CHANGE TRACKING AUTO option turns on automatic change tracking for the full-text index.

The ALTER FULLTEXT INDEX statement in the listing enables the full-text index and starts a full population. ALTER FULLTEXT INDEX is a flexible statement that can be used to add columns to, or remove columns from, a full-text index. You can also use it to enable or disable a full-text index, set the change-tracking options, start or stop a full-text index population, or change full-text index stoplist settings.

■ **Note** Stoplists are lists of words that are considered unimportant for purposes of FTS. These words are known as stopwords. Stopwords are language dependent, with the English system stoplist containing words like a, an, and, and the (and many others). SQL Server 2014 provides a system stoplist and allows you to create your own custom stoplists. We will discuss stoplists later in this chapter.

Full-Text Querying

After you create a full-text catalog and a full-text index, you can take advantage of FTS with SQL Server's FTS predicates and functions. SQL Server provides four ways to query a full-text index. The FREETEXT and CONTAINS predicates retrieve rows from a table that match a given FTS criteria, in much the same way that the EXISTS predicate returns rows that meet given criteria. The FREETEXTTABLE and CONTAINSTABLE functions return rowsets with two columns: a key column, which is a row identifier (the unique index value specified when the full-text index was created) and a rank column, which is a relevance rating.

The FREETEXT Predicate

The FREETEXT predicate offers the simplest method of using FTS to search character-based columns of a full-text index. FREETEXT searches for words that match inflectional forms and thesaurus expansions and replacements. The FREETEXT predicate accepts a column name or list of columns, a free-text search string, and an optional language identifier (a locale ID, or LCID). Because it is a predicate, FREETEXT can be used in the WHERE clause of a SELECT query or DML statement. All rows for which the FREETEXT predicate returns true (a match) are returned. Listing 11-3 shows a simple FREETEXT query that uses the full-text index created on the Production.ProductModel table in the previous section. The results are shown in Figure 11-10. The wildcard character (*) passed as a parameter to the FREETEXT predicate indicates that all columns participating in the full-text index should be searched for a match. The second FREETEXT parameter is the word you want to match.

Listing 11-3. Simple FREETEXT Full-Text Query

```
SELECT
    ProductModelID,
    Name,
    CatalogDescription,
    Instructions
FROM Production.ProductModel
WHERE FREETEXT(*, N'sock');
```

	ProductModelID	Name	CatalogDescription	Instructions
1	18	Mountain Bike Socks	NULL	NULL
2	24	Racing Socks	NULL	NULL

Figure 11-10. *Using FREETEXT to Find Socks*

The FREETEXT predicate automatically stems words to find inflectional forms. The query in Listing 11-3 returns rows that contain an inflectional form of the word sock—in this case, FTS finds two rows that contain the plural form of the word, socks. Notice that if you were to replace the word "socks" with "sox" you receive the same result set. This is because FREETEXT also performs FTS thesaurus expansions and replacements automatically, if a thesaurus file is available.

The integration of FTS with the SQL Server query engine results in a more efficient FTS experience. In SQL Server 2014, FTS can take advantage of optimized operators like the Table Valued Function [FulltextMatch] operator shown in Figure 11-11. The query plan shown is generated by the query in Listing 11-3.

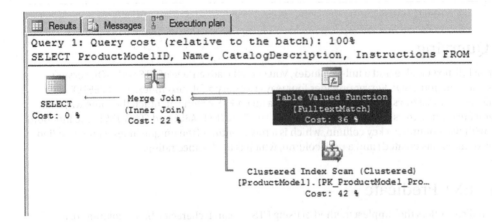

Figure 11-11. *FREETEXT Query Execution Plan*

FTS Performance Optimization

In previous releases of SQL Server, the FTS functionality was provided via an independent service known as MSFTESQL (Microsoft Full-Text Engine for SQL Server). Because it was completely separate from the SQL Server query engine, the MSFTESQL service could not take advantage of T-SQL operators to optimize performance. As an example, consider the following variation on the query in Listing 11-3:

```
SELECT
  ProductModelID,
  Name,
  CatalogDescription,
  Instructions
FROM Production.ProductModel
WHERE FREETEXT(*, N'sock')
AND ProductModelID < 100;
```

Imagine for a moment that the `Production.ProductModel` table has 1,000,000 rows that match the `FREETEXT` predicate. Versions of SQL Server prior to SQL Server 2008 were incapable of using the additional T-SQL `ProductModelID < 100` predicate in the `WHERE` clause to limit the rows accessed by the FTS service. The MSFTESQL service had to return all 1,000,000 rows from the `FREETEXT` predicate and then narrow them down. Beginning with SQL 2008 and continuing in SQL Server 2014, the FTS engine can work in tandem with the SQL Server query engine to optimize the query plan and limit the number of rows touched by the `FREETEXT` predicate.

■ **Tip** You'll see heavy use of the phrase inflectional forms throughout this section. Inflectional forms of words include verb conjugations like go, goes, going, gone, and went. Inflectional forms also include plural and singular noun variants of words, like bike and bikes. Searching for any word with `FREETEXT` automatically results in matches of all supported inflectional forms.

Listing 11-4 demonstrates a `FREETEXT` query that retrieves all rows that contain inflectional forms of the word ride in the `CatalogDescription` column. Another word for this process is called stemming. Inflectional forms that are matched in this query include the plural noun riders and the verb riding. In this `FREETEXT` query, the `CatalogDescription` column name is identified by name to restrict the search to a single column, and the LANGUAGE specifier is used to indicate LCID 1033, which is US English. The results are shown in Figure 11-12.

Listing 11-4. FREETEXT Query with Automatic Word Stemming

```
SELECT
  ProductModelID,
  Name,
  CatalogDescription,
  Instructions
FROM Production.ProductModel
WHERE FREETEXT(CatalogDescription, N'weld', LANGUAGE 1033);
```

	ProductModelID	Name	CatalogDescription	Instructions
1	19	Mountain-100	<?xml-stylesheet href="ProductDescription.xsl" t...	NULL
2	25	Road-150	<?xml-stylesheet href="ProductDescription.xsl" t...	NULL

Figure 11-12. *Automatic Stemming with FREETEXT*

You can't see the words that matched in the xml type CatalogDescription (there's not enough space on the page to reproduce the entire result). Rest assured that FREETEXT has located valid matches in the row. For the first match the XML has the text "The heat treated welded aluminum," while the second match has the text "it is welded and heat treated."

The CONTAINS Predicate

In addition to the FREETEXT predicate, SQL Server 2014 supports the CONTAINS predicate. CONTAINS allows more advanced full-text query options than the FREETEXT predicate. Just like FREETEXT, the CONTAINS predicate accepts a column name or list of columns, a search condition, and an optional language identifier as parameters. The CONTAINS predicate can search for simple strings like FREETEXT, but it also allows sophisticated search conditions that include word or phrase prefixes, words that are in close proximity to other words, inflectional word forms, thesaurus synonyms, and combinations of search criteria.

The simplest CONTAINS predicates are basic word searches, similar to FREETEXT. Unlike FREETEXT, however, the CONTAINS predicate does not automatically search for inflectional forms of words or thesaurus expansions and replacements. Listing 11-5 modifies Listing 11-4 to demonstrate a simple CONTAINS query. The results are shown in Figure 11-13. As you can see, a couple of rows that do not contain an exact match for the word weld are eliminated from the results.

Listing 11-5. Simple CONTAINS Query

```
SELECT
  ProductModelID ,
  Name,
  CatalogDescription,
  Instructions
FROM Production.ProductModel
WHERE CONTAINS (*, N'weld');
```

	ProductModelID	Name	CatalogDescription	Instructions
1	7	HL Touring Frame	NULL	<root xmlns="http://schemas.microsoft.com/sqlser...
2	10	LL Touring Frame	NULL	<root xmlns="http://schemas.microsoft.com/sqlser...
3	47	LL Touring Handlebars	NULL	<root xmlns="http://schemas.microsoft.com/sqlser...
4	48	HL Touring Handlebars	NULL	<root xmlns="http://schemas.microsoft.com/sqlser...

Figure 11-13. *Results of the Simple CONTAINS Query*

To use inflectional forms or thesaurus expansions and replacements with CONTAINS, use the FORMSOF generation term in your search condition. Listing 11-6 performs a CONTAINS search on the Name and CatalogDescription columns of the Production.ProductModel table. The results, which include matches for inflectional forms of the word sport, like sports and sporting, are shown in Figure 11-14.

Listing 11-6. Sample CONTAINS Query with FORMSOF Inflectional Generation Term

```
SELECT
  ProductModelID ,
  Name,
  CatalogDescription
FROM Production.ProductModel
WHERE CONTAINS
(
  (
    Name,
    CatalogDescription
  ),
  N'FORMSOF(INFLECTIONAL, sport)'
);
```

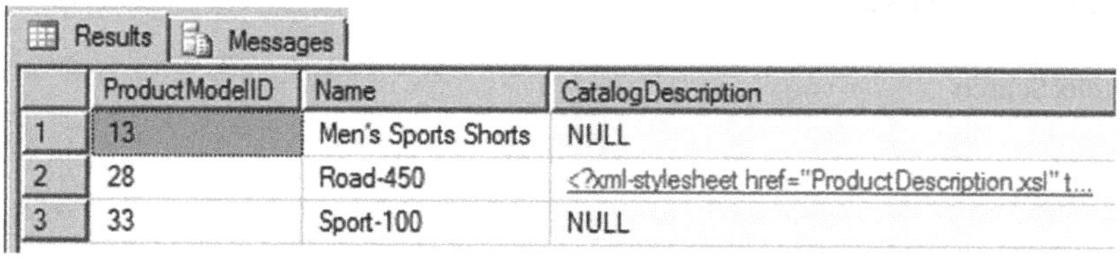

	Product ModelID	Name	Catalog Description
1	13	Men's Sports Shorts	NULL
2	28	Road-450	<?xml-stylesheet href="Product Description.xsl" t...
3	33	Sport-100	NULL

Figure 11-14. *Results of the CONTAINS Query with Inflectional FORMSOF Term*

The CONTAINS predicate also allows you to combine simple search terms like these with the AND (&), AND NOT (&!), and OR (|) Boolean operators. Listing 11-7 demonstrates combining two search terms in a CONTAINS predicate. The results of this sample query, which retrieves all rows containing inflectional forms of the word sport (like sports) or the word tube in the Name or CatalogDescription columns, are shown in Figure 11-15.

Listing 11-7. Compound CONTAINS Search Term

```
SELECT
  ProductModelID ,
  Name,
  CatalogDescription
FROM Production.ProductModel
WHERE CONTAINS
(
  (
    Name,
    CatalogDescription
  ),
  N'"tube" | FORMSOF (INFLECTIONAL, sport)'
);
```

	ProductModelID	Name	CatalogDescription
1	13	Men's Sports Shorts	NULL
2	19	Mountain-100	<?xml-stylesheet href="ProductDescription.xsl" t...
3	28	Road-450	<?xml-stylesheet href="ProductDescription.xsl" t...
4	33	Sport-100	NULL
5	34	Touring-1000	<?xml-stylesheet href="ProductDescription.xsl" t...
6	92	Mountain Tire Tube	NULL
7	93	Road Tire Tube	NULL
8	94	Touring Tire Tube	NULL

Figure 11-15. *Results of the CONTAINS Query with a Compound Search Term*

Listing 11-7 uses FORMSOF to return matches for inflectional forms. You can also use the FORMSOF (THESAURUS, ...) format to return matches for expansions and replacements of words, as defined in your language-specific thesaurus files.

CONTAINS also supports prefix searches using the wildcard asterisk (*) character. Place the search word or phrase, immediately followed by the wildcard character, in double quotes to specify a prefix search. Listing 11-8 demonstrates a simple prefix search to retrieve all rows that have a word starting with the prefix bot in the Name column. The results are shown in Figure 11-16.

Listing 11-8. CONTAINS Prefix Search

```
SELECT
  ProductModelID ,
  Name
FROM Production.ProductModel
WHERE CONTAINS (Name, N'"bot*"');
```

	ProductModelID	Name
1	95	LL Bottom Bracket
2	96	ML Bottom Bracket
3	97	HL Bottom Bracket
4	111	Water Bottle
5	112	Mountain Bottle Cage
6	113	Road Bottle Cage

Figure 11-16. *Results of the CONTAINS Prefix Search*

The CONTAINS predicate also supports the NEAR (~) keyword for proximity searches. NEAR will return matches for words that are close to one another in the source columns. Listing 11-9 demonstrates a NEAR proximity search that looks for instances of the word aluminum that occur in close proximity to the word jig in the Instructions column. The results are shown in Figure 11-17. This example is considered a generic proximity search.

Listing 11-9. CONTAINS Proximity Search

```
SELECT
  ProductModelID ,
  Name
FROM Production.ProductModel
WHERE CONTAINS (Instructions, N'aluminum NEAR jig');
```

	Product ModelID	Name
1	7	HL Touring Frame
2	10	LL Touring Frame
3	47	LL Touring Handlebars
4	48	HL Touring Handlebars

Figure 11-17. *CONTAINS Proximity Query Results*

■ **Tip** Avoid using generic proximity searches. These will be deprecated in future versions of SQL Server. Instead, use the custom proximity searches discussed later in this chapter.

SQL Server 2012 introduced a custom proximity search for the NEAR clause. It allows you to easily search for words within a customizable distance from one another. It also allows you to define the order of the phrases in your search. The distance is determined by the number of non-searchable words between the words included in your search. If we take the example in Listing 11-9 and convert it to a custom proximity search, we find that in order to get the same results we have to include a distance of three. This means that a maximum of three words exist between the words aluminum and jig. Listing 11-10 shows the revised code.

Listing 11-10. CONTAINS Custom Search

```
SELECT
  ProductModelID ,
  Name
FROM Production.ProductModel
WHERE CONTAINS(Instructions, 'NEAR((aluminum,jig), 3)');
```

Listing 11-10 gives you the same results as Figure 11-17. A distance of two will give you no results but any other number above three gives you the same results as the original. Keep in mind the distance between the words also includes stopwords. Remember stopwords are words usually not included in searches. Keep in mind too that the custom proximity clause is not limited to only two search words. You could have also included words like "bike," "weld," and "frame"—for example, NEAR((bike, weld, frame), 3). You can even include phrases like "bike riding" or "welding frame." Whatever you choose, the distance is still based on the distance between the first and last word listed in the condition.

By default the custom proximity search will ignore the order of the search words. In the example above, jig could be within a distance of three either before or after the word aluminum. If you want to control the order of the search words then you need add the TRUE clause in the NEAR statement. Listing 11-11 shows two examples. The first has jig before aluminum and the second has aluminum before jig. Notice that only the second example returns values.

Listing 11-11. Custom Search with TRUE Clause

```
SELECT
  ProductModelID ,
  Name
FROM Production.ProductModel
WHERE CONTAINS(Instructions, 'NEAR((jig, aluminum),3, TRUE)');

SELECT
  ProductModelID ,
  Name
FROM Production.ProductModel
WHERE CONTAINS(Instructions, 'NEAR((aluminum, jig),3, TRUE)');
```

The custom proximity search also allows for search conditions which combine multiple grouping of words using expressions like AND, OR, and AND NOT. The added flexibility of the SQL Server 2014 custom proximity search adds advanced features not available in the generic search. Going forward, all searches should be done using the custom properties.

The FREETEXTTABLE and CONTAINSTABLE Functions

SQL Server provides TVF-based counterparts to the FREETEXT and CONTAINS predicates, known as FREETEXTTABLE and CONTAINSTABLE. These functions operate like the similarly named predicates, but both functions return result sets consisting of a table with two columns, named KEY and RANK. The KEY column contains the key index values relating back to the unique index of matching rows in the source table, and the RANK column contains relevance rankings.

The FREETEXTTABLE function accepts the name of the table to search, a single column name or column list, a search string, and an optional language identifier just like the FREETEXT predicate. FREETEXTTABLE can also take an additional "top n by rank" parameter to limit the rows returned to a specific number of the highest-ranked rows. The results of FREETEXTTABLE are useful for joining back to the source table via the KEY column of the results. Listing 11-12 demonstrates a simple FREETEXTTABLE query that locates rows where the word aluminum appears in the Instructions column of the Production.ProductModel table. The results are joined back to the source table to return the ProductModelID and Name, as shown in Figure 11-18.

Listing 11-12. FREETEXTTABLE Results Joined to Source Table

```
SELECT
  ftt.[KEY],
  ftt.[RANK],
  pm.ProductModelID ,
  pm.Name FROM FREETEXTTABLE
(
  Production.ProductModel,
  Instructions,
  N'aluminum'
) ftt
INNER JOIN Production.ProductModel pm
  ON ftt.[KEY] = pm.ProductModelID;
```

Results | Messages

	KEY	RANK	ProductModelID	Name
1	7	567	7	HL Touring Frame
2	10	567	10	LL Touring Frame
3	47	636	47	LL Touring Handlebars
4	48	636	48	HL Touring Handlebars

Figure 11-18. *Results of the FREETEXTTABLE Query*

The CONTAINSTABLE function offers the advanced search capabilities of the CONTAINS predicate in a function form. The CONTAINSTABLE function accepts the name of the source table, a single column name or list of columns, and a CONTAINS-style search condition. Like FREETEXTTABLE, the CONTAINSTABLE function also accepts an optional language identifier and "top n by rank" parameter. Listing 11-13 demonstrates the CONTAINSTABLE function in a simple keyword search that retrieves KEY and RANK values for all rows containing inflectional forms of the word tours. The results are shown in Figure 11-19.

Listing 11-13. Simple CONTAINSTABLE Query

```
SELECT
  [KEY],
  [RANK]
FROM CONTAINSTABLE (
Production.ProductModel,
[Name],
N'FORMSOF(INFLECTIONAL, tours)'
);
```

Results | Messages

	KEY	RANK
1	7	64
2	10	64
3	34	64
4	35	64
5	36	64
6	43	64
7	44	64
8	47	64
9	48	64
10	53	64
11	65	64
12	66	64
13	67	64
14	91	64
15	94	64
16	120	64

Figure 11-19. *Results of the CONTAINSTABLE Query with Inflectional Forms*

CONTAINSTABLE supports all of the options supported by the CONTAINS predicate, including the ISABOUT term, which allows you to assign weights to the matched words it locates. With ISABOUT, you assign a weight value between 0.0 and 1.0 to each search word. CONTAINSTABLE applies the weight to the relevance rankings returned in the RANK column. Listing 11-14 shows two CONTAINSTABLE queries. The first query returns all products with the words aluminum or polish in their XML Instructions column. The second query uses ISABOUT to assign each of these words a weight between 0.0 and 1.0, which is then applied to the result RANK for each row. The results, shown in Figure 11-20, demonstrate how ISABOUT weights can rearrange the rankings of your CONTAINSTABLE query results.

Listing 11-14. ISABOUT in a CONTAINSTABLE Query

```
SELECT
  ct.[RANK],
  ct.[KEY],
  pm.[Name]
FROM CONTAINSTABLE
(
  Production.ProductModel,
  Instructions,
  N'aluminum OR polish'
) ct
INNER JOIN Production.ProductModel pm
  ON ct.[KEY] = pm.ProductModelID
ORDER BY ct.[RANK] DESC;

  SELECT
  ct.[RANK],
  ct.[KEY],
  pm.[Name] FROM CONTAINSTABLE
(
  Production.ProductModel,
  Instructions,
N'ISABOUT(aluminum WEIGHT(1.0 ), polish WEIGHT(0.1))'
) ct
INNER JOIN Production.ProductModel pm
  ON ct.[KEY] = pm.ProductModelID
ORDER BY ct.[RANK] DESC;
```

	RANK	KEY	Name
1	24	7	HL Touring Frame
2	24	10	LL Touring Frame
3	19	47	LL Touring Handlebars
4	19	48	HL Touring Handlebars

	RANK	KEY	Name
1	19	47	LL Touring Handlebars
2	19	48	HL Touring Handlebars
3	18	7	HL Touring Frame
4	18	10	LL Touring Frame

Figure 11-20. *Changing Result Set Rankings with ISABOUT*

Thesauruses and Stoplists

The FREETEXT predicate and FREETEXTTABLE function automatically perform word stemming for inflectional forms and thesaurus expansions and replacements. The CONTAINS predicate and CONTAINSTABLE function require you to explicitly specify that you want inflectional forms and thesaurus expansions and replacements with the FORMSOF term. While inflectional forms include verb conjugations and plural forms of words, thesaurus functionality is based on user-managed XML files that define word replacement and expansion patterns.

Each language-specific thesaurus is located in an XML file in the FTData directory of your SQL Server installation. If you installed SQL Server with the default settings then the directory would be located in the path C:\Program Files\Microsoft SQL Server\MSSQL12.MSSQLSERVER\MSSQL\FTData\. The thesaurus files are named using the format tsnnn.xml, where nnn is a three-letter code representing a specific language. The file name tsenu.xml, for instance, is the US English thesaurus. To demonstrate the FTS thesaurus capabilities, we'll begin by creating a new full-text index on the Production.Product table using the code in Listing 11-15.

Listing 11-15. Creating a Full-Text Index

```
CREATE  FULLTEXT  INDEX  ON  Production.Product
(
    Name  LANGUAGE  English,
    Color LANGUAGE English
)
KEY  INDEX PK_Product_ProductID
ON  (AdventureWorksFTCat)
WITH
(
    CHANGE_TRACKING AUTO,
    STOPLIST = SYSTEM
);
GO

ALTER FULLTEXT INDEX ON Production.Product
ENABLE;
GO
```

You can edit the thesaurus XML files with a simple text editor or a more advanced XML editor. For this example, we opened the tsenu.xml thesaurus file in Notepad, made the appropriate changes, and saved the file back to the MSSQLFTData directory. The contents of the tsenu.xml file, after our edits, are shown in Listing 11-16.

Listing 11-16. Tsenu.xml US English XML Thesaurus File

```
<XML  ID = "Microsoft  Search  Thesaurus">
    <thesaurus xmlns = "x-schema:tsSchema.xml">
        <diacritics_sensitive>0</diacritics_sensitive>
        <expansion>
        <sub>thin</sub>
        <sub>flat</sub>
        </expansion>
        <replacement>
        <pat>sapphire</pat>
```

```
        <pat>indigo</pat>
        <pat>navy</pat>
        <sub>blue</sub>
        </replacement>
    </thesaurus>
</XML>
```

After editing the XML thesaurus file, you can use the sys.spfulltextloadthesaurusfile stored procedure (SP) to reload the thesaurus file. This procedure accepts an integer LCID parameter, as shown in Listing 11-17. The LCID used in the listing is 1033, which specifies US English.

Listing 11-17. Reloading US English XML Thesaurus

```
EXEC sys.sp_fulltext_load_thesaurus_file 1033;
GO
```

■ **Note**   Starting in SQL Server 2008, reloading a thesaurus in SQL Server did not require an SQL Server service restart.

The diacritics_sensitive element of the thesaurus file indicates whether accent marks are replaced during expansion and replacement. For instance, if diacritics_sensitive is set to 0, the words cafe and café are considered equivalent for purposes of the thesaurus. If diacritics_sensitive is set to 1, however, these two words would be considered different.

The expansion element indicates substitutions that should be applied during the full-text query. The word being searched is expanded to match the other words in the expansion set. In the example, if the user queries for the word thin, the search is automatically expanded to include matches for the word flat, and vice versa. An expansion set can include as many substitutions as you care to define, and the thesaurus can contain as many expansion sets as you need. The sample FREETEXT query in Listing 11-18 shows the expansion sets in action, with partial results shown in Figure 11-21.

Listing 11-18. FREETEXT Query with Thesaurus Expansion Sets

```
SELECT
  ProductID,
  Name
FROM Production.Product
WHERE FREETEXT(*, N'flat');
```

	ProductID	Name
1	341	Flat Washer 1
2	342	Flat Washer 6
3	343	Flat Washer 2
4	344	Flat Washer 9
5	345	Flat Washer 4
6	346	Flat Washer 3
7	347	Flat Washer 8
8	348	Flat Washer 5
9	349	Flat Washer 7
10	359	Thin-Jam Hex Nut 9
11	360	Thin-Jam Hex Nut 10
12	361	Thin-Jam Hex Nut 1
13	362	Thin-Jam Hex Nut 2
14	363	Thin-Jam Hex Nut 15
15	364	Thin-Jam Hex Nut 16

Figure 11-21. Partial Results of the Full-text Query with Expansion Sets

The replacement section of the thesaurus file indicates replacements for words that are used in a full-text query. In the example, we've defined patterns like navy, sapphire, and indigo, which will be replaced with the word blue. The result is that a full-text query for these replacement patterns will be converted internally to a search for blue. Listing 11-19 shows a FREETEXT query that uses the replacement patterns defined in the thesaurus. You can use any of the replacement patterns defined in the thesaurus file in the full-text query to get the same result. Figure 11-22 shows the results.

Listing 11-19. FREETEXT Query with Thesaurus Replacement Patterns

```
SELECT
  ProductID,
  Name,
  Color
FROM Production.Product
WHERE FREETEXT(*, N'navy');
```

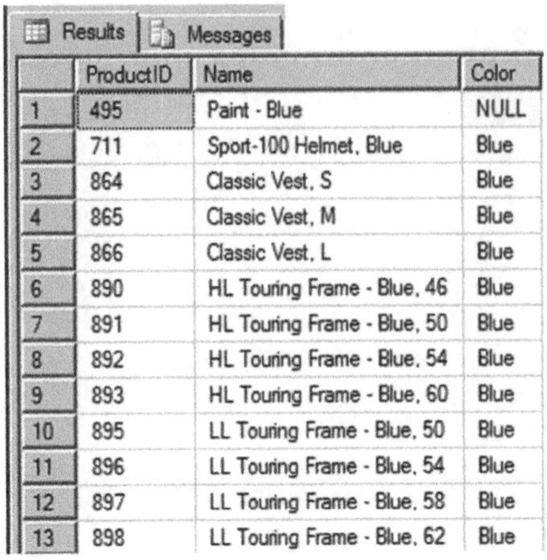

Results | Messages

	ProductID	Name	Color
1	495	Paint - Blue	NULL
2	711	Sport-100 Helmet, Blue	Blue
3	864	Classic Vest, S	Blue
4	865	Classic Vest, M	Blue
5	866	Classic Vest, L	Blue
6	890	HL Touring Frame - Blue, 46	Blue
7	891	HL Touring Frame - Blue, 50	Blue
8	892	HL Touring Frame - Blue, 54	Blue
9	893	HL Touring Frame - Blue, 60	Blue
10	895	LL Touring Frame - Blue, 50	Blue
11	896	LL Touring Frame - Blue, 54	Blue
12	897	LL Touring Frame - Blue, 58	Blue
13	898	LL Touring Frame - Blue, 62	Blue

Figure 11-22. *Partial Results of the Full-text Query with Replacement Sets*

Previous versions of FTS had system-defined lists of noise words, which provided a way to essentially ignore commonly occurring words that don't help the search. Commonly cited noise words included those like the, a, an, and others. The noise word implementation in previous versions stored the noise words in files in the file system.

SQL Server 2014 implements the classic noise words, known in FTS as stopwords. Stopwords are managed inside the SQL Server database using structures known as stoplists. You can use the system-supplied stoplists or create and manage your own language-specific stoplists with the `CREATE FULLTEXT STOPLIST`, `ALTER FULLTEXT STOPLIST`, and `DROP FULLTEXT STOPLIST` statements. The statement in Listing 11-20 creates a stoplist based on the system stoplist.

Listing 11-20. Creating a Full-Text Stoplist

```
CREATE FULLTEXT STOPLIST AWStoplist
FROM SYSTEM STOPLIST;
GO
```

Stoplists are more flexible than the old noise word lists since you can easily use T-SQL statements to add words to your stoplists. Consider AdventureWorks product model searches where the word "instructions" appears in several of the XML documents in the `Instructions` column. You can add the word instructions to the previously created stoplist with the `ALTER FULLTEXT STOPLIST` statement, and then associate the stoplist with the full-text index on the `Production.ProductModel` table via the `ALTER FULLTEXT INDEX` statement, as shown in Listing 11-21. This will effectively ignore the word instructions during full-text searches on this column.

Listing 11-21. Adding the Word "Instructions" to the Stoplist

```
ALTER FULLTEXT STOPLIST AWStoplist
ADD N'instructions' LANGUAGE English;
GO

ALTER FULLTEXT INDEX ON Production.ProductModel
SET STOPLIST AWStoplist;
GO
```

After application of the newly created stoplist, a full-text query against the `Production.ProductModel` table for the word instructions, as shown in Listing 11-22, will return no results.

Listing 11-22. Full-Text Query with Newly Created Stoplist

```
SELECT
  ProductModelID,
  Name
FROM Production.ProductModel
WHERE FREETEXT(*, N'instructions');
```

Stored Procedures and Dynamic Management Views and Functions

SQL Server 2014 provides access to many of the legacy FTS SPs available in previous releases of SQL Server. Most of these procedures have been deprecated, however, and have been replaced by fully integrated T-SQL statements and dynamic management views and functions.

SQL Server 2014 FTS uses the `sys.sp_fulltext_load_thesaurus_file` procedure that we introduced earlier in this chapter to load an XML thesaurus file. Another procedure is the `sys.sp_fulltext_resetfdhostaccount` procedure that updates the Windows username and password that SQL Server uses to start the filter daemon service.

A big issue for developers who used FTS in SQL Server 2005 and earlier was the lack of transparency. Basically everything that FTS did was well hidden from view, and developers and administrators had to troubleshoot FTS issues in the dark. SQL Server 2008 introduced some catalog views and dynamic management functions that made FTS more transparent, and this continues to be the case in SQL Server 2014.

If you're experiencing FTS query performance issues, the `sys.fulltext_index_fragments` catalog view can provide insight. This catalog view reports full-text index fragments and their status. You can use the information in this catalog view to decide if it's time to reorganize your full-text index.

The `sys.fulltext_stoplists` and `sys.fulltext_stopwords` catalog views let you see the user-defined stopwords and stoplists defined in the current database. The information returned by these catalog views is useful for troubleshooting issues with certain words being ignored (or not being ignored) in full-text queries. The `sys.fulltext_system_stopwords` catalog view returns a row for every stopword in the system stoplist, which is useful information to have if you want to use the system stoplist as the basis for your own stoplists.

The `sys.dm_fts_parser` function is a useful tool for troubleshooting full-text queries. This function accepts a full-text query string, an LCID, a stoplist ID, and an accent sensitivity setting. The result returned by the function shows the results produced by the word breaker and stemmer for any given full-text query. This information is very useful if you need to troubleshoot or just want to better understand exactly how the word breaker and stemmer affect your queries. Listing 11-23 is a simple demonstration of stemming the word had with the `sys.dm_fts_parser` function. Results are shown in Figure 11-23.

Listing 11-23. Using Sys.dm_fts_parser to See Word Breaking and Stemming

```
SELECT
  keyword,
  group_id,
  phrase_id,
  occurrence,
  special_term,
  display_term,
  expansion_type,
  source_term
```

```
FROM sys.dm_fts_parser
(
    N'FORMSOF(FREETEXT,had)',
    1033,
    NULL,
    0
);
```

	keyword	group_id	phrase_id	occurrence	special_term	display_term	expansion_type	source_term
1	0x0068006100073	1	0	1	Exact Match	has	2	had
2	0x0068006100760065	1	0	1	Exact Match	have	2	had
3	0x00680061007600650027007300	1	0	1	Exact Match	have's	2	had
4	0x0068006100760065000730073	1	0	1	Exact Match	haves	2	had
5	0x00680061007600650073000730027	1	0	1	Exact Match	haves'	2	had
6	0x0068006100760069006E0067	1	0	1	Exact Match	having	2	had
7	0x0068006100640	1	0	1	Exact Match	had	0	had

Figure 11-23. Results of Word-breaking and Stemming the Word "Had"

Statistical Semantics

When you created the index (see Figure 11-6) you had the option to select statistical semantics. Statistical semantics was new in SQL Server 2012 and it dramatically changed what it meant to search documents. Everything discussed up to now was focused on searching words within a document. If you needed to find all the words similar to "weld," you could find them by using FTS functions against text data stored in the SQL Server engine. But what if you wanted to find all the documents stored in your SQL Server database that were related to finance or a particular law case? Or, let's say, you needed to search through hundreds of resumes to determine which ones best fit a particular job application. This is where statistical semantics becomes helpful. Statistical semantics is used to search for the meaning of documents and not just their content.

The statistical semantic feature requires FTS but is installed as a separate feature. The install file is located on the SQL Server install disk. The 64bit version is located at ...\x64\Setup and the file name is SemanticLanguageDatabase.msi. The install wizard is straight-forward. The wizard extracts the semantic database files to a directory. The default directory is C:\Program Files\Microsoft Semantic Language Database. You will then want to copy or move these database files to another location, preferably the same location as your other database files, and then attach the database. Once the database is attached, run the command in Listing 11-24.

Listing 11-24. Initializing the Statistical Semantics Database

```
EXEC sp_fulltext_semantic_register_language_statistics_db @dbname = N'semanticsdb';
```

Once initialized, you can verify the database is ready by running the code in Listing 11-25. Figure 11-24 shows the results.

Listing 11-25. Verifying Active Statistical Semantics Database

```
SELECT * FROM sys.fulltext_semantic_language_statistics_database
```

	database_id	register_date	registered_by	version
1	9	2012-07-14 18:21:38.980	1	11.0.1153.1.1

Figure 11-24. Results of Querying the Semantics Database

From here you can now go back to the properties of the Production.ProductModel FTS index we created earlier in the chapter and checkmark the Statistical Semantics column as shown in Figure 11-25.

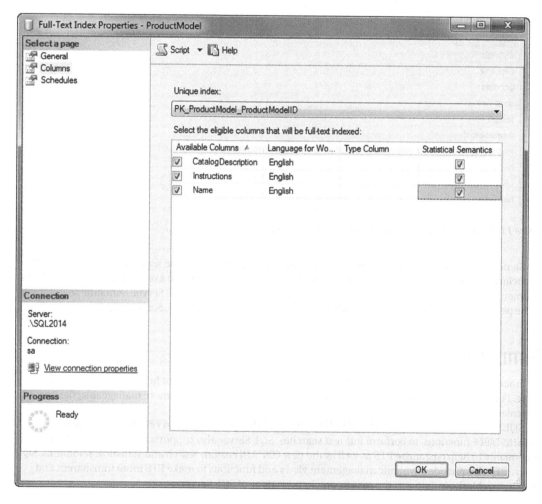

Figure 11-25. Enabling Statistical Semantics on Table Columns

Now that statistical semantics is installed we can do things like search for key phrases or find related documents. To find a key phrase we use the TVF semantickeyphrasetable. Searching for key phrases on the Production.ProductModel name column yields the results we see in Figure 11-26. Run the code in Listing 11-26 to get the results.

Listing 11-26. Using the Semantickeyphrasetable Function

```
SELECT TOP(10) KEYP_TBL.keyphrase
FROM SEMANTICKEYPHRASETABLE
    (
    Production.ProductModel,
        Name
    ) AS KEYP_TBL
ORDER BY KEYP_TBL.score DESC;
GO
```

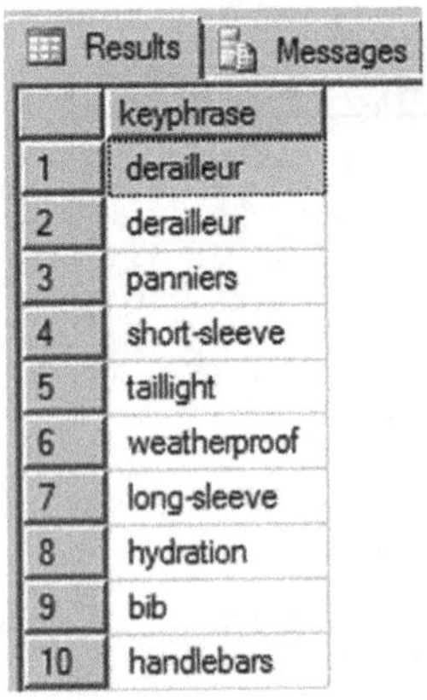

	Results	Messages
	keyphrase	
1	derailleur	
2	derailleur	
3	panniers	
4	short-sleeve	
5	taillight	
6	weatherproof	
7	long-sleeve	
8	hydration	
9	bib	
10	handlebars	

Figure 11-26. *Results from Semantickeyphrasetable Function*

Semantic searching offers some interesting possibilities and broadens the scope of traditional FTS. If you include the SQL Server 2014 FileTable feature then the possibilities widen even further. FileTable allows documents stored on a file system to be integrated and managed through SQL Server. Semantic searching can be performed against these and any other document managed by the SQL Server engine.

Summary

FTS functionality is highly integrated with SQL Server, providing more efficient full-text queries than ever before. Full-text indexes and stoplists are stored in the database, making FTS more manageable, flexible, and scalable.

SQL Server provides the powerful FREETEXT and CONTAINS predicates, and FREETEXTTABLE and CONTAINSTABLE functions, to perform full-text searches. SQL Server also supports thesaurus and stoplist functionality to help customize FTS as well as the new CONTAIN custom search and statistical semantics. SQL Server 2014 also provides dynamic management views and functions to make FTS more transparent and easier to troubleshoot than was the case in previous versions of SQL Server.

EXERCISES

1. [True/False] Stoplists and full-text indexes are stored in the database.
2. [Choose one] You can create a full-text index with which of the following methods:

    a. Using a wizard in SSMS

    b. Using the T-SQL CREATE FULLTEXT INDEX statement

    c. Both (a) and (b)

    d. None of the above

3. [Fill in the blanks] The FREETEXT predicate automatically performs word stemming and thesaurus _____ and _____.

4. [Fill in the blank] Stoplists contain stopwords, which are words that are _____ during full-text querying.

5. [True/False] The sys.dm_fts_parser dynamic management function shows the results produced by word breaking and stemming.

CHAPTER 12

XML

SQL Server 2014 continues the standard for XML integration included with the SQL Server 2008 release. SQL Server 2014 XML still offers tight integration with T-SQL through the xml data type, support for the World Wide Web Consortium (W3C) XQuery and XML Schema recommendations.

SQL Server 2014's tight XML integration and the xml data type provide streamlined methods of performing several XML-related tasks that used to require clunky code to interface with COM objects and other tools external to the SQL Server engine. This chapter discusses the xml data type and the XML tools built into T-SQL to take advantage of this functionality.

The new memory-optimized tables provided in SQL Server 2014, do not support xml data types. Currently, the row limit size is 8060 bytes and there is no off-row storage capability. If you have a need to relate to a row of data with an xml data type, we would recommend that the data be stored in a disk-based table with a pointer back to the memory-optimized table.

Legacy XML

T-SQL support for XML was introduced with the release of SQL Server 2000 via the FOR XML clause of the SELECT statement, the OPENXML rowset provider, and the sp_xml_preparedocument and sp_xml_removedocument system SPs. In this section, we'll discuss the legacy OPENXML, sp_xml_preparedocument, and sp_xml_removedocument functionality. Though these tools still exist in SQL Server 2014 and can be used for backward-compatibility scripts, they are awkward and kludgy to use.

OPENXML

OPENXML is a legacy XML function that provides a rowset view of XML data. The process of converting XML data to relational form is known as shredding. OPENXML is technically a rowset provider, which means its contents can be queried and accessed like a table. The legacy SQL Server XML functionality requires the sp_xml_preparedocument and sp_xml_removedocument system SPs to parse text into an XML document and clean up afterward. These procedures are used in conjunction with the OPENXML function to move XML data from its textual representation into a parsed internal representation of an XML document, and from there into a tabular format.

This method is rather clunky compared to the newer methods first introduced by SQL Server 2005, but you might need it if you're writing code that needs to be backward compatible. The OPENXML method has certain disadvantages based on its heritage, some of which are listed here:

OPENXML relies on COM to invoke the Microsoft XML Core Services Library (MSXML) to perform XML manipulation and shredding.

When it is invoked, MSXML assigns one-eighth of SQL Server's total memory to the task of parsing and manipulating XML data.

If you fail to call spxmlremovedocument after preparing an XML document with the spxmlpreparedocument procedure, it won't be removed from memory until the SQL Server service is restarted.

■ **Tip** We strongly recommend using xml data type methods like nodes(), value(), and query() to shred your XML data instead of using OPENXML. We'll discuss these xml data type methods later in this chapter, in the section titled "The XML Data Type Methods."

The sample query in Listing 12-1 is a simple demonstration of using OPENXML to shred XML data. The partial results of this query are shown in Figure 12-1.

Listing 12-1. Simple OPENXML Query

```
DECLARE @docHandle int;

DECLARE @xmlDocument nvarchar(max) = N'<Customers>
    <Customer CustomerID="1234" ContactName="Larry" CompanyName="APress">
        <Orders>
            <Order CustomerID="1234"    OrderDate="2006-04-25T13:22:18"/>
            <Order CustomerID="1234"    OrderDate="2006-05-10T12:35:49"/>
        </Orders>
    </Customer>
    <Customer CustomerID="4567" ContactName="Bill" CompanyName="Microsoft">
        <Orders>
            <Order CustomerID="4567"    OrderDate="2006-03-12T18:32:39"/>
            <Order CustomerID="4567"    OrderDate="2006-05-11T17:56:12"/>
        </Orders>
    </Customer>
</Customers>';

EXECUTE sp_xml_preparedocument @docHandle OUTPUT, @xmlDocument;

SELECT
        Id,
        ParentId,
        NodeType,
        LocalName,
        Prefix,
        NameSpaceUri,
        DataType,
        Prev,
        [Text]
FROM OPENXML(@docHandle, N'/Customers/Customer');

EXECUTE sp_xml_removedocument @docHandle;
GO
```

	Id	ParentId	NodeType	LocalName	Prefix	NameSpaceUri	DataType	Prev	Text
1	2	0	1	Customer	NULL	NULL	NULL	NULL	NULL
2	3	2	2	CustomerID	NULL	NULL	NULL	NULL	NULL
3	24	3	3	#text	NULL	NULL	NULL	NULL	1234
4	4	2	2	ContactName	NULL	NULL	NULL	NULL	NULL
5	25	4	3	#text	NULL	NULL	NULL	NULL	Larry
6	5	2	2	CompanyName	NULL	NULL	NULL	NULL	NULL
7	26	5	3	#text	NULL	NULL	NULL	NULL	APress
8	6	2	1	Orders	NULL	NULL	NULL	NULL	NULL
9	7	6	1	Order	NULL	NULL	NULL	NULL	NULL
10	8	7	2	CustomerID	NULL	NULL	NULL	NULL	NULL
11	27	8	3	#text	NULL	NULL	NULL	NULL	1234
12	9	7	2	OrderDate	NULL	NULL	NULL	NULL	NULL
13	28	9	3	#text	NULL	NULL	NULL	NULL	2006-04-25T13:22:18
14	10	6	1	Order	NULL	NULL	NULL	7	NULL

Figure 12-1. *Results of the OPENXML Query*

The first step in using OPENXML is to call the sp_xml_preparedocument SP to convert an XML-formatted string into an XML document:

```
DECLARE @docHandle int;

DECLARE @xmlDocument nvarchar(max) = N'<Customers>
    <Customer CustomerID="1234" ContactName="Larry" CompanyName="APress">
        <Orders>
            <Order CustomerID="1234"    OrderDate="2006-04-25T13:22:18"/>
            <Order CustomerID="1234"    OrderDate="2006-05-10T12:35:49"/>
        </Orders>
    </Customer>
    <Customer CustomerID="4567" ContactName="Bill" CompanyName="Microsoft">
        <Orders>
            <Order CustomerID="4567"    OrderDate="2006-03-12T18:32:39"/>
            <Order CustomerID="4567"    OrderDate="2006-05-11T17:56:12"/>
        </Orders>
    </Customer>
</Customers>';

EXECUTE sp_xml_preparedocument @docHandle OUTPUT, @xmlDocument;
```

The sp_xml_preparedocument procedure invokes MSXML to parse your XML document into an internal Document Object Model (DOM) tree representation of the nodes. The sp_xml_preparedocument procedure accepts up to three parameters, as follows:

- The first parameter, called hdoc, is an output parameter that returns an int handle to the XML document created by the SP.

- The second parameter is the original XML document. This parameter is known as xmltext and can be a char, nchar, varchar, nvarchar, text, ntext, or xml data type. If NULL is passed in or the xmltext parameter is omitted, an empty XML document is created. The default for this parameter is NULL.

- A third optional parameter, xpathnamespaces, specifies the namespace declarations used in OPENXML XPath expressions. Like xmltext, the xpath_namespaces parameter can be a char, nchar, varchar, nvarchar, text, ntext, or xml data type. The default xpath_namespaces value is <root xmlns:mp="urn:schemas-microsoft-com: xml-metaprop">.

The OPENXML rowset provider shreds the internal DOM representation of the XML document into relational format. The result of the rowset provider can be queried like a table or view, as shown following:

```
SELECT
    Id,
    ParentId,
    NodeType,
    LocalName,
    Prefix,
    NameSpaceUri,
    DataType,
    Prev,
    [Text]
FROM OPENXML(@docHandle, N'/Customers/Customer');
```

The OPENXML rowset provider accepts up to three parameters:

- The first parameter, hdoc, is the int document handle returned by the call to the sp_xml_preparedocument procedure.

- The second parameter, known as rowpattern, is an nvarchar XPath query pattern that determines which nodes of the XML document are returned as rows.

- The third parameter is an optional flags parameter. This tinyint value specifies the type of mapping to be used between the XML data and the relational rowset. If specified, flags can be a combination of the values listed in Table 12-1.

Table 12-1. *OPENXML Flags Parameter Options*

Value	Name	Description
0	DEFAULT	A flags value of 0 tells OPENXML to default to attribute-centric mapping. This is the default value if the flags parameter is not specified.
1	XML_ATTRIBUTES	A flags value of 1 indicates that OPENXML should use attribute-centric mapping.
2	XML_ELEMENTS	A flags value of 2 indicates that OPENXML should use element-centric mapping.
3	XML_ATTRIBUTES | XML_ELEMENTS	Combining the XML_ATTRIBUTES flag value with the XML_ELEMENTS flag value (logical OR) indicates that attribute-centric mapping should be applied first, and element-centric mapping should be applied to all columns not yet dealt with.
8		A flags value of 8 indicates that the consumed data should not be copied to the overflow property @mp:xmltext. This value can be combined (logical OR) with any of the other flags values.

The internal XML document generated by sp_xml_preparedocument is cached and will continue to take up SQL Server memory until it is explicitly removed with the sp_xml_removedocument procedure. The sp_xml_removedocument procedure accepts a single parameter, the int document handle initially generated by sp_xml_preparedocument:

```
EXECUTE sp_xml_removedocument @docHandle;
```

■ **Caution** Always call sp_xml_removedocument to free up memory used by XML documents created with sp_xml_createdocument. Any XML documents created with sp_xml_createdocument remain in memory until sp_xml_removedocument is called or the SQL Server service is restarted. Microsoft advises that not freeing up memory with sp_xml_removedocument could cause your server to run out of memory.

OPENXML Result Formats

The sample in Listing 12-1 returns a table in edge table format, which is the default OPENXML rowset format. According to BOL, "Edge tables represent the fine-grained XML document structure . . . in a single table" (http://msdn2.microsoft.com/en-us/library/ ms186918(SQL.11).aspx). The columns returned by the edge table format are shown in Table 12-2.

Table 12-2. *Edge Table Format*

Column Name	Data Type	Description
id	Bigint	The unique ID of the document node. The root element ID is 0.
parentid	Bigint	The identifier of the parent of the node. If the node is a top-level node, the parentid is NULL.
nodetype	Int	The column that indicates the type of the node. It can be 1 for an element node, 2 for an attribute node, or 3 for a text node.
localname	Nvarchar	The local name of the element or attribute, or NULL if the DOM object does not have a name.
prefix	Nvarchar	The namespace prefix of the node.
namespaceuri	Nvarchar	The namespace URI of the node, or NULL if there's no namespace.
datatype	Nvarchar	The data type of the element or attribute row, which is inferred from the inline DTD or inline schema.
prev	Bigint	The XML ID of the previous sibling element, or NULL if there is no direct previous sibling.
text	Ntext	The attribute value or element content.

OPENXML supports an optional WITH clause to specify a user-defined format for the returned rowset. The WITH clause lets you specify the name of an existing table or a schema declaration to define the rowset format. By adding a WITH clause to the OPENXML query in Listing 12-1, you can specify an explicit schema for the resulting rowset. This technique is demonstrated in Listing 12-2, with results shown in Figure 12-2. The differences between Listings 12-2 and 12-1 are shown in bold.

Listing 12-2. OPENXML and WITH Clause, Explicit Schema

```
DECLARE @docHandle int;

DECLARE @xmlDocument nvarchar(max) = N'<Customers>
    <Customer CustomerID="1234" ContactName="Larry" CompanyName="APress">
        <Orders>
            <Order CustomerID="1234"    OrderDate="2006-04-25T13:22:18"/>
            <Order CustomerID="1234"    OrderDate="2006-05-10T12:35:49"/>
        </Orders>
    </Customer>
    <Customer CustomerID="4567" ContactName="Bill" CompanyName="Microsoft">
        <Orders>
            <Order CustomerID="4567"    OrderDate="2006-03-12T18:32:39"/>
            <Order CustomerID="4567"    OrderDate="2006-05-11T17:56:12"/>
        </Orders>
    </Customer>
</Customers>';
EXECUTE sp_xml_preparedocument @docHandle OUTPUT, @xmlDocument;
```

```
SELECT
    CustomerID,
        CustomerName,
        CompanyName,
        OrderDate
FROM OPENXML(@docHandle, N'/Customers/Customer/Orders/Order')
WITH
(
        CustomerID nchar(4) N'../../@CustomerID',
        CustomerName nvarchar(50) N'../../@ContactName',
        CompanyName nvarchar(50) N'../../@CompanyName',
        OrderDate datetime
);

EXECUTE sp_xml_removedocument @docHandle;
GO
```

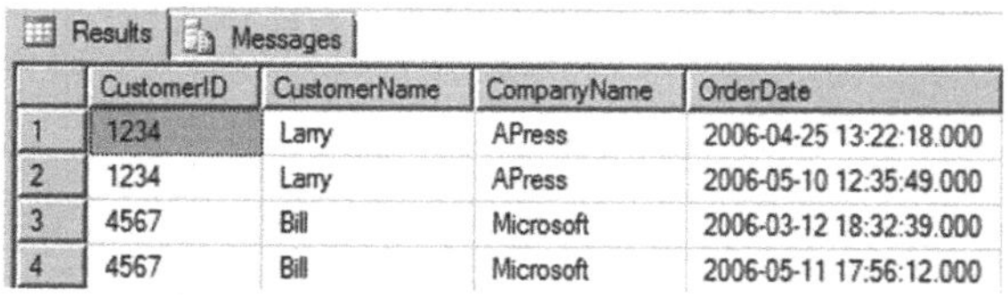

	CustomerID	CustomerName	CompanyName	OrderDate
1	1234	Larry	APress	2006-04-25 13:22:18.000
2	1234	Larry	APress	2006-05-10 12:35:49.000
3	4567	Bill	Microsoft	2006-03-12 18:32:39.000
4	4567	Bill	Microsoft	2006-05-11 17:56:12.000

Figure 12-2. *Results of OPENXML with an Explicit Schema Declaration*

The OPENXML WITH clause can also use the schema from an existing table to format the relational result set. This is demonstrated in Listing 12-3. The differences between Listing 12-3 and 12-2 are shown in bold.

Listing 12-3. OPENXML with WITH Clause, Existing Table Schema

```
DECLARE @docHandle int;

DECLARE @xmlDocument nvarchar(max) = N'<Customers>
    <Customer CustomerID="1234" ContactName="Larry" CompanyName="APress">
        <Orders>
            <Order CustomerID="1234"    OrderDate="2006-04-25T13:22:18"/>
            <Order CustomerID="1234"    OrderDate="2006-05-10T12:35:49"/>
        </Orders>
    </Customer>
    <Customer CustomerID="4567" ContactName="Bill" CompanyName="Microsoft">
        <Orders>
            <Order CustomerID="4567"    OrderDate="2006-03-12T18:32:39"/>
            <Order CustomerID="4567"    OrderDate="2006-05-11T17:56:12"/>
        </Orders>
    </Customer>
</Customers>';
```

```
EXECUTE sp_xml_preparedocument @docHandle OUTPUT, @xmlDocument;

CREATE TABLE #CustomerInfo
(
    CustomerID nchar(4) NOT NULL,
    ContactName nvarchar(50) NOT NULL,
    CompanyName nvarchar(50) NOT NULL
);

CREATE TABLE #OrderInfo
(
    CustomerID nchar(4) NOT NULL,
    OrderDate datetime NOT NULL
);

INSERT INTO #CustomerInfo
(
    CustomerID,
    ContactName,
    CompanyName
)
SELECT
    CustomerID,
    ContactName,
    CompanyName
FROM OPENXML(@docHandle, N'/Customers/Customer')
WITH #CustomerInfo;

INSERT INTO #OrderInfo
(
    CustomerID,
    OrderDate
)
SELECT
    CustomerID,
    OrderDate
FROM OPENXML(@docHandle, N'//Order')
WITH #OrderInfo;
SELECT
    c.CustomerID,
    c.ContactName,
    c.CompanyName,
    o.OrderDate
FROM #CustomerInfo c
INNER JOIN #OrderInfo  o
    ON c.CustomerID = o.CustomerID;

DROP TABLE #OrderInfo;
DROP TABLE #CustomerInfo;

EXECUTE sp_xml_removedocument @docHandle;
GO
```

The WITH clause used by each OPENXML query in Listing 12-3 specifies a table name. OPENXML uses the table's schema to define the relational format of the result returned.

FOR XML Clause

SQL Server 2000 introduced the FOR XML clause for use with the SELECT statement to efficiently convert relational data to XML format. The FOR XML clause is highly flexible and provides a wide range of options that give you fine-grained control over your XML result.

FOR XML RAW

The FOR XML clause appears at the end of the SELECT statement and can specify one of five different modes and several mode-specific options. The first FOR XML mode is RAW mode, which returns data in XML format with each row represented as a node with attributes representing the columns. FOR XML RAW is useful for ad hoc FOR XML queries while debugging and testing. The FOR XML RAW clause allows you to specify the element name for each row returned in parentheses immediately following the RAW keyword (if you leave it off, the default name, row, is used). The query in Listing 12-4 demonstrates FOR XML RAW, with results shown in Figure 12-3.

Listing 12-4. Sample FOR XML RAW Query

```
USE AdventureWorks2014;
GO

SELECT
    ProductID,
    Name,
    ProductNumber
FROM Production.Product
WHERE ProductID IN (770, 903)
FOR XML RAW;
```

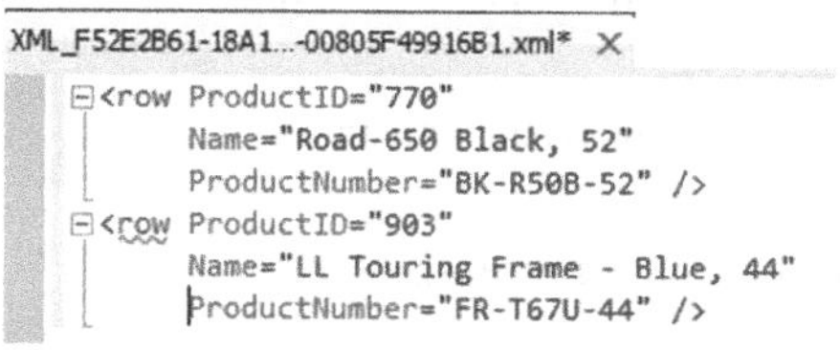

Figure 12-3. Results of the FOR XML RAW Query

The FOR XML clause modes support several additional options to control the resulting output. The options supported by all FOR XML modes are shown in Figure 12-4.

FOR XML Clause Options	XMLDATA*	XMLSCHEMA	ELEMENTS XSINIL	ELEMENTS ABSENT	BINARY BASE64	TYPE	ROOT	('ElementName')
FOR XML AUTO	●	●	●	●	●	●	●	
FOR XML RAW	●	●	●	●	●	●	●	●
FOR XML PATH			●	●	●	●	●	●
FOR XML EXPLICIT	●					●	●	●

*The XMLDATA option is deprecated. Use XMLSCHEMA instead.

Figure 12-4. FOR XML Clause Options

The options supported by FOR XML RAW mode include the following:

- The TYPE option specifies that the result should be returned as an xml data type instance. This is particularly useful when you use FOR XML in nested subqueries. By default, without the TYPE option, all FOR XML modes return XML data as a character string.

- The ROOT option adds a single top-level root element to the XML result. Using the ROOT option guarantees a well-formed XML (single root element) result.

- The ELEMENTS option specifies that column data should be returned as subelements instead of attributes in the XML result. The ELEMENTS option can have the following additional options:

- XSINIL specifies that columns with SQL nulls are included in the result with an xsi:nil attribute set to true.

- ABSENT specifies that no elements are created for SQL nulls. ABSENT is the default action for handling nulls.

- The BINARY BASE64 option specifies that binary data returned by the query should be represented in Base64-encoded form in the XML result. If your result contains any binary data, the BINARY BASE64 option is required.

- XMLSCHEMA returns an inline XML schema definition (the W3C XML Schema Recommendation is available at www.w3.org/XML/Schema).

- XMLDATA appends an XML-Data Reduced (XDR) schema to the beginning of your XML result. This option is deprecated and should not be used for future development. If you currently use this option, Microsoft recommends changing your code to use the XMLSCHEMA option instead.

As we discuss the other FOR XML modes, we will point out the options supported by each.

FOR XML AUTO

For a query against a single table, the AUTO keyword retrieves data in a format similar to RAW mode, but the XML node name is the name of the table and not the generic label row. For queries that join multiple tables, however, each XML element is named for the tables from which the SELECT list columns are retrieved. The order of the column names in the SELECT list determine the XML element nesting in the result. The FOR XML AUTO clause is called similarly to the FOR XML RAW clause, as shown in Listing 12-5. The results are shown in Figure 12-5.

Listing 12-5. FOR XML AUTO Query on a Single Table

```
USE AdventureWorks2014;
GO

SELECT
    ProductID,
    Name,
    ProductNumber
FROM Production.Product
WHERE ProductID IN (770, 903)
FOR XML AUTO;
```

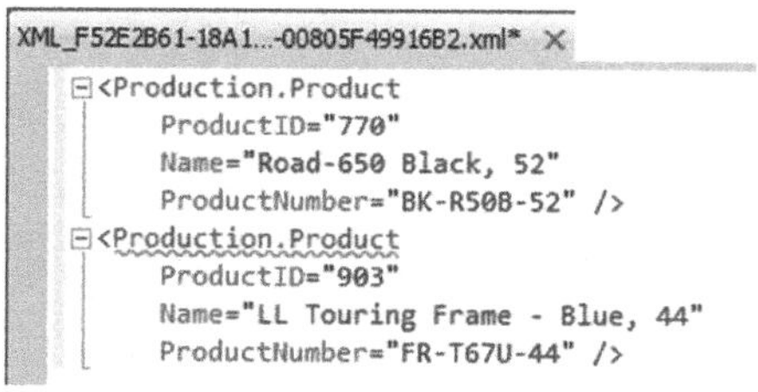

```
XML_F52E2B61-18A1...-00805F4991 6B2.xml*  ×
    ⊟<Production.Product
          ProductID="770"
          Name="Road-650 Black, 52"
          ProductNumber="BK-R50B-52" />
    ⊟<Production.Product
          ProductID="903"
          Name="LL Touring Frame - Blue, 44"
          ProductNumber="FR-T67U-44" />
```

Figure 12-5. *Results of the FOR XML AUTO Single-table Query*

Listing 12-6 demonstrates using FOR XML AUTO in a SELECT query that joins two tables. The results are shown in Figure 12-6.

Listing 12-6. FOR XML AUTO Query with a Join

```
SELECT
  Product.ProductID,
  Product.Name,
  Product.ProductNumber,
  Inventory.Quantity
FROM Production.Product Product
INNER JOIN Production.ProductInventory Inventory
ON Product.ProductID = Inventory.ProductID
WHERE Product.ProductID IN (770, 3)
FOR XML AUTO;
```

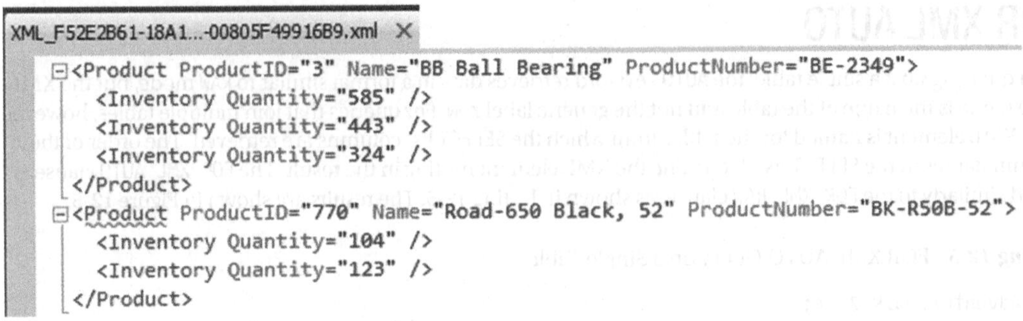

```
XML_F52E2B61-18A1...-00805F499169B9.xml   X
  ⊟<Product ProductID="3" Name="BB Ball Bearing" ProductNumber="BE-2349">
      <Inventory Quantity="585" />
      <Inventory Quantity="443" />
      <Inventory Quantity="324" />
   </Product>
  ⊟<Product ProductID="770" Name="Road-650 Black, 52" ProductNumber="BK-R50B-52">
      <Inventory Quantity="104" />
      <Inventory Quantity="123" />
   </Product>
```

Figure 12-6. *Results of the FOR XML AUTO Query with a Join*

The FOR XML AUTO statement can be further refined by adding the ELEMENTS option. Just as with the FOR XML RAW clause, the ELEMENTS option transforms the XML column attributes into subelements, as demonstrated in Listing 12-7, with results shown in Figure 12-7.

Listing 12-7. FOR XML AUTO Query with ELEMENTS Option

```
SELECT
  ProductID,
  Name,
  ProductNumber
FROM Production.Product
WHERE ProductID = 770
FOR XML AUTO, ELEMENTS;
```

```
XML_F52E2B61-18A1...-00805F499169B4.xml
  ⊟<Production.Product>
      <ProductID>770</ProductID>
      <Name>Road-650 Black, 52</Name>
      <ProductNumber>BK-R50B-52</ProductNumber>
   </Production.Product>
```

Figure 12-7. *Results of the FOR XML AUTO Query with the ELEMENTS Option*

The FOR XML AUTO clause can accept almost all of the same options as the FOR XML RAW clause. The only option that you can use with FOR XML RAW that's not available to FOR XML AUTO is the user-defined ElementName option, since AUTO mode generates row names based on the names of tables in the query.

FOR XML EXPLICIT

The FOR XML EXPLICIT clause is flexible but complex. This clause allows you to specify the exact hierarchy of XML elements and attributes in your XML result. This structure is specified in the SELECT statement itself using a special ElementName!TagNumber!AttributeName!Directive notation.

■ **Tip** The FOR XML PATH clause, described in the next section, also allows you to explicitly define your XML result structure. The FOR XML PATH clause accepts XPath-style syntax to define the structure and node names, however, and is much easier to use than FOR XML EXPLICIT. As a general recommendation, we would advise using FOR XML PATH instead of FOR XML EXPLICIT for new development and converting old FOR XML EXPLICIT queries to FOR XML PATH when possible.

In order to get FOR XML EXPLICIT to convert your relational data to XML format, there's a strict requirement on the results of the SELECT query—it must return data in universal table format that includes a Tag column defining the level of the current tag and a Parent column with the parent level for the current tag. The remaining columns in the query are the actual data columns. Listing 12-8 demonstrates a FOR XML EXPLICIT query that returns information about a product, including all of its inventory quantities, as a nested XML result. The results are shown in Figure 12-8.

Listing 12-8. FOR XML EXPLICIT Query

```
SELECT
        1 AS Tag,
        NULL AS Parent,
        ProductID AS [Products!1!ProductID!element],
        Name AS [Products!1!ProductName],
        ProductNumber AS [Products!1!ProductNumber],
        NULL AS [Products!2!Quantity]
        FROM Production.Product
        WHERE ProductID IN (770, 3)

UNION ALL

SELECT
  2 AS Tag,
  1 AS Parent,
  NULL,
  NULL,
  NULL,
  Quantity
FROM Production.ProductInventory
WHERE ProductID IN (770, 3)
  FOR XML EXPLICIT;
```

```
XML_F52E2B61-18A1...00805F49916B10.xml  ×
⊟<Products ProductName="BB Ball Bearing" ProductNumber="BE-2349">
   <ProductID>3</ProductID>
  </Products>
⊟<Products ProductName="Road-650 Black, 52" ProductNumber="BK-R50B-52">
   <ProductID>770</ProductID>
   <Products Quantity="585" />
   <Products Quantity="443" />
   <Products Quantity="324" />
   <Products Quantity="104" />
   <Products Quantity="123" />
  </Products>
```

Figure 12-8. *Results of the FOR XML EXPLICIT Query*

The FOR XML EXPLICIT query in Listing 12-8 defines the top-level elements with Tag = 1 and Parent = NULL. The next level is defined with Tag = 2 and Parent = 1, referencing back to the top level. Additional levels can be added by using the UNION keyword with additional queries that increment the Tag and Parent references for each additional level.

Each column of the query must be named with the ElementName!TagNumber!AttributeName!Directive format that we mentioned previously. As specified by this format, ElementName is the name of the XML element, in this case Products. TagNumber is the level of the element, which is 1 for top-level elements. AttributeName is the name of the attribute if you want the data in the column to be returned as an XML attribute. If you want the item to be returned as an XML element, use AttributeName to specify the name of the attribute, and set the Directive value to element. The Directive values that can be specified include the following:

- The hide directive value, which is useful when you want to retrieve values for sorting purposes but do not want the specified node included in the resulting XML.

- The element directive value, which generates an XML element instead of an attribute.

- The elementxsinil directive value, which generates an element for SQL null column values.

- The xml directive value, which generates an element instead of an attribute, but does not encode entity values.

- The cdata directive value, which wraps the data in a CDATA section and does not encode entities.

- The xmltext directive value, which wraps the column content in a single tag integrated with the document.

- The id, idref, and idrefs directive values, which allow you to create internal document links.

The additional options that the FOR XML EXPLICIT clause supports are BINARY BASE64, TYPE, ROOT, and XMLDATA. These options operate the same as they do in the FOR XML RAW and FOR XML AUTO clauses.

FOR XML PATH

The FOR XML PATH clause was first introduced in SQL Server 2005. It provides another way to convert relational data to XML format with a specific structure, but is much easier to use than the FOR XML EXPLICIT clause. Like FOR XML EXPLICIT, the FOR XML PATH clause makes you define the structure of the XML result. But the FOR XML PATH clause allows you to use a subset of the well-documented and much more intuitive XPath syntax to define your XML structure.

The FOR XML PATH clause uses column names to define the structure, as with FOR XML EXPLICIT. In keeping with the XML standard, column names in the SELECT statement with a FOR XML PATH clause are case sensitive. For instance, a column named Inventory is different from a column named INVENTORY. Any columns that do not have names are inlined, with their content inserted as XML content for xml data type columns or as a text node for other data types. This is useful for including the results of nameless computed columns or scalar subqueries in your XML result.

FOR XML PATH uses XPath-style path expressions to define the structure and names of nodes in the XML result. Because path expressions can contain special characters like the forward slash (/) and at sign (@), you will usually want to use quoted column aliases as shown in Listing 12-9. The results of this sample FOR XML PATH query are shown in Figure 12-9.

Listing 12-9. FOR XML PATH Query

```
SELECT
        p.ProductID AS "Product/@ID",
        p.Name AS "Product/Name",
        p.ProductNumber AS "Product/Number",
        i.Quantity AS "Product/Quantity"
FROM Production.Product p
        INNER JOIN Production.ProductInventory i
        ON p.ProductID = i.ProductID
        WHERE p.ProductID = 770
FOR XML PATH;
```

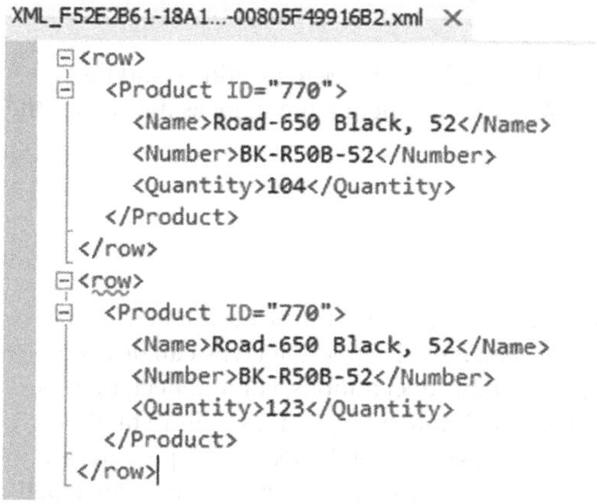

```
XML_F52E2B61-18A1...-00805F499168B2.xml  ×
  ⊟<row>
  ⊟    <Product ID="770">
           <Name>Road-650 Black, 52</Name>
           <Number>BK-R50B-52</Number>
           <Quantity>104</Quantity>
        </Product>
     </row>
  ⊟<row>
  ⊟    <Product ID="770">
           <Name>Road-650 Black, 52</Name>
           <Number>BK-R50B-52</Number>
           <Quantity>123</Quantity>
        </Product>
     </row>
```

Figure 12-9. *Results of the FOR XML PATH Query*

The FOR XML PATH clause imposes some rules on column naming, since the column names define not only the names of the XML nodes generated, but also the structure of the XML result. You can also use XPath node tests in your FOR XML PATH clauses. These rules and node tests are summarized in Table 12-3.

Table 12-3. *FOR XML PATH Column-naming Conventions*

Column Name	Result
text()	The string value of the column is added as a text node.
comment()	The string value of the column is added as an XML comment.
node()	The string value of the column is inserted inline under the current element.
*	This is the same as node().
data()	The string value of the column is inserted as an atomic value. Spaces are inserted between atomic values in the resulting XML.

(continued)

Table 12-3. (*continued*)

Column Name	Result
processing-instruction(name)	The string value of the column is inserted as an XML-processing instruction named name.
@name	The string value of the column is inserted as an attribute of the current element.
Name	The string value of the column is inserted as a subelement of the current element.
elem/name	The string value of the column is inserted as a subelement of the specified element hierarchy, under the element specified by elem.
elem/@name	The string value of the column is inserted as an attribute of the last element in the specified hierarchy, under the element specified by elem.

The FOR XML PATH clause supports the BINARY BASE64, TYPE, ROOT, and ELEMENTS options, and the user-defined ElementName options. The additional FOR XML PATH options operate the same as they do for the FOR XML AUTO and FOR XML RAW clauses.

The xml Data Type

SQL Server's legacy XML functionality can be cumbersome and clunky to use at times. Fortunately, SQL Server 2014 provides much tighter XML integration with its xml data type. The xml data type can be used anywhere that other SQL Server data types are used, including variable declarations, column declarations, SP parameters, and UDF parameters and return types. The T-SQL xml data type provides built-in methods that allow you to query and modify XML nodes. When you declare instances of the xml data type, you can create them as untyped (which is the default), or you can associate them with XML schemas to create typed xml instances. This section discusses both typed and untyped xml in T-SQL.

The xml data type can hold complete XML documents or XML fragments. An XML document must follow all the rules for well-formed XML, including the following:

- Well-formed XML must have at least one element.

- Every well-formed XML document has a single top-level, or root, element.

- Well-formed XML requires properly nested elements (tags cannot overlap).

- All tags must be properly closed in a well-formed XML document.

- Attribute values must be quoted in a well-formed XML document.

- Special characters in element content must be properly entitized, or converted to XML entities such as & for the ampersand character.

An XML fragment must conform to all the rules for well-formed XML, except that it may have more than one top-level element. The stored internal representation of an XML document or fragment stored in an xml variable or column maxes out at around 2.1 GB of storage.

Untyped xml

Untyped xml variables and columns are created by following them with the keyword xml in the declaration, as shown in Listing 12-10.

Listing 12-10. Untyped xml Variable and Column Declarations

```
DECLARE @x XML;
CREATE TABLE XmlPurchaseOrders
(
    PoNum int NOT NULL PRIMARY KEY,
    XmlPurchaseOrder xml );
```

Populating an xml variable or column with an XML document or fragment requires a simple assignment statement. You can implicitly or explicitly convert char, varchar, nchar, nvarchar, varbinary, text, and ntext data to xml. There are some rules to consider when converting from these types to xml:

- The XML parser always treats nvarchar, nchar, and nvarchar(max) data as a two-byte Unicode-encoded XML document or fragment.

- SQL Server treats char, varchar, and nvarchar(max) data as a single-byte-encoded XML document or fragment. The code page of the source string, variable, or column is used for encoding by default.

- The content of varbinary data is passed directly to the XML parser, which accepts it as a stream. If the varbinary XML data is Unicode encoded, the byte-order mark/encoding information must be included in the varbinary data. If no byte-order mark/encoding information is included, the default of UTF-8 is used.

Note The binary data type can also be implicitly or explicitly converted to xml, but it must be the exact length of the data it contains. The extra padding applied to binary variables and columns when the data they contain is too short can cause errors in the XML-parsing process. Use the varbinary data type when you need to convert binary data to XML.

Listing 12-11 demonstrates implicit conversion from nvarchar to the xml data type. The CAST or CONVERT functions can be used when an explicit conversion is needed.

Listing 12-11. Populating an Untyped xml Variable

```
DECLARE @x xml = N'<?xml version="1.0" ?>
<Address>
<Latitude>47.642737</Latitude>
<Longitude>-122.130395</Longitude>
<Street>ONE MICROSOFT WAY</Street>
<City>REDMOND</City>
<State>WA</State>
<Zip>98052</Zip>
<Country>US</Country>
</Address>';

SELECT @x;
```

Typed xml

To create a typed xml variable or column in SQL Server 2014, you must first create an XML schema collection with the CREATE XML SCHEMA COLLECTION statement. The CREATE XML SCHEMA COLLECTION statement allows you to specify a SQL Server name for your schema collection and an XML schema to add. Listing 12-12 shows how to create an XML schema collection.

Listing 12-12. Creating a Typed xml Variable

```
CREATE XML SCHEMA COLLECTION AddressSchemaCollection
    AS N'<?xml version="1.0" encoding="utf-16"  ?>
    <xsd:schema xmlns:xsd="http://www.w3.org/2001/XMLSchema">
        <xsd:element name="Address">
            <xsd:complexType>
                <xsd:sequence>
                    <xsd:element name="Latitude" type="xsd:decimal" />
                    <xsd:element name="Longitude" type="xsd:decimal" />
                    <xsd:element name="Street" type="xsd:string" />
                    <xsd:element name="City" type="xsd:string" />
                    <xsd:element name="State" type="xsd:string" />
                    <xsd:element name="Zip" type="xsd:string"  />
                    <xsd:element name="Country" type="xsd:string" />
                </xsd:sequence>
            </xsd:complexType>
        </xsd:element>
    </xsd:schema>';
GO
DECLARE @x XML (CONTENT AddressSchemaCollection);

SELECT @x =   N'<?xml version="1.0" ?>
        <Address>
                <Latitude>47.642737</Latitude>
                <Longitude>-122.130395</Longitude>
                <Street>ONE  MICROSOFT  WAY</Street>
                <City>REDMOND</City>
                <State>WA</State>
                <Zip>98052</Zip>
                <Country>US</Country>
        </Address>';

SELECT @x;

DROP  XML SCHEMA COLLECTION AddressSchemaCollection;
GO
```

The first step in creating a typed xml instance is to create an XML schema collection, as we did in Listing 12-12:

```
CREATE XML SCHEMA COLLECTION AddressSchemaCollection
        AS N'<?xml version="1.0" encoding="utf-16"  ?>
        <xsd:schema xmlns:xsd="http://www.w3.org/2001/XMLSchema">
                <xsd:element name="Address">
                        <xsd:complexType>
                                <xsd:sequence>
                                        <xsd:element name="Latitude" type="xsd:decimal" />
                                        <xsd:element name="Longitude" type="xsd:decimal" />
                                        <xsd:element name="Street" type="xsd:string" />
                                        <xsd:element name="City" type="xsd:string" />
                                        <xsd:element name="State" type="xsd:string" />
                                        <xsd:element name="Zip" type="xsd:string"  />
                                        <xsd:element name="Country" type="xsd:string" />
                                </xsd:sequence>
                        </xsd:complexType>
                </xsd:element>
        </xsd:schema>';
```

■ **Tip** The World Wide Web Consortium (W3C) maintains the standards related to XML schemas. The official XML Schema recommendations are available at www.w3.org/TR/xmlschema-1/ and www.w3.org/TR/xmlschema-2/. These W3C recommendations are an excellent starting point for creating your own XML schemas.

The next step is to declare the variable as xml type, but with an XML schema collection specification included:

```
DECLARE @x XML (CONTENT AddressSchemaCollection);
```

In the example, we used the CONTENT keyword before the schema collection name in the xml variable declaration. SQL Server offers two keywords, DOCUMENT and CONTENT, that represent facets you can use to constrain typed xml instances. Using the DOCUMENT facet in your typed xml variable or column declaration constrains your typed XML data so that it must contain only one top-level root element. The CONTENT facet allows zero or more top-level elements. CONTENT is the default if neither is specified explicitly.

The next step in the example is the assignment of XML content to the typed xml variable. During the assignment, SQL Server validates the XML content against the XML schema collection.

```
SELECT @x = N'<?xml version="1.0" ?>
        <Address>
                <Latitude>47.642737</Latitude>
                <Longitude>-122.130395</Longitude>
                <Street>ONE  MICROSOFT  WAY</Street>
                <City>REDMOND</City>
                <State>WA</State>
                <Zip>98052</Zip>
                <Country>US</Country>
        </Address>';

SELECT @x;
```

The DROP XML SCHEMA COLLECTION statement in the listing removes the XML schema collection from SQL Server.

```
DROP XML SCHEMA COLLECTION AddressSchemaCollection;
```

You can also add new XML schemas and XML schema components to XML schema collections with the ALTER XML SCHEMA COLLECTION statement.

The xml Data Type Methods

The xml data type has several methods for querying and modifying xml data. The built-in xml data type methods are summarized in Table 12-4.

Table 12-4. xml Data Type Methods

Method	Result
query(xquery)	Performs an XQuery query against an xml instance. The result returned is an untyped xml instance.
value(xquery, sql_type)	Performs an XQuery query against an xml instance and returns a scalar value of the specified SQL Server data type.
exist(xquery)	Performs an XQuery query against an xml instance and returns one of the following bit values: 1 if the xquery expression returns a nonempty result, 0 if the xquery expression returns an empty result, NULL if the xml instance is NULL.
modify(xml_dml)	Performs an XML Data Modification Language (XML DML) statement to modify an xml instance.
nodes(xquery) as table_name(column_name)	Performs an XQuery query against an xml instance and returns matching nodes as an SQL result set. The table_name and column_name specify aliases for the virtual table and column to hold the nodes returned. These aliases are mandatory for the nodes() method.

This section introduces each of these xml data type methods.

The query Method

The xml data type query() method accepts an XQuery query string as its only parameter. This method returns all nodes matching the XQuery as a single untyped xml instance. Conveniently enough, Microsoft provides sample typed xml data in the Resume column of the HumanResources.JobCandidate table. Though all of its xml is well formed with a single root element, the Resume column is faceted with the default of CONTENT.

Listing 12-13 shows how to use the query() method to retrieve names from the resumes in the HumanResources.JobCandidate table.

Listing 12-13. Using the Query Method on the HumanResources.JobCandidate Resume XML

```
SELECT Resume.query(N'declare namespace ns =
    "http://schemas.microsoft.com/sqlserver/2004/07/adventure-works/Resume";
/ns:Resume/ns:Name') AS [NameXML]
FROM HumanResources.JobCandidate;
```

The first thing to notice is the namespace declaration inside the XQuery query via the declare namespace statement. This is done because the Resume column's xml data declares a namespace. In fact, the namespace declaration used in the XQuery is exactly the same as the declaration used in the xml data. The declaration section of the XQuery looks like this:

```
declare namespace ns =
"http://schemas.microsoft.com/sqlserver/2004/07/adventure-works/Resume";
```

The actual query portion of the XQuery query is a simple path expression:

```
/ns:Resume/ns:Name
```

A sample of the results of Listing 12-13 are shown in Figure 12-10 (reformatted for easy reading).

```
NameXML 1.xml*  X
<ns:Name xmlns:ns="http://schemas.microsoft.com/sqlserver/2004/07/adventure-works/Resume">
    <ns:Name.Prefix />
    <ns:Name.First>Shai</ns:Name.First>
    <ns:Name.Middle />
    <ns:Name.Last>Bassli</ns:Name.Last>
    <ns:Name.Suffix />
</ns:Name>
<ns:Name xmlns:ns="http://schemas.microsoft.com/sqlserver/2004/07/adventure-works/Resume">
    <ns:Name.Prefix>Mr.</ns:Name.Prefix>
    <ns:Name.First>Max</ns:Name.First>
    <ns:Name.Middle />
    <ns:Name.Last>Benson</ns:Name.Last>
    <ns:Name.Suffix />
</ns:Name>
<ns:Name xmlns:ns="http://schemas.microsoft.com/sqlserver/2004/07/adventure-works/Resume">
    <ns:Name.Prefix>Mr.</ns:Name.Prefix>
    <ns:Name.First>Krishna</ns:Name.First>
    <ns:Name.Middle />
    <ns:Name.Last>Sunkammurali</ns:Name.Last>
    <ns:Name.Suffix />
</ns:Name>
```

Figure 12-10. *Retrieving Job Candidate Names with the Query Method (Partial Results)*

■ **Tip** SQL Server 2014 implements a subset of the W3C XQuery recommendation. Chapter 13 discusses SQL Server's XPath and XQuery implementations in detail. If you're just getting started with XQuery, additional resources include the W3C recommendation available at http://www.w3.org/standards/techs/xquery#w3c_all/, and on BOL at http://msdn.microsoft.com/en-us/library/ms189075.aspx.

The value Method

The xml data type's value() method performs an XQuery query against an xml instance and returns a scalar result. The scalar result of value() is automatically cast to the T-SQL data type specified in the call to value(). The sample code in Listing 12-14 uses the value() method to retrieve all last names from AdventureWorks job applicant resumes. The results are shown in Figure 12-11.

Listing 12-14. *xml Data Type Value Method Sample*

```
SELECT Resume.value (N'declare namespace ns =
    "http://schemas.microsoft.com/sqlserver/2004/07/adventure-works/Resume";
    (/ns:Resume/ns:Name/ns:Name.Last)[1]',
    'nvarchar(100)') AS [LastName]
FROM HumanResources.JobCandidate;
```

	LastName
1	Bassli
2	Benson
3	Sunkammurali
4	Jiang
5	D'Hers
6	Kleinerman
7	Penuchot
8	Wu
9	Yang
10	Yee
11	คณาพล
12	เบญจศร
13	บางสุบศรี

Figure 12-11. *Using the Value Method to Retrieve Job Candidate Last Names*

Like the query() method described previously, the value() method sample XQuery query begins by declaring a namespace:

```
declare namespace ns =
    "http://schemas.microsoft.com/sqlserver/2004/07/adventure-works/Resume";
```

The actual query portion of the XQuery query is a simple path expression:

```
(/ns:Resume/ns:Name/ns:Name.Last)[1]
```

Because value() returns a scalar value, the query is enclosed in parentheses with an XQuery numeric predicate [1] following it to force the return of a singleton atomic value. The second parameter passed into value() is the T-SQL data type that value() will cast the result to, in this case nvarchar. The value() method cannot cast its result to a SQL CLR user-defined type or an xml, image, text, ntext, or sql_variant data type.

The exist Method

The xml data type provides the exist() method for determining if an XML node exists in an xml instance, or if an existing XML node value meets a specific set of criteria. The example in Listing 12-15 uses the exist() method in a query to return all AdventureWorks job candidates that reported a bachelor's degree level of education. The results are shown in Figure 12-12.

Listing 12-15. xml Data Type Exist Method Example

```
SELECT Resume.value (N'declare namespace ns =
  "http://schemas.microsoft.com/sqlserver/2004/07/adventure-works/Resume";
  (/ns:Resume/ns:Name/ns:Name.Last) [1]',
  'nvarchar(100)') AS [BachelorsCandidate]
FROM HumanResources.JobCandidate
WHERE Resume.exist (N'declare namespace ns =
  "http://schemas.microsoft.com/sqlserver/2004/07/adventure-works/Resume";
  /ns:Resume/ns:Education/ns:Edu.Level [ . = "Bachelor" ]') = 1;
```

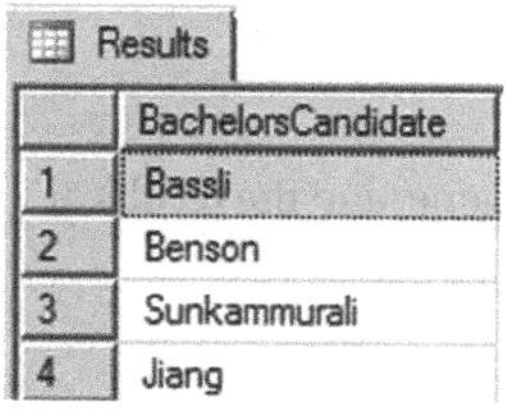

	BachelorsCandidate
1	Bassli
2	Benson
3	Sunkammurali
4	Jiang

Figure 12-12. *Using the Exist Method to Retrieve Bachelor's Degree Job Candidates*

The first part of the query borrows from the value() method example in Listing 12-13 to retrieve matching job candidate names:

```
SELECT Resume.value (N'declare namespace ns =
"http://schemas.microsoft.com/sqlserver/2004/07/adventure-works/Resume";
(/ns:Resume/ns:Name/ns:Name.Last) [1]',
'nvarchar(100)') AS [BachelorsCandidate] FROM HumanResources.JobCandidate
```

The exist() method in the WHERE clause specifies the xml match criteria. Like the previous sample queries, the exist() method XQuery query begins by declaring a namespace:

```
declare namespace ns =
"http://schemas.microsoft.com/sqlserver/2004/07/adventure-works/Resume";
```

The query itself compares the Edu.Level node text to the string Bachelor:

```
/ns:Resume/ns:Education/ns:Edu.Level [ . = "Bachelor" ]
```

If there is a match, the query returns a result and the exist() method returns 1. If there is no match, there will be no nodes returned by the XQuery query, and the exist() method will return 0. If the xml is NULL, exist() returns NULL. The query limits the results to only matching resumes by returning only those where exist() returns 1.

The nodes Method

The nodes() method of the xml data type retrieves XML content in relational format—a process known as shredding. The nodes() method returns a rowset composed of the xml nodes that match a given XQuery expression. Listing 12-16 retrieves product names and IDs for those products with the word Alloy in the Material node of their CatalogDescription column. The table queried is Production.ProductModel. Notice that the CROSS APPLY operator is used to perform the nodes() method on all rows of the Production.ProductModel table.

Listing 12-16. xml Data Type Nodes Example

```
SELECT
        ProductModelID,
        Name,
        Specs.query('.') AS Result
FROM Production.ProductModel
CROSS APPLY CatalogDescription.nodes('declare namespace ns =
"http://schemas.microsoft.com/sqlserver/2004/07/adventure-works/ProductModelDescription";
/ns:ProductDescription/ns:Specifications/Material/text()
  [ contains ( . , "Alloy" ) ]')
AS NodeTable(Specs);
```

The first part of the SELECT query retrieves the product model ID, the product name, and the results of the nodes() method via the query() method:

```
SELECT
  ProductModelId,
  Name,
  Specs.query('.') AS Result
FROM Production.ProductModel
```

One restriction of the nodes() method is that the relational results generated cannot be retrieved directly. They can only be accessed via the exist(), nodes(), query(), and value() methods of the xml data type, or checked with the IS NULL and IS NOT NULL operators.

The CROSS APPLY operator is used with the nodes() method to generate the final result set. The XQuery query used in the nodes() method begins by declaring a namespace:

```
CROSS APPLY CatalogDescription.nodes('declare namespace ns = "http://schemas.microsoft.
com/sqlserver/2004/07/adventure-works/ProductModelDescription";
```

The query portion is a path expression that retrieves XML nodes in which a Material node's text contains the word Alloy:

```
/ns:ProductDescription/ns:Specifications/Material/text() [ contains ( . , "Alloy" ) ]')
```

Notice that the nodes() method requires you to provide aliases for both the virtual table returned and the column that will contain the result rows. In this instance, we chose to alias the virtual table with the name NodeTable and the column with the name Specs.

```
AS NodeTable(Specs);
```

The modify Method

The xml data type modify() method can be used to modify the content of an xml variable or column. The modify() method allows you to insert, delete, or update xml content. The main restrictions on the modify() method is that it must be used in a variable SET statement or in the SET clause of an UPDATE statement. The example in Listing 12-17 demonstrates the modify() method on an untyped xml variable. The results are shown in Figure 12-13.

Listing 12-17. xml Data Type Modify Method Example

```
DECLARE @x xml = N'<?xml version="1.0" ?>
<Address>
  <Street>1 MICROSOFT WAY</Street>
  <City>REDMOND</City>
  <State>WA</State>
  <Zip>98052</Zip>
  <Country>US</Country>
  <Website>http://www.microsoft.com</Website>
</Address>';

SELECT @x;

SET @x.modify ('insert
(
  <CompanyName>Microsoft Corporation</CompanyName>,
  <Url>http://msdn.microsoft.com</Url>,
  <UrlDescription>Microsoft Developer Network</UrlDescription>
)
into (/Address)[1] ');

SET @x.modify('replace value of
  (/Address/Street/text())[1]
  with "ONE MICROSOFT WAY"
');

SET @x.modify('
delete /Address/Website
');

SELECT @x;
```

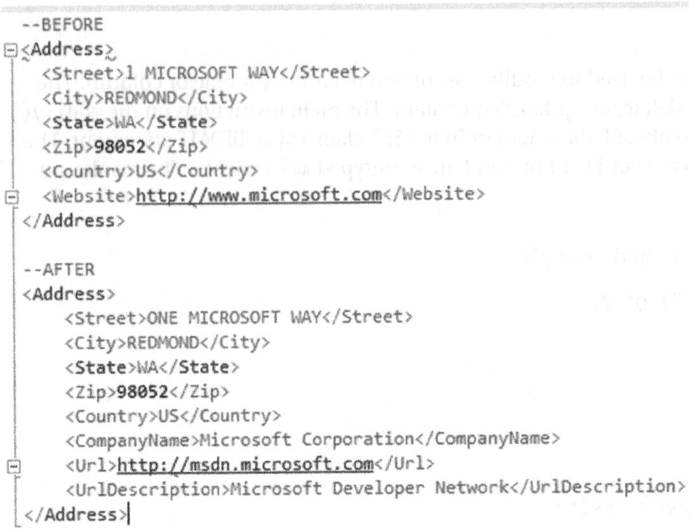

```
--BEFORE
<Address>
    <Street>1 MICROSOFT WAY</Street>
    <City>REDMOND</City>
    <State>WA</State>
    <Zip>98052</Zip>
    <Country>US</Country>
    <Website>http://www.microsoft.com</Website>
</Address>

--AFTER
<Address>
    <Street>ONE MICROSOFT WAY</Street>
    <City>REDMOND</City>
    <State>WA</State>
    <Zip>98052</Zip>
    <Country>US</Country>
    <CompanyName>Microsoft Corporation</CompanyName>
    <Url>http://msdn.microsoft.com</Url>
    <UrlDescription>Microsoft Developer Network</UrlDescription>
</Address>
```

Figure 12-13. *Before-and-after Results of the Modify Method*

■ **Tip** Although the SELECT and SET statements are similar in their functionality when applied to variables, the modify() method of the xml data type will not work in SELECT statements—even SELECT statements that assign values to variables. Use the SET statement as demonstrated in Listing 12-17 to use the modify() method on an xml variable.

The sample begins by creating an xml variable and assigning XML content to it:

```
DECLARE @x xml = N'<?xml version="1.0" ?> <Address>
<Street>1 MICROSOFT WAY</Street>
<City>REDMOND</City>
<State>WA</State>
<Zip>98052</Zip>
<Country>US</Country>
<Website>http://www.microsoft.com</Website> </Address>';
SELECT @x;
```

The XML DML insert statement inserts three new nodes into the xml variable, right below the top-level Address node:

```
SET @x.modify ('insert
(
  <CompanyName>Microsoft Corporation</CompanyName>]
  <Url>http://msdn.microsoft.com</Url>,
  <UrlDescription>Microsoft Developer&apos;s Network</UrlDescription>
)
into (/Address)[1] ');
```

372

The `replace value of` statement specified in the next `modify()` method updates the content of the Street node with the street address our good friends at Microsoft prefer: `ONE MICROSOFT WAY`, instead of `1 MICROSOFT WAY`.

```
SET @x.modify('replace value of (/Address/Street/text())[1]
  with "ONE MICROSOFT WAY"
');
```

Finally, the XML DML method `delete` statement is used to remove the old `<Website>` tag from the xml variable's content:

```
SET @x.modifyC
    delete /Address/Website
');

SELECT @x;
```

XML Indexes

SQL Server provides XML indexes to increase the efficiency of querying xml data type columns. XML indexes come in two flavors:

- Primary XML index: An XML column can have a single primary XML index declared on it. The primary XML index is different from the standard relational indexes most of us are used to. Rather, it is a persisted preshredded representation of your XML data. Basically, the XML data stored in a column with a primary XML index is converted to relational form and stored in the database. By persisting an xml data type column in relational form, you eliminate the implicit shredding that occurs with every query or manipulation of your XML data. In order to create a primary XML index on a table's xml column, a clustered index must be in place on the primary key columns for the table.

- Secondary XML index: Secondary XML indexes can also be created on a table's xml column. Secondary XML indexes are nonclustered relational indexes created on primary XML indexes. In order to create secondary XML indexes on an xml column, a primary XML index must already exist on that column. You can declare any of three different types of secondary XML index on your primary XML indexes:

  - The PATH index is a secondary XML index optimized for XPath and XQuery path expressions that rely heavily on path and node values. The PATH index creates an index on path and node values on the columns of the primary XML index. The path and node values are used as key columns for efficient path seek operations.

  - The VALUE index is optimized for queries by value where the path is not necessarily known. This type of index is the inverse of the PATH index, with the primary XML index node values indexed before the node paths.

  - The PROPERTY index is optimized for queries that retrieve data from other columns of a table based on the value of nodes or paths in the xml data type column. This type of secondary index is created on the primary key of the base table, node paths, and node values of the primary XML index.

Consider the example XQuery FLWOR (for, let, where, order by, return) expression in Listing 12-18 that retrieves the last, first, and middle names of all job applicants in the HumanResources.JobCandidate table with an education level of Bachelor. The results of this query are shown in Figure 12-14.

Listing 12-18. *Retrieving Job Candidates with Bachelor's Degrees*

```
SELECT Resume.query('declare namespace ns =
  "http://schemas.microsoft.com/sqlserver/2004/07/adventure-works/Resume";
for $m in /ns:Resume
where $m/ns:Education/ns:Edu.Level[. = "Bachelor" ]
return <Name>
    {
      data(($m/ns:Name/ns:Name.Last)[1]),
      data(($m/ns:Name/ns:Name.First)[1]),
      data(($m/ns:Name/ns:Name.Middle)[1])
    } </Name>')
FROM HumanResources.JobCandidate;
GO
```

	(No column name)
1	<Name>Bassli Shai </Name>
2	<Name>Benson Max </Name>
3	<Name>Sunkammurali Krishna </Name>
4	<Name>Jiang Stephen Y </Name>

Figure 12-14. Retrieving Candidate Names with a FLWOR Expression

We'll describe FLWOR expressions in greater detail, with examples, in Chapter 13. For the purposes of this discussion, however, the results are not as important as what's going on under the hood. This FLWOR expression is returning the last, first, and middle names of all candidates for which the Edu.Level node contains the value Bachelor. As shown in Figure 12-15, the execution cost of this query is 41.2849. Although the subtree cost is an arbitrary number, it represents the total cost in relationship to the batch. In this case the number is large enough in relationship to the batch to warrant investigation.

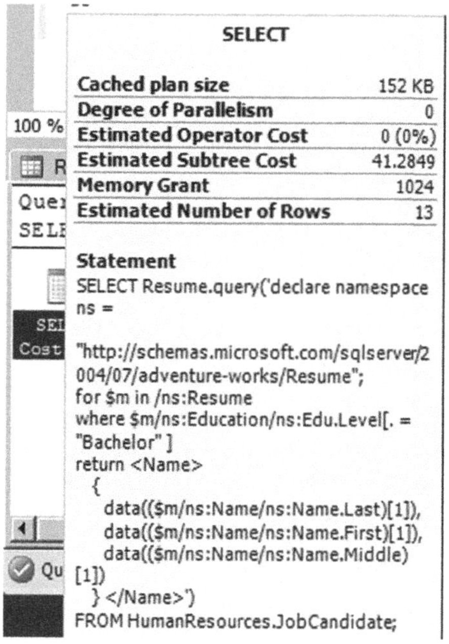

Figure 12-15. *The Execution Cost of the Query*

By far the most expensive part of this query is contained in a step called Table Valued Function [XML Reader with XPath Filter]. This is the main operator SQL Server uses to shred XML data on the fly whenever you query XML data. In this query plan, it is invoked two times at a cost of 13.052 each, and three more times at a cost of 4.89054 each, accounting for over 98 percent of the query plan cost (see Figure 12-16).

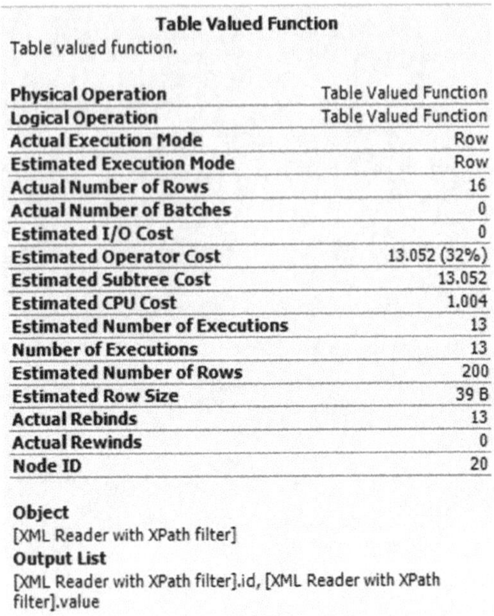

Table Valued Function

Table valued function.

Physical Operation	Table Valued Function
Logical Operation	Table Valued Function
Actual Execution Mode	Row
Estimated Execution Mode	Row
Actual Number of Rows	16
Actual Number of Batches	0
Estimated I/O Cost	0
Estimated Operator Cost	13.052 (32%)
Estimated Subtree Cost	13.052
Estimated CPU Cost	1.004
Estimated Number of Executions	13
Number of Executions	13
Estimated Number of Rows	200
Estimated Row Size	39 B
Actual Rebinds	13
Actual Rewinds	0
Node ID	20

Object
[XML Reader with XPath filter]
Output List
[XML Reader with XPath filter].id, [XML Reader with XPath filter].value

Figure 12-16. *Table Valued Function [XML Reader with XPath Filter] Cost*

Adding XML indexes to this column of the HumanResources.JobCandidate table significantly improves XQuery query performance by eliminating on-the-fly XML shredding. Listing 12-19 adds a primary and secondary XML index to the Resume column.

Listing 12-19. Adding XML Indexes to the Resume Column

```
CREATE PRIMARY XML INDEX PXML_JobCandidate
ON HumanResources.JobCandidate (Resume);
GO

CREATE XML INDEX IXML_Education
ON HumanResources.JobCandidate (Resume)
USING XML INDEX PXML_JobCandidate
FOR PATH;
GO
```

With the primary and secondary XML indexes in place, the query execution cost drops significantly from 41.2849 to 0.278555, as shown in Figure 12-17.

SELECT

Cached plan size	184 KB
Degree of Parallelism	0
Estimated Operator Cost	0 (0%)
Estimated Subtree Cost	0.278555
Estimated Number of Rows	13

Statement

SELECT Resume.query('declare namespace ns =

"http://schemas.microsoft.com/sqlserver/2004/07/adventure-works/Resume";
for $m in /ns:Resume
where $m/ns:Education/ns:Edu.Level[. =
"Bachelor"]
return <Name>
{
data(($m/ns:Name/ns:Name.Last)[1]),
data(($m/ns:Name/ns:Name.First)[1]),
data(($m/ns:Name/ns:Name.Middle)[1])
} </Name>')
FROM HumanResources.JobCandidate;

Figure 12-17. *The Query Execution Cost with XML Indexes*

The greater efficiency is brought about by the XML Reader with XPath Filter step being replaced with efficient index seek operators on both clustered and nonclustered indexes. The primary XML index eliminates the need to shred XML data at query time and the secondary XML index provides additional performance enhancement by providing a nonclustered index that can be used to efficiently fulfill the FLWOR expression where clause.

The CREATE PRIMARY XML INDEX statement in the example creates a primary XML index on the Resume column of the HumanResources.JobCandidate table. The primary XML index provides a significant performance increase by itself, since it eliminates on-the-fly XML shredding at query time.

CREATE PRIMARY XML INDEX PXML_JobCandidate ON HumanResources.JobCandidate (Resume);

The primary XML index is a prerequisite for creating the secondary XML index that will provide additional performance enhancement for XQuery queries that specify both a path and a predicate based on node content. The CREATE XML INDEX statement in the example creates the secondary XML PATH index.

CREATE XML INDEX IXML_Education ON HumanResources.JobCandidate (Resume) USING XML INDEX PXML_JobCandidate FOR PATH;

The USING XML INDEX clause of the CREATE XML INDEX statement specifies the name of the primary XML index on which to build the secondary XML index. The FOR clause determines the type of secondary XML index that will be created. You can specify a VALUE, PATH, or PROPERTY type as described previously.

The optional WITH clause of both of the XML index creation statements allows you to specify a variety of XML index creation options, as shown in Table 12-5.

Table 12-5. *XML Index Creation Options*

Option	Description
PAD_INDEX	This option specifies whether index padding is on or off. The default is OFF.
FILLFACTOR	This option indicates how full the leaf level index pages should be made during XML index creation or rebuild. Values of 0 and 100 are equivalent. The FILLFACTOR option is used in conjunction with the PAD_INDEX option.
SORT_IN_TEMPDB	This option specifies that intermediate sort results should be stored in tempdb. By default, SORT_IN_TEMPDB is set to OFF and intermediate sort results are stored in the local database.
STATISTICS_NORECOMPUTE	This option indicates whether distribution statistics are automatically recomputed. The default is OFF.
DROP_EXISTING	This option specifies that the preexisting XML index of the same name should be dropped before creating the index. The default is OFF.
ALLOW_ROW_LOCKS	This option allows SQL Server to use row locks when accessing the XML index. The default is ON.
ALLOW_PAGE_LOCKS	This option allows SQL Server to use page locks when accessing the XML index. The default is ON.
MAXDOP	This option determines the maximum degree of parallelism SQL Server can use during the XML index creation operation. MAXDOP can be one of the following values: 0: Uses up to the maximum number of processors available. 1: Uses only one processor; no parallel processing. 2 through 64: Restricts the number of processors used for parallel processing to the number specified or less.

XSL Transformations

One of the powerful features available to SQL Server 2014 is its ability to execute .NET Framework-based code via the SQL Common Language Runtime (SQL CLR). You can use standard .NET Framework classes to access XML-based functionality that is not supported directly within T-SQL. One useful feature that can be accessed via CLR Integration is the W3C Extensible Stylesheet Language Transformations (XSLT). As defined by the W3C, XSLT is a language designed for the sole purpose of "transforming XML documents into other XML documents." SQL Server 2014 provides access to XSL transformations via a combination of the built-in xml data type and the .NET Framework XslCompiledTransform class.

■ **Tip** The XSLT 1.0 standard is available at www.w3.org/TR/xslt.

You can access XSLT from SQL Server to perform server-side transformations of your relational data into other XML formats. I've chosen to use XHTML as the output format for this example, although some would argue that generating XHTML output is best done away from SQL Server, in the middle tier or presentation layer. Arguments can also be made for performing XSL transformations close to the data, for efficiency reasons. I'd like to put those arguments aside for the moment, and focus on the main purpose of this example, demonstrating that additional XML functionality is available to SQL Server via SQL CLR. Listing 12-20 demonstrates the first step in the process of performing server-side XSL transformations using FOR XML to convert relational data to an xml variable.

Listing 12-20. Using FOR XML to Convert Relational Data to Populate an xml Variable

```
DECLARE @xml xml =
(
    SELECT
        p.ProductNumber AS "@Id",
        p.Name AS "Name",
        p.Color AS "Color",
        p.ListPrice AS "ListPrice",
        p.SizeUnitMeasureCode AS "Size/@UOM",
        p.Size AS "Size",
        p.WeightUnitMeasureCode AS "Weight/@UOM",
        p.Weight AS "Weight",
        (
        SELECT COALESCE(SUM(i.Quantity), 0)
        FROM Production.ProductInventory i
        WHERE i.ProductID = p.ProductID
        ) AS "QuantityOnHand"
    FROM Production.Product p
    WHERE p.FinishedGoodsFlag = 1
    ORDER BY p.Name
    FOR XML PATH ('Product'),
        ROOT ('Products')
);

SELECT @xml;
```

The resulting xml document looks like Figure 12-18.

```
<Products>
    <Product Id="ST-1401">
        <Name>All-Purpose Bike Stand</Name>
        <ListPrice>159.0000</ListPrice>
        <QuantityOnHand>144</QuantityOnHand>
    </Product>
    <Product Id="CA-1098">
        <Name>AWC Logo Cap</Name>
        <Color>Multi</Color>
        <ListPrice>8.9900</ListPrice>
        <QuantityOnHand>288</QuantityOnHand>
    </Product>
    <Product Id="CL-9009">
        <Name>Bike Wash - Dissolver</Name>
        <ListPrice>7.9500</ListPrice>
        <QuantityOnHand>36</QuantityOnHand>
    </Product>
    <Product Id="LO-C100">
        <Name>Cable Lock</Name>
        <ListPrice>25.0000</ListPrice>
        <QuantityOnHand>252</QuantityOnHand>
    </Product>
```

Figure 12-18. *Partial Results of the FOR XML Product Query*

The next step is to create the XSLT style sheet to specify the transformation and assign it to an xml data type variable. Listing 12-21 demonstrates a simple XSLT style sheet to convert XML data to HTML.

Listing 12-21. XSLT Style Sheet to Convert Data to HTML

```
DECLARE @xslt xml = N'<?xml version="1.0" encoding="utf-16"?>
<xsl:stylesheet version="1.0"
        xmlns:xsl="http://www.w3.org/1999/XSL/Transform">
<xsl:template match="/Products">
<html>
        <head>
            <title>AdventureWorks Product Listing Report</title>
            <style type="text/css">
        tr.row-heading  {
            background-color: 000099;
            color: ffffff;
            font-family: tahoma, arial, helvetica, sans-serif;
            font-size:  12px;
        }
        tr.row-light {
            background-color:  ffffff;
            font-family: tahoma, arial, helvetica, sans-serif;
            font-size: 12px;
        }
        tr.row-dark  {
            background-color:  00ffff;
            font-family: tahoma,  arial, helvetica, sans-serif;
            font-size: 12px;
        }
        td.col-right {
            text-align: right;
        }
        </style>
</head>
<body>
    <table>
      <tr  class="row-heading">
        <th>ID</th>
        <th>Product  Name</th>
        <th>On  Hand</th>
        <th>List Price</th>
        <th>Color</th>
        <th>Size</th>
        <th>Weight</th>
      </tr>
      <xsl:for-each  select="Product">
          <xsl:element name="tr">
            <xsl:choose>
                <xsl:when test="position() mod 2 = 0">
                    <xsl:attribute name="class">row-light</xsl:attribute>
                </xsl:when>
```

```
            <xsl:otherwise>
                <xsl:attribute name="class">row-dark</xsl:attribute>
            </xsl:otherwise>
            </xsl:choose>
            <td><xsl:value-of select="@Id"/></td>
            <td><xsl:value-of select="Name"/></td>
            <td class="col-right">
                <xsl:value-of select="QuantityOnHand"/>
            </td>
            <td class="col-right"><xsl:value-of select="ListPrice"/></td>
            <td><xsl:value-of select="Color"/></td>
            <td class="col-right">            <xsl:value-of select="Size"/>
                <xsl:value-of select="Size/@UOM"/>
            </td>
            <td class="col-right">
                <xsl:value-of select="Weight"/>
                <xsl:value-of select="Weight/@UOM"/>
            </td>
        </td>
    </xsl:element>
  </xsl:for-each>
   </table>
 </body>
</html>
</xsl:template>
</xsl:stylesheet>';
```

■ **Tip**   We won't dive into the details of XSLT style sheet creation in this book, but information can be found at the official W3C XSLT 1.0 standard site, at http://www.w3.org/TR/xslt20/. The book Pro SQL Server 2008 XML (Apress, 2008) also offers a detailed discussion of XSLT on SQL Server.

The final step is to create an SQL CLR SP that accepts the raw XML data and the XSLT style sheet, performs the XSL transformation, and writes the results to an HTML file. The SQL CLR SP code is shown in Listing 12-22.

Listing 12-22. SQL CLR SP for XSL Transformations

```
using System.Data.SqlTypes;
using System.Xml;
using System.Xml.Xsl;

namespace Apress.Samples
{
public partial class XSLT
{
[Microsoft.SqlServer.Server.SqlProcedure]
public static void XmlToHtml
(
SqlXml RawXml,
```

```
SqlXml XslStyleSheet,
SqlString OutputPage
)

{
// Create and load the XslCompiledTransform object
XslCompiledTransform xslt = new XslCompiledTransform();
XmlDocument xmldoc1 = new XmlDocument();
xmldocl.LoadXml(XslStyleSheet.Value);
xslt.Load(xmldoc1);

// Create and load the Raw XML document
XmlDocument xml = new XmlDocument();
xml.LoadXml(RawXml.Value);

// Create the XmlTextWriter for output to HTML document
XmlTextWriter htmlout = new XmlTextWriter
(
OutputPage.Value,
System.Text.Encoding.Unicode
);

// Perform the transformation
xslt.Transform
(
xml,
htmlout
);

// Close the XmlTextWriter
htmlout.Close();
}
    }
};
```

SQL CLR Security Settings

There are a few administrative details you need to take care of before you deploy SQL CLR code to SQL
Server. The first thing to do is set the database to trustworthy mode with the ALTER DATABASE statement, as
shown following:

ALTER DATABASE AdventureWorks2014 SET TRUSTWORTHY ON;

A better alternative to setting your database to trustworthy mode is to sign your assemblies with a
certificate. While signing SQL CLR assemblies is beyond the scope of this book, authors Robin Dewson and
Julian Skinner cover this topic in their book Pro SQL Server 2005 Assemblies (Apress, 2005). The book covers
SQL 2005 but the topics are still relevant and applicable to SQL Server 2014.

For the example in Listing 12-22, which accesses the local file system, you also need to set the CLR
assembly permission level to External. You can do this through Visual Studio, as shown in the following
illustration, or you can use WITH PERMISSION_SET clause of the CREATE ASSEMBLY or ALTER ASSEMBLY
statements in T-SQL.

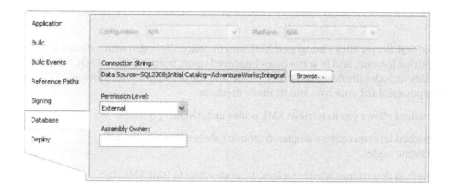

For SQL CLR code that doesn't require access to external resources or unmanaged code, a permission level of Safe is adequate. For SQL CLR assemblies that need access to external resources like hard drives or network resources, External permissions are the minimum required. Unsafe permissions are required for assemblies that access unsafe or unmanaged code. Always assign the minimum required permissions when deploying SQL CLR assemblies to SQL Server.

Finally, make sure the SQL Server service account has permissions to any required external resources. For this example, the service account needs permissions to write to the c:\Documents and Settings\ All Users\Documents directory.

After you have deployed the SQL CLR assembly to SQL Server and set the appropriate permissions, you can call the XmlToHtml procedure to perform the XSL transformation, as shown in Listing 12-23. The resulting HTML file is shown in Figure 12-19.

Listing 12-23. Performing a SQL CLR XSL Transformation

```
EXECUTE XmlToHtml @xml,
    gxslt,
    'c:\Documents and SettingsXAll Users\Documents\adventureworks-inventory.html';
```

Figure 12-19. Results of the XML-to-HTML Transformation

Summary

In this chapter, we discussed SQL Server 2014's integrated XML functionality. We began with a discussion of legacy XML functionality carried forward, and in some cases improved upon, from the days of SQL Server 2005. This legacy functionality includes the flexible FOR XML clause and the OPENXML rowset provider.

We then discussed the powerful xml data type and its many methods:

- The query() method allows you to retrieve XML nodes using XQuery queries.

- The value() method lets you retrieve singleton atomic values using XQuery path expressions to locate nodes.

- The exist() method determines whether a specific node exists in your XML data.

- The modify() method allows you to use XML DML to modify your XML data directly.

- The nodes() method makes shredding XML data simple.

We also presented SQL Server's primary and secondary XML indexes, which are designed to optimize XML query performance. Finally, we touched on SQL Server's SQL CLR integration and demonstrated how to use it to access .NET Framework XML functionality not directly available through the T-SQL language.

In the next chapter, we will continue the discussion of SQL Server XML by introducing XPath and XQuery support, including a more detailed discussion of the options, functions, operators, and expressions available for querying and manipulating XML on SQL Server.

EXERCISES

1. [Choose all that apply] SQL Server's FOR XML clause supports which of the following modes:

   a. FOR XML RAW

   b. FOR XML PATH

   c. FOR XML AUTO

   d. FOR XML EXPLICIT

   e. FOR XML RECURSIVE

2. [Fill in the blank] By default, the OPENXML rowset provider returns data in _____ table format.

3. [True/False] The xml data type query() method returns its results as an untyped xml data type instance.

4. [Choose one] A SQL Server primary XML index performs which of the following functions:

   f. It creates a nonclustered index on your xml data type column or variable.

   g. It creates a clustered index on your xml data type column or variable.

   h. It stores your xml data type columns in a preshredded relational format.

   i. It stores your xml data type columns using an inverse index format.

5. [True/False] When you perform XQuery queries against an xml data type column with no primary XML index defined on it, SQL Server automatically shreds your XML data to relational format.

6. [True/False] You can utilize define an XML data type column on a memory-optimized table in SQL Server 2014.

7. [True/False] You can access additional XML functionality on SQL Server through the .NET Framework via SQL Server's SQL CLR integration.

5. [True/False] When you perform XQuery queries against an xml data type column with no primary XML index defined on it, SQL Server automatically shreds your XML data to relational format.

6. [True/False] You can utilize define an XML data type column on a memory-optimized table in SQL Server 2014.

7. [True/False] You can access additional XML functionality on SQL Server through the .NET Framework via SQL Server's SQL CLR integration.

CHAPTER 13

■ ■ ■

Xquery and XPath

As we described in Chapter 12, SQL Server 2014 continues the high level of XML integration begun in SQL Server 2005. As part of that integration, SQL Server's xml data type provides built-in functionality for shredding XML data into relational format, querying XML nodes and singleton atomic values via XQuery, and modifying XML data via XML Data Modification Language (XML DML). This chapter focuses on how to get the most out of SQL Server's implementation of the powerful and flexible XPath and XQuery standards.

The XML data model represents a departure from the relational model SQL Server developers know so well. XML is not a replacement for the relational model, but it does nicely complement relational data. XML is very useful for sharing data with a wide variety of web services and message systems including MSMQ and disparate systems, and highly structured XML data from remote data sources is often shredded to relational format for easy storage and querying. The SQL Server 2014 xml data type and XML-specific query and conversion tools represent a marriage of some of the best features of relational database and XML technologies.

■ **Note**   This chapter is not meant to be a comprehensive guide to XPath and XQuery, but rather an introduction to SQL Server's XPath and XQuery implementations, which are both subsets of the W3C XPath 2.0 and XQuery 1.0 recommendations. In addition to the discussion in this chapter, Appendix B provides a reference to the XQuery Data Model (XDM) type system as implemented by SQL Server.

XPath and FOR XML PATH

The FOR XML PATH clause of the SELECT statement uses XPath 2.0-style path expressions to specify the structure of the XML result. Listing 13-1 demonstrates a simple FOR XML PATH query that returns the names and e-mail addresses of people in the AdventureWorks database. Partial results are shown in Figure 13-1, which you can display by clicking on the XML within the column.

Listing 13-1. Retrieving Names and E-mail Addresses with FOR XML PATH

```
SELECT
        p.BusinessEntityID AS "Person/ID",
        p.FirstName AS "Person/Name/First",
        p.MiddleName AS "Person/Name/Middle",
        p.LastName AS "Person/Name/Last",
        e.EmailAddress AS "Person/Email"
FROM Person.Person p INNER JOIN Person.EmailAddress e
ON p.BusinessEntityID = e.BusinessEntityID
FOR XML PATH, ROOT('PersonEmailAddress');
```

Figure 13-1. *Partial Results of Retrieving Names and E-mail Addresses with FOR XML PATH*

Because they are used specifically to define the structure of an XML result, FOR XML PATH XPath expressions are somewhat limited in their functionality. Specifically, you cannot use features that contain certain filter criteria or use absolute paths. Briefly, here are the restrictions:

- A FOR XML PATH XPath expression may not begin or end with the /step operator, and it may not begin with, end with, or contain //.

- FOR XML PATH XPath expressions cannot specify axis specifiers such as child:: or parent::.

- The . (context node) and .. (context node parent) axis specifiers are not allowed.

- The functions defined in Part 4 of the XPath specification, Core Function Library, are not allowed.

- Predicates, which are used to filter result sets, are not allowed. [position() = 4] is an example of a predicate.

Basically, the FOR XML PATH XPath subset allows you to specify the structure of the resulting XML relative to the implicit root node. This means that advanced functionality of XPath expressions above and beyond defining a simple relative path expression is not allowed. In general, XPath 2.0 features that can be used to locate specific nodes, return sets of nodes, or filter result sets are not allowed with FOR XML PATH.

By default, FOR XML PATH uses the name row for the root node of each row it converts to XML format. The results of FOR XML PATH also default to an element-centric format, meaning that results are defined in terms of element nodes.

In Listing 12-1, we've aliased the column names using the XPath expressions that define the structure of the XML result. Because the XPath expressions often contain characters that are not allowed in SQL identifiers, you will probably want to use quoted identifiers.

SELECT p.BusinessEntityID AS "Person/ID", p.FirstName AS "Person/Name/First", p.MiddleName AS "Person/Name/Middle", p.LastName AS "Person/Name/Last", e.EmailAddress AS "Person/Email"

XPath expressions are defined as a path separated by step operators. The step operator (/) indicates that a node is a child of the preceding node. For instance, the XPath expression Person/ID in the example indicates that a node named ID will be created as a child of the node named Person in a hierarchical XML structure.

XPath Attributes

Alternatively, you can define a relational column as an attribute of a node. Listing 13-2 modifies Listing 13-1 slightly to demonstrates this. We've shown the differences between the two listings in bold print. Partial results are shown in Figure 13-2, reformatted slightly for easier reading.

Listing 13-2. FOR XML PATH Creating XML Attributes

```
SELECT p.BusinessEntityID  AS "Person/@ID",
               e.EmailAddress AS "Person/@Email",
               p.FirstName AS "Person/Name/First",
               p.MiddleName AS "Person/Name/Middle",
               p.LastName AS "Person/Name/Last"
FROM Person.Person p INNER JOIN Person.EmailAddress e
ON p.BusinessEntityID = e.BusinessEntityID FOR XML PATH;
```

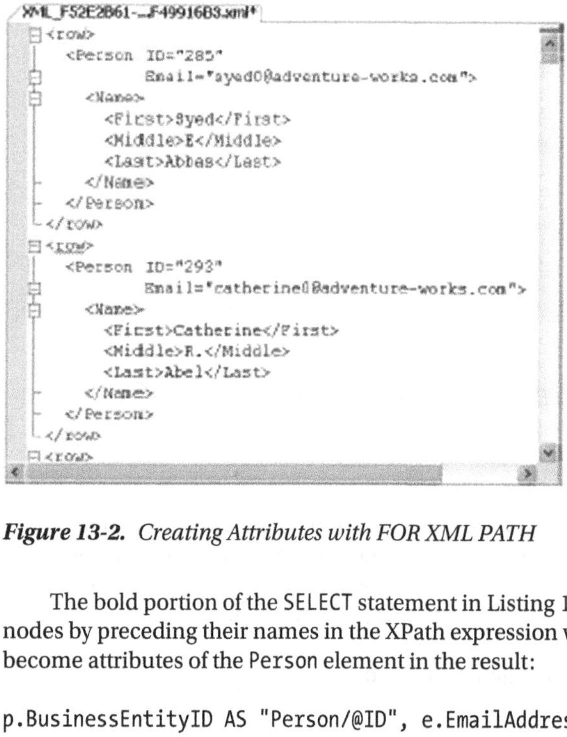

Figure 13-2. *Creating Attributes with FOR XML PATH*

The bold portion of the SELECT statement in Listing 13-2 generates XML attributes of the ID and Email nodes by preceding their names in the XPath expression with the @ symbol. The result is that ID and Email become attributes of the Person element in the result:

```
p.BusinessEntityID AS "Person/@ID", e.EmailAddress AS "Person/@Email",
```

Columns without Names and Wildcards

Some of the other XPath expression features you can use with FOR XML PATH include columns without names and wildcard expressions, which are turned into inline content. The sample in Listing 13-3 demonstrates this.

Listing 13-3. Using Columns without Names and Wildcards with FOR XML PATH

```
SELECT p.BusinessEntityID AS "*", ',' + e.EmailAddress,
p.FirstName AS "Person/Name/First",
p.MiddleName AS "Person/Name/Middle",
p.LastName AS "Person/Name/Last" FROM Person.Person p INNER JOIN Person.EmailAddress e
ON p.BusinessEntityID = e.BusinessEntityID FOR XML PATH;
```

In this example, the XPath expression for BusinessEntityID is the wildcard character *. The second column is defined as ',' + EmailAddress and the column is not given a name. Both of these columns are turned into inline content immediately below the row element, as shown in Figure 13-3. This is particularly useful functionality when creating lists within your XML data, or when your XML data conforms to a schema that looks for combined, concatenated, or list data in XML text nodes.

Figure 13-3. *Columns without Names and Wildcard Expressions in FOR XML PATH*

Element Grouping

As you saw in the previous examples, FOR XML PATH groups together nodes that have the same parent elements. For instance, the First, Middle, and Last elements are all children of the Name element. They are grouped together in all of the examples because of this. However, as shown in Listing 13-4, this is not the case when these elements are separated by an element with a different parent element.

Listing 13-4. Two Elements with a Common Parent Element Separated

```
SELECT p.BusinessEntityID AS "@ID",
            e.EmailAddress AS "@EmailAddress",
            p.FirstName AS "Person/Name/First",
            pp.PhoneNumber AS "Phone/BusinessPhone",
            p.MiddleName AS "Person/Name/Middle",
            p.LastName AS "Person/Name/Last"
FROM Person.Person p
INNER JOIN Person.EmailAddress e
ON p.BusinessEntityID = e.BusinessEntityID
INNER JOIN  Person.PersonPhone pp
ON p.BusinessEntityID = pp.BusinessEntityID
AND pp.PhoneNumberTypeID = 3 FOR XML PATH;
```

The results of this query include a new Phone element as a direct child of the Person element. Because this new element is positioned between the Person/Name/First and Person/Name/Middle elements, FOR XML PATH creates two separate Person/Name elements: one to encapsulate the First element, and another to encapsulate the Middle and Last elements, as shown in Figure 13-4.

Figure 13-4. *Breaking Element Grouping with FOR XML PATH*

The data Function

The FOR XML PATH XPath expression provides support for a function called data(). If the column name is specified as data(), the value is treated as an atomic value in the generated XML. If the next item generated is also an atomic value, FOR XML PATH appends a space to the end of the data returned. This is useful for using subqueries to create lists of items, as in Listing 13-5, which demonstrates use of the data() function.

Listing 13-5. The FOR XML PATH XPath data Node Test

```
SELECT DISTINCT soh.SalesPersonID AS "SalesPerson/@ID", (
        SELECT soh2.SalesOrderID AS "data()"
        FROM Sales.SalesOrderHeader soh2
        WHERE soh2.SalesPersonID = soh.SalesPersonID FOR XML PATH ('') ) AS
        "SalesPerson/@Orders",
        p.FirstName AS "SalesPerson/Name/First",
        p.MiddleName AS "SalesPerson/Name/Middle",
        p.LastName AS "SalesPerson/Name/Last",
        e.EmailAddress AS "SalesPerson/Email"
        FROM Sales.SalesOrderHeader soh
        INNER JOIN Person.Person p
                ON p.BusinessEntityID = soh.SalesPersonID
        INNER JOIN Person.EmailAddress e
                ON p.BusinessEntityID = e.BusinessEntityID
        WHERE soh.SalesPersonID IS NOT NULL FOR XML PATH;
```

This sample retrieves all SalesPerson ID numbers from the Sales.SalesOrderHeader table (eliminating NULLs for simplicity) and retrieves their names in the main query. The subquery uses the data() function to retrieve a list of each salesperson's sales order numbers and places them in a space-separated list in the Orders attribute of the SalesPerson element. A sample of the results is shown in Figure 13-5.

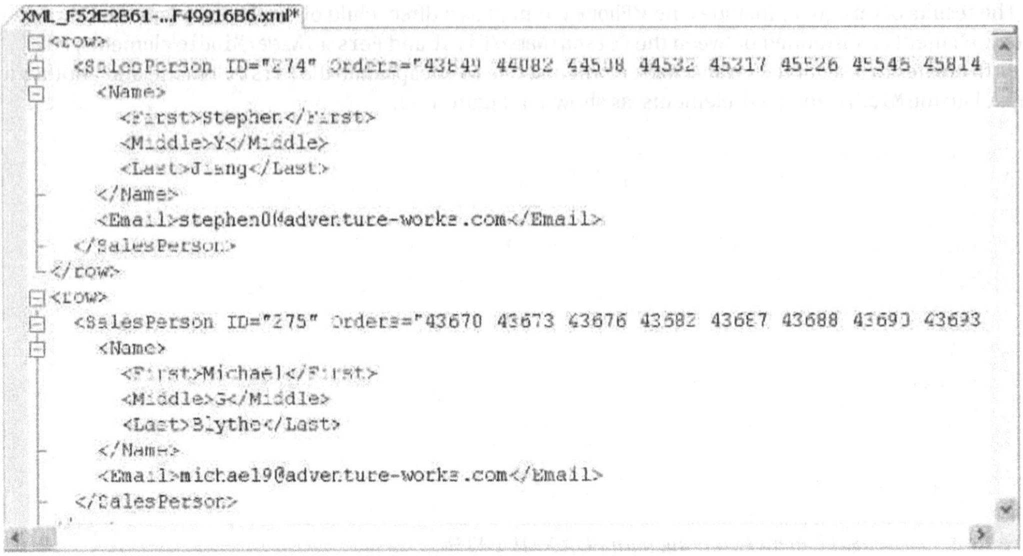

Figure 13-5. Creating Lists with the data Node Test

Node Tests and Functions

The SQL Server 2014 FOR XML PATH expression provides access to both the text() function and the data() node test. In terms of FOR XML PATH, the text() function returns the data in the text node as inline text with no separator. The data() node test returns the data in the XML text node as a space-separated concatenated list.

In XQuery expressions, the data() node test, the text() function, and the related string() function all return slightly different results. The following code snippet demonstrates their differences:

```
DECLARE @x xml;
SET @x = N'<a>123<b>456</b><c>789</c></a><a>987<b>654</b><c>321</c></a>';
SELECT @x.query('/a/text()');
SELECT @x.query('data(/a)');
SELECT @x.query('string(/a[1])');
```

The text() function in this example returns the concatenated text nodes of the <a> elements; in this example, it returns 123987.

The data() node test returns the concatenated XML text nodes of the <a> elements and all their child elements. In this example, data() returns 123456789 987654321, the concatenation of the <a> elements and the <b> and <c> subelements they contain. The data() node test puts a space separator between the <a> elements during the concatenation.

The string() function is similar to the data() node test in that it concatenates the data contained in the specified element and all child elements. The string() function requires a singleton node instance, which is why we specified string(/a[i]) in the example. The result of the string() function used in the example is 123456789. We'll discuss the text() and string() functions in greater detail later in this chapter.

XPath and NULL

In all of the previous examples, FOR XML PATH maps SQL NULL to a missing element or attribute. Consider the results of Listing 13-1 for Kim Abercrombie, shown in Figure 13-6. Because her MiddleName in the table is NULL, the Name/Middle element is missing from the results.

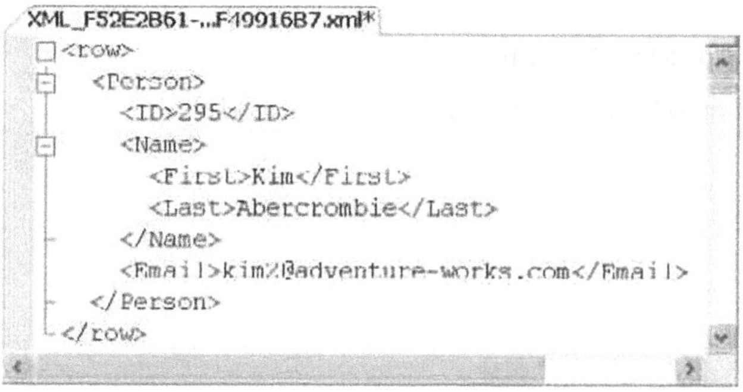

Figure 13-6. *NULL Middle Name Eliminated from the FOR XML PATH Results*

If you want SQL NULL-valued elements and attributes to appear in the final results, use the ELEMENTS XSINIL option of the FOR XML clause, as shown in Listing 13-6.

Listing 13-6. FOR XML with the ELEMENTS XSINIL Option

```
SELECT
p.BusinessEntityID AS "Person/ID",
p.FirstName AS "Person/Name/First",
p.MiddleName AS "Person/Name/Middle",
p.LastName AS "Person/Name/Last",
e.EmailAddress AS "Person/Email" FROM Person.Person p INNER JOIN Person.EmailAddress e
ON p.BusinessEntityID = e.BusinessEntityID FOR XML PATH,
ELEMENTS XSINIL;
```

With the ELEMENTS XSINIL option, Kim's results now look like the results shown in Figure 13-7. The FOR XML PATH clause adds a reference to the xsi namespace, and elements containing SQL NULL are included but marked with the xsi:nil="true" attribute.

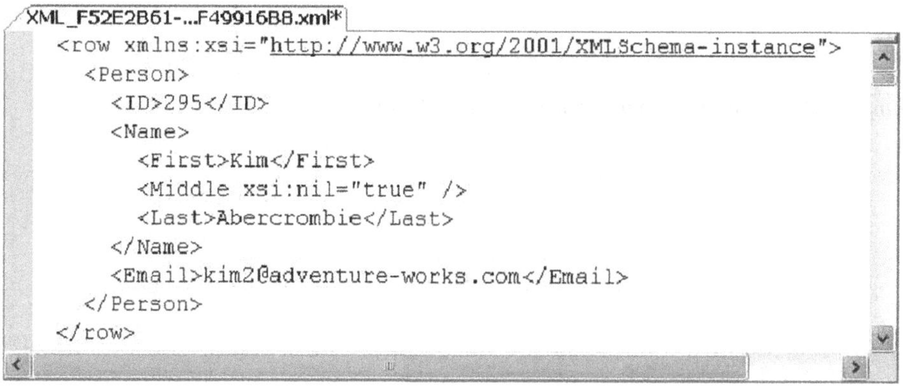

Figure 13-7. *NULL Marked with the xsi:nil Attribute*

The WITH XMLNAMESPACES Clause

Namespace support is provided for FOR XML clauses and other XML functions by the WITH XMLNAMESPACES clause. The WITH XMLNAMESPACES clause is added to the front of your SELECT queries to specify XML namespaces to be used by FOR XML clauses or xml data type methods. Listing 13-7 demonstrates the use of the WITH XMLNAMESPACES clause with FOR XML PATH.

Listing 13-7. Using WITH XMLNAMESPACES to Specify Namespaces

```
WITH XMLNAMESPACES('http://www.apress.com/xml/sampleSqlXmlNameSpace' as ns)
SELECT
p.BusinessEntityID AS "ns:Person/ID",
p.FirstName AS "ns:Person/Name/First",
p.MiddleName AS "ns:Person/Name/Middle",
p.LastName AS "ns:Person/Name/Last",
e.EmailAddress AS "ns:Person/Email"
FROM Person.Person p
INNER JOIN Person.EmailAddress e
ON p.BusinessEntityID = e.BusinessEntityID
FOR XML PATH;
```

The WITH XMLNAMESPACES clause in this example declares a namespace called ns with the URI http://www.apress.com/xml/sampleSqlXmlNameSpace. The FOR XML PATH clause adds this namespace prefix to the Person element, as indicated in the XPath expressions used to define the structure of the result. A sample of the results is shown in Figure 13-8.

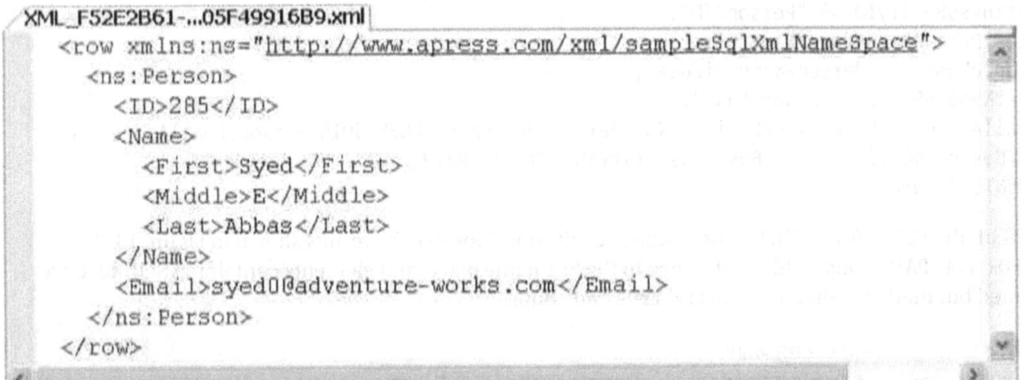

Figure 13-8. Adding an XML Namespace to the FOR XML PATH Results

Node Tests

In addition to the previous options, the FOR XML PATH XPath implementation supports four node tests, including the following:

- The text() node test turns the string value of a column into a text node.

- The comment() node test turns the string value of a column into an XML comment.

- The node() node test turns the string value of a column into inline XML content; it is the same as using the wildcard * as the name.

- The processing-instruction(name) node test turns the string value of a column into an XML-processing instruction with the specified name.

Listing 13-8 demonstrates use of XPath node tests as column names in a FOR XML PATH query. The results are shown in Figure 13-9.

Listing 13-8. FOR XML PATH Using XPath Node Tests

```
SELECT
p.NameStyle AS "processing-instruction(nameStyle)",
p.BusinessEntityID AS "Person/@ID",
p.ModifiedDate AS "comment()",
pp.PhoneNumber AS "text()",
FirstName AS "Person/Name/First",
MiddleName AS "Person/Name/Middle",
LastName AS "Person/Name/Last",
EmailAddress AS "Person/Email"
FROM Person.Person p
INNER JOIN Person.EmailAddress e
ON p.BusinessEntityID = e.BusinessEntityID
INNER JOIN Person.PersonPhone pp
ON p.BusinessEntityID = pp.BusinessEntityID
FOR XML PATH;
```

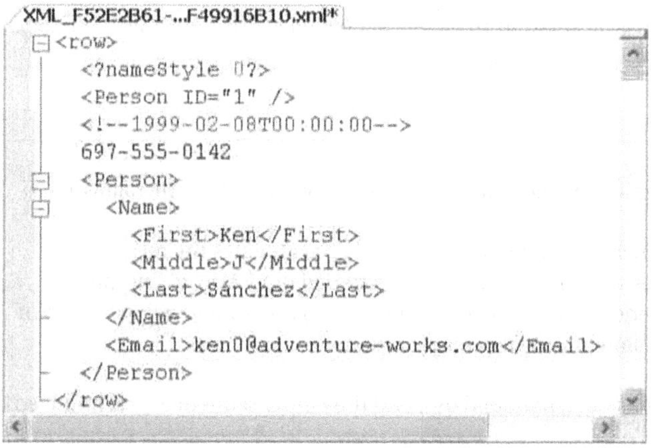

```
XML_F52E2B61-...F49916B10.xml*
<row>
    <?nameStyle 0?>
    <Person ID="1" />
    <!--1999-02-08T00:00:00-->
    697-555-0142
    <Person>
      <Name>
         <First>Ken</First>
         <Middle>J</Middle>
         <Last>Sánchez</Last>
      </Name>
      <Email>ken0@adventure-works.com</Email>
    </Person>
</row>
```

Figure 13-9. *Using Node Tests with FOR XML PATH*

In this example, the NameStyle column value is turned into an XML-processing instruction called nameStyle, the ModifiedDate column is turned into an XML comment, and the contact PhoneNumber is turned into a text node for each person in the AdventureWorks database.

XQuery and the xml Data Type

XQuery represents the most advanced standardized XML querying language to date. Designed as an extension to the W3C XPath 2.0 standard, XQuery is a case-sensitive, declarative, functional language with a rich type system based on the XDM. The SQL Server 2014 xml data type supports querying of XML data using a subset of XQuery via the query() method. Before diving into the details of the SQL Server implementation, we are going to start this section with a discussion of XQuery basics.

Expressions and Sequences

XQuery introduces several advances on the concepts introduced by XPath and other previous XML query tools and languages. Two of the most important concepts in XQuery are expressions and sequences. A sequence is an ordered collection of items—either nodes or atomic values. The word ordered, as it applies to sequences, does not necessarily mean numeric or alphabetic order. Sequences are generally in document order (the order in which their contents appear in the raw XML document or data) by default, unless you specify a different ordering. The roughly analogous XPath 1.0 structure was known as a node set, a name that implies ordering was unimportant. Unlike the relational model, however, the order of nodes is extremely important to XML. In XML, the ordering of nodes and content provides additional context and can be just as important as the data itself. The XQuery sequence was defined to ensure that the importance of proper ordering is recognized. There are also some other differences that we will cover later in this section.

Sequences can be returned by XQuery expressions or created by enclosing one of the following in parentheses:

- Lists of items separated by the comma operator (,)

- Range expressions

- Filter expressions

■ **Tip**   Range expressions and the range expression keyword to are not supported in SQL Server 2014 XQuery. If you are converting an XQuery with range expressions like (1 to 10), you will have to modify it to run on SQL Server 2014.

A sequence created as a list of items separated by the comma operator might look like the following:
(1, 2, 3, 4, (5, 6), 7, 8, (), 9, 10)

The comma operator evaluates each of the items in the sequence and concatenates the result. Sequences cannot be nested, so any sequences within sequences are "flattened out." Also, the empty sequence (a sequence containing no items, denoted by empty parentheses: ()) is eliminated. Evaluation of the previous sample sequence results in the following sequence of ten items:
(1, 2, 3, 4, 5, 6, 7, 8, 9, 10)

Notice that the nested sequence (5, 6) has been flattened out, and the empty sequence () is removed during evaluation.

■ **Tip** SQL Server 2014 XQuery does not support the W3C-specified sequence operators union, intersect, and except. If you are porting XQuery code that uses these operators, it will have to be modified to run on SQL Server 2008.

Another method of generating a sequence is with a filter expression. A filter expression is a primary expression followed by zero or more predicates. An example of a filter expression to generate a sequence might look like the following:

(//Coordinates/*/text())

An important property of sequences is that a sequence of one item is indistinguishable from a singleton atomic value. So the sequence (1.0) is equivalent to the singleton atomic value 1.0.

Sequences come in three flavors: empty sequences, homogeneous sequences, and heterogeneous sequences. Empty sequences are sequences that contain no items. As mentioned before, the empty sequence is annotated with a set of empty parentheses: ().

Homogeneous sequences are sequences of one or more items of the same or compatible types. The examples already given are all examples of homogenous sequences.

Heterogeneous sequences are sequences of two or more items of incompatible types, or singleton atomic types and nodes. The following is an example of a heterogeneous sequence:

("Harry", 299792458, xs:date("2006-12-29Z"))

SQL Server does not allow heterogeneous sequences that mix nodes with singleton atomic values. Trying to declare the following sequence results in an error:

(<tag/>, "you are it!")

■ **Note** Singleton atomic values are defined as values that are in the value space of the atomic types. The value space is the complete set of values that can be expressed with a given type. For instance, the complete value space for the xs:boolean type is true and false. Singleton atomic values are indivisible for purposes of the XDM standard (although you can extract portions of their content in some situations). Values that fall into this space are decimals, integers, dates, strings, and other primitive data types.

Primary expressions are the building blocks of XQuery. An expression in XQuery evaluates to a singleton atomic value or a sequence. Primary expressions can be any of several different items, including the following:

- Literals: These include string and numeric data type literals. String literals can be enclosed in either single or double quotes and may contain the XML-defined entity references >, <, &, ", and ', or Unicode character references such as €, which represents the euro symbol (€).

- Variable references: These are XML-qualified names (QNames) preceded by a $ sign. A variable reference is defined by its local name. Note that SQL Server 2012 does not support variable references with namespace URI prefixes, which are allowed under the W3C recommendation. An example of a variable reference is $count.

- Parenthesized expressions: These are expressions enclosed in parentheses. Parenthesized expressions are often used to force a specific order of operator evaluation. For instance, in the expression (3 + 4) * 2, the parentheses force the addition to be performed before the multiplication.

- Context item expressions: These are expressions that evaluate to the context item. The context item is the node or atomic value currently being referenced by the XQuery query engine.

- Function calls: These are composed of a QName followed by a list of arguments in parentheses. Function calls can reference built-in functions. SQL Server 2014 does not support XQuery user-defined functions.

The query Method

The query() method can be used to query and retrieve XML nodes from xml variables or xml-typed columns in tables, as demonstrated in Listing 13-9, with partial results shown in Figure 13-10.

Listing 13-9. Retrieving Job Candidates with the query Method

```
SELECT Resume.query
(
N'//*:Name.First,
//*:Name.Middle,
//*:Name.Last,
//*:Edu.Level'
)
FROM HumanResources.JobCandidate;
```

xmlresult1.xml
```
<p1:Name.First xmlns:p1="http://schemas.microsoft.com/sqlserver/2004/07/adventure-works/Resume">Shai</p1:Name.First>
<p2:Name.Middle xmlns:p2="http://schemas.microsoft.com/sqlserver/2004/07/adventure-works/Resume" />
<p3:Name.Last xmlns:p3="http://schemas.microsoft.com/sqlserver/2004/07/adventure-works/Resume">Bassli</p3:Name.Last>
<p4:Edu.Level xmlns:p4="http://schemas.microsoft.com/sqlserver/2004/07/adventure-works/Resume">Bachelor</p4:Edu.Level>
```

Figure 13-10. *Sample Job Candidate Returned by the query Method*

The simple XQuery query retrieves all first names, middle names, last names, and education levels for all AdventureWorks job candidates. The XQuery path expressions in the example demonstrate some key XQuery concepts, including the following:

- The first item of note is the // axis at the beginning of each path expression. This axis notation is defined as shorthand for the descendant-or-self::node(), which we'll describe in more detail in the next section. This particular axis retrieves all nodes with a name matching the location step, regardless of where it occurs in the XML being queried.

- In the example, the four node tests specified are Name.First, Name.Middle, Name.Last, and Edu.Level. All nodes with the names that match the node tests are returned no matter where they occur in the XML.

- The * namespace qualifier is a wildcard that matches any namespace occurring in the XML. Each node in the result node sequence includes an xmlns namespace declaration.

- This XQuery query is composed of four different paths denoting the four different node sequences to be returned. They are separated from one another by commas.

Location Paths

The location path determines which nodes should be accessed by XQuery. Following a location path from left to right is generally analogous to moving down and to the right in your XML node tree (there are exceptions, of course, which we discuss in the section on axis specifiers). If the first character of the path expression is a single forward slash (/), then the path expression is an absolute location path, meaning that it starts at the root of the XML. Listing 13-10 demonstrates the use of an XQuery absolute location path. The results are shown in Figure 13-11.

Listing 13-10. Querying with an Absolute Location Path

```
DECLARE @x xml = N'<?xml version = "1.0"?>
<Geocode>
<Info ID = "1">
<Coordinates Resolution = "High">
<Latitude>37.859609</Latitude>
<Longitude>-122.291673</Longitude>
</Coordinates>
<Location Type = "Business">
<Name>APress, Inc.</Name>
</Location>
</Info>
<Info ID = "2">
<Coordinates Resolution = "High">
<Latitude>37.423268</Latitude>
<Longitude>-122.086345</Longitude>
</Coordinates>
<Location Type = "Business">
<Name>Google, Inc.</Name>
</Location>
</Info>
</Geocode>';
SELECT @x.query(N'/Geocode/Info/Coordinates');
```

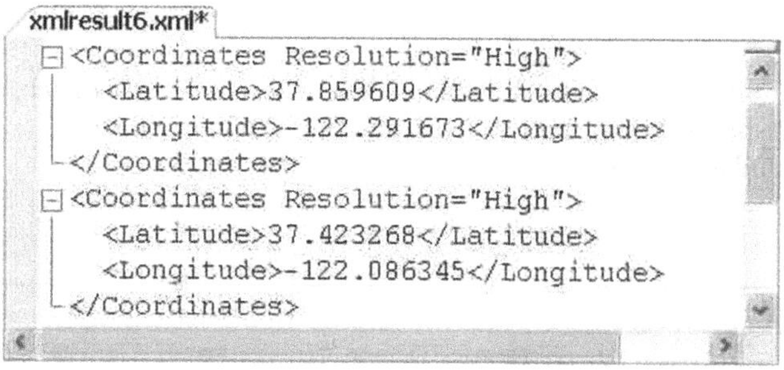

Figure 13-11. *Absolute Location Path Query Result*

■ **Tip** The left-hand forward slash actually stands for a conceptual root node that encompasses your XML input. The conceptual root node doesn't actually exist, and can neither be viewed in your XML input nor accessed or manipulated directly. It's this conceptual root node that allows XQuery to properly process XML fragments that are not well formed (i.e., XML with multiple root nodes) as input. Using a path expression that consists of only a single forward slash returns every node below the conceptual root node in your XML document or fragment.

Listing 13-10 defines an `xml` variable and populates it with an XML document containing geocoding data for a couple of businesses. We've used an absolute location path in the query to retrieve a node sequence of the latitude and longitude coordinates for the entire XML document.

A relative location path indicates a path relative to the current context node. The context node is the current node being accessed by the XQuery engine at a given point when the query is executed. The context node changes during execution of the query. Relative location paths are specified by excluding the leading forward slash, as in the following modification to Listing 13-10:

```
SELECT @x.query(N'Geocode/Info/Coordinates');
```

And, as previously mentioned, using a double forward slash (//) in the lead position returns nodes that match the node test anywhere they occur in the document. The following modification to Listing 13-10 demonstrates this:

```
SELECT @x.query(N'//Coordinates');
```

In addition, the wildcard character (*) can be used to match any node by name. The following example retrieves the root node, all of the nodes on the next level, and all `Coordinates` nodes below that:

```
SELECT @x.query(N'//*/*/Coordinates');
```

Because the XML document in the example is a simple one, all the variations of Listing 13-10 return the same result. For more complex XML documents or fragments, the results of different relative location paths could return completely different results.

Node Tests

The node tests in the previous example are simple name node tests. For a name node test to return a match, the nodes must have the same names as those specified in the node tests. In addition to name node tests, SQL Server 2014 XQuery supports four node kind tests, as listed in Table 13-1.

Table 13-1. Supported Node Tests

Node Kind Test	Description
`comment()`	Returns true for a comment node only.
`node()`	Returns true for any kind of node.
`processing-instruction("name")`	Returns true for a processing instruction node. The name parameter is an optional string literal. If it is included, only processing instruction nodes with that name are returned; if not included, all processing instructions are returned.
`text()`	Returns true for a text node only.

■ **Tip**   Keep in mind that XQuery, like XML, is case sensitive. This means your node tests and other identifiers must all be of the proper case. The identifier `PersonalID`, for instance, does not match `personalid` in XML or XQuery. Also note that your database collation case sensitivity settings do not affect XQuery queries.

Listing 13-11 demonstrates use of the `processing-instruction()` node test to retrieve the processing instruction from the root level of a document for one product model. The results are shown in Figure 13-12.

Listing 13-11. Sample Processing-instruction Node Test

```
SELECT CatalogDescription.query(N'/processing-instruction()') AS Processing_Instr
FROM Production.ProductModel
WHERE ProductModelID = 19;
```

Figure 13-12. Results of the Processing-instruction Node Test Query

The sample can be modified to retrieve all XML comments from the source by using the `comment()` node test, as in Listing 13-12. The results are shown in Figure 13-13.

Listing 13-12. Sample comment Node Test

```
SELECT CatalogDescription.query(N'//comment()') AS Comments
FROM Production.ProductModel
WHERE ProductModelID = 19;
```

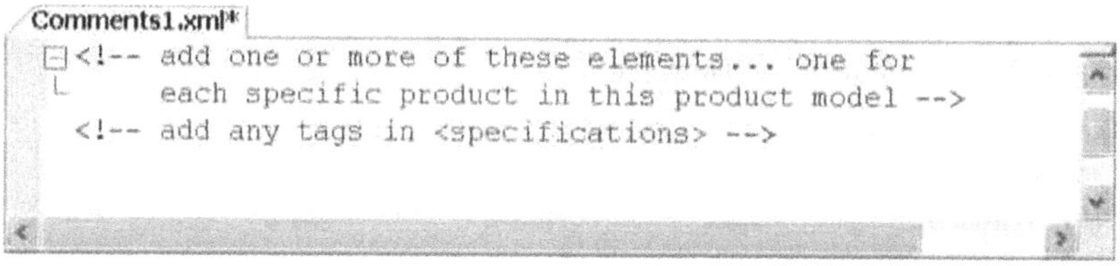

Figure 13-13. Results of the comment Node Test Query

Listing 13-13 demonstrates use of another node test, `node()`, to retrieve the specifications for product model 19. Results are shown in Figure 13-14.

Listing 13-13. Sample node Node Test

```
SELECT CatalogDescription.query(N'//*:Specifications/node()') AS Specifications
FROM Production.ProductModel
WHERE ProductModelID = 19;
```

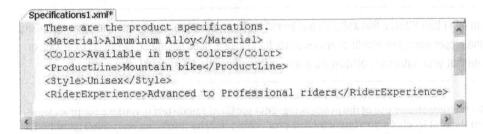

Figure 13-14. *Results of the node Node Test Query*

SQL Server 2014 XQuery does not support other node kind tests specified in the XQuery recommendation. Specifically, the `schema-element()`, `schema-attribute()`, and `document-node()` kind tests are not implemented. SQL Server 2013 also doesn't provide support for type tests, which are node tests that let you query nodes based on their associated type information.

Namespaces

You might notice that the first node of the result shown in Figure 13-14 is not enclosed in XML tags. This node is a text node located in the `Specifications` node being queried. You might also notice that the * namespace wildcard mentioned previously is used in this query. This is because namespaces are declared in the XML of the `CatalogDescription` column. Specifically the root node declaration looks like this:

```
<pl:ProductDescription xmlns:pl="http://schemas.microsoft.com/sqlserver/2004↵
07/adventure-works/ProductModelDescription" xmlns:wm="http://schemas.microsoft.com/
sqlserver/2004/07/↵
adventure-works/ProductModelWarrAndMain" xmlns:wf="http://www.adventure-works.com/
schemas/OtherFeatures" xmlns:html="http://www.w3.org/1999/xhtml" ProductModelID="19"
ProductModelName="Mountain 100">
```

The `Specifications` node of the XML document is declared with the `pi` namespace in the document. Not using a namespace in the query at all, as shown in Listing 13-14, results in an empty sequence being returned (no matching nodes).

Listing 13-14. Querying CatalogDescription with No Namespaces

```
SELECT CatalogDescription.query(N'//Specifications/node()') AS Specifications
FROM Production.ProductModel
WHERE ProductModelID = 19;
```

In addition to the wildcard namespace specifier, you can use the XQuery prolog to define namespaces for use in your query. Listing 13-15 shows how the previous example can be modified to include the p1 namespace with a namespace declaration in the prolog.

Listing 13-15. Prolog Namespace Declaration

```
SELECT CatalogDescription.query
(
N'declare namespace
p1 = "http://schemas.microsoft.com/sqlserver/2004/07/adventure-works/
ProductModelDescription";
//p1:Specifications/node()'
)
FROM Production.ProductModel
WHERE ProductModelID = 19;
```

The keywords declare namespace allow you to declare specific namespaces that will be used in the query. You can also use the declare default element namespace keywords to declare a default namespace, as in Listing 13-16.

Listing 13-16. Prolog Default Namespace Declaration

```
SELECT CatalogDescription.query
(
N'declare default element namespace
"http://schemas.microsoft.com/sqlserver/2004/07/adventure-works/ProductModelDescription";
//Specifications/node()'
)
FROM Production.ProductModel
WHERE ProductModelID = 19;
```

Declaring a default namespace with the declare default element namespace keywords allows you to eliminate namespace prefixes in your location paths (for steps that fall within the scope of the default namespace, of course). Listings 13-15 and 13-16 both generate the same result as the query in Listing 13-13.

■ **Tip**   You can also use the T-SQL WITH XMLNAMESPACES clause, described previously in this chapter, to declare namespaces for use by xml data type methods.

SQL Server defines an assortment of predeclared namespaces that can be used in your queries. With the exception of the xml namespace, you can redeclare these namespaces in your queries using the URIs of your choice. The predeclared namespaces are listed in Table 13-2.

Table 13-2. *SQL Server Predeclared XQuery Namespaces*

Namespace	URI	Description
Fn	http://www.w3.org/2005/xpath-functions	XQuery 1.0, XPath 2.0, XSLT 2.0 functions and operators namespace.
Sqltypes	http://schemas.microsoft.com/sqlserver/2004/sqltypes	This namespace provides SQL Server 2005 to base type mapping.
Xdt	http://www.w3.org/2005/xpath-datatypes/	XQuery 1.0/XPath 2.0 data types namespace.
Xml	http://www.w3.org/XML/1998/namespace	Default XML namespace.
Xs	http://www.w3.org/2001/XMLSchema	XML schema namespace.
Xsi	http://www.w3.org/2001/	XML schema instance namespace; XMLSchema-instance.

■ **Tip** The W3C-specified local functions namespace, local (http://www.w3.org/2005/xquery-local-functions), is not predeclared in SQL Server. SQL Server 2014 does not support XQuery user-defined functions.

Another useful namespace is http://www.w3.org/2005/xqt-errors, which is the namespace for XPath and XQuery function and operator error codes. In the XQuery documentation, this URI is bound to the namespace err, though this is not considered normative.

Axis Specifiers

Axis specifiers define the direction of movement of a location path step relative to the current context node. The XQuery standard defines several axis specifiers, which can be defined as forward axes or reverse axes. SQL Server 2014 supports a subset of these axis specifiers, as listed in Table 13-3.

Table 13-3. *SQL 2014 Supported Axis Specifiers*

Axis Name	Direction	Description
child::	Forward	Retrieves the children of the current context node.
descendant::	Forward	Retrieves all descendents of the current context node, recursive style. This includes children of the current node, children of the children, and so on.
self::	Forward	Contains just the current context node.
descendant-or-self::	Forward	Contains the context node and children of the current context node.
attribute::	Forward	Returns the specified attribute(s) of the current context node. This axis specifier may be abbreviated using an at sign (@).
parent::	Reverse	Returns the parent of the current context node. This axis specifier may be abbreviated as two periods (..).

In addition, the context-item expression, indicated by a single period (.), returns the current context item (which can be either a node or an atomic value). The current context item is the current node or atomic value being processed by the XQuery engine at any given point during query execution.

■ **Note**   The following axes, defined as optional axes by the XQuery 1.0 specification, are not supported by SQL Server 2014: `following-sibling::`, `following::`, `ancestor::`, `preceding-sibling::`, `preceding::`, `ancestor-or-self::`, and the deprecated `namespace::`. If you are porting XQuery queries from other sources, they may have to be modified to avoid these axis specifiers.

In all of the examples so far, the axis has been omitted, and the default axis of `child::` is assumed by XQuery in each step. Because `child::` is the default axis, the two queries in Listing 13-17 are equivalent.

Listing 13-17. Query with and Without Default Axes

```
SELECT CatalogDescription.query(N'//*:Specifications/node()') AS Specifications
FROM Production.ProductModel
WHERE ProductModelID = 19;
SELECT CatalogDescription.query(N'//child::*:Specifications/child::node()')
AS Specifications
FROM Production.ProductModel
WHERE ProductModelID = 19;
```

Listing 13-18 demonstrates the use of the `parent::` axis to retrieve `Coordinates` nodes from the sample XML.

Listing 13-18. Sample Using the parent:: Axis

```
DECLARE @x xml = N'<?xml version = "1.0"?>
<Geocode>
<Info ID = "1">
<Coordinates Resolution = "High">
<Latitude>37.859609</Latitude>
<Longitude>-122.291673</Longitude>
</Coordinates>
<Location Type = "Business">
<Name>APress, Inc.</Name>
</Location>
</Info>
<Info ID = "2">
<Coordinates Resolution = "High">
<Latitude>37.423268</Latitude>
<Longitude>-122.086345</Longitude>
</Coordinates>
<Location Type = "Business">
<Name>Google, Inc.</Name>
</Location>
</Info>
</Geocode>';
SELECT @x.query(N'//Location/parent::node()/Coordinates');
```

This particular query locates all Location nodes, then uses the parent:: axis to retrieve their parent nodes (Info nodes), and finally returns the Coordinates nodes, which are children of the Info nodes. The end result is shown in Figure 13-15.

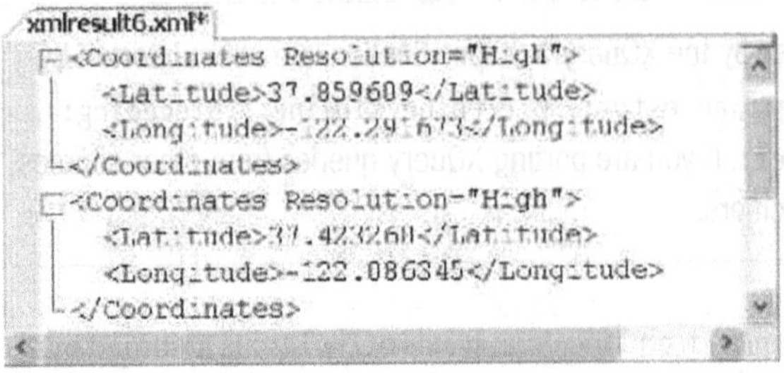

Figure 13-15. *Retrieving Coordinates Nodes with the parent:: Axis*

Dynamic XML Construction

The XQuery 1.0 recommendation is based on XPath 2.0, which is in turn based largely on XPath 1.0. The XPath 1.0 recommendation was designed to consolidate many of the best features of both the W3C XSLT and XPointer recommendations. One of the benefits of XQuery's lineage is its ability to query XML and dynamically construct well-formed XML documents from the results. Consider the example in Listing 13-19, which uses an XQuery direct constructor to create an XML document. Figure 13-16 shows the results.

Listing 13-19. XQuery Dynamic XML Construction

```
DECLARE @x xml = N'<?xml version = "1.0"?>
<Geocode>
        <Info ID = "1">
        <Location Type = "Business">
        <Name>APress,  Inc.</Name>
        </Location>
        </Info>
        <Info ID = "2">
        <Location Type = "Business">
        <Name>Google,  Inc.</Name>
        </Location>
        </Info>
</Geocode>';
SELECT  @x.query(N'<Companies>
        {
        //Info/Location/Name
        }
</Companies>');
```

Figure 13-16. *Dynamic Construction of XML with XQuery*

The direct constructor in the XQuery example looks like this:

```
<Companies>
{
//Info/Location/Name
}
</Companies>
```

The `<Companies>` and `</Companies>` opening and closing tags in the direct constructor act as the root tag for the XML result. The opening and closing tags contain the content expression, which consists of the location path used to retrieve the nodes. The content expression is wrapped in curly braces between the `<Companies>` and `</Companies>` tags:

```
{
//Info/Location/Name
}
```

■ **Tip** If you need to output curly braces in your constructed XML result, you can escape them by doubling them up in your query using {{ and }}.

You can also use the `element`, `attribute`, and `text` computed constructors to build your XML result, as demonstrated in Listing 13-20, with the result shown in Figure 13-17.

Listing 13-20. Element and Attribute Dynamic Constructors

```
SELECT CatalogDescription.query
(
N'declare namespace
p1 = "http://schemas.microsoft.com/sqlserver/2004/07/adventure-works/ProductModelDescription";
//p1:Specifications/node()'
)
FROM Production.ProductModel
WHERE ProductModelID = 19;

DECLARE @x xml = N'<?xml version = "1.0"?>
<Geocode>
<Info ID = "1">
<Location Type = "Business">
<Name>APress, Inc.</Name>
<Address>
```

```
<Street>2560 Ninth St, Ste 219</Street>
<City>Berkeley</City>
<State>CA</State>
<Zip>94710-2500</Zip>
<Country>US</Country>
</Address>
</Location>
</Info>
</Geocode>';
SELECT @x.query
(
N'element Companies
{
element FirstCompany
{
attribute CompanyID
{
(//Info/@ID)[1]
},
(//Info/Location/Name)[1]
}
}'
);
```

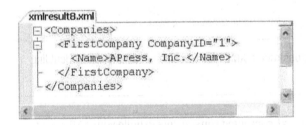

Figure 13-17. Results of the XQuery Computed Element Construction

The element Companies computed element constructor creates the root Companies node.
The FirstCompany node is constructed as a child node using another element constructor:

```
element Companies
{
element FirstCompany
{
...
}
}
```

The content expressions of the FirstCompany elements are where the real action takes place:

```
element FirstCompany
{
attribute CompanyID
{
(//Info/@ID)[1]
},
(//Info/Location/Name)[1]
}
```

The CompanyID dynamic attribute constructor retrieves the ID attribute from the first Info node. The predicate [1] in the path ensures that only the first //Info/@ID is returned. This path location could also be written like this:

```
//Info[1]/@ID
```

The second path location retrieves the first Name node for the first Location node of the first Info node. Again, the [1] predicate ensures that only the first matching node is returned. The path is equivalent to the following:

```
//Info[1]/Location[1]/Name[1]
```

To retrieve the second node, change the predicate to [2], and so on.

■ **Tip** By definition, a predicate that evaluates to a numeric singleton value (such as the integer constant 1) is referred to as a numeric predicate. The effective Boolean value is true only when the context position is equal to the numeric predicate expression. When the numeric predicate is 3, for instance, the predicate truth value is true only for the third context position. This is a handy way to limit the results of an XQuery query to a single specific node.

XQuery Comments

XQuery comments (not to be confused with XML comment nodes) are used to document your queries inline. You can include them in XQuery expressions by enclosing them with the (: and :) symbols (just like the smiley face emoticon). Comments can be used in your XQuery expressions anywhere ignorable whitespace is allowed, and they can be nested. XQuery comments have no effect on query processing. The following example modifies the query in Listing 13-19 to include XQuery comments:

```
SELECT @x.query ( N'<Companies> (: This is the root node :) {
//Info/Location/Name (: Retrieves all company names (: ALL of them :) :) } </Companies>' );
```

You will see XQuery comments used in some of the examples later in this chapter.

Data Types

XQuery maintains the string value and typed value for all nodes in the referenced XML. XQuery defines the string value of an element node as the concatenated string values of the element node and all its child element nodes. The type of a node is defined in the XML schema collection associated with the xml variable or column. As an example, the built-in AdventureWorks Production.ManuInstructionsSchemaCollection XML schema collection defines the LocationID attribute of the Location element as an xsd:integer:

```
<xsd:attribute name="LocationID" type="xsd:integer" use="required" />
```

Every instance of this attribute in the XML of the Instructions column of the Production. ProductModel table must conform to the requirements of this data type. Typed data can also be manipulated according to the functions and operators defined for this type. For untyped XML, the typed data is defined as xdt:untypedAtomic. A listing of XDM data types available to SQL Server via XQuery is given in Appendix B.

Predicates

An XQuery predicate is an expression that evaluates to one of the xs:boolean values true or false. In XQuery, predicates are used to filter the results of a node sequence, discarding nodes that don't meet the specified criteria from the results. Predicates limit the results by converting the result of the predicate expression into an xs:boolean value, referred to as the predicate truth value. The predicate truth value is determined for each item of the input sequence according to the following rules:

1. If the type of the expression is numeric, the predicate truth value is true if the value of the predicate expression is equal to the context position; otherwise for a numeric predicate, the predicate truth value is false.

2. If the type of the expression is a string, the predicate is false if the length of the expression is 0. For a string type expression with a length greater than 0, the predicate truth value is true.

3. If the type of the expression is xs:boolean, the predicate truth value is the value of the expression.

4. If the expression results in an empty sequence, the predicate truth value is false.

5. If the value of the predicate expression is a node sequence, the predicate truth value is true if the sequence contains at least one node; otherwise it is false.

Queries that include a predicate return only nodes in a sequence for which the predicate truth value evaluates to true. Predicates are composed of expressions, conveniently referred to as predicate expressions, enclosed in square brackets ([ ]). You can specify multiple predicates in a path, and they are evaluated in order of occurrence from left to right.

■ **Note**   The XQuery specification says that multiple predicates are evaluated from left to right, but it also gives some wiggle room for vendors to perform predicate evaluations in other orders, allowing them to take advantage of vendor-specific features such as indexes and other optimizations. You don't have to worry too much about the internal evaluation order of predicates, though. No matter what order predicates are actually evaluated in, the end results have to be the same as if the predicates were evaluated left to right.

Value Comparison Operators

As we mentioned, the basic function of predicates is to filter results. Results are filtered by specified comparisons, and XQuery offers a rich set of comparison operators. These operators fall into three main categories: value comparison operators, general comparison operators, and node comparison operators. Value comparison operators compare singleton atomic values only. Trying to compare sequences with value comparison operators results in an error. The value comparison operators are listed in Table 13-4.

Table 13-4. *Value Comparison Operators*

Operator	Description
Eq	Equal
Ne	Not equal
Lt	Less than
Le	Less than or equal to
Gt	Greater than
Ge	Greater than or equal to

Value comparisons follow a specific set of rules:

1. The operands on the left and right sides of the operator are atomized.

2. If either atomized operand is an empty sequence, the result is an empty sequence.

3. If either atomized operand is a sequence with a length greater than 1, an error is raised.

4. If either atomized operand is of type xs:untypedAtomic, it is cast to xs:string.

5. If the operands have compatible types, they are compared using the appropriate operator. If the comparison of the two operands using the chosen operator evaluates to true, the result is true; otherwise the result is false. If the operands have incompatible types, an error is thrown.

Consider the value comparison examples in Listing 13-21, with results shown in Figure 13-18.

Listing 13-21. Value Comparison Examples

```
DECLARE @x xml = N'<?xml version = "1.0" ?>
<Animal>
Cat
</Animal>';
SELECT @x.query(N'9 eq 9.0 (: 9 is equal to 9.0 :)');
SELECT @x.query(N'4 gt 3 (: 4 is greater than 3 :)');
SELECT @x.query(N'(/Animal/text())[1] lt "Dog" (: Cat is less than Dog :)') ;
```

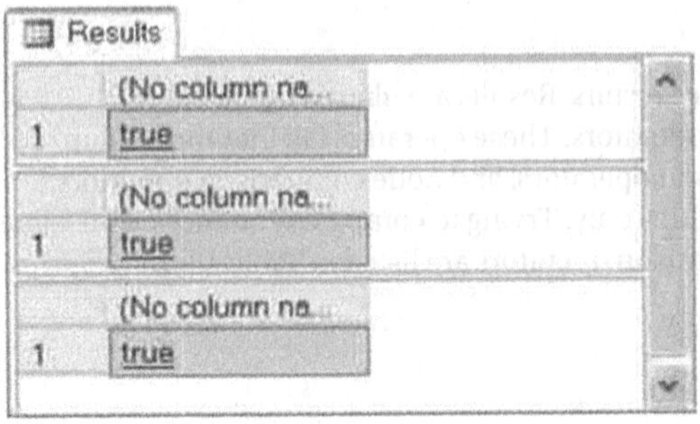

Figure 13-18. *Results of the XQuery Value Comparisons*

Listing 13-22 attempts to compare two values of incompatible types, namely an xs:decimal type value and an xs:string value. The result is the error message shown in the results following.

Listing 13-22. Incompatible Type Value Comparison

```
DECLARE @x xml = N'';
SELECT @x.query(N'3.141592 eq "Pi"') ;


Msg 2234, Level 16, State 1, Line 2
XQuery [query()]: The operator "eq" cannot be applied to "xs:decimal" and "xs:string" operands.
```

General Comparison Operators

General comparisons are existential comparisons that work on operand sequences of any length. Existential simply means that if one atomized value from the first operand sequence fulfills a value comparison with at least one atomized value from the second operand sequence, the result is true. The general comparison operators will look familiar to programmers who are versed in other computer languages, particularly C-style languages. The general comparison operators are listed in Table 13-5.

Table 13-5. *General Comparison Operators*

Operator	Description
=	Equal
!=	Not equal
<	Less than
>	Greater than
<=	Less than or equal to
>=	Greater than or equal to

Listing 13-23 demonstrates comparisons using general comparisons on XQuery sequences. The results are shown in Figure 13-19.

Listing 13-23. General Comparison Examples

```
DECLARE @x xml = '';
SELECT @x.query('(3.141592, 1) = (2, 3.141592) (: true :) ');
SELECT @x.query('(1.0, 2.0, 3.0) = 1 (: true :) ');
SELECT @x.query('("Joe", "Harold") < "Adam" (: false :) ');
SELECT @x.query('xs:date("1999-01-01") < xs:date("2006-01-01") (: true :)');
```

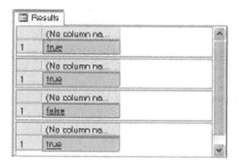

Figure 13-19. General XQuery Comparison Results

Here's how the general comparison operators work. The first query compares the sequences (3.141592, 1) and (2, 3.141592) using the = operator. The comparison atomizes the two operand sequences and compares them using the rules for the equivalent value comparison operators. Since the atomic value 3.141592 exists in both sequences, the equality test result is true.

The second example compares the sequence (1.0, 2.0, 3.0) to the atomic value 1. The atomic values 1.0 and 1 are compatible types and are equal, so the equality test result is true. The third query returns false because neither of the atomic values Doe or Harold are lexically less than the atomic value Adam.

The final example compares two xs:date values. Since the date 1999-01-01 is less than the date 2006-01-01, the result is true.

Xquery Date Format

The XQuery implementation in SQL Server 2005 had a special requirement concerning xs:date, xs:time, xs:dateTime, and derived types. According to a subset of the ISO 8601 standard that SQL Server 2005 uses, date and time values had to include a mandatory time offset specifier. SQL Server 2014 does not strictly enforce this rule. When you leave the time offset information off an XQuery date or time value, SQL Server 2014 defaults to the zero meridian (Zspecifier).

SQL Server 2014 also differs from SQL Server 2005 in how it handles time offset information. In SQL Server 2005, all dates were automatically normalized to coordinated universal time (UTC). SQL Server 2014 stores the time offset information you indicate when specifying a date or time value. If a time zone is provided, it must follow the date or time value, and can be either of the following:

The capital letter Z, which stands for the zero meridian, or UTC. The zero meridian runs through Greenwich, England.

An offset from the zero meridian in the format [+/-]hh:mm. For instance, the US Eastern Time zone would be indicated as -05:00.

Here are a few sample ISO 8601 formatted dates and times acceptable to SQL Server, with descriptions:

1999-05-16: May 16,1999, no time, UTC

09:15:00-05:00: No date, 9:15 am, US and Canada Eastern time

2003-12-25T20:00:00-08:00: December 25, 2003, 8:00 pm, US and Canada Pacific time

2004-07-06T23:59:59.987+01:00: July 6, 2004,11:59:59.987 pm (.987 is fractional seconds), Central European time

Unlike the homogenous sequences in Listing 13-23, a heterogeneous sequence is one that combines nodes and atomic values, or atomic values of incompatible types (such as xs:string and xs:decimal). Trying to perform a general comparison with a heterogeneous sequence causes an error in SQL Server, as demonstrated by Listing 13-24.

Listing 13-24. General Comparison with Heterogeneous Sequence

```
DECLARE @x xml = '';
SELECT @x.query('(xs:date("2006-10-09"), 6.02E23) > xs:date("2007-01-01")');
```

The error generated by Listing 13-24 looks like the following:

```
Msg 9311, Level 16, State 1, Line 3
XQuery [queryQ]: Heterogeneous sequences are not allowed in V, found
'xs:date' and 'xs:double'.
```

SQL Server also disallows heterogeneous sequences that mix nodes and atomic values, as demonstrated by Listing 13-25.

Listing 13-25. Mixing Nodes and Atomic Values in Sequences

```
DECLARE @x xml = '';
SELECT @x.query('(1, <myNode>Testing</myNode>)');
```

Trying to mix and match nodes and atomic values in a sequence like this results in an error message indicating that you tried to create a sequence consisting of atomic values and nodes, similar to the following:

```
Msg 2210, Level 16, State 1, Line 3
XQuery [queryQ]: Heterogeneous sequences are not allowed: found
'xs:integer' and 'element(myl\lode,xdt:untyped)'
```

Node Comparisons

The third type of comparison that XQuery allows is a node comparison. Node comparisons allow you to compare XML nodes in document order. The node comparison operators are listed in Table 13-6.

Table 13-6. *Node Comparison Operators*

Operator	Description
Is	Node identity equality
<<	Left node precedes right node
>>	Left node follows right node

The is operator compares two nodes to each other and returns true if the left node is the same node as the right node. Note that this is not a test of the equality of node content but rather of the actual nodes themselves based on an internally generated node ID. Consider the sample node comparisons in Listing 13-26 with results shown in Figure 13-20.

Listing 13-26. Node Comparison Samples

```
DECLARE @x xml = N'<?xml version = "1.0"?>
<Root>
<NodeA>Test Node</NodeA>
<NodeA>Test Node</NodeA>
<NodeB>Test Node</NodeB>
</Root>';
SELECT @x.query('((/Root/NodeA)[1] is (//NodeA)[1]) (: true :)');
SELECT @x.query('((/Root/NodeA)[1] is (/Root/NodeA)[2]) (: false :)');
SELECT @x.query('((/Root/NodeA)[2] << (/Root/NodeB)[1]) (: true :)');
```

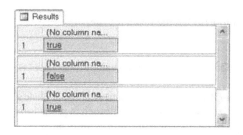

Figure 13-20. *Results of the XQuery Node Comparisons*

The first query uses the is operator to compare (/Root/NodeA)[1] to itself. The [1] numeric predicate at the end of the path ensures that only a single node is returned for comparison. The right-hand and left-hand expressions must both evaluate to a singleton or empty sequence. The result of this comparison is true only because (/Root/NodeA)[1] is the same node returned by the (//NodeA)[1] path on the right-hand side of the operator.

The second query compares (/Root/NodeA)[1] with (/Root/NodeA)[2]. Even though the two nodes have the same name and content, they are in fact different nodes. Because they are different nodes, the is operator returns false.

The final query retrieves the second NodeA node with the path (/Root/NodeA)[2]. Then it uses the " operator to determine if this node precedes the NodeB node from the path (/Root/NodeB)[1]. Since the second NodeA precedes NodeB in document order, the result of this comparison is true.

A node comparison results in an xs:boolean value or evaluates to an empty sequence if one of the operands results in an empty sequence. This is demonstrated in Listing 13-27.

Listing 13-27. Node Comparison That Evaluates to an Empty Sequence

```
DECLARE @x xml = N'<?xml version = "1.0"?>
<Root>
<NodeA>Test Node</NodeA>
</Root>';
SELECT @x.query('((/Root/NodeA)[1] is (/Root/NodeZ)[1]) (: empty sequence :)');
```

The result of the node comparison is an empty sequence because the right-hand path expression evaluates to an empty sequence (because no node named NodeZ exists in the XML document).

Conditional Expressions (if...then...else)

As shown in the previous examples, XQuery returns xs:boolean values or empty sequences as the result of comparisons. XQuery also provides support for the conditional if...then...else expression. The if...then...else construct returns an expression based on the xs:boolean value of another expression. The format for the XQuery conditional expression is shown in the following:

```
if (test-expression) then then-expression else else-expression
```

In this syntax, test-expression represents the conditional expression that is evaluated, the result of which will determine the returned result. When evaluating test-expression, XQuery applies the following rules:

1. If test-expression results in an empty sequence, the result is false.

2. If test-expression results in an xs:boolean value, the result is the xs:boolean value of the expression.

3. If test-expression results in a sequence of one or more nodes, the result is true.

4. If these steps fail, a static error is raised.

If test-expression evaluates to true, then-expression is returned. If test-expression evaluates to false, else-expression is returned.

The XQuery conditional is a declarative expression. Unlike the C# if...else statement and Visual Basic's If...Then...Else construct, XQuery's conditional if...then...else doesn't represent a branch in procedural logic or a change in program flow. It acts like a function that accepts a conditional expression as input and returns an expression as a result. In this respect, XQuery's if...then...else has more in common with the SQL CASE expression and the C# ?: operator than the if statement in procedural languages. In the XQuery if...then...else, syntax parentheses are required around test-expression, and the else clause is mandatory.

Arithmetic Expressions

XQuery arithmetic expressions provide support for the usual suspects—standard mathematical operators found in most modern programming languages, including the following:

- Multiplication (*)

- Division (div)

- Addition (+)

- Subtraction (-)

- Modulo (mod)

Integer Division in XQuery

SQL Server 2014 XQuery does not support the idiv integer division operator. Fortunately, the W3C XQuery recommendation defines the idiv operator as equivalent to the following div expression:

```
($arg1 div $arg2) cast as xs:integer?
```

If you need to convert XQuery code that uses idiv to SQL Server, you can use the div and cast operators as shown to duplicate idiv functionality.

XQuery also supports the unary plus (+) and unary minus (-) operators. Because the forward slash character is used as a path separator in XQuery, the division operator is specified using the keyword div. The modulo operator, mod, returns the remainder of division.

Of the supported operators, unary plus and unary minus have the highest precedence. Multiplication, division, and modulo are next. Binary addition and subtraction have the lowest precedence. Parentheses can be used to force the evaluation order of mathematical operations.

XQuery Functions

XQuery provides several built-in functions defined in the XQuery Functions and Operators specification (sometimes referred to as F&O), which is available at www.w3.org/TR/ xquery-operators/. Built-in XQuery functions are in the predeclared namespace fn.

■ **Tip** The fn namespace does not have to be specified when calling a built-in function. Some people leave it off to improve readability of their code.

We've listed the XQuery functions that SQL Server 2014 supports in Table 13-7.

Table 13-7. *Supported Built-in XQuery Functions*

Function	Description
fn:avg(x)	Returns the average of the sequence of numbers x. For example, fn:avg((10, 20, 30, 40, 50)) returns 30.
fn:ceiling(n)	Returns the smallest number without a fractional part that is not less than n. For example, fn:ceiling(1.1) returns 2.
fn:concat (s1, s2, ...)	Concatenates zero or more strings and returns the concatenated string as a result. For example, fn:concat("hi", ",", "how are you?") returns "hi, how are you?".
fn:contains (s1, s2,)	Returns true if the string s1 contains the string s2. For example, fn:contains("fish", "is") returns true.
fn:count(x)	Returns the number of items in the sequence x. For example, fn:count((1, 2, 4, 8, 16)) returns 5.
fn:data(a)	Returns the typed value of each item specified by the argument a. For example, fn:data((3.141592, "hello")) returns "3.141592 hello".
fn:distinct-values(x)	Returns the sequence x with duplicate values removed. For example, fn:distinct-values((1, 2, 3, 4, 5, 4, 5)) returns "1 2 3 4 5".

(continued)

Table 13-7. *(continued)*

Function	Description
fn:empty(i)	Returns true if i is an empty sequence; returns false otherwise. For example, fn:empty((1, 2, 3)) returns false.
fn:expanded-QName(u, l)	Returns an xs:QName. The arguments u and l represent the xs:QName's namespace URI and local name, respectively.
fn:false()	Returns the xs:boolean value false. For example, fn:false() returns false.
fn:floor(n)	Returns the largest number without a fractional part that is not greater than n. For example, fn:floor(1.1) returns 1.
fn:id(x)	Returns the sequence of element nodes with ID values that match one or more of the IDREF values supplied in x. The parameter x is treated as a whitespace-separated sequence of tokens.
fn:last()	Returns the index number of the last item in the sequence being processed. The first index in the sequence has an index of 1.
fn:local-name(n)	Returns the local name, without the namespace URI, of the specified node n.
fn:local-name-from-QName(q)	Returns the local name part of the xs:QName argument q. The value returned is an xs:NCName.
fn:max(x)	Returns the item with the highest value from the sequence x. For example, fn:max((1.0, 2.5, 9.3, 0.3, -4.2)) returns 9.3.
fn:min(x)	Returns the item with the lowest value from the sequence x. For example, fn:min(("x", "q", "u", "e", "r", "y")) returns "e".
fn:namespace-uri(n)	Returns the namespace URI of the specified node n.
fn:namespace-uri-from-QName(q)	Returns the namespace URI part of the xs:QName argument q. The value returned is an xs:NCName.
fn:not(b)	Returns true if the effective Boolean value of b is false; returns false if the effective Boolean value is true. For example, fn:not(xs:boolean("true")) returns false.
fn:number(n)	Returns the numeric value of the node indicated by n. For example, fn:number("/Root/NodeA[1]").
fn:position()	Returns the index number of the context item in the sequence currently being processed.
fn:round(n)	Returns the number closest to n that does not have a fractional part. For example, fn:round(10.5) returns 11.
fn:string(a)	Returns the value of the argument a, expressed as an xs:string. For example, fn:string(3.141592) returns "3.141592".
fn:string-length(s)	Returns the length of the string s. For example, fn:string- length("abcdefghij") returns 10.
fn:substring (s, m, n)	Returns n characters from the string s, beginning at position m. If n is not specified, all characters from position m to the end of the string are returned. The first character in the string is position 1. For example, fn:substring("Money", 2, 3) returns "one".
fn:sum(x)	Returns the sum of the sequence of numbers in x. For example, fn:sum((1, 4, 9, 16, 25)) returns 55.
fn:true()	Returns the xs:boolean value true. For example, fn:true() returns true.

In addition, two functions from the `sql:` namespace are supported. The `sql:column` function allows you to expose and bind SQL Server relational column data in XQuery queries. This function accepts the name of an SQL column and exposes its values to your XQuery expressions. Listing 13-28 demonstrates the `sql:column` function.

Listing 13-28. The sql:column Function

```
DECLARE @x xml = N'';
SELECT @x.query(N'<Name>
<ID>
{
sql:column("p.BusinessEntityID")
}
</ID>
<FullName>
{
sql:column("p.FirstName"),
sql:column("p.MiddleName"),
sql:column("p.LastName")
}
</FullName>
</Name>')
FROM Person.Person p
WHERE p.BusinessEntityID <= 5
ORDER BY p.BusinessEntityID;
```

The result of this example, shown in Figure 13-21, is a set of XML documents containing the `BusinessEntityID` and full name of the first five contacts from the `Person.Person` table.

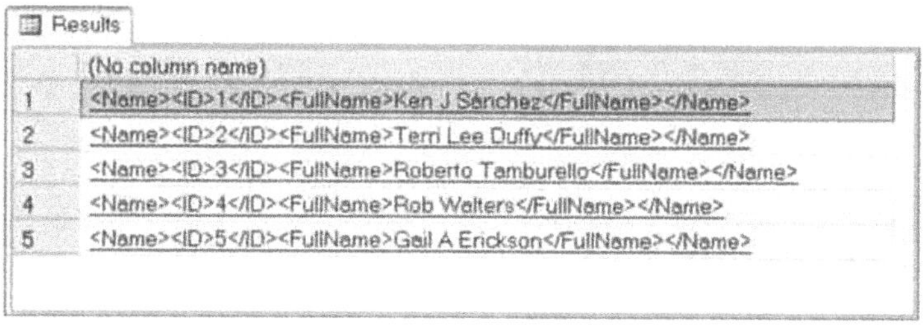

	(No column name)
1	<Name><ID>1</ID><FullName>Ken J Sánchez</FullName></Name>
2	<Name><ID>2</ID><FullName>Terri Lee Duffy</FullName></Name>
3	<Name><ID>3</ID><FullName>Roberto Tamburello</FullName></Name>
4	<Name><ID>4</ID><FullName>Rob Walters</FullName></Name>
5	<Name><ID>5</ID><FullName>Gail A Erickson</FullName></Name>

Figure 13-21. *Results of the sql:column Function Query*

The `sql variable` function goes another step, allowing you to expose T-SQL variables to XQuery. This function accepts the name of a T-SQL variable and allows you to access its value in your XQuery expressions. Listing 13-29 is an example that combines the `sql:column` and `sql:variable` functions in a single XQuery query.

Listing 13-29. XQuery sql:column and sql:variable Functions Example

```
/* 10% discount */
DECLARE @discount NUMERIC(3, 2);
SELECT @discount = 0.10;
DECLARE @x xml;
SELECT @x = '';
SELECT @x.query('<Product>
<Model-ID> { sql:column("ProductModelID") }</Model-ID>
<Name> { sql:column("Name") }</Name>
<Price> { sql:column("ListPrice") } </Price>
<DiscountPrice>
{ sql:column("ListPrice") -
(sql:column("ListPrice") * sql:variable("@discount") ) }
</DiscountPrice>
</Product>
')
FROM Production.Product p
WHERE ProductModelID = 30;
```

The XQuery generates XML documents using the sql:column function to retrieve the ListPrice from the Production.Product table. It also uses the sql:variable function to calculate a discount price for the items retrieved. Figure 13-22 shows partial results of this query (formatted for easier reading):

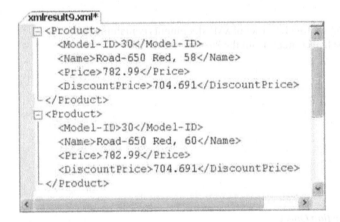

Figure 13-22. *Partial Results of the Query with the sql:column and sql:variable Functions*

Constructors and Casting

The XDM provides constructor functions to dynamically create instances of several supported types. The constructor functions are all in the format xs:TYP(value), where TYP is the XDM type name. Most of the XDM data types have constructor functions; however, the following types do not have constructors in SQL Server XQuery: xs:yearMonthDuration, xs:dayTimeDuration, xs: QName, xs:NMTOKEN, and xs:NOTATION.

The following are examples of XQuery constructor functions:

```
xs:boolean("1")      (: returns true :)
xs:integer(1234)     (: returns 1234 :)
xs:float(9.8723E+3)  (: returns 9872.3 :)
xs:NCName("my-id")   (: returns the NCName "my-id" :)
```

Numeric types can be implicitly cast to their base types (or other numeric types) by XQuery to ensure proper results of calculations. The process of implicit casting is known as type promotion. For instance, in the following sample expression, the xs:integer type value is promoted to an xs:decimal to complete the calculation:

```
xs:integer(100) + xs:decimal(100.99)
```

■ **Note** Only numeric types can be implicitly cast. String and other types cannot be implicitly cast by XQuery.

Explicit casting is performed using the cast as keywords. Examples of explicit casting include the following:

```
xs:string("98d3f4") cast as xs:hexBinary? (: 98d3f4 :)
100 cast as xs:double?  (: 1.0E+2 :)
"0" cast as xs:boolean? (: true :)
```

The ? after the target data type is the optional occurrence indicator. It is used to indicate that an empty sequence is allowed. SQL Server XQuery requires the ? after the cast as expression. SQL Server BOL provides a detailed description of the XQuery type casting rules at http://msdn.microsoft.com/en-us/library/ms191231.aspx.

The instance of Boolean operator allows you to determine the type of a singleton value. This operator takes a singleton value on its left side and a type on its right. The xs:boolean value true is returned if the atomic value represents an instance of the specified type. The following examples demonstrate the instance of operator:

```
10 instance of xs:integer (: returns true :) 100 instance of xs:decimal (: returns true :)
"hello" instance of xs:bytes  (: returns false :)
```

The ? optional occurrence indicator can be appended after the data type to indicate that the empty sequence is allowable (though it is not mandatory, as with the cast as operator), as in this example:

```
9.8273 instance of xs:double? (: returns true :)
```

FLWOR Expressions

FLWOR expressions provide a way to iterate over a sequence and bind intermediate results to variables. FLWOR is an acronym for the keywords that define this type of expression: for, let, where, order by, and return. This section discusses XQuery's powerful FLWOR expressions.

The for and return Keywords

The for and return keywords have long been a part of XPath, though in not nearly so powerful a form as the XQuery FLWOR expression. The for keyword specifies that a variable is iteratively bound to the results of the specified path expression. The result of this iterative binding process is known as a tuple stream. The XQuery for expression is roughly analogous to the T-SQL SELECT statement. The for keyword must, at a minimum, have a matching return clause after it. The sample in Listing 13-30 demonstrates a basic for expression.

Listing 13-30. Basic XQuery for...return Expression

```
SELECT CatalogDescription.query(N'declare namespace ns =
"http://schemas.microsoft.com/sqlserver/2004/07/adventure-works/ProductModelDescription";
for $spec in //ns:ProductDescription/ns:Specifications/*
return fn:string($spec)') AS Description FROM Production.ProductModel WHERE ProductModelID = 19;
```

The for clause iterates through all elements returned by the path expression. It then binds the elements to the $spec variable. The tuple stream that is bound to $spec consists of the following nodes in document order:

```
$spec = <Material>Almuminum Alloy</Material>
$spec = <Color>Available in most colors</Color>
$spec = <ProductLine>Mountain bike</ProductLine>
$spec = <Style>Unisex</Style>
$spec = <RiderExperience>Advanced to Professional riders</RiderExperience>
```

The return clause applies the fn:string function to the $spec variable to return the string value of each node as it is bound. The results look like the following:

```
Almuminum Alloy Available in most colors Mountain bike Unisex Advanced to Professional
riders.
```

The sample can be modified to return an XML result, using the techniques described previously in the "Dynamic XML Construction" section. Listing 13-31 demonstrates with results shown in Figure 13-23.

Listing 13-31. XQuery for...return Expression with XML Result

```
SELECT CatalogDescription.query (

N'declare namespace ns =
"http://schemas.microsoft.com/sqlserver/2004/07/adventure-works/ProductModelDescription";
for $spec in //ns:ProductDescription/ns:Specifications/* return <detail> {
$spec/text() } </detail>' ) AS Description
FROM Production.ProductModel WHERE ProductModelID = 19;
```

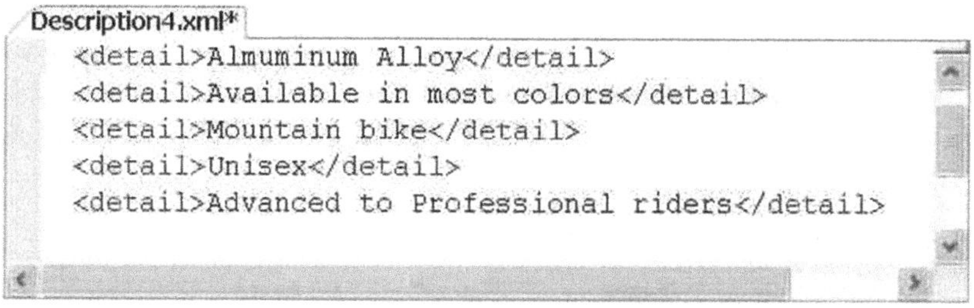

Figure 13-23. *Results of the for...return Expression with XML Construction*

XQuery allows you to bind multiple variables in the for clause. When you bind multiple variables, the result is the Cartesian product of all possible values of the variables. SQL Server programmers will recognize the Cartesian product as being equivalent to the SQL CROSS JOIN operator. Listing 13-32 modifies the previous example further to generate the Cartesian product of the Specifications and Warranty child node text.

Listing 13-32. XQuery Cartesian Product with for Expression

```
SELECT CatalogDescription.query(N'declare namespace ns =
"http://schemas.microsoft.com/sqlserver/2004/07/adventure-works/ProductModelDescription";
for $spec in //ns:ProductDescription/ns:Specifications/*,
$feat in //ns:ProductDescription/*:Features/*:Warranty/node()
return <detail>
{
$spec/text()
} +
{
fn:string($feat/.)
}
</detail>'
) AS Description
FROM Production.ProductModel
WHERE ProductModelID = 19;
```

The $spec variable is bound to the same nodes shown previously. A second variable binding, for the variable $feat, is added to the for clause in this example. Specifically, this second variable is bound to the child nodes of the Warranty element, as shown following:

```
<pl:WarrantyPeriod>3 years</pl:WarrantyPeriod> <pl:Description>parts and
labor</pl:Description
```

The Cartesian product of the text nodes of these two tuple streams consists of ten possible combinations. The final result of the XQuery expression is shown in Figure 13-24 (formatted for easier reading).

Description6.xml*

```
<detail>Almuminum Alloy + 3 years</detail>
<detail>Almuminum Alloy + parts and labor</detail>
<detail>Available in most colors + 3 years</detail>
<detail>Available in most colors + parts and labor</detail>
<detail>Mountain bike + 3 years</detail>
<detail>Mountain bike + parts and labor</detail>
<detail>Unisex + 3 years</detail>
<detail>Unisex + parts and labor</detail>
<detail>Advanced to Professional riders + 3 years</detail>
<detail>Advanced to Professional riders + parts and labor</detail>
```

Figure 13-24. Cartesian Product XQuery

A bound variable can be used immediately after it is bound, even in the same for clause. Listing 13-33 demonstrates this.

Listing 13-33. Using a Bound Variable in the for Clause

```
SELECT CatalogDescription.query
(
N'declare namespace ns =
"http://schemas.microsoft.com/sqlserver/2004/07/adventure-works/ProductModelDescription";
for $spec in //ns:ProductDescription/ns:Specifications,
$color in $spec/Color
return <color>
{
$color/text()
}
</color>'
) AS Color
FROM Production.ProductModel
WHERE ProductModelID = 19;
```

In this example, the $spec variable is bound to the Specifications node. It is then used in the same for clause to bind a value to the variable $color. The result is shown in Figure 13-25.

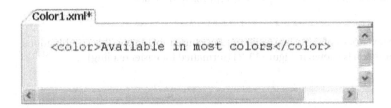

Color1.xml*

```
<color>Available in most colors</color>
```

Figure 13-25. Binding a Variable to Another Bound Variable in the for Clause

The where Keyword

The where keyword specifies an optional clause to filter tuples generated by the for clause. The expression in the where clause is evaluated for each tuple, and those for which the effective Boolean value evaluates to false are discarded from the final result. Listing 13-34 demonstrates use of the where clause to limit the results to only those tuples that contain the letter A. The results are shown in Figure 13-26.

Listing 13-34. where Clause Demonstration

```
SELECT CatalogDescription.query
(
N'declare namespace ns =
"http://schemas.microsoft.com/sqlserver/2004/07/adventure-works/ProductModelDescription";
for $spec in //ns:ProductDescription/ns:Specifications/*
where $spec[ contains( . , "A" ) ]
return <detail>
{
$spec/text()
}
</detail>'
) AS Detail
FROM Production.ProductModel
WHERE ProductModelID = 19;
```

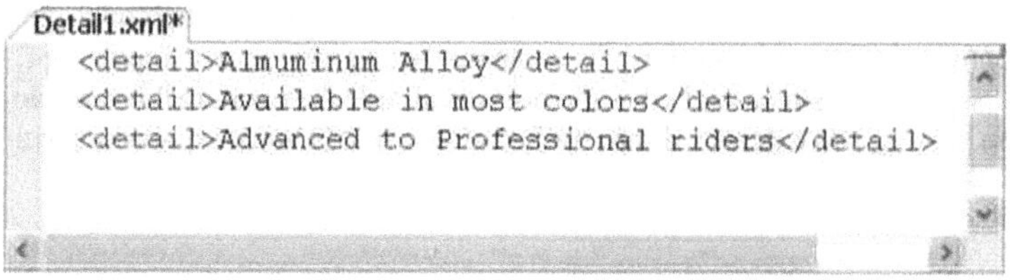

Detail1.xml*
```
<detail>Almuminum Alloy</detail>
<detail>Available in most colors</detail>
<detail>Advanced to Professional riders</detail>
```

Figure 13-26. *Results of a FLWOR Expression with the where Clause*

The functions and operators described previously in this chapter (such as the contains function used in the example) can be used in the where clause expression to limit results as required by your application.

The order by Keywords

The order by clause is an optional clause of the FLWOR statement. The order by clause reorders the tuple stream generated by the for clause, using criteria that you specify. The order by criteria consists of one or more ordering specifications that are made up of an expression and an optional order modifier. Ordering specifications are evaluated from left to right.

The optional order modifier is either ascending or descending to indicate the direction of ordering. The default is ascending, as shown in Listing 13-35. The sample uses the order by clause to sort the results in descending (reverse) order. The results are shown in Figure 13-27.

Listing 13-35. order by Clause

```
SELECT CatalogDescription.query(N'declare namespace ns =
"http://schemas.microsoft.com/sqlserver/2004/07/adventure-works/ProductModelDescription";
for $spec in //ns:ProductDescription/ns:Specifications/*
order by $spec/. descending
return <detail> { $spec/text() } </detail>') AS Detail
FROM Production.ProductModel
WHERE ProductModelID = 19;
```

```
Detail2.xml*
    <detail>Unisex</detail>
    <detail>Mountain bike</detail>
    <detail>Available in most colors</detail>
    <detail>Almuminum Alloy</detail>
    <detail>Advanced to Professional riders</detail>
```

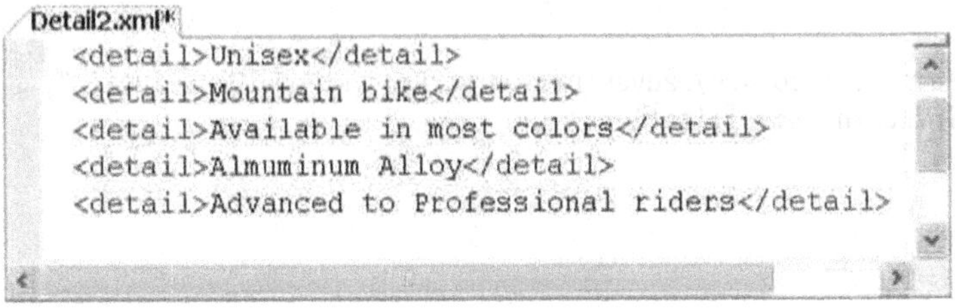

Figure 13-27. *Results of a FLWOR Expression with the order by Clause*

The let Keyword

SQL Server 2012 added support for the FLWOR expression let clause. The let clause allows you to bind tuple streams to variables inside the body of the FLWOR expression. You can use the let clause to name repeating expressions. SQL Server XQuery inserts the expression assigned to the bound variable everywhere the variable is referenced in the FLWOR expression. Listing 13-36 demonstrates the let clause in a FLWOR expression, with results shown in Figure 13-28.

Listing 13-36. let Clause

```
SELECT CatalogDescription.query
(
N'declare namespace ns =
"http://schemas.microsoft.com/sqlserver/2004/07/adventure-works/ProductModelDescription";
for $spec in //ns:ProductDescription/ns:Specifications/*
let $val := $spec/text()
order by fn:string($val[1]) ascending
return <spec>
{
$val
}
</spec>'
) AS Detail
FROM Production.ProductModel
WHERE ProductModelID = 19;
```

Detail9.xml*

```
<spec>Advanced to Professional riders</spec>
<spec>Almuminum Alloy</spec>
<spec>Available in most colors</spec>
<spec>Mountain bike</spec>
<spec>Unisex</spec>
```

Figure 13-28. *Results of a FLWOR Expression with the let Clause*

UTF-16 Support

When SQL Server stores unicode data types with nchar and nvarchar it stores using UCS-2 encoding (UCS – Universal Character Set), meaning it counts every 2-byte character as single character. In recent years the charater limit was increased to 31 bits, and it would be difficult to store these characters given the fact that we only have 2 bytes per character. This led to the problem of SQL Server not handling some of the characters properly. In the previous versions of SQL Server, even though SQLXML supports UTF-16, the string functions only supported for UCS-2 unicode values. This means that even though the data can be stored and retrieved without losing the property, some of the string operations such as string length or substring functions provided wrong results since they don't recognize surrogate pairs.

Let's review this with an example, and in our case, let's say we have to store UTF-16 encoding such as musical symbol drum cleff-1 as a part of a name in our database. Drum-cleff-1 is represented by surrogate values 0xD834 and 0xDD25. Let's say we calculate the length of the string to see if SQL Server checks for surrogate pairs. Listing 13-37 demonstrates the creation of the sample row for our usage and Listing 13-38 uses the row that was created using Listing 13-37 to demonstrate UTF-16 encoding handling in SQL Server. Results for Listing 13-38 are shown in Figure 13-29.

Listing 13-37. Create Record to Demonstrate UTF-16

```
declare @BusinessEntityId int
INSERT INTO Person.BusinessEntity(rowguid, ModifiedDate)
VALUES (NEWID(),CURRENT_TIMESTAMP)
SET @BusinessEntityId = SCOPE_IDENTITY()
INSERT INTO [Person].[Person]
           ([BusinessEntityID]
           ,[PersonType]
           ,[NameStyle]
           ,[Title]
           ,[FirstName]
           ,[MiddleName]
           ,[LastName]
           ,[Suffix]
           ,[EmailPromotion]
           ,[AdditionalContactInfo]
           ,[Demographics]
           ,[rowguid]
           ,[ModifiedDate])
```

```
VALUES
            (@BusinessEntityId,
            'EM',
            0,
            NULL,
            N'T' + nchar(0xD834) + nchar(0xDD25),
            'J',
            'Kim',
            NULL,
            0,
            NULL,
            '<IndividualSurvey xmlns="http://schemas.microsoft.com/sqlserver/2004/07/
              adventure-works/IndividualSurvey"><TotalPurchaseYTD>0</TotalPurchaseYTD>
              </IndividualSurvey>',
            NEWID(),
            CURRENT_TIMESTAMP)
```

Listing 13-38. SQL Server to Check for Presence of Surrogates

```
SELECT
p.NameStyle AS "processing-instruction(nameStyle)",
p.BusinessEntityID AS "Person/@ID",
p.ModifiedDate AS "comment()",
FirstName AS "Person/Name/First",
Len(FirstName) AS "Person/FirstName/Length",
MiddleName AS "Person/Name/Middle",
LastName AS "Person/Name/Last"
FROM Person.Person p
WHERE BusinessEntityID = 20778
FOR XML PATH;
```

```
<row>
   <?nameStyle 0?>
   <Person ID="20778" />
   <!--2012-08-04T02:48:40.307-->
   <Person>
     <Name>
        <First>T◻</First>
     </Name>
     <FirstName>
        <Length>3</Length>
     </FirstName>
     <Name>
        <Middle>J</Middle>
        <Last>Kim</Last>
     </Name>
   </Person>
</row>
```

Figure 13-29. *Results of SQL Server UTF-16 Surrogate Pair*

From Figure 13-29, you can see that the query returns the column length to be 3 whereas the length should be 2 because length function calculates the number of characters and we have 2 characters in our string. Since the surrogate pair is not recognized, the number of characters is listed as 3 instead of 2.

To mitigate the above issue, in SQL Server 2014 there is full support for UTF-16/UCS-4, meaning the Xquery handles the surrogate pairs properly and returns the correct results for string operations and the operators such as =,==,<,>=and LIKE. Note that some of the string operators may already be surrogate aware. However since some of the applications are already developed and being used based on the older behavior, SQL Server 2012 added a new set of flags to the collation names to indicate that the collation is UTF-16 aware. The _SC (Supplementary Characters) flag will be appended to the version 100 collation names and it be applicable for nchar, nvarchar, and sql_variant data types.

Let's modify the code snippet we have from Listing 13-38 and add the _SC collation to the query to see how SQL Server calculates the column length properly. In this example let's include the supplementary characters collation so that SQL Server is UTF-16 aware. The modified code snippet is shown in Listing 13-39 and results are shown in Figure 13-30.

Listing 13-39. Surroage Pair with UTF-16 and _SC collation

```
SELECT
p.NameStyle AS "processing-instruction(nameStyle)",
p.BusinessEntityID AS "Person/@ID",
p.ModifiedDate AS "comment()",
FirstName AS "Person/Name/First",
Len(FirstName COLLATE Latin1_General_100_CS_AS_SC) AS "Person/FirstName/Length",
MiddleName AS "Person/Name/Middle",
LastName AS "Person/Name/Last"
FROM Person.Person p
WHERE BusinessEntityID = 20778
FOR XML PATH;
```

```
<row>
  <?nameStyle 0?>
  <Person ID="20778" />
  <!--2012-08-04T02:48:40.307-->
  <Person>
    <Name>
      <First>T▨</First>
    </Name>
    <FirstName>
      <Length>2</Length>
    </FirstName>
    <Name>
      <Middle>J</Middle>
      <Last>Kim</Last>
    </Name>
  </Person>
</row>
```

Figure 13-30. Results of SQL Server UTF-16 Surrogate Pair with _SC collation

Figure 13-30 demonstrates that by using supplementary characters collation, SQL Server now is UTF-16 aware, and it calculates the column length as it should: we see the proper value of 2 for the column length.

To maintain backward compatibility SQL Server is surrogate pair aware only when the compatibility mode is set to SQL11 or higher. If the compatability mode is set to SQL10 or lower, the fn:string-length and fn:substring will not be surrogate aware and the older behavior will continue.

Summary

This chapter has expanded the discussion of SQL Server XML functionality that we began in Chapter 12. In particular, we focused on the SQL Server implementations of XPath and XQuery. We provided a more detailed discussion of the SQL Server FOR XML PATH clause XPath implementation, including XPath expression syntax, axis specifiers, and supported node tests. We also discussed SQL Server support for XML namespaces via the WITH XMLNAMESPACES clause.

We used the majority of this chapter to detail SQL Server support for XQuery, which provides a powerful set of expression types, functions, operators, and support for the rich XDM data type system. SQL Server support for XQuery has improved with the release of SQL Server 2014, including new options like the FLWOR expression let clause, support for date and time literals without specifying explicit time offsets, and UTF-16 support and Supplementary Characters collation.

The next chapter discusses SQL Server 2014 catalog views and dynamic management views and functions that provide a way to look under the hood of your databases and server instances.

EXERCISES

1. [True/False] The FOR XML PATH clause supports a subset of the W3C XPath recommendation.

2. [Choose one] Which of the following symbols is used in XQuery and XPath as an axis specifier to identify XML attributes:

   a. An at sign (@)

   b. An exclamation point (!)

   c. A period (.)

   d. Two periods (..)

3. [Fill in the blanks] The context item, indicated by a single period (.) in XPath and XQuery, specifies the current _____ or scalar _____ being accessed at any given point in time during query execution.

4. [Choose all that apply] You can declare namespaces for XQuery expressions in SQL Server using which of the following methods:

   e. The T-SQL WITH XMLNAMESPACES clause

   f. The XQuery declare default element namespace statement

   g. The T-SQL CREATE XML NAMESPACE statement

   h. The XQuery declare namespace statement

5. [Fill in the blanks] In XQuery, you can dynamically construct XML via _____ constructors or _____ constructors.

6. [True/False] SQL Server 2012 supports the for, let, where, order by, and return clauses of XQuery FLWOR expressions.

7. [Fill in the blanks] _SC collation enables SQL Server to be _____.

8. [Choose all that apply] SQL Server supports the following types of XQuery comparison operators:

    i. Array comparison operators

    j. General comparison operators

    k. Node comparison operators

    l. Value comparison operators

■ ■ ■

CHAPTER 14

Catalog Views and Dynamic
aent Views

SQL Server has always offered access to metadata describing databases, tables, views, and other database objects. Prior to the introduction of catalog views in SQL Server 2005, the primary methods of accessing this metadata included system tables, system SPs, INFORMATION_SCHEMA views, and SQL Distributed Management Objects (SQL-DMO). Catalog views provide access to a richer set of detailed information than any of these options provided in previous SQL Server releases. SQL Server even includes catalog views that allow you to access server-wide configuration metadata.

■ **Note** Metadata is simply data that describes data. SQL Server 2014 databases are largely "self-describing." The data describing the objects, structures, and relationships that form a database are stored in the database itself. This data describing the database structure and objects is what we refer to as *metadata*.

SQL Server 2014 also provides dynamic management views (DMVs) and dynamic management functions (DMFs) that allow you to access server-state information. The SQL Server DMVs and DMFs provide a relational tabular view of internal SQL Server data structures that would otherwise be inaccessible. SQL Server 2014 provides a new set of DMVs specifically focused on the memory, performance, and space usage of memory-optimized tables. Examples of metadata that can be accessed include information about the state of internal memory structures, the contents of caches and buffers, and statuses of processes and components. You can use the information returned by DMVs and DMFs to diagnose server problems, monitor server health, and tune performance. This chapter discusses catalog views, DMVs, and DMFs.

Catalog Views

Catalog views provide insight into database objects and server-wide configuration options in much the same way that system tables, system SPs, and INFORMATION_SCHEMA views did in previous releases of SQL Server. Catalog views offer advantages over these older methods of accessing database and server metadata, including the following:

- Catalog views, unlike system SPs, can be used in queries with results joined to other catalog views or tables. You can also limit the results returned by catalog views with a WHERE clause.

- Catalog views offer SQL Server–specific information that isn't available through the INFORMATION_SCHEMA views. The reason is that although INFORMATION_SCHEMA views are still included in SQL Server to comply with the ISO standard, they may not be regularly updated. So it's advisable to use catalog views to access metadata instead of the system SPs or INFORMATION_SCHEMA views.

- Catalog views provide richer information than system tables and simplify data access from system tables regardless of schema changes in the underlying system tables. There are also more catalog views available than legacy system tables because some catalog views inherit rows from other catalog views.

Many catalog views follow an inheritance model in which some catalog views are defined as extensions to other catalog views. The sys.tables catalog view, for instance, inherits columns from the sys.objects catalog view. Some catalog views, such as sys.allcolumns, are defined as the union of two other catalog views. In this example, the sys.allcolumns catalog view is defined as the union of the sys.columns and sys.systemcolumns catalog views.

SQL Server supplies a wide range of catalog views that return metadata about all different types of database objects and server-configuration options, SQL CLR assemblies, XML schema collections, the SQL Server resource governor, change tracking, and more. Rather than give a complete list of all the available catalog views, this section provides some usage examples and descriptions of the functionality available through catalog views.

■ **Tip** BOL details the complete list of available catalog views (there are more than 100 of them) at http://msdn.microsoft.com/en-us/library/ms174365.aspx.

Table and Column Metadata

Way back in the pre-SQL Server Integration Services (SSIS) days, we spent a good deal of our time creating custom ETL (extract, transform, and load) solutions. One of the problems we faced was the quirky nature of the various bulk-copy APIs available. Unlike SQL Server DML statements like INSERT, which specify columns to populate by name, the available bulk-copy APIs require you to specify columns to populate by their ordinal position. This can lead to all kinds of problems if the table structure changes (for example, if new columns are added, columns are removed, or the order of existing columns is changed). One way to deal with this type of disconnect is to create your own function that maps column names to ordinal positions. You can use catalog views to access exactly this type of functionality. In Listing 14-1, you join the sys.schemas, sys.tables, sys.columns, and sys.types catalog views to return column-level metadata about the AdventureWorks Person.Address table. The results are shown in Figure 14-1.

Listing 14-1. Retrieving Column-level Metadata with Catalog Views

```
SELECT
s.name AS schema_name,
t.name AS table_name,
t.type_desc AS table_type,
c.name AS column_name,
c.column_id,
ty.name AS data_type_name,
c.max_Length,
c.precision,
```

```
c.scale,
c.is_nullable FROM sys.schemas s INNER JOIN sys.tables t
ON s.schema_id = t.schema_id INNER JOIN sys.columns c
ON t.object_id = c.object_id INNER JOIN sys.types ty
ON c.system_type_id = ty.system_type_id AND c.user_type_id = ty.user_type_id WHERE
s.name = 'Person'
AND t.name = 'Address';
```

	schema_name	table_name	table_type	column_name	column_id	data_type_name	max_Length	precision	scale	is_nullable
1	Person	Address	USER_TABLE	AddressID	1	int	4	10	0	0
2	Person	Address	USER_TABLE	AddressLine1	2	nvarchar	120	0	0	0
3	Person	Address	USER_TABLE	AddressLine2	3	nvarchar	120	0	0	1
4	Person	Address	USER_TABLE	City	4	nvarchar	60	0	0	0
5	Person	Address	USER_TABLE	StateProvinceID	5	int	4	10	0	0
6	Person	Address	USER_TABLE	PostalCode	6	nvarchar	30	0	0	0
7	Person	Address	USER_TABLE	SpatialLocation	7	geography	-1	0	0	1
8	Person	Address	USER_TABLE	rowguid	8	uniqueidentifier	16	0	0	0
9	Person	Address	USER_TABLE	ModifiedDate	9	datetime	8	23	3	0

Figure 14-1. *Retrieving column-level metadata*

This type of metadata is also useful for administrative applications or dynamic queries that need to run against several different tables for which you don't necessarily know the structure in advance.

Whether it's for administrative applications, bulk loading, or dynamic queries that need to run against several different tables, SQL Server catalog views can provide structure and attribute information for database objects. SQL Server 2014 provides several methods of retrieving metadata.

Querying Permissions

Another administrative task that can be performed through catalog views is querying and scripting database object permissions. Listing 14-2 begins this demonstration by creating a couple of new users named jack and jill in the AdventureWorks database. The jill user is assigned permissions to human resources–related objects, and jack is assigned permissions to production objects.

Listing 14-2. Creating the jack and jill Users

```
CREATE USER jill WITHOUT LOGIN;
CREATE USER jack WITHOUT LOGIN;
GRANT SELECT, INSERT
ON Schema::HumanResources TO jill;
GRANT SELECT
ON dbo.ufnGetContactInformation TO jill;
GRANT EXECUTE
ON HumanResources.uspUpdateEmployeeLogin TO jill;
DENY SELECT
ON Schema::Sales TO jill;
DENY SELECT
ON HumanResources.Shift (ModifiedDate) TO jill;
GRANT SELECT, UPDATE, INSERT, DELETE
ON Schema::Production TO jack WITH GRANT OPTION;
```

You grant and deny permissions to these users on a wide selection of objects for demonstration purposes. The query in Listing 14-3 is a modified version of an example first published by SQL Server MVP Louis Davidson. The code uses the sys.databasepermissions, sys.databaseprincipals, and sys.objects catalog views to query the permissions granted and denied to database principals in the database. The results are shown in Figure 14-2.

Listing 14-3. Querying Permissions on AdventureWorks Objects

```
WITH Permissions (
permission,
type,
obj_name,
db_principal,
grant_type,
schema_name ) AS
(
    SELECT dp.permission_name,
        CASE dp.class_desc
        WHEN 'OBJECT_OR_COLUMN' THEN
        CASE
        WHEN  minor_id  >  0  THEN  'COLUMN'
        ELSE  o.type_desc
        END
        ELSE dp.class_desc
        END,
        CASE dp.class_desc
        WHEN  'SCHEMA'  THEN  SCHEMA_NAME(dp.major_id)
        WHEN 'OBJECT_OR_COLUMN' THEN
        CASE
        WHEN  dp.minor_id  =  0  THEN object_name(dp.major_id)
        ELSE
        (
        SELECT object_name(o.object_id) + '.'+ c.name
        FROM sys.columns c
        WHERE  c.object_id  =  dp.major_id
        AND  c.column_id  =  dp.minor_id
        )
        END
        ELSE '**UNKNOWN**'
        END,
        dpr.name,
        dp.state_desc,
        SCHEMA_NAME(o.schema_id)
    FROM  sys.database_permissions  dp
    INNER JOIN sys.database_principals dpr
        ON  dp.grantee_principal_id  =  dpr.principal_id
    LEFT  JOIN  sys.objects  o
        ON o.object_id = dp.major_id
    WHERE dp.major_id > 0
)
```

```
SELECT
    p.permission,
    CASE type
        WHEN 'SCHEMA' THEN 'Schema::' + obj_name
        ELSE schema_name + '.' + obj_name
    END  AS  name,
    p.type,
    p.db_principal,
    p.grant_type
FROM Permissions p
ORDER  BY
    p.db_principal,
    p.permission;
GO
```

	permission	name	type	db_principal	grant_type
1	DELETE	Schema::Production	SCHEMA	jack	GRANT_WITH_GRANT_OPTION
2	INSERT	Schema::Production	SCHEMA	jack	GRANT_WITH_GRANT_OPTION
3	SELECT	Schema::Production	SCHEMA	jack	GRANT_WITH_GRANT_OPTION
4	UPDATE	Schema::Production	SCHEMA	jack	GRANT_WITH_GRANT_OPTION
5	EXECUTE	HumanResources.uspUpdateEmployeeLogin	SQL_STORED_PROCEDURE	jill	GRANT
6	INSERT	Schema::HumanResources	SCHEMA	jill	GRANT
7	SELECT	Schema::HumanResources	SCHEMA	jill	GRANT
8	SELECT	HumanResources.Shift.ModifiedDate	COLUMN	jill	DENY
9	SELECT	dbo.ufnGetContactInformation	SQL_TABLE_VALUED_FUNCTION	jill	GRANT
10	SELECT	Schema::Sales	SCHEMA	jill	DENY

Figure 14-2. *Results of the permissions query*

As you can see in Figure 14-2, the query retrieves the explicit permissions granted to and denied from the jack and jill database principals. These permissions are shown for each object along with information about the objects themselves. This simple example can be expanded to perform additional tasks, such as scripting object permissions.

■ **Tip** *Explicit permissions* are permissions explicitly granted or denied through T-SQL GRANT, DENY, and REVOKE statements. The effective permissions of a principal are a combination of the principal's explicit permissions, permissions inherited from the roles or groups to which the principal belongs, and permissions implied by other permissions. You can use the sys.fn_my_permissions system function to view your effective permissions.

Dynamic Management Views and Functions

In addition to catalog views, SQL Server 2014 provides more than 204 DMVs and DMFs that give you access to internal server-state information. DMVs and DMFs are designed specifically for the benefit of database administrators (DBAs), but they can also provide developers with extremely useful insights into the internal workings of SQL Server. Having access to this server-state information can enhance the server-management and -administration experience and help to identify potential problems and performance issues (for which developers are increasingly sharing responsibility).

SQL Server provides DMVs and DMFs that are scoped at the database level and at the server level. All DMVs and DMFs are in the sys schema, and their names all start with dm*. There are several categories of DMVs and DMFs, with most being grouped together using standard name prefixes. Table 14-1 lists some of the most commonly used categories. The majority of the new system views related to SQL Server 2014 memory-optimized tables contain the abbreviation %xtp% in the object name.

Table 14-1. *Commonly Used DMV and DMF Categories*

Names	Description
sys.dm_cdc_*	Contains information about Change Data Capture (CDC) transactions and log sessions
sys.dm_exec_*	Returns information related to user code execution
sys.dm_fts_*	Retrieves information about integrated full-text search (iFTS) functionality
sys.dm_os_*	Displays low-level details such as locks, memory usage, and scheduling
sys.dm_tran_*	Provides information about current transactions and lock resources
sys.dm_io_*	Allows you to monitor network and disk I/O
sys.dm_db_*	Returns information about databases and database-level objects
sys.dm_db_xtp*	Returns information about database-level memory-optimized objects (new in SQL Server 2014)
sys.dm_xtp*	Returns information related to memory-optimized objects (new in SQL Server 2014)

Chapter 5 gave an example of DMV and DMF usage with an SP that extracts information from the SQL Server query-plan cache. This section explores more uses for DMVs and DMFs.

Index Metadata

SQL Server metadata is useful for performing tedious administrative tasks like identifying potential performance issues, updating statistics, and rebuilding indexes. Creating a customized procedure to perform these tasks gives you the ability to create scripts that are flexible and target the maintenance tasks being performed, which isn't an option available with the standard maintenance plan. Listing 14-4 uses catalog views to identify all tables in the AdventureWorks database with clustered or nonclustered indexes defined on them. The procedure then generates T-SQL ALTER INDEX statements to rebuild all the indexes defined on these tables and also updates the statistics and recompiles stored procedures and triggers. We have kept this example fairly simple, although it can be used as a basis for more complex index-rebuilding procedures that make decisions based on various scenarios like rebuilding indexes for all the databases in the server and that also consider factors such as LOB to reindex the objects. Figure 14-3 shows the ALTER INDEX statements created by the procedure.

Listing 14-4. Stored Procedure to Rebuild Table Indexes

```
CREATE PROCEDURE dbo.RebuildIndexes
    @db sysname = 'Adventureworks',
    @online bit = 1,
    @maxfrag int = 10,
    @rebuildthreshold int = 30,
    @WeekdayRebuildOffline int = 1
AS
BEGIN;
    SET NOCOUNT ON;
    DECLARE
        @objectid int,
        @indexid int,
        @indextype nvarchar(60),
        @schemaname nvarchar(130),
        @objectname nvarchar(130),
        @indexname nvarchar(130),
        @frag float,
        @sqlcommand nvarchar(4000);


    -- Select tables and indexes from the
    -- sys.dm_db_index_physical_stats function based on the threshold defined
    SELECT
        object_id AS objectid,
        index_id AS indexid,
        index_type_desc AS indextype,
        avg_fragmentation_in_percent AS frag
    INTO
        #reindexobjects
    FROM
        sys.dm_db_index_physical_stats(DB_ID(@db), NULL, NULL, NULL, 'LIMITED')
    WHERE
        avg_fragmentation_in_percent > @maxfrag
        AND index_id > 0


    -- Declare the cursor for the list of objects to be processed.
    DECLARE objects CURSOR FOR
        SELECT o.* FROM #reindexobjects o
        INNER JOIN sys.indexes i ON i.object_id = o.objectid
        WHERE i.is_disabled = 0 AND i.is_hypothetical = 0;


    -- Open the cursor.
    OPEN objects;


    WHILE (1=1)
    BEGIN;
        FETCH NEXT FROM objects INTO @objectid, @indexid, @indextype, @frag;
        IF @@FETCH_STATUS < 0 BREAK;
        SELECT @objectname = QUOTENAME(o.name), @schemaname = QUOTENAME(s.name)
```

```
        FROM sys.objects AS o
        JOIN sys.schemas AS s ON s.schema_id = o.schema_id
        WHERE o.object_id = @objectid;

        SELECT @indexname = QUOTENAME(name)
        FROM sys.indexes
        WHERE object_id = @objectid AND index_id = @indexid;

        SET @sqlcommand = N'ALTER INDEX ' + @indexname + N' ON ' +
                    @schemaname + N'.' + @objectname;

        IF @frag > @rebuildthreshold
        BEGIN;
            SET @sqlcommand = @sqlcommand + N' REBUILD';

            IF (DATEPART(WEEKDAY, GETDATE()) <> @WeekdayRebuildOffline)
AND ((@indextype Like 'HEAP') OR (@indextype like '%CLUSTERED%'))
            SET @sqlcommand = @sqlcommand + N' WITH (ONLINE = ON)';
        END;
        ELSE
            SET @sqlcommand = @sqlcommand + N' REORGANIZE';
        PRINT N'Executing: ' + @sqlcommand;
        EXEC (@sqlcommand) ;
    END;

    -- Close and deallocate the cursor.
    CLOSE objects;
    DEALLOCATE objects;

    --  UPDATE STATISTICS & SP_RECOMPILE
    DECLARE tablelist CURSOR FOR
        SELECT distinct OBJECT_NAME(o.objectid) FROM #reindexobjects o;

    -- Open the cursor.
    OPEN tablelist;

    FETCH NEXT FROM tablelist INTO @objectname;

    -- Loop through the partitions.
    WHILE @@FETCH_STATUS = 0
    BEGIN;
        --Update Statistics
        SET @sqlcommand = ' UPDATE STATISTICS ' + @objectname;
        PRINT N'Executing: ' + @sqlcommand;
        EXEC (@sqlcommand) ;

        --Recompile Stored Procedures and Triggers
        SET @sqlcommand = ' EXEC sp_recompile ' + @objectname;
        PRINT N'Executing: ' + @sqlcommand;
```

```
        EXEC (@sqlcommand) ;
        FETCH NEXT FROM tablelist INTO @objectname;
    END;

    CLOSE tablelist;
    DEALLOCATE tablelist;
    DROP TABLE #reindexobjects;
END;
GO
```

```
🗋 Messages
Executing: ALTER INDEX [PK_DatabaseLog_DatabaseLogID] ON [dbo].[DatabaseLog] REORGANIZE
Executing: ALTER INDEX [PK_DatabaseLog_DatabaseLogID] ON [dbo].[DatabaseLog] REORGANIZE
Executing: ALTER INDEX [PK_ProductInventory_ProductID_LocationID] ON [Production].[ProductInventory] REORGANIZE
Executing: ALTER INDEX [PK_SpecialOfferProduct_SpecialOfferID_ProductID] ON [Sales].[SpecialOfferProduct] REBUILD WITH (ONLINE = ON)
Executing: ALTER INDEX [PK_SpecialOfferProduct_SpecialOfferID_ProductID] ON [Sales].[SpecialOfferProduct] REBUILD WITH (ONLINE = ON)
Executing: ALTER INDEX [PK_SpecialOfferProduct_SpecialOfferID_ProductID] ON [Sales].[SpecialOfferProduct] REBUILD WITH (ONLINE = ON)
Executing: ALTER INDEX [PXML_ProductModel_CatalogDescription] ON [Production].[ProductModel] REBUILD
Executing: ALTER INDEX [PXML_ProductModel_CatalogDescription] ON [Production].[ProductModel] REBUILD
Executing: ALTER INDEX [PXML_ProductModel_CatalogDescription] ON [Production].[ProductModel] REBUILD
Executing: ALTER INDEX [PXML_ProductModel_CatalogDescription] ON [Production].[ProductModel] REBUILD
Executing: ALTER INDEX [PXML_ProductModel_CatalogDescription] ON [Production].[ProductModel] REBUILD
Executing: ALTER INDEX [PXML_ProductModel_Instructions] ON [Production].[ProductModel] REBUILD
Executing: ALTER INDEX [PXML_ProductModel_Instructions] ON [Production].[ProductModel] REBUILD
Executing: ALTER INDEX [PXML_ProductModel_Instructions] ON [Production].[ProductModel] REBUILD
Executing: ALTER INDEX [PXML_ProductModel_Instructions] ON [Production].[ProductModel] REBUILD
Executing: ALTER INDEX [PXML_ProductModel_Instructions] ON [Production].[ProductModel] REBUILD
Executing: ALTER INDEX [PK_StateProvince_StateProvinceID] ON [Person].[StateProvince] REBUILD WITH (ONLINE = ON)
Executing: ALTER INDEX [PK_StateProvince_StateProvinceID] ON [Person].[StateProvince] REBUILD WITH (ONLINE = ON)
Executing: ALTER INDEX [PK_StateProvince_StateProvinceID] ON [Person].[StateProvince] REBUILD WITH (ONLINE = ON)
Executing: ALTER INDEX [PK_StateProvince_StateProvinceID] ON [Person].[StateProvince] REBUILD WITH (ONLINE = ON)
Executing: ALTER INDEX [PK_ProductModelProductDescriptionCulture_ProductModelID_ProductDescriptionID_CultureID] ON [Production].[Produc
Executing: ALTER INDEX [AK_BillOfMaterials_ProductAssemblyID_ComponentID_StartDate] ON [Production].[BillOfMaterials] REORGANIZE
Executing: ALTER INDEX [AK_BillOfMaterials_ProductAssemblyID_ComponentID_StartDate] ON [Production].[BillOfMaterials] REORGANIZE
```

Figure 14-3. *ALTER INDEX statements to rebuild indexes on AdventureWorks tables*

The procedure in Listing 14-4 uses the DMV `sys.dm_db_index_physical_stats` to retrieve a list of all tables in the database that have indexes defined on them based on the thresholds defined for fragmentation:

```
SELECT
object_id AS objectid,
    index_id AS indexid,
    index_type_desc AS indextype,
    avg_fragmentation_in_percent AS frag
INTO
    #reindexobjects
FROM
    sys.dm_db_index_physical_stats(DB_ID(@db), NULL, NULL, NULL, 'LIMITED')
WHERE
    avg_fragmentation_in_percent > @maxfrag
    AND index_id > 0
```

The procedure then uses the cursor to loop through the active indexes. Depending on the index-rebuild thresholds, the procedure determines whether the index has to be rebuilt or reorganized. The procedure also takes into consideration whether the process can be performed online or offline, based on the day of the week.

For example, you may consider rebuilding the index offline during weekends when the database isn't too active. The procedure then executes ALTER INDEX statements for each index:

```
DECLARE objects CURSOR FOR
    SELECT o.* FROM #reindexobjects o
    INNER JOIN sys.indexes i ON i.object_id = o.objectid
    WHERE i.is_disabled = 0 AND i.is_hypothetical = 0;

-- Open the cursor.
OPEN objects;

WHILE (1=1)
BEGIN;
    FETCH NEXT FROM objects INTO @objectid, @indexid, @indextype, @frag;
    IF @@FETCH_STATUS < 0 BREAK;
    SELECT @objectname = QUOTENAME(o.name), @schemaname = QUOTENAME(s.name)
    FROM sys.objects AS o
    JOIN sys.schemas AS s ON s.schema_id = o.schema_id
    WHERE o.object_id = @objectid;

    SELECT @indexname = QUOTENAME(name)
    FROM sys.indexes
    WHERE object_id = @objectid AND index_id = @indexid;

    SET @sqlcommand = N'ALTER INDEX ' + @indexname + N' ON ' +
                        @schemaname + N'.' + @objectname;

    IF @frag > @rebuildthreshold
    BEGIN;
        SET @sqlcommand = @sqlcommand + N' REBUILD';

        IF (DATEPART(WEEKDAY, GETDATE()) <> @WeekdayRebuildOffline)
            AND ((@indextype Like 'HEAP') OR (@indextype like '%CLUSTERED%'))
        SET @sqlcommand = @sqlcommand + N' WITH (ONLINE = ON)';
    END;
    ELSE
        SET @sqlcommand = @sqlcommand + N' REORGANIZE';
    PRINT N'Executing: ' + @sqlcommand;
    EXEC (@sqlcommand) ;
END;

-- Close and deallocate the cursor.
CLOSE objects;
DEALLOCATE objects;
```

Next, the procedure uses the cursor to loop through the objects, updates the statistics, and recompiles the stored procedures and triggers:

```
DECLARE tablelist CURSOR FOR
    SELECT distinct OBJECT_NAME(o.objectid) FROM #reindexobjects o;

-- Open the cursor.
OPEN tablelist;

FETCH NEXT FROM tablelist INTO @objectname;

-- Loop through the partitions.
WHILE @@FETCH_STATUS = 0
BEGIN;
    --Update Statistics
    SET @sqlcommand = ' UPDATE STATISTICS ' + @objectname;
    PRINT N'Executing: ' + @sqlcommand;
    EXEC (@sqlcommand) ;

    --Recompile Stored Procedures and Triggers
    SET @sqlcommand = ' EXEC sp_recompile ' + @objectname;
    PRINT N'Executing: ' + @sqlcommand;
    EXEC (@sqlcommand) ;
    FETCH NEXT FROM tablelist INTO @objectname;
END;

CLOSE tablelist;
DEALLOCATE tablelist;
```

The procedure then cleans up the temporary objects that were created:

```
DROP TABLE #reindexobjects;
```

Session Information

The sys.dm_exec_sessions DMV returns one row per session on the server. The information returned is similar to that returned by the sp_who2 system SP. You can use this DMV to retrieve information that includes the database ID, session ID, login name, client program name, CPU time and memory usage, transaction isolation level, and session settings like ANSI_NULLS and ANSI_PADDING. Listing 14-5 is a simple query against the sys.dm_exec_sessions DMV. Partial results are shown in Figure 14-4.

Listing 14-5. Retrieving Session Information

```
SELECT
db_name(database_id) dbname,
session_id,
host_name,
program_name,
client_interface_name,
```

```
login_name,
cpu_time,
CASE WHEN ansi_nulls = O THEN 'OFF' ELSE 'ON' END ansi_nulls,
CASE WHEN ansi_padding = O THEN 'OFF' ELSE 'ON' END ansi_padding
 FROM sys.dm_exec_sessions;
```

	dbname	session_id	host_name	program_name	client_interface_name	login_name	cpu_time	ansi_nulls	ansi_padding
35	master	51	SQL2012	Microsoft SQ...	.Net SqlClient Data P...	sqluser01	0	ON	ON
36	master	52	SQL2012	Microsoft SQ...	.Net SqlClient Data P...	sqluser01	0	ON	ON
37	Repor...	53	SQL2012	Report Server	.Net SqlClient Data P...	NT SERV...	0	ON	ON
38	Repor...	54	SQL2012	Report Server	.Net SqlClient Data P...	NT SERV...	0	ON	ON
39	master	55	SQL2012	Microsoft SQ...	.Net SqlClient Data P...	sqluser01	0	ON	ON
40	Repor...	56	SQL2012	Report Server	.Net SqlClient Data P...	NT SERV...	0	ON	ON
41	master	57	SQL2012	Microsoft SQ...	.Net SqlClient Data P...	sqluser01	0	ON	ON
42	master	58	SQL2012	Microsoft SQ...	.Net SqlClient Data P...	sqluser01	0	ON	ON
43	master	59	SQL2012	Microsoft SQ...	.Net SqlClient Data P...	sqluser01	0	ON	ON
44	master	60	SQL2012	Microsoft SQ...	.Net SqlClient Data P...	sqluser01	30	ON	ON
45	master	61	SQL2012	Microsoft SQ...	.Net SqlClient Data P...	sqluser01	0	ON	ON
46	master	62	SQL2012	Microsoft SQ...	.Net SqlClient Data P...	sqluser01	0	ON	ON

Figure 14-4. *Retrieving session information with* `sys.dm_exec_sessions`

You can also use `sys.dm_exec_sessions` to retrieve summarized information about sessions. Listing 14-6 presents summary information for every current session on the server. The results are shown in Figure 14-5.

Listing 14-6. Retrieving Summarized Session Information

```
SELECT
login_name,
SUM(cpu_time) AS tot_cpu_time,
SUM(memory_usage) AS tot_memory_usage,
AVG(total_elapsed_time) AS avg_elapsed_time,
SUM(reads) AS tot_reads,
SUM(writes) AS tot_writes,
SUM(logical_reads) AS tot_logical_reads,
COUNT(session_id) as tot_sessions
FROM sys.dm_exec_sessions WHERE session_id > 50
GROUP BY login_name;
```

	login_name	tot_cpu_time	tot_memory_usage	avg_elapsed_time	tot_reads	tot_writes	tot_logical_reads	tot_sessions
1	NT SERVICE\ReportServer$SQL2012	0	4	0	0	0	14	2
2	sqluser01	36288	12	23164	11914	21727	188065	7

Figure 14-5. *Summary session information*

Connection Information

In addition to session information, you can retrieve connection information via the sys.dm_exec_connections DMV. This DMV returns connection information for every session with a sessionid greater than 50 (values of 50 and below are used exclusively by the server). Listing 14-7 uses the DMV to retrieve connection information; the results are shown in Figure 14-6. Notice that this DMV also returns client network address, port, and authentication scheme information with no fuss.

Listing 14-7. Retrieving Connection Information

```
SELECT
Session_id,
client_net_address,
auth_scheme,
net_transport,
client_tcp_port,
local_tcp_port,
connection_id
FROM sys.dm_exec_connections;
```

	session_id	client_net_address	auth_scheme	net_transport	client_tcp_port	local_tcp_port	connection_id
1	51	192.168.1.13	SQL	TCP	59238	53906	D598D7DC-D0A3-4707-BCFD-030518A98908
2	52	192.168.1.13	SQL	TCP	57084	53906	C42E4F70-DE13-496E-A7E3-E372DC3DE54F
3	53	192.168.1.13	SQL	TCP	57336	53906	755666E1-1507-4C60-9011-8C1653237EA2
4	54	192.168.1.13	SQL	TCP	59469	53906	7F2B5CB6-4D35-4ABA-9C81-C93DFB018916
5	55	<local machine>	NTLM	Shared memory	NULL	NULL	6EED30DE-19A9-4555-B946-B67B0AADE1C5
6	56	192.168.1.13	SQL	TCP	53841	53906	9B8C66BE-F4A5-469A-A8D9-D8D12D890710
7	57	<local machine>	NTLM	Shared memory	NULL	NULL	E4490733-602D-44AE-878F-CDCE76C5B893
8	59	192.168.1.13	SQL	TCP	59243	53906	01B8011D-C2A3-4150-B794-ACD2CF3FE199
9	60	192.168.1.13	SQL	TCP	59290	53906	AAE03F98-6C65-4CA9-828E-474CB06D2B22

Figure 14-6. *Connection information retrieved via DMV*

Currently Executing SQL

The sys.dm_exec_requests DMV allows you to see all currently executing requests on SQL Server. When you combine the DMV sys.dm_exec_requests with sys.dm_exec_sessions, you can get information about the SQL statements that are executing at that point in time and whether the session is being blocked. You can use these DMVs to return the details of currently executing SQL, as shown in Listing 14-8. Partial results are shown in Figure 14-7.

■ **Tip**   The sys.dm_exec_requests DMV can be used to retrieve additional information for currently executing requests for CPU time, reads, writes, and the amount of granted memory, among others. The information returned is similar to what is returned by the sys.dm_exec_sessions DMV described previously in this section, but on a per-request basis instead of a per-session basis.

Listing 14-8. Querying Currently Executing SQL Statements

```
SELECT
s.session_id,
r.request_id,
r.blocking_session_id,
DB_NAME(r.database_id) as database_name,
r.[user_id],
r.status AS request_status,
s.status AS session_status,
s.login_time,
s.is_user_process,
ISNULL (s.[host_name], '') AS [host_name],
ISNULL (s.[program_name], '') AS [program_name],
ISNULL (s.login_name, '') AS login_name,
ISNULL (r.wait_type, '')  AS wait_type,
ISNULL (r.last_wait_type, '') AS last_wait_type,
ISNULL (r.wait_resource, '')  AS wait_resource,
r.transaction_id,
r.open_transaction_count,
r.cpu_time AS request_cpu_time,
r.logical_reads AS request_logical_reads,
r.reads AS request_reads,
r.writes AS request_writes,
r.total_elapsed_time AS request_total_elapsed_time,
r.start_time AS request_start_time,
r.wait_time AS request_wait_time,
s.memory_usage,
s.cpu_time AS session_cpu_time,
s.total_elapsed_time AS session_total_elapsed_time,
s.last_request_start_time AS session_last_request_start_time,
s.last_request_end_time AS session_last_request_end_time,
r.command,
r.sql_handle
FROM sys.dm_exec_sessions s
LEFT OUTER MERGE JOIN sys.dm_exec_requests r
ON s.session_id = r.session_id
WHERE r.session_id <> @@SPID AND
    ((r.session_id IS NOT NULL AND (s.is_user_process = 1 OR
r.status NOT IN ('background', 'sleeping'))) OR
    (s.session_id IN (SELECT DISTINCT blocking_session_id
FROM sys.dm_exec_requests WHERE blocking_session_id != 0)))
OPTION (FORCE ORDER);
```

	session_id	request_id	blocking_session_id	database_name	user_id	request_status	session_status	login_time	is_user_process	host_name	program_name
1	66	0	0	AdventureWorks	1	suspended	running	2012-07-09 04:14:23.660	1	SQL2012	Microsoft SQL Server Management
2	67	0	65	AdventureWorks	1	suspended	running	2012-07-09 18:18:29.137	1	SQL2012	Microsoft SQL Server Management

Figure 14-7. *Currently executing SQL statements*

The procedure in Listing 14-8 uses `sys.dm_exec_sessions` to retrieve the session details and `sys.dm_exec_requests` to retrieve the request statistics. The field `session_id` returns the ID for the current session that is being executed, and `blocking_session_id` returns the head blocker. If the query isn't being blocked, `blocking_session_id` is 0.

The query filter then returns all active sessions. If there is blocking for a session, the query filter also returns the head blocker, even if the session is inactive:

```
((r.session_id IS NOT NULL AND (
    s.is_user_process = 1 OR r.status
    NOT IN ('background', 'sleeping'))) OR
(s.session_id IN (
    SELECT DISTINCT blocking_session_id
    FROM sys.dm_exec_requests
    WHERE blocking_session_id != 0)))
```

The query hint `OPTION (FORCE ORDER)` has been added to suppress warning messages.

As you can see in the results shown in Figure 14-7, there were two active sessions in the SQL Server 2014 instance when we ran this query. Session ID 67 is blocked by session ID 65, and the `request_wait_time` field returns the wait time for session ID 67 (which is currently blocked) in milliseconds. You can review the columns `wait_type` and `wait_resource` to understand what the session is waiting on and resolve the blocking issue. If you have more active sessions in your server, the query will report them all.

Memory-Optimized System Views

SQL Server 2014 introduces a series of new views to assist with the management of memory-optimized objects; see Table 14-2. These system views allow you to better monitor memory usage, garbage collection, index usage, and transaction statistics related to memory-optimized objects. Disk-based tables have a counterpart view that lets you monitor disk-based tables in a similar fashion.

Table 14-2. *Memory-Optimized System Views*

System View	Description
dm_db_xtp_checkpoint_files	Displays information about checkpoint files, including file size, physical location, state, and lsn information
dm_db_xtp_checkpoint_stats	Returns statistics about In-Memory OLTP checkpoint operations in the current database
dm_db_xtp_gc_cycle_stats	Outputs the current state of committed transactions that have deleted one or more rows from the garbage-collection cycles
dm_db_xtp_hash_index_stats	Returns statistics that are useful for understanding, managing, and tuning hash index bucket counts
dm_db_xtp_index_stats	Contains statistics collected since the last database restart, specifically tracking memory-optimized objects that aren't tracked in other system views
dm_db_xtp_memory_consumers	Returns one row of memory information about memory-optimized objects, which the database engine uses at a granular level

(continued)

Table 14-2. *(continued)*

System View	Description
dm_db_xtp_merge_requests	Monitors database merge requests that were generated by SQL Server or manually triggered using the sys.sp_xtp_merge_checkpoint_files system procedure
dm_db_xtp_nonclustered_index_stats	Returns statistics about the usage of nonclusted indexes in memory-optimized tables in the current database. The statistics are reset after a database restart, because in-memory objects are recreated after a restart
dm_db_xtp_object_stats	Monitors the number of operations made against in-memory tables, regardless of the success or failure of the operation
dm_db_xtp_table_memory_stats	Returns the memory usage for each table and index created in memory, expressed in KB
dm_db_xtp_transactions	Returns the current active transactions for in-memory objects
dm_xtp_gc_queue_stats	Returns information about the garbage-collection worker queue process and statistics, per schedulers/cores on the machine
dm_xtp_gc_stats	Returns overall statistics information about the current behavior of the In-Memory OLTP garbage-collection process
dm_xtp_system_memory_consumers	Returns system-level memory consumers for in-memory OLTP, expressed in bytes
dm_xtp_transaction_stats	Returns information about the transactions that have run since the server started

Most Expensive Queries

The sys.dm_exec_query_stats DMV allows you to see the aggregated performance statistics for the cached query plans. This DMV contains one row for each query plan; it has more than one row for stored procedures containing multiple statements. You can use this DMV in conjunction with sys.dm_exec_sql_text, which shows the SQL statement text based on the SQL handle, and sys.dm_exec_query_plan, which shows the showplan in an XML format to retrieve the most expensive queries for the cached query plans in the server (see Listing 14-9). Partial results are shown in Figure 14-8. You can use the columns min_rows, max_rows, total_rows, and last_rows to analyze the row statistics for the query plan since it was last compiled. For example, if you have a long-running query, and you're trying to analyze the cause for the query's slowness, this information will help you to understand the maximum number of rows and average numbers of rows returned by the query over time and to tune the query.

Listing 14-9. Querying the Most Expensive Queries

```
SELECT
    DB_Name(qp.dbid) AS [DB],
    qp.dbid AS [DBID],
    qt.text,
    SUBSTRING(qt.TEXT,
```

```
            (qs.statement_start_offset/2)+1,
                ((CASE qs.statement_end_offset
                    WHEN -1
                        THEN DATALENGTH(qt.TEXT)
                        ELSE qs.statement_end_offset
                    END - qs.statement_start_offset)/2)+1) AS stmt_text,
        qs.execution_count,
        qs.total_rows,
        qs.min_rows,
        qs.max_rows,
        qs.last_rows,
        qs.total_logical_reads/qs.execution_count AS avg_logical_reads,
        qs.total_physical_reads/qs.execution_count AS avg_physical_reads,
        qs.total_logical_writes/qs.execution_count AS avg_writes,
        (qs.total_worker_time/1000)/qs.execution_count AS avg_CPU_Time_ms,
        qs.total_elapsed_time/qs.execution_count/1000 AS avg_elapsed_time_ms,
qs.last_execution_time,
        qp.query_plan AS [Plan]
FROM sys.dm_exec_query_stats qs
    CROSS APPLY sys.dm_exec_sql_text(qs.sql_handle) qt
        CROSS APPLY sys.dm_exec_query_plan(qs.plan_handle) qp
ORDER BY
execution_count DESC, qs.total_logical_reads desc, total_rows desc;
```

	DB	DBID	text	stmt_text	execution_count	total_rows	min_rows	max_rows	last_rows	avg_logical_reads	avg_physical_reads	avg_write
157	AdventureWorks	7	SELECT r.name AS [Name] FROM sys.database_principals...	SELECT r.name AS [Name] FROM sys.database_princip...	3	0	0	0	0	30	0	0
158	AdventureWorks	7	SELECT SCHEMA_NAME(s.schema_id) AS [Schema], s.na...	SELECT SCHEMA_NAME(s.schema_id) AS [Schema], s...	3	0	0	0	0	45	0	0
159	AdventureWorks	7	SELECT SCHEMA_NAME(obj.schema_id) AS [Schema], obj...	SELECT SCHEMA_NAME(obj.schema_id) AS [Schema]...	3	0	0	0	0	474	2	0
160	AdventureWorks	7	SELECT execution_count, SUBSTRING (qt.text,qs.state...	SELECT execution_count, SUBSTRING (qt.text.qs.sta...	2	2571	1285	1286	1286	205	0	0
161	AdventureWorks	7	CREATE PROCEDURE Sales.GetSalesRunningTotal (@Ye...	WITH RunningTotalCTE AS (SELECT soh S...	2	1379	0	1379	1379	477176	0	4
162	master	1	select object_id as id, null as id2, case when |...	select object_id as id, null as id2, case when ...	2	134	67	67	67	514	0	0
163	master	1	SELECT s.name AS [Name], s.alias AS [Alias], s.lcid AS [L...	SELECT s.name AS [Name], s.alias AS [Alias], s.lcid AS...	2	68	34	34	34	0	0	0
164	master	1	select object_id as id, null as id2, case when |...	select perms.class as class, objectproperty(perms.m...	2	26	13	13	13	105	0	0
165	AdventureWorks	7	SELECT TOP 10 BusinessEntityID, FirstName, LastName FR...	SELECT TOP 10 BusinessEntityID, FirstName, LastName ...	2	20	10	10	10	2	8	0
166	AdventureWorks	7	SELECT soh.SalesOrderNumber, sr.[Name] AS Reason...	SELECT soh.SalesOrderNumber, sr.[Name] AS Reaso...	2	18	9	9	9	34	8	0
167	master	1	SELECT r.name AS [Name] FROM sys.server_principals r W...	SELECT r.name AS [Name] FROM sys.server_principals r ...	2	18	9	9	9	71	0	0

Figure 14-8. *Most expensive queries*

You can use the DMV sys.dm_exec_query_stats and sys.dm_exec_sql_text to view the queries that are blocked in the server, as shown in Listing 14-10. Partial results are shown in Figure 14-9.

Listing 14-10. Querying the Most-Blocked Queries

```
SELECT TOP 50
(total_elapsed_time - total_worker_time) / qs.execution_count AS average_time_blocked,
total_elapsed_time - total_worker_time AS total_time_blocked,
qs.execution_count,
qt.text blocked_query,
DB_NAME(qt.dbid) dbname
FROM sys.dm_exec_query_stats qs
CROSS APPLY sys.dm_exec_sql_text(qs.sql_handle) qt
ORDER BY average_time_blocked DESC;
```

449

	average_time_blocked	total_time_blocked	execution_count	blocked_query	dbname
1	27473428307	27473428307	1	begin tran select * from production.product	NULL
2	2059109419	2059109419	1	SELECT * FROM Sales.SalesOrderDetail sod INNER JOI...	NULL
3	385547097	385547097	1	begin tran select * from production.product	NULL
4	376854960	376854960	1	create procedure select_product AS select * from producti...	AdventureWorks
5	5173840	10347681	2	SELECT * FROM Sales.SalesOrderDetail sod INNER JO...	NULL
6	628700	628700	1	SELECT DB_Name(qp.dbid) AS [DB], qt.text, SUBSTRI...	NULL
7	437365	874731	2	create procedure sys.sp_updatestats @resample char(8)='...	NULL
8	395732	395732	1	SELECT DB_Name(qp.dbid) AS [DB], qt.text, SUBSTRI...	NULL
9	331527	331527	1	SELECT DB_Name(qp.dbid) AS [DB], qt.text, SUBSTRI...	NULL
10	191252	191252	1	begin tran select * from production.product	NULL
11	123674	2720833	22	create procedure sys.sp_updatestats @resample char(8)='...	NULL
12	98655	2170428	22	create procedure sys.sp_updatestats @resample char(8)='...	NULL
13	48444	48444	1	select * from production.product	NULL
14	32058	1442613	45	create procedure sys.sp_updatestats @resample char(8)='...	NULL
15	5732	126108	22	create procedure sys.sp_updatestats @resample char(8)='...	NULL
16	15	93	6	select r.session_id, r.request_id, s.cpu_time, s.memory_u...	NULL
17	5	17	3	create procedure sys.sp_who2 --- 1995/11/03 10:16 @I...	NULL
18	1	1	1	CREATE PROCEDURE [dbo].[AnnounceOrGetKey] @Mac...	ReportServer$SQL2012

Figure 14-9. *Most-blocked queries*

As you can see in Figure 14-9, the dbname field lists the database name for some queries and doesn't return the database name for other queries. The reason is that sql_handle identifies only the text that is being submitted to the server. Because only the text is submitted to the server, the query text may be generic enough that it can be submitted to multiple databases; and in this case, sql_handle can't identify the database name. However, if a stored procedure resides in a database, the database name can be identified and retrieved. In Figure 14-9, if you look at the rows 1 and 4, you can see that both queries reference the same select statement—the difference is that row 4 uses a stored procedure, whereas row 1 uses a batch SQL query. The database name was retrieved for row 4, but for row 1 it wasn't.

Tempdb Space

The tempdb system database holds a position of prominence for DBAs. The tempdb database constitutes a global server-wide resource shared by all sessions, connections, and databases for temporary storage on a single SQL Server instance. An improperly managed tempdb can bring a SQL Server instance to its knees. Listing 14-11 demonstrates a simple usage of sys.dm_db_file_space_usage to report free and used space in tempdb. The database_id for the system database tempdb is 2. The results are shown in Figure 14-10.

Listing 14-11. Querying Free and Used Space in tempdb

```
SELECT
db_name(database_id) AS Database_Name,
SUM(unallocated_extent_page_count) AS free_pages,
SUM(unallocated_extent_page_count) * 8.0 AS free_KB,
SUM(user_object_reserved_page_count) AS user_object_pages,
SUM(user_object_reserved_page_count) * 8.0 AS user_object_pages,
SUM(internal_object_reserved_page_count) AS internal_object_pages,
SUM(internal_object_reserved_page_count) * 8.0 AS internal_object_KB
FROM sys.dm_db_file_space_usage
WHERE database_id = 2
GROUP BY database_id;
```

	database_name	free_pages	free_KB	user_object_pages	user_object_pages	internal_object_pages	internal_object_KB
1	tempdb	6568	52544.0	112	896.0	24	192.0

Figure 14-10. *Free and used space in* tempdb

The tempdb can run out of space for various reasons—perhaps the objects created in the tempdb haven't been dropped, or the application is performing sort operations that take up all the space allocated for the tempdb. When troubleshooting tempdb space usage, it's important to understand space allocation for the objects that currently reside in the tempdb. In addition to the sys.dm_db_file_space_usage DMV, SQL Server 2014 provides the sys.dm_db_partition_stats DMV, which returns detailed allocations per table. This DMV returns results based on the execution database context. The DMV returns details about how much space has been reserved for the in-row, LOB data and variable-length data; the row-overflow data and how much has been used; and the row count. If the table isn't partitioned, then the partition number is returned as 1. Listing 14-12 demonstrates a simple usage of sys.dm_db_partition_stats to report the user objects in the tempdb and the details of the rowcount, reserved pages, used pages, and index type. Figure 14-11 shows partial result sets for the query.

Listing 14-12. Querying User Object Allocations in tempdb

```
SELECT object_name(o.object_id) AS Object,
    CASE
        WHEN index_id = 0 then 'heap'
        WHEN index_id = 1 then 'clustered index'
        WHEN index_id > 1 then 'nonclustered index'
    END AS IndexType,
    SUM(reserved_page_count) AS ReservedPages,
    SUM(used_page_count) AS UsedPages,
    SUM(case when (index_id < 2) then row_count else 0 end) AS Rows
FROM sys.dm_db_partition_stats p JOIN sys.objects o ON p.object_id = o.object_id
WHERE type_desc = 'USER_TABLE'
GROUP BY o.object_id,index_id
ORDER BY sum(used_page_count) DESC;
```

	Object	IndexType	ReservedPages	UsedPages	Rows
1	#SalesOrderDetail_____ ...	heap	1498	1496	121317
2	#Product_____ ...	heap	16	14	504
3	#B8B161C1	heap	2	2	0
4	#B9A585FA	heap	0	0	0
5	#BF5E5F50	heap	0	0	0
6	#A59E8D4D	clustered index	0	0	0
7	#AD3FAF15	clustered index	0	0	0
8	#B01C1BC0	clustered index	0	0	0
9	#B5D4F516	clustered index	0	0	0
10	#AF27F787	heap	0	0	0
11	#1_____ ...	heap	0	0	0
12	#B2046432	heap	0	0	0
13	#B7BD3D88	heap	0	0	0
14	#A0528389	heap	0	0	0
15	#A146A7C2	heap	0	0	0

Figure 14-11. *User object allocations in* tempdb

In addition, you can use the DMV's sys.dm_db_session_space_usage and sys.dm_db_task_space_usage to return details about tempdb space usage based on a specific session or task to further narrow the specific offender that consumes most tempdb space. Listing 14-13 uses the sys.dm_db_session_space_usage and sys.dm_db_task_space_usage DMVs to return the session_id, the request associated with the session, and the object page allocation. Figure 14-12 shows a partial result set.

Listing 14-13. Querying User Object Allocations in the tempdb per Session

```
SELECT s.session_id, request_id,
SUM(s.internal_objects_alloc_page_count+
t.internal_objects_alloc_page_count)*8.0 AS internal_obj_pages_kb,
    SUM(s.user_objects_alloc_page_count) as user_obj_pages
FROM sys.dm_db_session_space_usage s JOIN sys.dm_db_task_space_usage t
ON s.session_id = t.session_id
GROUP BY s.session_id, request_id;
```

	session_id	request_id	internal_obj_pages_kb	user_obj_pages
29	15	0	0.0	0
30	3	0	0.0	0
31	20	0	0.0	0
32	17	0	0.0	0
33	5	0	0.0	0
34	62	0	0.0	0
35	19	0	0.0	0
36	10	0	0.0	0
37	67	0	3712.0	0
38	24	0	0.0	0
39	12	0	0.0	0

Figure 14-12. *User object allocations in* tempdb *with session data*

Server Resources

The sys.dm_os* DMVs and functions allow you to query detailed information about your server and resources. This is useful for retrieving the server restart time or machine and configuration details such as whether you're using hyperthreading. The sys.dm_os_sys_info DMV returns details about server resources, information about whether the SQL Server instance is physical or virtual, and details of the virtualization environment. The value in the column virtual_machine_type_desc can be None, Hypervisor, or Other. None means the server is physical, and Hypervisor means the instance is running in the hypervisor.

Listing 14-14 retrieves server configuration information, including the number of logical CPUs on the server, the ratio of logical to physical CPUs, physical and virtual memory available to the server, the last server restart time, and the hyperthreading ratio. The results are shown in Figure 14-13.

Listing 14-14. Retrieving Low-level Configuration Information

```
SELECT
cpu_count AS logical_CPUs,
hyperthread_ratio,
physical_memory_kb / 1048576.00 AS physical_MB,
virtual_memory_kb / 1048576.00 AS virtual_MB,
sqlserver_start_time,
virtual_machine_type_desc
FROM sys.dm_os_sys_info;
```

logical_CPUs	hyperthread_ratio	physical_MB	virtual_MB	sqlserver_start_time	virtual_machine_type_desc
8	8	15.9290771484	8191.9998779296	2012-07-01 00:13:54.260	NONE

Figure 14-13. *Server configuration details*

Another useful DMV, sys.dm_os_volume_stats, returns volume information for the mount points as well. You can check to see whether the volume attribute is read-only or get the space utilization before performing a bulk operation. Checking the volume attribute can come in handy when you work with the Scalable Shared Database (SSD). SSD lets you attach a read-only volume to multiple SQL Server instances to help scale out the database.

Listing 14-15 demonstrates a simple query that lists the volume information for all databases including the database name, file name, and volume ID and mount points, along with the space used. Partial results are shown in Figure 14-14.

Listing 14-15. Returning Volume Information for All Databases

```
SELECT
    DB_NAME(f.database_id) AS DBName,
    f.name AS FileName,
    volume_mount_point,
    volume_id,
    logical_volume_name,
    total_bytes,
    available_bytes,
    CAST(CAST(available_bytes AS FLOAT)/ CAST(total_bytes AS FLOAT) AS DECIMAL(18,1)) *
    100 AS [Space Used %],
    v.is_read_only
FROM sys.master_files  f
    CROSS APPLY sys.dm_os_volume_stats(f.database_id, f.file_id) v
ORDER BY f.database_id DESC;
```

	DBName	FileName	volume_mount_point	volume_id	logical_volume_name	total_bytes	available_bytes	Space Used %	is_read_only
5	AdventureWorks	AdventureWorks2012_Log	D:\	\\?\Volume{28d047e9-92b1-11e0-9bdf-806e6f6e6963}\	Data	750152888320	48394203136	10.0	0
6	AdventureWorks	AdventureWorks2012_Data	D:\	\\?\Volume{28d047e9-92b1-11e0-9bdf-806e6f6e6963}\	Data	750152888320	48394203136	10.0	0
7	ReportServer$SQL2012TempDB	ReportServer$SQL2012TempDB_log	C:\	\\?\Volume{c86e3599-91ef-11e0-9b3a-806e6f6e6963}\		319965622272	44772450304	10.0	0
8	ReportServer$SQL2012TempDB	ReportServer$SQL2012TempDB	C:\	\\?\Volume{c86e3599-91ef-11e0-9b3a-806e6f6e6963}\		319965622272	44772450304	10.0	0
9	ReportServer$SQL2012	ReportServer$SQL2012_log	C:\	\\?\Volume{c86e3599-91ef-11e0-9b3a-806e6f6e6963}\		319965622272	44772450304	10.0	0
10	ReportServer$SQL2012	ReportServer$SQL2012	C:\	\\?\Volume{c86e3599-91ef-11e0-9b3a-806e6f6e6963}\		319965622272	44772450304	10.0	0
11	msdb	MSDBLog	C:\	\\?\Volume{c86e3599-91ef-11e0-9b3a-806e6f6e6963}\		319965622272	44772450304	10.0	0
12	msdb	MSDBData	C:\	\\?\Volume{c86e3599-91ef-11e0-9b3a-806e6f6e6963}\		319965622272	44772450304	10.0	0
13	model	modellog	C:\	\\?\Volume{c86e3599-91ef-11e0-9b3a-806e6f6e6963}\		319965622272	44772450304	10.0	0
14	model	modeldev	C:\	\\?\Volume{c86e3599-91ef-11e0-9b3a-806e6f6e6963}\		319965622272	44772450304	10.0	0
15	tempdb	tempdev1	C:\	\\?\Volume{c86e3599-91ef-11e0-9b3a-806e6f6e6963}\		319965622272	44772450304	10.0	0
16	tempdb	templog	C:\	\\?\Volume{c86e3599-91ef-11e0-9b3a-806e6f6e6963}\		319965622272	44772450304	10.0	0
17	tempdb	tempdev	C:\	\\?\Volume{c86e3599-91ef-11e0-9b3a-806e6f6e6963}\		319965622272	44772450304	10.0	0

Figure 14-14. *Returning volume information for all databases*

When the SQL Server process creates a dump file or mini dumps, you have to browse through the SQL Server error logs to locate the dump file and start investigating the issue. To facilitate your locating the dump file, SQL Server 2012 introduced a DMV called sys.dm_server_memory_dumps. This DMV stores all the SQL Server dumps so that you can easily locate the dump file path along with the file's name, size, and creation date.

Listing 14-16 demonstrates a query that lists the details of the SQL dumps; the results are shown in Figure 14-15. You can see that the server has two SQL mini dumps; the path to the dumps and the creation time make it simple to locate the dump files. You can also correlate the dumps to the application log files to determine the code that caused each dump.

Listing 14-16. Listing SQL Server Dumps

```
select * from sys.dm_server_memory_dumps
```

	filename	creation_time	size_in_bytes
1	C:\Program Files\Microsoft SQL Server\MSSQL11.SQL2012\MSSQL\LOG\SQLDump0001.mdmp	2012-07-13 01:01:12.6701082 -04:00	9567615
2	C:\Program Files\Microsoft SQL Server\MSSQL11.SQL2012\MSSQL\LOG\SQLDump0002.mdmp	2012-07-13 01:01:58.3781082 -04:00	9551681

Figure 14-15. *Returning SQL Server dump details*

Another useful DMV is sys.dm_server_registry, which lists all SQL Server registry settings. For example, suppose you're calling CLR procedures in the code, and you want to check whether trace flag 6527 is not enabled for the SQL Server instance so that you can make sure SQL Server will generate memory dump on the first occurrence of an out-of-memory exception. This DMV makes it easier for you to perform that check. Listing 14-17 demonstrates the query usage, and Figure 14-16 shows a partial result set.

Listing 14-17. Listing SQL Server Instance Registry Settings

```
select * from sys.dm_server_registry
```

	registry_key	value_name	value_data
1	HKLM\SYSTEM\CurrentControlSet\Services\MSSQL$SQL2012	ObjectName	NT Service\MSSQL$SQL2012
2	HKLM\SYSTEM\CurrentControlSet\Services\MSSQL$SQL2012	ImagePath	"C:\Program Files\Microsoft SQL Server\MSSQL11.S...
3	HKLM\SYSTEM\CurrentControlSet\Services\MSSQL$SQL2012	Start	2
4	HKLM\SYSTEM\CurrentControlSet\Services\SQLAgent$SQL2012	ObjectName	NT Service\SQLAgent$SQL2012
5	HKLM\SYSTEM\CurrentControlSet\Services\SQLAgent$SQL2012	ImagePath	"C:\Program Files\Microsoft SQL Server\MSSQL11.S...
6	HKLM\SYSTEM\CurrentControlSet\Services\SQLAgent$SQL2012	Start	3
7	HKLM\SYSTEM\CurrentControlSet\Services\SQLAgent$SQL2012	DependOnService	MSSQL$SQL2012
8	HKLM\Software\Microsoft\Microsoft SQL Server\MSSQL11.SQL2012\MSSQLServer\CurrentVersion	CurrentVersion	11.0.2100.60
9	HKLM\Software\Microsoft\Microsoft SQL Server\MSSQL11.SQL2012\MSSQLServer\Parameters	SQLArg0	-dC:\Program Files\Microsoft SQL Server\MSSQL11.S...
10	HKLM\Software\Microsoft\Microsoft SQL Server\MSSQL11.SQL2012\MSSQLServer\Parameters	SQLArg1	-eC:\Program Files\Microsoft SQL Server\MSSQL11.S...
11	HKLM\Software\Microsoft\Microsoft SQL Server\MSSQL11.SQL2012\MSSQLServer\Parameters	SQLArg2	-lC:\Program Files\Microsoft SQL Server\MSSQL11.S...
12	HKLM\Software\Microsoft\Microsoft SQL Server\MSSQL11.SQL2012\MSSQLServer\SuperSocketNetLib\AdminCon...	TcpDynamicPorts	52573
13	HKLM\Software\Microsoft\Microsoft SQL Server\MSSQL11.SQL2012\MSSQLServer\SuperSocketNetLib\AdminCon...	DisplayName	TCP/IP
14	HKLM\Software\Microsoft\Microsoft SQL Server\MSSQL11.SQL2012\MSSQLServer\SuperSocketNetLib\Np	Enabled	1

Figure 14-16. *Returning SQL Server instance registry keys and values*

Unused Indexes

Another important aspect of managing a database is determining which indexes are used and which ones aren't. Indexes consume storage space, and the query optimizer uses them to efficiently access data as well. If an index isn't being used, then the storage space that is being consumed by that index is an overhead. SQL Server provides the sys.dm_db_index_usage_stats DMV to report which indexes have been used since the SQL Server service was last started. When a query accesses the indexes, the objective is to seek. If the index has a high number of user_scans, then it's a candidate for tuning so an index seek can take place. If the index has a high number of updates and few or no seeks, lookups, or scans, you can safely assume that the index isn't being used, and hence it can be removed.

Listing 14-18 presents a query that lists all indexes that haven't been used since the service was last restarted for the AdventureWorks database. Partial results are shown in Figure 14-17.

Listing 14-18. Listing Unused Indexes

```
USE AdventureWorks;
SELECT
    DB_NAME() AS DatabaseName,
    OBJECT_SCHEMA_NAME(i.object_id, s.database_id) AS SchemaName,
    OBJECT_NAME(i.object_id) AS TableName,
    i.name AS IndexName,
    user_updates,
    user_seeks,
    user_scans,
    user_lookups,
    system_updates,
    last_user_seek,
    last_user_update
FROM sys.indexes i
    LEFT JOIN sys.dm_db_index_usage_stats s ON s.object_id = i.object_id AND
    i.index_id = s.index_id
WHERE s.database_id = DB_ID()
ORDER BY last_user_update DESC;
```

Figure 14-17. *Indexes that haven't been usrd Recently*

As you can see in Figure 14-17, the query returns index-usage details for the table and the corresponding index. `user_scans` returns the number of times the index has been scanned. `user_seeks` returns the number of times index seeks have taken place. `user_lookups` returns the number of times the index has been used in bookmark lookups. `user_updates` returns the number of times the index has been updated, and `system_updates` returns the number of times the index was updated by the system. In the figure, you can see that the indexes `AK_Product_Name` and `IX_vProductAndDescription` have `user_updates` but no `user_seeks/scans/lookups`, which means these indexes haven't been used since the last system restart.

Although the indexes listed by this query haven't been used since the last restart, that's no guarantee that they won't be used in the future. Instead of deleting the index based on the queries, if you gather index usage information like this on a regular basis, you can develop a picture of index usage patterns. You can use this information to optimize existing indexes and redesign or drop irrelevant indexes.

Wait Stats

Finally, let's look at one of the DMVs that will help you quickly narrow down IO, CPU, network, locking, or memory performance issues. The `sys.dm_os_wait_stats` DMV can help you understand why SQL Server has been waiting for a resource since the server was restarted. For example, your application team may notice a performance issue and conclude that multiple processes are blocking each other; however, the real issue could be the delay associated with the log cache being flushed to the disk.

Listing 14-19 shows a query to list the top 20 waits since the server was restarted or the statistics were cleared. Partial results are shown in Figure 14-18.

Listing 14-19. Listing the Top 20 Wait Types for the SQL Server Instance

```
SELECT TOP 20
  wait_type,
  wait_time_ms / 1000 wait_time_secs,
  CONVERT(DECIMAL(12,2), wait_time_ms * 100.0
              / SUM(wait_time_ms) OVER()) Per_waiting
FROM sys.dm_os_wait_stats
ORDER BY wait_time_ms DESC;
```

	wait_type	wait_time_secs	Per_waiting
1	FT_IFTS_SCHEDULER_IDLE_WAIT	3124291	22.85
2	SQLTRACE_INCREMENTAL_FLUSH_SLEEP	1050835	7.68
3	LOGMGR_QUEUE	1050824	7.68
4	DIRTY_PAGE_POLL	1050820	7.68
5	REQUEST_FOR_DEADLOCK_SEARCH	1050809	7.68
6	HADR_FILESTREAM_IOMGR_IOCOMPLETION	1050793	7.68
7	XE_TIMER_EVENT	1050784	7.68
8	LAZYWRITER_SLEEP	1050734	7.68
9	CHECKPOINT_QUEUE	1038432	7.59
10	XE_DISPATCHER_WAIT	1024516	7.49
11	BROKER_TO_FLUSH	563389	4.12
12	SLEEP_TASK	492562	3.60
13	BROKER_TASK_STOP	61528	0.45
14	PREEMPTIVE_DEBUG	12877	0.09
15	CLR_AUTO_EVENT	114	0.00
16	LCK_M_X	77	0.00
17	SLEEP_SYSTEMTASK	45	0.00
18	CHKPT	45	0.00
19	SLEEP_MASTERDBREADY	45	0.00

Figure 14-18. *Top 20 wait types for the SQL Server instance*

INFORMATION_SCHEMA Views

INFORMATION_SCHEMA views provide yet another method of retrieving metadata in SQL Server 2014. Defined by the SQL-92 standard, INFORMATION_SCHEMA views provide the advantage of being cross-platform compatible with other SQL-92-compliant database platforms. One of the major disadvantages is that they leave out a lot of platform-specific metadata like detailed SQL CLR assembly information. Also, unlike some of the catalog views that are server wide, all INFORMATION_SCHEMA views are database specific. The INFORMATION_SCHEMA views are listed in Table 14-3.

Table 14-3. INFORMATION_SCHEMA Views

Name	Description
CHECK_CONSTRAINTS	Returns a row of descriptive information for each check constraint in the current database.
COLUMN_DOMAIN_USAGE	Returns a row of metadata for each column in the current database that has an alias data type.
COLUMN_PRIVILEGES	Returns a row of information for each column in the current database with a privilege that has been granted by, or granted to, the current user of the database.
COLUMNS	Returns descriptive information for each column that can be accessed by the current user in the current database.
CONSTRAINT_COLUMN_USAGE	Returns one row of metadata for each column in the current database that has a constraint defined on it, on each table-type object for which the current user has permissions.
CONSTRAINT_TABLE_USAGE	Returns one row of information for each table in the current database that has a constraint defined on it for which the current user has permissions.
DOMAIN_CONSTRAINTS	Returns a row of descriptive information for each alias data type in the current database that the current user can access and that has a rule bound to it.
DOMAINS	Returns a row of descriptive metadata for each alias data type in the current database that the current user can access.
KEY_COLUMN_USAGE	Returns a row of metadata for each column that is constrained by a key for which the current user has permissions in the current database.
PARAMETERS	Returns a row of descriptive information for each parameter for all user-defined functions (UDFs) and SPs that can be accessed by the current user in the current database. For UDFs, the results also contain a row with return value information.
REFERENTIAL_CONSTRAINTS	Returns a row of metadata for each FOREIGN KEY constraint defined in the current database, on objects for which the current user has permissions.
ROUTINE_COLUMNS	Returns a row of descriptive information for each column returned by table-valued functions (TVFs) defined in the current database. This INFORMATION_SCHEMA view only returns information about TVFs for which the current user has access.
ROUTINES	Returns a row of metadata for each SP and function in the current database that is accessible to the current user.
SCHEMATA	Returns a row of information for each schema defined in the current database.
TABLE_CONSTRAINTS	Returns a row of metadata for each table constraint in the current database on table-type objects for which the current user has permissions.
TABLE_PRIVILEGES	Returns a row of descriptive metadata for each table privilege that is either granted by, or granted to, the current user in the current database.

(continued)

Table 14-3. (*continued*)

Name	Description
TABLES	Returns a row of metadata for each table in the current database for which the current user has permissions.
VIEW_COLUMN_USAGE	Returns a row of information for each column in the current database that is used in a view definition, on objects for which the current user has permissions.
VIEW_TABLE_USAGE	Returns a row of information for each table that the current user has permissions for in the current database. The tables returned are those for which the current user has permissions.
VIEWS	Returns a row of metadata for each view that can be accessed by the current user in the current database.

■ **Note** Some of the changes made in SQL Server 2012 and 2014 can break backward compatibility with SQL Server 2008, 2005, or 2000 INFORMATION_SCHEMA views and applications that rely on them. Also note that SQL Server 6.5 and earlier don't implement INFORMATION_SCHEMA views. Check BOL for specific change information if your application uses INFORMATION_SCHEMA and requires backward compatibility.

Retrieving column information with the INFORMATION_SCHEMA.COLUMNS view is similar to using the sys.columns catalog view. Listing 14-20 demonstrates this, with results shown in Figure 14-19.

Listing 14-20. Retrieving Column Data with INFORMATION_SCHEMA.COLUMNS

```
SELECT
c.COLUMN_NAME,
c.ORDINAL_POSITION FROM
INFORMATION_SCHEMA.COLUMNS c WHERE c.TABLE_SCHEMA = 'Person'
AND c.TABLE_NAME = 'Person' ORDER BY c.ORDINAL_POSITION;
```

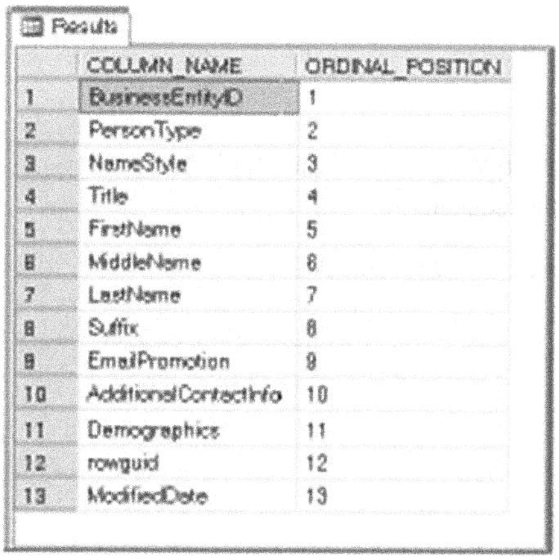

	COLUMN_NAME	ORDINAL_POSITION
1	BusinessEntityID	1
2	PersonType	2
3	NameStyle	3
4	Title	4
5	FirstName	5
6	MiddleName	6
7	LastName	7
8	Suffix	8
9	EmailPromotion	9
10	AdditionalContactInfo	10
11	Demographics	11
12	rowguid	12
13	ModifiedDate	13

Figure 14-19. *Column metadata retrieved via* INFORMATION_SCHEMA

INFORMATION_SCHEMA views are useful for applications that require cross-platform or high levels of ISO compatibility. Because they're ISO compliant, INFORMATION_SCHEMA views don't report a lot of platform-specific metadata. The ISO standard has also not kept up with the demand for access to server-wide metadata, so there is no standard server-scoped equivalent to INFORMATION_SCHEMA.

Summary

This chapter has discussed catalog views, which allow you to query database and server-wide metadata. Catalog views let you retrieve comprehensive information about databases, database objects, and database configuration. You also saw some scenarios for using catalog views and code examples that demonstrated their utility.

The chapter also introduced DMVs and DMFs, which provide an amazing level of detailed insight into the inner workings of SQL Server. SQL Server 2014 supports the DMVs and DMFs introduced in SQL Server 2005 and introduces several more to support SQL Server 2014 functionality like memory-optimized tables. Although DMVs and DMFs are targeted to fulfill the needs of DBAs, the information they provide can be valuable to developers who are troubleshooting performance problems or other issues.

Finally, the chapter briefly discussed the ISO standard INFORMATION_SCHEMA metadata views. The INFORMATION_SCHEMA views provide less detail than catalog views and are scoped at the database level only, but they do provide the advantage of cross-platform portability when that is a requirement. Because they have to conform to the ISO SQL standard, however, they leave out a lot of useful platform-specific metadata.

The next chapter discusses CLR integration and the improvements that were first introduced in Server 2012.

EXERCISES

1. [Fill in the blank] "Metadata" is defined as "data that describes _____."

2. [Fill in the blank] _____ provide insight into database objects and server-wide configuration options.

3. [Choose one] Many catalog views are defined using what model?

   a. European model

   b. Inheritance model

   c. First In, First Out model

   d. Procedural model

4. [True/False] Dynamic management views and functions provide access to internal SQL Server data structures that would be otherwise inaccessible.

5. [Choose all that apply] The advantages provided by INFORMATION_SCHEMA views include:

   a. ISO SQL standard compatibility

   b. Access to server-scoped metadata

   c. Cross-platform compatibility

   d. Operating system configuration metadata

CHAPTER 15

■ ■ ■

.NET Client Programming

Which is more important: an efficient database or a well-designed client application that connects to the database? In our estimation, they're both equally important. After all, your database can be very well designed and extremely efficient, but that won't matter to the end user if the client application they use to connect to your database is slow and unresponsive. This book focuses on SQL Server server-side development functionality, but we've decided to take a moment to introduce some of the tools available to create efficient SQL Server client applications. The .NET Framework, in particular, offers several options to make SQL Server 2014 client connectivity simple and efficient. This chapter discusses using ADO. NET and the .NET SqlClient as a basis for building your own easy-to-use, cutting-edge SQL Server client applications, and you venture into modern O/RM trends with LINQ to SQL and Entity Framework.

ADO.NET

The System.Data.* namespaces consist of classes and enumerations that form the ADO.NET architecture, the .NET Framework's primary tool for database access. You can use the classes in the System.Data.* namespaces to connect to your databases and access them in real time, or in a disconnected fashion via the DataSet, DataTable, and DataAdapter classes. The following are some of the more commonly used namespaces for SQL Server data access, some of which you saw in Chapter 14 when you had a look at SQL Server .NET Integration:

- The System.Data namespace provides access to classes that implement the ADO. NET architecture, such as DataSet and DataTable.

- The System.Data.Common namespace provides access to classes that are shared by .NET Framework data-access providers, such as the DbProviderFactory class.

- The primary namespace for native SQL Server connectivity is System.Data. SqlClient. This namespace includes classes that provide optimized access to SQL Server (version 7.0 and higher) via SQL Server Native Client. The classes in this namespace are designed specifically to take advantage of SQL Server–specific features and don't work with other data sources.

- The System.Data.Odbc namespace provides managed access to old-fashioned ODBC drivers. ODBC was developed in the early 1990s as a one-size-fits-all standard for connecting to a wide array of varied data sources. Because of its mission of standardizing data access across a variety of data sources, ODBC provides a generally "plain vanilla" interface that sometimes doesn't take advantage of SQL Server or other database management system (DBMS) platform-specific features. This means ODBC isn't as efficient as the SQL client, but it provides a useful option for connecting to assorted data sources such as Excel spreadsheets and other DBMSs.

- Microsoft also provides the System.Data.OleDb namespaces, which can connect to a variety of data sources, including SQL Server. It's an option for applications that need to access data on multiple platforms, such as both SQL Server and Microsoft Access. OLEDB has been recently deprecated by Microsoft in favor of the more standard ODBC, even though OLEDB was created after ODBC.

- The System.Data.SqlTypes namespace provides .NET classes representing native, nullable SQL Server data types. These .NET SQL Server–specific data types for the most part use the same internal representation as the equivalent SQL Server native data types, helping to reduce precision-loss problems. Using these types can also speed up SQL Server connectivity, because it helps eliminate implicit conversions. And these data types, unlike the standard .NET value types, have built-in NULL-handling capability. Table 15-1 lists the .NET SqlTypes types and their corresponding native T-SQL data types.

Table 15-1. *System.Data.SqlTypes Conversions*

System.Data.SqlTypes Class	Native T-SQL Data Type
SqlBinary	binary, image, timestamp, varbinary
SqlBoolean	bit
SqlByte	tinyint
SqlDateTime	datetime, smalldatetime
SqlDecimal	decimal, numeric
SqlDouble	float
SqlGuid	uniqueidentifier
SqlInt16	smallint
SqlInt32	int
SqlInt64	bigint
SqlMoney	money, smallmoney
SqlSingle	real
SqlString	char, nchar, ntext, nvarchar, text, varchar
SqlXml	xml

■ **Note** At the time of this writing, there are no .NET SqlTypes types corresponding to the SQL Server data types introduced in SQL Server 2008 (such as date, time, datetimeoffset, and datetime2).

The .NET SQL Client

The .NET native SQL client (SQLNCLI) is the most efficient way to connect to SQL Server from a client application. With the possible exceptions of upgrading legacy code and designing code that must access non-SQL Server data sources, the native SQL client is the client connectivity method of choice. The main classes for establishing a connection, sending SQL commands, and retrieving results with SqlClient are listed in Table 15-2.

Table 15-2. *Commonly Used Native SQL Client Classes*

System.Data.SqlClient Class	Description
SqlCommand	Represents an SQL statement or SP to execute.
SqlCommandBuilder	Automatically generates single-table commands to reconcile changes made to an ADO.NET DataSet.
SqlConnection	Establishes a connection to SQL Server.
SqlConnectionStringBuilder	Builds connection strings for use by SqlConnection objects.
SqlDataAdapter	Wraps a set of SqlCommand objects and an SqlConnection that can be used to fill an ADO.NET DataSet and update an SQL Server database.
SqlDataReader	Provides methods to read a forward-only stream of rows from an SQL Server database.
SqlException	Provides access to SQL Server–specific exceptions. This class can be used to capture an SQL Server error or warning.
SqlParameter	Represents a parameter to an SqlCommand.
SqlParameterCollection	A collection of SqlParameter objects associated with an SqlCommand.
SqlTransaction	Enables an SQL Server transaction to be initiated and managed from a client.

Connected Data Access

Listing 15-1 demonstrates SqlClient data access via an SqlDataReader instance. This is the type of access you might use in an ASP.NET page to quickly retrieve values for a drop-down list, for example. This example is written to run as a C# console application. The SQL Server connection string defined in the sqlconnection variable should be modified to suit your local SQL Server environment and security.

Listing 15-1. SqlDataReader Example

```
using System;
using System.Data.SqlClient;

namespace Apress.Examples
{
    class Listing15_1
    {
        static void Main(string[] args)
        {
            string sqlconnection = @"DATA SOURCE=SQL2014;" +
                "INITIAL CATALOG=AdventureWorks;" +
                "INTEGRATED SECURITY=SSPI;";

            string sqlcommand = "SELECT " +
                "    DepartmentId, " +
                "    Name, " +
                "    GroupName " +
                " FROM HumanResources.Department " +
                " ORDER BY DepartmentId";
```

```
        try
        {
            connection = new SqlConnection(sqlconnection);
            connection.Open();
            command = new SqlCommand(sqlcommand, connection);
            datareader = command.ExecuteReader();

            while (datareader.Read())
            {
                Console.WriteLine
                    (
                        "{0}\t{1}\t{2}",
                        datareader["DepartmentId"].ToString(),
                        datareader["Name"].ToString(),
                        datareader["GroupName"].ToString()
                    );
            }
        }
        catch (SqlException ex)
        {
            Console.WriteLine(ex.Message);
        }
        finally
        {
            connection.Close();
        }
        Console.Write("Press a Key to Continue...");
        Console.ReadKey();
    }
}
}
```

This example is a very simple console application that retrieves the list of departments from the HumanResources.Department table of the AdventureWorks database and writes the data to the display. The example begins by importing the System and System.Data.SqlClient namespaces. Although not required, importing the namespaces saves some keystrokes and helps make code more readable by eliminating the need to prefix the classes and enumerations used with their associated namespaces:

```
using System;
using System.Data.SqlClient;
```

The body of the class defines the SQL Server connection string and the T-SQL command that retrieves the department data. The DATA_SOURCE connection string option is set at the server named SQL2014; change it accordingly to match your own server name. When defining the connection string, you prefix the string with the @ sign, to create a verbatim string literal. This is useful because a verbatim string literal doesn't interpret special characters like \. Without that, if you declares a named instance as a data source, such as YOUR_SERVER\SQL2014, you would have to escape it like this: YOUR_SERVER\\SQL2014. With a verbatim string literal, the \ doesn't need to be escapedL

```
string sqlconnection = @"DATA SOURCE=SQL2014;" +
        "INITIAL CATALOG=AdventureWorks;" +
        "INTEGRATED SECURITY=SSPI;";

    string sqlcommand = "SELECT " +
    "   DepartmentId, " +
    "   Name, " +
    "   GroupName " +
    " FROM HumanResources.Department " +
    " ORDER BY DepartmentId";

    SqlConnection connection = null;
```

The SqlConnection connection string is composed of a series of key/value pairs separated by semicolons, as shown in the following:

```
DATA SOURCE=SQL2014;INITIAL CATALOG=AdventureWorks;INTEGRATED SECURITY=SSPI;
```

Some of the commonly used SqlConnection connection string keys are listed in Table 15-3.

Table 15-3. *SqlConnection Connection String Keys*

Connection String Keys	Description
AttachDBFileName	Name of the full path to an attachable primary database file (MDF file).
Connection Timeout	Length of time (in seconds) to wait for a server connection before stopping the attempt.
Data Source	Name or IP address of an SQL Server instance to connect to. Use the server\instance format for named instances. A port number can be added to the end of the name or network address by appending it with a comma.
Encrypt	Indicates that SSL encryption will be used to communicate with SQL Server.
Initial Catalog	Name of the database to connect to once a server connection is established.
Integrated Security	When true, yes, or sspi, Windows integrated security is used to connect. When false or no, SQL Server security is used.
MultipleActiveResultSets	When true, a connection can enable multiple active result sets (MARS). When false, all result sets from a batch must be processed before any other batch can be executed on the connection.
Password	Password for the SQL Server account used to log in. Using integrated security is recommended over SQL Server account security.
Persist Security Info	When false or no, sensitive security information (like a password) isn't returned as part of the connection if the connection has been opened. The recommended setting is false.
User ID	SQL Server account user ID used to log in. Integrated security is recommended over SQL Server account security.

■ **Note** The www.connectionstrings.com/ web site is a handy reference of connection strings for all major database servers.

The next section of code is enclosed in a try...catch block because of the possibility that a database connection or other error might occur. If an error does occur, control is passed to the catch block and the error message is displayed. The try...catch block includes the finally block, which cleans up the database connection whether an exception is thrown or not:

```
try
{
    ...
}
catch  (SqlException ex)
{
    Console.WriteLine(ex.Message);
}
finally
{
    connection.Close();
}
```

When connecting to SQL Server from a client application, it's a very good idea to code defensively with try...catch blocks. Defensive coding simply means trying to anticipate the problems that may occur and making sure your code handles them. Following this practice in database client applications can save you a lot of headaches down the road. Some of the possible errors you may encounter in SQL Server client applications include problems connecting to SQL Server, trying to access tables and other database objects that have been changed or no longer exist, and returning NULL when you expect other values.

In the example's try...catch block, the SqlConnection is instantiated and opened using the connection string defined previously. Then an SqlCommand is created on the open connection and executed with the ExecuteReader() method. The ExecuteReader() method returns an SqlDataReader instance, which allows you to retrieve result-set rows in an efficient forward-only fashion. This example uses SqlDataReader in a while loop to quickly retrieve all rows and display them on the console:

```
try
{
    connection = new SqlConnection(sqlconnection);
    connection.Open();
    command = new SqlCommand(sqlcommand, connection);
    datareader = command.ExecuteReader();

    while (datareader.Read())
    {
        Console.WriteLine
        (
            "{0}\t{1}\t{2}",
            datareader["DepartmentId"].ToString(),
            datareader["Name"].ToString(),
            datareader["GroupName"].ToString()
        );
    }
}
```

The results of the simple client utility from Listing 15-1 are shown in Figure 15-1.

```
1        Engineering      Research and Development
2        Tool Design      Research and Development
3        Sales   Sales and Marketing
4        Marketing        Sales and Marketing
5        Purchasing       Inventory Management
6        Research and Development        Research and Development
7        Production       Manufacturing
8        Production Control      Manufacturing
9        Human Resources Executive General and Administration
10       Finance Executive General and Administration
11       Information Technology  Executive General and Administration
12       Document Control        Quality Assurance
13       Quality Assurance       Quality Assurance
14       Facilities and Maintenance      Executive General and Administration
15       Shipping and Receiving  Inventory Management
16       Executive       Executive General and Administration
Press a Key to Continue...
```

Figure 15-1. *Querying the database table and iterating the result set*

Disconnected Datasets

The example in Listing 15-1 demonstrated the forward-only read-only SqlDataReader, which provides an efficient interface for data retrieval but is far less flexible than ADO.NET disconnected datasets. A disconnected dataset is an in-memory cache of a dataset. It provides flexibility because you don't need a constant connection to the database in order to query and manipulate the data. Listing 15-2 demonstrates how to use the SqlDataAdapter to fill a DataSet and print the results. The differences between Listing 15-2 and Listing 15-1 are shown in bold.

Listing 15-2. Using SqlDataReader to Fill a DataSet

```csharp
using System;
using System.Data;
using System.Data.SqlClient;

namespace Apress.Examples
{
    class Listing15_2
    {
        static void Main(string[] args)
        {
            string sqlconnection = @"DATA SOURCE=SQL2014;" +
                "INITIAL CATALOG=AdventureWorks;" +
                "INTEGRATED SECURITY=SSPI;";
```

467

```csharp
string sqlcommand = "SELECT " +
    "    DepartmentId, " +
    "    Name, " +
    "    GroupName " +
    " FROM HumanResources.Department " +
    " ORDER BY DepartmentId";

SqlDataAdapter adapter = null;
DataSet dataset = null;

try
{
    adapter = new SqlDataAdapter(sqlcommand, sqlconnection);
    dataset = new DataSet();
    adapter.Fill(dataset);

    foreach (DataRow row in dataset.Tables[0].Rows)
    {
        Console.WriteLine
          (
            "{0}\t{1}\t{2}",
            row["DepartmentId"].ToString(),
            row["Name"].ToString(),
            row["GroupName"].ToString()
          );
    }
}
catch (SqlException ex)
{
    Console.WriteLine(ex.Message);
}
finally
{
    if (dataset != null)
        dataset.Dispose();
    if (adapter != null)
        adapter.Dispose();
}
Console.Write("Press a Key to Continue...");
Console.ReadKey();
        }
    }
}
```

The second version of the application, in Listing 15-2, generates the same results as Listing 15-1. The first difference is that this example imports the System.Data namespace, because the DataSet class is a member of System.Data. Again, this isn't required, but it does save wear and tear on your fingers by eliminating the need to prefix System.Data classes and enumerations with the namespace:

```csharp
using System;
using System.Data;
using System.Data.SqlClient;
```

The SQL connection-string and query-string definitions are the same in both examples. Listing 15-2 departs from Listing 15-1 by declaring an SqlDataAdapter and a DataSet instead of an SqlConnection, SqlCommand, and SqlDataReader:

```
SqlDataAdapter adapter = null;
DataSet dataset = null;
```

The code to retrieve the data creates a new SqlDataAdapter and DataSet and then populates the DataSet via the Fill() method of the SqlDataAdapter:

```
adapter = new SqlDataAdapter(sqlcommand, sqlconnection);
dataset = new DataSet();
adapter.Fill(dataset);
```

The main loop iterates through each DataRow in the single table returned by the DataSet and writes the results to the console:

```
foreach (DataRow row in dataset.Tables[0].Rows)
{
    Console.WriteLine
    (
        "{0}\t{1}\t{2}",
        row["DepartmentId"].ToString(),
        row["Name"].ToString(),
        row["GroupName"].ToString()
    );
}
```

The balance of the code handles exceptions, performs cleanup by disposing of the DataSet and SqlDataAdapter, and waits for a keypress before exiting:

```
if (dataset != null)
    dataset.Dispose();
if (adapter != null)
    adapter.Dispose();
```

Parameterized Queries

ADO.NET provides a safe method for passing parameters to an SP or SQL statement, known as parameterization. The "classic" Visual Basic 6/VBScript method of concatenating parameter values directly into a long SQL query string is inefficient and potentially unsafe (see the "SQL Injection and Performance" sidebar later in this chapter for more information). A concatenated string query might look like this:

```
string sqlstatement = "SELECT  " +
    "    BusinessEntityID, " +
    "    LastName, " +
    "    FirstName, " +
    "    MiddleName " +
    "FROM Person.Person " +
    "WHERE LastName = N'" + name + "';";
```

The value of the name variable can contain additional SQL statements, leaving SQL Server wide open to SQL injection attacks. Let's imagine that the name variable used here comes directly from a text box where the user can enter the name. An attacker could enter some special characters in order to tamper with the generated query, as in the following:

```
string name = "';
DELETE FROM Person.Person; --";
```

This value for the name variable results in the following dangerous SQL statements being executed on the server:

```
SELECT
    BusinessEntityID,
    LastName,
    FirstName,
    MiddleName
FROM Person.Person
WHERE  LastName = N'';
DELETE  FROM  Person.Person;  -- ';
```

Parameterized queries avoid SQL injection by sending the parameter values to the server separately from the SQL statement. Listing 15-3 demonstrates a simple parameterized query. (The results are shown in Figure 15-2.)

Listing 15-3. Parameterized SQL Query

```
using System;
using System.Data;
using System.Data.SqlClient;

namespace Apress.Examples
{
    class Listing15_3
    {
        static void Main(string[] args)
        {

            string name = "SMITH";
            string sqlconnection = @"SERVER=SQL2014; " +
                "INITIAL CATALOG=AdventureWorks; " +
                "INTEGRATED SECURITY=SSPI;";

            string sqlcommand = "SELECT " +
                "   BusinessEntityID, " +
                "   FirstName, " +
                "   MiddleName, " +
                "   LastName " +
                "FROM Person.Person " +
                "WHERE LastName = @name";

            SqlConnection connection = null;
            SqlCommand command = null;
            SqlDataReader datareader = null;
```

```
try
{
    connection = new SqlConnection(sqlconnection);
    connection.Open();
    command = new SqlCommand(sqlcommand, connection);
    command.Parameters.Add("@name", SqlDbType.NVarChar, 50).Value = name;
    datareader = command.ExecuteReader();
    while (datareader.Read())
    {
        Console.WriteLine
            (
              "{0}\t{1}\t{2}\t{3}",
              datareader["BusinessEntityID"].ToString(),
              datareader["LastName"].ToString(),
              datareader["FirstName"].ToString(),
              datareader["MiddleName"].ToString()
            );
    }
}
catch (Exception ex)
{
    Console.WriteLine(ex.Message);
}
finally
{
    connection.Close();
}
Console.WriteLine("Press any key...");
Console.ReadKey();
    }
  }
}
```

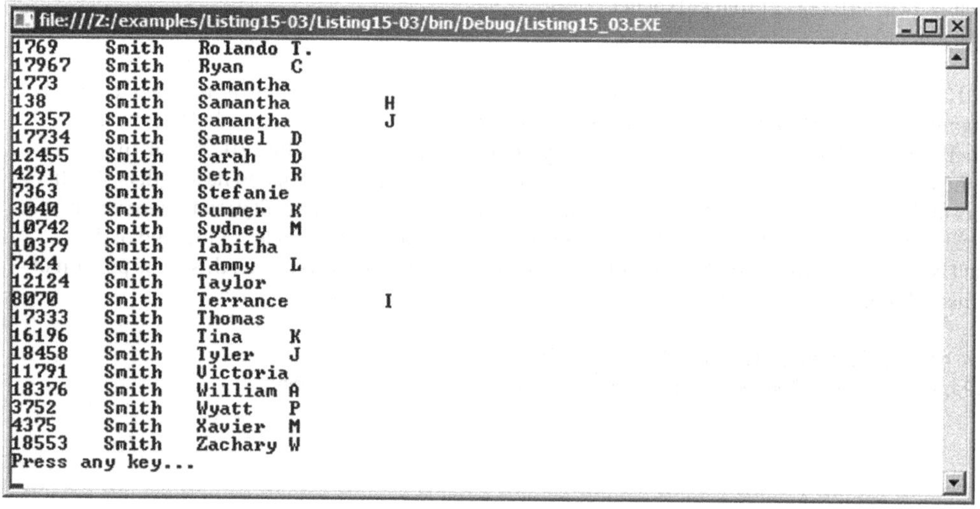

Figure 15-2. *Results of the parameterized query*

Listing 15-3 retrieves and prints the contact information for all people in the AdventureWorks
Person.Person table whose last name is Smith. The example begins by importing the appropriate
namespaces. The System.Data namespace is referenced here because it contains the SqlDbType
enumeration that is used to declare parameter data types:

```
using System;
using System.Data;
using System.Data.SqlClient;
```

The program declares a variable to hold the parameter value, the SqlClient connection string, a
parameterized SQL SELECT statement, and the SqlConnection, SqlCommand, and SqlDataReader objects:

```
string name = "SMITH";
string sqlconnection = @"SERVER=SQL2014; " +
    "INITIAL CATALOG=AdventureWorks; " +
    "INTEGRATED SECURITY=SSPI;";

string sqlcommand = "SELECT " +
    "  BusinessEntityID, " +
    "  FirstName, " +
    "  MiddleName, " +
    "  LastName " +
    "FROM Person.Person " +
    "WHERE LastName = @name";

SqlConnection connection = null;
SqlCommand command = null;
SqlDataReader datareader = null;
```

As in the previous examples, try...catch is used to capture runtime exceptions. The parameterized
SQL SELECT statement contains a reference to an SQL Server parameter named @name. Next, a connection is
established to the AdventureWorks database:

```
connection = new SqlConnection(sqlconnection);
connection.Open();
```

An SqlCommand is created using the previously defined query string, and a value is assigned to the
@name parameter. Every SqlCommand exposes an SqlParameterCollection property called Parameters.
The Add method of the Parameters collection allows you to add parameters to the SqlCommand. In this
example, the parameter added is named @name; it's an nvarchar type parameter, and its length is 50. The
parameters in the Parameters collection are passed along to SQL Server with the SQL statement when
the ExecuteReader(), ExecuteScalar(), ExecuteNonQuery(), or ExecuteXmlReader() method of the
SqlCommand is called. The addition of a Parameter object to the SqlCommand is critical; this is the portion of
the code that inhibits SQL injection attacks:

```
command = new SqlCommand(sqlcommand, connection);
command.Parameters.Add("@name", SqlDbType.NVarChar, 50).Value = name;
```

In this instance, the ExecuteReader() method is called to return the results via SqlDataReader instance, and a while loop is used to iterate over and display the results:

```
datareader = command.ExecuteReader();
while (datareader.Read())
{
    Console.WriteLine
    (
        "{0}\t{1}\t{2}\t{3}",
        datareader["BusinessEntityID"].ToString(),
        datareader["LastName"].ToString(),
        datareader["FirstName"].ToString(),
        datareader["MiddleName"].ToString()
    );
}
```

SQL INJECTION AND PERFORMANCE

SQL developers and DBAs have long known of the potential security risks that SQL injection attacks can pose. You often hear about exploits based on SQL injections. As an example, in 2011, hackers claimed in a press release to have stolen the personal information of 1 million users on the Sony Pictures web site via a single SQL injection attack. So if developers and DBAs have known all about the evils of SQL injection for years, why are so many databases being compromised?

The problem isn't that people don't know what SQL injection is. Most DBAs and developers instinctively shudder at the sound of those two little words. Instead, it appears that many developers either don't know how or are just not motivated to properly code to defend against this vicious attack. A lot of injection-susceptible code was written on the Visual Basic 6 and classic ASP platforms, where query parameterization was a bit of a hassle. Many programmers have carried their bad coding habits over to .NET, despite the fact that query parameterization with SqlClient is easier than ever.

As an added benefit, when you properly parameterize your queries, you can get a performance boost. When SQL Server receives a parameterized query, it automatically caches the query plan generated by the optimizer. On subsequent executions of the same parameterized query, SQL Server can use the cached query plan. Concatenated string queries without parameterization generally can't take advantage of cached query-plan reuse, so SQL Server must regenerate the query plan every time the query is executed. Keep these benefits in mind when developing SQL Server client code.

Additionally, using stored procedures instead of ad hoc queries built in the client code solves almost all SQL injection threats and allows the best possible query-plan reuse, unless you create dynamic SQL in the procedure with the EXECUTE() command.

Nonquery, Scalar, and XML Querying

The examples covered so far in this chapter have all been SQL SELECT queries that return rows. SQL statements that don't return result sets are classified by .NET as nonqueries. Examples of nonqueries include UPDATE, INSERT, and DELETE statements, as well as DDL statements like CREATE INDEX and ALTER TABLE. The .NET Framework provides the ExecuteNonQuery() method of the SqlCommand class to execute statements such as these. Listing 15-4 is a code snippet that shows how to execute a nonquery using the ExecuteNonQuery() method of SqlCommand.

Listing 15-4. Executing a Nonquery

```
SqlCommand command = new SqlCommand
  (
    "CREATE TABLE #temp " +
    "  ( " +
    "    Id INT NOT NULL PRIMARY KEY, " +
    "    Name NVARCHAR(50) " +
    "  );", connection
  );
command.ExecuteNonQuery();
```

The example creates a temporary table named #temp with two columns. Because the statement is a DDL statement that returns no result set, the ExecuteNonQuery() method is used.

In addition to queries that return no result sets, some queries return a result set consisting of a single row and a single column. For these queries, .NET provides a shortcut method of retrieving the value. The ExecuteScalar() method retrieves the single value returned as a scalar value as a .NET Object. Using this method, you can avoid the hassle of creating an SqlDataReader instance and iterating it to retrieve a single value. Listing 15-5 is a code snippet that demonstrates the ExecuteScalar() method.

Listing 15-5. Using ExecuteScalar to Retrieve a Row Count

```
SqlCommand command = new SqlCommand
  (
    "SELECT COUNT(*) " +
    "FROM Person.Person;", sqlconnection
  );
Object count = command.ExecuteScalar();
```

If you call ExecuteScalar() on an SqlCommand that returns more than one row or column, only the first row of the first column is retrieved. Your best bet is to make sure you only call ExecuteScalar() on queries that return a single scalar value (one row, one column) to avoid possible confusion and problems down the road.

■ **Tip**　You may find that using the ExecuteNonQuery() method with scalar OUTPUT parameters is more efficient than the ExecuteScalar() method for servers under heavy workload.

An additional technique for retrieving results in .NET is the ExecuteXmlReader() method. This method of the SqlCommand object uses an XmlReader to retrieve XML results, such as those generated by a SELECT query with the FOR XML clause. Listing 15-6 demonstrates a modified version of the code in Listing 15-3 that uses the ExecuteXmlReader() method. Differences between this listing and Listing 15-3 are in bold.

Listing 15-6. Reading XML Data with ExecuteXmlReader()

```
using System;
using System.Data;
using System.Data.SqlClient;
using System.Xml;

namespace Apress.Examples
{
    class Listing15_6
    {
        static void Main(string[] args)
        {
            string name = "SMITH";
            string sqlconnection = @"SERVER=SQL2014; " +
                "INITIAL CATALOG=AdventureWorks; " +
                "INTEGRATED SECURITY=SSPI;";

            string sqlcommand = "SELECT " +
                "  BusinessEntityID, " +
                "  FirstName, " +
                "  COALESCE(MiddleName, '') AS MiddleName, " +
                "  LastName " +
                "FROM Person.Person " +
                "WHERE LastName = @name " +
                "FOR XML AUTO;";

            SqlConnection connection = null;
            SqlCommand command = null;
            XmlReader xmlreader = null;

            try
            {
                connection = new SqlConnection(sqlconnection);
                connection.Open();
                command = new SqlCommand(sqlcommand, connection);
                SqlParameter par = command.Parameters.Add("@name", SqlDbType.NVarChar, 50);
                par.Value = name;
                xmlreader = command.ExecuteXmlReader();
                while (xmlreader.Read())
                {
                    Console.WriteLine
                    (
                      "{0}\t{1}\t{2}\t{3}",
                      xmlreader["BusinessEntityID"].ToString(),
                      xmlreader["LastName"].ToString(),
                      xmlreader["FirstName"].ToString(),
                      xmlreader["MiddleName"].ToString()
                    );
                }
            }
```

```
        catch (Exception ex)
        {
            Console.WriteLine(ex.Message);
        }
        finally
        {
            if (xmlreader != null)
                xmlreader.Close();
            if (command != null)
                command.Dispose();
            if (connection != null)
                connection.Dispose();
        }
        Console.WriteLine("Press any key...");
        Console.ReadKey();
    }
  }
}
```

The first difference between this listing and Listing 15-3 is the addition of the System.Xml namespace, because the XmlReader class is being used:

```
using System;
using System.Data;
using System.Data.SqlClient;
using System.Xml;
```

The SQL SELECT statement is also slightly different. For one thing, the COALESCE() function is used on the MiddleName column to replace NULL middle names with empty strings. The FOR XML clause leaves NULL attributes out of the generated XML by default. Missing attributes would generate exceptions when trying to display the results. The FOR XML AUTO clause is used in the SELECT query to inform SQL Server that it needs to generate an XML result:

```
string sqlcommand = "SELECT " +
  "  BusinessEntityID, " +
  "  FirstName, " +
  "  COALESCE(MiddleName, '') AS MiddleName, " +
  "  LastName " +
  "FROM Person.Person " +
  "WHERE LastName = @name " +
  "FOR XML AUTO;";
```

The try...catch block uses the ExecuteXmlReader() method instead of the ExecuteReader() method. The loop that displays the results is very similar to Listing 15-3 as well. The main difference in this listing is that an XmlReader is used in place of an SqlDataReader:

```
xmlreader = command.ExecuteXmlReader();
while (xmlreader.Read())
{
    Console.WriteLine
    (
```

```
        "{0}\t{1}\t{2}\t{3}",
        xmlreader["BusinessEntityID"].ToString(),
        xmlreader["LastName"].ToString(),
        xmlreader["FirstName"].ToString(),
        xmlreader["MiddleName"].ToString()
    );
}
```

The remaining code in the example performs exception handling and proper cleanup, as in the other example listings.

SqlBulkCopy

SQL Server provides tools such as SQL Server Integration Services (SSIS) and the Bulk Copy Program (BCP) to help populate your databases from external data sources. Some applications can benefit from built-in .NET bulk-load functionality. The .NET Framework (versions 2.0 and higher) SqlClient implements the SqlBulkCopy class to make efficient bulk loading easy. SqlBulkCopy can be used to load data from a database table, an XML table, a flat file, or any other type of data source you choose. The SqlBulkCopy example in Listing 15-7 loads US Postal Service ZIP code data from a tab-delimited flat file into an SQL Server table. A sample of the source text file is shown in Table 15-4.

Table 15-4. *Sample Tab-Delimited ZIP Code Data*

ZIP Code	Latitude	Longitude	City	State
99546	54.2402	–176.7874	ADAK	AK
99551	60.3147	–163.1189	AKIACHAK	AK
99552	60.3147	–163.1189	AKIAK	AK
99553	55.4306	–162.5581	AKUTAN	AK
99554	62.1172	–163.2376	ALAKANUK	AK
99555	58.9621	–163.1189	ALEKNAGIK	AK

The complete sample ZIP code file is included with the downloadable source code for this book. The target table is built with the CREATE TABLE statement in Listing 15-7. You need to execute this statement to create the target table in the AdventureWorks database (or another target database if you choose).

Listing 15-7. Creating the ZipCodes Target Table

```
CREATE TABLE dbo.ZipCodes
(
    ZIP CHAR(5) NOT NULL PRIMARY KEY,
    Latitude NUMERIC(8, 4) NOT NULL,
    Longitude NUMERIC(8, 4) NOT NULL,
    City NVARCHAR(50) NOT NULL,
    State CHAR(2) NOT NULL
)
GO
```

The code presented in Listing 15-8 uses the SqlBulkCopy class to bulk-copy the data from the flat file into the destination table.

477

Listing 15-8. SqlBulkCopy Class Example

```csharp
using System;
using System.Data;
using System.Data.SqlClient;
using System.Data.SqlTypes;
using System.Diagnostics;
using System.IO;
using System.Globalization;

namespace Apress.Example
{
    class Listing15_8
    {
        static string sqlconnection = "DATA SOURCE=SQL2014; " +
          "INITIAL CATALOG=AdventureWorks; " +
          "INTEGRATED SECURITY=SSPI;";

        static string sourcefile = "c:\\ZIPCodes.txt";

        static DataTable loadtable = null;

        static void Main(string[] args)
        {
            Stopwatch clock = new Stopwatch();
            clock.Start();
            int rowcount = DoImport();
            clock.Stop();
            Console.WriteLine("{0} Rows Imported in {1} Seconds.",
              rowcount, (clock.ElapsedMilliseconds / 1000.0));
            Console.WriteLine("Press a Key...");
            Console.ReadKey();
        }

        static int DoImport()
        {
            using (SqlBulkCopy bulkcopier = new SqlBulkCopy(sqlconnection))
            {
                bulkcopier.DestinationTableName = "dbo.ZIPCodes";
                try
                {
                    LoadSourceFile();
                    bulkcopier.WriteToServer(loadtable);
                }
                catch (SqlException ex)
                {
                    Console.WriteLine(ex.Message);
                }
            }
            return loadtable.Rows.Count;
        }
```

```csharp
static void LoadSourceFile()
{
    loadtable = new DataTable();
    DataColumn loadcolumn = new DataColumn();
    DataRow loadrow = null;

    loadcolumn.DataType = typeof(SqlString);
    loadcolumn.ColumnName = "ZIP";
    loadcolumn.Unique = true;
    loadtable.Columns.Add(loadcolumn);

    loadcolumn = new DataColumn();
    loadcolumn.DataType = typeof(SqlDecimal);
    loadcolumn.ColumnName = "Latitude";
    loadcolumn.Unique = false;
    loadtable.Columns.Add(loadcolumn);

    loadcolumn = new DataColumn();
    loadcolumn.DataType = typeof(SqlDecimal);
    loadcolumn.ColumnName = "Longitude";
    loadcolumn.Unique = false;
    loadtable.Columns.Add(loadcolumn);

    loadcolumn = new DataColumn();
    loadcolumn.DataType = typeof(SqlString);
    loadcolumn.ColumnName = "City";
    loadcolumn.Unique = false;
    loadtable.Columns.Add(loadcolumn);

    loadcolumn = new DataColumn();
    loadcolumn.DataType = typeof(SqlString);
    loadcolumn.ColumnName = "State";
    loadcolumn.Unique = false;
    loadtable.Columns.Add(loadcolumn);

    using (StreamReader stream = new StreamReader(sourcefile))
    {
        string record = stream.ReadLine();
        while (record != null)
        {
            string[] cols = record.Split('\t');
            loadrow = loadtable.NewRow();
            loadrow["ZIP"] = cols[0];
            loadrow["Latitude"] = decimal.Parse(cols[1], CultureInfo.InvariantCulture);
            loadrow["Longitude"] = decimal.Parse(cols[2], CultureInfo.InvariantCulture);
            loadrow["City"] = cols[3];
            loadrow["State"] = cols[4];
            loadtable.Rows.Add(loadrow);
            record = stream.ReadLine();
        }
    }
}
```

The code begins by importing required namespaces, declaring the Apress.Example namespace, and declaring the module name. The System.IO namespace is imported for the StreamReader, and the System.Diagnostics namespace is imported for the Stopwatch class so that the program can report the import time. The System.Globalization namespace gives you access to the CultureInfo class to allow a safe conversion of decimal columns:

```
using System;
using System.Data;
using System.Data.SqlClient;
using System.Diagnostics;
using System.IO;
using System.Globalization;
```

The class defines an SQL connection string, the source file name, and a DataTable:

```
static string sqlconnection = @"DATA SOURCE=SQL2014; " +
    "INITIAL CATALOG=AdventureWorks; " +
    "INTEGRATED SECURITY=SSPI;";

static string sourcefile = "c:\\ZIPCodes.txt";

static DataTable loadtable = null;
```

The class contains three functions: Main(), DoImport(), and LoadSourceFile(). The Main() function begins by starting a Stopwatch to time the import process. Then it invokes the DoImport() function that performs the actual import and reports back the number of rows. Finally, the Stopwatch is stopped and the number of rows imported and number of seconds elapsed are displayed:

```
static void Main(string[] args)
{
    Stopwatch clock = new Stopwatch();
    clock.Start();
    int rowcount = DoImport();
    clock.Stop();
    Console.WriteLine("{0} Rows Imported in {1} Seconds.",
        rowcount, (clock.ElapsedMilliseconds / 1000.0));
    Console.WriteLine("Press a Key...");
    Console.ReadKey();
}
```

The second function, DoImport(), initializes an instance of the SqlBulkCopy class. It then calls the LoadSourceFile() function to populate the DataTable with data from the source flat file. The populated DataTable is passed into the WriteToServer() method of the SqlBulkCopy object. This method performs a bulk copy of all the rows in the DataTable to the destination table. The DoImport() function ends by returning the number of rows loaded into the DataTable:

```
static int DoImport()
{
    using (SqlBulkCopy bulkcopier = new SqlBulkCopy(sqlconnection))
    {
        bulkcopier.DestinationTableName = "dbo.ZIPCodes";
        try
        {
            LoadSourceFile();
```

```
            bulkcopier.WriteToServer(loadtable);
        }
        catch (SqlException ex)
        {
            Console.WriteLine(ex.Message);
        }
    }
    return loadtable.Rows.Count;
}
```

The third and final function, LoadSourceFile(), initializes the structure of the DataTable and loads the source file data into it:

```
static void LoadSourceFile()
{
    loadtable = new DataTable();
    DataColumn loadcolumn = new DataColumn();
    DataRow loadrow = null;

    loadcolumn.DataType = typeof(SqlString);
    loadcolumn.ColumnName = "ZIP";
    loadcolumn.Unique = true;
    loadtable.Columns.Add(loadcolumn);

    loadcolumn = new DataColumn();
    loadcolumn.DataType = typeof(SqlDecimal);
    loadcolumn.ColumnName = "Latitude";
    loadcolumn.Unique = false;
    loadtable.Columns.Add(loadcolumn);

    loadcolumn = new DataColumn();
    loadcolumn.DataType = typeof(SqlDecimal);
    loadcolumn.ColumnName = "Longitude";
    loadcolumn.Unique = false;
    loadtable.Columns.Add(loadcolumn);

    loadcolumn = new DataColumn();
    loadcolumn.DataType = typeof(SqlString);
    loadcolumn.ColumnName = "City";
    loadcolumn.Unique = false;
    loadtable.Columns.Add(loadcolumn);

    loadcolumn = new DataColumn();
    loadcolumn.DataType = typeof(SqlString);
    loadcolumn.ColumnName = "State";
    loadcolumn.Unique = false;
    loadtable.Columns.Add(loadcolumn);

    using (StreamReader stream = new StreamReader(sourcefile))
    {
        string record = stream.ReadLine();
        while (record != null)
```

```
        {
            string[] cols = record.Split('\t');
            loadrow = loadtable.NewRow();
            loadrow["ZIP"] = cols[0];
            loadrow["Latitude"] = decimal.Parse(cols[1], CultureInfo.InvariantCulture);
            loadrow["Longitude"] = decimal.Parse(cols[2], CultureInfo.InvariantCulture);
            loadrow["City"] = cols[3];
            loadrow["State"] = cols[4];
            loadtable.Rows.Add(loadrow);
            record = stream.ReadLine();
        }
    }
  }
 }
}
```

You do an explicit conversion to decimals for latitude and longitude from the strings extracted from the file. Using the decimal.Parse() method ensures that the conversion understands the . (dot) as a decimal separator even if the code is run on a machine configured for a culture where the decimal separator isn't a dot, such as in French.

After it completes, Listing 15-8 reports the number of rows bulk-loaded and the amount of time required, as shown in Figure 15-3.

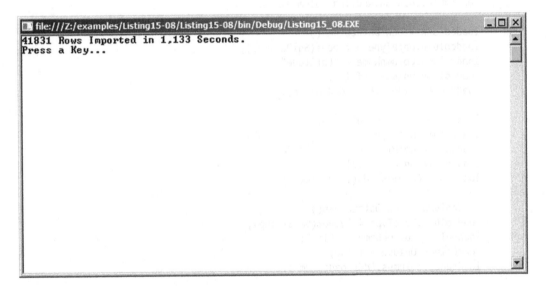

Figure 15-3. *Report of bulk-copy rows imported and the time required*

You can perform a simple SELECT statement like the one shown in Listing 15-9 to verify that the destination table was properly populated. Partial results are shown in Figure 15-4.

Listing 15-9. Verifying Bulk-Copy Results

```
SELECT
    ZIP,
    Latitude,
    Longitude,
    City,
State FROM dbo.ZipCodes;
```

	ZIP	Latitude	Longitude	City	State
1	00501	40.9223	-72.6371	HOLTSVILLE	NY
2	00544	40.9223	-72.6371	HOLTSVILLE	NY
3	01001	42.1405	-72.7887	AGAWAM	MA
4	01002	42.3671	-72.4646	AMHERST	MA
5	01003	42.3696	-72.6360	AMHERST	MA
6	01004	42.3845	-72.5132	AMHERST	MA
7	01005	42.3292	-72.1395	BARRE	MA
8	01007	42.2803	-72.4021	BELCHERTOWN	MA
9	01008	42.1778	-72.9584	BLANDFORD	MA
10	01009	42.2061	-72.3405	BONDSVILLE	MA
11	01010	42.1086	-72.2045	BRIMFIELD	MA
12	01011	42.2943	-72.9528	CHESTER	MA

Figure 15-4. *ZIP codes bulk-loaded into the database*

Multiple Active Result Sets

Prior to SQL Server 2005, client-side applications were limited to one open result set per connection to SQL Server. The workaround was to fully process or cancel all open result sets on a single connection before retrieving a new result set, or to open multiple connections, each with its own single open result.

SQL Server 2014, like SQL Server 2005, allows you to use multiple active result sets (MARS) functionality. MARS lets you process multiple open result sets over a single connection. Listing 15-10 demonstrates how to use MARS to perform the following tasks over a single connection:

1. Open a result set, and begin reading it.

2. Stop reading the result set after a few rows.

3. Open a second result set, and read it to completion.

4. Resume reading the first result set.

Listing 15-10. Opening Two Result Sets over a Single Connection

```
using System;
using System.Data;
using System.Data.SqlClient;

namespace Apress.Examples
{
    class MARS
    {
        static string sqlconnection = @"SERVER=SQL2014; " +
            "INITIAL CATALOG=AdventureWorks; " +
            "INTEGRATED SECURITY=SSPI; " +
            "MULTIPLEACTIVERESULTSETS=true; ";

        static string sqlcommand1 = "SELECT " +
            "  DepartmentID, " +
            "  Name, " +
            "  GroupName " +
            "FROM HumanResources.Department; ";

        static string sqlcommand2 = "SELECT " +
            "  ShiftID, " +
            "  Name, " +
            "  StartTime, " +
            "  EndTime " +
            "FROM HumanResources.Shift; ";

        static SqlConnection connection = null;
        static SqlCommand command1 = null;
        static SqlCommand command2 = null;
        static SqlDataReader datareader1 = null;
        static SqlDataReader datareader2 = null;

        static void Main(string[] args)
        {
            try
            {
                connection = new SqlConnection(sqlconnection);
                connection.Open();
                command1 = new SqlCommand(sqlcommand1, connection);
                command2 = new SqlCommand(sqlcommand2, connection);
                datareader1 = command1.ExecuteReader();
                datareader2 = command2.ExecuteReader();
                int i = 0;

                Console.WriteLine("===========");
                Console.WriteLine("Departments");
                Console.WriteLine("===========");
```

```csharp
        while (datareader1.Read() && i++ < 3)
        {
            Console.WriteLine
            (
              "{0}\t{1}\t{2}",
              datareader1["DepartmentID"].ToString(),
              datareader1["Name"].ToString(),
              datareader1["GroupName"].ToString()
            );
        }

        Console.WriteLine("======");
        Console.WriteLine("Shifts");
        Console.WriteLine("======");
        while (datareader2.Read())
        {
            Console.WriteLine
            (
              "{0}\t{1}\t{2}\t{3}",
              datareader2["ShiftID"].ToString(),
              datareader2["Name"].ToString(),
              datareader2["StartTime"].ToString(),
              datareader2["EndTime"].ToString()
            );
        }

        Console.WriteLine("======================");
        Console.WriteLine("Departments, Continued");
        Console.WriteLine("======================");
        while (datareader1.Read())
        {
            Console.WriteLine
            (
              "{0}\t{1}\t{2}",
              datareader1["DepartmentID"].ToString(),
              datareader1["Name"].ToString(),
              datareader1["GroupName"].ToString()
            );
        }
    }
    catch (SqlException ex)
    {
        Console.WriteLine(ex.Message);
    }
    finally
    {
        if (datareader1 != null)
            datareader1.Dispose();
        if (datareader2 != null)
            datareader2.Dispose();
        if (command1 != null)
            command1.Dispose();
```

```
            if (command2 != null)
                command2.Dispose();
            if (connection != null)
                connection.Dispose();
        }
        Console.WriteLine("Press a key to end...");
        Console.ReadKey();
    }
  }
}
```

Listing 15-10 begins by importing the necessary namespaces:

```
using System;
using System.Data;
using System.Data.SqlClient;
```

The class first declares an SQL connection string and two SQL query strings. It also declares an SqlConnection, two SqlCommand objects, and two SqlDataReader objects. The connection is then opened, and two SqlCommands are created on the single connection to retrieve the two result sets:

```
static string sqlconnection = @"SERVER=SQL2014; " +
    "INITIAL CATALOG=AdventureWorks; " +
    "INTEGRATED SECURITY=SSPI; " +
    "MULTIPLEACTIVERESULTSETS=true; ";

static string sqlcommand1 = "SELECT " +
    "  DepartmentID, " +
    "  Name, " +
    "  GroupName " +
    "FROM HumanResources.Department; ";

static string sqlcommand2 = "SELECT " +
    "  ShiftID, " +
    "  Name, " +
    "  StartTime, " +
    "  EndTime " +
    "FROM HumanResources.Shift; ";

static SqlConnection connection = null;
static SqlCommand command1 = null;
static SqlCommand command2 = null;
static SqlDataReader datareader1 = null;
static SqlDataReader datareader2 = null;
```

The key to enabling MARS is the MULTIPLEACTIVERESULTSETS=true key/value pair in the connection string. The Main function creates and opens the SqlConnection, the SqlCommand objects, and the SqlDataReader objects required to create two active result sets over one connection:

```
connection = new SqlConnection(sqlconnection);
connection.Open();
command1 = new SqlCommand(sqlcommand1, connection);
command2 = new SqlCommand(sqlcommand2, connection);
datareader1 = command1.ExecuteReader();
datareader2 = command2.ExecuteReader();
```

The balance of the code loops through the result sets, displaying the data on the console. The code interrupts the first result set after three rows are consumed, consumes the second result set in its entirety, and then finishes the first result set, all over a single connection. The results are shown in Figure 15-5.

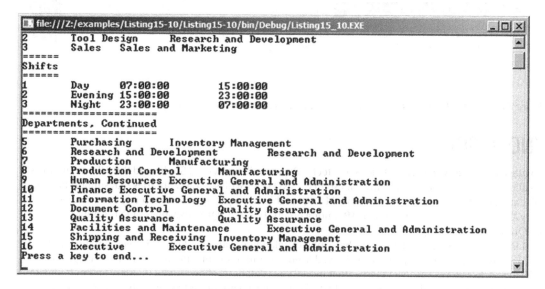

Figure 15-5. *Results of iterating over two active result sets over one connection*

Removing the MULTIPLEACTIVERESULTSETS=true option from the connection string, as shown in the code snippet in Listing 15-11, results in the invalid operation exception in Figure 15-6 being thrown.

Listing 15-11. SQL Connection String without MARS Enabled

```
static string sqlconnection = "SERVER=SQL_2014; " + "INITIAL CATALOG=AdventureWorks; " +
"INTEGRATED SECURITY=SSPI; ";
```

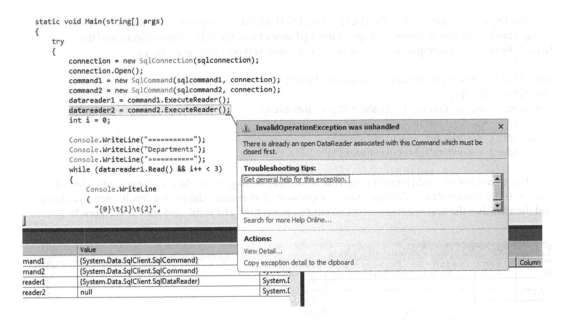

Figure 15-6. *Trying to open two result sets on one connection without MARS*

LINQ to SQL

Language Integrated Query (LINQ) is a set of technologies built into Visual Studio and the .NET Framework that allows you to query data from any data source. LINQ ships with standard libraries that support querying SQL databases, XML, and objects. Additional LINQ-enabled data providers have already been created to query Amazon.com, NHibernate, and LDAP, among others. LINQ to SQL encapsulates LINQ's built-in support for SQL database querying.

LINQ to SQL provides two things: a basic object/relational mapping (O/RM) implementation for the .NET Framework, and a query language derived from SQL but more integrated into the .NET language. LINQ to SQL lets you create .NET classes that model your database, allowing you to query and manipulate data using object-oriented methodologies. Instead of enclosing queries into strings that you send to the server, you write them with the LINQ syntax. As objects are recognized through the O/RM mapping, the syntax is recognized directly like any other .NET language construct. It helps to decrease the so-called object/relational impedance mismatch between object-oriented languages and SQL (in other words, the impossibility of gracefully integrating one language into the other).

This section introduces LINQ to SQL. For an in-depth introduction, we recommend the book *LINQ for Visual C# 2008* by Fabio Claudio Ferracchiati (Apress, 2008).

■ **Tip** In addition to Ferracchiati's *LINQ for Visual C#* books, Apress publishes several other books on LINQ. You can view the list at http://www.apress.com/catalogsearch/result/?q=LINQ&submit=Go. The MSDN web site (http://msdn.microsoft.com) also has several LINQ resources available.

Using the Designer

Visual Studio includes a LINQ to SQL designer that makes mapping database schema to a .NET representation a relatively painless process. The LINQ to SQL designer can be accessed in Visual Studio by adding a new LINQ to SQL Classes item to your .NET project, as shown in Figure 15-7. Note that some importance is placed on the file name you choose, because the .NET data context class (the main LINQ to SQL class) created is based on the name you choose (without the .dbml extension). In this case, we chose the name AdventureWorks.dbml.

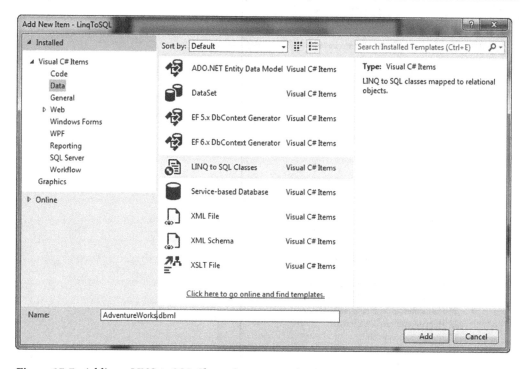

Figure 15-7. *Adding a LINQ to SQL Classes item to a project*

Once the LINQ to SQL Classes item has been added, you need to create a Microsoft SQL Server SqlClient connection that points to your server and database. You can add a data connection through the Visual Studio SQL Server Object Explorer, as shown in Figure 15-8.

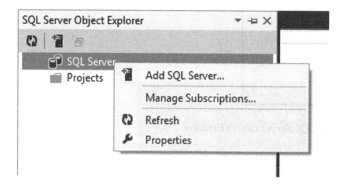

Figure 15-8. *Adding a connection through the SQL Server Object Explorer*

When you've added the connection to your database, the SQL Server Object Explorer displays the tables and other objects contained in the database. You can select tables and SPs and drag them from the SQL Server Object Explorer onto the O/RM designer surface. Figure 15-9 shows the selection of two tables, Person.Person and Person.EmailAddress, in the SQL Server Object Explorer.

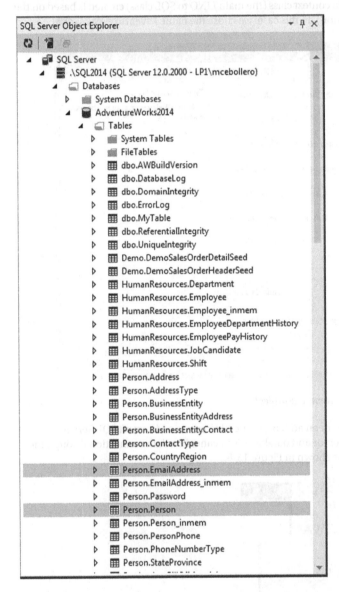

Figure 15-9. Viewing and selecting tables in the SQL Server Object Explorer

Once the tables have been dragged onto the O/RM designer surface, Visual Studio provides a visual representation of the classes it creates to model the database and the relationships between them. Figure 15-10 shows the designer surface with the Person.Person and Person.EmailAddress tables added to it.

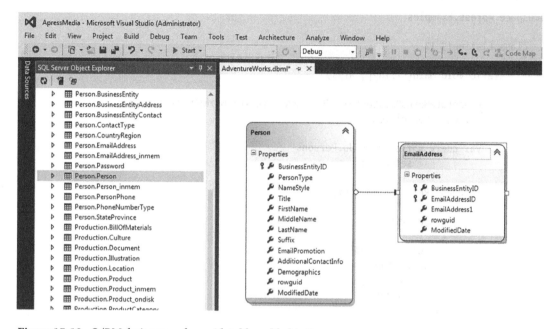

Figure 15-10. *O/RM designer surface with tables added to it*

Querying with LINQ to SQL

Once you've created your LINQ to SQL O/RM classes with the designer, it's time to write queries. Not only does LINQ allow you to query any data source including SQL, but it's also integrated directly into Visual Basic and C# via dedicated keywords. These new LINQ-specific keywords include from, select, where, and others that will seem eerily familiar to SQL developers. These keywords, combined with some other features, provide a powerful mechanism for performing declarative queries directly in your procedural code.

Basic LINQ to SQL Querying

The first LINQ to SQL query example, in Listing 15-12, queries the Persons property of the AdventureWorksDataContext class.

Listing 15-12. Querying Persons with LINQ to SQL

```
using System;
using System.Linq;

namespace Apress.Examples
{
    class Listing15_12
    {
        static void Main(string[] args)
        {
            AdventureWorksDataContext db = new AdventureWorksDataContext();
            db.Log = Console.Out;

            var query = from p in db.Persons
                        select p;

            foreach (Person p in query)
            {
                Console.WriteLine
                  (
                    "{0}\t{1}\t{2}",
                    p.FirstName,
                    p.MiddleName,
                    p.LastName
                  );
            }
            Console.WriteLine("Press a key to continue...");
            Console.ReadKey();
        }
    }
}
```

The first thing to notice about this example is the namespace declarations. Because you're using LINQ to SQL, you have to import the System.Linq namespace. This namespace gives access to the LINQ IQueryable interface, providing objects that can be enumerated in a foreach loop, like IEnumerable:

```
using System;
using System.Linq;
```

The Main() method of the program begins by creating an instance of the AdventureWorksDataContext, which you query against. Notice that you set the Log property of the AdventureWorksDataContext instance to Console.Out. This displays the actual SQL query that LINQ to SQL generates on the console:

```
AdventureWorksDataContext db = new AdventureWorksDataContext();
db.Log = Console.Out;
```

After the AdventureWorksDataContext class is instantiated, querying with the new C# keywords is as simple as assigning a query to a variable. This example takes advantage of the .NET anonymous types feature. Anonymous types allow you to declare variables without an explicit type using the var keyword. When you declare a variable using anonymous types, the compiler automatically infers the type at compile time. This is an important distinction from Object and variant data types, which represent general-purpose types that are determined at runtime. The query is simple, using the from...in clause to indicate the source of the data and the select keyword to return objects. As you can see, the LINQ to SQL syntax has a different order than the SQL syntax. The select keyword comes at the end of the statement:

```
var query = from p in db.Persons
            select p;
```

The final part of this example uses a foreach loop to iterate over all the Person objects returned by the query and print the names to the display. Partial results of this query are shown in Figure 15-11:

```
foreach (Person p in query)
{
    Console.WriteLine
    (
        "{0}\t{1}\t{2}",
        p.FirstName,
        p.MiddleName,
        p.LastName
    );
}
```

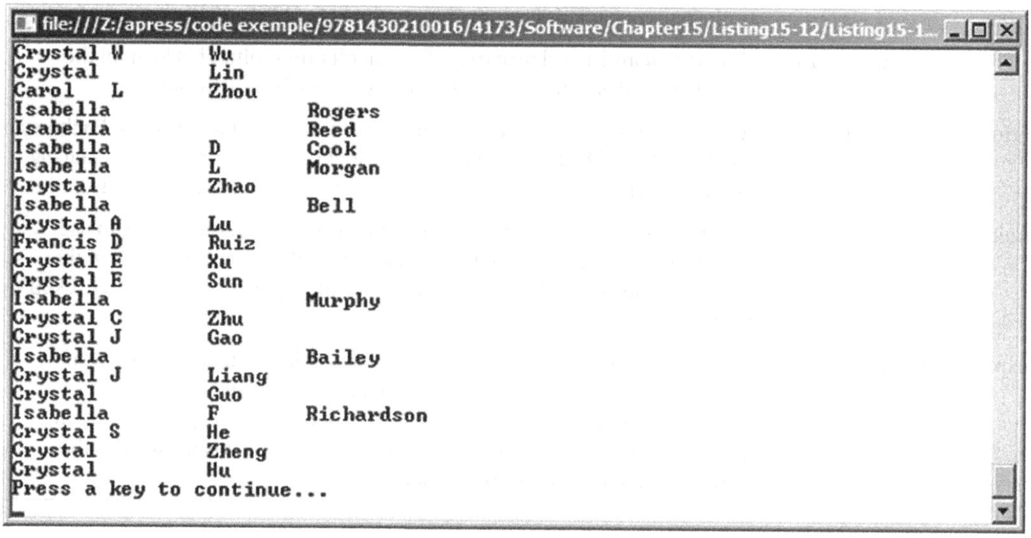

Figure 15-11. Querying Persons with LINQ to SQL

As mentioned previously, you can use the Log attribute of the data context class to output the SQL code generated by LINQ to SQL. This is useful for debugging or finding out more about how LINQ to SQL works internally. The SQL query generated by Listing 15-12 is shown in Listing 15-13 (reformatted for readability).

Listing 15-13. LINQ to SQL–Generated SQL Query

```
SELECT [t0].[BusinessEntityID], [t0].[PersonType],
            [t0].[NameStyle], [t0].[Title], [t0].[FirstName],
            [t0].[MiddleName], [t0].[LastName], [t0].[Suffix],
            [t0].[EmailPromotion], [t0].[AdditionalContactInfo],
            [t0].[Demographics], [t0].[rowguid], [t0].[ModifiedDate]
    FROM [Person].[Person] AS [t0]
```

LINQ to SQL provides several clauses in addition to from and select. Table 15-5 is a summary of some commonly used LINQ to SQL query operators. The discussion of LINQ to SQL query operators continues in the sections that follow.

Table 15-5. *Useful LINQ Standard Query Operators*

Function	Keyword	Description
Restriction	where	Restricts/filters the results returned by a query, returning only the items that match the where predicate condition. You can think of this as equivalent to the WHERE clause in SQL.
Projection	select	Defines/restricts the attributes that should be returned in the result collection. The select keyword approximates the SQL SELECT clause.
Join	join	Performs an inner join of two sequences based on matching keys from both sequences. This is equivalent to the SQL INNER JOIN clause.
Join	join...into	Can accept an into clause to perform a left outer join. This form of the join keyword is equivalent to the SQL LEFT OUTER JOIN clause.
Ordering	orderby	Accepts a comma-separated list of keys to sort your query results. Each key can be followed by the ascending or descending keyword. The ascending keyword is the default. This is equivalent to the SQL ORDER BY clause.
Grouping	group	Allows you to group results by a specified set of key values. You can use the group...into syntax to perform additional query operations on the grouped results. The behavior of this keyword approximates the SQL GROUP BY clause.
Subexpressions	let	Allows you to store subexpressions in a variable during the query. You can use the variable in subsequent query clauses. SQL doesn't have an equivalent for this statement, although subqueries can approximate the behavior in some instances. The best equivalent for this keyword is the XQuery FLWOR expression let clause.

The where Clause

The where clause allows you to restrict the results returned by a query, as shown in Listing 15-14. Replacing the query in Listing 15-12 with this query restricts the Person objects returned to only those with the letters *smi* in their last names.

Listing 15-14. Querying Persons with "smi" in Their Last Names

```
var query = from p in db.Persons
            where p.LastName.Contains("SMI")
            select p;
```

The SQL code generated by this LINQ to SQL query is slightly different from the previous SQL query, as shown in Listing 15-15.

Listing 15-15. LINQ to SQL-Generated SQL Query with a WHERE Clause

```
exec sp_executesql
     N'SELECT [t0].[BusinessEntityID], [t0].[PersonType],
                  [t0].[NameStyle], [t0].[Title], [t0].[FirstName],
                  [t0].[MiddleName], [t0].[LastName],
                  [t0].[Suffix], [t0].[EmailPromotion],
                  [t0].[AdditionalContactInfo], [t0].[Demographics],
                  [t0].[rowguid], [t0].[ModifiedDate]
         FROM [Person].[Person] AS [t0]
       WHERE [t0].[LastName]
                  LIKE @p0',N'@p0 nvarchar(5)',@p0=N'%SMI%'
```

One interesting aspect to this query is that LINQ to SQL converts the Contains method of the Person object's LastName property to an SQL LIKE predicate. This is important because it means LINQ to SQL is smart enough to realize that it doesn't have to retrieve an entire table, instantiate objects for every row of the table, and then use .NET methods to limit the results on the client. This can be a significant performance enhancement over the alternative. Furthermore, it uses sp_executesql to parameterize the query.

Another interesting feature that LINQ to SQL provides is query parameterization. In this instance, the generated SQL query includes a parameter named @p0 that is defined as an nvarchar(5) parameter and assigned a value of %SMI%.

The orderby Clause

LINQ to SQL also provides result ordering via the orderby clause. You can use the orderby keyword in a query to specify the attributes to sort by. Listing 15-16 builds on the query in Listing 15-14 by adding an orderby clause that sorts results by the LastName and FirstName attributes of the Person object.

Listing 15-16. Ordering LINQ to SQL Query Results

```
var query = from p in db.Persons
            where p.LastName.Contains("SMI")
            orderby p.LastName, p.FirstName
            select p;
```

Replacing the query in Listing 15-12 with this query returns all Person objects whose last names contain the letters *smi*, and sorts the objects by their last and first names. The generated SQL query is shown in Listing 15-17. It's similar to the previous query except that LINQ to SQL has added an SQL ORDER BY clause.

Listing 15-17. LINQ to SQL-Generated SQL Query with an ORDER BY Clause

```
exec sp_executesql
      N'SELECT [to].[BusinessEntityID], [to].[PersonType],
                     [to].[NameStyle], [to].[Title], [to].[FirstName],
                     [to].[MiddleName], [to].[LastName],
                     [to].[Suffix], [to].[EmailPromotion],
                     [to].[AdditionalContactInfo], [to].[Demographics],
                     [to].[rowguid], [to].[ModifiedDate]
            FROM [Person].[Person] AS [to]
         WHERE [to].[LastName] LIKE @p0
         ORDER BY [to].[LastName], [to].[FirstName]',N'@p0 nvarchar(5)',@p0=N'%SMI%'
```

The join Clause

LINQ to SQL also provides the join clause, which allows you to perform inner joins in your queries. An inner join relates two entities, like Person and EmailAddress in the example, based on common values of an attribute. The LINQ to SQL join operator essentially works the same way as the SQL INNER JOIN operator. Listing 15-18 demonstrates a LINQ to SQL join query.

Listing 15-18. Retrieving Persons and Related E-mail Addresses

```
using System;
using System.Linq;

namespace Apress.Examples
{
    class Listing15_18
    {
        static void Main(string[] args)
        {
            AdventureWorksDataContext db = new AdventureWorksDataContext();
            db.Log = Console.Out;

            var query = from p in db.Persons
                        join e in db.EmailAddresses
                        on p.BusinessEntityID equals e.BusinessEntityID
                        where p.LastName.Contains("SMI")
                        orderby p.LastName, p.FirstName
                        select new
                        {
                            LastName = p.LastName,
                            FirstName = p.FirstName,
                            MiddleName = p.MiddleName,
                            EmailAddress = e.EmailAddress1
                        };

            foreach (var q in query)
            {
                Console.WriteLine
                    (
                        "{0}\t{1}\t{2}\t{3}",
```

```
                q.FirstName,
                q.MiddleName,
                q.LastName,
                q.EmailAddress
            );
    }
    Console.WriteLine("Press a key to continue...");
    Console.ReadKey();
        }
    }
}
```

THE EQUALS OPERATOR AND NON-EQUIJOINS

C# uses the `equals` keyword in the LINQ `join...on` clause instead of the familiar `==` operator. This is done for clarity. The LINQ `from...join` pattern maps directly to the `Enumerable.Join()` LINQ query operator, which requires two delegates that are used to compute values for comparison. The delegate/key on the left side of the operator consumes the outer sequence, and the right delegate/key consumes the inner sequence. The decision was made to use the `equals` keyword to clarify this concept primarily because implementing a full query processor for LINQ would have resulted in significant overhead. To perform other types of non-equijoins in LINQ, you can use a combination of the LINQ `GroupJoin` operator and the `where` clause.

The LINQ to SQL query in Listing 15-18 uses the `join` operator to identify the entities to join and the `on` clause specifies the join criteria. In this example, the `Person` and `EmailAddress` entities are joined based on their `BusinessEntityID` attributes. Because the query needs to return some attributes of both entities, the `select` clause creates a new anonymous type on the fly. Partial results of the join query are shown in Figure 15-12:

```
var query = from p in db.Persons
            join e in db.EmailAddresses
            on p.BusinessEntityID equals e.BusinessEntityID
            where p.LastName.Contains("SMI")
            orderby p.LastName, p.FirstName
            select new
            {
                LastName = p.LastName,
                FirstName = p.FirstName,
                MiddleName = p.MiddleName,
                EmailAddress = e.EmailAddress1
            };
```

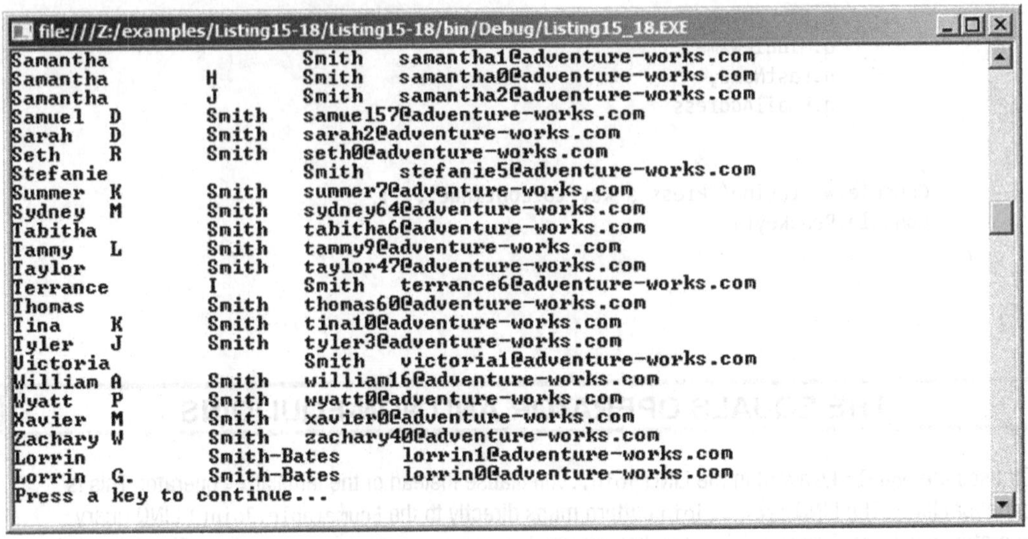

```
file:///Z:/examples/Listing15-18/Listing15-18/bin/Debug/Listing15_18.EXE
Samantha                Smith   samantha1@adventure-works.com
Samantha        H       Smith   samantha0@adventure-works.com
Samantha        J       Smith   samantha2@adventure-works.com
Samuel  D       Smith   samuel57@adventure-works.com
Sarah   D       Smith   sarah2@adventure-works.com
Seth    R       Smith   seth0@adventure-works.com
Stefanie                Smith   stefanie5@adventure-works.com
Summer  K       Smith   summer7@adventure-works.com
Sydney  M       Smith   sydney64@adventure-works.com
Tabitha         Smith   tabitha6@adventure-works.com
Tammy   L       Smith   tammy9@adventure-works.com
Taylor          Smith   taylor47@adventure-works.com
Terrance        I       Smith   terrance6@adventure-works.com
Thomas          Smith   thomas60@adventure-works.com
Tina    K       Smith   tina10@adventure-works.com
Tyler   J       Smith   tyler3@adventure-works.com
Victoria                Smith   victoria1@adventure-works.com
William A       Smith   william16@adventure-works.com
Wyatt   P       Smith   wyatt0@adventure-works.com
Xavier  M       Smith   xavier0@adventure-works.com
Zachary W       Smith   zachary40@adventure-works.com
Lorrin          Smith-Bates     lorrin1@adventure-works.com
Lorrin  G.      Smith-Bates     lorrin0@adventure-works.com
Press a key to continue...
```

Figure 15-12. *Retrieving* Person *names and related e-mail addresses*

The SQL query generated by LINQ to SQL includes an SQL `INNER JOIN` clause and only retrieves the columns required by the query, as shown in Listing 15-19.

Listing 15-19. LINQ to SQL-Generated SQL Query with an `INNER JOIN` Clause

```
exec sp_executesql
      N'SELECT [t0].[LastName], [t0].[FirstName],
                        [t0].[MiddleName], [t1].[EmailAddress]
          FROM [Person].[Person] AS [t0]
        INNER JOIN [Person].[EmailAddress] AS [t1]
                        ON [t0].[BusinessEntityID] = [t1].[BusinessEntityID]
        WHERE [t0].[LastName] LIKE @p0
        ORDER BY [t0].[LastName], [t0].[FirstName]',N'@p0 nvarchar(5)',@p0=N'%SMI%'
```

Deferred Query Execution

LINQ to SQL uses a query execution pattern known as deferred query execution. When you declare a LINQ to SQL query, .NET creates an expression tree. The expression tree is essentially a data structure that acts as a guide that LINQ to SQL can use to execute your query. The expression tree doesn't contain the data retrieved by the query, but rather the information required to execute the query. Deferred query execution causes the execution of the query to be delayed until the data returned by the query is actually needed—when you iterate the results in a `foreach` loop, for instance. You can view deferred query execution in action by placing breakpoints on the `foreach` loops of the code examples in the previous sections. LINQ to SQL will not generate and output its SQL code until after the `foreach` loop iteration begins. This is shown in Figure 15-13.

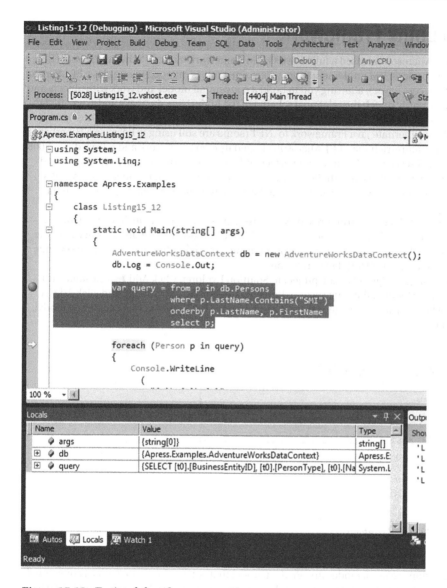

Figure 15-13. *Testing deferred query execution*

Deferred query execution is an important concept that every LINQ to SQL developer needs to be familiar with. If the value of a variable that the query depends on changes between the time the query is declared and the time it's executed, the query can return unexpected results.

From LINQ to Entity Framework

After LINQ was designed, Microsoft released a full blown O/RM framework named Entity Framework (EF). LINQ provides only a very basic O/RM implementation, where one table is mapped to one class. EF offers an abstraction level (a Data Access Layer), allowing you to build a conceptual model and work with objects and collections that don't necessarily match the relational schema of the underlying database and aren't tied to a physical implementation. Before EF, developers who wanted to work with an O/RM in .NET mostly used NHibernate, the port of the Hibernate Java Framework to .NET (some are still using it, because NHibernate is for now more mature and feature-rich than EF). Microsoft created its own framework and released it in 2008 with the .NET framework 3.5 service pack 1. It wasn't perfect and got a lot of criticism. In 2010, the second version, Entity Framework 4, was released with the .NET framework 4 (the version number was obviously chosen to match the .NET framework version) and corrected most of the problems encountered with the first release.

Entity Framework 4 maps database structures to .NET classes that you manipulate in your client application like any other classes. There is no contact with SQL code and no need for any knowledge of the database structure or physical implementation, matching a business model rather than a physical schema. This is called the Entity Data Model (EDM). Let's create one.

In a Visual Studio C# project, right-click the project in Solution Explorer. Click Add ➤ New Item, and select ADO.NET Entity Data Model in the Data section. Enter a name for the data model, and click Add. A wizard opens and asks whether you want to generate the model from a database or create an empty model, as shown in Figure 15-14.

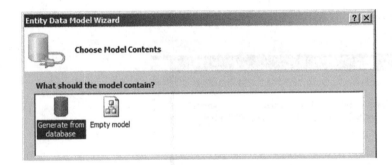

Figure 15-14. *Choosing EF model contents*

The Empty Model option creates a model-first EF data model that you could use to model a conceptual schema, create EF classes, and generate database tables later. In this case, choose Generate From Database, and click Next. The next step allows you to choose or create a data connection to SQL Server. After that, you select the database objects you want to use in your model. You can add tables, views, and stored procedure results, as shown in Figure 15-15.

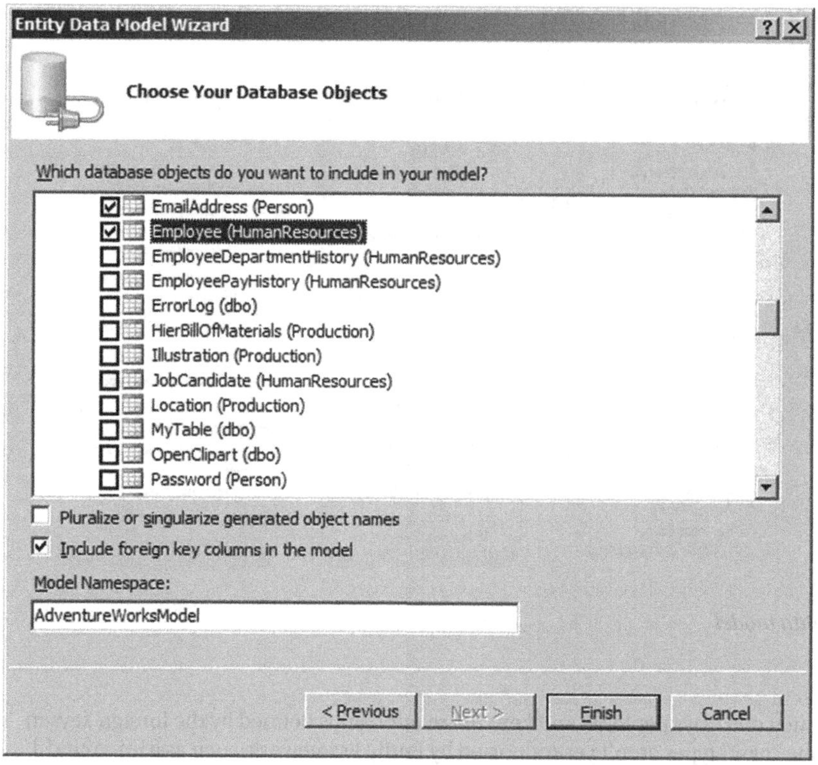

Figure 15-15. *Selecting database objects*

Select the following tables:

- HumanResources.Employee

- Person.Person

- Person.BusinessEntity

- Person.EmailAddress

- Person.PersonPhone

- Person.PhoneNumberType

The page shown in Figure 15-15 has a check box labeled Pluralize Or Singularize Generated Object Names. This allows you to automatically apply English language rules to name entities and entity sets. If the names of your database tables are in plural form, EF creates entity classes in plural that will look confusing in your code. The EntityType generated from the tables keeps the plural. Look at this code example:

```
Employees Employee = new Employees();
```

What does the Employees class represent? A single entity, so it should be Employee. But if the database table is named Employees, EF uses this name to build the entity. If Pluralize Or Singularize Generated Object Names is checked, EF removes the s.

When the tables are selected, click Finish to let the wizard create the data model. The model generated is shown in Figure 15-16.

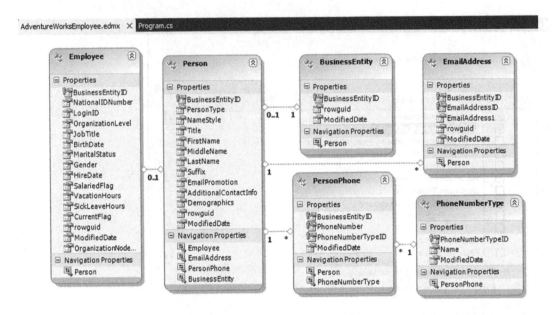

Figure 15-16. *The entity data model*

As you can see, EF created one class per table and kept the relationships defined by the foreign keys in your database schema. Some "new" types aren't yet supported by Entity Framework, such as hierarchyid and spatial types. If you created the EDM from the example, you get a warning about the OrganizationNode column of the HumanResources.Employee table, which is a hierarchyid type column and can't be imported into the EDM. To include the string representation of the OrganizationNode column, you can create a computed column in HumanResources.Employee as shown in Listing 15-20.

Listing 15-20. Creating a Computed Column to Show a hierarchyid Representation in the EDM

```
ALTER TABLE [HumanResources].[Employee]
ADD OrganizationNodeString AS OrganizationNode.ToString() PERSISTED;
```

■ **Note**   The future release of Entity Framework 5 will integrate spatial data types.

In each class of the EDM, you can see a list of properties that are the tables' columns, as well as navigation properties that reference the association between entities. For instance, the PersonPhone entity has a navigation property referencing the PhoneNumberType entity, and the PhoneNumberType entity has a navigation property referencing the PersonPhone entity. Each entity that is part of an association is called an end, and the properties that define the values of the association are called roles. If you click the line joining the two entities in the EDM that represents the association, you see the association's properties, as shown in Figure 15-17.

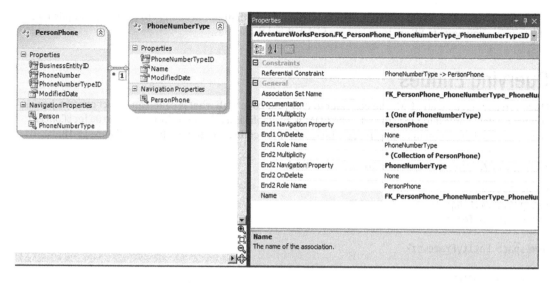

Figure 15-17. *The properties of an association between entities*

The multiplicity of properties allow you to define the cardinality of each role, and the OnDelete properties reflect whether a cascading option has been defined on the foreign key in the database.

■ **Caution**   Do not set OnDelete to cascade in your EDM if there is no cascading option in the foreign key at the database level. EF will assume that the DELETE is taken care of by the database engine. It will only delete associated objects if they're in memory.

We have said that the EDM isn't tied to a physical implementation. Entity Framework maintains three layers for better abstraction. At design time, all the information is stored in an .edmx file, but at runtime, EF separates the model into three XML files that have different structures, as detailed in Table 15-6.

Table 15-6. *Entity Framework Abstraction Layers*

File extension	Name	Description
.csdl	Conceptual Schema Definition Language	Defines a conceptual model that is agnostic regarding the database physical implementation. It defines entities, relationships, and functions.
.ssdl	Store Schema Definition Language	Describes the storage model of the conceptual schema. It defines the name of the underlying tables and columns, and the queries used to retrieve the data from the database.
.msl	Mapping Specification Language	Maps the CSDL attributes to the SSDL columns.

These levels allow you to switch the backend database with minimal change to your client application. The requests you write to EF are translated to SQL behind the scenes.

Querying Entities

Once you have created an EDM, you can refer to it in your code with what is called an object context, just as you have a data context in LINQ to SQL. The EDM is available as a class inheriting from the `ObjectContext` class. Let's see it in action in Listing 15-21. The result of the code execution is shown in Figure 15-18.

Listing 15-21. Using an EF Object Context in C# Code

```
using System;
using System.Linq;
using System.Text;

namespace EntityFramework
{
    class Program
    {
        static void Main(string[] args)
        {
            using (var ctx = new AdventureWorksEntitiesEmployee())
            {
                var qry = from e in ctx.Employee
                            where e.Gender == "F"
                            select new
                            {
                                e.Person.FirstName,
                                e.Person.LastName,
                                e.BirthDate
                            };

                foreach (var emp in qry.Take(5)) {
                    Console.WriteLine("{0} {1}, born {2}",
                                emp.FirstName,
                                emp.LastName,
                                emp.BirthDate.ToLongDateString()
                    );
                }
                Console.Read();
            }
        }
    }
}
```

```
Terri Duffy, born Wednesday, 01 September 1965
Gail Erickson, born Tuesday, 29 October 1946
Diane Margheim, born Sunday, 06 July 1980
Gigi Matthew, born Wednesday, 21 February 1973
Janice Galvin, born Wednesday, 29 June 1983
```

Figure 15-18. *The result of the code execution*

The code in Listing 15-21 is a console application. It returns five lines of employees. First, you create an instance of the AdventureWorksEntitiesEmployee class, which inherits from ObjectContext. It gives you access to entities present in the AdventureWorksEntitiesEmployee EDM. The context allows you to access its entities, to define and execute queries, and to apply modifications to data. You enclose the context instantiation in a using block in order to ensure that the instance will be freed no matter what happens in the block:

```
using (var ctx = new AdventureWorksEntitiesEmployee())
{
    ...
}
```

You can use LINQ queries against entities. This functionality is called LINQ to Entities, and it's very much like LINQ to SQL. In LINQ to SQL you would write this:

```
var qry = from e in ctx.Employee
          join p in ctx.Person on e.BusinessEntityId equals p.BusinessEntityId
          where e.Gender == "F"
          select new
          {
              p.FirstName,
              p.LastName,
              e.BirthDate
          };
```

But in Entity Framework, you can take advantage of navigation properties, which are properties of an entity that give access to the other end of an association. A navigation property returns either one entity or a collection of entities, depending on the cardinality of the relationship. Here, because the association is 0..1, there can be only one person associated with an employee, so it returns only one entity reference. You can directly use its properties to retrieve the FirstName and LastName. Additionally, to limit the number of properties returned by the query, you create an anonymous type (a class without a name), declared on the fly with a new {...} construct to retrieve only Person.FirstName, Person.LastName, and Employee.BirthDate:

```
var qry = from e in ctx.Employee
          where e.Gender == "F"
          select new
    {
        e.Person.FirstName,
        e.Person.LastName,
        e.BirthDate
    };
```

505

Using the anonymous type improves performance. In Listing 15-22 you can see the T-SQL query generated by EF that is retrieved using SQL Server Profiler.

Listing 15-22. T-SQL Query Generated by EF

```
SELECT TOP (5)
[Extent1].[BusinessEntityID] AS [BusinessEntityID],
[Extent2].[FirstName] AS [FirstName],
[Extent3].[LastName] AS [LastName],
[Extent1].[BirthDate] AS [BirthDate]
FROM    [HumanResources].[Employee] AS [Extent1]
INNER JOIN [Person].[Person] AS [Extent2] ON [Extent1].[BusinessEntityID] =
[Extent2].[BusinessEntityID]
LEFT OUTER JOIN [Person].[Person] AS [Extent3] ON [Extent1].[BusinessEntityID] =
[Extent3].[BusinessEntityID]
WHERE N'F' = [Extent1].[Gender]
```

You can see that only the needed columns are selected. That reduces the cost of the query and the amount of data that needs to be carried by the query back to the client.

Then, you can simply loop into the query's result, because the query returns an IQueryable descendant object. To limit the number of rows returned, you call the method Take() on the IQueryable, which translates to a SELECT TOP, as you can see in the generated T-SQL in Listing 15-22. You can also see that deferred execution is working in Entity Framework. Finally, you format the BirthDate column/property to display a user-friendly birth date:

```
foreach (var emp in qry.Take(5)) {
    Console.WriteLine("{0} {1}, born {2}",
        emp.FirstName,
        emp.LastName,
        emp.BirthDate.ToLongDateString()
    );
}
```

So that you can see the result in the console before it disappears, you add a call to Console.Read(), which makes the console wait until a key is pressed.

The context can also give you direct access to entities in the form of an ObjectSet. You can think of an ObjectSet as a kind of result set. You can directly call an ObjectSet and enumerate through it. So, the code in Listing 15-21 can be rewritten as in Listing 15-23.

Listing 15-23. Using an EF ObjectSet

```
using System;
using System.Linq;
using System.Text;

namespace EntityFramework
{
    class Program
    {
        static void Main(string[] args)
        {
            using (var ctx = new AdventureWorksEntitiesEmployee())
            {
```

```
            foreach (var emp in ctx.Employee.Where(e => e.Gender == "F").Take(5))
            {
                Console.WriteLine("{0} {1}, born {2}",
                                emp.Person.FirstName,
                                emp.Person.LastName,
                                emp.BirthDate.ToLongDateString()
                );
            }
            Console.Read();
          }
        }
      }
}
```

Listing 15-23 directly uses the Employee ObjectSet. You can still filter it by using its Where() method. In contrast to the LINQ query approach, this is called a method-based query. The Where() method takes a lambda expression as its parameter. Lambda expressions are a way to express parameters with a syntax derived from Lambda calculus, a formal notation in mathematical logic. You can use LINQ queries or method-based querying; choose what feels more natural to you.

Finally, Listing 15-24 shows an example of data modification with Entity Framework. The result is shown in Figure 15-19.

Listing 15-24. Modifying Data in EF

```
using System;
using System.Linq;
using System.Text;

namespace EntityFramework
{
    class Program
    {
        static void Main(string[] args)
        {
            using (var ctx = new AdventureWorksEntitiesEmployee())
            {
                var newP = new BusinessEntity {
                    ModifiedDate = DateTime.Now,
                    rowguid = Guid.NewGuid()
                };

                Console.WriteLine("BusinessEntityID before insert : {0}",
                                newP.BusinessEntityID);

                ctx.BusinessEntities.AddObject(newP);
                ctx.SaveChanges();
```

```
                Console.WriteLine("BusinessEntityID after insert :  {0}",
                                    newP.BusinessEntityID);
            }

            Console.Read();
        }
    }
}
```

```
BusinessEntityID before insert : 0
BusinessEntityID after insert :  20780
```

Figure 15-19. *The result of the code execution*

There are several ways to insert new data. This example uses the object-initializer syntax, available since .NET 3.5. In the object-initializer block, you assign values to the two properties of the BusinessEntity entity that need to be populated. The ModifiedDate property is a datetime, so you use the DateTime.Now property to set the current date and time; the rowguid property stores a uniqueidentifier, so you use the Guid. NewGuid() method to retrieve a value. When the object is fully populated, you can add it to the entity by using the AddObject() method:

```
var newP = new BusinessEntity {
    ModifiedDate = DateTime.Now,
    rowguid = Guid.NewGuid()
};
...
ctx.BusinessEntities.AddObject(newP);
```

The changes made to entities are stored in a collection in the context and are applied to the underlying database only when the SaveChanges() method of the context is called. To see what happens with the BusinessEntityId identity column, you return its value before and after the call to SaveChanges(). The key value is automatically set by EF to match the identity value generated by SQL Server. The query issued by EF when you call SaveChanges() is shown in Listing 15-25.

Listing 15-25. The DML Query Generated by EF

```
exec sp_executesql
        N'insert [Person].[BusinessEntity]([rowguid], [ModifiedDate])
          values (@0, @1)
           select [BusinessEntityID]
             from [Person].[BusinessEntity]
          where @@ROWCOUNT > 0
             and [BusinessEntityID] = scope_identity()',
        N'@0 uniqueidentifier,@1 datetime2(7)',
          @0='92EEC64E-BD11-4936-97C3-6528B5D1D97D',
          @1='2012-05-21 15:14:05.3493966'
```

As you can see, a SELECT is issued after the INSERT operation to retrieve the identity value and return it to EF.

This section has only scratched the surface of Entity Framework. You have to be aware of it, even if you don't do any client coding, because it's the way of the future in .NET data access. The question of whether this a good or bad thing is, fortunately (we admit a bit of cowardice here), outside the scope of this book. The thinking behind LINQ and EF is to abstract out database access and to hide the T-SQL language from developers, which is considered a pain by many client-side developers. This trend pushes toward considering DBMSs to be just data stores. In this model, objects like views and stored procedures have less importance, and the craftsmanship of writing good T-SQL queries seems outdated. This has advantages and pitfalls, the more important of the latter being performance issues in complex queries. The best way to address this problem is to become proficient in EF; and to start on that path, you can read *Pro Entity Framework 4.0* by Scott Klein (Apress, 2010).

Summary

Although the focus of this book is server-side development, a good database is useful only if end users can access the data contained in it efficiently. That's where an efficient and well-designed client-side application comes in. This chapter discussed several options available for connecting to SQL Server 2014 from .NET.

The chapter began with a discussion of the ADO.NET namespaces and the .NET SQL Server Native Client (SqlClient), including connected data access, which requires constant database connectivity, and disconnected datasets, which allow users to cache data locally and connect to a database as needed. Although .NET offers other options for connecting to SQL Server, including OLE DB and ODBC, the primary method of connecting to SQL Server (version 7.0 and higher) is encapsulated in ADO.NET and the System. Data.SqlClient namespace.

You also learned about parameterized queries, including the topics of security and SQL injection. Other topics covered included the various methods and options that .NET provides to query SQL Server, bulk-copy data into SQL Server, and open multiple result sets over a single active database connection.

You rounded out this chapter with a discussion of the O/RM functionalities provided by .NET and Visual Studio. Visual Studio's built-in visual designer and automated class generation can make light work of many O/RM applications. The ability to abstract out database access and to write declarative LINQ to SQL queries directly in procedural code elevates data querying to the level of a first-class programming concept.

EXERCISES

1. [True/False] The System.Data.SqlClient namespace provides optimized access to SQL Server via the SQL Server Native Client library.

2. [Choose one] Which of the following concepts allows for local caching of data, with establishment of database connections on an as-needed basis?

    a. Connected data access

    b. Disconnected datasets

    c. Casual data access

    d. Partial datasets

3. [Choose all that apply] Which of the following are benefits of query parameterization?

   a. Protection against SQL injection attacks

   b. Conversion of lead to gold

   c. Increased efficiency through query plan reuse

   d. Decreased power consumption by at least 25%

4. [True/False] Turning on MARS by setting MULTIPLEACTIVERESULTSETS=true in your connection string allows you to open two result sets but requires at least two open connections.

5. [True/False] Visual Studio includes a drag-and-drop visual O/RM designer.

6. [Choose one] LINQ to SQL uses which of the following query execution patterns?

   a. Instant query execution

   b. Fast-forward query execution

   c. Random query execution

   d. Deferred query execution

CHAPTER 16

■ ■ ■

CLR Integration Programming

One of the most prominent enhancements to SQL Server 2005 was the introduction of the integrated SQL Common Language Runtime, named SQL CLR at that time. What is now called CLR integration is an SQL Server–specific version of the .NET Common Language Runtime, which allows you to run .NET-managed code in the database. CLR integration programming is a broad subject that could easily fill an entire book, and in fact it does—*Pro SQL Server 2005 Assemblies*, by Robin Dewson and Julian Skinner (Apress, 2005), is an excellent resource for in-depth coverage of CLR integration programming. This chapter discusses the methods used to extend SQL Server functionality in the past and explains the basics of the CLR integration programming model in SQL Server 2014.

The Old Way

In versions of SQL Server prior to the 2005 release, developers could extend SQL Server functionality by writing extended stored procedures (XPs). Writing high-quality XPs required a strong knowledge of the Open Data Services (ODS) library and the poorly documented C-style Extended Stored Procedure API. Anyone who attempted the old style of XP programming can tell you it was a complex undertaking, in which a single misstep could easily result in memory leaks and corruption of the SQL Server process space. Additionally, the threading model used by XPs required SQL Server to rely on the operating system to control threading in the XP. This could lead to many issues, such as unresponsiveness of XP code.

■ **Caution** XPs have been deprecated since SQL Server 2005. Use CLR integration instead of XPs for SQL Server 2014 development.

Earlier SQL Server releases also allowed you to create OLE Automation server objects via the sp_OACreate SP. Creating OLE Automation servers can be complex and awkward as well. OLE Automation servers created with sp_OACreate can result in memory leaks and in some instances corruption of the SQL Server process space.

Another option in previous versions of SQL Server was to code all business logic exclusively in physically separate business objects. Although this method is preferred by many developers and administrators, it can result in extra network traffic and a less robust security model than can be achieved through tight integration with the SQL Server security model.

The CLR Integration Way

The CLR integration programming model provides several advantages over older methods of extending SQL Server functionality via XPs, OLE Automation, or external business objects. These advantages include the following:

- A managed code base that runs on the CLR integration .NET Framework is managed by the SQL Server Operating System (SQL OS). This means SQL Server can properly manage threading, memory usage, and other resources accessed via CLR integration code.

- Tight integration of the CLR into SQL Server means SQL Server can provide a robust security model for running code and maintain stricter control over database objects and external resources accessed by CLR code.

- CLR integration is more thoroughly documented in more places than the Extended Stored Procedure API ever was (or presumably ever will be).

- CLR integration doesn't tie you to the C language-based Extended Stored Procedure API. In theory, the .NET programming model doesn't tie you to any one specific language (although you can't use dynamic languages like IronPython in CLR integration).

- CLR integration allows access to the familiar .NET namespaces, data types, and managed objects, easing development.

- CLR integration introduces SQL Server–specific namespaces that allow direct access to the underlying SQL Server databases and resources, which can be used to limit or reduce network traffic generated by using external business objects.

There's a misperception expressed by some that CLR integration is a replacement for T-SQL altogether. CLR integration isn't a replacement for T-SQL, but rather a supplement that works hand in hand with T-SQL to make SQL Server 2014 more powerful than ever. So when should you use CLR code in your database? There are no hard and fast rules concerning this, but here are some general guidelines:

- Existing custom XPs on older versions of SQL Server are excellent candidates for conversion to SQL Server CLR integration assemblies—that is, if the functionality provided isn't already part of SQL Server 2014 T-SQL (for example, encryption).

- Code that accesses external server resources, such as calls to xpcmdshell, are also excellent candidates for conversion to more secure and robust CLR assemblies.

- T-SQL code that performs lots of complex calculations and string manipulations can be a strong candidate for conversion to CLR integration assemblies.

- Highly procedural code with lots of processing steps might be considered for conversion.

- External business objects that pull large amounts of data across the wire and perform a lot of processing on that data might be considered for conversion. You might first consider these business objects for conversion to T-SQL SPs, especially if they don't perform much processing on the data in question.

On the flip side, here are some general guidelines for items that should not be converted to CLR integration assemblies

- External business objects that pull relatively little data across the wire, or that pull a lot of data across the wire but perform little processing on that data, are good candidates for conversion to T-SQL SPs instead of CLR assemblies.

- T-SQL code and SPs that don't perform many complex calculations or string manipulations generally won't benefit from conversion to CLR assemblies.

- T-SQL can be expected to always be faster than CLR integration for set-based operations on data stored in the database.

- You might not be able to integrate CLR assemblies into databases that are hosted on an Internet Service Provider's (ISP's) server, if the ISP didn't allow CLR integration at the database-server level. This is mainly for security reasons and because there can be less control of the code in an assembly.

- CLR integration isn't supported on the SQL Azure platform.

As with T-SQL SPs, the decision about whether and to what extent to use CLR integration in your databases depends on your needs, including organizational policies and procedures. The recommendations presented here are guidelines of instances that can make good business cases for conversion of existing code and creation of new code.

CLR Integration Assemblies

CLR integration exposes .NET managed code to SQL Server via assemblies. An assembly is a compiled .NET managed code library that can be registered with SQL Server using the CREATE ASSEMBLY statement. Publicly accessible members of classes in the assemblies are then referenced in the appropriate CREATE statements, described later in this chapter. Creating a CLR integration assembly requires that you do the following:

1. Design and program .NET classes that publicly expose the appropriate members.

2. Compile the .NET classes into managed code DLL manifest files containing the assembly.

3. Register the assembly with SQL Server via the CREATE ASSEMBLY statement.

4. Register the appropriate assembly members via the appropriate CREATE FUNCTION, CREATE PROCEDURE, CREATE TYPE, CREATE TRIGGER, or CREATE AGGREGATE statements.

CLR integration provides additional SQL Server–specific namespaces, classes, and attributes to facilitate development of assemblies. Visual Studio 2010, Visual Studio 2011, and Visual Studio 13 also include an SQL Server project type that assists in quickly creating assemblies. In addition, to maximize your SQL Server development possibilities with Visual Studio, you can install the SQL Server Data Tools (SSDT) from the Microsoft Data Developer Center web site (http://msdn.microsoft.com/en-us/data/tools.aspx) which provides an integrated environment for database developers in Visual Studio by allowing you to create and manage database objects and data and to execute T-SQL queries directly.

Perform the following steps to create a new assembly using Visual Studio 2013:

1. Select File ➤ New Project from the menu.

2. Go to Installed ➤ Templates ➤ SQL Server, as shown in Figure 16-1.

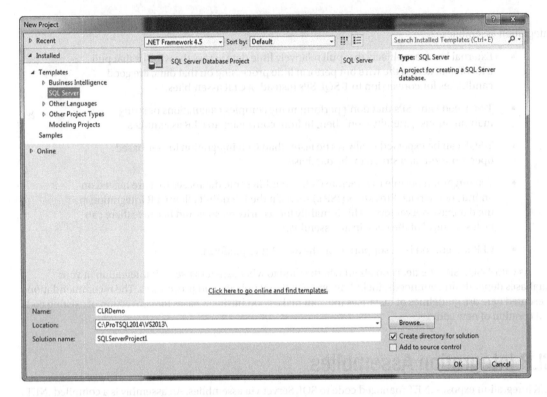

Figure 16-1. *Visual Studio 2013 New Project dialog box*

3. A new SQL Server database project is created in the SQL Server 2014 target platform. You can verify the target platform by selecting Project ➤ CLRDemo Properties, as shown in Figure 16-2. This brings up the properties of your current project, where you can verify the target platform; see Figure 16-3.

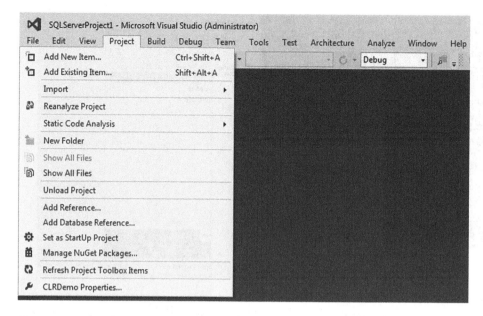

Figure 16-2. *Database project properties menu*

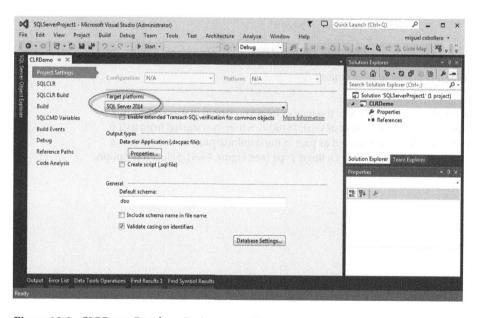

Figure 16-3. *CLRDemo Database Project properties*

4. Highlight the project name in the Solution Explorer, right-click, and choose Add ➤ New Item (Ctrl+Shift+A), as shown in Figure 16-4.

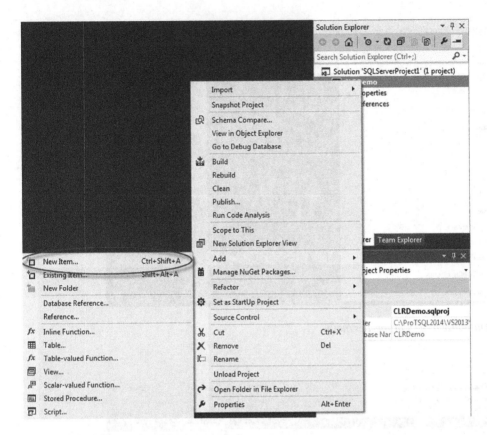

Figure 16-4. Adding a new item to your project

5.   Visual Studio asks you to select the type of item you would like to add. This is different from preview version of Visual Studio, where you started from a CLR Project type. This is now treated as part of the database project, and there is a new option: SQL CLR C# User Defined Type (see Figure 16-5). Select this option.

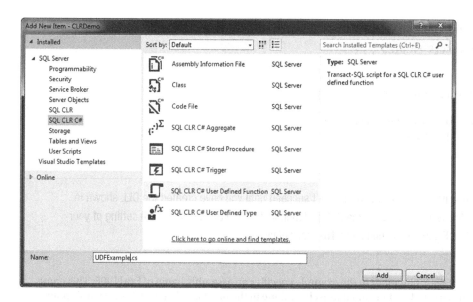

Figure 16-5. Adding a new SQL CLR C# User Defined Type to your project

6. Visual Studio automatically generates a template for the item you select in the language of your choice, complete with the appropriate Imports statements in VB.NET or using in C#.

In addition to the standard .NET namespaces and classes, CLR integration implements some SQL Server-specific namespaces and classes to simplify interfacing your code with SQL Server. Some of the most commonly used namespaces include the following:

- System, which includes the base .NET data types and the Object base class from which all .NET classes inherit.

- System.Data, which contains the DataSet class and other classes for ADO.NET data management.

- System.Data.SqlClient, which contains the SQL Server-specific ADO.NET data provider.

- System.Data.SqlTypes, which contains SQL Server data types. This is important because (unlike the standard .NET data types) these types can be set to SQL NULL and are defined to conform to the same operator rules, behaviors, precision, and scale as their SQL Server type counterparts.

- Microsoft.SqlServer.Server, which contains the SqlContext and SqlPipe classes that allow assemblies to communicate with SQL Server.

Once the assembly is created and compiled, it's registered with SQL Server via the CREATE ASSEMBLY statement. Listing 16-1 demonstrates a CREATE ASSEMBLY statement that registers a CLR integration assembly with SQL Server from an external DLL file. The DLL file used in the example isn't supplied in precompiled form in the sample downloads for this book available on the Apress web site, but you can compile it yourself from the code introduced in Listing 16-2. CLR integration isn't enabled by default, so you also need to enable it at the server level. Here, you do that using the sp_configure system stored procedure prior to running the CREATE ASSEMBLY statement. (CREATE ASSEMBLY would succeed even if CLR integration was disabled; an error would be raised by SQL Server only when a CLR integration code module was called by a user later.) The RECONFIGURE statement applies the configuration change immediately.

Listing 16-1. Registering a CLR Integration Assembly with SQL Server

```
EXEC sp_configure 'CLR Enabled';
RECONFIGURE;

CREATE ASSEMBLY ApressExamples
AUTHORIZATION dbo
FROM N'C:\MyApplication\CLRDemo.DLL'
WITH PERMISSION_SET = SAFE;
GO
```

■ **Note** The second portion of Listing 16-1 won't succeed until you have created the DLL shown in Listing 16-2. Additionally, the location of the DLL is dependent on the Build Output Path setting of your database project. See Figure 16-6 and Figure 16-7 for details.

The CREATE ASSEMBLY statement in the example specifies an assembly name of EmailUDF. This name must be a valid SQL Server identifier, and it must be unique in the database. You use this assembly name when referencing the assembly in other statements.

The AUTHORIZATION clause specifies the owner of the assembly, in this case dbo. If you leave out the AUTHORIZATION clause, it defaults to the current user.

The FROM clause in this example specifies the full path to the external DLL file. Alternatively, you can specify a varbinary value instead of a character file name. If you use a varbinary value, SQL Server uses it, as it's a long binary string representing the compiled assembly code, and no external file needs to be specified.

Finally, the WITH PERMISSION_SET clause grants a set of Code Access Security (CAS) permissions to the assembly. Valid permission sets include the following:

- The SAFE permission set is the most restrictive, preventing the assembly from accessing system resources outside of SQL Server. SAFE is the default.

- EXTERNAL_ACCESS allows assemblies to access some external resources, such as files, the network, the registry, and environment variables.

- UNSAFE allows assemblies unlimited access to external resources, including the ability to execute unmanaged code.

After the assembly is installed, you can use variations of the T-SQL database object-creation statements (such as CREATE FUNCTION or CREATE PROCEDURE) to access the methods exposed by the assembly classes. These statements are demonstrated individually in the following sections.

User-Defined Functions

CLR integration UDFs that return scalar values are similar to standard .NET functions. The primary differences from standard .NET functions are that the SqlFunction attribute must be applied to the main function of CLR integration functions if you're using Visual Studio to deploy your function or if you need to set additional attribute values like IsDeterministic and DataAccess. Listing 16-2 demonstrates a scalar UDF that accepts an input string value and a regular expression pattern and returns a bit value indicating a match (1) or no match (0). The UDF is named EmailMatch() and is declared as a method of the UDFExample class in the Apress.Example namespace used for all the examples in this chapter.

Listing 16-2. Regular Expression Match UDF

```
using System.Data.SqlTypes;
using System.Text.RegularExpressions;

namespace Apress.Examples
{
    public static class UDFExample
    {
        private static readonly Regex email_pattern = new Regex
        (
        // Everything before the @ sign (the "local part")
        "^[a-z0-9!#$%&'*+/=?^_`{|}~-]+(?:\\.[a-z0-9!#$%&'*+/=?^_`{|}~-]+)*" +

        // Subdomains after the @ sign
        "@(?:[a-z0-9](?:[a-z0-9-]*[a-z0-9])?\\.)+" +

        // Top-level domains
        "(?:[a-z]{2}|com|org|net|gov|mil|biz|info|mobi|name|aero|jobs|museum)\\b$"
        );

        [Microsoft.SqlServer.Server.SqlFunction
        (
        IsDeterministic = true
        )]
        public static SqlBoolean EmailMatch(SqlString input)
        {
            SqlBoolean result = new SqlBoolean();
            if (input.IsNull)
                result = SqlBoolean.Null;
            else
                result = (email_pattern.IsMatch(input.Value.ToLower()) == true)
                ? SqlBoolean.True : SqlBoolean.False;
            return result;
        }
    }
}
```

In order to compile this code, you must build your database project (see Figure 16-6). Doing so creates the DLL that you deploy to your database.

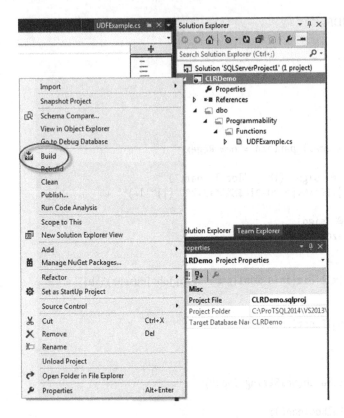

Figure 16-6. *Build your project, to compile the UDF*

The location of your DLL output is dependent on the build configuration of your database project. You can change the location to suit your needs. Figure 16-7 shows how to specify where your objects should reside when the project is built.

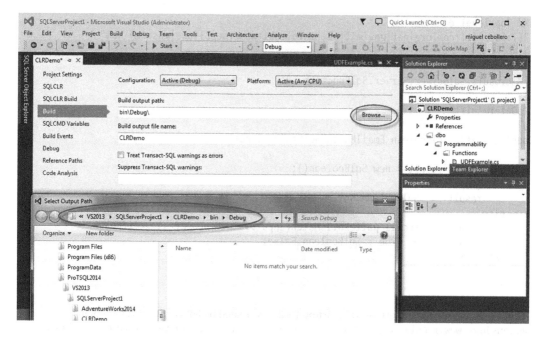

Figure 16-7. *Build location of objects in your project*

The first part of Listing 16-2 specifies the required namespaces to import. This UDF uses the
System.Data.SqlTypes and System.Text.RegularExpressions namespaces:

```
using System.Data.SqlTypes;
using System.Text.RegularExpressions;
```

The UDFExample class and the EmailMatch function it exposes are both declared static. CLR integration
functions need to be declared as static. A static function is shared among all instances of the class. Here,
the class itself is also static, so it can't be instantiated; this allows the class to be loaded more quickly and
its memory to be shared between SQL Server sessions. The function is decorated with the Microsoft.
SqlServer.Server.SqlFunction attribute with the IsDeterministic property set to true to indicate the
function is a deterministic CLR integration method. The function body is relatively simple. It accepts an
SqlString input string value. If the input string is NULL, the function returns NULL; otherwise the function
uses the .NET Regex.IsMatch function to perform a regular expression match. If the result is a match, the
function returns a bit value of 1; otherwise it returns 0:

```
public static class UDFExample
{
    private static readonly Regex email_pattern = new Regex
    (
    // Everything  before  the  @  sign  (the  "local  part")
    "^[a-z0-9!#$%&'*+/=?^_`{|}~-]+(?:\\.[a-z0-9!#$%&'*+/=?^_`{|}~-]+)*" +

    // Subdomains  after  the  @  sign
    "@(?:[a-z0-9](?:[a-z0-9-]*[a-z0-9])?\\.)+" +
```

```
// Top-level domains
"(?:[a-z]{2}|com|org|net|gov|mil|biz|info|mobi|name|aero|jobs|museum)\\b$"
);

[Microsoft.SqlServer.Server.SqlFunction
(
IsDeterministic = true
)]
public static SqlBoolean EmailMatch(SqlString input)
{
    SqlBoolean result = new SqlBoolean();
    if (input.IsNull)
        result = SqlBoolean.Null;
    else
        result = (email_pattern.IsMatch(input.Value.ToLower()) == true)
        ? SqlBoolean.True : SqlBoolean.False;
    return result;
}
}
```

The regular expression pattern used in Listing 16-2 was created by Jan Goyvaerts of Regular-Expressions.info (www.regular-expressions.info). Jan's regular expression validates e-mail addresses according to RFC 2822, the standard for e-mail address formats. Although not perfect, Jan estimates that this regular expression matches over 99% of "e-mail addresses in actual use today." Performing this type of e-mail address validation using only T-SQL statements would be cumbersome, complex, and inefficient.

■ **Tip** It's considered good practice to use the SQL Server data types for parameters and return values to CLR Integration methods (SqlString, SqlBoolean, SqlInt32, and so on). Standard .NET data types have no concept of SQL NULL and will error out if NULL is passed in as a parameter, calculated in the function, or returned from the function.

After the assembly is installed via the CREATE ASSEMBLY statement you wrote in Listing 16-1, the function is created with the CREATE FUNCTION statement using the EXTERNAL NAME clause, as shown in Listing 16-3.

Listing 16-3. Creating a CLR UDF from the Assembly Method

```
CREATE FUNCTION dbo.EmailMatch (@input nvarchar(4000))
RETURNS bit
WITH EXECUTE AS CALLER
AS
EXTERNAL NAME ApressExamples.[Apress.Examples.UDFExample].EmailMatch
GO
```

After this, the CLR function can be called like any other T-SQL UDF, as shown in Listing 16-4. The results are shown in Figure 16-8.

Listing 16-4. Validating E-mail Addresses with Regular Expressions

```
SELECT
    'nospam-123@yahoo.com' AS Email,
    dbo.EmailMatch (N'nospam-123@yahoo.com') AS Valid
UNION
SELECT
    '123@456789',
    dbo.EmailMatch('123@456789')
UNION
    SELECT 'BillyG@HOTMAIL.COM',
    dbo.EmailMatch('BillyG@HOTMAIL.COM');
```

	Email	Valid
1	123@456789	0
2	BillyG@HOTMAIL.COM	1
3	nospam-123@yahoo.com	1

Figure 16-8. Results of e-mail address validation with regular expressions

■ **Tip** Normally you can automate the process of compiling your assembly, registering it with SQL Server, and installing the CLR Integration UDF with Visual Studio's Build and Deploy option. You can also test the CLR Integration UDF with the Visual Studio Debug and Start Debugging option. This doesn't work with Visual Studio 2010, because it doesn't recognize SQL Server 2012, which was released after Visual Studio. In Visual Studio 11 and 2013, you can deploy the assembly with Visual Studio. This is just a detail; it's straightforward to copy the assembly on the server and register it manually with CREATE ASSEMBLY as shown in Listing 16-1.

As mentioned previously, CLR UDFs also allow tabular results to be returned to the caller. This example demonstrates another situation in which CLR integration can be a useful supplement to T-SQL functionality: accessing external resources such as the file system, network resources, or even the Internet. Listing 16-5 uses a CLR function to retrieve the Yahoo Top News Stories RSS feed and return the results as a table. Table-valued CLR UDFs are a little more complex than scalar functions. This code could be added to the same Visual Studio project that you created for the first CLR function example. Here you create another class named YahooRSS.

Listing 16-5. Retrieving the Yahoo Top News Stories RSS Feed

```
using System;
using System.Collections;
using System.Data.SqlTypes;
using Microsoft.SqlServer.Server;
using System.Xml;
```

```csharp
namespace Apress.Examples {
    public partial class YahooRSS {

        [Microsoft.SqlServer.Server.SqlFunction (
            IsDeterministic = false,
            DataAccess = DataAccessKind.None,
            TableDefinition = "title nvarchar(256),"
            + "link nvarchar(256), "
            + "pubdate datetime, "
            + "description nvarchar(max)",
            FillRowMethodName = "GetRow" )
        ]
        public static IEnumerable GetYahooNews() {
            XmlTextReader xmlsource =
                new XmlTextReader("http://rss.news.yahoo.com/rss/topstories");
            XmlDocument newsxml = new XmlDocument();
            newsxml.Load(xmlsource);
            xmlsource.Close();
            return newsxml.SelectNodes("//rss/channel/item");
        }

        private static void GetRow (
            Object o,
            out SqlString title,
            out SqlString link,
            out SqlDateTime pubdate,
            out SqlString description )
        {
            XmlElement element = (XmlElement)o;
            title = element.SelectSingleNode("./title").InnerText;
            link = element.SelectSingleNode("./link").InnerText;
            pubdate = DateTime.Parse(element.SelectSingleNode("./pubDate").InnerText);
            description = element.SelectSingleNode("./description").InnerText;
        }
    }
}
```

Before stepping through the source listing, let's address security, because this function accesses the Internet. Because the function needs to access an external resource, it requires EXTERNAL_ACCESS permissions. In order to deploy a non-SAFE assembly, one of two sets of conditions must be met:

- The database must be marked TRUSTWORTHY, and the user installing the assembly must have EXTERNAL ACCESS ASSEMBLY or UNSAFE ASSEMBLY permission.

- Or the assembly must be signed with an asymmetric key or certificate associated with a login that has proper permissions.

To meet the first set of requirements, do the following:

1. Execute the ALTER DATABASE AdventureWorks SET TRUSTWORTHY ON; statement.

2. In Visual Studio, select Project ➤ CLRDemo Properties ➤ SQLCLR, and change the permission level to EXTERNAL_ACCESS (see Figure 16-9).

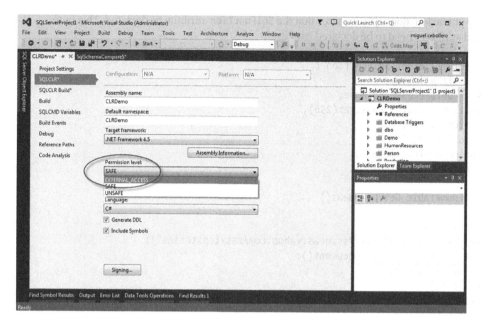

Figure 16-9. *Alter the permission level of your database project SQLCLR*

3. If you manually import the assembly into SQL Server, specify the `EXTERNAL_ ACCESS` permission set when issuing the `CREATE ASSEMBLY` statement, as shown in Listing 16-6.

Listing 16-6. `CREATE ASSEMBLY` with `EXTERNAL_ACCESS` Permission Set

```
CREATE ASSEMBLY ApressExample
AUTHORIZATION dbo
FROM N'C:\MyApplication\CLRDemo.DLL'
WITH PERMISSION_SET = EXTERNAL_ACCESS;
```

As mentioned previously, signing assemblies is beyond the scope of this book. You can find additional information on signing assemblies in this MSDN Data Access Technologies blog entry: `http://blogs.msdn.com/b/dataaccesstechnologies/archive/2011/10/29/deploying-sql-clr-assembly-using-asymmetric-key.aspx`.

The code listing begins with the `using` statements. This function requires the addition of the `System.Xml` namespace in order to parse the RSS feed and the `System.Collections` namespace to allow the collection to be searched, among other functionality specific to collections:

```
using System;
using System.Collections;
using System.Data.SqlTypes;
using Microsoft.SqlServer.Server;
using System.Xml;
```

The primary public function again requires that the SqlFunction attribute be declared. This time several additional attributes need to be declared with it:

```
[Microsoft.SqlServer.Server.SqlFunction (
    IsDeterministic = false,
    DataAccess = DataAccessKind.None,
    TableDefinition = "title nvarchar(256),"
    + "link nvarchar(256), "
    + "pubdate datetime, "
    + "description nvarchar(max)",
    FillRowMethodName = "GetRow" )
]
public static IEnumerable GetYahooNews()
{
    XmlTextReader xmlsource =
        new XmlTextReader("http://rss.news.yahoo.com/rss/topstories");
    XmlDocument newsxml = new XmlDocument();
    newsxml.Load(xmlsource);
    xmlsource.Close();
    return newsxml.SelectNodes("//rss/channel/item");
}
```

You specifically set the IsDeterministic attribute to false this time to indicate that the contents of an RSS feed can change between calls, making this UDF nondeterministic. Because the function doesn't read data from system tables using the in-process data provider, the DataAccess attribute is set to DataAccessKind.None. This CLR TVF also sets the additional TableDefinition attribute defining the structure of the result set for Visual Studio. In addition, it needs the FillRowMethodName attribute to designate the fill-row method. The fill-row method is a user method that converts each element of an IEnumerable object into an SQL Server result set row.

The public function is declared to return an IEnumerable result. This particular function opens an XmlTextReader that retrieves the Yahoo Top News Stories RSS feed and stores it in an XmlDocument. The function then uses the SelectNodes method to retrieve news story summaries from the RSS feed. The SelectNodes method generates an XmlNodeList. The XmlNodeList class implements the IEnumerable interface. This is important because the fill-row method is fired once for each object returned by the IEnumerable collection returned (in this case, the XmlNodeList).

The GetRow method is declared as a C# void function, which means no value is returned by the function; the method communicates with SQL Server via its out parameters. The first parameter is an Object passed by value—in this case, an XmlElement. The remaining parameters correspond to the columns of the result set. The GetRow method casts the first parameter to an XmlElement (the parameter can't be directly an XmlElement because the fill-row method signature must have an Object as the first parameter). It then uses the SelectSingleNode method and InnerText property to retrieve the proper text from individual child nodes of the XmlElement, assigning each to the proper columns of the result set along the way:

```
private static void GetRow (
    Object o,
    out SqlString title,
    out SqlString link,
    out SqlDateTime pubdate,
    out SqlString description )
```

```
{
    XmlElement element = (XmlElement)o;
    title = element.SelectSingleNode("./title").InnerText;
    link = element.SelectSingleNode("./link").InnerText;
    pubdate = DateTime.Parse(element.SelectSingleNode("./pubDate").InnerText);
    description = element.SelectSingleNode("./description").InnerText;
}
```

The CLR TVF can be called with a SELECT query, as shown in Listing 16-7. The results are shown in Figure 16-10.

Listing 16-7. Querying a CLR Integration TVF

```
CREATE FUNCTION dbo.GetYahooNews()
RETURNS TABLE(title nvarchar(256), link nvarchar(256), pubdate datetime, description
nvarchar(max))
AS EXTERNAL NAME ApressExamples.[Apress.Examples.YahooRSS].GetYahooNews
GO

SELECT
    title,
    link,
    pubdate,
    description
FROM dbo.GetYahooNews();
```

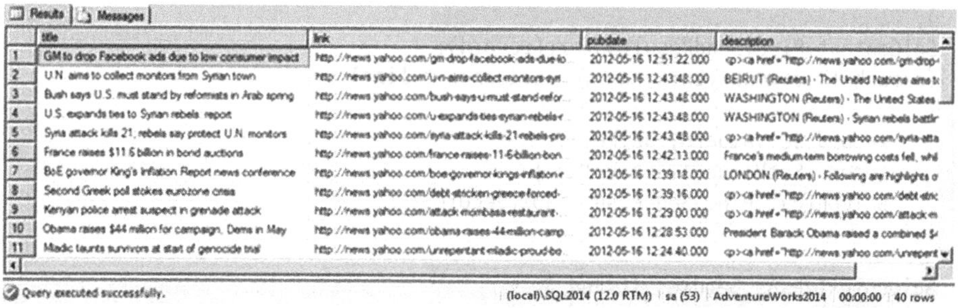

Figure 16-10. Retrieving the Yahoo RSS feed with the GetYahooNews() function

Stored Procedures

CLR integration SPs provide an alternative to extend SQL Server functionality when T-SQL SPs just won't do. Of course, like other CLR integration functionality, there is a certain amount of overhead involved with CLR SPs, and you can expect them to be less efficient than comparable T-SQL code for set-based operations. On the other hand, if you need to access .NET functionality or external resources, or if you have code that is computationally intensive, CLR integration SPs can provide an excellent alternative to straight T-SQL code.

Listing 16-8 shows how to use CLR integration to retrieve operating system environment variables and return them as a recordset via an SP. In the Apress.Examples namespace, you create a SampleProc class.

Listing 16-8. Retrieving Environment Variables with a CLR Stored Procedure

```
using System;
using System.Collections;
using System.Data;

using System.Data.SqlClient;
using System.Data.SqlTypes;
using Microsoft.SqlServer.Server;
namespace Apress.Examples
{
    public partial class SampleProc
    {
        [Microsoft.SqlServer.Server.SqlProcedure()]
        public static void GetEnvironmentVars()
        {
            try
            {
                SortedList environment_list = new SortedList();
                foreach (DictionaryEntry de in Environment.GetEnvironmentVariables())
                {
                    environment_list[de.Key] = de.Value;
                }

                SqlDataRecord record = new SqlDataRecord (
                    new SqlMetaData("VarName", SqlDbType.NVarChar, 1024),
                    new SqlMetaData("VarValue", SqlDbType.NVarChar, 4000)
                );
                SqlContext.Pipe.SendResultsStart(record);
                foreach (DictionaryEntry de in environment_list)
                {
                    record.SetValue(0, de.Key);
                    record.SetValue(1, de.Value);
                    SqlContext.Pipe.SendResultsRow(record);
                }

                SqlContext.Pipe.SendResultsEnd();
            }
            catch (Exception ex)
            {
                SqlContext.Pipe.Send(ex.Message);
            }
        }
    }
};
```

As with the previous CLR integration examples, appropriate namespaces are imported at the top:

```
using System;
using System.Collections;
using System.Data;
using System.Data.SqlClient;
using System.Data.SqlTypes;
using Microsoft.SqlServer.Server;
```

The GetEnvironmentVars() method is declared as a public void function. The SqlProcedure() attribute is applied to the function in this code to indicate to Visual Studio that this is a CLR SP. The body of the SP is wrapped in a try...catch block to capture any .NET exceptions, which are returned to SQL Server. If an exception occurs in the .NET code, it's sent back to SQL Server via the SqlContext.Pipe.Send method:

```
public partial class SampleProc
{
    [Microsoft.SqlServer.Server.SqlProcedure()]
    public static void GetEnvironmentVars()
    {
        try
        {
            ...
        }
        catch (Exception ex)
        {
            SqlContext.Pipe.Send(ex.Message);
        }
    }
};
```

THROWING READABLE EXCEPTIONS

When you need to raise an exception in a CLR SP, you have two options. For code readability reasons, I've chosen the simpler option of allowing exceptions to bubble up through the call stack. This results in .NET Framework exceptions being returned to SQL Server. The .NET Framework exceptions return a lot of extra information, like call stack data, however.

If you want to raise a nice, simple SQL Server–style error without all the extra .NET Framework exception information, you can use a method introduced in the book *Pro SQL Server 2005*, by Thomas Rizzo et al. (Apress, 2005). This second method involves using the ExecuteAndSend() method of the SqlContext.Pipe to execute a T-SQL RAISERROR statement. This method is shown in the following C# code snippet:

```
try {
    SqlContext.Pipe.ExecuteAndSend("RAISERROR ('This is a T-SQL Error', 16, 1);");
}
catch
{
    // do nothing
}
```

The ExecuteAndSend() method call executes the RAISERROR statement on the current context connection. The try...catch block surrounding the call prevents the .NET exception generated by the RAISERROR to be handled by .NET and reported as a new error. Keep this method in mind if you want to raise SQL Server–style errors instead of returning the verbose .NET Framework exception information to SQL Server.

As the procedure begins, all the environment variable names and their values are copied from the .NET Hashtable returned by the Environment.GetEnvironmentVariables() function to a .NET SortedList. In this procedure, I chose to use the SortedList to ensure that the results are returned in order by key. I added the SortedList for display purposes, but it's not required. Greater efficiency can be gained by iterating the Hashtable directly without a SortedList:

```
SortedList environment_list = new SortedList();
foreach (DictionaryEntry de in Environment.GetEnvironmentVariables())
{
    environment_list[de.Key] = de.Value;
}
```

The procedure uses the SqlContext.Pipe to return results to SQL Server as a result set. The first step of using the SqlContext.Pipe to send results back is to set up an SqlRecord with the structure that you wish the result set to take. For this example, the result set consists of two nvarchar columns: VarName, which contains the environment variable names; and VarValue, which contains their corresponding values:

```
SqlDataRecord record = new SqlDataRecord (
    new SqlMetaData("VarName", SqlDbType.NVarChar, 1024),
    new SqlMetaData("VarValue", SqlDbType.NVarChar, 4000)
);
```

Next, the function calls the SendResultsStart() method with the SqlDataRecord to initialize the result set:

```
SqlContext.Pipe.SendResultsStart(record);
```

Then it's a simple matter of looping through the SortedList of environment variable key/value pairs and sending them to the server via the SendResultsRow() method:

```
foreach (DictionaryEntry de in environment_list) {
    record.SetValue(0, de.Key);
    record.SetValue(1, de.Value);
    SqlContext.Pipe.SendResultsRow(record);
}
```

The SetValue() method is called for each column of the SqlRecord to properly set the results, and then SendResultsRow() is called for each row. After all the results have been sent to the client, the SendResultsEnd() method of the SqlContext.Pipe is called to complete the result set and return the SqlContext.Pipe to its initial state:

```
SqlContext.Pipe.SendResultsEnd();
```

The GetEnvironmentVars CLR SP can be called using the T-SQL EXEC statement, shown in Listing 16-9. The results are shown in Figure 16-11.

Listing 16-9. Executing the GetEnvironmentVars CLR Procedure

```
CREATE PROCEDURE dbo.GetEnvironmentVars
AS EXTERNAL NAME ApressExamples.[Apress.Examples.SampleProc].GetEnvironmentVars;
GO

EXEC dbo.GetEnvironmentVars;
```

	VarName	VarValue
1	ALLUSERSPROFILE	C:\ProgramData
2	APPDATA	C:\Users\MSSQLSERVER\AppData\Roaming
3	CommonProgramFiles	C:\Program Files\Common Files
4	CommonProgramFiles(x86)	C:\Program Files (x86)\Common Files
5	CommonProgramW6432	C:\Program Files\Common Files
6	COMPLUS_MDA	InvalidVariant;RaceOnRCWCleanup;InvalidFunctionP...
7	COMPUTERNAME	SQL2012
8	ComSpec	C:\Windows\system32\cmd.exe
9	FP_NO_HOST_CHECK	NO
10	LOCALAPPDATA	C:\Users\MSSQLSERVER\AppData\Local
11	NUMBER_OF_PROCESSORS	1
12	OS	Windows_NT

Figure 16-11. *Retrieving environment variables with CLR*

User-Defined Aggregates

User-defined aggregates (UDAs) are an exciting addition to SQL Server's functionality. UDAs are similar to the built-in SQL aggregate functions (SUM, AVG, and so on) in that they can act on entire sets of data at once, as opposed to one item at a time. An SQL CLR UDA has access to .NET functionality and can operate on numeric, character, date/time, or even user-defined data types. A basic UDA has four required methods:

- The UDA calls its Init() method when the SQL Server engine prepares to aggregate. The code in this method can reset member variables to their start state, initialize buffers, and perform other initialization functions.

- The Accumulate() method is called as each row is processed, allowing you to aggregate the data passed in. The Accumulate() method might increment a counter, add a row's value to a running total, or possibly perform other more complex processing on a row's data.

- The Merge() method is invoked when SQL Server decides to use parallel processing to complete an aggregate. If the query engine decides to use parallel processing, it creates multiple instances of your UDA and calls the Merge() method to join the results into a single aggregation.

- Terminate() is the final method of the UDA. It's called after all rows have been processed and any aggregates created in parallel have been merged. The Terminate() method returns the final result of the aggregation to the query engine.

■ **Tip** In SQL Server 2005, there was a serialization limit of 8,000 bytes for an instance of an SQL CLR UDA, making certain tasks harder to perform using a UDA. For instance, creating an array, a hash table, or another structure to hold intermediate results during an aggregation (like aggregates that calculate a statistical mode or median) could cause a UDA to very quickly run up against the 8,000-byte limit and throw an exception for large datasets. SQL Server 2008, 2012, and 2014 don't have this limitation.

Creating a Simple UDA

The example UDA in Listing 16-10 determines the statistical range for a set of numbers. The statistical range for a given set of numbers is the difference between the minimum and maximum values of the set. The UDA determines the minimum and maximum values of the set of numbers passed in and returns the difference.

Listing 16-10. Sample Statistical Range UDA

```
using System;
using System.Data;
using System.Data.SqlClient;
using System.Data.SqlTypes;
using Microsoft.SqlServer.Server;

namespace Apress.Examples {
    [Serializable]
    [Microsoft.SqlServer.Server.SqlUserDefinedAggregate(Format.Native)]

    public struct Range
    {
        SqlDouble min, max;

        public void Init() {
            min = SqlDouble.Null;
            max = SqlDouble.Null;
        }

        public void Accumulate(SqlDouble value)
        {
            if (!value.IsNull) {
                if (min.IsNull || value < min)
                {
                    min = value;
                }
```

```
                    if (max.IsNull || value > max)
                    {
                        max = value;
                    }
                }
            }

        public void Merge(Range group)
        {
            if (min.IsNull || (!group.min.IsNull && group.min < min))
            {
                min = group.min;
            }
            if (max.IsNull || (!group.max.IsNull && group.max > max))
            {
                max = group.max;
            }
        }

        public SqlDouble Terminate() {
            SqlDouble result = SqlDouble.Null;
            if (!min.IsNull && !max.IsNull)
            {
                result = max - min;
            }

            return result;
        }
    }
}
```

This UDA begins, like the previous CLR integration assemblies, by importing the proper namespaces:

```
using System;
using System.Data;
using System.Data.SqlClient;
using System.Data.SqlTypes;
using Microsoft.SqlServer.Server;
```

Next, the code declares the struct that represents the UDA. The attributes Serializable and SqlUserDefinedAggregate are applied to the struct. You use the Format.Native serialization format for this UDA. Because this is a simple UDA, Format.Native provides the best performance and is the easiest to implement. More complex UDAs that use reference types require Format.UserDefined serialization and must implement the IBinarySerialize interface:

```
[Serializable]
[Microsoft.SqlServer.Server.SqlUserDefinedAggregate(Format.Native)]
public struct Range
{
}
```

The struct declares two member variables, min and max, which hold the minimum and maximum values encountered during the aggregation process:

```
SqlDouble min, max;
```

The mandatory Init() method in the aggregate body initializes the min and max member variables to SqlDouble.Null:

```
public void Init() {
    min = SqlDouble.Null;
    max = SqlDouble.Null;
}
```

The Accumulate() method accepts a SqlDouble parameter. This method first checks that the value isn't NULL (NULL is ignored during aggregation). Then it checks to see if the value passed in is less than the min variable (or if min is NULL) and, if so, assigns the parameter value to min. The method also checks max and updates it if the parameter value is greater than max (or if max is NULL). In this way, the min and max values are determined on the fly as the query engine feeds values into the Accumulate() method:

```
public void Accumulate(SqlDouble value)
    {
        if (!value.IsNull) {
            if (min.IsNull || value < min)
            {
                min = value;
            }

            if (max.IsNull || value > max)
            {
                max = value;
            }
        }
    }
```

The Merge() method merges a Range structure that was created in parallel with the current structure. The method accepts a Range structure and compares its min and max variables to those of the current Range structure. It then adjusts the current structure's min and max variables based on the Range structure passed into the method, effectively merging the two results:

```
public void Merge(Range group)
{
    if (min.IsNull || (!group.min.IsNull && group.min < min))
    {
        min = group.min;
    }
    if (max.IsNull || (!group.max.IsNull && group.max > max))
    {
        max = group.max;
    }
}
```

The final method of the UDA is the Terminate() function, which returns an SqlDouble result. This function checks for min or max results that are NULL. The UDA returns NULL if either min or max is NULL. If neither min nor max is NULL, the result is the difference between the max and min values:

```
public SqlDouble Terminate() {
    SqlDouble result = SqlDouble.Null;
    if (!min.IsNull && !max.IsNull)
    {
        result = max - min;
    }

    return result;
}
```

■ **Note**   The Terminate() method must return the same data type that the Accumulate() method accepts. If these data types don't match, an error will occur. Also, as mentioned previously, it's best practice to use the SQL Server–specific data types, because the standard .NET types will choke on NULL.

Listing 16-11 is a simple test of this UDA. The test determines the statistical range of unit prices that customers have paid for AdventureWorks products. Information like this, on a per-product or per-model basis, can be paired with additional information to help the AdventureWorks sales teams set optimal price points for their products. The results are shown in Figure 16-12.

Listing 16-11. Retrieving Statistical Ranges with a UDA

```
CREATE AGGREGATE Range (@value float) RETURNS float
EXTERNAL NAME ApressExamples.[Apress.Examples.Range];
GO

SELECT
    ProductID,
    dbo.Range(UnitPrice) AS UnitPriceRange
FROM Sales.SalesOrderDetail
WHERE UnitPrice > 0
GROUP BY ProductID;
```

	ProductID	UnitPriceRange
1	707	19.2445
2	708	19.2445
3	709	0.95
4	710	0
5	711	19.2445
6	712	4.6679
7	713	0
8	714	22.4955
9	715	25.9563
10	716	22.111
11	717	100.8241
12	718	100.8241

Figure 16-12. *Results of the range aggregate applied to unit prices*

■ **Caution** This UDA is an example. It's faster to use regular T-SQL aggregation functions for this type of calculation, especially if you have a large number of rows to process.

Creating an Advanced UDA

You can create more advanced CLR aggregates that use reference data types and user-defined serialization. When creating a UDA that uses reference (nonvalue) data types such as ArrayLists, SortedLists, and Objects, CLR integration imposes the additional restriction that you can't mark the UDA for Format.Native serialization. Instead, these aggregates have to be marked for Format.UserDefined serialization, which means the UDA must implement the IBinarySerialize interface, including both the Read and Write methods. Basically, you have to tell SQL Server how to serialize your data when using reference types. There is a performance impact associated with Format.UserDefined serialization as opposed to Format.Native.

Listing 16-12 is a UDA that calculates the statistical median of a set of numbers. The statistical median is the middle number of an ordered group of numbers. If the set contains an even number of values, the statistical median is the average (mean) of the middle two numbers in the set.

Listing 16-12. UDA to Calculate the Statistical Median

```
using System;
using System.Collections.Generic;
using System.Data;
using System.Data.SqlTypes;
using System.Runtime.InteropServices;
using Microsoft.SqlServer.Server;

namespace Apress.Examples {
    [Serializable]
    [Microsoft.SqlServer.Server.SqlUserDefinedAggregate (
        Format.UserDefined,
        IsNullIfEmpty = true,
        MaxByteSize = -1 )]
```

```csharp
[StructLayout(LayoutKind.Sequential)]

public struct Median : IBinarySerialize
{
    List<double> temp; // List of numbers

    public void Init()
    {
        // Create new list of double numbers
        this.temp = new List<double>();
    }

    public void Accumulate(SqlDouble number)
    {
        if (!number.IsNull) // Skip over NULLs
        {
            this.temp.Add(number.Value); // If number is not NULL, add it to list
        }
    }

    public void Merge(Median group)
    {
        // Merge two sets of numbers
        this.temp.InsertRange(this.temp.Count, group.temp);
    }

    public SqlDouble Terminate() {
        SqlDouble result = SqlDouble.Null; // Default result to NULL
        this.temp.Sort(); // Sort list of numbers

        int first, second; // Indexes to middle two numbers

        if (this.temp.Count % 2 == 1)
        {
            // If there is an odd number of values get the middle number twice
            first = this.temp.Count / 2;
            second = first;
        }
        else
        {
            // If there is an even number of values get the middle two numbers
            first = this.temp.Count / 2 - 1;
            second = first + 1;
        }

        if (this.temp.Count > 0) // If there are numbers, calculate median
        {
            // Calculate median as average of middle number(s)
            result = (SqlDouble)( this.temp[first] + this.temp[second] ) / 2.0;
        }

        return result;
    }

    #region IBinarySerialize Members
```

```
        // Custom serialization read method
        public void Read(System.IO.BinaryReader r)
        {
            // Create a new list of double values
            this.temp = new List<double>();

            // Get the number of values that were serialized
            int j = r.ReadInt32();

            // Loop and add each serialized value to the list
            for (int i = 0; i < j; i++)
            {
                this.temp.Add(r.ReadDouble());
            }
        }

        // Custom serialization write method
        public void Write(System.IO.BinaryWriter w)
        {
            // Write the number of values in the list
            w.Write(this.temp.Count);

            // Write out each value in the list
            foreach (double d in this.temp)
            {
                w.Write(d);
            }
        }

        #endregion
    }
}
```

This UDA begins, like the other CLR integration examples, with namespace imports. You add the System.Collections.Generic namespace this time so you can use the .NET List<T> strongly typed list:

```
using System;
using System.Collections.Generic;
using System.Data;
using System.Data.SqlTypes;
using System.Runtime.InteropServices;
using Microsoft.SqlServer.Server;
```

The Median structure in the example is declared with the Serializable attribute to indicate that it can be serialized, and the StructLayout attribute with the LayoutKind.Sequential property to force the structure to be serialized in sequential fashion for a UDA that has a Format different from Native. The SqlUserDefinedAggregate attribute declares three properties, as follows:

- Format.UserDefined indicates that the UDA implements serialization methods through the IBinarySerialize interface. This is required because the List<T> reference type is being used in the UDA.

- IsNullIfEmpty is set to true, indicating that NULL will be returned if no rows are passed to the UDA.

- MaxByteSize is set to -1 so that the UDA can be serialized if it's greater than 8,000 bytes. (The 8,000-byte serialization limit was a strict limit in SQL Server 2005 that prevented serialization of large objects, like large ArrayList objects, in the UDA).

Because Format.UserDefined is specified on the Median structure, it must implement the IBinarySerialize interface. In the body of the struct, you define a List<double> named temp that holds an intermediate temporary list of numbers passed into the UDA:

```
[Serializable]
[Microsoft.SqlServer.Server.SqlUserDefinedAggregate (
    Format.UserDefined,
    IsNullIfEmpty = true,
    MaxByteSize = -1 )]
[StructLayout(LayoutKind.Sequential)]
public struct Median : IBinarySerialize
{
    List<double> temp; // List of numbers
    ...
}
```

The Read() and Write() methods of the IBinarySerialize interface are used to deserialize and serialize the list, respectively:

```
#region IBinarySerialize Members

// Custom serialization read method
public void Read(System.IO.BinaryReader r)
{
    // Create a new list of double values
    this.temp = new List<double>();

    // Get the number of values that were serialized
    int j = r.ReadInt32();

    // Loop and add each serialized value to the list
    for (int i = 0; i < j; i++)
    {
        this.temp.Add(r.ReadDouble());
    }
}
```

```
// Custom serialization write method
public void Write(System.IO.BinaryWriter w)
{
    // Write the number of values in the list
    w.Write(this.temp.Count);

    // Write out each value in the list
    foreach (double d in this.temp)
    {
        w.Write(d);
    }
}
```

#endregion

The Init method of the UDA initializes the temp list by creating a new List<double> instance:

```
public void Init() {
    // Create new list of double numbers
    this.temp = new List<double>();
}
```

The Accumulate() method accepts a SqlDouble number and adds all non-NULL values to the temp list. Although you can include NULLs in your aggregate results, keep in mind that T-SQL developers are used to the NULL handling of built-in aggregate functions like SUM and AVG. In particular, developers are used to their aggregate functions discarding NULL. This is the main reason you eliminate NULL in this UDA:

```
public void Accumulate(SqlDouble number)
{
    if (!number.IsNull) // Skip over NULLs
    {
        this.temp.Add(number.Value); // If number is not NULL, add it to list
    }
}
```

The Merge() method in the example merges two lists of numbers if SQL Server decides to calculate the aggregate in parallel. If so, the server passes a list of numbers into the Merge() method. This list of numbers must then be appended to the current list. For efficiency, you use the InsertRange() method of List<T> to combine the lists:

```
public void Merge(Median group)
{
    // Merge two sets of numbers
    this.temp.InsertRange(this.temp.Count, group.temp);
}
```

The Terminate() method of the UDA sorts the list of values and then determines the indexes of the middle values. If there is an odd number of values in the list, there is only a single middle value; if there is an even number of values in the list, the median is the average of the middle two values. If the list contains no values (which can occur if every value passed to the aggregate is NULL), the result is NULL; otherwise the Terminate() method calculates and returns the median:

```
public SqlDouble Terminate() {
    SqlDouble result = SqlDouble.Null; // Default result to NULL
    this.temp.Sort(); // Sort list of numbers

    int first, second; // Indexes to middle two numbers

    if (this.temp.Count % 2 == 1)
    {
        // If there is an odd number of values get the middle number twice
        first = this.temp.Count / 2;
        second = first;
    }
    else
    {
        // If there is an even number of values get the middle two numbers
        first = this.temp.Count / 2 - 1;
        second = first + 1;
    }

    if (this.temp.Count > 0) // If there are numbers, calculate median
    {
        // Calculate median as average of middle number(s)
        result = (SqlDouble)( this.temp[first] + this.temp[second] ) / 2.0;
    }

    return result;
}
```

Listing 16-13 demonstrates the use of this UDA to calculate the median UnitPrice from the Sales.SalesOrderDetail table on a per-product basis. The results are shown in Figure 16-13.

Listing 16-13. Calculating the Median Unit Price with a UDA

```
CREATE AGGREGATE dbo.Median (@value float) RETURNS float
EXTERNAL NAME ApressExamples.[Apress.Examples.Median];
GO

SELECT
    ProductID,
    dbo.Median(UnitPrice) AS MedianUnitPrice
FROM Sales.SalesOrderDetail
GROUP BY ProductID;
```

	ProductID	Median Unit Price
1	707	34,99
2	708	34,99
3	709	5,7
4	710	5,7
5	711	34,99
6	712	8,99
7	713	49,99
8	714	29,994
9	715	29,994
10	716	29,994
11	717	780,8182
12	718	780,8182

Figure 16-13. Median unit price for each product

CLR Integration User-Defined Types

SQL Server 2000 had built-in support for user-defined data types, but they were limited in scope and functionality. The old-style user-defined data types had the following restrictions and capabilities:

- They had to be derived from built-in data types.

- Their format and/or range could only be restricted through T-SQL rules.

- They could be assigned a default value.

- They could be declared as NULL or NOT NULL.

SQL Server 2014 provides support for old-style user-defined data types and rules, presumably for backward compatibility with existing applications. The AdventureWorks database contains examples of old-style user-defined data types, like the dbo.Phone data type, which is an alias for the varchar(25) data type.

■ **Caution** Rules (CHECK constraints that can be applied to user-defined data types) have been deprecated since SQL Server 2005 and will be removed from a future version. T-SQL user-defined data types are now often referred to as alias types.

SQL Server 2014 supports a far more flexible solution to your custom data type needs in the form of CLR user-defined types. CLR integration user-defined types allow you to access the power of the .NET Framework. Common examples of CLR UDTs include mathematical concepts like points, vectors, complex numbers, and other types not built into the SQL Server type system. In fact, CLR UDTs are so powerful that Microsoft has begun including some as standard in SQL Server. These CLR UDTs include the spatial data types geography and geometry, and the hierarchyid data type.

CLR UDTs are useful for implementing data types that require special handling and that implement their own special methods and functions. Complex numbers, which are a superset of real numbers, are one example. Complex numbers are represented with a "real" part and an "imaginary" part in the format a+bi, where a is a real number representing the real part of the value, b is a real number representing the imaginary part, and the literal letter i after the imaginary part stands for the imaginary number i, which is the square root of -1. Complex numbers are often used in math, science, and engineering to solve difficult abstract problems. Some examples of complex numbers include 101.9+3.7i, 98+12i, -19i, and 12+0i (which can also be represented as 12). Because their format is different from real numbers and calculations with them require special functionality, complex numbers are a good candidate for CLR. The example in Listing 16-14 implements a complex number CLR UDT.

■ **Note**   To keep the example simple, only a partial implementation is reproduced here. The sample download file includes the full version of this CLR UDT that includes basic operators as well as additional documentation and implementations of many more mathematical operators and trigonometric functions.

Listing 16-14. Complex Numbers UDT

```
using System;
using System.Data.SqlTypes;
using Microsoft.SqlServer.Server;
using System.Text.RegularExpressions;

namespace Apress.Examples
{
    [Serializable]
    [Microsoft.SqlServer.Server.SqlUserDefinedType
      (
        Format.Native,
        IsByteOrdered = true
      )]
    public struct Complex : INullable
    {

        #region "Complex Number UDT Fields/Components"

        private bool m_Null;
        public Double real;
        public Double imaginary;

        #endregion

        #region "Complex Number Parsing, Constructor, and Methods/Properties"

        private static readonly Regex rx = new Regex(
          "^(?<Imaginary>[+-]?([0-9]+|[0-9]*\\.[0-9]+))[i|I]$|" +
          "^(?<Real>[+-]?([0-9]+|[0-9]*\\.[0-9]+))$|" +
          "^(?<Real>[+-]?([0-9]+|[0-9]*\\.[0-9]+))" +
          "(?<Imaginary>[+-]?([0-9]+|[0-9]*\\.[0-9]+))[i|I]$");
```

```
    public static Complex Parse(SqlString s)
    {
        Complex u = new Complex();
        if (s.IsNull)
            u = Null;
        else
        {
            MatchCollection m = rx.Matches(s.Value);
            if (m.Count == 0)
                throw (new FormatException("Invalid Complex Number Format."));
            String real_str = m[0].Groups["Real"].Value;
            String imaginary_str = m[0].Groups["Imaginary"].Value;
            if (real_str == "" && imaginary_str == "")
                throw (new FormatException("Invalid Complex Number Format."));
            if (real_str == "")
                u.real = 0.0;
            else
                u.real = Convert.ToDouble(real_str);
            if (imaginary_str == "")
                u.imaginary = 0.0;
            else
                u.imaginary = Convert.ToDouble(imaginary_str);
        }
        return u;
    }

    public override String ToString()
    {
        String sign = "";
        if (this.imaginary >= 0.0)
            sign = "+";
        return this.real.ToString() + sign + this.imaginary.ToString() + "i";
    }

    public bool IsNull
    {
        get
        {
            return m_Null;
        }
    }

    public static Complex Null
    {
        get
        {
            Complex h = new Complex();
            h.m_Null = true;
            return h;
        }
    }
```

```
    public Complex(Double r, Double i)
    {
        this.real = r;
        this.imaginary = i;
        this.m_Null = false;
    }

    #endregion

    #region "Complex Number Basic Operators"

    // Complex number addition

    public static Complex operator +(Complex n1, Complex n2)
    {
        Complex u;
        if (n1.IsNull || n2.IsNull)
            u = Null;
        else
            u = new Complex(n1.real + n2.real, n1.imaginary + n2.imaginary);
        return u;
    }

    #endregion

    #region "Exposed Mathematical Basic Operator Methods"

    // Add complex number n2 to n1
    public static Complex CAdd(Complex n1, Complex n2)
    {
        return n1 + n2;
    }

    // Subtract complex number n2 from n1
    public static Complex Sub(Complex n1, Complex n2)
    {
        return n1 - n2;
    }

    #endregion

    // other complex operations are available in the source code

    }
}
```

The code begins with the required namespace imports and the namespace declaration for the example:

```
using System;
using System.Data.SqlTypes;
using Microsoft.SqlServer.Server;
using System.Text.RegularExpressions;
```

Next is the declaration of the structure that represents an instance of the UDT. The Serializable, Format.Native, and IsByteOrdered=true attributes and attribute properties are all set on the UDT. In addition, all CLR UDTs must implement the INullable interface. INullable requires that the IsNull and Null properties be defined:

```
[Serializable]
[Microsoft.SqlServer.Server.SqlUserDefinedType
  (
    Format.Native,
    IsByteOrdered = true
  )]
public struct Complex : INullable
{
    ...
}
```

Table 16-1 shows a few of the common attributes that are used in CLR integration UDT definitions.

Table 16-1. Common CLR UDT Attributes

Attribute	Property	Value	Description
Serializable	n/a	n/a	Indicates that the UDT can be serialized and deserialized.
SqlUserDefinedType	Format.Native	n/a	Specifies that the UDT uses native format for serialization. The native format is the most efficient format for serialization/deserialization, but it imposes some limitations. You can only expose .NET value data types (Char, Integer, and o on) as the fields. You can't expose reference data types (Strings, Arrays, and so on).
SqlUserDefinedType	Format. UserDefined	n/a	Specifies that the UDT uses a user-defined format for serialization. When this is specified, your UDT must implement the IBinarySerialize interface, and you're responsible for supplying the Write() and Read() methods that serialize and deserialize your UDT.
SqlUserDefinedType	IsByteOrdered	true/false	Allows comparisons and sorting of UDT values based on their binary representation. This is also required if you intend to create indexes on columns defined as a CLR UDT type.
SqlUserDefinedType	IsFixedLength	true/false	Should be set to true if the serialized instance of your UDT is a fixed length.
SqlUserDefinedType	MaxByteSize	<= 8000 or -1	The maximum size of your serialized UDT instances in bytes. This value must be between 1 and 8,000; or it can be -1 for a maximum size of 2.1 GB.

The public and private fields are declared in the body of the Complex structure. The real and imaginary public fields represent the real and imaginary parts of the complex number, respectively. The m_Null field is a bool value that is set to true if the current instance of the complex type is NULL and is set to false otherwise:

```
#region "Complex Number UDT Fields/Components"

private bool m_Null;
public Double real;
public Double imaginary;

#endregion
```

The first method declared in the UDT is the Parse method (required by all UDTs), which takes a string value from SQL Server and parses it into a complex number. Parse uses a .NET regular expression to simplify parsing a bit:

```
private static readonly Regex rx = new Regex(
    "^(?<Imaginary>[+-]?([0-9]+|[0-9]*\\.[0-9]+))[i|I]$|" +
    "^(?<Real>[+-]?([0-9]+|[0-9]*\\.[0-9]+))$|" +
    "^(?<Real>[+-]?([0-9]+|[0-9]*\\.[0-9]+))" +
    "(?<Imaginary>[+-]?([0-9]+|[0-9]*\\.[0-9]+))[i|I]$");

public static Complex Parse(SqlString s)
{
    Complex u = new Complex();
    if (s.IsNull)
        u = Null;
    else
    {
        MatchCollection m = rx.Matches(s.Value);
        if (m.Count == 0)
            throw (new FormatException("Invalid Complex Number Format."));
        String real_str = m[0].Groups["Real"].Value;
        String imaginary_str = m[0].Groups["Imaginary"].Value;
        if (real_str == "" && imaginary_str == "")
            throw (new FormatException("Invalid Complex Number Format."));
        if (real_str == "")
            u.real = 0.0;
        else
            u.real = Convert.ToDouble(real_str);
        if (imaginary_str == "")
            u.imaginary = 0.0;
        else
            u.imaginary = Convert.ToDouble(imaginary_str);
    }
    return u;
}
```

The regular expression (a.k.a. regex) uses named groups to parse the input string into Real and/or Imaginary named groups. If the regex is successful, at least one (if not both) of these named groups will be populated. If unsuccessful, both named groups will be empty and an exception of type FormatException will be thrown. If at least one of the named groups is properly set, the string representations are converted to Double type and assigned to the appropriate UDT fields. Table 16-2 shows some sample input strings and the values assigned to the UDT fields when they're parsed.

Table 16-2. Complex Number-Parsing Samples

Complex Number	Real	Imaginary	m_Null
100+11i	100.0	11.0	false
99.9	99.9	0.0	false
3.7-9.8i	3.7	-9.8	false
2.1i	0.0	2.1	false
-9-8.2i	-9.0	-8.2	false
NULL			true

The ToString() method is required for all UDTs as well. This method converts the internal UDT data to its string representation. In the case of complex numbers, ToString() needs to perform the following steps:

1. Convert the real part to a string.

2. Append a plus sign (+) if the imaginary part is 0 or positive.

3. Append the imaginary part.

4. Append the letter i to indicate that it does in fact represent a complex number.

Notice that if the imaginary part is negative, no sign is appended between the real and imaginary parts, because the sign is already included in the imaginary part:

```
public override String ToString()
{
    String sign = "";
    if (this.imaginary >= 0.0)
        sign = "+";
    return this.real.ToString() + sign + this.imaginary.ToString() + "i";
}
```

The IsNull and Null properties are both required by all UDTs. IsNull is a bool property that indicates whether a UDT instance is NULL. The Null property returns a NULL instance of the UDT type. One thing you need to be aware of any time you invoke a UDT (or any CLR integration object) from T-SQL is SQL NULL. For purposes of the Complex UDT, you take a cue from T-SQL and return a NULL result any time a NULL is passed in as a parameter to any UDT method. So a Complex value plus NULL returns NULL, as does a Complex value divided by NULL, and so on. Notice that a lot of code in the complete Complex UDT listing is specifically designed to deal with NULL:

```
public bool IsNull
{
    get
    {
        return m_Null;
    }
}
```

```
public static Complex Null
{
    get
    {
        Complex h = new Complex();
        h.m_Null = true;
        return h;
    }
}
```

This particular UDT includes a constructor function that accepts two Double type values and creates a UDT instance from them:

```
public Complex(Double r, Double i)
{
    this.real = r;
    this.imaginary = i;
    this.m_Null = false;
}
```

■ **Tip**   For a UDT designed as a .NET structure, a constructor method isn't required. In fact, a default constructor (that takes no parameters) isn't even allowed. To keep later code simple, I added a constructor method to this example.

In the next region, you define a few useful complex number constants and expose them as static properties of the Complex UDT:

```
#region "Useful Complex Number Constants"

// The property "i" is the Complex number 0 + 1i. Defined here because
// it is useful in some calculations

public static Complex i
{
    get
    {
        return new Complex(0, 1);
    }
}

...

#endregion
```

To keep this listing short but highlight the important points, the sample UDT shows only the addition operator for complex numbers. The UDT overrides the + operator. Redefining operators makes it easier to write and debug additional UDT methods. These overridden .NET math operators aren't available to T-SQL code, so the standard T-SQL math operators won't work on the UDT:

```
// Complex number addition

public static Complex operator +(Complex n1, Complex n2)
{
    Complex u;
    if (n1.IsNull || n2.IsNull)
        u = Null;
    else
        u = new Complex(n1.real + n2.real, n1.imaginary + n2.imaginary);
    return u;
}
```

Performing mathematical operations on UDT values from T-SQL must be done via explicitly exposed methods of the UDT. These methods in the Complex UDT are CAdd and Div, for complex number addition and division, respectively. Note that I chose CAdd (which stands for "complex number add") as a method name to avoid conflicts with the T-SQL reserved word ADD. I won't go too deeply into the inner workings of complex numbers, but I chose to implement the basic operators in this listing because some (like complex number addition) are straightforward operations, whereas others (like division) are a bit more complicated. The math operator methods are declared as static, so they can be invoked on the UDT data type itself from SQL Server instead of on an instance of the UDT:

```
#region "Exposed Mathematical Basic Operator Methods"

// Add complex number n2 to n1
public static Complex CAdd(Complex n1, Complex n2)
{
    return n1 + n2;
}

// Subtract complex number n2 from n1
public static Complex Sub(Complex n1, Complex n2)
{
    return n1 - n2;
}

#endregion
```

■ **Note** Static methods of a UDT (declared with the `static` keyword in C# or the `Shared` keyword in Visual Basic) are invoked from SQL Server using a format like this: `Complex::CAdd(@n1, @n2)`. Nonshared, or instance, methods of a UDT are invoked from SQL Server using a format similar to this: `@>n1.CAdd(@n2)`. The style of method you use (shared or instance) is a determination you need to make on a case-by-case basis.

Listing 16-15 demonstrates how the `Complex` UDT can be used; the results are shown in Figure 16-14.

Listing 16-15. Using the Complex Number UDT

```
CREATE TYPE dbo.Complex
EXTERNAL NAME ApressExamples.[Apress.Examples.Complex];
GO

DECLARE @c complex = '+100-10i',
  @d complex = '5i';
SELECT 'ADD: ' + @c.ToString() + ' , ' + @d.ToString() AS Op,
  complex::CAdd(@c, @d).ToString() AS Result
UNION
SELECT 'DIV: ' + @c.ToString() + ' , ' + @d.ToString(),
  complex::Div(@c, @d).ToString()
UNION
SELECT 'SUB: ' + @c.ToString() + ' , ' + @d.ToString(),
  complex::Sub(@c, @d).ToString()
UNION
SELECT 'MULT: ' + @c.ToString() + ' , ' + @d.ToString(),
  complex::Mult(@c, @d).ToString()
UNION
SELECT 'PI:  ',
  complex::Pi.ToString();
```

	Op	Result
1	ADD: 100-10i , 0+5i	100-5i
2	DIV: 100-10i , 0+5i	-2-20i
3	MULT: 100-10i , 0+5i	50+500i
4	PI:	3.14159265358979+0i
5	SUB: 100-10i , 0+5i	100-15i

Figure 16-14. *Performing operations with the `Complex` UDT*

In addition to the basic operations, the `Complex` class can be easily extended to support several more advanced complex number operators and functions. The code sample download file contains a full listing of an expanded `Complex` UDT, including all the basic math operators, as well as logarithmic and exponential functions (`Log()`, `Power()`, etc.) and trigonometric and hyperbolic functions (`Sin()`, `Cos()`, `Tanh()`, etc.) for complex numbers.

Triggers

Finally, you can also create .NET triggers. This is logical; after all, triggers are just a specialized type of stored procedures. There are few examples of really interesting .NET triggers. Most of what you want to do in a trigger can be done with regular T-SQL code. When SQL Server 2005 was released, you saw an example of a .NET trigger on a location table that calls a web service to find the coordinates of a city and adds them to a coordinates column. This could at first sound like a cool idea, but if you remember that a trigger is fired in the scope of the DML statement's transaction, you can guess that the latency added to every insert and update on the table might be a problem. Usually, you try to keep the trigger impact as light as possible. Listing 16-16 presents an example of a .NET trigger based on your previous regular expression UDF. It tests an e-mail inserted or modified on the AdventureWorks Person.EmailAddress table, and rolls back the transaction if it doesn't match the pattern of a correct e-mail address. Let's see it in action.

Listing 16-16. Trigger to Validate an E-mail Address

```
using System;
using System.Data;
using System.Data.SqlClient;
using Microsoft.SqlServer.Server;
using System.Text.RegularExpressions;
using System.Transactions;

namespace Apress.Examples
{
    public partial class Triggers
    {
        private static readonly Regex email_pattern = new Regex
        (
            // Everything before the @ sign (the "local part")
            "^[a-z0-9!#$%&'*+/=?^_`{|}~-]+(?:\\.[a-z0-9!#$%&'*+/=?^_`{|}~-]+)*" +

            // Subdomains after the @ sign
            "@(?:[a-z0-9](?:[a-z0-9-]*[a-z0-9])?\\.)+" +

            // Top-level domains
            "(?:[a-z]{2}|com|org|net|gov|mil|biz|info|mobi|name|aero|jobs|museum)\\b$"
        );

        [Microsoft.SqlServer.Server.SqlTrigger(
            Name = "EmailAddressTrigger",
            Target = "[Person].[EmailAddress]",
            Event = "FOR INSERT, UPDATE")]
        public static void EmailAddressTrigger()
        {
            SqlTriggerContext tContext = SqlContext.TriggerContext;

            // Retrieve the connection that the trigger is using.
            using (SqlConnection cn
                = new SqlConnection(@"context connection=true"))
            {
                SqlCommand cmd;
                SqlDataReader r;

                cn.Open();

                cmd = new SqlCommand(@"SELECT EmailAddress FROM INSERTED", cn);
                r = cmd.ExecuteReader();
```

```
            try
            {
                while (r.Read())
                {
                    if (!email_pattern.IsMatch(r.GetString(0).ToLower()))
                        Transaction.Current.Rollback();
                }
            }
            catch (SqlException ex)
            {
                // Catch the expected exception.
            }
            finally
            {
                r.Close();
                cn.Close();
            }
        }
    }
}
```

As you now are used to, you first declare your .NET namespaces. To manage the transaction, you have to declare the System.Transactions namespace. In your Visual Studio project, it might not be recognized. You need to right-click the project in the Solution Explorer and select "add reference." Then, go to the SQL Server tab, and check "System.Transactions for framework 4.0.0.0."

Then, like in your previous UDF, you declare the Regex object. The trigger body follows. In the function's decoration, you name the trigger, and you declare for which target table it's intended. You also specify at what events it will fire.

```
[Microsoft.SqlServer.Server.SqlTrigger(
    Name = "EmailAddressTrigger",
    Target = "[Person].[EmailAddress]",
    Event = "FOR INSERT, UPDATE")]
public static void EmailAddressTrigger()
{ ...
```

Then, you declare an instance of the SqlTriggerContext class. This class exposes a few properties that give information about the trigger's context, like what columns are updated, what the action is that fired the trigger, and in case of a DDL trigger, it also gives access to the EventData XML structure containing all the execution details.

```
SqlTriggerContext tContext = SqlContext.TriggerContext;
```

The next line opens the so-called context connection to SQL Server. There is only one way to access the content of a table: with a T-SQL SELECT statement. Even a .NET code executed in SQL Server can't escape from this rule. To be able to retrieve the e-mails that have been inserted or updated, you need to open a connection to SQL Server and query the inserted virtual table. For that, you use a special type of connection available in CLR integration named the context connection, which is designed to be faster than a regular network or local connection. Then you use a data reader to retrieve the e-mails in the EmailAddress column. You loop through the results and apply the regular expression pattern to each address. If it doesn't match, you roll back the transaction by using the Transaction.Current.Rollback()

method. You need to protect the rollback by a try ... catch block, because it will throw an ambiguous exception, stating that "Transaction is not allowed to roll back in a user defined routine, trigger or aggregate because the transaction is not started in that CLR level." This can be safely ignored. Another error will be raised even if the try ... catch block is there, and it must be dealt with at the T-SQL level. You see that in your example later on.

```
using (SqlConnection cn
    = new SqlConnection(@"context connection=true"))
{
    SqlCommand cmd;
    SqlDataReader r;

    cn.Open();

    cmd = new SqlCommand(@"SELECT EmailAddress FROM INSERTED", cn);
    r = cmd.ExecuteReader();
    try
    {
        while (r.Read())
        {
            if (!email_pattern.IsMatch(r.GetString(0).ToLower()))
                Transaction.Current.Rollback();
        }
    }
    catch (SqlException ex)
    {
        // Catch the expected exception.
    }
    finally
    {
        r.Close();
        cn.Close();
    }
}
```

Now that the trigger is written, let's try it out. When the assembly is compiled and added to the AdventureWorks database using CREATE ASSEMBLY, you can add the trigger to the Person.EmailAddress table, as shown in Listing 16-17.

Listing 16-17. Creation of the CLR Trigger to Validate an E-mail Address

```
CREATE TRIGGER atr_Person_EmailAddress_ValidateEmail
ON Person.EmailAddress
AFTER INSERT, UPDATE
AS EXTERNAL NAME ApressExamples.[Apress.Examples.Triggers].EmailAddressTrigger;
```

You now try to update a line to an obviously invalid e-mail address in Listing 16-18. The result is shown in Figure 16-15.

Listing 16-18. Setting an Invalid E-mail Address

```
UPDATE Person.EmailAddress
SET EmailAddress = 'pro%sql@apress@com'
WHERE EmailAddress = 'dylan0@adventure-works.com';
```

```
 Messages
  Msg 3991, Level 16, State 1, Procedure atr_Person_EmailAddress_ValidateEmail, Line 1
  The context transaction which was active before entering user defined routine, trigger or aggregate
  "atr_Person_EmailAddress_ValidateEmail" has been ended inside of it, which is not allowed.
  Change application logic to enforce strict transaction nesting.
  The statement has been terminated.
```

Figure 16-15. *Result of the Trigger's Action*

As you can see, the trigger worked and rolled back the UPDATE attempt, but the error message generated for the CLR code isn't very user-friendly. You need to catch the exception in your T-SQL statement. A modified UPDATE dealing with that is shown in Listing 16-19.

Listing 16-19. UPDATE Statement Modified to Handle the Error

```
BEGIN TRY
    UPDATE Person.EmailAddress
    SET EmailAddress = 'pro%sql@apress@com'
    WHERE EmailAddress = 'dylan0@adventure-works.com';
END TRY
BEGIN CATCH
    IF ERROR_NUMBER() = 3991
        RAISERROR('invalid email address', 16, 10)
END CATCH
```

This CLR trigger is an example, and it might not be the best solution to your e-mail checking needs, for two reasons: firstly because you need to handle the CLR error in your calling code, which forces us to enclose every statement modifying the EmailAddress in a try ... catch block, and secondly because of performance considerations. Your CLR code loops through a DataReader and checks it line per line. A set-oriented T-SQL trigger like the one shown in Listing 16-20 will certainly be faster, especially if there are many rows affected by the INSERT or UPDATE statement.

Listing 16-20. T-SQL Trigger to Validate an E-mail Address

```
CREATE TRIGGER atr_Person_EmailAddress_ValidateEmail
ON Person.EmailAddress
AFTER INSERT, UPDATE
AS BEGIN
    IF @@ROWCOUNT = 0 RETURN

    IF EXISTS (SELECT * FROM inserted WHERE dbo.EmailMatch(EmailAddress) = 0)
    BEGIN
        RAISERROR('an email is invalid', 16, 10)
        ROLLBACK TRANSACTION
    END

END;
```

Summary

SQL Server 2005 introduced SQL CLR integration, allowing you to create UDFs, UDAs, SPs, UDTs, and triggers in managed .NET code. SQL Server 2008 improved on CLR integration by allowing UDTs and UDAs to have a maximum size of 2.1 GB (the size of large object (LOB) size limit), which is still the case in SQL Server 2014.

In this chapter, you talked about CLR integration usage considerations and scenarios when CLR integration code might be considered a good alternative to strict T-SQL. You also discussed assemblies and security, including the SAFE, EXTERNAL_ACCESS, and UNSAFE permission sets that can be applied on a per-assembly basis.

Finally, you provided several examples of CLR integration code that cover a wide range of possible uses, including the following:

- CLR integration can be invaluable when access to external resources is required from the server.

- CLR integration can be useful when non-table specific aggregations are required.

- CLR integration simplifies complex data validations that would be complex and difficult to perform in T-SQL.

- CLR integration allows you to supplement SQL Server's data typing system with your own specialized data types that define their own built-in methods and properties.

This chapter has served as an introduction to CLR integration programming. For in-depth CLR integration programming information, I highly recommend Pro SQL Server 2005 Assemblies, by Robin Dewson and Julian Skinner (Apress, 2005). Though written for SQL Server 2005, much of the information it contains is still relevant to SQL Server 2014. In the next chapter, you introduce client-side .NET connectivity to SQL Server 2014.

EXERCISES

1. [Choose all that apply] SQL Server 2014 provides support for which of the following CLR integration objects:

    a. UDFs

    b. UDAs

    c. UDTs

    d. SPs

    e. Triggers

    f. User-defined catalogs

2. [True/False] SQL Server 2014 limits CLR integration UDAs and UDTs to a maximum size of 8000 bytes.

3. [Choose one] SAFE permissions allow your CLR integration code to

    g. Write to the file system

    h. Access network resources

    i. Read the computer's registry

    j. Execute managed .NET code

    k. All of the above

4. [True/False] CLR integration UDAs and UDTs must be defined with the Serializable attribute.

5. [Fill in the blank] A CLR integration UDA that is declared as Format.UserDefined must implement the _____ interface.

6. [Choose all that apply] A CLR integration UDA must implement which of the following methods?

    l. Init

    m. Aggregate

    n. Terminate

    o. Merge

    p. Accumulate

CHAPTER 17

■ ■ ■

Data Services

Today's systems are disparate, and large enterprises have widely heterogeneous environments, with Windows and non-Windows platforms for application development. Developers, whether they're enterprise developers, web developers, independent software vendor (ISV)) developers, or DBAs, have different needs and different ways of accessing the data that resides in SQL Server. For example, ISV developers look for stability in the platform, enterprise developers look for rich development tooling experience and interoperability, and web developers want the latest rich development experience. Similarly, what a PHP developer needs is very different from what a .NET developer needs. To achieve the rich development experience, developers can choose from various data access libraries such as ADO.NET, SQL Server 2014 Native Client (SNAC), JDBC, ODBC, and PHP, based on the application's requirements. Since SQL Server 2000, the platform has supported interoperability with Windows and non-Windows environments. SQL Server 2000 started supporting Java development using JDBC drivers. PHP application development support was added to SQL Server with SQL Server 2005. With SQL Server 2014, support for ODBC driver for Linux has been added. This simplifies PHP or other application development on Linux to a greater extent.

The model of choice to address distributed computing and heterogeneous environments today is the Service Oriented Architecture (SOA) paradigm. There have been different ways to generate services from query results over the SQL Server versions. Microsoft is now concentrating on a powerful and very flexible framework named Windows Communication Foundation (WCF). In this chapter, you see how to use WCF Data Services to provide services and trendy RESTful resources from your databases. Bear with us for the explanation of these concepts.

But first, the data access libraries support a powerful new SQL Server 2014 feature named Local Database runtime (LocalDB). Let's look at this very interesting way to ship solutions with an embedded database.

SQL Server 2014 Express LocalDB

Developers always look for simple way to install and embed SQL Server with third-party applications or to use a small database engine to connect to diverse remote-data storage types. When you wanted to meet any of these requirements for creating applications prior to SQL Server 2012, the only option was to use SQL Server Express Edition. However, developers didn't want to go through tons of screens to install the SQL Server. On top of this, they had to worry about security and management of the SQL Server instance they had just installed.

Starting with SQL Server 2012, SQL Server simplifies the experience for developers by introducing LocalDB, which was temporarily called Serverless SQL Server during SQL Server 2012 development. The goal of this new feature is to simplify installation and provide a database as a file without any administration overhead while providing the same feature sets as SQL Server Express Edition.

■ **Note** Database as a file means LocalDB allows the use of SQL Server, a traditional client-server application, in a local context, more or less like local applications such as Microsoft Access and SQLite.

The installation of LocalDB is simplified to a great extent, with no prerequisites, no reboots, and no options to select. There is only one global installation, meaning only one set of binaries is installed per major version of SQL Server for all LocalDB instances; there is no constantly running service or agent in the box. The instance of LocalDB is started when the application connects to it and stopped when the application closes the connection.

You can download LocalDB from the same page as the old-fashioned SQL Server 2014 Express Edition, at www.microsoft.com/en-us/download/details.aspx?id=42299. Two builds are available: ENU\x64\SqlLocalDB.MSI for 64-bit systems and ENU\x86\SqlLocalDB.MSI for 32-bit systems. MSI files are Microsoft Installer packages that you can run by double-clicking and typing like any executable in a cmd or PowerShell session. MSI installations are usually graphical wizard-driven installations. The LocalDB installation doesn't require any user choice, so you can simply perform a silent install by using the following command:

```
SQLLocalDB.msi /Quiet
```

Once LocalDB is installed, you can create and manage the instances by using SQLLocalDB.exe, found in %Program Files%\Microsoft SQL Server\110\Tools\Binn. From now on, each time you call SQLLocalDB.exe, it will be in this directory context. Because it isn't in the path, you need to tell your shell where to find the tool.

■ **Note**   The LocalDB runtime, which is nothing more than a specific sqlserver.exe binary, can be found in %Program Files%\Microsoft SQL Server\120\LocalDB\Binn.

You can use the following command to find out the details of the existing instances:

```
SQLLocalDB.exe info
```

To create a LocalDB instance, you can use SQLLocaldb.exe and specify the name of the instance and the version number with the create option. The commands listed next first create an SQL Server 2014 LocalDB instance named SQLSrvWebApp1 and then start the instance. Finally, you use the info command to list the existing instances. The results are shown in Figure 17-1.

```
SQLLocalDB.exe create SQLSrvWebApp1 12.0
SQLLocalDB.exe start SQLSrvWebApp1
SQLLocalDB.exe info
```

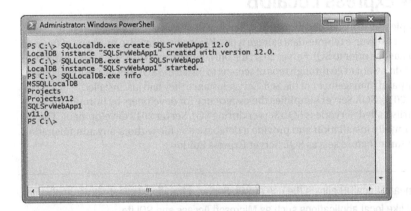

Figure 17-1. Query to create and start a LocalDB instance named SQLSrvWebApp1

You may have guessed that if you want to drop an instance, you can use the SQLLocalDB.exe delete command.

There are two types of LocalDB instances: automatic and named. Automatic instances are created by default. There can be only one automatic instance per major version of SQL Server. For SQL Server 2014, the automatic instance name is v12.0 (which is the internal version number of the SQL Server 2014 RTM release); the intent for this instance is that it be public and shared by many applications. Named instances are created explicitly by the user and are managed by a single application. So, if you have a small web application that needs to start small and be implemented in the enterprise, the better option is to create a named instance when it's small so that you can isolate and manage the application.

To connect to a LocalDB instance with your SQL server Native Client, OLEDB, or ODBC provider, you mention the (localdb) keyword in the connection string. Here are some examples of connection strings that connect to an automatic instance (first line) and named instance (second line):

```
New SQLConnection("Server=(localDB)\v12.0;AttachDBFile=
    C:\Program Files\Microsoft SQL Server\Data Files\AppDB1.mdf")'
```

```
New SQLConnection("Server=(localDB)\WebApp1;AttachDBFile=
    C:\Program Files\Microsoft SQL Server\Data Files\WebApp1DB.mdf")'
```

This code invokes LocalDB as a child process and connects to it. LocalDB runs as an application when you initiate a connection from the client, and if the database isn't used by the client application for more than 5 minutes, LocalDB is shut down to save system resources.

LocalDB is supported in ODBC, SQL Native Client, and OLEDB client providers. If these client providers encounter Server=(localdb)\<instancename>, they know to call the LocalDB instance if it already exists or to start the instance automatically as part of the connection attempt.

Likewise, you can connect to a LocalDB instance using SQL Server Management Studio (the Express or full version) or the sqlcmd command-line tool, by using the same (localdb) keyword as the server name, as shown in the following:

```
sqlcmd -S (localdb)\SQLSrvWebApp1
```

For this to work, you need to make sure the LocalDB instance is started. You can test it by using the info command along with the instance name, as shown next. The result of the command is shown in Figure 17-2. The instance's state is visible on the State: line:

```
SQLLocalDB.exe info SQLSrvWebApp1
```

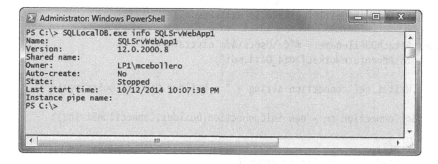

Figure 17-2. *Results of the SQLLocalDB.exe info SQLSrvWebApp1 command when the instance is stopped*

You can see in Figure 17-2 that the instance is running. If it had stopped, you could start it using the start command (shown earlier), and then you would be able to connect to it.

■ **Note**   Connecting to the (localdb) keyword is supported in .NET version 4.0.2 onward. If you're using an older .NET version, you can connect to a LocalDB instance, but you need to use the named pipe address that is returned by the SQLLocalDB.exe info command. You can see that address In Figure 17-2. The server's address in this case is np:\\.\pipe\LOCALDB#ECOF7CB5\tsql\query: that's what you would need to enter in the Server address box for an SSMS connection, or after the –S parameter when calling sqlcmd.

The authentication and security model of LocalDB is simplified. The current user is sysadmin and is the owner of the databases attached to the instance. No other permission is applied. Because the LocalDB processes run under a user's account, this also implies that the database files you want to use on this instance must be in a directory where the user has read and write permissions. Also, whereas SQL Server hides the physical details of the database storage, LocalDB follows another approach: it gives access to a database file. A LocalDB connection string supports the AttachDbFileName property, which allows you to attach a database file during connection. The C# console application in Listing 17-1 illustrates how to use the database as a file approach with LocalDB.

Listing 17-1. Console Application to Connect to a LocalDB Instance

```
using System;
using System.Data.SqlClient;
using System.Text;

namespace localdbClient
{
    class Program
    {
        static void Main(string[] args)
        {
            try
            {
                SqlConnectionStringBuilder builder =
                    new SqlConnectionStringBuilder(@"Server=(localdb)
                        \SQLSrvWebApp1;Integrated Security=true");

                builder.AttachDBFilename = @"C:\Users\Administrator
                \Documents\AdventureWorksLT2014_Data.mdf";

                Console.WriteLine("connection string = " + builder.ConnectionString);

                using (SqlConnection cn = new SqlConnection(builder.ConnectionString))
                {
                    cn.Open();
                    SqlCommand cmd = cn.CreateCommand();
                    cmd.CommandText = "SELECT Name FROM sys.tables;";
                    SqlDataReader rd = cmd.ExecuteReader();
```

```
            while(rd.Read())
            {
                Console.WriteLine(rd.GetValue(0));
            }
            rd.Close();
            cn.Close();
        }
        Console.WriteLine("Press any key to finish.");
        Console.ReadLine();
    }
    catch (Exception ex)
    {
        Console.WriteLine(ex.Message);
        Console.WriteLine("Press any key to finish.");
        Console.ReadLine();
    }
    }
  }
}
```

The interesting element of the code in Listing 17-1 is the connection-string builder. You first create a SqlConnectionStringBuilder to connect to the (localdb)\SQLSrvWebApp1 LocalDB, and then you use the connection builder's AttachDBFilename property to attach the AdventureWorksLT2014 data file to your LocalDB:

```
SqlConnectionStringBuilder builder =
    new SqlConnectionStringBuilder(@"Server=(localdb)
        \SQLSrvWebApp1;Integrated Security=true");
builder.AttachDBFilename = @"C:\Users\Administrator\Documents\AdventureWorksLT2014_Data.mdf";
```

The AdventureWorksLT2014_Data.mdf file is in the Documents directory, so you have full permissions over it. When connecting, you are automatically in the database's context, as you can see by executing the code. A list of the first ten tables in the AdventureWorksLT database is returned, as shown in Figure 17-3. The generated connection string is also printed in the figure.

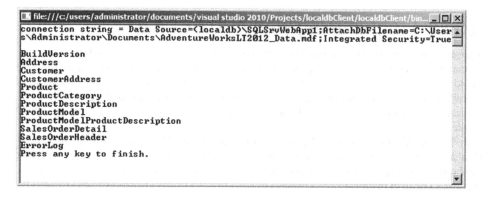

Figure 17-3. *Results of the LocalDB client program execution*

Databases attached to LocalDB can be thought of as personal databases—thus the database as a file approach. You can of course use all T-SQL DDL commands to create a database and the tables in it. You just need to specify for the database files a location on which you have permissions. If you create a database without specifying a location, LocalDB chooses your user directory. For example, the following command

```
CREATE DATABASE ApressDb;
```

creates .mdf and .ldf files in your personal directory, as shown in Figure 17-4.

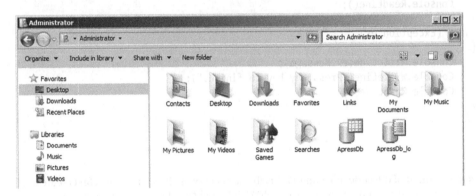

Figure 17-4. *The ApressDb database files*

You should obviously specify a dedicated location when you create a LocalDB database. The databases created or attached to a LocalDB instance will stay attached until you detach or remove them, even if you attached one during a connection with the AttachDBFilename command. So, you theoretically don't need to attach it every time you connect. However, if you use the AttachDBFilename command, the name of the database in LocalDB is the full path of the database file.

```
select name FROM sys.databases;
```

It's easier to keep the AttachDBFilename option in the connection string that allows you to attach the database if it isn't already attached, and enter the database context at connection time, thus providing a smoother experience from the developer's point of view.

Asynchronous Programming with ADO.NET 4.5

Let's take a simple scenario of an application requirement to upload multiple files or the need to create reports with pagination. In either scenario, using a synchronous model in the application can cause the client and server to slow down considerably and result in higher memory utilization due to I/O operations. In cases like this, writing the calls asynchronously instead of synchronously can improve the user experience; however, the current model has some issues with manageability and debugging capabilities with asynchronous code.

Starting with .NET 4.5, the new Async .NET pattern is extended to ADO.NET. Now the connection operations SqlDataReader and SqlBulkCopy can use the asynchronous capabilities. For example, let's take the simple case shown in Listing 17-2 that opens a connection and runs a stored procedure named dbo. GetProducts against a LocalDB instance.

Listing 17-2. ADO.NET Code to Run a Stored Procedure Synchronously

```
private void ExecuteSP()
{
    SqlConnectionStringBuilder cnString = new SqlConnectionStringBuilder();
    cnString.DataSource = @"(localdb)\v12.0";
    cnString.IntegratedSecurity = true;

    using (SqlConnection cn = new SqlConnection(cnString.ConnectionString))
    {
        cn.Open();
        SqlCommand cmd = new SqlCommand("EXEC dbo.GetProducts", cn);
        cmd.ExecuteReader();
    }
}
```

This code opens the connection to the database synchronously and runs the stored procedure, waiting until the entire resultset is returned. Instead of waiting for the process to complete, it would be more efficient to perform this operation asynchronously. Listing 17-3 shows the code from Listing 17-2 modified for asynchronous execution. Changes appear in bold.

Listing 17-3. ADO.NET Code to Run Stored Procedure Asynchronously

```
private async Task ExecuteSP()
{
    SqlConnectionStringBuilder cnString = new SqlConnectionStringBuilder();
    cnString.DataSource = @"(localdb)\v12.0";
    cnString.IntegratedSecurity = true;

    using (SqlConnection cn = new SqlConnection(cnString.ConnectionString))
    {
        await cn.OpenAsync();
        SqlCommand cmd = new SqlCommand("EXEC dbo.GetProducts", cn);
        await cmd.ExecuteReaderAsync();
    }
}
```

If you compare the code in Listings 17-2 and 17-3, the structure has not changed; however, by including the keyword await and modifying a few keywords, you retain readability and manageability while adding the asynchronous capability.

Every possibility for improving performance on the client side is interesting. Keep in mind, of course, that the best way to ensure optimal performance in database querying is to improve the structure and code on the server side.

ODBC for Linux

For many years, and over many SQL Server versions, developers who wanted to access SQL Server from non-Windows environments had only one option: using a free library named FreeTDS that was originally created to access Sybase servers.

■ **Note** TDS stands for Tabular Data Stream and is the network layer protocol used by Sybase and SQL Server to exchange packets between the database server and the client library. As you may know, SQL Server was in its early days a joint development between Sybase and Microsoft.

FreeTDS is fine and works well, but it doesn't cover the newer data types and functionalities SQL Server has to offer, like XML, date, time, and datetime2, or FILESTREAM data types, or features like multiple active resultsets (MARS). So, Linux developers wanting to access SQL Server from PHP or any CGI application had to stick to a limited set of functionalities. If you ever wrote PHP code to access SQL Server in a Linux environment, you may have used the integrated PHP MSSQL functions that call the php5-odbc library. It's nothing more than a layer using FreeTDS behind the scenes.

In an effort to provide a wider range of possibilities for accessing SQL Server, Microsoft decided to change its data-access strategy, which was previously in favor of OLEDB, by aligning with ODBC for native access to SQL Server. Open Database Connectivity (ODBC) is an API first designed by Microsoft that became a kind of de facto standard for heterogeneous database access. It allows access to different data sources from many languages and environments.

Along with this change of strategy, Microsoft developed an ODBC driver for Linux that was released in March 2012. You can download it from www.microsoft.com/en-us/download/details.aspx?id=28160.

Linux is available though many distributions, which have their own core applications, distribution mechanisms, and directory organization. At the time of this writing, Microsoft offers 64-bit packages for the Red Hat Enterprise distribution only. A 32-bit version is planned. Red Hat Enterprise doesn't necessarily have the most widespread distribution, and many companies use other distributions, such as Debian, Ubuntu, CentOS, and so on. The Microsoft ODBC driver can be installed from other distributions, providing you have a way to install the libraries the ODBC driver is using.

■ **Caution** In the Linux world, most of the tools used are open source and can be compiled directly on the system, to link to the available version of the libraries used in the code. But the ODBC driver for SQL Server isn't open source, and only the binaries are available to download. That's why you need to ensure that you get the proper version of the libraries used by the ODBC driver installed on the Linux box.

Let's look at a short example using Ubuntu Server. Ubuntu is a very popular distribution that is based on Debian, another widespread Linux distribution.

The driver you can download at the address previously mentioned is compressed in the tar.gz format, the common compression format in Linux. Once downloaded, you can extract it by opening a shell, going to the directory where the compressed file is, and executing the following command:

```
tar xvzf sqlncli-11.0.1790.0.tar.gz
```

The tar command extracts the archive into a new directory named here sqlncli-11.0.1790.0 on the version of the ODBC driver.

■ **Note** The xvzf set of options used with the tar command is commonly used to extract tar.gz archives. x means eXtract, and v means Verbose; these options allow the extraction's details to be printed on the shell output. z tells tar that it needs to deal with a gzip archive; and f tells tar that the name of the file to extract will follow.

The archive is extracted into a directory. You enter it using the cd (change directory) command:

```
cd sqlncli-11.0.1790.0
```

The steps to install the driver on Ubuntu are valid at the time of this writing with the current driver release, which is sqlncli-11.0.1790.0 for Red Hat Enterprise 6, and the current Ubuntu version, which is 12.04 Precise Pangolin. The driver being installed is correct at the time of writing, but Linux minor and major version upgrades occur regularly. This means the Microsoft driver may be out of date, or you may need a later version when a new one is brought out. However, we're demonstrating on Ubuntu 12.04 with the 11.0.1790.0 Microsoft driver, and although in future releases the process may vary, we can hopefully guide you in a general way.

According to its documentation, the unixodbc version needed to run the driver is 2.3.0. Using the apt-cache tool that manages the cache of Debian and Ubuntu packages, you can check the current unixodbc version on your system:

```
apt-cache show unixodbc
```

The show option returns details about a package, and on Debian and Ubuntu, the name of the package is simply unixodbc. The result is shown in Figure 17-5.

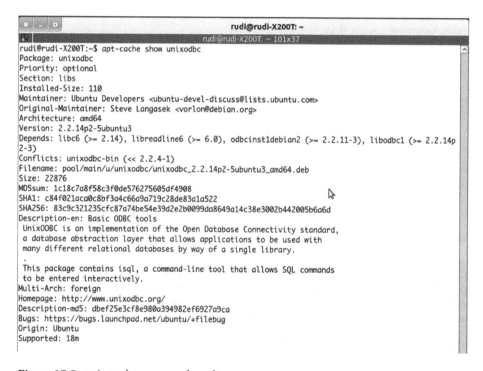

Figure 17-5. apt-cache *command result*

The current version on our Ubuntu is 2.2.14. The libsqlncli downloaded from Microsoft includes a script that downloads and builds the required unixodbc version. So you first uninstall the current unixodbc using the apt-get command, and then you install the newer unixodbc using the Microsoft script. Also, you need to prefix the commands with the sudo instruction to execute them with super user (su) privileges, as follows:

```
sudo apt-get remove unixodbc
sudo bash ./build_dm.sh
```

There is a catch here: at the time of this writing, the build_dm.sh script (as well as the install.sh script that you see shortly) has a flaw. If you open it in a text editor, you'll see on its first line that it declares itself as a script written for the sh Linux shell, using what is called the *shebang syntax*, as follows:

```
#!/bin/sh
```

This allows the file to be executed without mentioning the interpreter on the command line. The shebang line is read, and the proper interpreter is called. The problem here is that the script is declared as being an sh script, whereas it is in fact a bash script. sh and bash are two different Linux shells. So, to make the shell work, you need to run it explicitly with bash. A partial result of the build_dm.sh command is shown in Figure 17-6.

```
The script is provided as a convenience to you as-is, without any express
or implied warranties of any kind.  Microsoft is not liable for any issues
arising out of your use of the script.

Enter 'YES' to have this script continue: YES

Verifying processor and operating system ................................... OK
Verifying wget is installed ................................................ OK
Verifying tar is installed ................................................. OK
Verifying make is installed ................................................ OK
Downloading unixODBC 2.3.0 DriverManager ................................... OK
Unpacking unixODBC 2.3.0 DriverManager ..................................... OK
Configuring unixODBC 2.3.0 DriverManager ................................... OK
Building unixODBC 2.3.0 DriverManager ...................................... OK
Build of the unixODBC 2.3.0 DriverManager complete.

Run the command 'cd /tmp/unixODBC.22830.6255.24287/unixODBC-2.3.0; make install' to install the drive
r manager.
```

Figure 17-6. *build_dm.sh command result*

The unixodbc driver manager is built and copied to a directory in /tmp. The script tells you what to do next: go there and use the make install command to copy the binaries at the right place. What it doesn't say is that you need administrative privileges to run both commands (shown on the same line in Figure 17-6, separated by a semicolon). So, you need to run the commands as follows:

```
sudo cd /tmp/unixODBC.22830.6255.24287/unixODBC-2.3.0
sudo make install
```

Now that the driver manager is installed, you can go to the next step: installing the Microsoft driver. The first thing to do is to check the versions of the libraries requested by the driver. You can use the ldd command, which returns the shared libraries dependencies of a binary, to check the libraries used by the driver:

```
ldd lib64/libsqlncli-11.0.so.1790.0
```

.so (shared object) is the common extension for shared libraries on Linux. On our system, the command returns the results shown in Figure 17-7.

Figure 17-7. *Results of the* ldd *command*

In Figure 17-7, you see that most of the libraries are found, except the SSL libraries libcrypto.so.10 and libssl.so.10. Here, 10 stands for the dynamic shared objects' version number. You need to find out whether any versions of these libraries are available on your system. To do that, you use the find command as follows:

```
find / -name libcrypto.so.* -print
```

As you might have guessed, the find command searches for files. You ask it to start its search at the root of the file system (/), to search for libcrypto.so.*, and to print the result. We found this reference: /lib/x86_64-linux-gnu/libcrypto.so.1.0.0. That looks like what you need, but how do you allow the driver to see it? You create a symbolic link—you could call it a shortcut—with the name requested by the driver, which is a pointer to the installed library. The following commands do just that:

```
sudo ln -s /lib/x86_64-linux-gnu/libcrypto.so.1.0.0 /lib/x86_64-linux-gnu/libcrypto.so.10
sudo ln -s /lib/x86_64-linux-gnu/libssl.so.1.0.0 /lib/x86_64-linux-gnu/libssl.so.10
```

You use the ln command to create a link, and the -s option specifies that you create a symbolic link.

Now you can install the driver. In the driver's directory, the install.sh shell script allows you to copy the files to the /opt/microsoft/sqlncli location and create the symbolic links in the path to let the driver and its tools be recognized on your system. The /opt directory is chosen as the install path because it's where applications not installed with the distribution are supposed to go:

```
sudo bash ./install.sh install --force
```

Once again you use sudo to run the script under administrative privileges, and you use bash explicitly. The --force option is needed on this distribution to prevent dependency checks performed by the script from canceling the installation process.

The installation script runs quickly, and when it's finished, you can test the ODBC driver by using the two tools installed with it: a Linux version of the bcp (Bulk Copy) tool, and a Linux version of the sqlcmd shell. Symbolic links are created by the installation script in the path, so you can use sqlcmd wherever you are in the file system. An example of starting sqlcmd follows:

```
sqlcmd -S SQL2014 -U apress -P @press!
```

This command connects to the SQL2014 server using the SQL login apress, with password @press!. If you receive an error saying that the library libcrypto.so.10 (or any library used by the ODBC driver) isn't found, you may have to investigate and install the library or use the symbolic link technique described earlier.

Note that here you connect using an SQL login and not integrated security. That's logical, you might think: you're on Linux, not logged in to a Windows domain, so how could integrated security work? Well, it can—not fully, but it can. For that, your Linux box must have Kerberos properly configured, which is out of the scope of this book; please refer to this documentation entry for a high-level description of the requirements for it to work: http://msdn.microsoft.com/en-us/library/hh568450. Note that you can't impersonate an account, and you're limited to the Linux machine system account.

JDBC

To use the JDBC component, first download it from http://msdn.microsoft.com/en-us/sqlserver/aa937724.aspx. The driver is a JDBC 4 driver that is available to download as a Windows self-extract executable or a tar.gz compressed file for non-Windows environments. Once the file is uncompressed, you have a directory with two jar files and other resources such as documentation. Put the sqljdbc4.jar file, which is the JDBC 4 driver, in your Java classpath. The classpath is the path where Java searches for classes to run or to import.

Java development is a broad subject, so we don't give many details here, but let's look at a short example of using the JDBC driver, mainly to illustrate the use of the connection string. JDBC connection can be done using a connection string, also called a connection URL. In the case of SQL Server, it's very similar to the ADO.NET or ODBC connection string. The general form of the string is as follows:

```
jdbc:sqlserver://[serverName[\instanceName][:portNumber]][;property=value[;property=value]]
```

Other methods, like setting properties of a Connection object, can be used; this example uses the connection-string method.

Listing 17-4 shows a short but complete example of a Java class that lets you connect to SQL Server and run a query. To make it more interesting, we assumed that we were in an environment using AlwaysOn Availability Groups, and we added the failoverPartner option in the connection string to allow for reconnecting to a mirror if the first server didn't respond.

Listing 17-4. Java Example Using the Microsoft JDBC Driver

```java
import java.sql.*;

public class ApressExample {

    public static void main(String[] args) {

        String connectionUrl = "jdbc:sqlserver://SQL2014;integratedSecurity=true;databaseName=
        AdventureWorks2014;failoverPartner=SQL2014B";
        Connection cn = null;
        String qry = "SELECT TOP 10 FirstName, LastName FROM Person.Contact";

        try {
            cn = DriverManager.getConnection(connectionUrl);
            runQuery(cn, qry);
        } catch (SQLException se) {
            try {
                System.out.println("Connection to principal server failed, trying the
                mirror server.");
                cn = DriverManager.getConnection(connectionUrl);
                runQuery(cn, qry);
            } catch (Exception e) {
                e.printStackTrace();
            }
        } catch (Exception e) {
            e.printStackTrace();
        } finally {
            if (cn != null) try { cn.close(); } catch(Exception e) { }
        }
    }

    private static void runQuery(Connection cn, String SQL) {
        Statement stmt = null;
        ResultSet rs = null;

        try {
            stmt = cn.createStatement();
            rs = stmt.executeQuery(SQL);

            while (rs.next()) {
                System.out.println(rs.getString(0));
            }
            rs.close();
            stmt.close();
        } catch (Exception e) {
            e.printStackTrace();
        } finally {
            if (rs != null) try { rs.close(); } catch(Exception e) {}
            if (stmt != null) try { stmt.close(); } catch(Exception e) {}
        }
    }
}
```

■ **Note** If your application accesses SQL Server with AlwaysOn that listens in multiple subnets with the JDBC driver, it's important to set the keyword `MultiSubnetFailover=True` in the connection string. The reason is that JDBC drivers don't iterate through multiple IP addresses; if the network name listens to multiple IP addresses, the JDBC driver spawns parallel connections to the IP addresses and listens to the first one that responds.

For this example to work, save it in a file named `ApressExample.java`, and compile it with the Java compiler (`javac.exe` on Windows) after making sure the `sqljdbc4.jar` file is in the Java classpath. You could also indicate the path of the driver in the `javac` command line, as shown in the following example:

```
javac.exe -classpath "C:\sqljdbc_4.0\enu\sqljdbc4.jar" c:\apress\ApressExample.java
```

The compilation results in an `ApressExample.class` file that you can run with `java.exe`. Once again, the JDBC driver must be in the classpath for it to work. The classpath is an environment variable, and an example of setting it for the session and running the java class in a `cmd` session on Windows is shown next. You must be in the directory where the `ApressExample.class` file is, for it to work:

```
set classpath=c:\sqljdbc_4.0\enu\sqljdbc4.jar;.;%classpath%
java ApressExample
```

The first line adds the path of the `sqljdbc4.jar` file and the current directory to the classpath environment variable, so it will find the JDBC driver and the `ApressExample` class. The second line runs the code example.

Now that you can run the example, let's come back to its content. The first thing you do in the code is import the `java.sql` classes so you have the `Connection`, `Statement,` and other JDBC classes handy. In the `main()` method of the `ApressExample` class, you define the connection string and set the server's address as well as the mirroring server's address. We chose to be authenticated by Windows, using Integrated Security:

```
String connectionUrl = "jdbc:sqlserver://SQL2014;integratedSecurity=true;databaseName=Advent
ureWorks2014;failoverPartner=SQL2014B";
```

If you know JDBC, you may be surprised not to find a `Class.forName()` call, as shown in the following snippet:

```
Class.forName("com.microsoft.sqlserver.jdbc.SQLServerDriver");
```

The `Class.forName()` instruction is used to load the JDBC driver and register it to the JDBC `DriverManager`. This isn't required anymore if you use JDBC 4, because in JDBC 4, drivers can be loaded magically just by being on the classpath.

The rest of the code is a pretty standard Java example. Let's concentrate on the line that opens the connection:

```
cn = DriverManager.getConnection(connectionUrl);
```

It's enclosed in a `try catch` block, in order to catch a connection failure. If such a failure happens, the catch block runs the exact same connection command. This is to allow automatic reconnection in case of a failover. At the second connection attempt, the JDBC driver—once again magically—tries with the address defined in the `failoverpartner` option. This second attempt must also be enclosed in a `try catch` block, in case the other server doesn't answer either. Because you have to write the connection code twice, we chose here to move the code that uses the connection to run a query in a private method of the class, in order to call it from the `main()` method.

Service-Oriented Architecture and WCF Data Services

If you're a die-hard T-SQL developer who doesn't venture much into Microsoft client-side code and all the frameworks and libraries, you may crack a smile while reading the few next paragraphs. T-SQL developers are used to dealing with a stable and old-fashioned technology with no fancy names, which could give the impression that it's so old and solid that it will never change. On the client side, however, things are constantly moving. A history of data-access methods and what are today called *data services*, because of the Service Oriented Architecture (SOA) paradigm, could fill a book, and that book would be full of twists and turns. In the early days of SQL Server, the data-access libraries were the native dblib DLL and the ODBC API. This was superseded by OLEDB, then by the SQL Server Native Client. Today, we're returning to ODBC to align with a de facto standard, as you saws in the "ODBC for Linux" section.

On the subject of data services, before the concept ever existed, developers talked about *distributed applications*: applications that are broken into components and that span multiple computers, allowing distant interoperability. The components exchanged information using a broker like Distributed Component Object Model(DCOM) or Common Object Request Broker Architecture (CORBA) and used a Remote Procedure Call (RPC) model. With the release of the .NET framework, Microsoft developed a replacement for creating distributed .NET components, called .NET Remoting. But the distributed components model had some shortcomings: mainly, the network protocols used were not tailored for the Web, and it was sometimes tricky to allow distant computers behind firewalls to work together. Also, you had to implement a unique technology, whether it was DCOM, CORBA, .NET Remoting, or others. Moreover, in the case of DCOM and .NET Remoting, you had to develop on Windows and run Microsoft operating systems and technologies on every end.

The SOA paradigm gained attention and popularity because it addressed these limitations. The goal of SOA was to use standard and widely used protocols like HTTP and SMTP to exchange information between the components of a distributed application—except that SOA uses different terminology. The components are *services*, a term that emphasizes their loosely coupled and independent nature; and the distributed application model is named *Service Oriented Architecture*. Using protocols like HTTP allows you to take advantage of existing and proven technologies and infrastructures available on all platforms and designed for the Internet. To ensure that the information exchanged is understood on every platform, text-based structures like XML and JavaScript Object Notation (JSON) are used to generate messages that are created and consumed by these services, which are called *web services* (WS) because of their use of the HTTP protocol. These messages are exchanged mostly using a protocol named SOAP (originally an acronym for Simple Object Access Protocol). SOAP is an envelope in which XML messages are enclosed; it defines a set of properties and functionalities for the message.

So far so good, but a new model started to gain popularity in the last decade: Representational State Transfer (REST). It's is a set of architectural principles for building services called *resources*. A REST resource is defined by an *address*, which is an Internet address in the form of a uniform resource identifier (URI—a more generic term for what is called an URL in the HTTP protocol). To call the resource, a REST client uses standard HTTP verbs like GET and PUT to send and receive messages. So, with REST, you use a model close to what a Web browser would do to call resources; that makes it interesting mainly because it lets you use proven technologies on both sides, and it offers natively the scalability of the web technologies. Because REST is more about offering resources than exchanging messages per se, this model is sometimes called *Resource Oriented Architecture* (ROA), and a system implementing this model is said to be *RESTful*.

With SOA quickly replacing distributed components, libraries or frameworks were needed in the Microsoft world to build web services. The first generation of these tools was called ASP.NET Web Services (ASMX) and was released for .NET 1.0. It was quickly completed by Web Services Enhancement (WSE), which added some SOAP WS specifications. That was another programming model to learn, and it was still limited because it didn't implement all the SOA possibilities like the REST model. To build XML messages, you used the .NET XML libraries; or, using SQL Server 2000, you generated the XML directly using the FOR XML clause, and you enclosed it in a SOAP message using client code. In SQL Server, you could also use an ISAPI extension to provide XML responses directly from SQL server through IIS, without using ASMX.

When SQL Server 2005 was released, the ISAPI extension was replaced by an integrated HTTP endpoint capability. SQL Server was then able to act natively as an HTTP server, to receive and send back SOAP messages. Today, this feature has been removed from SQL Server 2014, because it didn't offer a complete enough environment to build web services. As a matter of fact, ASMX didn't offer all of what was needed, either. So, Microsoft decided to build a complete and flexible framework to handle all interoperability technologies, which it now calls *Connected Systems*. That framework is named *Windows Communication Foundation* (WCF).

WCF is integrated into .NET and is the way to go when talking about web services, REST, distributed components, and message queuing in the Microsoft world. WCF offers several layers that provide everything needed to create connected systems. They're schematized in Figure 17-8.

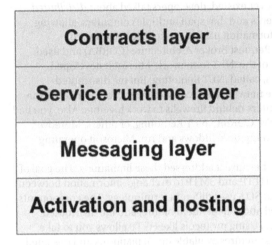

Figure 17-8. *The WCF layers stack*

The contracts layer consists of the contracts (or interfaces) definition classes that allow services to publish and agree on the content of the information they exchange. You can define data contracts, message contacts, service contracts, and so on. The service runtime layer offers all the behaviors necessary to implement the services, like transaction behavior, parameter filtering, and so on. The messaging layer offers encoders and channels to handle the more physical and concrete exchange of messages and services. And finally, the activation and hosting layer lets you run the services, as an EXE, a Windows service, a COM+ application, and so on.

WCF can be used to create services or remoting applications or to implement message queuing. Here, we of course concentrate on a specific feature of WCF that provides a very simple way to publish data as REST resources: WCF Data Services.

■ **Note**   Here again, the name of the technology has changed several times in a few years. In 2007, we heard about project Astoria, which aimed to deliver a framework for creating and consuming data services using SOA. When it was released in 2008 along with .NET 3.5, its final name was ADO.NET Data Services, which was later changed to WCF Data Services.

WCF Data Services supports the concept of REST for accessing data remotely. As we briefly said before, REST-style services provide simple URI-based querying, α simpler mechanism than the SOAP protocol. WCF Data Services translates regular HTTP requests into create, read, update, and delete (CRUD) operations against a data source, and it exchanges data by using the Open Data (OData) protocol, an open web protocol for querying and updating data. WCF Data Services uses an HTTP request-to-CRUD operation mapping, as shown in Table 17-1.

Table 17-1. *HTTP Requests to WCF Data Services Operations*

HTTP Request	WCF Data Services Operation
GET	Query the data source; retrieve data.
POST	Create a new entity and insert it into the data source.
PUT	Update an entity in the data source.
DELETE	Delete an entity from the data source.

Creating a WCF Data Service

As with a web service, the first step to creating a WCF data service is to create a new ASP.NET web application project, as shown in Figure 17-9.

Figure 17-9. *Creating an ASP.NET web application in Visual Studio 2010*

Defining the Data Source

Once you have created a web application project, you need to add a source for your data. The easiest way is to add an ADO.NET entity data model (EDM) by right-clicking the project in Solution Explorer, choosing Add a New Item in Visual Studio, and selecting the ADO.NET Entity Data Model template on the Data page of the Add New Item window, as shown in Figure 17-10. This launches the ADO.NET Entity Data Model Wizard.

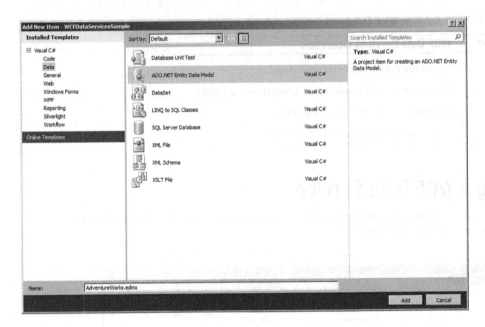

Figure 17-10. *Adding an ADO.NET EDM item to your web application*

Chapter 15 covers the Entity Framework, so we don't need to go into details her. You're generating an EDM from tables in the AdventureWorks database. Include the `Production.Product`, `Production.ProductPhoto`, and `Production.ProductProductPhoto` tables of the database, as shown in Figure 17-11.

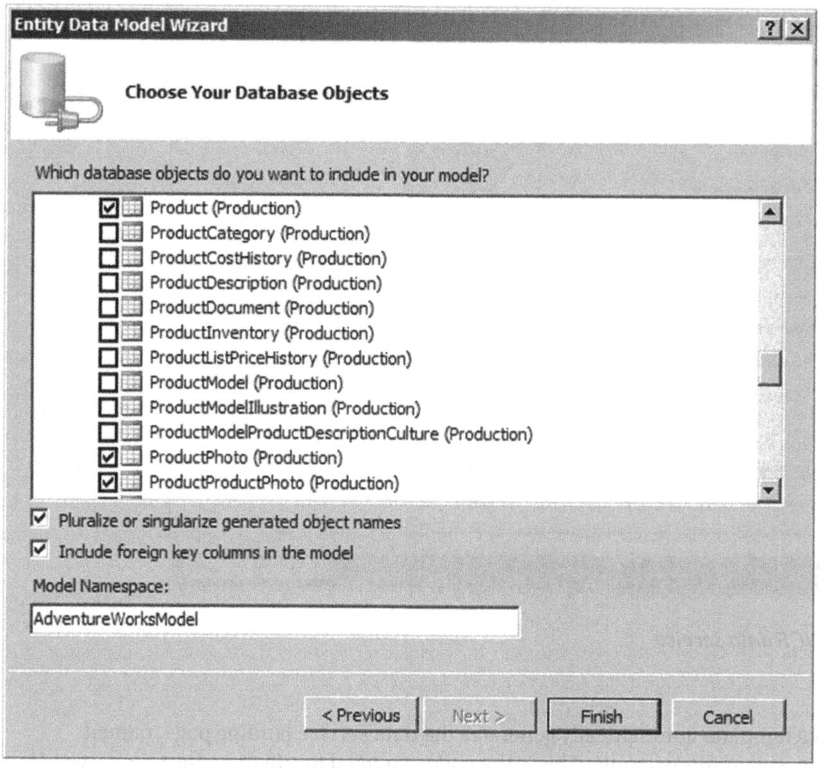

Figure 17-11. *Adding tables to the EDM*

Once you've added tables to your EDM, you can view them in the Entity Data Model Designer, as you have seen previously.

Creating the Data Service

The next step after you've defined your EDM is to add a WCF data service item to your project through the New Item menu option. The Add New Item window is shown in Figure 17-12 with the WCF Data Service template highlighted.

Figure 17-12. *Adding a WCF data service*

The WCF Data Service template automatically generates the data service landing page, named
ProductPhotoDataService.svc in this example. This is the page you need to call to request the service. Its
source file, named ProductPhotoDataService.svc.cs in this example, uses the System.Data.Services
namespace and contains a class definition for the service that defines access rules for entity sets and
service operations. The class defined in this file requires some modification by hand where you see the
automatically generated TODO comments. You must define the data source class—the EF entities class—and
at a minimum you must set the entity access rules as shown in Listing 17-5.

Listing 17-5. AdventureWorksDataService Class Definition Using System.Data.Services;

```
using System;
using System.Collections.Generic;
using System.Data.Services;
using System.Data.Services.Common;
using System.Linq;
using System.ServiceModel.Web;
using System.Web;

namespace WCFDataServicesSample
{
    public class ProductPhotoDataService : DataService<AdventureWorksEntities>
    {
        // This method is called only once to initialize service-wide policies.
        public static void InitializeService(DataServiceConfiguration config)
        {
            config.SetEntitySetAccessRule("Products", EntitySetRights.AllRead);
            config.SetEntitySetAccessRule("ProductPhotoes", EntitySetRights.AllRead);
```

```
        config.SetEntitySetAccessRule("ProductProductPhotoes", EntitySetRights.AllRead);
        config.DataServiceBehavior.MaxProtocolVersion = DataServiceProtocolVersion.V2;
      }
   }
}
```

■ **Caution**   You can use the wildcard character (*) to set rights for all entities and service operations at once, but Microsoft strongly recommends against this. Although it's useful for testing purposes, in a production environment this can lead to serious security problems.

Listing 17-5 mentions the entity set names that were pluralized by EF, which is why the code includes the Photoes faulty plural form. Feel free to correct it in the entity model source. You set the access rules to AllRead, meaning the service allows queries by key or queries for all contents of the entity set. The rights allowed are shown in Table 17-2.

Table 17-2. *Service Entity and Operation Access Rights*

Access Rights	Entity/Operation	Description
All	Both	Allows full read/write access to the entity and full read access to operations.
AllRead	Both	Allows full read access to the entity or operation. It's shorthand for ReadSingle and ReadMultiple access rights combined with a logical OR (|) operation.
AllWrite	Entity	Allows full write access to the entity. It's shorthand for WriteAppend, WriteUpdate, and WriteDelete access rights combined with a logical OR (|) operation.
None	Both	Allows no read or write access, and doesn't appear in the services metadata document.
ReadSingle	Both	Allows for queries by key against an entity set.
ReadMultiple	Both	Allows for queries for the entire contents of the set.
WriteAppend	Entity	Allows new resources to be appended to the set.
WriteDelete	Entity	Allows existing resources to be deleted from the set.
WriteUpdate	Entity	Allows existing resources to be updated in the set.

You can test your WCF data service by running it in Debug mode from Visual Studio. Visual Studio opens a browser window with the address set to the start page for your project. Change it to the address of the data service, which in our case is http://localhost:59560/ProductPhotoDataService.svc.

■ **Note**   You can also set your WCF data service page (.svc extension) as the project start page. In that case, you can delete the Default.aspx page in the project, because it's not needed.

Your start address and port number will most likely be different. The WCF data service responds to your request with a listing of entities for which you have access, as shown in Figure 17-13.

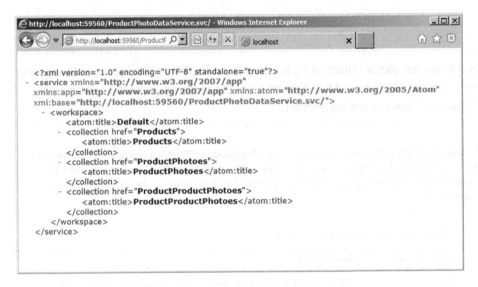

Figure 17-13. *Calling the page for the WCF data service*

■ **Tip** WCF Data Services supports two payload types. The *payload type* is the standard format for incoming request data and outgoing results data. WCF Data Services supports both JSON and the Atom Publishing Protocol for payloads. If you call the page for your WCF data service and the results look like a nonsensical syndication feed instead of standard XML, you need to turn off the feed-reading view in your browser. In Internet Explorer 7, you can uncheck the Tools ➤ Internet Options ➤ Content ➤ Settings ➤ Turn On Feed Reading View option.

Once you've confirmed that the WCF data service is up and running, you can query the service using a combination of path expression–style syntax in the URI to locate entities and query string parameters to further restrict and control output. The following are some examples of WCF data service queries:

- `http://localhost:59560/ProductPhotoDataService.svc/Products`: This query retrieves all Product entities.

- `http://localhost:59560/ProductPhotoDataService.svc/Products(749)`: This query retrieves the Product entities with a primary key value of 749. The primary key of the Product entity is ProductID.

- `http://localhost:59560/ProductPhotoDataService.svc/Products?$skip=10&$top=10`: This query skips the first ten Product entities and retrieves the following ten (items 11 through 20) in key order.

- `http://localhost:59560/ProductPhotoDataService.svc/Products?$top=20&$orderby=Name`: This query retrieves the first 20 Product entities ordered (sorted) by the Name attribute.

- `http://localhost:59560/ProductPhotoDataService.svc/`
  `Products?$filter=ListPrice gt 1000&$expand=ProductProductPhotoes/`
  `ProductPhoto`: This query retrieves all `Product` entities with a `ListPrice` attribute
  that is greater than 1,000. The results include related `ProductProductPhoto` and
  `ProductPhoto` entities expanded inline. Note that in the expanded option, you need
  to mention first the entity set and then the entities linked to the set, which is why you
  have `ProductProductPhotoes` and then `ProductPhoto`.

This is just a small sampling of the types of REST-style queries you can create using WCF Data Services.
In fact, WCF Data Services supports several query string options, as shown in Table 17-3.

Table 17-3. *Query String Options*

Option	Description
$expand	Expands results to include one or more related entities inline in the results.
$filter	Restricts the results returned by applying an expression to the last entity set identified in the URI path. The $filter option supports a simple expression language that includes logical, arithmetic, and grouping operators, and an assortment of string, date, and math functions.
$orderby	Orders (sorts) results by the attributes specified. You can specify multiple attributes separated by commas, and each attribute can be followed by an optional asc or desc modifier indicating ascending or descending sort order, respectively.
$skip	Skips a given number of rows when returning results.
$top	Restricts the number of entities returned to the specified number.

Creating a WCF Data Service Consumer

Once you have a WCF data service up and running, creating a consumer application is relatively simple.
For this example, you create a simple .NET application that calls the service to display the image and details
of products selected from a drop-down list.

The first step in building a consumer application is to create classes based on your EDM. Instead
of doing so manually, you can generate the creation of these classes by using the Add Service Reference
command in Visual Studio, which automatically generates C# or Visual Basic classes for use in client
applications. For this example, we created an ASP.NET web application, right-clicked the project in the
Solution Explorer, and chose the Add Service Reference command. In the Add Service Reference Window,
we added the WCF data service address and clicked Go. Visual Studio queried the service's metadata.
Figure 17-14 shows the result of this request.

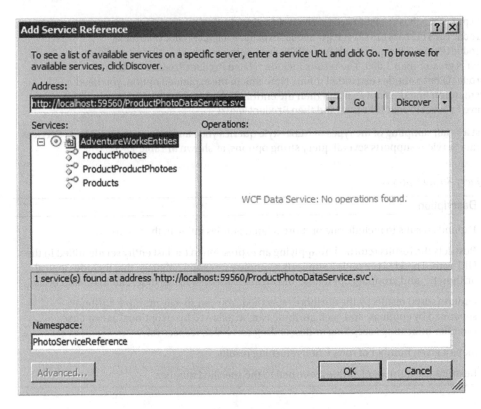

Figure 17-14. Adding a service reference in Visual Studio 2010

Step two of the process is to create the Default.aspx page of the client application. This page performs the necessary calls to the service. You aren't tied to a web application, however; you can just as easily call ADO.NET data services from Windows applications, Silverlight applications, or any other platform that can initiate HTTP requests (although object deserialization on platforms that don't support .NET classes could pose a bit of a challenge). For this client application, we simply added a drop-down list, an image control, and a table to the web form. Then we wired up the page load and drop-down list-selection-change events. The code is shown in Listing 17-6, with results shown in Figure 17-15.

Listing 17-6. ASP.NET Client Application Default.aspx Page

```
using System;
using System.Collections.Generic;
using System.Linq;
using System.Web;
using System.Web.UI;
using System.Web.UI.WebControls;
using WCFdsClient.PhotoServiceReference;
using System.Data.Services.Client;
```

```
namespace WCFdsClient
{
    public partial class _Default : System.Web.UI.Page
    {
        protected void Page_Load(object sender, EventArgs e)
        {
            PopulateDropDown();
        }

        private void PopulateDropDown()
        {
            AdventureWorksEntities ctx = new AdventureWorksEntities(
                new Uri ("http://localhost:59560/ProductPhotoDataService.svc")
                );

            var qry = from p in ctx.Products
                        where p.FinishedGoodsFlag
                        orderby p.Name
                        select p;

            foreach (Product p in qry) {
                ProductDropDown.Items.Add(new ListItem(p.Name, p.ProductID.ToString()));
            }

            string id = ProductDropDown.SelectedValue;
            UpdateImage(id);
        }

        private void UpdateImage(string id) {
            ProductImage.ImageUrl = string.Format("GetImage.aspx?id={0}", id);
        }

        protected void ProductDropDownlist_SelectedIndexChanged(object sender, EventArgs e)
        {
            string id = ProductDropDown.SelectedValue;

            AdventureWorksEntities ctx = new AdventureWorksEntities(
                new Uri("http://localhost:59560/ProductPhotoDataService.svc")
                );

            var qry = from p in ctx.Products
                        where p.ProductID == Convert.ToInt32(id)
                        select p;

            //DataServiceQuery<Product> qry = ctx.CreateQuery<Product>(string.Format("/
            Product({0})", id));

            foreach (Product p in qry)
            {
                TableProduct.Rows[0].Cells[1].Text = p.Class;
                TableProduct.Rows[1].Cells[1].Text = p.Color;
                TableProduct.Rows[2].Cells[1].Text = p.Size + " " + p.SizeUnitMeasureCode;
```

```
                    TableProduct.Rows[3].Cells[1].Text = p.Weight + " " +
                    p.WeightUnitMeasureCode;
                    TableProduct.Rows[4].Cells[1].Text = p.ListPrice.ToString();
                    TableProduct.Rows[5].Cells[1].Text = p.ProductNumber;
                }
            UpdateImage(id);
        }

    }

}
```

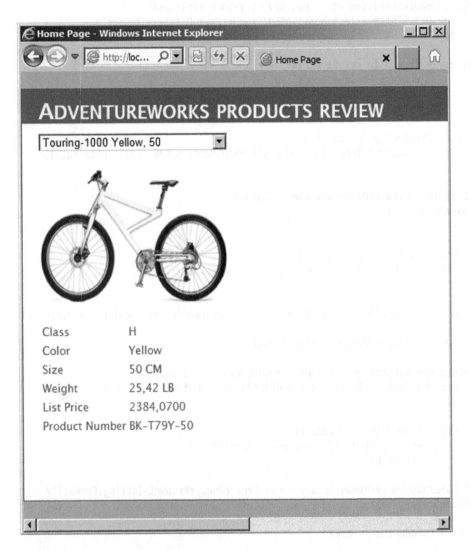

Figure 17-15. Calling the WCF data service from a consumer application

The first part of the code imports the necessary namespaces. The System.Data.Services.Client namespace is required to create WCF Data Services client queries. You need to add a reference to the System.Data.Services.Client component library to your project. The WCFdsClient.PhotoServiceReference namespace is a reference to the EDM classes' namespace:

```
using WCFdsClient.PhotoServiceReference;
using System.Data.Services.Client;
```

The PageLoad event of the Default.aspx page calls a little function called PopulateDropDown that populates the drop-down list with the names and IDs of all "finished goods" products that AdventureWorks keeps in its database:

```
PopulateDropDown();
```

The PopulateDropDown function begins by creating an instance of the AdventureWorksEntities EDM data context that points to the URI of the WCF data service. You saw data contexts in Chapter 15. Here, in WCF Data Services, the object is a sibling named a DataServiceContext:

```
AdventureWorksEntities ctx = new AdventureWorksEntities(
    new Uri ("http://localhost:59560/ProductPhotoDataService.svc")
);
```

Next, this function uses a LINQ query on the AdventureWorksEntities DataServiceContext that returns a DataServiceOuery. The query filters the Product entities whose FinishedGoodsFlag attributes are set to true. Results are sorted by the Name attribute:

```
var qry = from p in ctx.Products
          where p.FinishedGoodsFlag
          orderby p.Name
          select p;
```

The query returns an IEnumerable result that can be iterated using foreach. In this example, the Name and ProductID attributes are iterated and added to the drop-down list:

```
foreach (Product p in qry) {
    ProductDropDown.Items.Add(new ListItem(p.Name, p.ProductID.ToString()));
}
```

Finally, the product image is updated based on the value selected in the drop-down list:

```
string id = ProductDropDown.SelectedValue;
UpdateImage(id);
```

You also wire the SelectedIndexChanged event of the drop-down list so that the image and other data being displayed are updated when the user selects a new product. The first thing this function does is retrieve the currently selected value from the drop-down list:

```
string id = ProductDropDown.SelectedValue;
```

Then, as with the `PopulateDropDown` function, this function queries the WCF data service to retrieve the product selected from the drop-down list:

```
AdventureWorksEntities ctx = new AdventureWorksEntities(
    new Uri("http://localhost:59560/ProductPhotoDataService.svc")
);

var qry = from p in ctx.Products
          where p.ProductID == Convert.ToInt32(id)
          select p;
```

Next, the function iterates the results and updates the display, including the summary information table and the product image:

```
foreach (Product p in qry)
{
    TableProduct.Rows[0].Cells[1].Text = p.Class;
    TableProduct.Rows[1].Cells[1].Text = p.Color;
    TableProduct.Rows[2].Cells[1].Text = p.Size + " " + p.SizeUnitMeasureCode;
    TableProduct.Rows[3].Cells[1].Text = p.Weight + " " + p.WeightUnitMeasureCode;
    TableProduct.Rows[4].Cells[1].Text = p.ListPrice.ToString();
    TableProduct.Rows[5].Cells[1].Text = p.ProductNumber;
}
UpdateImage(id);
```

The `UpdateImage` function, called by two of the event handlers in this example, consists of a single line that changes the URL of the product image:

```
ProductImage.ImageUrl = string.Format("GetImage.aspx?id={0}", id);
```

■ **Note** In order to actually show the images on a web page, we had to resort to an old ASP.NET trick. Because the images are stored in the database, we had to create a second page in the project called `GetImage.aspx` to retrieve the appropriate image. This method calls the WCF data service and returns the binary product photo image as a JPEG image. We won't go into the details here because they're not essential to understanding WCF Data Services, but the source code is available in the downloadable sample files for the curious.

Now that you've seen how to create a basic WCF data service consumer, let's review some of the SQL Server 2014 features supported in ADO.NET 4.5. ADO.NET 4.5 enables support for null bit compression using sparse columns to optimize data transfer over the wire. Imagine a table in which more than half the columns are nullable and have null values for all the rows. When you use null bit compression and a sparse column schema, you can save on storage as well as optimize data transfer over the wire.

ADO.NET 4.5 also adds support for LocalDB. Remember that LocalDB needs to be started for your code to be able to access it.

Summary

SQL Server 2012 introduced an addition to SQL Server Express named LocalDB that lets you use databases as files in applications and simplifies embedding database capabilities in local, easy-to-deploy applications. At the same time, SQL Server data-access libraries keep improving, providing a heterogeneous environment with Linux systems and Java code.

In SQL Server 2005, Microsoft introduced HTTP SOAP endpoints, which allowed developers to expose SPs and UDFs in the database as web service methods. Because it wasn't a full-featured and solid enough implementation, and also because Microsoft wants to focus on a unified framework for connected systems, HTTP endpoints have been removed from SQL Server 2014.

The chapter ended with an introduction to WCF Data Services. With built-in support for entity data models and the powerful ADO.NET EDM designer, REST-style querying, and both the JSON and Atom payload formats, WCF Data Services can provide a lightweight alternative to SOAP-based web services and is a good way to provide interoperability across systems.

EXERCISES

1. [True/False] A LocalDB instance can be run as a Windows service.

2. [True/False] You can't access an XML data-type column if you access SQL Server from a Linux computer.

3. [True/False] HTTP SOAP endpoints can be created in SQL Server 2014.

4. [Fill in the blank] Visual Studio 2010 and 2012 provide a _____ project template to create new web services.

5. [True/False] Visual Studio 2012 includes a graphical EDM designer.

6. [Choose one] WCF Data Services accepts which type of query requests?

   a. SQL queries

   b. XSLT queries

   c. REST-style queries

   d. English language queries

Summary

■ ■ ■

Error Handling and Dynamic SQL

Prior to SQL Server 2005, error handling was limited almost exclusively to the @@error system function and the RAISERROR statement, or it was performed through client-side exception handling. T-SQL in SQL Server 2014 still provides access to these tools, but it also supports modern structured error handling similar to that offered by other high-level languages such as C++, C#, and Visual Basic. This chapter discusses legacy T-SQL error-handling functionality and the newer structured error-handling model in T-SQL. The chapter introduces tools useful for debugging server-side code, including T-SQL statements and the Visual Studio IDE.

The chapter also discusses dynamic SQL, which is often more difficult to debug and manage than standard (nondynamic) T-SQL statements. Dynamic SQL, although a useful tool, also has security implications, as you'll see.

Error Handling

SQL Server 2012 provided several improvements in error handling over SQL Server 2008 and prior releases that have been carried into SQL Server 2014. This section discusses legacy error handling, SQL Server 2008 TRY...CATCH structured error handling, as well as the THROW statement introduced in SQL 2014.

■ **Note** It may seem odd to still be referring in 2014 to an error-handling mechanism introduced in SQL Server 2000. The reality is that you're likely to encounter the @@error statement in much of your code; and despite certain limitations and restrictions, it remains useful for error handling.

Legacy Error Handling

In SQL Server 2000, the primary method of handling exceptions was through the @@error system function. This function returns an int value representing the current error code. An @@error value of 0 means no error occurred. One of the major limitations of this function is that it's automatically reset to 0 after every successful statement. This means you can't have any statements between the code you think might produce an exception and the code that checks the value of @@error. It also means that after @@error is checked, it's automatically reset to 0, so you can't both check the value of @@error and return @@error from in an SP. Listing 18-1 demonstrates an SP that generates an error and attempts to print the error code from within the procedure and return the value of @@error to the caller.

Listing 18-1. Incorrect Error Handling with @@error

```
CREATE PROCEDURE dbo.TestError (@e int OUTPUT)
AS

BEGIN
  INSERT INTO Person.Person(BusinessEntityID)
  VALUES (1);

  PRINT N'Error code in procedure = ' + CAST(@@error AS nvarchar(10));

  SET @e = @@error;
END
GO

DECLARE @ret int,
  @e int;

EXEC @ret = dbo.TestError @e OUTPUT;
PRINT N'Returned error code = ' + CAST(@e AS nvarchar(10));
PRINT N'Return value = ' + CAST(@ret AS nvarchar(10));
```

The TestError procedure in Listing 18-1 demonstrates one problem with @@error. The result of executing the procedure should be similar to the following:

```
Msg 515, Level 16, State 2, Procedure TestError, Line 4
Cannot insert the value NULL into column 'PersonType', table
'AdventureWorks.Person.Person'; column does not allow nulls. INSERT fails.
The statement has been terminated.
Error code in procedure = 515
Returned error code = 0
Return value = -6
```

As you can see, the error code generated by the failed INSERT statement is 515 when printed in the SP, but a value of 0 (no error) is returned to the caller via the OUTPUT parameter. The problem is with the following line in the SP:

```
PRINT N'Error code in procedure = ' + CAST(@@error AS nvarchar(10));
```

The PRINT statement automatically resets the value of @@error after it executes, meaning you can't test or retrieve the same value of @@error afterward (it will be 0 every time). The workaround is to store the value of @@error in a local variable immediately after the statement you suspect might fail (in this case, the INSERT statement). Listing 18-2 demonstrates this method of using @@error.

Listing 18-2. Corrected Error Handling with @@error

```
CREATE PROCEDURE dbo.TestError2 (@e int OUTPUT)
AS
BEGIN
  INSERT INTO Person.Person(BusinessEntityID)
  VALUES (1);

SET @e = @@error;

  PRINT N'Error code in procedure = ' + CAST(@e AS nvarchar(10));
END
GO

DECLARE @ret int,
  @e int;
EXEC @ret = dbo.TestError2 @e OUTPUT;
PRINT N'Returned error code = ' + CAST(@e AS nvarchar(10));
PRINT N'Return value = ' + CAST(@ret AS nvarchar(10));
```

By storing the value of @@error immediately after the statement you suspect might cause an error, you can test or retrieve the value as often as you like for further processing. The following is the result of the new procedure:

```
Msg 515, Level 16, State 2, Procedure TestError2, Line 4
Cannot insert the value NULL into column 'PersonType', table 'AdventureWorks.Person.Person';
column does not allow nulls. INSERT fails.
The statement has been terminated.
Error code in procedure = 515
Returned error code = 515
Return value = -6
```

In this case, the proper @@error code is both printed and returned to the caller by the SP. Also of note is that the SP return value is automatically set to a nonzero value when the error occurs.

The RAISERROR Statement

RAISERROR is a T-SQL statement that allows you to throw an exception at runtime. The RAISERROR statement accepts a message ID number or message string, severity level, state information, and optional argument parameters for special formatting codes in error messages. Listing 18-3 uses RAISERROR to throw an exception with a custom error message, a severity level of 17, and a state of 127.

Listing 18-3. Raising a Custom Exception with RAISERROR

```
RAISERROR ('This is an exception.', 17, 127);
```

When you pass a string error message to the RAISERROR statement, as in Listing 18-3, a default error code of 50000 is raised. If you specify a message ID number instead, the number must be between 13000 and 2147483647, and it can't be 50000. The severity level is a number between 0 and 25, with each level representing the seriousness of the error. Table 18-1 lists the severity levels recognized by SQL Server.

Table 18-1. *SQL Server Error Severity Levels*

Range	Description
0–10	Informational messages
11–18	Errors
19–25	Fatal errors

■ **Tip** Only members of the `sysadmin` fixed server role of users with `ALTER TRACE` permissions can specify severity levels greater than 18 with `RAISERROR`, and the `WITH LOG` option must be used.

The state value passed to `RAISERROR` is a user-defined informational value between 1 and 127. The state information can be used to help locate specific errors in your code when using `RAISERROR`. For instance, you can use a state of 1 for the first `RAISERROR` statement in a given SP and a state of 2 for the second `RAISERROR` statement in the same SP. The state information provided by `RAISERROR` isn't as necessary in SQL Server 2014 because you can retrieve much more descriptive and precise information from the functions available in CATCH blocks.

The `RAISERROR` statement supports an optional `WITH` clause for specifying additional options. The `WITH LOG` option logs the error raised to the application log and the SQL error log, the `WITH NOWAIT` option sends the error message to the client immediately, and the `WITH SETERROR` option sets the `@@error` system function (in a CATCH block) to an indicated message ID number. This should be used with a severity of 10 or less to set `@@error` without causing other side effects (for example, batch termination).

`RAISERROR` can be used in a TRY or CATCH block to generate errors. In the TRY block, if `RAISERROR` generates an error with a severity between 11 and 19, control passes to the CATCH block. For errors with a severity of 10 or lower, processing continues in the TRY block. For errors with a severity of 20 or higher, the client connection is terminated and control doesn't pass to the CATCH block. For these high-severity errors, the error is returned to the caller.

Try...Catch Exception Handling

SQL Server 2014 supports the TRY...CATCH model of exception handling, which is common in other modern programming languages and was first introduced in SQL Server 2008. In the T-SQL TRY...CATCH model, you wrap the code you suspect could cause an exception in a `BEGIN TRY...END TRY` block. This block is immediately followed by a `BEGIN CATCH...END CATCH` block that is invoked only if the statements in the TRY block cause an error. Listing 18-4 demonstrates TRY...CATCH exception handling with a simple SP.

Listing 18-4. Sample TRY...CATCH Error Handling

```
CREATE PROCEDURE dbo.TestError3 (@e int OUTPUT)
AS
BEGIN

  SET @e = 0;

  BEGIN TRY
  INSERT INTO Person.Address (AddressID)
  VALUES (1);
END TRY
```

```
BEGIN CATCH
    SET @e = ERROR_NUMBER();
    PRINT N'Error Code = ' + CAST(@e AS nvarchar(10));
    PRINT N'Error Procedure = ' + ERROR_PROCEDURE();
    PRINT N'Error Message = ' + ERROR_MESSAGE();
END CATCH

END
GO

DECLARE @ret   int,
    @e int;
EXEC @ret  = dbo.TestError3 @e OUTPUT;
PRINT N'Error code = ' + CAST(@e AS nvarchar(10));
PRINT N'Return value = ' + CAST(@ret AS nvarchar(10));
```

The result is similar to Listing 18-2, but SQL Server's TRY...CATCH support gives you more control and flexibility over the output, as shown here:

```
(0 row(s) affected)
Error Code = 544
Error Procedure = TestError3
Error Message = Cannot insert explicit value for identity column in table
'Address' when IDENTITY_INSERT is set to OFF.
Returned error code = 544
Return value = -6
```

The T-SQL statements in the BEGIN TRY...END TRY block execute normally. If the block completes without error, the T-SQL statements between the BEGIN CATCH...END CATCH block are skipped. If an exception is thrown by the statements in the TRY block, control transfers to the statements in the BEGIN CATCH...END CATCH block.

The CATCH block exposes several functions for determining exactly what error occurred and where it occurred. Listing 18-4 uses some of these functions to return additional information about the exception thrown. These functions are available only between the BEGIN CATCH...END CATCH keywords, and only during error handling when control has been transferred to the CATCH block by an exception thrown in a TRY block. If used outside of a CATCH block, all of these functions return NULL. The functions available are listed in Table 18-2.

Table 18-2. *CATCH Block Functions*

Function Name	Description
ERROR_LINE()	Returns the line number on which the exception occurred
ERROR_MESSAGE()	Returns the complete text of the generated error message
ERROR_PROCEDURE()	Returns the name of the SP or trigger where the error occurred
ERROR_NUMBER()	Returns the number of the error that occurred
ERROR_SEVERITY()	Returns the severity level of the error that occurred
ERROR_STATE()	Returns the state number of the error that occurred

TRY...CATCH blocks can be nested. You can have TRY...CATCH blocks in other TRY blocks or CATCH blocks to handle errors that might be generated in your exception-handling code.

You can also test the state of transactions in a CATCH block by using the XACT_STATE function. It's strongly recommended that you test your transaction state before issuing a COMMIT TRANSACTION or ROLLBACK TRANSACTION statement in your CATCH block, to ensure consistency. Table 18-3 lists the return values for XACT_STATE and how you should handle each in your CATCH block.

Table 18-3. *XACT_STATE Function Return Values*

XACT_STATE	Meaning
-1	An uncommittable transaction is pending. Issue a ROLLBACK TRANSACTION statement.
0	No transaction is pending. No action is necessary.
1	A committable transaction is pending. Issue a COMMIT TRANSACTION statement.

The T-SQL TRY...CATCH method of error handling has certain limitations attached to it. For one, TRY...CATCH can only capture errors that have a severity greater than 10 that don't close the database connection. The following errors aren't caught:

- Errors with a severity of 10 or lower (informational messages) aren't caught.

- Errors with a severity of 20 or higher (connection-termination errors) aren't caught, because they close the database connection immediately.

- Most compile-time errors, such as syntax errors, aren't caught by TRY...CATCH, although there are exceptions (for example, when using dynamic SQL).

- Statement-level recompilation errors, such as object-name resolution errors, aren't caught, due to SQL Server's deferred-name resolution.

Also keep in mind that errors captured by a TRY...CATCH block aren't returned to the caller. You can, however, use the RAISERROR statement (described in the next section) to return error information to the caller.

TRY_PARSE, TRY_CONVERT, and TRY_CAST

SQL Server 2012 introduced additional enhancements to the TRY command. The TRY_PARSE, TRY_CONVERT, and TRY_CAST functions offer error-handling simplicity to some common T-SQL problems. For example, the TRY_PARSE function attempts to convert a string value to a date type or numeric type. If the attempt fails, SQL returns a NULL value. In previous versions of SQL Server, you used CAST or CONVERT and had to write code to capture any errors. The syntax for the TRY_PARSE command is as follows:

```
TRY_PARSE ( string_value AS data_type [ USING culture ] )
```

The culture statement allows you to specify the language format used for the conversion. This is set regardless of the default SQL Server collation. If no culture is specified, the command uses the default language on the server. Listing 18-5 shows a few examples. The output is shown in Figure 18-1.

Listing 18-5. Examples of TRY_PARSE

```
DECLARE @fauxdate AS varchar(10)
DECLARE @realdate AS VARCHAR(10)

SET @fauxdate = 'iamnotadate'
SET @realdate = '01/05/2012'

SELECT TRY_PARSE(@fauxdate AS DATE);

SELECT TRY_PARSE(@realdate AS DATE);

SELECT TRY_PARSE(@realdate AS DATE USING 'Fr-FR');

SELECT IIF(TRY_PARSE(@realdate AS DATE) IS NULL, 'False', 'True')
```

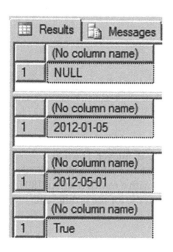

Figure 18-1. *Output of the TRY_PARSE function*

The first query attempts to convert a non-date string to a date and fails by returning NULL. The second query succeeds and returns the date 2012-05-01. The third query returns the same date but converts it to the French date format. The final query shows how you can use conditional processing to return any value you want based on whether the conversion succeeds or fails.

The next function is TRY_CONVERT. It has the same functionality as the CONVERT function but returns NULL instead of an error if the conversion fails. You can use TRY_CONVERT when you want to test the possibility of converting one data type to another data type. The syntax is as follows:

```
TRY_CONVERT ( data_type [ ( length ) ], expression [, style ] )
```

data_type is the data type you want to convert the expression into, and style determines formatting. Listing 18-6 shows several examples, and Figure 18-2 shows the output.

Listing 18-6. TRY_CONVERT Examples

```
DECLARE @sampletext AS VARCHAR(10)

SET @sampletext = '123456'

SELECT TRY_CONVERT(INT, @ sampletext);

SELECT TRY_CONVERT(DATE, @ sampletext);

SELECT IIF(TRY_CONVERT(binary, @ sampletext) IS NULL, 'FALSE', 'TRUE');
```

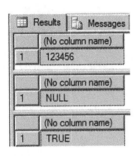

Figure 18-2. *Output of TRY_CONVERT*

The listing sets the variable to a text value, which can easily be converted to an integer. The first TRY_CONVERT successfully performs the conversion, but the second fails because the text value can't implicitly be converted to a date. The final example shows that the conversion succeeded with a return result of TRUE.

Now let's look at TRY_CAST. It's the technical equivalent of TRY_CONVERT, but the format is different. The syntax for TRY_CAST is the following:

```
TRY_CAST ( expression AS data_type [ ( length ) ] )
```

Listing 18-7 uses the same examples as Listing 18-5 but changes the syntax to use TRY_CAST. The output is the same as in Figure 18-2.

Listing 18-7. Examples Using TRY_CAST

```
DECLARE @sampletext AS VARCHAR(10)

SET @sampletext = '123456'

SELECT TRY_CAST(@sampletext AS INT);

SELECT TRY_CAST(@sampletext AS DATE);

SELECT IIF(TRY_CAST(@sampletext AS BINARY) IS NULL, 'FALSE', 'TRUE');
```

■ **Tip**   Although they're useful, keep in mind a couple of things about TRY_PARSE, TRY_CONVERT, and TRY_CAST. Parsing strings can be a costly process, so use the functions sparingly. Microsoft recommends using TRY_PARSE only for converting strings to date or numeric values. For all other conversions, use CAST or CONVERT. Also keep in mind that TRY_CONVERT and TRY_CAST throw errors for explicit conversions—these conversions aren't possible. For a chart of implicit and explicit conversions, see Books Online (BOL) at http://msdn.microsoft.com/en-us/library/ms191530.aspx.

Throw Statement

SQL Server 2014 introduced the THROW statement. It's similar to what you find in programming languages like C++ and C# and can be used instead of RAISERROR. A primary benefit of using THROW instead of RAISERROR is that it doesn't require an error message ID to exist in sys.messages. The THROW statement can occur either in a CATCH block or outside the TRY...CATCH statements. If no parameters are defined, then THROW must be in the CATCH block. Listing 18-8 shows examples of both. It uses the same INSERT statements as the previous examples.

Listing 18-8.   Examples of the THROW Statement

```
--1. Using THROW without parameters

     BEGIN TRY
   INSERT INTO Person.Address (AddressID)
   VALUES (1);
   END TRY
   BEGIN CATCH
   PRINT 'This is an error';
   THROW
   END CATCH ;

--2. Using THROW with parameters

  THROW 52000,  'This is also an error',  1

    BEGIN TRY
       INSERT INTO Person.Address (AddressID)
   VALUES (1);
   END TRY
   BEGIN CATCH
   THROW
   END CATCH
```

```
(0 row(s) affected)
This is an error
Msg 544, Level 16, State 1, Line 2
Cannot insert explicit value for identity column in table 'Address' when
IDENTITY INSERT is set to OFF.

MSG 52000, Level 16, State 1, Line 1
```

597

There are a couple of things to notice: First, the only severity level returned by THROW is 16. The statement doesn't allow for any other level, which is another difference between THROW and RAISERROR. Also notice that any statement prior to the THROW statement in the CATCH block must end in a semicolon. This is yet another reason to make sure all your block statements terminate in semicolons.

If you're accustomed to using THROW in other programming languages, you should find this a helpful addition to SQL Server 2014.

Debugging Tools

In procedural languages like C#, debugging code is somewhat easier than in declarative languages like T-SQL. In procedural languages, you can easily follow the flow of a program, setting breakpoints at each atomic step of execution. In declarative languages, however, a single statement can perform dozens or hundreds of steps in the background, most of which you probably aren't even aware of at execution time. The good news is that the SQL Server team didn't leave us without tools to debug and troubleshoot T-SQL code. The unpretentious PRINT statement provides a very simple and effective method of debugging.

PRINT Statement Debugging

The PRINT statement is a simple and useful server-side debugging tool. Simply printing constants and variable values to standard output during script or SP execution often provides enough information to quickly locate problem code. PRINT works from within SPs and batches, but it doesn't work in UDFs because of the built-in restrictions on functions causing side effects. Consider the example code in Listing 18-9, which tries to achieve an end result where @i is equal to 10. The end result of the code is not @>i = 10, so the listing has a couple of PRINT statements to uncover the reason.

Listing 18-9. Debugging Script with PRINT

```
DECLARE @i int;
PRINT N'Initial value of @i = ' + COALESCE(CAST(@i AS nvarchar(10)), N'NULL');
SET @i += 10;
PRINT N'Final value of @i = ' + COALESCE(CAST(@i AS nvarchar(10)), N'NULL');
```

The result, shown in Figure 18-3, indicates that the desired end result isn't occurring because I failed to initialize the variable @i to 0 at the beginning of the script. The initial value of @>i is NULL, so the end result is NULL. Once you've identified the issue, fixing it is a relatively simple matter in this case.

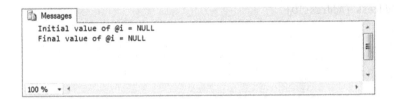

Figure 18-3. Results of PRINT statement debugging

In addition to the PRINT statement, you can use the RAISERROR statement with a NOWAIT clause to send a message or status indication immediately to the client. Whereas PRINT waits for the buffer to flush, RAISERROR with the NOWAIT clause sends the message immediately.

Trace Flags

SQL Server 2014 provides several trace flags that can help with debugging, particularly when you suspect you have a problem with SQL Server settings. Trace flags can turn on or off specific SQL Server behavior or temporarily change other server characteristics for a server or session. As an example, trace flag 1204 returns the resources and types of locks participating in a deadlock, and the current command affected.

■ **Tip**   Many trace flags are undocumented and may only be revealed to you by Microsoft Product Support Services when you report a specific issue; but those that are documented can provide very useful information. BOL provides a complete list of documented SQL Server 2014 trace flags under "Trace Flags."

Turning on or off a trace flag is as simple as using the DBCC TRACEON and DBCC TRACEOFF statements, as shown in Listing 18-10.

Listing 18-10. Turning Trace Flag 1204 On and Off

```
DBCC TRACEON (1204, -1);
GO

DBCC TRACEOFF (1204, -1);
GO
```

Trace flags may report information via standard output, the SQL Server log, or additional log files created for that specific trace flag. Check BOL for specific information about the methods that specific trace flags report back to you.

SSMS Integrated Debugger

SQL Server 2005 did away with the integrated user interface debugger in SSMS, although it was previously a part of Query Analyzer (QA). Apparently, the thought was that Visual Studio would be the debugging tool of choice for stepping through T-SQL code and setting breakpoints in SPs. Integrated SSMS debugging was brought back in SQL Server 2012 and is carried forward in SQL Server 2014. The SSMS main menu contains several debugging actions accessible through the new Debug menu, as shown in Figure 18-4.

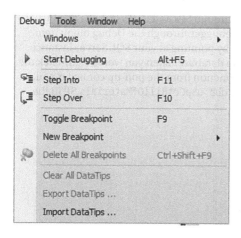

Figure 18-4. *The SSMS Debug menu*

The options are similar to those available when debugging Visual Studio projects. From this menu, you can start debugging, step into/over your code one statement at a time, and manage breakpoints. Figure 18-5 shows an SSMS debugging session that has just hit a breakpoint in the body of a SP.

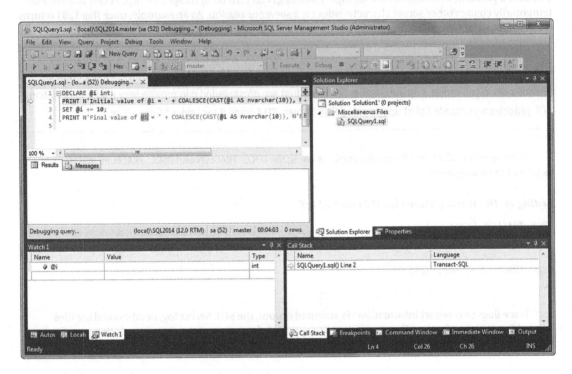

Figure 18-5. *Stepping into code with the SSMS debugger*

The SSMS debugger provides several windows that provide additional debugging information, including the Call Stack, Breakpoints, Command, Output, Locals, and Watch windows.

Visual Studio T-SQL Debugger

Visual Studio 2013 also offers an excellent facility for stepping through SPs and UDFs just like any Visual Basic or C# application. You can access Visual Studio's T-SQL debugger through the Debug menu item. Prior to SQL Server 2014, the debug functionality was available by pointing at your SQL Server instance and the SP or function you wish to debug under the appropriate database. Then you would right-click the procedure or function and select Debug Procedure or Debug Function from the pop-up context menu. Figure 18-6 demonstrates by selecting Debug Procedure for the dbo.uspGetBillOfMaterials SP in the AdventureWorks 2012 database.

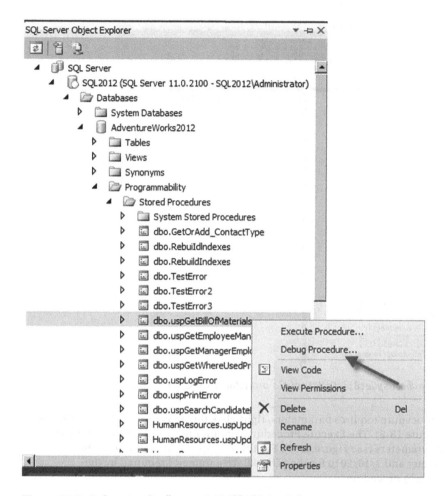

Figure 18-6. Debugging the dbo.uspGetBillOfMaterials procedure in SQL Server 2012

■ **Tip**   It's much easier to configure Visual Studio T-SQL debugging on a locally installed instance of SQL Server than to set up remote debugging. BOL offers information about setting up both local and remote SQL Server debugging, in the article "Debugging SQL" (http://msdn.microsoft.com/en-us/library/cc646024.aspx).

SQL Server 2014 debug functionality is now only available via the toolbar or menu item. The right-click debugging functionality was removed from the SQL Server Object Explorer. Figure 18-7 demonstrates the location of the Debug menu and toolbar items.

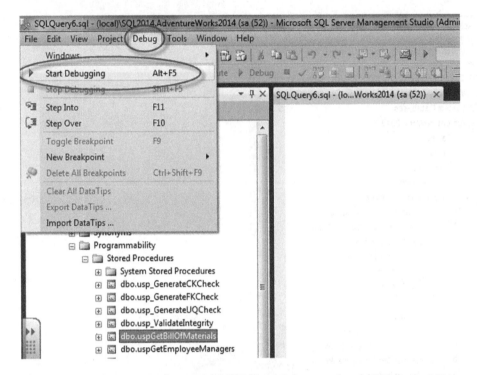

Figure 18-7. *Debugging the* dbo.uspGetBillOfMaterials *procedure in SQL Server 2014*

If your function or procedure requires parameters, right-click the procedure and select Execute Stored Procedure (see Figure 18-8). The Execute Procedure window opens and asks you to enter values for the required parameters (see Figure 18-9). For this example, I entered 770 for the @StartProductID parameter and 7/10/2010 for the @CheckDate parameter required by the dbo.uspGetBillOfMaterials procedure.

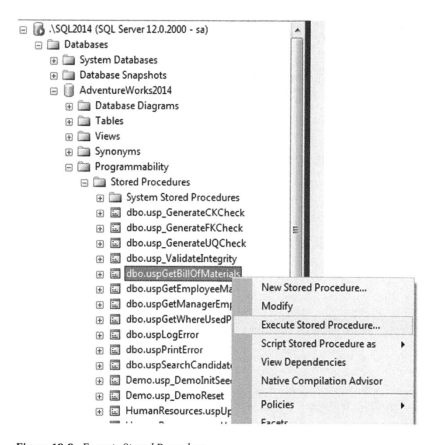

Figure 18-8. *Execute Stored Procedure*

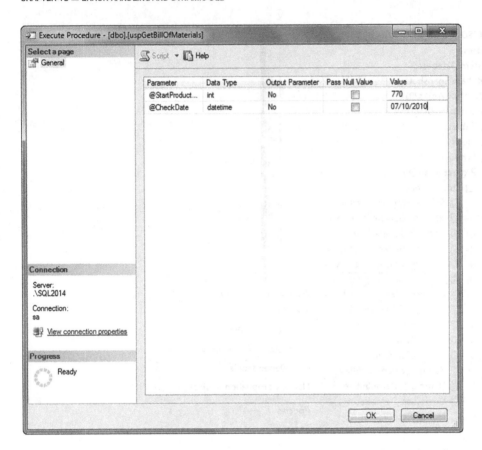

Figure 18-9. *Entering parameter values*

After you enter the parameters, the procedure begins running. You must choose to run the procedure in Debug mode to be able to step through the code. Visual Studio shows the script and highlights each line in yellow as you step through it, as shown in Figure 18-10.

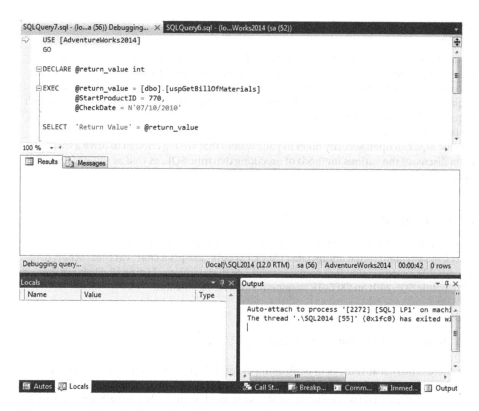

Figure 18-10. Stepping through an SP in Debug mode

In Debug mode, you can set breakpoints by clicking the left border and using the Continue (F5), Stop Debugging (Shift+F5), Step Over (F10), Step Into (F11), and Step Out (Shift+F11) commands, just like when you debug C# or Visual Basic programs. You can also add watches and view locals to inspect parameter and variable values as your code executes. Any result sets and return values from the SP are shown in the Visual Studio Output window, as in Figure 18-11.

	ProductAssemblyID	ComponentID	ComponentDesc	TotalQuantity	StandardCost	ListPrice	BOMLevel	RecursionLevel
1	770	517	LL Road Seat Assembly	2.00	98.77	133.34	1	0
2	770	738	LL Road Frame - Black. 52	1.00	204.6251	337.22	1	0
3	770	806	ML Headset	1.00	45.4168	102.29	1	0
4	770	811	LL Road Handlebars	1.00	19.7758	44.54	1	0
5	770	826	LL Road Rear Wheel	2.00	49.9789	112.565	1	0
6	770	894	Rear Derailleur	1.00	53.9282	121.46	1	0
7	770	907	Rear Brakes	2.00	47.286	106.50	1	0
8	770	938	LL Road Pedal	2.00	17.9776	40.49	1	0
9	770	948	Front Brakes	1.00	47.286	106.50	1	0

	Return Value
1	0

Query executed successfully. (local)\SQL2014 (12.0 RTM) sa (56) AdventureWorks2014 00:02:30 46 rows

Figure 18-11. The Visual Studio Output window

Dynamic SQL

SQL Server MVP Erland Sommarskog said it best: "dynamic SQL is a curse and a blessing".[1] Put simply, dynamic SQL is a means of constructing SQL statements as strings in your server-side (or even client-side) applications and executing them dynamically on the fly. When used properly, dynamic SQL can be used to generate complex queries at runtime, in some cases to improve performance, and to do tasks that just aren't possible (or are extremely difficult) in standard, nondynamic T-SQL.

The downside is that there are numerous ways to shoot yourself in the foot with dynamic SQL. If not used properly, dynamic SQL can open security holes in your system that are big enough to drive a truck through. This section discusses the various methods of executing dynamic SQL, as well as some of the risks and rewards that Erland alludes to.

The EXECUTE Statement

The most basic form of server-side dynamic SQL is achieved by passing an SQL query or other instruction as a string to the EXECUTE statement (often abbreviated EXEC). EXECUTE accepts a char, varchar, nchar, or nvarchar constant, variable, or expression that contains valid T-SQL statements. Listing 18-11 shows the most basic form of dynamic SQL with an EXECUTE statement and a string constant.

Listing 18-11. Basic EXECUTE Statement

```
EXECUTE (N'SELECT ProductID FROM Production.Product');
```

As you can see, there is no real advantage to performing dynamic SQL on a string constant. A simple SELECT statement without the EXECUTE would perform the same function and return the same result. The true power of dynamic SQL is that you can build an SQL statement or query dynamically and execute it. Listing 18-12 demonstrates how this can be done.

Listing 18-12. More Complex Dynamic SQL Example

```
DECLARE @min_product_id int = 500;
DECLARE @sql_stmt nvarchar(128) =
    N'SELECT ProductID ' +
    N'FROM Production.Product ' +
    N'WHERE ProductID >= ' + CAST(@min_product_id AS nvarchar(10));
EXECUTE (@sql_stmt);
```

Now that you've seen this simple code sample, let's explore all the things that are wrong with it.

SQL Injection and Dynamic SQL

In Listing 18-12, the variable @sqlstmt contains the dynamic SQL query. The query is built dynamically by appending the minimum product ID to the WHERE clause. This isn't the recommended method of performing this type of query, and it's shown here to make a point.

One of the problems with this method is that you lose some of the benefits of cached query-plan execution. SQL Server 2014 has some great features that can help in this area, including parameter sniffing and the ability to turn on forced parameterization, but there are many exceptions to SQL Server's ability to automatically parameterize queries or clauses. To guarantee efficient reuse of cached query execution plans as the text of your query changes, you should parameterize queries yourself.

---

[1] The Curse and Blessings of Dynamic SQL by Erland Sommarskog; http://www.sommarskog.se/dynamic_sql.html

But the big problem here is SQL injection. Although not really a problem when appending an integer value to the end of a dynamic query (as in Listing 18-12), SQL injection can provide a back door for hackers trying to access or destroy your data when you concatenate strings to create dynamic SQL queries. Take a look at the innocent-looking dynamic SQL query in Listing 18-13. You see how a hacker could wreak havoc with this query after the listing.

Listing 18-13. Basic Dynamic SQL Query with a String Appended

```
DECLARE @product_name nvarchar(50) = N'Mountain';
DECLARE @sql_stmt NVARCHAR(128) = N'SELECT ProductID, Name ' +
      N'FROM Production.Product ' +
      N'WHERE Name LIKE ''' +
      @product_name + N'%''';
EXECUTE (@sql_stmt);
```

This query returns the product IDs and names of all products that begin with the word Mountain. The problem is with how SQL Server interprets the concatenated string. The EXECUTE statement sees the following result after all the string concatenations are done:

```
SELECT ProductID, Name
FROM  Production.Product
WHERE Name LIKE 'Mountain%'
```

A simple substitution for @productname can execute other unwanted statements on your server. This is especially true with data coming from an external source (for example, from the front end or application layer). Consider the following change to Listing 18-13:

```
DECLARE @product_name nvarchar(50) =
    N'''; DROP TABLE Production.Product; --'
```

As before, the string concatenations result in a statement to be executed. However, this time the statement passed to EXECUTE looks as follows:

```
SELECT  ProductID,  Name
FROM   Production.Product
WHERE Name LIKE '';
DROP  TABLE Production.Product; --%'
```

The simple dynamic SQL query is now two queries, the second of which drops the Production.Product table from the database! Now consider if the value of the @productname variable had been retrieved from a user interface, like a web page. A malicious hacker could easily issue arbitrary INSERT, UPDATE, DELETE, DROP TABLE, TRUNCATE TABLE, or other statements to destroy data or open a back door into your system. Depending on how secure your server is, hackers may be able to use SQL injection to grant themselves administrator rights, retrieve and modify data stored in your server's file system, take control of your server, or access network resources.

The only justification for using the string-concatenation method with EXECUTE is if you have to dynamically name the tables or columns in your statements. This is far rarer than many people think. In fact, the only time this is usually necessary is if you need to dynamically generate SQL statements around database, table, or column names—if you're creating a dynamic pivot table-type query or coding an administration tool for SQL Server, for instance.

If you must use string concatenation with the EXECUTE method, be sure to take the following precautions with the strings being passed in from the user interface:

- Don't ever trust data from the front end. Always validate the data. If you're expecting only the letters A through Z and the numbers 0 through 9, reject all other characters in the input data.

- Disallow apostrophes, semicolons, parentheses, and double hyphens (--) in the input if possible. These characters have special significance to SQL Server and should be avoided. If you must allow these characters, scrutinize the input thoroughly before using them.

- If you absolutely must allow apostrophes in your data, escape them (double them) before accepting the input.

- Reject strings that contain binary data, escape sequences, and multiline comment markers (/* and */).

- Validate XML input data against an XML schema when possible.

- Take extra-special care when input data contains xp_ or sp_, because it may indicate an attempt to run procedures or XPs on your server.

■ **Tip**   If you're concatenating one-part table and object names into SQL statements on the server side, you can use the QUOTENAME function to safely quote them. QUOTENAME doesn't work for two-, three-, and four-part names, however.

Usually, data validations like the ones listed previously are performed on the client side, on the front end, in the application layer, or in the middle tiers of multitier systems. In highly secure and critical applications, it may be important to also perform server-side validations or some combination of client- and server-side validations. Triggers and check constraints can perform this type of validation on data before it's inserted into a table, and you can create UDFs or SPs to perform validations on dynamic SQL before executing it. Listing 18-14 shows a simple UDF that uses the Numbers table created in Chapter 4 to perform basic validation on a string, ensuring that it contains only the letters A through Z, the digits 0 through 9, and the underscore character _, which is a common validation used on usernames, passwords, and other simple data.

Listing 18-14. Simple T-SQL String-Validation Function

```
CREATE  FUNCTION  dbo.ValidateString  (@string  nvarchar(4000))
RETURNS int
AS
BEGIN
    DECLARE @result int = 0;
    WITH Numbers (Num)
    AS
    (
        SELECT 1
        UNION ALL
        SELECT Num + 1
        FROM Numbers
        WHERE Num <= LEN(@string)
    )
```

```
    SELECT @result = SUM
    (
        CASE
        WHEN  SUBSTRING(@string,  n.Num,  1)  LIKE N'[A-ZO-9\_]' ESCAPE '\'
        THEN  0
        ELSE 1
        END
    )
    FROM Numbers n
    WHERE n.Num <= LEN(@string)
    OPTION (MAXRECURSION 0);
    RETURN @result;
END
GO
```

The function in Listing 18-14 uses a common table expression (CTE) to validate each character in the given string. The result is the total number of invalid characters in the string: a value of 0 indicates that all the characters in the string are valid. More complex validations can be performed with the LIKE operator or procedural code to ensure that data is in a prescribed format as well.

Troubleshooting Dynamic SQL

A big disadvantage of using dynamic SQL is in debugging and troubleshooting code. Complex dynamic SQL queries can be difficult to troubleshoot, and very simple syntax or other errors can be hard to locate. Fortunately there is a fairly simple fix for that: write your troublesome query directly in T-SQL, replacing parameters with potential values. Highlight the code, and parse—or execute—it. Any syntax errors are detected and described by SQL Server immediately. Fix the errors, and repeat until all errors have been fixed. Then and only then revert the values back to their parameter names and put the statement back in dynamic SQL.

Another handy method of troubleshooting is to print the dynamic SQL statement before executing it. Highlight, copy, and attempt to parse or run it in SSMS. You should be able to quickly and easily locate any problems and fix them as necessary.

One of the restrictions on dynamic SQL is that it can't be executed in a UDF. This restriction is in place because UDFs can't produce side effects that change the database. Dynamic SQL offers infinite opportunities to circumvent this restriction, so it's simply not allowed.

The sp_executesql Stored Procedure

The sp_executesql SP provides a second method of executing dynamic SQL. When used correctly, it's safer than the EXECUTE method for concatenating strings and executing them. Like EXECUTE, sp_executesql takes a string constant or variable as a SQL statement to execute. Unlike EXECUTE, the SQL statement parameter must be an nchar or nvarchar.

The sp_executesql procedure offers a distinct advantage over the EXECUTE method: you can specify your parameters separately from the SQL statement. When you specify the parameters separately instead of concatenating them into one large string, SQL Server passes the parameters to sp_executesql separately. SQL Server then substitutes the values of the parameters in the parameterized SQL statement. Because the parameter values aren't concatenated into the SQL statement, sp_executesql protects against SQL injection attacks. sp_executesql parameterization also improves reuse of the query execution plan cache, which helps with performance.

A limitation of this approach is that you can't use the parameters in your SQL statement in place of table, column, or other object names. Listing 18-15 shows how to parameterize the previous example.

Listing 18-15. Dynamic SQL sp_executesql Parameterized

```
DECLARE @product_name NVARCHAR(50) = N'Mountain%';
DECLARE @sql_stmt NVARCHAR(128) = N'SELECT ProductID, Name ' +
        N'FROM Production.Product ' +
        N'WHERE Name LIKE @name';
EXECUTE  sp_executesql @sql_stmt,
        N'@name NVARCHAR(50)',
        @name = @product_name;
```

■ **Tip** It's strongly recommended that you use parameterized queries whenever possible when using dynamic SQL. If you can't parameterize (for example, you need to dynamically change the table name in a query), be sure to thoroughly validate the incoming data.

Dynamic SQL and Scope

Dynamic SQL executes in its own batch. This means variables and temporary tables created in a dynamic SQL statement or statement batch aren't directly available to the calling routine. Consider the example in Listing 18-16.

Listing 18-16. Limited Scope of Dynamic SQL

```
DECLARE @sql_stmt NVARCHAR(512) = N'CREATE TABLE #Temp_ProductIDs ' +
    N'(' +
    N'    ProductID int NOT NULL PRIMARY KEY' +
    N'); ' +
    N'INSERT INTO #Temp_ProductIDs (ProductID) ' +
    N'SELECT ProductID ' +
    N'FROM Production.Product;' ;

EXECUTE (@sql_stmt);

SELECT  ProductID
FROM #Temp_ProductIDs;
```

The #Temp_ProductIDs temporary table is created in a dynamic SQL batch, so it isn't available outside of the batch. This causes the following error message to be generated:

```
(504 row(s) affected)
Msg 208, Level 16, State 0, Line 9
Invalid object name '#Temp_ProductIDs'.
```

The message (504 row(s) affected) indicates that the temporary-table creation and INSERT INTO statement of the dynamic SQL executed properly and without error. The problem is with the SELECT statement after EXECUTE. Because the #Temp_ProductIDs table was created in the scope of the dynamic SQL statement, the temporary table is dropped immediately when the dynamic SQL statement completes. This means that once SQL Server reaches the SELECT statement, the #Temp_ProductIDs table no longer exists. One way to work around this issue is to create the temporary table before the dynamic SQL executes. The dynamic SQL is able to access and update the temporary table created by the caller, as shown in Listing 18-17.

Listing 18-17. Creating a Temp Table Accessible to Dynamic SQL

```
CREATE  TABLE  #Temp_ProductIDs
(
    ProductID int NOT NULL PRIMARY KEY
);

DECLARE @sql_stmt NVARCHAR(512) = N'INSERT INTO #Temp_ProductIDs (ProductID) ' +
        N'SELECT ProductID ' +
        N'FROM Production.Product;' ;

EXECUTE (@sql_stmt);

SELECT  ProductID
FROM  #Temp_ProductIDs;
```

Table variables and other variables declared by the caller aren't accessible to dynamic SQL, however. Variables and table variables have well-defined scope: they're only available to the batch, function, or procedure in which they're created, not to dynamic SQL or other called routines.

Client-Side Parameterization

Parameterization of dynamic SQL queries isn't just a good idea on the server side; it's also a great idea to parameterize queries instead of building dynamic SQL strings on the client side. In addition to the security implications, query parameterization provides reuse of cached query execution plans, making queries more efficient than their concatenated string counterparts. Microsoft .NET languages provide the tools necessary to parameterize queries from the application layer in the System.Data.SqlClient and System.Data namespaces. Chapter 16 discussed parameterization on the client side.

Summary

SQL Server has long supported simple error handling using the @@error system function to retrieve error information and the RAISERROR statement to throw exceptions. SQL Server 2014 continues to support these methods of handling errors, but it also provides modern, structured TRY...CATCH and THROW exception handling similar to other modern languages. T-SQL TRY...CATCH exception handling includes several functions that expose error-specific information in the CATCH block. SQL Server 2012 introduced a more streamlined error-handling approach to common programming scenarios by introducing TRY_PARSE, TRY_CONVERT, and TRY_CAST functions.

In addition to the SSMS integrated debugger, which can be accessed through the Debug menu, SQL Server and Visual Studio provide tools that are useful for troubleshooting and debugging your T-SQL code. These include simple tools like the PRINT statement and trace flags, and even more powerful tools like Visual Studio debugging, which lets you set breakpoints, step into code, and use much of the same functionality that is useful when debugging C# and Visual Basic programs.

This chapter also discussed dynamic SQL, a tool that is very useful and powerful in its own right but is often incorrectly used. Misuse of dynamic SQL can expose your databases, servers, and other network resources, leaving your IT infrastructure vulnerable to SQL injection attacks. Improper use of dynamic SQL can also impact application performance. SQL injection and query performance are the two most compelling reasons to take extra precautions when using dynamic SQL.

The next chapter gives an overview of SQL Server 2014 query performance tuning.

EXERCISES

1. [Fill in the blank] The _____ system function automatically resets to 0 after every successful statement execution.

2. [Choose one] Which of the following functions, available only in the CATCH block in SQL Server, returns the severity level of the error that occurred?

    a. ERR_LEVEL()

    b. EXCEPTION_SEVERITY()

    c. EXCEPTION_LEVEL()

    d. ERROR_SEVERITY()

3. [True/False] The RAISERROR statement allows you to raise errors in SQL Server.

4. [True/False] Visual Studio provides integrated debugging, which allows you to step into T-SQL functions and SPs and set breakpoints.

5. [Choose all that apply] The potential problems with dynamic SQL include which of the following?

    a. Potential performance issues

    b. SQL injection attacks

    c. General exception errors caused by interference with graphics drivers

    d. All of the above

CHAPTER 19

■ ■ ■

Performance Tuning

In most production environments, database and server optimization have long been the domain of DBAs. This includes server settings, hardware optimizations, index creation and maintenance, and many other responsibilities. SQL developers, however, are responsible for ensuring that their queries perform optimally. SQL Server is truly a developer's DBMS, and as a result the developer responsibilities can overlap with those of the DBA. This overlap includes recommending database design and indexing strategies, troubleshooting poorly performing queries, and making other performance-enhancement recommendations. This chapter discusses various tools and strategies for query optimization and performance enhancement and tuning queries.

SQL Server Storage

SQL Server is designed to abstract away many of the logical and physical aspects of storage and data retrieval. In a perfect world, you wouldn't have to worry about such things—you would be able to just "set it and forget it." Unfortunately, the world isn't perfect, and how SQL Server stores data can have a noticeable impact on query performance. Understanding SQL Server storage mechanisms is essential to properly troubleshooting performance issues. With that in mind, this section offers a brief overview of how SQL Server stores your data.

■ **Tip**   This section gives only a summarized description of how SQL Server stores data. The best detailed description of the SQL Server storage engine internals is in the book *Inside Microsoft SQL Server 2012 Internals*, by Kalen Delaney et al. (Microsoft Press, 2012).

Files and Filegroups

SQL Server stores databases in files. Each database consists of at least two files: a database file with an `.mdf` extension and a log file with an `.ldf` extension. You can also add additional files to a SQL Server database, normally with an `.ndf` extension.

Filegroups are logical groupings of files for administration and allocation purposes. By default, SQL Server creates all database files in a single primary filegroup. You can add filegroups to an existing database or specify additional filegroups at creation time. When creating in-memory optimized tables, you're required to create a new filegroup with the `CONTAINS MEMORY_OPTIMIZED_DATA` syntax. Chapter 6 covers in-memory optimized tables and provides a more detailed discussion of the requirements for the new filegroup type. There are significant performance benefits to using multiple filegroups, which come from placing the different filegroups on different physical drives. It's common practice to increase performance by placing data files in a separate filegroup and physical drive from nonclustered indexes. It's also common to place log files on a separate physical drive from both data and nonclustered indexes.

Understanding how physical separation of files improves performance requires an explanation of the read/write patterns involved with each type of information that SQL Server stores. Database data generally uses a random-access read/write pattern. The hard drive head constantly repositions itself to read and write user data to the database. Nonclustered indexes are also usually random-access in nature; the hard drive head repositions itself to traverse the nonclustered index. Once nodes that match the query criteria are found in the nonclustered index, if columns must be accessed that aren't in the nonclustered index, the hard drive must again reposition itself to locate the actual data stored in the data file. The transaction log file has a completely different access pattern than either data or nonclustered indexes: SQL Server writes to the transaction log in a serial fashion. These conflicting access patterns can result in *head thrashing*, or constant repositioning of the hard drive head to read and write these different types of information. Dividing your files by type and placing them on separate physical drives helps improve performance by reducing head thrashing and allowing SQL Server to perform I/O activities in parallel.

You can also place multiple data files in a single filegroup. When you create a database with multiple files in a single filegroup, SQL Server uses a proportional fill strategy across the files as data is added to the database. This means SQL Server tries to fill all files in a filegroup at approximately the same time. Log files, which aren't part of a filegroup, are filled using a serial strategy. If you add additional log files to a database, they won't be used until the current log file is filled.

■ **Tip**   You can move a table from its current filegroup to a new filegroup by dropping the current clustered index on the table and creating a new clustered index, specifying the new filegroup in the CREATE CLUSTERED INDEX statement.

Space Allocation

When reading data, SQL Server uses a random-access file to locate the data that resides in a specific location rather than reading the data from the beginning. To enable the random-access file, the system should have consistently sized allocation units in the file structure. SQL Server allocates space in the database in units called *extents* and *pages* to accomplish this. A page is an 8 KB block of contiguous storage. An extent consists of eight logically contiguous pages, or 64 KB of storage. SQL Server has two types of extents: *uniform extents*, which are owned completely by a single database object, and *mixed extents*, which can be shared by up to eight different database objects. When a new table or index is created, the pages are allocated from mixed extents. When the table or index grows beyond eight pages, then the allocations are done in uniform extents to make the space allocation efficient.

This physical limitation on the size of pages is the reason for the historic limitations on data types such as varchar and nvarchar (up to 8,000 and 4,000 characters, respectively) and row size (8,060 bytes). It's also why special handling is required internally for LOB data types such as varchar(max), varbinary(max), and xml, because the data they contain can span many pages.

SQL Server keeps track of allocated extents with what are termed *allocation maps*: *global allocation map* (GAM) pages and *shared global allocation map* (SGAM) pages. GAM pages use bits to track all extents that have been allocated. SGAM pages use bits to track mixed extents with one or more free pages available. *Index allocation map* (IAM) pages track all the extents used by an index or table, and they're used to navigate through data pages. *Page free space* (PFS) pages track the free space on each page that stores LOB values. The combination of GAM and SGAM pages allows SQL Server to quickly allocate free extents, uniform/full mixed extents, and mixed extents with free pages as necessary, whereas IAM and PFS are used to decide when an object needs extent allocation.

The behavior of the SQL Server storage engine can have a direct bearing on performance. For instance, consider the code in Listing 19-1, which creates a table with narrow rows. Note that SQL Server can optimize storage for variable-length data types like varchar and nvarchar, so this example forces the issue by using fixed-length char data types.

Listing 19-1. Creating a Narrow Table

```
CREATE TABLE dbo.SmallRows
(
    Id  int NOT NULL,
    LastName nchar(50) NOT NULL,
    FirstName nchar(50) NOT NULL,
    MiddleName nchar(50) NULL
);

INSERT  INTO  dbo.SmallRows
(
    Id,
    LastName,
    FirstName,
    MiddleName
)
SELECT
    BusinessEntityID,
    LastName,
    FirstName,
    MiddleName
FROM Person.Person;
```

The rows in the dbo.SmallRows table are 304 bytes wide. This means SQL Server can fit about 25 rows on a single 8 KB page. You can verify this with the undocumented sys.fn_PhysLocFormatter function, as shown in Listing 19-2. Partial results are shown in Figure 19-1. The sys.fn_PhysLocFormatter function returns the physical locator in the form (fileipage:slot). As you can see in the figure, SQL Server fits 25 rows on each page (rows are numbered 0 to 24).

■ **Note** The sys.fn_PhysLocFormatter function is undocumented and not supported by Microsoft. It's used here for demonstration purposes, because it's handy for looking at row allocations on pages; but don't use it in production code.

Listing 19-2. Looking at Data Allocations for the SmallRows Table

```
SELECT
    sys.fn_PhysLocFormatter(%%physloc%%) AS [Row_Locator],
    Id
FROM dbo.SmallRows;
```

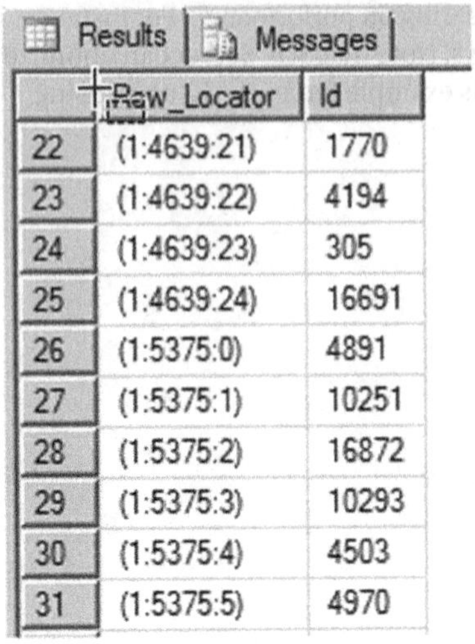

	Raw_Locator	Id
22	(1:4639:21)	1770
23	(1:4639:22)	4194
24	(1:4639:23)	305
25	(1:4639:24)	16691
26	(1:5375:0)	4891
27	(1:5375:1)	10251
28	(1:5375:2)	16872
29	(1:5375:3)	10293
30	(1:5375:4)	4503
31	(1:5375:5)	4970

Figure 19-1. SQL Server fits 25 rows per page for the dbo.SmallRows table

By way of comparison, the code in Listing 19-3 creates a table with wide rows—3,604 bytes wide, to be exact. The final SELECT query retrieves the row-locator information, demonstrating that SQL Server can fit only two rows per page for the dbo.LargeRows table. The results are shown in Figure 19-2.

Listing 19-3. Creating a Table with Wide Rows

```
CREATE TABLE dbo.LargeRows
(
    Id  int NOT NULL,
    LastName nchar(600) NOT NULL,
    FirstName nchar(600) NOT NULL,
    MiddleName nchar(600) NULL
);

INSERT  INTO  dbo.LargeRows
(
    Id,
    LastName,
    FirstName,
    MiddleName
)
SELECT
    BusinessEntityID,
    LastName,
    FirstName,
    MiddleName
FROM Person.Person;
```

```
SELECT
    sys.fn_PhysLocFormatter(%%physloc%%) AS [Row_Locator],
    Id
FROM dbo.LargeRows;
```

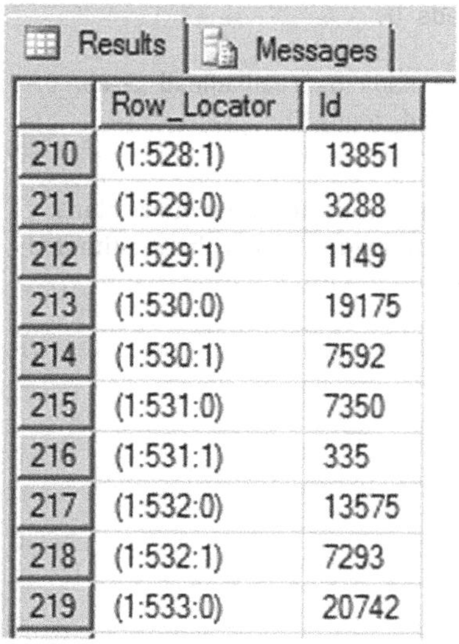

	Row_Locator	Id
210	(1:528:1)	13851
211	(1:529:0)	3288
212	(1:529:1)	1149
213	(1:530:0)	19175
214	(1:530:1)	7592
215	(1:531:0)	7350
216	(1:531:1)	335
217	(1:532:0)	13575
218	(1:532:1)	7293
219	(1:533:0)	20742

Figure 19-2. SQL Server fits only two rows per page for the dbo.LargeRows table

Now that you've created two tables with different row widths, the query in Listing 19-4 queries both tables with STATISTICS IO turned on to demonstrate the difference this makes to your I/O.

Listing 19-4. I/O Comparison of Narrow and Wide Tables

```
SET  STATISTICS IO ON;
SELECT
    Id,
    LastName,
    FirstName,
    MiddleName
FROM dbo.SmallRows;

SELECT
    Id,
    LastName,
    FirstName,
    MiddleName
FROM dbo.LargeRows;
```

The results returned, shown next, demonstrate a significant difference in both logical reads and read-ahead reads:

```
(19972 row(s) affected)
Table 'SmallRows'. Scan count 1, logical reads 799, physical reads 0, read-ahead reads 8,
lob logical reads 0, lob physical reads 0, lob read-ahead reads 0.
(19972 row(s) affected)
Table 'LargeRows'. Scan count 1, logical reads 9986, physical reads 0, read-ahead reads
10002, lob logical reads 0, lob physical reads 0, lob read-ahead reads 0.
```

The extra I/Os incurred by the query on the dbo.LargeRows table significantly affect the query plan's estimated I/O cost. The query plan for the dbo.SmallRows query is shown in Figure 19-3, with an estimated I/O cost of 0.594315.

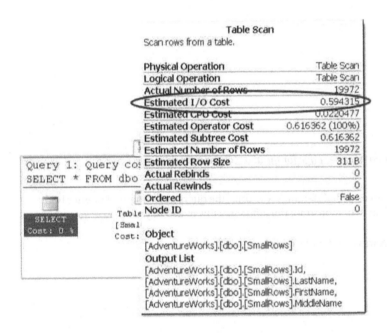

Figure 19-3. *Estimated I/O cost for the dbo.SmallRows query*

The query against the dbo.LargeRows table is significantly costlier, with an estimated I/O cost of 7.39942—nearly 12.5 times greater than the dbo.SmallRows query. Figure 19-4 shows the higher cost for the dbo.LargeRows query.

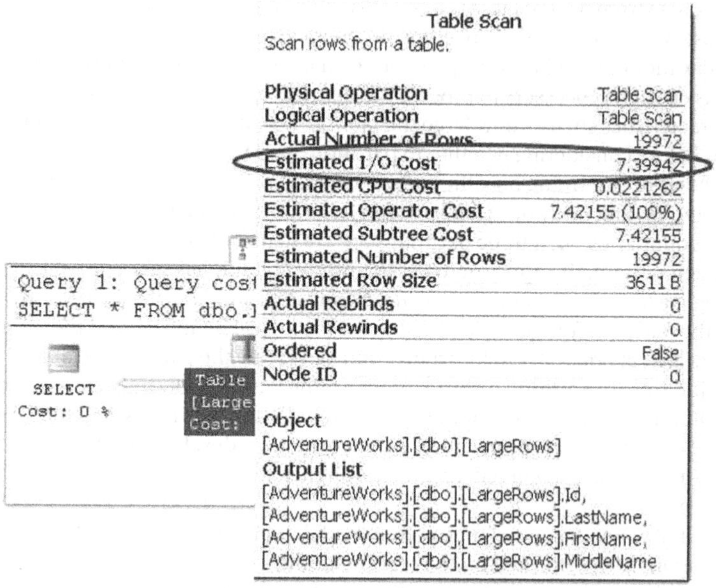

Table Scan

Scan rows from a table.

Physical Operation	Table Scan
Logical Operation	Table Scan
Actual Number of Rows	19972
Estimated I/O Cost	7.39942
Estimated CPU Cost	0.0221262
Estimated Operator Cost	7.42155 (100%)
Estimated Subtree Cost	7.42155
Estimated Number of Rows	19972
Estimated Row Size	3611 B
Actual Rebinds	0
Actual Rewinds	0
Ordered	False
Node ID	0

Object
[AdventureWorks].[dbo].[LargeRows]
Output List
[AdventureWorks].[dbo].[LargeRows].Id,
[AdventureWorks].[dbo].[LargeRows].LastName,
[AdventureWorks].[dbo].[LargeRows].FirstName,
[AdventureWorks].[dbo].[LargeRows].MiddleName

Query 1: Query cost
SELECT * FROM dbo.]

SELECT
Cost: 0 %

Table
[Large
Cost:

Figure 19-4. Estimated I/O cost for the dbo.LargeRows query

As you can see from these simple examples, SQL Server has to read significantly more pages when a table is defined with wide rows. This increased I/O cost can cause a significant performance drain when performing SQL Server queries—even those queries that are otherwise highly optimized. You can minimize the cost of I/O by minimizing the width of columns where possible and always using the appropriate data type for the job. In the examples given, a variable-width character data type (varchar) would significantly reduce the storage requirements of the sample tables. Although I/O cost is often a secondary consideration for developers and DBAs, and frequently is addressed only after slow queries begin to cause drag on a system, it's a good idea to keep the cost of I/O in mind when initially designing your tables.

Partitions

Partitioning the tables and indexes by range was introduced in SQL Server 2005. This functionality allows the data to be partitioned into rowsets based on the partitioning column value and the partitions can be placed into one more filegroups in the database to improve the performance of the query and manageability while treating them as a single object.

Partitioning is defined by a partition scheme that maps the partitions defined by the partition function to a set of files or filegroups that you define. A partition function specifies how the index or the table is partitioned. The column value used to define the partition can be of any data type except LOB data or timestamp. SQL Server 2008 supports 1,000 partitions by default, which meets most application needs; however, in some cases, due to industry regulations, you need to retain the daily data for more than 3 years. In those cases, you need the database to support more than 1,000 partitions. SQL Server 2008 R2 introduced support for 15,000 partitions, but you need to run a stored procedure to enable this support. SQL Server 2014 provides support for 15,000 partitions by default and also provides native support for high-availability and disaster-recovery features such as AlwaysOn, replication, database mirroring, and log shipping.

Partitioning is useful for grouping data from a large table into smaller chunks so that the data can be maintained independently for database operations such as speeding up queries (primarily with scans), loading data, reindexing, and so on. Partitioning can improve query performance when the partitioning key is part of the query and the system has enough processors to process the query. Not all tables need to be partitioned; you should consider characteristics such as how large the table is, how it's being accessed, and query performance against the tables before considering whether to partition the data.

The first step in partitioning a table is to determine how the rows in the table will be divided between the partitions, using a *partition function*. To effectively design a partition function, you need to specify logical boundaries. If you specify two boundaries, then three partitions are created; and, depending on whether the data is being partitioned left or right, the upper or lower boundary condition is set.

The partition function defines logical boundaries, and the *partition scheme* defines the physical location (filegroups) for them. Once the partition function is defined to set the logical boundary and the partition scheme is defined to map the logical boundary to filegroups, you can create the partitioned table.

Like the table, you can partition indexes. To partition a clustered index, the partition key must be specified in the clustered index. Partitioning a nonclustered index doesn't require the partition key; if the partition key isn't specified, then SQL Server includes the partition columns in the index. Indexes that are defined with partitioned tables can be aligned or nonaligned; an index is aligned if the table and the index logically have the same partition strategy.

In general, partitioning is most useful when data has a time component. Large tables such as order details—where most of the DML operations are performed on the current month's data and previous months are simply used for selects—may be good candidates to partition by month. This enables the queries to modify the data found in a single partition rather than scanning though the entire table to locate the data to be modified, hence enhancing query performance.

Partitions can be split or merged easily in a sliding-window scenario. You can split or merge partitions only if all the indexes are aligned and the partition scheme and functions match. Partition alignment doesn't mean both objects have to use the same partition function; but if both objects have the same partition scheme, functions, and boundaries, they're considered to be aligned. When both objects have the same partitioning scheme or filegroups, they're *storage aligned*. Storage alignment can be physical or logical; in both cases, query performance is improved.

Data Compression

In addition to minimizing the width of columns by using the appropriate data type for the job, SQL Server 2014 provides built-in data-compression functionality. By compressing your data directly in the database, SQL Server can reduce I/O contention and minimize storage requirements. There is some CPU overhead associated with compression and decompression of data during queries and DML activities, but data compression is particularly useful for historical data storage where access and manipulation demands aren't as high as they might be for the most recent data. This section discusses the types of compression that SQL Server supports as well as the associated overhead and recommended usage of each.

Row Compression

SQL Server 2005 introduced an optimization to the storage format for the decimal data type in SP 2. The vardecimal type provides optimized variable-length storage for decimal data, which often results in significant space savings—particularly when decimal columns contain a lot of zeros. This optimization is internal to the storage engine, so it's completely transparent to developers and end users. In SQL Server 2008, this optimization was expanded to include all fixed-length numeric, date/time, and character data types, in a feature known as *row compression*.

> ■ **Note** The vardecimal compression options and SPs to manage this feature, including sp_db_vardecimal_storage_format and sp_estimated_rowsize_reduction_for_vardecimal, are deprecated, because SQL Server 2014 rolls this functionality into the new row-compression feature.

SQL Server 2014 provides the useful sp_estimate_data_compression_savings procedure to estimate the savings you get from applying compression to a table. Listing 19-5 estimates the space saved by applying row compression to the Production.TransactionHistory table. This particular table contains fixed-length int, datetime, and money columns. The results are shown in Figure 19-5.

Listing 19-5. Estimating Row-Compression Space Savings

```
EXEC sp_estimate_data_compression_savings 'Production',
    'TransactionHistory',
    NULL,
    NULL,
    'ROW';
```

	object_name	schema_name	index_id	partition_number	size_with_current_compression_setting(KB)	size_with_requested_compression_setting(KB)	sample_size_with_current_compression_setting(KB)	sample_size_with_requested_compression_setting(KB)
1	TransactionHistory	Production	1	1	6480	4216	6488	4224
2	TransactionHistory	Production	2	1	1592	1168	1760	1296
3	TransactionHistory	Production	3	1	2040	1576	2648	2056

Figure 19-5. *Row compression space savings estimate for a table*

> ■ **Note** We changed the names of the last four columns in this example so they would fit in the image. The abbreviations are size_cur_cmp for Size with current compression setting (KB), size_req_cmp for Size with requested compression setting (KB), size_sample_cur_cmp for Sample size with current compression setting (KB), and size_sample_req_cmp for Sample size with requested compression setting (KB).

The results shown in Figure 19-5 indicate that the current size of the clustered index (index_id = 1) is about 6.1 MB, whereas the two nonclustered indexes (index_id = 1 and 2) total about 2.9 MB. SQL Server estimates that it can compress this table down to a size of about 4.0 MB for the clustered index and 2.6 MB for the nonclustered indexes.

> ■ **Tip** If your table doesn't have a clustered index, the heap is indicated in the results with an index_id of 0.

You can turn on row compression for a table with the DATACOMPRESSION = ROW option of the CREATE TABLE and ALTER TABLE DDL statements. Listing 19-6 turns on row compression for the Production.TransactionHistory table.

Listing 19-6. Turning on Row Compression for a Table

```
ALTER TABLE Production.TransactionHistory REBUILD
WITH (DATA_COMPRESSION = ROW);
```

You can verify that the ALTER TABLE statement has applied row compression to your table with the sp_spaceused procedure, as shown in Listing 19-7. The results are shown in Figure 19-6.

Listing 19-7. Viewing Space Used by a Table after Applying Row Compression

```
EXEC sp_spaceused N'Production.TransactionHistory';
```

	name	rows	reserved	data	index_size	unused
1	TransactionHistory	113443	7384 KB	4152 KB	2978 KB	258 KB

Figure 19-6. Space used by the table after applying row compression

As you can see in the figure, the size of the data used by the Production.TransactionHistory table has dropped to about 4.0 MB. The indexes aren't automatically compressed by the ALTER TABLE statement. To compress the nonclustered indexes, you need to issue ALTER INDEX statements with the DATA_COMPRESSION = ROW option. You can use the DATA_COMPRESSION = NONE option to turn off row compression for a table or index.

Row compression uses variable-length formats to store fixed-length data, and SQL Server stores an offset value in each record for each variable-length value it stores. Prior to SQL Server 2008, this offset value was fixed at 2 bytes of overhead per variable-length value. SQL Server 2008 introduced a new record format that uses a 4-bit offset for variable-length columns that are 8 bytes in length or less.

Page Compression

SQL Server 2014 also has the capability to compress data at the page level using two methods: *column-prefix compression* and *page-dictionary compression*. Whereas row compression is good for minimizing the storage requirements for highly unique fixed-length data at the row level, page compression helps minimize the storage space required by duplicated data stored in pages.

The column-prefix compression method looks for repeated prefixes in columns of data stored on a page. Figure 19-7 shows a sample page from a table, with repeated prefixes in columns underlined.

BusinessEntityID	FirstName	LastName
18069 (0x00004E95)	Alexander	Smith
15854 (0x00003DEE)	Alexandra	Smith
16058 (0x00003EBA)	Alexis	Smith
18863 (0x000049AF)	Andrew	Smith
18118 (0x00004EC6)	Austin	Smith

Figure 19-7. Page with repeated column prefixes identified

To compress the column prefixes identified in Figure 19-7, SQL Server creates an *anchor record*. This is a row in the table just like any other row, except that it serves the special purpose of storing the longest value in the column containing a duplicated column prefix. The anchor record is later used by the storage engine to re-create the full representations of the compressed column values when they're accessed. This special type of record is accessible only internally by the storage engine and can't be retrieved or modified directly by normal queries or DML operations. Figure 19-8 shows the column prefix–compressed version of the page from Figure 19-7.

	BusinessEntityID		FirstName	LastName
Anchor Record	18069	(0x00004695)	Alexander	Smith
	[NULL]	[NULL]	[NULL]	[NULL]
	[2] 15854	[2] 3DEE)	[7] ra	[NULL]
	[2] 16058	[2] 3EBA)	[4] is	[NULL]
	[2] 18863	[2] 49AF)	[1] ndrew	[NULL]
	[3] 198	[3] C6)	[1] ustin	[NULL]

Figure 19-8. *Page with column-prefix compression applied*

There are several items of note in the column prefix–compressed page shown in Figure 19-8. First, the anchor record has been added to the page. Column-prefix compression uses byte patterns to indicate prefixes, making the column-prefix method data-type agnostic. In this instance, the BusinessEntityID column is an int data type; but as you can see, it takes advantage of data-type compression as well. The BusinessEntityID column values are shown in both int and varbinary formats to demonstrate that they're compressed as well.

The next interesting feature of column-prefix compression is that SQL Server replaces the prefix of each column with an indicator of how many bytes need to be prepended from the anchor-record value to re-create the original value. NULL is used to indicate that the value in the table is the full anchor-record value.

■ **Note**   The storage engine uses metadata associated with each value to indicate the difference between an actual NULL in the column and a NULL indicating a placeholder for the anchor-record value.

In the example, each column in the first row is replaced with NULLs that act as placeholders for the full anchor-record values. The second row's BusinessEntityID column indicates that the first 2 bytes of the value should be replaced with the first 2 bytes of the BusinessEntityID anchor-record column. The FirstName column of this row indicates that the first 7 bytes of the value should be replaced with the first 7 bytes of the FirstName anchor-record column, and so on.

Page-dictionary compression is the second type of compression that SQL Server uses to compress pages. It creates an on-page dictionary of values that occur multiple times across any columns and rows on the page. It then replaces those duplicate values with indexes into the dictionary. Consider Figure 19-9, which shows a data page with duplicate values.

BusinessEntityID		FirstName	LastName
1585	(0x00003DEB)	Maurizio	Macagno
3150	(0x00000C4E)	Adriana	Arthur
17387	(0x000043EB)	Austin	Martin
10935	(0x00002AB7)	Arthur	Martin
16756	(0x00004174)	Martin	Fernandez

Figure 19-9. *Uncompressed page with duplicate values across columns and rows*

The duplicate values Arthur and Martin are added to the dictionary and replaced in the data page with indexes into the dictionary. The value Martin is replaced with the index value (0) everywhere it occurs in the data page, and the value Arthur is replaced with the index value (1). This is demonstrated in Figure 19-10.

	BusinessEntityID		FirstName	LastName
Dictionary	(0)=Martin, (1)=Arthur			
	1585	(0x00003DEB)	Maurizio	Macagno
	3150	(0x00000C4E)	Adriana	(1)
	17387	(0x000043EB)	Austin	(0)
	10935	(0x00002AB7)	(1)	(0)
	16756	(0x00004174)	(0)	Fernandez

Figure 19-10. *Page compressed with page-dictionary compression*

When SQL Server performs page compression on data pages and leaf-index pages, it first applies row compression, and then it applies page-dictionary compression.

■ **Note**   For performance reasons, SQL Server doesn't apply page-dictionary compression to non-leaf index pages.

You can estimate the savings you'll get through page compression with the sp_estimate_data_compression_savings procedure, as shown in Listing 19-8. The results are shown in Figure 19-11.

Listing 19-8. Estimating Data-Compression Savings with Page Compression

```
EXEC sp_estimate_data_compression_savings 'Person',
    'Person',
    NULL,
    NULL,
    'PAGE';
```

	object_name	schema_name	index_id	partition_number	size_with_current_compression_setting(KB)	size_with_requested_compression_setting(KB)	sample_size_with_current_compression_setting(KB)	sample_size_with_requested_compression_setting(KB)
1	Person	Person	1	1	30672	18816	30672	18816
2	Person	Person	2	1	848	400	1008	480
3	Person	Person	5	1	1000	448	1000	448
4	Person	Person	3	1	544	560	784	816

Figure 19-11. *Page compression space savings estimate*

As you can see in Figure 19-11, SQL Server estimates that it can use page compression to compress the Person.Person table from 29.8 MB in size down to about 18.2 MB—a considerable savings. You can apply page compression to a table with the ALTER TABLE statement, as shown in Listing 19-9.

Listing 19-9. Applying Page Compression to the Person.Person Table

```
ALTER TABLE Person.Person REBUILD
WITH (DATA_COMPRESSION = PAGE);
```

As with row compression, you can use the sp_spaceused procedure to verify how much space page compression saves you.

Page compression is great for saving space, but it doesn't come without a cost. Specifically, you pay for the space savings with increased CPU overhead for SELECT queries and DML statements. So, when should you use page compression? Microsoft makes the following recommendations:

- If the table or index is small in size, then the overhead you incur from compression probably won't be worth the extra CPU overhead.

- If the table or index is heavily accessed for queries and DML actions, the extra CPU overhead can significantly impact performance. It's important to identify usage patterns when deciding whether to compress the table or index.

- Use the sp_estimate_data_compression_savings procedure to estimate space savings. If the estimated space savings is insignificant (or nonexistent), then the extra CPU overhead will probably outweigh the benefits.

Sparse Columns

In addition to row compression and page compression, SQL Server provides *sparse columns*, which let you optimize NULL value storage in columns: when a NULL value is stored in the column, it takes up 0 bytes. . The trade-off (and you knew there would be one) is that the cost of storing non-NULL values goes up by 4 bytes for each value. Microsoft recommends using sparse columns when doing so will result in at least 20% to 40% space savings. For an int column, for instance, at least 64% of the values must be NULL to achieve a 40% space savings with sparse columns.

To demonstrate sparse columns in action, let's use a query that generates columns with a lot of NULLs in them. The query shown in Listing 19-10 creates a pivot-style report that lists the CustomerID numbers associated with every sales order down the right side of the results, and a selection of product names from the sales orders. The intersection of each CustomerID and product name contains the number of each item ordered by each customer. A NULL indicates that a customer didn't order an item. Partial results of this query are shown in Figure 19-12.

Listing 19-10. Pivot Query that Generates Columns with Many NULLs

```
SELECT
    CustomerID,
    [HL Road Frame - Black, 58],
    [HL Road Frame - Red, 58],
    [HL Road Frame - Red, 62],
    [HL Road Frame - Red, 44],
    [HL Road Frame - Red, 48],
    [HL Road Frame - Red, 52],
    [HL Road Frame - Red, 56],
    [LL Road Frame - Black, 58]
FROM
(
    SELECT soh.CustomerID, p.Name AS ProductName,
        COUNT
        (
        CASE  WHEN  sod.LineTotal  IS  NULL  THEN  NULL
        ELSE 1
        END
        ) AS  NumberOfItems
        FROM Sales.SalesOrderHeader soh
        INNER JOIN Sales.SalesOrderDetail sod
        ON soh.SalesOrderID = sod.SalesOrderID
        INNER JOIN Production.Product p
        ON  sod.ProductID  =  p.ProductID
        GROUP BY
        soh.CustomerID,
        sod.ProductID,
        p.Name
) src
PIVOT
(
    SUM(NumberOfItems) FOR ProductName
    IN
    (
    "HL Road Frame - Black, 58",
    "HL  Road  Frame  -  Red, 58",
    "HL  Road  Frame  -  Red, 62",
    "HL  Road  Frame  -  Red, 44",
    "HL  Road  Frame  -  Red, 48",
    "HL  Road  Frame  -  Red, 52",
    "HL  Road  Frame  -  Red, 56",
    "LL Road Frame - Black, 58"
    )
) AS  pvt;
```

	CustomerID	HL Road Frame - Black, 58	HL Road Frame - Red, 58	HL Road Frame - Red, 62	HL Road Frame - Red, 44
19112	30111	NULL	NULL	NULL	NULL
19113	30112	NULL	NULL	1	2
19114	30113	NULL	NULL	NULL	NULL
19115	30114	NULL	NULL	NULL	NULL
19116	30115	NULL	NULL	NULL	NULL
19117	30116	NULL	NULL	NULL	NULL
19118	30117	NULL	NULL	2	2
19119	30118	NULL	NULL	NULL	NULL

Figure 19-12. *Pivot query that returns the number of each item ordered by each customer*

Listing 19-11 creates two similar tables to hold the results generated by the query in Listing 19-10. The tables generated by the CREATE TABLE statements in Listing 19-11 have the same structure, except that SparseTable includes the keyword SPARSE in its column declarations, indicating that these are sparse columns.

Listing 19-11. Creating Sparse and Nonsparse Tables

```
CREATE TABLE NonSparseTable
(
    CustomerID int NOT NULL PRIMARY KEY,
    "HL Road Frame - Black, 58" int NULL,
    "HL  Road  Frame  -  Red,  58"  int NULL,
    "HL  Road  Frame  -  Red,  62"  int NULL,
    "HL  Road  Frame  -  Red,  44"  int NULL,
    "HL  Road  Frame  -  Red,  48"  int NULL,
    "HL  Road  Frame  -  Red,  52"  int NULL,
    "HL  Road  Frame  -  Red,  56"  int NULL,
    "LL Road Frame - Black, 58" int NULL
);
CREATE  TABLE  SparseTable
(
    CustomerID int NOT NULL PRIMARY KEY,
    "HL  Road  Frame  -  Black,  58"  int  SPARSE  NULL,
    "HL  Road  Frame  -  Red,  58"  int  SPARSE NULL,
    "HL  Road  Frame  -  Red,  62"  int  SPARSE NULL,
    "HL  Road  Frame  -  Red,  44"  int  SPARSE NULL,
    "HL  Road  Frame  -  Red,  48"  int  SPARSE NULL,
    "HL  Road  Frame  -  Red,  52"  int  SPARSE NULL,
    "HL  Road  Frame  -  Red,  56"  int  SPARSE NULL,
    "LL  Road  Frame  -  Black,  58"  int  SPARSE  NULL
);
```

After using the query in Listing 19-10 to populate these two tables, you can use the sp_spaceused procedure to see the space savings that sparse columns provide. Listing 19-12 executes sp_spaceused on these two tables, both of which contain identical data. The results shown in Figure 19-13 demonstrate that the SparseTable takes up only about 25% of the space used by the NonSparseTable, because NULL values in sparse columns take up no storage space.

Listing 19-12. Calculating the Space Savings of Sparse Columns

```
EXEC sp_spaceused N'NonSparseTable';
EXEC sp_spaceused N'SparseTable';
```

name	rows	reserved	data	index_size	unused
1	NonSparseTable	19119	904 KB	872 KB	16 KB	16 KB

name	rows	reserved	data	index_size	unused
1	SparseTable	19119	328 KB	256 KB	16 KB	56 KB

Figure 19-13. Space savings provided by sparse columns

Sparse Column Sets

In addition to sparse columns, SQL Server provides support for XML sparse column sets. An XML column set is defined as an xml data type column, and it contains non-NULL sparse column data from the table. An XML sparse column set is declared using the COLUMNSET FOR ALLSPARSECOLUMNS option on an xml column. As a simple example, the AdventureWorks Production.Product table contains several products that don't have associated size, color, or other descriptive information. Listing 19-13 creates a table called Production.SparseProduct that defines several sparse columns and a sparse column set.

Listing 19-13. Creating and Populating a Table with a Sparse Column Set

```
CREATE TABLE Production.SparseProduct
(
    ProductID int NOT NULL PRIMARY KEY,
    Name    dbo.Name   NOT   NULL,
    ProductNumber nvarchar(25) NOT NULL,
    Color nvarchar(15) SPARSE NULL,
    Size  nvarchar(5)  SPARSE  NULL,
    SizeUnitMeasureCode nchar(3) SPARSE NULL,
    WeightUnitMeasureCode nchar(3) SPARSE NULL,
    Weight decimal(8, 2) SPARSE NULL,
    Class nchar(2) SPARSE NULL,
    Style nchar(2) SPARSE NULL,
    SellStartDate datetime NOT NULL,
    SellEndDate datetime SPARSE NULL,
    DiscontinuedDate datetime SPARSE NULL,
    SparseColumnSet xml COLUMN_SET FOR ALL_SPARSE_COLUMNS
);
GO

INSERT INTO Production.SparseProduct
(
    ProductID,
    Name,
    ProductNumber,
    Color,
    Size,
    SizeUnitMeasureCode,
```

```
        WeightUnitMeasureCode,
        Weight,
        Class,
        Style,
        SellStartDate,
        SellEndDate,
        DiscontinuedDate
)
SELECT
        ProductID,
        Name,
        ProductNumber,
        Color,
        Size,
        SizeUnitMeasureCode,
        WeightUnitMeasureCode,
        Weight,
        Class,
        Style,
        SellStartDate,
        SellEndDate,
        DiscontinuedDate
FROM   Production.Product;
GO
```

You can view the sparse column set in XML form with a query like the one in Listing 19-14. The results in Figure 19-14 show that the first five products don't have any sparse column data associated with them, so the sparse column data takes up no space. By contrast, products 317 and 318 both have Color and Class data associated with them.

Listing 19-14. Querying a XML Sparse Column Set as XML

```
SELECT TOP(7)
ProductID,
SparseColumnSet FROM Production.SparseProduct;
```

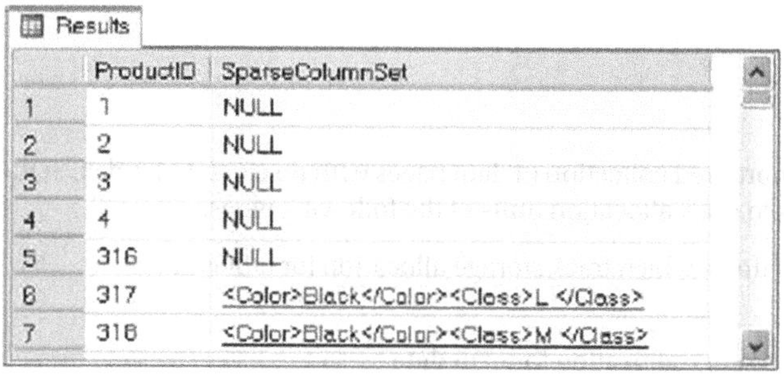

	ProductID	SparseColumnSet
1	1	NULL
2	2	NULL
3	3	NULL
4	4	NULL
5	316	NULL
6	317	<Color>Black</Color><Class>L </Class>
7	318	<Color>Black</Color><Class>M </Class>

Figure 19-14. *Viewing sparse column sets in XML format*

Although SQL Server manages sparse column sets using XML, you don't need to know XML to access sparse column set data. In fact, you can access the columns defined in sparse column sets using the same query and DML statements you've always used, as shown in Listing 19-15. The results of this query are shown in Figure 19-15.

Listing 19-15. Querying Sparse Column Sets by Name

```
SELECT
    ProductID,
    Name,
    ProductNumber,
    SellStartDate,
    Color,
    Class
FROM  Production.SparseProduct
WHERE ProductID IN (1, 317);
```

	ProductID	Name	ProductNum..	SellStartDate	Color	Class
1	1	Adjustable Race	AR-5381	1998-06-01 00:00:00.000	NULL	NULL
2	317	LL Crankarm	CA-5965	1998-06-01 00:00:00.000	Black	L

Figure 19-15. *Querying sparse column sets with SELECT queries*

Sparse column sets provide the benefits of sparse columns, with NULLs taking up no storage space. However, the downside is that non-NULL sparse columns that are a part of a column set are stored in XML format, adding some storage overhead as compared with their nonsparse, non-NULL counterparts.

Indexes

Your query performance may begin to lag over time for several reasons. It may be that database usage patterns have changed significantly, or the amount of data stored in the database has increased significantly, or the database has fallen out of maintenance. Whatever the reason, the knee-jerk reaction of many developers and DBAs is to throw indexes at the problem. Although indexes are indeed useful for increasing performance, they consume resources, both in storage and maintenance. Before creating new indexes all over your database, it's important to understand how they work. This section provides an overview of SQL Server's indexing mechanisms.

Heaps

In SQL Server parlance, a *heap* is simply an unordered collection of data pages with no clustered index. SQL Server uses index allocation map (IAM) pages to track allocation units of the following types:

- Heap or B-tree (HOBT) allocation units, which track storage allocation for tables and indexes
- LOB allocation units, which track storage allocation for LOB data
- Small LOB (SLOB) allocation units, which track storage allocation for row-overflow data

As any DBA will tell you, a table scan, which is SQL Server's "brute force" data-retrieval method, is a bad thing (although not necessarily the worst thing that can happen). In a table scan, SQL Server literally scans every data page that was allocated by the heap. Any query against the heap causes a table-scan operation.

To determine which pages have been allocated for the heap, SQL Server must refer back to the IAM. A table scan is known as an *allocation order scan* because it uses the IAM to scan the data pages in the order in which they were allocated by SQL Server.

Heaps are also subject to fragmentation, and the only way to eliminate fragmentation from the heap is to copy the heap to a new table, create a clustered index on the table, or perform periodic maintenance to keep the index from being fragmented. Forward pointers introduce another performance-related issue to heaps. When a row with variable-length columns is updated with row length larger than the page size, the updated row may have to be moved to a new page. When SQL Server must move the row in a heap to a new location, it leaves a forward pointer to the new location at the old location. If the row is moved again, SQL Server leaves another forward pointer, and so on. Forward pointers result in additional I/Os, making table scans even less efficient (and you thought that wasn't possible!). Table scans aren't entirely bad if you have to perform row0based operations or if you're querying against tables with small data sets such as lookup tables, where adding an index creates maintenance overhead.

■ **Tip**   Querying a heap with no clustered or nonclustered indexes always results in a costly table scan.

Clustered Indexes

If a heap is an unordered collection of data pages, how do you impose order on the heap? The answer is a *clustered index*. A clustered index turns an unordered heap into a collection of data pages ordered by the specified clustered-index columns. Clustered indexes are managed in the database as B-tree structures.

The top level of the clustered index B-tree is known as the *root node*, the bottom-level nodes are known as *leaf nodes*, and all nodes in between the root node and leaf nodes are collectively referred to as *intermediate nodes*. In a clustered index, the leaf nodes contain the actual data rows for a table, and all leaf nodes point to the next and previous leaf nodes, forming a doubly linked list. The clustered index holds a special position in SQL Server indexing because its leaf nodes contain the actual table data. Because the page chain for the data pages can be ordered only one way, there can be only one clustered index defined per table. The query optimizer uses the clustered index for seeks, because the data can be found directly at the leaf level if a clustered index is used. The clustered-index B-tree structure is shown in Figure 19-16.

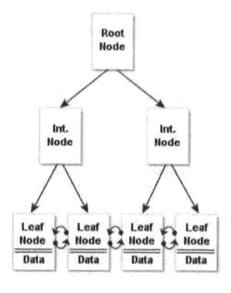

Figure 19-16. *Clustered index B-tree structure*

Guaranteed Order

Despite the fact that the data pages in a clustered index are ordered by the clustered-index columns, you can't depend on table rows being returned in clustered-index order unless you specify an ORDER BY clause in your queries. There are a couple of reasons for this, including the following:

- Your query may join multiple tables, and the optimizer may choose to return results in another order based on indexes on another table.

- The optimizer may use an allocation-order scan of your clustered index, which will return results in the order in which data pages were allocated.

The bottom line is that the SQL query optimizer may decide that, for whatever reason, it's more efficient to return results unordered or in an order other than clustered-index order. Because of this, you can't depend on results always being returned in the same order without an explicit ORDER BY clause. I've seen many cases of developers being bitten because their client-side code expected results in a specific order, and after months of receiving results in the correct order, the optimizer decided that returning results in a different order would be more efficient. Don't fall victim to this false optimism—use ORDER BY when ordered results are important.

Many are under the impression that a clustered-index scan is the same thing as a table scan. In one sense, this is correct—when SQL Server performs an unordered clustered-index scan, it refers back to the IAM to scan the data pages of the clustered index using an allocation-order scan, just like a table scan.

However, SQL Server has another option for clustered indexes: the *ordered clustered index scan*. In an ordered clustered-index scan, or *leaf-level scan*, SQL Server can follow the doubly linked list at the leaf-node level instead of referring back to the IAM. The leaf-level scan has the benefit of scanning in clustered-index order. Table scans don't have the option of a leaf-level scan because the leaf-level pages aren't ordered or linked.

Clustered indexes also eliminate the performance problems associated with forward pointers in the heap, although you do have to pay attention to fragmentation, page splits, and fill factor when you have a clustered index on your table. *Fill factor* determines how many rows can be filled in the index page. When the index page is full and new rows need to be inserted, SQL Server creates a new index page and transfers rows to the new page from the previous page; this is called as *page split*. You can reduce page splits by setting the proper fill factor to determine how much free space there is in the index pages.

So when should you use a clustered index? As a general rule, we like to put a clustered index on nearly every table we create, although it isn't a requirement to have clustered indexes for all tables. You have to decide which columns you wish to create in your clustered indexes. Here are some general recommendations for columns to consider in your clustered index design:

- Columns that provide a high degree of uniqueness. Monotonically increasing columns, such as IDENTITY and SEQUENCE columns, are ideal because they also reduce the overhead associated with page splits that result from insert and update operations.

- Columns that return a range of values using operators like >=, <, and BETWEEN. When you use a range query on clustered index columns, after the first match is found, the remaining values are guaranteed to be linked/adjacent in the B-tree.

- Columns that are used in queries that return large result sets of data from those columns.

- Columns that are used in the ON clause of a JOIN. Usually, these are primary-key or foreign-key columns. SQL Server creates a unique clustered index on the column when the primary key is added to the table.

- Columns that are used in GROUP BY or ORDER BY clauses. A clustered index on these columns can help SQL Server improve performance when ordering query result sets.

You should also make your clustered indexes as narrow as possible (often a single int or uniqueidentifier column), because this decreases the number of levels that must be traversed and hence reduces I/O. Another reason is that they're automatically appended to all nonclustered indexes on the same table as row locators, so keeping the clustered-index key small reduces the size of nonclustered indexes as well.

Nonclustered Indexes

Nonclustered indexes provide another tool for indexing relational data in SQL Server. Like clustered indexes, SQL Server stores nonclustered indexes as B-tree structures. Unlike clustered indexes, however, each leaf node in a nonclustered index contains the nonclustered key value and a row locator. The table rows are stored apart from the nonclustered index—in the clustered index if one is defined on the table or in a heap if the table has no clustered index. Figure 19-17. shows the nonclustered index B-tree structure. Recall from the previous section on clustered indexes that data rows can only be stored in one sorted order, and this is achieved via a clustered index. Order can only be achieved via the clustered index.

If a table has a clustered index, all nonclustered indexes defined on the table automatically include the clustered-index columns as the row locator. If the table is a heap, SQL Server creates row locators to the rows from the combination of the file identifier, page number, and slot on the page. Therefore, if you add a clustered index at a later date, be aware that you need to rebuild your nonclustered indexes to use the clustered-index column as a row locator rather than file identifier.

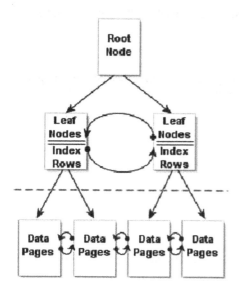

Figure 19-17. *Nonclustered index B-tree structure*

Nonclustered indexes are associated with the RID-lookup and key-lookup operations. *RID lookups* are bookmark lookups into the heap using row identifiers (RIDs), whereas *key lookups* are bookmark lookups on tables with clustered indexes. Once SQL Server locates the index rows that fulfill a query, if the query requires more columns than the nonclustered index covers, then the query engine must use the row locator to find the rows in the clustered index or the heap to retrieve necessary data. These are the operations referred to as RID and key lookups, and they're costly—so costly, in fact, that many performance-tuning operations are based on eliminating them.

■ **Note** Prior versions of SQL Server had the bookmark lookup operation. In SQL Server 2014, this operation has been split into two distinct operations—the RID lookup and the key lookup—to differentiate between bookmark lookups against heaps and clustered indexes.

One method of dealing with RID and key lookups is to create covering indexes. A *covering index* is a nonclustered index that contains all the columns necessary to fulfill a given query or set of queries. If a nonclustered index doesn't cover a query, then for each row, SQL Server has to look up the row to retrieve values for the columns that aren't included in the nonclustered index. If you perform the lookup using RID, there is extra I/O for each row in the result set. But when you define a covering index, the query engine can determine that all the information it needs to fulfill the query is stored in the nonclustered index rows, so it doesn't need to perform a lookup operation.

SQL Server offers the option to INCLUDE columns in the index. An included column isn't an index key, so it allows the columns to appear on the leaf pages of the nonclustered index and hence improves query performance.

■ **Tip** Prolific author and SQL Server MVP Adam Machanic defines a clustered index as a covering index for every possible query against a table. This definition provides a good tool for demonstrating that there's not much difference between clustered and nonclustered indexes, and it helps to reinforce the concept of index covering.

The example query in Listing 19-16 shows a simple query against the Person.Person table that requires a bookmark lookup, which is itself shown in the query plan in Figure 19-18.

Listing 19-16. Query Requiring a Bookmark Lookup

```
SELECT
BusinessEntityID,
LastName,
FirstName,
MiddleName,
Title FROM Person.Person WHERE LastName = N'Duffy';
```

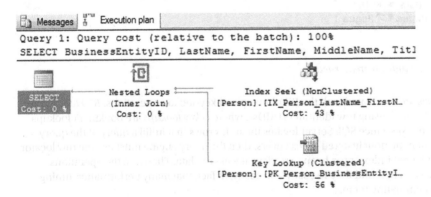

Figure 19-18. Bookmark lookup in the query plan

So why is there a bookmark lookup (referenced as a key lookup operator in the query plan)? The answer lies in the query. This particular query uses the LastName column in the WHERE clause to limit results, so the query engine decides to use the IX_Person_LastName_FirstName_MiddleName nonclustered index to fulfill the query. This nonclustered index contains the LastName, FirstName, and MiddleName columns, as well as the BusinessEntityID column, which is defined as the clustered index. The lookup operation is required because the SELECT clause also specifies that the Title column needs to be returned in the result set. Because the Title column isn't included in the covering index, SQL Server has to refer back to the table's data pages to retrieve it.

Creating an index with the Title column included in the nonclustered index as shown in Listing 19-17 removes the lookup operation from the query plan for the query in Listing 19-16. As shown in Figure 19-19, the IX_Covering_Person_LastName_FirstName_MiddleName index covers the query.

■ **Tip**   Another alternative to eliminate this costly lookup operation would be to modify the nonclustered index used in the example to include the Title column, which would create a covering index for the query.

Listing 19-17. Query Using a Covering Index

```
CREATE NONCLUSTERED INDEX [IX_Covering_Person_LastName_FirstName_MiddleName] ON
[Person].[Person]
(
    [LastName] ASC,
    [FirstName] ASC,
    [MiddleName] ASC
) INCLUDE (Title)
WITH (PAD_INDEX = OFF, STATISTICS_NORECOMPUTE = OFF, SORT_IN_TEMPDB = OFF, DROP_EXISTING =
OFF, ONLINE = OFF, ALLOW_ROW_LOCKS = ON, ALLOW_PAGE_LOCKS = ON) ON [PRIMARY]
GO
```

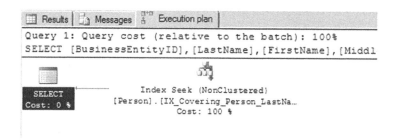

Figure 19-19. The covering index eliminates the lookup operation

You can define up to 999 nonclustered indexes per table. You should carefully plan your indexing strategy and try to minimize the number of indexes you define on a single table. Nonclustered indexes can require a substantial amount of additional storage, and there is a definite overhead involved in automatically updating them whenever the table data changes. When deciding how many indexes to add to a table, consider the usage patterns carefully. Tables with data that doesn't change—or rarely changes—may derive greater benefit from having lots of indexes defined on them than tables whose data is modified often.

Nonclustered indexes are useful for the following types of queries:

- Queries that return one row, or a few rows, with high selectivity.

- Queries that can use an index with high selectivity (generally greater than 95%). *Selectivity* is a measure of the unique key values in an index. SQL Server often ignores indexes with low selectivity.

- Queries that return small ranges of data that would otherwise result in a clustered index or table scan. These types of queries often use simple equality predicates (=) in the WHERE clause.

- Queries that are completely covered by the nonclustered index.

Filtered Indexes

In SQL Server 2014, filtered indexes provide a way to create more targeted indexes that require less storage and can support more efficient queries. *Filtered indexes* are optimized nonclustered indexes that allow you to easily add filtering criteria to restrict the rows included in the index with a WHERE clause. A filtered index improves the performance of queries because the index is smaller than a nonclustered index, and the statistics are more accurate because they cover only the rows in the filtered index. Adding a filtered index to a table where a nonclustered index is unnecessary reduces disk storage for the nonclustered index, and the statistics update the cost as well. Listing 19-18 creates a filtered index on the Size column of the Production.Product table that excludes NULL.

Listing 19-18. Creating and Testing a Filtered Index on the Production.Product Table

```
CREATE NONCLUSTERED INDEX IX_Product_Size
ON Production.Product
(
Size,
SizeUnitMeasureCode )
WHERE Size IS NOT NULL;
GO
SELECT
ProductID,
Size,
SizeUnitMeasureCode FROM Production.Product WHERE Size = 'L';
GO
```

■ **Tip**   Filtered indexes are particularly well suited for indexing non-NULL values of sparse columns.

Optimizing Queries

One of the more interesting tasks that SQL developers and DBAs must perform is optimizing queries. To borrow an old cliché, query optimization is as much art as science. There are a lot of moving parts in the SQL query engine, and your task is to give the optimizer as much good information as you can so that it can make good decisions at runtime.

Performance is generally measured in terms of response time and throughput, defined as follows:

- Response time is the time it takes SQL Server to complete a task such as a query.

- Throughput is a measure of the volume of work that SQL Server can complete in a fixed period of time, such as the number of transactions per minute.

Several other factors affect overall system performance but are outside the scope of this book. Application responsiveness, for instance, depends on several additional factors like network latency and UI architecture, both of which are beyond SQL Server's control. This section talks about how to use query plans to diagnose performance issues.

Reading Query Plans

When you submit a T-SQL script or statement to the SQL Server query engine, SQL Server compiles your code into a query plan. The query plan is composed of a series of physical and logical operators that the optimizer has chosen to complete your query. The optimizer bases its choice of operators on a wide array of factors like data-distribution statistics, cardinality of tables, and availability of useful indexes. SQL Server uses a cost-based optimizer, meaning the execution plan it chooses will have the lowest estimated cost.

SQL Server can return query plans in a variety of formats. My preference is the graphical query execution plan, which is used in examples throughout the book. Figure 19-20 shows a query plan for a simple query that joins two tables.

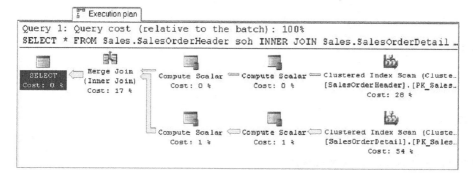

Figure 19-20. *Query execution plan for an inner join query*

You can generate a graphical query plan for a given query by selecting Query ➤ Include Actual Execution Plan from the SSMS menu and then running your SQL statements. Alternatively, you can select Query ➤ Display Estimated Execution Plan without running the query.

A graphical query plan is read from right to left and top to bottom. It contains arrows indicating the flow of data through the query plan. The arrows show the relative amount of data being moved from one operator to the next, with wider arrows indicating larger numbers of rows, as shown in Figure 19-20. You can position the mouse pointer on top of any operator or arrow in the graphical query plan to display a pop-up with additional information about the operator or data flow between operators, such as the number of rows being acted on and the estimated row size. You can also right-click an operator or arrow and select Properties from the pop-up menu to view even more descriptive information.

In addition you can right-click in the Execution Plan window and select Save Execution Plan As to save your graphical execution plan as an XML query plan. Query plans are saved with a .sqlplan file extension and can be viewed in graphical format in SSMS by double-clicking the file. This is particularly useful for troubleshooting queries remotely, because your users or other developers can save the graphical query plan and e-mail it to you, and you can open it up in a local instance of SSMS for further investigation.

Actual or Estimated?

Estimated execution plans are useful in determining the optimizer's intent. The word *estimated* in the name can be a bit misleading because all query plans are based on the optimizer's estimates of your data distribution, table cardinality, and more.

There are some differences between estimated and actual query plans, however. Because an actual query plan is generated as your T-SQL statements are executed, the optimizer can add information to the query plan as it runs. This additional information includes items like actual rebinds and rewinds, values that return the number of times the init() method is called in the plan, and the actual number of rows.

When dealing with temporary objects, actual query plans have better information available concerning which operators are being used. Consider the following simple script, which creates, populates, and queries a temporary table:

```
CREATE TABLE #t1 (
BusinessEntityID int NOT NULL,
LastName nvarchar(50),
FirstName nvarchar(50),
MiddleName nvarchar(50) );
CREATE INDEX t1_LastName ON #t1 (LastName);
INSERT INTO #t1 (
BusinessEntityID,
LastName,
FirstName,
MiddleName )
SELECT
BusinessEntityID,
LastName,
FirstName,
MiddleName FROM Person.Person;
SELECT
BusinessEntityID,
LastName,
FirstName,
MiddleName FROM #t1 WHERE LastName = N'Duffy';
DROP TABLE #t1;
```

In the estimated query plan for this code, the optimizer indicates that it will use a table scan, as shown next, to fulfill the SELECT query at the end of the script:

The actual query plan, however, uses a much more efficient nonclustered index seek with a bookmark lookup operation to retrieve the two relevant rows from the table, as shown here:

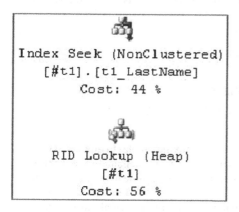

The difference between the estimated and actual query plans in this case is the information available at the time the query plan is generated. When the estimated query plan is created, there is no temporary table and no index on the temporary table, so the optimizer guesses that a table scan will be required. When the actual query plan is generated, the temporary table and its nonclustered index both exist, so the optimizer comes up with a better query plan.

In addition to graphical query plans, SQL Server supports XML query plans and text query plans, and it can report additional runtime statistics. This additional information can be accessed using the statements shown in Table 19-1.

Table 19-1. *Statements to Generate Query Plans*

Statement	Description
SET SHOWPLAN_ALL ON/OFF	Returns a text-based estimated execution plan without executing the query
SET SHOWPLAN_TEXT ON/OFF	Returns a text-based estimated execution plan without executing the query, but the information returned may be less than what you get from choosing SHOWPLAN_ALL.
SET SHOWPLAN_XML ON/OFF	Returns an XML-based estimated execution plan without executing the query
SET STATISTICS IO ON/OFF	Returns statistics information about logical I/O operations during execution of a query
SET STATISTICS PROFILE ON/OFF	Returns actual query execution plans in result sets following the result set generated by each query executed
SET STATISTICS TIME ON/OFF	Returns statistics about the time required to parse, compile, and execute statements at runtime

Once the query is compiled, it can be executed, and the execution need not necessarily happen after the query is compiled. So, if the query is executed several days after it has been compiled, the underlying data may have changed, and the plan that has been compiled may not be optimal during the execution time. So, when this query is being executed SQL Server first checks to see if the plan is still valid. If the query optimizer decides that the plan is suboptimal, a few statements or the entire batch will be recompiled to produce a different plan. These compilations are called *recompilations*; and although sometimes it's necessary to recompile queries, this process can slow down query or batch executions considerably, so it's optimal to reduce recompilations.

Some causes for recompilations are as follows:

- Schema changes such as adding or dropping columns, constraints, indexes, statistics, and so on

- Running sp_recompile on a stored procedure or trigger

- Using set options after the batch has started, such as ANSI_NULL_DFLT_OFF, ANSI_NULLS, ARITHABORT, and so on

One of the main causes for excessive recompilations is the use of temporary tables in queries. If you create a temporary table in StoredProcA and reference the temporary table in a statement in StoredProcB, then the statement must be recompiled every time StoredProcA runs. A table variable may be a good option to replace a temporary table for a small number of rows.

Sometimes you may experience suboptimal query performance, and there are several causes. One of the common causes is using *nonSearch ARGumentable* (nonSARGable) expressions in WHERE clauses or joins, which prevents SQL Server from using the index. Using these expressions can slow queries significantly as well. Some nonSARGable expressions are inequality expression comparisons, functions, implicit data-type conversions, and the LIKE keyword. Often these expressions can be rewritten to use an index. Consider the following simple script, which finds names starting with *C*:

```
SELECT Title, FirstName, LastName  FROM person.person WHERE SUBSTRING(FirstName, 1,1) = 'C'
```

This query causes a table scan. But if the query is rewritten as follows, the optimizer will use a clustered seek if a proper index exists in the table, hence improving performance:

```
SELECT Title, FirstName, LastName  FROM person.person WHERE FirstName LIKE 'C%'
```

Sometimes you do have to use functions in queries for calculations. In these cases, if you replace the function with an indexed computed column, the SQL Server query optimizer can generate a plan that will use an index. SQL Server can match an expression to the computed column to use statistics; however, the expression should match the computed column definition exactly.

Methodology

The methodology that has served me well when troubleshooting performance issues involves the following eight steps:

1. *Recognize the issue.* Before you can troubleshoot a performance issue, you must first determine that there is an actual issue. Recognizing an issue can begin with something as simple as end users complaining that their applications are running slowly.

2. *Identify the source.* Once you've recognized that there is an issue, you need to identify it as a SQL Server-related problem. For instance, if you receive reports of database-enabled applications running slowly, it's important to narrow the source of the problem. If the issue is related to network bandwidth or latency, for instance, it can't be resolved through simple query optimization. If it's a T-SQL issue, you can use tools like SQL Profiler and query plans to identify the problematic code.

3. *Review the baseline.* Once you've identified the issue and the source, evaluate the baseline. For instance, if the end user is complaining that the application runs slowly, you need to understand the definition of *slow* and also whether the issue is reproducible. *Slow* could mean reports aren't rendered within 1 minute, or it could mean reports aren't rendered within 10 milliseconds. Without a proper baseline, you have nothing to compare to and can't ascertain whether the issue really exists.

4. *Analyze the code.* Once you've identified T-SQL code as the source of the problem, it's time to dig deeper and analyze the root cause of the problem. The operators returned in graphical query plans provide an excellent indicator of the source of many problems. For example, you may spot a costly clustered index scan operator where you expected a more efficient nonclustered index seek.

5. *Define possible solutions.* After the issues have been identified in the code, it's time to come up with potential solutions. If bookmark-lookup operations are slowing query performance, for instance, you may determine that adding a new nonclustered index or modifying an existing one is a possible fix for the issue. Another possible solution might be changing the query to return fewer columns that are already covered by an index.

6. *Evaluate the solutions.* A critical step after defining possible solutions is to evaluate the practicality of those solutions. Many things affect whether a solution is practical. For instance, you may be forbidden to change indexes on production servers, in which case adding or modifying indexes to solve an issue may be impractical. On the other hand, your client applications may depend on all the columns currently being returned in the query's result sets, so changing the query to return fewer columns may not be a workable solution.

   During this step of the process, you also need to determine the impact of your solutions on other parts of the system. Adding or modifying an index on the server to solve a query performance problem may fix the problem for a single query, but it may also introduce new performance problems for other queries or DML statements. These conflicting needs should be evaluated.

7. *Implement the solution.* During this step of the process, you actually apply your solution. You'll most likely have a subprocess here in which you apply the solution first to a development environment and then to a quality assurance (QA) environment, and finally promote it to the production environment.

8. *Examine the impact of the solution.* After implementing your solution, you should revisit it to ensure that it fixes the problem. This is a very important step that many people ignore—they revisit their solutions only when another issue occurs. By scheduling a time to revisit your solution, you can take a proactive approach and head off problems before they affect end users.

Scalability is another important factor to consider when writing T-SQL. *Scalability* is a measure of how well your code works under increasing demands. For instance, a query may provide acceptable performance when the source table contains 100,000 rows and 10 end users simultaneously querying. However, the same query may suffer performance problems when the table grows to 1,000,000 rows and the number of end users grows to 100. Increasing stress on a system tends to uncover scalability and performance issues that weren't previously apparent in your code base. As pressure on your database grows, it's important to monitor changing access patterns and increasing demands on the system to proactively handle issues before they affect end users.

It's also important to understand when an issue isn't really a problem, or at least not one that requires a great deal of attention. As a general rule, we like to apply the 80/20 rule when optimizing queries: as a rule of thumb, focus your efforts on optimizing the 20% of code that is executed 80% of the time. If you have an SP that takes a long time to execute but is run only once a day, and a second procedure that takes a significant amount of time but is run 10,000 times a day, you'd be well served to focus your efforts on the latter procedure.

Waits

Your main goal in designing and writing an application is to enable users to get accurate result sets in an efficient way. So, when you come across a performance issue, the place to start is the query. For any given session, the query or thread can be in one of two states: it's either running or waiting on something. When the query is running, it may be compiling or executing. And when the query is waiting, it may be waiting for I/O, network, memory, locks or latches, and so on, or it may be forced to wait to make sure the process yields for other processes. Whatever the case, when the query is waiting on a resource, SQL Server logs the wait type for the resource the query is waiting on. You can then use this information to understand why query performance is affected.

To help you better understand resource usage, you need to be familiar with three performance metrics that can play a role in query performance: CPU, Duration, and Logical Reads. *CPU* is essentially the worker time spent to execute the query; *Duration* is the time the worker thread takes to execute the query, which includes the time it takes to wait for the resources as well as the time it takes to execute the query; and *Logical Reads* is the number of data pages read by the query execution from the buffer pool or memory. If the page doesn't exist in the buffer pool, then SQL Server performs a physical read to read the page into the buffer pool. Because you're measuring query performance, logical reads are considered to measure performance, not physical reads. You can calculate wait time using the formula Duration – CPU.

Using wait stats is a methodology that can help you identify opportunities to tune query performance, and SQL Server 2014 has 649 wait types. Let's say your application has some users read from the table and other users write to the same table. At any given time, if rows are being inserted into the table, the query that is trying to read those rows has to stop processing because the resource is unavailable. Once the row insertion is completed, the read process gets a signal that the resource is available for this process; and when a scheduler is available to process the read thread, the query is processed. The time SQL Server spends to acquire the system resource in this example is called a *wait*. The time SQL Server spends waiting for the process to be signed when the resource is available is called *resource wait time*. Once the process is signaled, the process has to wait for the scheduler to be available before the process can continue, and this is called *signal wait time*. Resource wait time and signal wait time combined give the wait time in milliseconds.

You can query the wait types using the DMVs sys.dm_os_waiting_tasks, sys.dm_os_wait_stats, and sys.dm_exec_requests. sys.dm_os_waiting_tasks and sys.dm_exec_requests return details about which tasks are waiting currently, whereas sys.dm_os_wait_stats lists the aggregate of the waits since the instance was last restarted. So, you need to check sys.dm_os_waiting_tasks for a query performance analysis.

Let's look at an example of how waits can help you tune queries. You might have come across a situation where you're trying to insert a set of rows into a table, but the insert process hangs and isn't responsive. When you query sp_who2, it doesn't show any blocking; however, the insert process waits for a long time before it completes. Let's see how you can use wait stats to debug this scenario. Listing 19-19 is a script that inserts rows into a waitsdemo table created in AdventureWorks with user session ID 54.

Listing 19-19. Script to Demonstrate Waits

```
use adventureworks
go
CREATE TABLE [dbo].[waitsdemo](
    [Id] [int] NOT NULL,
    [LastName] [nchar](600) NOT NULL,
    [FirstName] [nchar](600) NOT NULL,
    [MiddleName] [nchar](600) NULL
) ON [PRIMARY]

GO

declare @id int = 1
while (@id <= 50000)
begin
    insert into waitsdemo
        select @id,'Foo', 'User',NULL
    SET @id = @id + 1
end
```

To identify why the insert query is being blocked, you can query the sys.dm_exec_requests and sys. dm_exec_sessions DMVs to see the processes that are currently executing and also query the DMV sys. dm_os_waiting_tasks to see the list of processes that are currently waiting. The DMV queries are shown in Listing 19-20, and partial results are shown in Figure 19-21. In this example, the insert query using session ID 54 is waiting on the shrinkdatabase task with session ID 98.

Listing 19-20. DMV to Query Current Processes and Waiting Tasks

```
--List waiting user requests
SELECT
er.session_id, er.wait_type, er.wait_time,
er.wait_resource, er.last_wait_type,
er.command,et.text,er.blocking_session_id
FROM sys.dm_exec_requests AS er
JOIN sys.dm_exec_sessions AS es
ON es.session_id = er.session_id
AND es.is_user_process = 1
CROSS APPLY sys.dm_exec_sql_text(er.sql_handle) AS et
GO
--List waiting user tasks
SELECT
wt.waiting_task_address, wt.session_id, wt.wait_type,
wt.wait_duration_ms, wt.resource_description
FROM sys.dm_os_waiting_tasks AS wt
JOIN sys.dm_exec_sessions AS es
ON wt.session_id = es.session_id
AND es.is_user_process = 1
GO
-- List user tasks
SELECT
t.session_id, t.request_id, t.exec_context_id,
```

```
t.scheduler_id, t.task_address,
t.parent_task_address
FROM sys.dm_os_tasks AS t
JOIN sys.dm_exec_sessions AS es
ON t.session_id = es.session_id
AND es.is_user_process = 1
GO
```

	session_id	wait_type	wait_time	wait_resource	last_wait_type	command	text
1	54	WRITELOG	0		WRITELOG	INSERT	declare @id int = 1,@FirstName nchar(100) = 'Foo',@LastName nchar(100) = 'User' while (@id <= 50000) begin insert into
2	57	NULL	0		MISCELLANEOUS	SELECT	select er.session_id, er.wait_type, er.wait_time, er.wait_resource, er.last_wait_type, er.command,st.text, er.blocking_session_i
3	98	PAGEIOLATCH_SH	84	7:1:38527	PAGEIOLATCH_SH	DbccFilesCompact	DBCC SHRINKDATABASE(N'AdventureWorks')

	waiting_task_address	session_id	wait_type	wait_duration_ms	resource_description
1	0x00000004FB02DC38	54	WRITELOG	10	NULL

	session_id	request_id	exec_context_id	scheduler_id	task_address	parent_task_address
1	54	0	0	3	0x00000004FB02DC38	NULL
2	57	0	0	4	0x00000004FB035C38	NULL
3	98	0	0	5	0x00000004E3FC4558	NULL

Figure 19-21. Results of sys.dm_os_waiting_tasks

The results show that process 54 is indeed waiting; the wait type is writelog, which means the I/O to the log files is slow. When you correlate this to session_id 98, which is the shrinkdatabase task, you can identify that the root cause for the performance issue with the insert query is the shrinkdatabase process. Once the shrinkdatabase operation completes, the insert query starts to process, as shown in Figure 19-22.

	session_id	wait_type	wait_time	wait_resource	last_wait_type	command	text	blocking_session_id
1	54	WRITELOG	0		WRITELOG	INSERT	declare @id int = 1,@FirstName nchar(100) = ...	0
2	57	NULL	0		MISCELLANEOUS	SELECT	select er.session_id, er.wait_type, er.wait_time, ...	0

	waiting_task_address	session_id	wait_type	wait_duration_ms	resource_description
1	0x00000004FB02D868	54	WRITELOG	2	NULL

	session_id	request_id	exec_context_id	scheduler_id	task_address	parent_task_address
1	54	0	0	3	0x00000004FB02D868	NULL
2	57	0	0	4	0x00000004FB035868	NULL

Figure 19-22. Results of a DMV to show the blocking thread

Not all wait types need to be monitored constantly. Some wait types, like broker_* and clr_*, can be ignored if you aren't using a service broker or CLR in your databases. This example only touched the tip of the iceberg; waits can be a powerful mechanism to help you identify and resolve query performance issues.

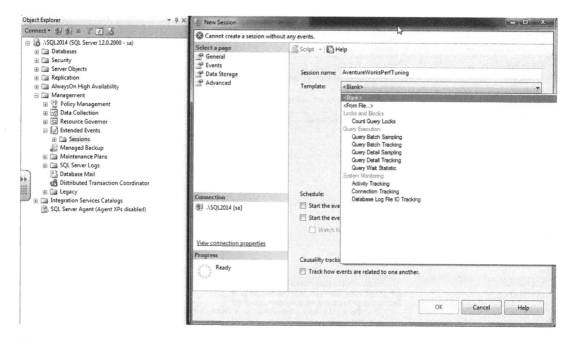

Figure 19-23. *New XEvents session*

Extended Events

Extended Events (XEvents) is a diagnostic system that can help you troubleshoot performance problems with SQL Server. It was first introduced in SQL 2008 and then went through a complete makeover in SQL Server 2012, with additional event types, a new user interface, and templates similar to SQL Server Profiler. Let's review the XEvents user interface first and then look at how you can troubleshoot with it.

The XEvents user interface is integrated with Management Studio; there is a separate Extended Events node in the tree. To start a new XEvents session, expand the Management node and then expand Extended Events. Right-click Sessions, and then click New Session. Figure 19-23 shows the XEvents user interface.

XEvents offers a rich diagnostic framework that is highly scalable and lets you collect small or large amounts of data to troubleshoot performance issues. It has the same capabilities as SQL Profiler; so, you may ask, why should you use XEvents and not SQL Profiler? Anybody who has worked with SQL Server can tell you that SQL Profiler adds significant resource overhead when tracing the server, which can sometimes bring the server to its knees. The reason for this overhead is that when you use SQL Profiler to trace activities on the server, all the events are streamed to the client and filtered based on criteria set by you on the client side; many resources are required to process the events. With XEvents, filtering happens on the server side, so events that are needed aren't sent to the client—hence you get better performance with a process that is less chatty. Another reason to begin using XEvents is that SQL Profiler has been marked for deprecation.

XEvents sessions can be based on predefined templates, or you can create a session by choosing specific events. You can also autostart an XEvents session on server startup—a feature that isn't available in SQL Profiler. Figure 19-24 shows the autostart option.

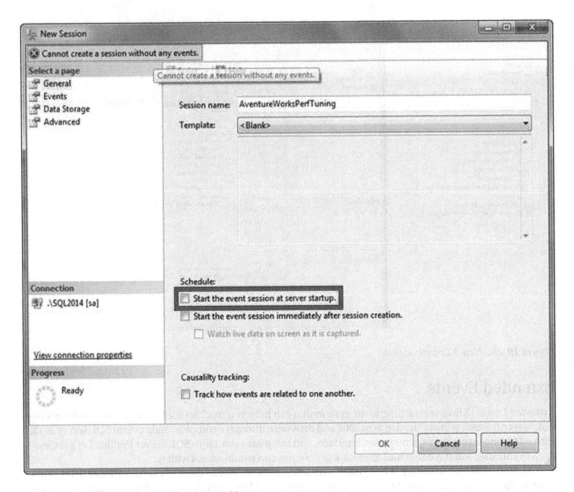

Figure 19-24. *Object Explorer database table pop-up context menu*

The Events library lists all searchable events, categorized and grouped based on events. You can search events based on their names and/or descriptions. Once you select the events you want to track, you can set filter criteria. After the filters have been defined, you can select the fields you want to track. The common fields that are tracked are selected by default. Figure 19-25 shows a sample session to capture SQL statements for performance tuning.

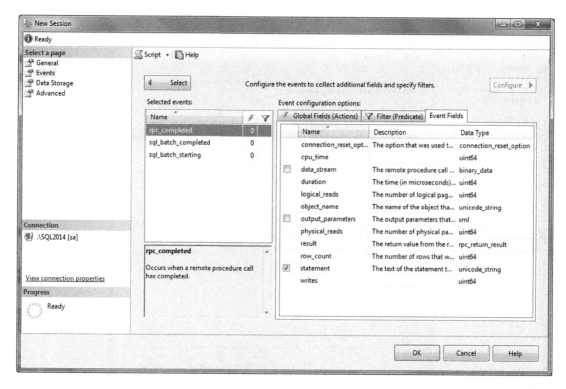

Figure 19-25. *Sample XEvents session configuration for SQL performance tuning*

After you've defined all the criteria, you can set the target depending on what you want to do with the data: capture it to a file, forward it to in-memory targets, or write it to a live reader. Figure 19-26 shows the possible targets for a session.

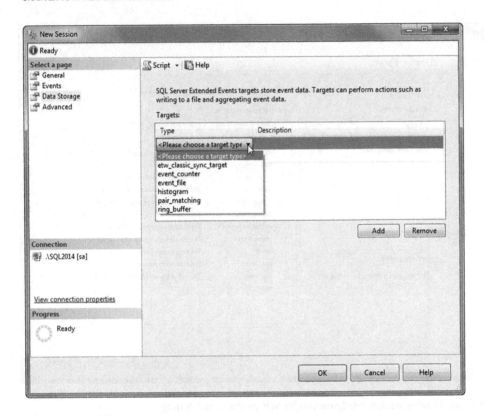

Figure 19-26. *XEvents target type*

Figure 19-27 shows the results of XEvents streaming the SQL statements' live data for the performance-tuning session.

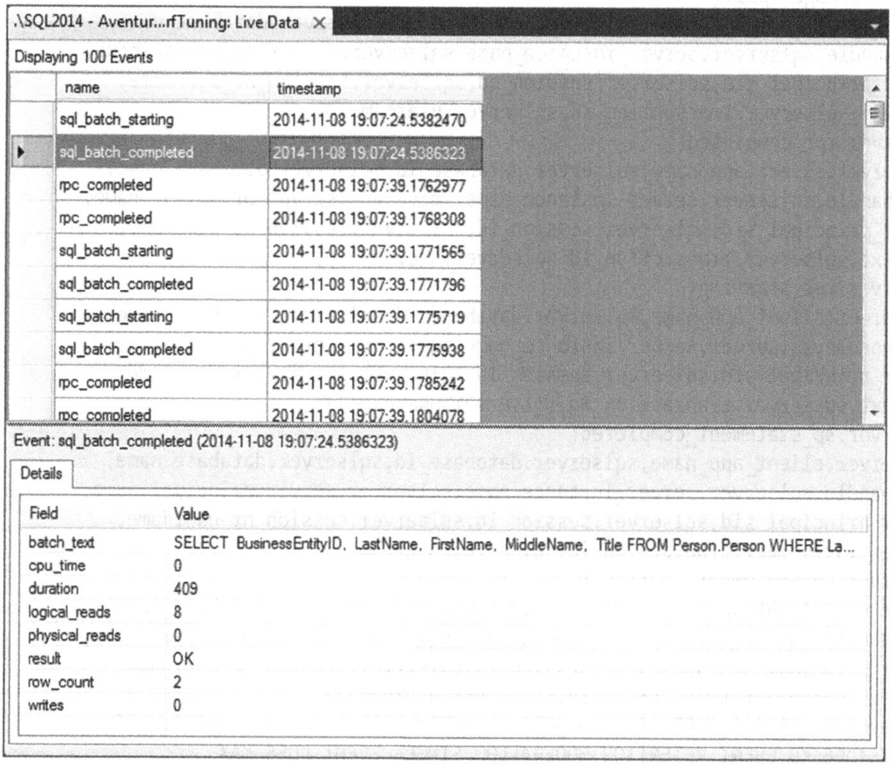

Figure 19-27. *Sample data from the XEvents session for SQL performance tuning*

Now let's consider a common problem: a business user is complaining that an application is slow and there is a lot of blocking. You need to figure out where the problem is, given that the application is third-party software. The challenge is to identify a piece of application functionality and the queries behind this functionality that are causing the performance issue. You have multiple areas to investigate, including clients, network, blocking, CPU, and I/O issues. One way to approach the problem is to run the Performance Monitor (perfmon) tool, start a profiler trace, and try to tie the application issue to the server metrics; but there is no direct way to get the details on the query chain of the lead blocker that causes and follows the blocking issue without using XEvents.

If the application is built on the latest ODBC drivers or the new ADO.NET 4.5, the application will attach a ConnectionId identifier. This is a guide to the server when the connections are made, which makes the process of tracing or correlating activities between client and server much simpler. Along with this, the client sends another identifier called ActivityId, which provides information about the process that is currently executing. With ConnectionId and ActivityId, you have the information required to build a complete image of the activities taking place in the server; and you can effectively trace the server activities to identify the bottlenecks.

XEvents makes common problems like page splits or locking much easier to identify and resolve with proper code changes. To track page splits, you can set up an XEvents session using a script like that shown in Listing 19-21.

Listing 19-21. XEvents Session Script to Troubleshoot Login Timeouts

```
CREATE EVENT SESSION [Troubleshoot page split] ON SERVER
ADD EVENT sqlserver.page_split(
    ACTION(sqlserver.client_app_name,sqlserver.database_id,sqlserver.database_name,
sqlserver.plan_handle,sqlserver.server_instance_name,sqlserver.server_principal_name,
sqlserver.server_principal_sid,sqlserver.session_id,sqlserver.session_nt_username,
sqlserver.sql_text,sqlserver.transaction_id,sqlserver.username)),
ADD EVENT sqlserver.rpc_completed(
    ACTION(sqlserver.client_app_name,sqlserver.database_id,sqlserver.database_name,
sqlserver.plan_handle,sqlserver.server_instance_name,sqlserver.server_principal_name,
sqlserver.server_principal_sid,sqlserver.session_id,sqlserver.session_nt_username,
sqlserver.sql_text,sqlserver.transaction_id,sqlserver.username)),
ADD EVENT sqlserver.rpc_starting(
    ACTION(sqlserver.client_app_name,sqlserver.database_id,sqlserver.database_name,
sqlserver.plan_handle,sqlserver.server_instance_name,sqlserver.server_principal_name,
sqlserver.server_principal_sid,sqlserver.session_id,sqlserver.session_nt_username,
sqlserver.sql_text,sqlserver.transaction_id,sqlserver.username)),
ADD EVENT sqlserver.sp_statement_completed(
    ACTION(sqlserver.client_app_name,sqlserver.database_id,sqlserver.database_name,
sqlserver.plan_handle,sqlserver.server_instance_name,sqlserver.server_principal_name,
sqlserver.server_principal_sid,sqlserver.session_id,sqlserver.session_nt_username,
sqlserver.sql_text,sqlserver.transaction_id,sqlserver.username)),
ADD EVENT sqlserver.sp_statement_starting(
    ACTION(sqlserver.client_app_name,sqlserver.database_id,sqlserver.database_name,
sqlserver.plan_handle,sqlserver.server_instance_name,sqlserver.server_principal_name,
sqlserver.server_principal_sid,sqlserver.session_id,sqlserver.session_nt_username,
sqlserver.sql_text,sqlserver.transaction_id,sqlserver.username))
ADD TARGET package0.event_file(SET filename=N'C:\Temp\Troubleshoot page split.xel')
WITH (MAX_MEMORY=4096 KB,EVENT_RETENTION_MODE=ALLOW_SINGLE_EVENT_LOSS,MAX_
DISPATCH_LATENCY=30 SECONDS,MAX_EVENT_SIZE=0 KB,MEMORY_PARTITION_MODE=NONE,TRACK_
CAUSALITY=OFF,STARTUP_STATE=OFF)
GO
```

Now you can start the XEvents session created in Listing 19-21 and begin identifying the queries and the session details that cause these page splits. This will help you narrow down the issue very quickly and troubleshoot the cause.

Summary

SQL Server stores data in 8 KB pages that it allocates in contiguous groups of 8 pages each, which are known as extents. In a perfect world, SQL Server's logical and physical storage mechanisms wouldn't make a difference to you as a developer. In the real world, however, an understanding of storage engine operation is important for maximizing performance. This chapter began an overview of the SQL Server storage engine and how it affects performance.

Indexes are the primary means of increasing query performance on SQL Server. We continued the discussion by addressing the concepts of heaps, clustered indexes, and nonclustered indexes, with details of how each affects the overall performance of your queries and DML statements.

Optimizing queries depends on maximizing two critical aspects: response time and throughput. SQL Server provides query plans and statistics, in addition to other external tools, to help diagnose performance issues. The chapter wrapped up with a suggested methodology for dealing with performance issues. Using a methodology like the eight-step process described here can help you quickly narrow down the source of performance issues; define, evaluate, and implement solutions; and take a proactive approach in addressing future performance-related issues.

Using troubleshooting techniques such as wait stats and DMVs can help you locate performance issues and provide information you can use to derive a complete picture of what is going on in the system. Combining this with a high-performance event-monitoring infrastructure such as Extended Events gives you proactive capabilities for monitoring servers so you can identify issues and resolve them in a timely fashion.

We hope you've enjoyed reading this book as much as we've enjoyed bringing it to you. We wish you all the best in your T-SQL development efforts and hope you find this book helpful in your development endeavors.

EXERCISES

1. [Choose all that apply] SQL Server 2014 uses which of the following types of files to store database information?

    a. Data files (.mdf extension)

    b. Transaction log files (.ldf extension)

    c. Additional data files (.ndf extension)

    d. Rich text files (.rtf extension)

2. [True/False] In-Memory tables are created in the default PRIMARY filegroup.

3. [True/False] SQL Server stores data in 8 KB storage units known as pages.

4. [Choose one] Eight contiguous 8 KB pages of storage in SQL Server are known as which of the following?

    a. A filegroup

    b. A chunk

    c. An extent

    d. A file

5. [Fill in the blank] A heap is an _____ collection of data pages.

6. [Fill in the blank] Clustered indexes and nonclustered indexes are managed by SQL Server as _____ structures.

7. [Fill in the blank] _____ sessions can be used to trace waits.

8. [Choose one] An optimized nonclustered index is a {filtered | parameterized | unsorted} index

9. [Choose all that apply] SQL Server performance is measured using which of the following terms?

    a. Throughput

    b. Luminescence

    c. Response time

    d. All of the above

a collaborator that the eight-step process described here can help you quickly narrow down the source of performance issues, define baselines and implement solutions, and take a proactive approach in addressing future performance-related issues.

Using multiple sophisticated techniques such as wait stats and DMVs can help you locate performance and profile information you can use to derive a complete picture of what is going on in the system. Combining this with high-performance event-monitoring infrastructure such as extended events gives you proactive capabilities for monitoring servers so you can identify issues and resolve them in a timely fashion. We hope you've enjoyed reading this book as we've enjoyed bringing it to you. We wish you all the best in your T-SQL development efforts and hope can help be helpful in your development endeavors.

EXERCISES

1. [Choose all that apply] SQL Server 2014 uses which of the following types of files to store database information?

   a. Data files (.mdf extension)

   b. Transaction log files (.ldf extension)

   c. Multiple data files (.ndf extension)

   d. None of the above

2. [True/False] In-Memory tables are created in the default PRIMARY filegroup.

3. [True/False] SQL Server stores data in 8 KB storage units known as pages.

4. [Choose one] Eight contiguous 8 KB pages of storage in SQL Server are known as which of the following?

   a. A filegroup

   b. A table

   c. An extent

   d. A file

5. [Fill in the blank] A heap is an _____ collection of data pages.

6. [Fill in the blank] Clustered indexes and nonclustered indexes are managed by SQL Server as _____ structures.

7. [Fill in the blank] _____ sessions can be used to trace waits.

8. [Choose one] An optimized nonclustered index is a (filtered / partitioned / unindexed) index.

9. [Choose all that apply] SQL Server performance is measured using which of the following terms?

   a. Throughput

   b. Luminescence

   c. Response time

   d. All of the above

Exercise Answers

This appendix contains the answers to the exercises at the end of each chapter. The answers are grouped by chapter and numbered to match the associated exercises in the corresponding chapter.

Chapter 1

1. Imperative languages require you to provide the computer with step-by-step directions to perform a task—essentially, you tell the computer how to achieve the end result. Declarative languages allow you to tell the computer what the end result should be and trust the computer to take appropriate action to achieve it.

2. ACID stands for "atomicity, consistency, isolation, durability." These represent the basic properties of a database that guarantee reliability of data storage, processing, and manipulations.

3. The seven index types that SQL Server supports are clustered indexes; nonclustered indexes; XML indexes; spatial indexes; full-text indexes; and two in-memory table index types, nonclustered hash index and memory-optimized nonclustered index.

4. All of the following are restrictions on all SQL Server UDFs: (1) they cannot perform DML or DDL statements, (2) they cannot change the state of the database (no side effects), (3) they cannot use dynamic SQL, and (4) they cannot utilize certain nondeterministic functions.

5. False. All newly declared variables are set to NULL on creation. You should always initialize newly created variables immediately after creation.

Chapter 2

1. SSDT is an integrated project-oriented development environment for database and application development. SSDT is the replacement for Business Intelligence Development Studio (BIDS).

2. The correct answers are A, B, C, and D. SQL Server 2014 SSMS provides integrated Object Explorer, IntelliSense, code snippets, and a customizable keyboard mapping scheme.

3. SSIS is considered an ETL (extract, transform, load) tool.

4. True. SQLCMD scripting variables can be set via command-line options and environment variables, and in script via the SQLCMD :setvar command.

5. The correct answer is D, All of the Above. BCP can generate format files that can be used with the SSIS Bulk Insert task, with the T-SQL BULK INSERT statement, or with BCP itself. BCP can also import data into tables without a format file and export data from a table to a file.

6. You can query Extended Events trace files directly. With a SQL Profiler trace, you have to load the captured trace data to a table and then query it. Direct querying against Profiler trace data is not supported.

7. SQL Server 2005, SQL Server 2008, SQL Server 2008 R2, SQL Server 2012, SQL Server 2014, and SQL Azure.

Chapter 3

1. True. SQL 3VL supports the three Boolean results true, false, and unknown.

2. The correct answer is A. In SQL, NULL represents an unknown or a missing value. NULL does not represent a numeric value of 0 or a zero-length string.

3. False. SQL's BEGIN...END construct defines a statement block but does not limit the scope of variables declared within the statement block. This is contrary to the behavior of C#'s curly braces ({ }).

4. The BREAK statement forces a WHILE loop to terminate immediately.

5. False. TRY...CATCH can't capture syntax errors, errors that cause a broken connection, or errors with severity of 10 or less, among others.

6. SQL CASE expressions come in both simple and searched CASE expression forms.

7. The correct answers are A and B. T-SQL provides support for read-only cursors and forward-only cursors. There is no such thing as a backward-only cursor or a write-only cursor.

8. The following code modifies the example in Listing 3-10 to return the total sales (TotalDue) by region in pivot-table format. The required change to the code is shown in bold:

```
-- Declare variables DECLARE @sql nvarchar(4000);
DECLARE @temp_pivot table (
    TerritoryID int NOT NULL PRIMARY KEY,
    CountryRegion nvarchar(20) NOT NULL,
    CountryRegionCode nvarchar(3) NOT NULL
);
-- Get column names from source table rows INSERT INTO @temp_pivot
(TerritoryID,
CountryRegion,
CountryRegionCode) SELECT TerritoryID,
```

```
Name,
CountryRegionCode FROM Sales.SalesTerritory GROUP BY TerritoryID, Name,
CountryRegionCode;
-- Generate dynamic SOL query SET @sql = N'SELECT' + SUBSTRING(
(
SELECT N', SUM(CASE WHEN t.TerritoryID = ' + CAST(TerritoryID AS
NVARCHAR(3)) +
N' THEN soh.TotalDue ELSE 0 END) AS ' + QUOTENAME(CountryRegion) AS "*"
FROM @temp_pivot
FOR XML PATH('') ), 2, 4000) +
N' FROM Sales.SalesOrderHeader soh ' +
N' INNER JOIN Sales.SalesTerritory t ' +
N' ON soh.TerritoryID = t.TerritoryID; ' ;
-- Print and execute dynamic SQL PRINT @sql;
EXEC (@sql);
```

Chapter 4

1. SQL Server supports three types of T-SQL UDFs: scalar UDFs, multistatement
    TVFs, and inline TVFs.

2. True. The RETURNS NULL ON NULL INPUT option is a performance-enhancing
    option that automatically returns NULL if any of the parameters passed into a
    scalar UDF are NULL.

3. False. The ENCRYPTION option performs a simple code obfuscation that is easily
    reverse-engineered. In fact, several programs and scripts are available online that
    allow anyone to decrypt your code with the push of a button.

4. The correct answers are A, B, and D. Multistatement TVFs (as well as all other
    TVFs) do not allow you to execute PRINT statements, call RAISERROR, or create
    temporary tables. In multistatement TVFs, you can declare table variables.

5. The following code creates a deterministic scalar UDF that accepts a float
    parameter, converts it from degrees Fahrenheit to degrees Celsius, and returns a
    float result. Notice that the WITH SCHEMABINDING option is required to make this
    scalar UDF deterministic:

```
CREATE FUNCTION dbo.FahrenheitToCelsius (@Degrees float)
RETURNS float
WITH SCHEMABINDING
AS
BEGIN
RETURN (@Degrees - 32.0) * (5.0 / 9.0); END;
```

Chapter 5

1. False. The SP RETURN statement can return only an int scalar value.

2. One method of proving that two SPs that call each other recursively are limited to 32 levels of recursion in total is shown here. Differences from the code in the original listing are shown in bold:

```
CREATE PROCEDURE dbo.FirstProc (@i int)
AS
BEGIN
PRINT @i;
SET @i += 1;
EXEC dbo.SecondProc @i;
END; GO
CREATE PROCEDURE dbo.SecondProc (@i int)
AS
BEGIN
PRINT @i;
SET @i += 1;
EXEC dbo.FirstProc @i; END; GO
EXEC dbo.FirstProc 1;
```

3. The correct answer is D. Table-valued parameters must be declared READONLY.

4. The correct answers are A and B. You can use the sprecompile system SP or the WITH RECOMPILE option to force SQL Server to recompile an SP. FORCE RECOMPILE and DBCC RECOMPILEALLSPS are not valid options/statements.

Chapter 6

1. The correct answers are A and B. Developer Edition, Enterprise Edition, and Evaluation Edition of the software support the new in-memory features.

2. False. BIN2 collation on a string data type column is necessary only if it is being used in an index or an ORDER BY clause.

3. The correct answers is C, range index. There is no concept of a clustered index on an in-memory table, and hash indexes are best suited for single-item point lookups.

4. True. By default, if the durability option for a memory-optimized table is not specified, it defaults to durable (SCHEMA_AND_DATA).

5. False. All memory-optimized tables require an index, but only tables that are durable (SCHEMA_AND_DATA option) require a primary key constraint.

6. The correct answers are A, B, and C. Execute as Owner, Self, and User are valid execution contexts. The only listed execution context that is not valid is EXECUTE AS CALLER. This execution context does not allow SQL Server to hardcode execution rights at the time the stored procedure is compiled.

Chapter 7

1. True. In DDL triggers, the EVENTDATA function returns information about the DDL event that fired the trigger.

2. True. In a DML trigger, an UPDATE event is treated as a DELETE followed by an INSERT, so both the deleted and inserted virtual tables are populated for UPDATE events.

3. False. DML triggers are not available for SQL Server 2014 in-memory tables.

4. The correct answers are A, C, and E. SQL Server 2014 supports logon triggers, DDL triggers, and DML triggers.

5. The SET NOCOUNT ON statement prevents extraneous rows affected messages.

6. The correct answer is A. The COLUMNSUPDATED function returns a varbinary string with bits set to represent affected columns.

7. True. @@ROWCOUNT at the beginning of a trigger returns the number of rows affected by the DML statement that fired the trigger.

8. False. You cannot create any AFTER triggers on a view.

Chapter 8

1. True. Symmetric keys can be used to encrypt data or other symmetric keys.

2. The correct answers are A, B, and E. SQL Server 2012 provides native support for DES, AES, and RC4 encryption. Although the Loki and Blowfish algorithms are real encryption algorithms, SQL Server does not provide native support for them.

3. False. SQL Server 2014 T-SQL provides no BACKUP ASYMMETRIC KEY statement.

4. You must turn on the EKM provider-enabled option with spconfigure to activate EKM on your server.

5. False. TDE automatically encrypts the tempdb database, but it does not encrypt the model and master databases.

6. True. SQL Server automatically generates random initialization vectors when you encrypt data with symmetric encryption.

Chapter 9

1. True. When a CTE is not the first statement in a batch, the statement preceding it must end with a semicolon statement terminator.

2. The correct answers are A, B, and D. Recursive CTEs require the WITH keyword, an anchor query, and a recursive query. SQL Server does not support an EXPRESSION keyword.

3. The MAXRECURSION option can accept a value between 0 and 32767.

4. The correct answer is E, All of the Above. SQL Server supports the ROWNUMBER, RANK, DENSE_RANK, and NTILE functions.

5. False. You cannot use ORDER BY with the OVER clause when used with aggregate functions.

6. True. When PARTITION BY and ORDER BY are both used in the OVER clause, PARTITION BY must appear first.

7. The names of all columns returned by a CTE must be unique.

8. The default framing clause is RANGE BETWEEN UNBOUNDED PRECEDING AND CURRENT ROW.

9. True. When Orderby is not specified, there is no starting or ending point for the boundary. So, the entire partition is used for the window frame.

Chapter 10

1. False. European language accents are included in the ANSI-encoded characters. You need Unicode for non-Latin characters.

2. The correct answers are A, C, and D. image and (n)text have been deprecated since SQL Server 2005.

3. False. The date data type does not store time zone information. Use the datetimeoffset data type if you need to store time zone information with your date/time data.

4. The hierarchyid data type uses the materialized path model to represent hierarchies in the database.

5. The correct answer is B. The geography data type requires Polygon objects to have a counterclockwise orientation. Also, spatial objects created with the geography data type must be contained in a single hemisphere.

6. The correct answer is B. The SWITCHOFFSET function adjusts a given datetimeoffset value to another specified time offset.

7. True. FILESTREAM functionality utilizes NTFS functionality to provide streaming BLOB data support.

8. The column is named path_locator. It is a hierarchyid type column.

Chapter 11

1. True. Stoplists and full-text indexes are stored in the database.

2. The correct answer is C. You can create a full-text index using the wizard in SSMS or the T-SQL CREATE FULLTEXT INDEX statement.

3. The FREETEXT predicate automatically performs word stemming and thesaurus replacements and expansions.

4. Stoplists contain stopwords, which are words that are ignored during full-text querying.

5. True. The `sys.dmftsparser` dynamic-management function shows the results produced by word breaking and stemming.

Chapter 12

1. The correct answers are A, B, C, and D. The SQL Server FOR XML clause supports the FOR XML RAW, FOR XML PATH, FOR XML AUTO, and FOR XML EXPLICIT modes. FOR XML RECURSIVE is not a valid FOR XML mode.

2. OPENXML returns results in edge table format by default.

3. True. The xml data type query() method returns results as untyped xml instances.

4. The correct answer is C. A SQL Server primary XML index stores xml data type columns in a preshredded relational format.

5. True. When you haven't defined a primary XML index on an xml data type column, performing XQuery queries against the column causes SQL Server to perform on-the-fly shredding of your XML data. This can result in a severe performance penalty.

6. True. Additional XML functionality, available through the .NET Framework, can be accessed via SQL Server's SQL CLR integration.

Chapter 13

1. True. The FOR XML PATH clause supports a subset of the W3C XPath recommendation for explicitly specifying your XML result structure.

2. The correct answer is A. The at sign (@) is used to identify attribute nodes in both XPath and XQuery.

3. The context item (indicated by a single period) specifies the current node or scalar value being accessed at any given point in time during query execution.

4. The correct answers are A, B, and D. You can declare XML namespaces for SQL Server XQuery expressions with the WITH XMLNAMESPACES clause, the declare default element namespace statement, or the declare namespace statement. There is no CREATE XML NAMESPACE statement.

5. In XQuery, you can dynamically construct XML via direct constructors or computed constructors.

6. True. SQL Server 2014 supports all five clauses of FLWOR expressions: for, let, where, order by, and return. Note that SQL Server 2005 did not support the let clause.

7. _SC collation enables SQL Server to be UTF-16 aware.

8. The correct answers are B, C, and D. XQuery provides three types of comparison operators: general comparison operators, node comparison operators, and value comparison operators.

Chapter 14

1. Metadata is "data that describes data."

2. Catalog views provide insight into database objects and server-wide configuration options.

3. The correct answer is B. Many catalog views are defined using an inheritance model. In the inheritance model, catalog views inherit columns from other catalog views. Some catalog views are also defined as the union of two other catalog views.

4. True. Dynamic-management views and functions provide access to internal SQL Server data structures that would be otherwise inaccessible. DMVs and DMFs present these internal data structures in relational tabular format.

5. The correct answers are A and C. INFORMATION_SCHEMA views provide the advantages of ISO SQL standard compatibility and, as a consequence, cross-platform compatibility.

Chapter 15

1. True. The System.Data.SqlClient namespace provides support for the SQL Server Native Client library, which provides optimized access to SQL Server.

2. The correct answer is B. Disconnected datasets cache required data locally and allow you to connect to a database only as needed.

3. The correct answers are A and C. The benefits of query parameterization include protection against SQL injection attacks and increased efficiency through query plan reuse.

4. False. When you turn on MARS, you can open two or more result sets over a single open connection. MARS requires only one open connection.

5. True. Visual Studio provides a visual O/RM designer with a drag-and-drop interface.

6. The correct answer is D. LINQ to SQL uses deferred query execution, meaning it does not execute your query until the data returned by the query is actually needed.

Chapter 16

1. The correct answers are A, B, C, D, and E. SQL Server 2014 provides support for SQL CLR UDFs, UDAs, UDTs, SPs, and triggers.

2. False. SQL Server 2014 expands the limit on MaxByteSize for UDAs and UDTs to more than 2 billion bytes. In SQL Server 2005, there was an 8,000-byte limit on the size of UDAs and UDTs.

3. The correct answer is D. SAFE permissions allow SQL CLR code to execute managed .NET code. EXTERNALACCESS permissions are required to write to the file system, access network resources, and read the computer's registry.

4. True. SQL CLR UDAs and UDTs must be declared with the Serializable attribute.

5. A SQL CLR UDA that is declared as Format.UserDefined must implement the IBinarySerialize interface.

6. The correct answers are A, C, D, and E. A SQL CLR UDA is required to implement the following methods: Init, Terminate, Merge, and Accumulate. The Aggregate method is not a required method for UDAs.

Chapter 17

1. False. A LocalDB instance cannot run as a service.

2. False. You can access XML columns from Linux by using the Microsoft ODBC driver for Linux.

3. False. HTTP SOAP endpoints were deprecated in SQL Server 2008.

4. Visual Studio 2010 and 2012 provides the ASP.NET Web Service template for creating new web services.

5. True. Visual Studio includes a built-in graphical EDM designer beginning with SP 1.

6. The correct answer is C. WCF Data Services accepts REST-style queries in requests.

Chapter 18

1. The @@error system function automatically resets to 0 after every successful statement execution.

2. The correct answer is D. The ERROR_SEVERITY() function, available only in the CATCH block in SQL Server, returns the severity level of the error that occurred.

3. True. The RAISERROR statement allows you to raise errors in SQL Server.

4. True. Visual Studio provides integrated debugging of T-SQL functions and SPs. Using Visual Studio, you can step into T-SQL code and set breakpoints.

5. The correct answers are A and B. The potential problems with dynamic SQL include performance issues caused by lack of query plan reuse, and exposure to SQL injection attacks.

Chapter 19

1. The correct answers are A, B, and C. SQL Server 2014 uses data files with an .mdf extension, transaction log files with an .ldf extension, and additional data files with an .ndf extension.

2. False. In-memory optimized tables must be created in a memory-optimized filegroup, specified by the CONTAINS MEMORY_OPTIMIZED_DATA syntax when creating the filegroup.

3. True. SQL Server stores data in 8 KB storage units known as pages.

4. The correct answer is C. Eight contiguous 8 KB pages of storage in SQL Server are known as an extent.

5. A heap is an unordered collection of data pages.

6. Clustered indexes and nonclustered indexes are managed by SQL Server as B-tree structures.

7. Extended Events sessions can be used to trace waits.

8. An optimized nonclustered index is called a filtered index.

9. The correct answers are A and C. SQL Server performance is measured in terms of throughput and response time.

APPENDIX B

■ ■ ■

XQuery Data Types

SQL Server 2014 supports the data types defined in the XQuery Data Model (XDM). The supported data types are listed with their definitions in Table B-1. The diagram in Figure B-1 is a quick reference showing the relationships between the XDM data types.

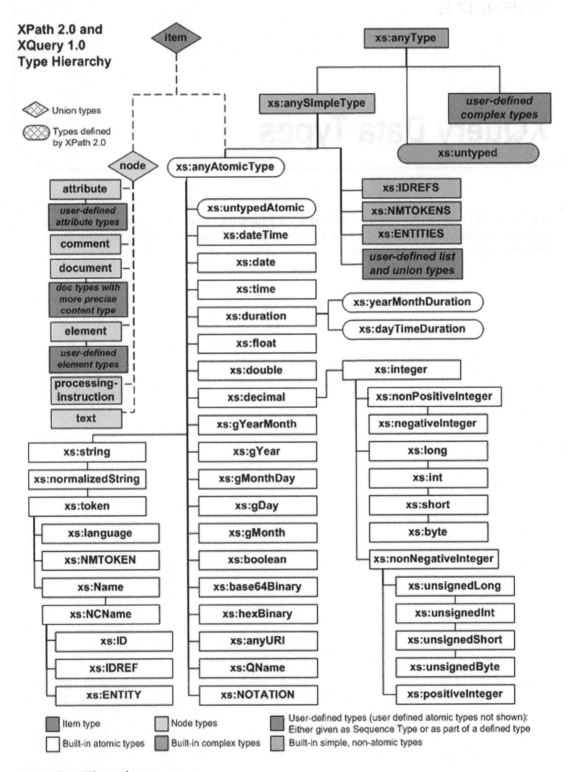

Figure B-1. *XQuery data type system*

Table B-1. *XQuery Data Types*

Type	Description
Base Types	
xs:anySimpleType	Base type for all simple built-in types.
xs:anyType	Base type for xs:anySimpleType and complex built-in types.
Date/Time Types	
xs:date	Represents a Gregorian calendar–based date value exactly one day in length, in the format yyyy-mm-dd[time_offset]. time_offset can be a capital Z for zero-meridian (UTC) or in the format +/-hh:mm to represent a UTC offset. An example of a valid xs:date is 2006-12-25Z, which represents December 25, 2006, UTC time.
xs:dateTime	Represents a Gregorian calendar–based date and time value with precision to 1/1000th of a second. The format is yyyy-mm-ddThh: mm:ss.sss[time_ offset]. Time is specified using a 24-hour clock. As with xs:date, time_offset can be a capital Z (UTC) or a UTC offset in the format +/-hh:mm. A valid xs:dateTime value is 2006-10-30T13:00: 59.500-05:00, which represents October 30, 2006, 1:00:59.5 PM, US Eastern Standard time. Unlike in SQL Server 2005, in SQL Server 2012 the xs:dateTime type maintains the time zone information you assign instead of automatically converting all date/time values to a single time zone. The time zone also isn't mandatory in SQL Server 2012.
xs:duration	Represents a Gregorian calendar–based temporal (time- based) duration, using the format PyyyyYmmMddDThhHmmMss.sssS. P0010Y03M12DT00H00M00.000S, for instance, represents 10 years, 3 months, 12 days.
xs:gDay	Represents a Gregorian calendar–based day. The format is dd[time_offset] (notice the three preceding hyphen [-] characters). The time_offset is optional. A valid xs:gDay value is 09Z, which stands for the ninth day of the month, UTC time.
xs:gMonth	Represents a Gregorian calendar–based month. The format is --mm[time_ offset] (notice the two preceding hyphen characters). time_offset is optional. A valid xs:gMonth value is -12, which stands for December.
xs:gMonthDay	Represents a Gregorian calendar–based month and day. The format is --mm-dd[time_offset] (notice the two preceding hyphens). The time_offset is optional. A valid xs:gMonthDay value is --02-29 for February 29.
xs:gYear	Represents a Gregorian calendar–based year. The format is yyyy[time_ offset]. The time_offset is optional. The year can also have a preceding hyphen character indicating a negative (BCE—"before the Christian Era") year as opposed to a positive (CE—"Christian Era") date. A valid xs:gYear value is -0044 for 44 BCE. Notice that all four digits are required in the year representation, even for years that can be normally represented with fewer than four digits.
xs:gYearMonth	Represents a Gregorian calendar–based year and month. The format is yyyy-mm[time_offset]. The time_offset is optional and can be Z or a UTC offset. A valid xs:gYearMonth value is 2001-01 for January 2001.

(continued)

Table B-1. *(continued)*

Type	Description
xs:time	Represents a time value with precision to 1/1000th of a second, using a 24-hour clock representation. The format is hh:mm:ss.sss [time_offset]. As with other temporal data types, time_offset can be Z (UTC) or a UTC offset in the format +/-hh:mm. A valid xs:time value is 23:59:59.000-06:00, which represents 11:59:59 PM, US Central Standard time. The canonical representation of midnight in 24-hour format is 00:00:00.

Binary Types

Type	Description
xs:base64Binary	Represents Base64-encoded binary data. Base64-encoding symbols are defined in RFC 2045 (www.ietf.org/rfc/rfc2045.txt) as A through Z, a through z, 0 through 9, +, /, and the trailing = sign. Whitespace characters are also allowed, and lowercase letters are considered distinct from uppercase letters. An example of a valid xs:base64Binary value is QVByZXNzIEJvb2tzIEFuZCBTUUwwgU 2V⊠ydmVyIDIwMDU=.
xs:hexBinary	Represents hexadecimal-encoded binary data. The symbols defined for encoding data in hexadecimal format are 0 through 9, A through F, and a through f. Upper- and lowercase letters A through F are considered equivalent by this data type. An example of a valid xs:hexBinary value is 6170726573732E636F6D.

Boolean Type

Type	Description
xs:Boolean	Represents a Boolean binary truth value. The values supported are true (1) and false (0). An example of a valid xs:boolean value is true.

Numeric Types

Type	Description
xs:byte	Represents an 8-bit signed integer in the range -128 to +127.
xs:decimal	Represents an exact decimal value up to 38 digits in length. These numbers can have up to 28 digits before the decimal point and up to 10 digits after the decimal point. A valid xs:decimal value is 8372.9381.
xs:double	Represents a double-precision floating-point value patterned after the IEEE standard for floating-point types. The representation of values is similar to xs:float values nE[+/-]e, where n is the mantissa followed by the letter E or e and an exponent e. The range of valid values for xs:double is approximately -1.79E+308 to -2.23E-308 for negative numbers, 0, and +2.23E-308 to +1.79E+308 for positive numbers.
xs:float	Represents an approximate single-precision floating point value per the IEEE 754-1985 standard. The format for values of this type is nEe, where n is a decimal mantissa followed by the letter E or e and an exponent. The value represents n·10e. The range for xs:float values is approximately -3.4028e+38 to -1.401298E-45 for negative numbers, 0, and +1.401298E-45 to +3.4028e+38 for positive numbers. The special values -INF and +INF represent negative and positive infinity. SQL Server doesn't support the XQuery-specified special value NaN, which stands for "not a number." A valid xs:float value is 1.98E+2.

(continued)

Table B-1. *(continued)*

Type	Description
xs:int	Represents a 32-bit signed integer in the range -2147483648 to +2147483647.
xs:integer	Represents an integer value up to 28 digits in length. A valid xs:integer value is 76372.
xs:long	Represents a 64-bit signed integer in the range -9223372036854775808 to +9223372036854775807.
xs:negativeInteger	Represents a negative nonzero integer value derived from the xs:integer type. It can be up to 28 digits in length.
xs:nonNegativeInteger	Represents a positive or zero integer value derived from the xs:integer type. It can be up to 28 digits in length.
xs:nonPositiveInteger	Represents a negative or zero integer value derived from the xs:integer type. It can be up to 28 digits in length.
xs:positiveInteger	Represents a positive nonzero integer value derived from the xs:integer type. It can be up to 28 digits in length.
xs:short	Represents a 16-bit signed integer in the range -37268 to +32767.
xs:unsignedByte	Represents an unsigned 8-bit integer in the range 0 to 255.
xs:unsignedInt	Represents an unsigned 32-bit integer in the range 0 to +4294967295.
xs:unsignedLong	Represents an unsigned 64-bit integer in the range 0 to +18446744073709551615.
xs:unsignedShort	Represents an unsigned 16-bit integer in the range 0 to +65535.
String Types	
xs:ENTITIES	A space-separated list of ENTITY types.
xs:ENTITY	Equivalent to the ENTITY type from the XML 1.0 standard. The lexical space has the same construction as an xs:NCName.
xs:ID	Equivalent to the ID attribute type from the XML 1.0 standard. An xs:ID value has the same lexical construction as an xs:NCName.
xs:IDREF	Represents the IDREF attribute type from the XML 1.0 standard. The lexical space has the same construction as an xs:NCName.
xs:IDREFS	A space-separated list of IDREF attribute types.
xs:language	A language identifier string representing natural language identifiers as specified by RFC 3066 (www.ietf.org/rfc/rfc3066.txt). A complete list of language codes is maintained by the IANA registry at www.iana.org/assignments/language-subtag-registry. Language identifiers must conform to the regular expression pattern [a-zA- Z]{1,8}(-[a-zA-Z0-9]{1,8})*. An example of a valid language identifier is tlh, which is the identifier for the Klingon language.

(continued)

Table B-1. *(continued)*

Type	Description
xs:Name	An XML name string. A name string must match the XML-specified production for Name. Per the standard, a Name must begin with a letter, an underscore, or a colon, and may then contain a combination of letters, numbers, underscores, colons, periods, hyphens, and various other characters designated in the XML standard as combining characters and extenders. Refer to the XML standard at www.w3.org/TR/2000/WD-xml-2e-20000814#NT-Name for specific information about these additional allowable Name characters.
xs:NCName	A noncolonized name. The format for an xs:NCName is the same as for xs:Name, but without colon characters.
xs:NMTOKEN	An NMTOKEN type from the XML 1.0 standard. An xs:NMTOKEN value is composed of any combination of letters, numbers, underscores, colons, periods, hyphens, and XML combining characters and extenders.
xs:NMTOKENS	A space-separated list of xs:NMTOKEN values.
xs:normalizedString	An XML whitespace-normalized string, which is one that doesn't contain the whitespace characters #x9 (tab), #xA (line feed), and #xD (carriage return).
xs:string	An XML character string.
xs:token	An XML whitespace-normalized string with the following additional restrictions on #x20 (space) characters: it can have no leading or trailing spaces, and it can't contain any sequences of two space characters in a row.

Glossary

ACID

An acronym for atomicity, consistency, isolation, durability. These four concepts of transactional data stores, including SQL databases, ensure data integrity.

adjacency list model

The representation of all arcs or edges of a graph as a list. In SQL, this is often implemented as a self-referential table in which each row maintains a pointer to its parent node in the graph.

ADO.NET Data Services

Also known as Project Astoria. ADO.NET Data Services provides middle-tier support for accessing SQL Server databases through REST-style queries and entity data models (EDMs).

anchor query

The nonrecursive query specified in the body of a common table expression.

application programming interface (API)

A well-defined interface provided by an application or service to support requests and communications from other applications.

assembly

In SQL Server, a .NET assembly is a compiled SQL CLR executable or DLL.

asymmetric encryption

Encryption that requires two different keys: one to encrypt data and another to decrypt it. The most common form of asymmetric encryption is public key encryption, in which the two keys are mathematically related.

atomic, list, and union data types

The XML Schema 1.1 Part 2: Data Types specification working draft (http://www.w3.org/TR/xmlschema11-2/) defines no built-in union data types.

Atomic data types are indivisible data types that derive from the xs:anyAtomicType type. Examples include xs:boolean, xs:date, and xs:integer.

list data types are constructed of sequences of other types.

union data types are constructed from the ordered union of two or more data types, or a restricted subset of a data type.

axis

Specifier that indicates the relationship between the nodes selected by the location step and the context node. Examples of axis specifiers include child, parent, and ancestor.

Bulk Copy Program (BCP)

A command-line utility supplied with SQL Server for the purpose of quickly loading large datasets into tables.

catalog view

View that returns a SQL Server database and server-specific metadata.

certificate

An electronic document consisting of an asymmetric key with additional metadata such as an expiration date and a digital signature that allows it to be verified by a third party like a certificate authority (CA).

check constraint

A condition placed on a table that restricts the range of valid values for one or more columns.

closed-world assumption (CWA)

A logic formalism stating that what is not known to be true, is false. SQL databases violate the CWA through the introduction of NULLs.

clustered index

An index that contains a table's row data in its leaf-level nodes.

comment

In XQuery, code that is ignored during processing. XQuery comments are denoted by the (: and :) delimiters in XQuery queries. They should not be confused with XML comment nodes, which are designated with <!-- and --> delimiters.

T-SQL allows single-line comments that begin with -- or multiline comments enclosed in /* and */ delimiters.

computed constructor

An alternative way to create XML nodes by specifying the type of node to be created through the use of special keywords.

content expression

Part of a computed constructor, enclosed in braces, that generates XML node content.

context item expression

An expression that evaluates to the context node.

context node

The node currently being processed. Each node of each set/sequence returned by a step in a location path is used in turn as a context node. Subsequent steps define their axes in relation to the current context node. For instance, with the sample XPath expression /Root/Person/Address, the Root node is the first context node. All Person nodes returned below Root become the context node in turn, and the Address nodes are retrieved relative to these context nodes.

database encryption key

An encryption key used by Transparent Data Encryption to encrypt entire SQL Server databases.

database master key

A database-level encryption key used to secure other keys in the database.

data domain

For a column, all valid values that may be stored in that column. The data domain can be restricted through the use of data types, check constraints, referential integrity/foreign key constraints, and triggers.

data page

The smallest unit of storage that SQL Server can allocate. The data page consists of 8 KB of logically contiguous storage.

datum

A set of reference points against which position can be measured. A geodetic datum is often associated with a model of the shape of the Earth to define a geographic coordinate system.

empty sequence

An XPath 2.0/XQuery 1.0 sequence containing zero items.

entity data model (EDM)

An abstract logical representation of a physical database, used to implement database connectivity in the middle or client tiers.

Extended Events (XEvents)

A lightweight diagnostic system that can help you troubleshoot performance problems with SQL Server.

extensible key management (EKM)

A SQL Server 2012 encryption option that allows you to physically store encryption keys on third-party hardware security modules (HSMs).

extent

SQL Server's basic allocation unit of storage. An extent is 64 KB in size and consists of eight logically contiguous data pages, each of which is 8 KB in size.

Extract, Transform, Load (ETL)

Processes that involve pulling data from disparate data sources, cleaning and scrubbing the data, manipulating it (transform), and storing it in the database.

facet

A schema component used to constrain data types. A couple of commonly used facets are whiteSpace, which controls how whitespace in string values is handled, and length, which restricts values to a specific number of units in length.

filter expression

A primary expression followed by zero or more predicates.

FLWOR expression

Expressions that support iteration and binding variables. FLWOR is an acronym for the XQuery keywords for, let, where, order by, and return.

foreign key constraint

A logical coupling of two SQL tables through the values of specified columns.

full-text catalog

A logical grouping of SQL Server full-text indexes for management purposes.

full-text index

Index that enables advanced text-based searches to be performed against a database table.

full-text search (FTS)

The SQL Server 2012 implementation of the SQL Server full-text search engine with the SQL Server query engine.

Functions and Operators (F&O)

The XQuery 1.0 and XPath 2.0 Functions and Operators specification, available at www.w3.org/TR/xquery-operators/.

general comparison

An existentially quantified XQuery comparison that may be applied to operand sequences of any length. In general comparisons, the nodes are atomized and the atomic values of both operands are compared using value comparisons. If any of the value comparisons evaluate to true, the result is true.

Geography Markup Language (GML)

A standard for the representation of geographic data using XML.

grouping set

A SQL Server 2012 feature that allows you to define sets of grouping columns in your queries.

hash

The result of applying a mathematical function or transformation to data to generate a smaller "fingerprint" of the data. Generally, the most useful hash functions are one-way, collision-free hashes that guarantee a high level of uniqueness in their results.

heap

An unordered collection of data pages. Any table without a clustered index is a heap.

heterogeneous sequence

An XQuery sequence of atomic values of different types and/or XML nodes. SQL Server XQuery doesn't support heterogeneous sequences consisting of atomic values and nodes.

homogenous sequence

An XQuery sequence consisting entirely of nodes or entirely of singleton atomic values of compatible data types.

indirect recursion

Recursion by a trigger that occurs when a trigger fires, causing another trigger of the same type to fire, which causes the first trigger to fire again.

inflectional forms

Are the different tenses of a verb or the singular and plural forms of nouns. SQL Server integrated full-text search (FTS) can search for inflectional forms of a word, including verb tenses and plural forms of nouns.

initialization vector (IV)

A block of bits that is used to obfuscate the first block of data during the encryption process.

Language Integrated Query (LINQ)

A set of features that adds native data source-agnostic querying capabilities to .NET languages using a declarative syntax.

location path

A series of steps separated by the solidus (forward slash) character, evaluated from left to right. A path is an XPath or XQuery expression that addresses a specific subset of nodes in an XML document. Each step on a location path generates a sequence of items. Location paths can be relative or absolute. Absolute location paths begin with a single solidus character; relative location paths do not.

logon trigger

A trigger that fires in response to a server LOGON event.

materialized path model

A model for storing hierarchical data, in which the entire path to the root node is stored with each node in the hierarchy.

Multiple Active Result Sets (MARS)

A feature that allows you to simultaneously open multiple result sets on a single open connection.

nested sets model

A model in which hierarchical data is represented as a collection of sets containing other sets. The lower and upper bounds of each set define the contents of the set.

node

In the Document Object Model (DOM), everything in an XML document is a node. The entire document is a tree-like structure that makes connections between the arbitrary attributes or nodes. XPath 2.0 and XQuery 1.0 treat XML data as a hierarchical tree structure, similar to (but not exactly the same as) the Document Object Model (DOM) that web programmers often use to manipulate HTML and XML. XPath and XQuery XML trees are composed of the seven types of nodes defined in the W3C XQuery 1.0 and XPath 2.0 Data Model (XDM), full descriptions of which are available at www.w3.org/TR/xpath-datamodel/#node-identity. These node types include the following:

- Attribute nodes represent XML attributes.

- Comment nodes encapsulate XML comments.

- Document nodes encapsulate XML documents.

- Element nodes encapsulate XML elements.

- Namespace nodes represent the binding of a namespace URI to a namespace prefix (or the default namespace).

- Processing instruction nodes encapsulate processing instructions.

- Text nodes encapsulate XML character content.

XPath 1.0 defines the node types it uses in Part 5 of the XPath 1.0 specification. The main difference between XPath 1.0 nodes and XDM nodes is that XPath 1.0 defines the root node of a document in place of the document nodes of the XDM. Another major difference is that in the XDM, element nodes are either explicitly or implicitly (based on content) assigned type information.

node comparison

Comparison of nodes in XQuery based on their document order or identity.

node test

A condition that must be true for each node generated by a step. A node test can be based on the name of the node, the kind of node, or the type of node.

nonclustered index

An index that stores the clustering key or row ID of the row data in its leaf nodes, depending on whether the table is a clustered table or a heap.

object-relational mapping (O/RM)

A technique for mapping data between relational databases and object-oriented programming languages.

open-world assumption (OWA)

A logic formalism stating that the truth of a statement is independent of whether it's known to be true.

optional occurrence indicator

The ? character, when used in conjunction with the cast as keywords. It indicates that the empty sequence is allowed.

parameterization

The act of using named or positional markers in place of constant values in a T-SQL query or statement. The actual values are passed to SQL Server independently of the actual query.

path expression

See location path.

predicate

In T-SQL, an expression that evaluates to a SQL truth value. Predicates are used to control program flow and to limit the results of queries and the effect of statements.

An XQuery predicate is an expression enclosed in brackets ([ ]) that is used to filter a sequence. The predicate expressions are generally comparison expressions of some sort (equality, inequality, and so on).

predicate truth value

In XQuery, a Boolean value derived from the result of an expression through a set of rules defined in the XQuery recommendation.

primary expression

The basic primitive of the XQuery language. A primary expression can be a literal, a variable reference, a context item expression, a data type constructor, or a function call.

query plan

A sequence of logical and physical operators and data flows that the SQL query optimizer returns for use by the query processor to retrieve or modify data.

recompilation

The process of compiling a new query plan for a given query, statement, or stored procedure when a plan already exists in the query-plan cache. Recompilation can be triggered by SQL Server due to changes that have occurred since the prior query plan was generated for the statement, or it can be forced by user actions and T-SQL options.

recursion

A method of defining functions, common table expressions, procedures, or triggers in such a way that they call themselves or cause themselves to be called multiple times.

row constructor

A SQL Server 2012 feature that allows you to specify multiple rows in a single VALUES clause of the INSERT statement.

scalar function

A function that returns a single atomic value as its result.

searched CASE expression

An expression that allows you to specify one or more SQL predicates in WHEN clauses.

sequence

An ordered collection of zero or more items, as defined in XPath 2.0 and XQuery 1.0. The word ordered is important, because it differentiates a sequence from a set, which, as most T-SQL programmers know (or quickly come to realize), is unordered. XPath 1.0 defined its results in terms of node sets, which are unordered and can't contain duplicates. XQuery changes this terminology to node sequences, which recognize the importance of node order in XML and can contain duplicates.

server certificate

A certificate created in the master database for the purpose of encrypting an entire database via transparent data encryption (TDE).

service master key (SMK)

An encryption key managed at the SQL Server service level. The SMK is used to encrypt all other keys in the SQL Server encryption key hierarchy.

shredding

The process of converting XML data into relational style rows and columns.

simple CASE expression

An expression defined with constants or value expressions in its WHEN clauses. The simple CASE evaluates to a series of simple equality expressions.

SOAP

Simple Object Access Protocol, an XML-based protocol designed for exchanging structured information in distributed, decentralized environments.

spatial data

Data used to represent objects and points on the Earth.

spatial index

A mechanism for increasing the efficiency of geographic calculations such as the distance between points, or whether an object contains another point or object.

SQL Server Data Tools

A set of tools that provides an integrated environment for database and application development.

SQL injection

A technique that exploits security vulnerabilities in the application layer and middle tier, allowing users to execute arbitrary SQL statements on a server.

step

In XQuery, a part of a path expression that generates a sequence of items and then filters the sequence. Each step is composed of an axis, a node test, and zero or more predicates.

table type

An alias type that defines a table structure for use with table-valued parameters.

three-valued logic (3VL)

A logic system that the SQL language supports with three truth values: true, false, and unknown.

transparent data encryption (TDE)

A SQL Server 2012 feature that allows you to encrypt an entire database at once.

untyped XML

An XML data instance that is not associated with an XML schema collection.

user-defined aggregate (UDA)

A SQL CLR routine that applies a function or calculation to an entire set of values.

user-defined type (UDT)

A SQL CLR-based data type.

value comparison

A comparison of single values in XQuery.

well-formed XML

XML data that follows the W3C XML recommendation for well-formed data. It includes a single root element and properly nested elements, and it's properly entitized.

well-known text (WKT)

A plain-text format for defining geospatial data.

windowing functions

Functions that can partition and possibly order datasets before they're applied to the dataset partitions.

World Wide Web Consortium (W3C)

A standards body with the stated mission of "developing interoperable technologies … to lead the Web to its full potential."

XML

Extensible Markup Language, a restricted form of Standardized General Markup Language (SGML) designed to be easily served, received, and processed on the Web.

XML schema

The basic data types utilized by XQuery. Part 2 of the XML Schema 1.1 standard defines XML Schema data types.

XPath

XML Path Language, an expression language designed to allow processing of values that conform to the XPath Data Model (XDM).

XQuery

XML Query Language, an XML query language designed to retrieve and interpret data from diverse XML sources.

XQuery/XPath Data Model (XDM)

The XQuery 1.0 and XPath 2.0 Data Model, defined by the W3C at www.w3.org/TR/2006/PR-xpath-datamodel-20061121/. See XQuery.

XSL

Extensible Stylesheet Language, a language for expressing style sheets, consisting of a language for transforming XML documents and an XML vocabulary for specifying formatting semantics. See XSLT.

XSLT

XSL Transformations, a language for transforming XML documents into other XML documents. For instance, XSLT can be used to transform an XML document into an XHTML document. See XSL.

SQLCMD Quick Reference

SQLCMD is the standard text-based tool for executing batches of T-SQL on SQL Server. As a text-based tool, SQLCMD provides a lightweight but powerful tool for automating T-SQL batches. This appendix is designed as a quick reference to SQLCMD. The descriptions of many of the features and the functionality given here differ from BOL in some instances; the descriptions provided in this appendix are based on extensive testing of SQLCMD.

Command-Line Options

SQLCMD provides several command-line options to provide flexibility in connecting to SQL Server and executing T-SQL batches in a database. The full format for SQLCMD is shown here:

```
sqlcmd [ [-U login_id ] [-P password ] | [-E] ] [-C]
[-S server [\instance] ] [-d db_name] [-H workstation]
[-l login timeout] [-t query timeout] [-h headers] [-s column_separator] [-w column_width]
[-a packet_size] [-I] [-L[c] ] [-W] [-r[o|1]] [-q "query"] [-Q "query" and exit]
[-c batch_term] [-e] [-m error Level] [-V Severity Level] [-b] [-N]  [-K]
[-i input_file [,input_file2 [, ...] ] ] [-o output_file] [-u]
[-v var = "value" [,var2 = "value2"] [,...] ] [-X[1 ] [-x] [-?]
[-z new_password] [-Z new_password] [-f codepage | i:in_codepage [,o:out_codepage] ]
[-k[1|2] ] [-y display_width] [-Y display_width]
[-p[1 ] [-R] [-A]
```

The available command-line options are listed in Table D-1. The SQLCMD command-line options are case sensitive, so, for example, -v is a different option from -V.

Table D-1. *SQLCMD Command-Line Options*

Option	Description
-?	Displays the SQLCMD help/syntax screen.
-A	Tells SQLCMD to log in to SQL Server with a dedicated administrator connection. This type of connection is usually used for troubleshooting.
-a packet_size	Requests communications with a specific packet size. The default is 4096. packet_size must be in the range 512 to 32767.
-b	Specifies that SQLCMD exits on an error and returns an ERRORLEVEL value to the operating system. When this option is set, a SQL error of severity 11 or greater returns an ERRORLEVEL of 1; an error or message of severity 10 or less returns an ERRORLEVEL of 0. If the -V option is also used, SQLCMD reports only the errors with a severity greater than or equal to the severity_level (level 11 or greater) specified with the -V option.
-c batch_term	Specifies the batch terminator. By default, it's the GO keyword. Avoid using special characters and reserved words as the batch terminator.
-C	Specifies that the server certificate can be trusted implicitly without validation used by the client.
-d db_name	Specifies the database to use after SQLCMD connects to SQL Server. Alternatively, you can set this option via the SQLCMDDBNAME environment variable. If the database specified doesn't exist, SQLCMD exits with an error.
-E	Uses a trusted connection (Windows authentication mode) to connect to SQL Server. This option ignores the SQLCMDUSER and SQLCMDPASSWORD environment variables, and you can't use it with the -U and -P options.
-e	Prints (echoes) input scripts to the standard output device (usually the screen by default).

(continued)

Table D-1. *(continued)*

Option	Description
-f codepage | i:in_ codepage [,oout_ codepage]	Specifies the code pages for input and output. If i: is specified, in_codepage is the input code page. If o: is specified, out_codepage is the output code page. If i: and o: aren't specified, the codepage supplied is the code page for both input and output. To specify a code page, use its numeric identifier. The following code pages are supported by SQL Server 2005:

Code Page Number	Code Page Name
437	MS-DOS US English
850	Multilingual (MS-DOS Latin1)
874	Thai
932	Japanese
936	Chinese (Simplified)
949	Korean
950	Chinese(Traditional)
1250	Central European
1251	Cyrillic
1252	Latin1 (ANSI)
1253	Greek
1254	Turkish
1255	Hebrew
1256	Arabic
1257	Baltic
1258	Vietnamese

Option	Description
-H workstation	The -H option sets the workstation name. You can use -H to differentiate between sessions with commands such as sp_who.
-h headers	Specifies the number of rows of data to print before a new column header is generated. The value must be from -1 (no headers) to 2147483647. The default value of 0 prints headings once for each set of results.
-I	Sets the connection QUOTED_IDENTIFIER option to ON. Turning on the QUOTED_IDENTIFIER option makes SQL Server follow the ANSI SQL-92 rules for quoted identifiers. This option is set to OFF by default.
-i input_file [,input_ file2] [,...]	Specifies that SQLCMD should use files that contain batches of T-SQL statements for input. The files are processed in order from left to right. If any of the files don't exist, SQLCMD exits with an error. You can use the GO batch terminator in your SQL script files.
-k [1|2]	-k removes control characters from the output. If 1 is specified, control characters are replaced one for one with spaces. If 2 is specified, consecutive control characters are replaced with a single space.

(continued)

Table D-1. *(continued)*

Option	Description
-K	Specifies the intent of the application workload that is connecting to the server that is a secondary replica in the AlwaysOn availability group. The only value that can be specified currently is ReadOnly.
-L [c]	-L returns a listing of available SQL Server machines on the network and local computer. If the -Lc format is used, a "clean" listing is returned without heading information. The listing is limited to a maximum of 3,000 servers. Note that because of the way SQL Server broadcasts to gather server information, any servers that don't respond in a timely manner aren't included in the list. You can't use the -L option with other options.
-l timeout	Specifies the login timeout. The timeout value must be from 0 to 65534. The default value is 8 seconds, and a value of 0 is no timeout (infinite).
-m error_level	Defines an error-message customization level. Only errors with a severity greater than the specified level are displayed. If error_level is -1, all messages are returned, even informational messages.
-N	Specifies that the client connection is encrypted.
-o output_file	Specifies the file to which SQLCMD should direct output. If -o isn't specified, SQLCMD defaults to standard output (usually the screen).
-P password	Specifies a password to log in to SQL Server when using SQL authentication mode. If -P is omitted, SQLCMD looks for the SQLCMDPASSWORD environment variable to get the password to log in. If the SQLCMDPASSWORD environment variable isn't found, SQLCMD prompts you for the password to log in using SQL authentication mode. If neither -P nor -U is specified and the corresponding environment variables aren't set, SQLCMD attempts to log in using Windows authentication mode.
-p [1]	-p prints performance statistics for each result set. Specifying 1 produces colon-separated output.
-Q "query" and -q "query"	Both execute a SQL query/command from the command line. -q remains in SQLCMD after query completion. -Q exits SQLCMD after completion.
-R	Specifies client regional settings for currency and date/time formatting.
-r [0|1]	-r redirects error-message output to the standard error-output device—the monitor by default. If 1 is specified, all error messages and informational messages are redirected. If 0 or no number is specified, only error messages with a severity of 11 or greater are redirected. The redirection doesn't work with the -o option; it does work if standard output is redirected with the Windows command-line redirector (>).
-S server [\instance]	Specifies the SQL Server server or named instance to which SQLCMD should connect. If this option isn't specified, SQLCMD connects to the default SQL Server instance on the local machine.

(continued)

Table D-1.   (*continued*)

Option	Description
`-s column_separator`	Sets the column-separator character. By default, the column separator is a space character. `Column_separator` can be enclosed in quotes, which is useful if you want to use a character that the operating system recognizes as a special character, such as the greater-than sign (`>`).
`-t timeout`	Specifies the SQL query/command timeout in seconds. The timeout value must be in the range 0 to 65535. If `-t` isn't specified, or if it's set to 0, queries/commands don't time out.
`-U login_id`	Specifies the user login ID to log in to SQL Server using SQL authentication mode. If the `-U` option is omitted, SQLCMD looks for the `SQLCMDUSER` environment variable to get the login password. If the `-U` option is omitted, SQLCMD attempts to use the current user's Windows login name to log in.
`-u`	Specifies that the output of SQLCMD is in Unicode format. Use this option with the `-o` option.
`-V severity_level`	Specifies the lowest severity level that SQLCMD reports back. Errors and messages of a severity less than `severity_level` are reported as 0. `Severity_level` must be in the range 1 to 25. In a command-line batch file, `-V` returns the severity level of any SQL Server errors encountered via the `ERRORLEVEL` so that your batch file can take appropriate action.
`-v var = "value"` `[,var2 = "value2"]` `[,...]`	Sets scripting variables that SQLCMD can use in your scripts to the specified values. Scripting variables are described later in this appendix.
`-W`	Removes trailing spaces from a column. You can use this option with the `-s` option when preparing data that is to be exported to another application. You can't use `-W` in conjunction with the `-Y` or `-y` option.
`-w column_width`	Specifies the screen width for output. The width value must be in the range 9 to 65535. The default of 0 is equivalent to the width of the output device. For screen output, the default is the width of the screen. For files, the default width is unlimited.
`-X [1]`	`-X` disables options that can compromise security in batch files. Specifically, `-X` does the following: • Disables the SQLCMD:`!!` and `:ED` commands • Prevents SQLCMD from using operating system environment variables • Disables the SQLCMD startup script If a disabled command is encountered, SQLCMD issues a warning and continues processing. If the optional 1 is specified with `-X`, SQLCMD exits with an error when a disabled command is encountered. Descriptions of SQLCMD commands, script variables, environment variables, and the startup script are detailed later in this appendix.
`-x`	Forces SQLCMD to ignore scripting variables.

(*continued*)

Table D-1. *(continued)*

Option	Description
-Y display_width	Limits the number of characters returned for the char, nchar, varchar (8,000 bytes or less), nvarchar (4,000 bytes or less), and sql_variant data types.
-y display_width	Limits the number of characters returned for variable-length data types such as varchar(max), varbinary(max), xml, text, and fixed-length or variable-length user-defined types (UDTs).
-Z new_password and -z new_password	When used with SQL authentication (the -U and -P options), -Z and -z change the SQL login password. If the -P option isn't specified, SQLCMD prompts you for the current password. -z changes the password and enters interactive mode. -Z exits SQLCMD immediately after the password is changed.

Scripting Variables

SQLCMD supports scripting variables, which allow you to dynamically replace script content at execution time. This lets you use a single script in multiple scenarios. By using scripting variables, for instance, you can execute a single script against different servers or databases without modification. SQLCMD allows you to set your own custom scripting variables with the -v command-line option. If more than one scripting variable is specified with the same name, the variable with the highest precedence (according to the following list) is used:

1. System-level environment variables have the highest precedence.

2. User-level environment variables are next.

3. Variables set via the command shell SET option are next.

4. Variables set via the SQLCMD -v command-line option are next.

5. Variables set inside a SQLCMD batch via the :SETVAR command have the lowest precedence.

■ **Note** The -X and -x options disable startup-script execution and environment-variable access, respectively. -x also prevents SQLCMD from dynamically replacing scripting-variable references in your code with the appropriate values. This is a feature designed for secure environments where scripting-variable usage could compromise security.

SQLCMD also provides several predefined scripting variables, which are listed in Table D-2. You can set the predefined read-only SQLCMD scripting variables via the command shell SET option or through SQLCMD command-line options; you can't alter them from within a SQLCMD script with :SETVAR.

Table D-2. *SQLCMD Scripting Variables*

Name	Default	Read/Write	Description
SQLCMDCOLSEP		Read/write	Column separator character. See the -s command-line switch (in Table D-1).
SQLCMDCOLWIDTH	0	Read/write	Output column width. See the -w command-line switch.
SQLCMDDBNAME		Read-only	Default database name. See the -d command-line switch.
SQLCMDERRORLEVEL	0	Read/write	Level of error-message customization. See the -m command-line switch.
SQLCMDHEADERS	0	Read/write	Number of lines to print between result set headers. See the -h command-line switch.
SQLCMDINI		Read-only	SQLCMD startup script.
SQLCMDLOGINTIMEOUT	8	Read/write	Login timeout setting (in seconds). See the -l command-line switch.
SQLCMDMAXFIXEDTYPEWIDTH	256	Read/write	Fixed-width data type display limit. See the -Y command-line switch.
SQLCMDMAXVARTYPEWIDTH	0	Read/write	Variable-length data type display limit. See the -y command-line switch.
SQLCMDPACKETSIZE	4096	Read-only	Packet size being used for SQL communications. See the -a command-line switch.
SQLCMDPASSWORD		N/A	SQL Server login password. See the -P command-line switch.
SQLCMDSERVER	server name	Read-only	SQL Server/instance name. See the -S command-line switch.
SQLCMDSTATTIMEOUT	0	Read/write	Query/command timeout setting (in seconds). See the -t command-line switch.
SQLCMDUSER		Read-only	SQL Server login username. See the -U command-line switch.
SQLCMDWORKSTATION		Read-only	SQL Server workstation name. See the -H command-line switch.
SQLCMDEDITOR	" "	Read-only	SQLCMD default editor.

Commands

SQLCMD recognizes a set of commands that aren't part of T-SQL. These SQLCMD commands aren't recognized by other query tools; they're not even recognized by SSMS (except when you run it in SQLCMD mode). SQLCMD commands all begin on a line with a colon (:) to identify them as different from T-SQL statements. You can intersperse SQLCMD commands within your T-SQL scripts. Table D-3 lists the SQLCMD commands available.

■ **Tip**   For backward compatibility with older osql scripts, you can enter the following commands without a colon prefix: !!, ED, RESET, EXIT, and QUIT. Also, SQLCMD commands are case insensitive, they must appear at the beginning of a line, and they must be on their own line. A SQLCMD command can't be followed on the same line by a T-SQL statement or another SQLCMD command.

Table D-3. *SQLCMD Commands*

Command	Description
:!!	Invokes the command shell. This command executes the specified operating system command in the command shell.
:CONNECT server [\instance] [-ltimeout] [-Uuser [-Ppassword]]	Connects to a SQL Server instance. The server name (server) and instance name (\instance) are specified in the command. When :CONNECT is executed, the current connection is closed. You can use the following options with the :CONNECT command: -l specifies the login timeout (specified in seconds; 0 equals no timeout); -U specifies the SQL authentication username; and -P specifies the SQL authentication password.
:ED	Starts the text editor to edit the current batch or the last executed batch. The SQLCMDEDITOR environment variable defines the application used as the SQLCMD editor. The default is the Windows EDIT utility.
:ERROR destination	Redirects error messages to the specified destination. destination can be a file name, STDOUT for standard output, or STDERR for standard error output.
:EXIT [()|(query)]	Has three forms: :EXIT alone immediately exits without executing the batch and with no return code. :EXIT() executes the current batch and exits with no return code. :EXIT(query) executes the batch, including the query specified, and returns the first value of the first result row of the query as a 4-byte integer to the operating system.
GO [n]	The batch terminator. It executes the statements in the cache. If n is specified, GO executes the statement n times.
:HELP	Displays a list of SQLCMD commands.
:LIST	Lists the contents of the current batch of statements in the statement cache.
:LISTVAR	Lists all the SQLCMD scripting variables (that have been set) and their current values.
:ON ERROR action	Specifies the action SQLCMD should take when an error is encountered. action can be one of two values: EXIT stops processing and exits, returning the appropriate error code. IGNORE disregards the error and continues processing.

(continued)

Table D-3. *(continued)*

Command	Description
`:OUT destination`	Redirects output to the specified `destination`. `destination` can be a file name, `STDOUT` for standard output, or `STDERR` for standard error output. Output is sent to `STDOUT` by default.
`:PERFTRACE destination`	Redirects performance trace/timing information to the specified `destination`. `destination` can be a file name, `STDOUT` for standard output, or `STDERR` for standard error output. Trace information is sent to `STDOUT` by default.
`:QUIT`	Quits SQLCMD immediately.
`:R filename`	Reads in the contents of the specified file and appends it to the statement cache.
`:RESET`	Resets/clears the statement cache.
`:SERVERLIST`	Lists all SQL Server instances on the local machine and any servers broadcasting on the local network. If SQLCMD doesn't receive timely responses from a server on the network, it may not be listed.
`:SETVAR var [value]`	Allows you to set or remove SQLCMD scripting variables. To remove a SQLCMD scripting variable, use the `:SETVAR var` format. To set a SQLCMD scripting variable to a value, use the `:SETVAR var value` format.
`:XML ON|OFF`	Indicates to SQLCMD that you expect XML output from SQL Server (that is, the `SELECT` statement's `FOR XML` clause). Use `:XML ON` before your SQL batch is run and `:XML OFF` after the batch has executed (after the `GO` batch terminator).

Index

A

Accumulate() method, 531, 534, 540
ACID. *See* Atomicity, consistency, isolation,
    durability (ACID)
ACM. *See* Association for Computing
    Machinery (ACM)
Adjacency list model, 669
ADO.NET
    4.5, asynchronous programming, 564–565
    code
        run stored procedure asynchronously, 565
        run stored procedure synchronously, 565
    data services, 669
    System.Data.Common, 461
    System.Data namespace, 461
    System.Data.Odbc, 461
    System.Data.OleDb, 462
    System.Data.SqlClient, 461
    System.Data.SqlTypes, 462
AdventureWorks
    BOM, 285, 287
    CREATE DATABASE, 302
    DataService Class, 578–579
    LT2014 data file, 563
    sample database, 44
American National Standards
    Institute (ANSI), 1
Analytic functions
    CUME_DIST and PERCENT_RANK
        functions, 259–261
    FIRST_VALUE and LAST_VALUE, 265–266
    LAG and LEAD, 263–265
    PERCENTILE_CONT and
        PERCENTILE_DISC function, 262–263
Anchor query, 669
ANSI. *See* American National Standards
    Institute (ANSI)
ANSI-encoded characters, 658
Application programming interface (API), 119, 669
ApressDb database files, 564
apt-cache command, 567

B

Association for Computing Machinery (ACM), 1
Asymmetric encryption, 669
Asymmetric keys
    algorithms and limits, 216
    ALTER ASYMMETRIC KEY, 217
    AsymKeyID function, 219
    DecryptByAsymKey, 217
    DMK, 218
    EncryptByAsymKey function, 217
    HSM, 220
    public and private keys, 216
    SignByAsymKey function, 219
    varbinary signature, 219
Asynchronous programming
    code structure, 564–565
    stored procedure, 564
Atomic data types, 670
Atomicity, consistency, isolation,
    durability (ACID), 653, 669
AUTHORIZATION clause, 518
AUTO mode, 357–358

BACKUP ASYMMETRIC KEY statement, 657
BCP. *See* Bulk Copy Program (BCP)
Best practices, SPs
    API, 119
    BEGIN/END TRANSACTION, 118
    CLR, 117
    DBMSs, 119
    dbo.sp_help, 119
    functionality, 119
    modularization and security, 118
    nullability, 118
    query optimization, 118
    scalar function, 117
    SELECT statements, 117
    UNION ALL operator, 118
BIDS. *See* Business Intelligence Development
    Studio (BIDS)

Bill of materials (BOM)
   AdventureWorks, 285–287
   hierarchyid, 285, 290
   recursive CTE, 240–241
BOL. *See* Books Online (BOL)
BomChildren, 287
Books Online (BOL), 43–44
BREAK statement, 654
build_dm.sh command, 568
Bulk Copy Program (BCP), 42, 670
Business Intelligence Development Studio (BIDS), 653
Bw-tree architecture, 170

■ **C**

Cartesian product XQuery, 424
CASE expressions
   CHOOSE function, 66–67
   COALESCE and NULLIF functions, 67–68
   IIF statement, 65–66
   pivot tables, 59–65
   search expression, 58–59
   simple expression, 56–58, 678
CASE-style pivot table, 60
CatalogDescription with no namespaces, 402
Catalog views
   advantages, 433
   inheritance model, 434
   metadata, 433
   querying permissions, 435, 437
   SQL Server database and server-specific
      metadata, 670
   table and column metadata, 434
Certificate authority (CA), 670
Certificates
   CertID function, 213
   CREATE CERTIFICATE statement, 211–212
   DecryptByCert function, 213
   decryption functions, 213
   DER, 212
   EncryptByCert function, 213
   EXECUTABLE FILE clause, 212
   FROM ASSEMBLY clause, 212
   public/private key, 211
   SignByCert function, 215
   SQL Server, 212
   TestCertificate, 213
   varbinary, 213
   varchar, 213
Change data capture (CDC)
   built-in auditing functionality, 182
   DML audit
      action table, 185
      CASE expression, 185
      CREATE TRIGGER statement, 184

      logging table, 182–183
      @@ROWCOUNT function, 184
      row insertion, 186
      SELECT statement, 185
      SET NOCOUNT ON, 185
      testing, 187–188
      trigger logging table, 183–184
      UPDATE statement, 188
   nested and recursive triggers, 189
   sharing data, 188
   UPDATE() and COLUMNS_UPDATED()
      functions, 190–192, 194
Check constraint, 670
CHOOSE statement, 67
Closed-world assumption (CWA), 49, 670
CLRDemo Database Project properties, 515
CLR integration program
   advantages, 512
   assemblies
      AUTHORIZATION clause, 518
      CLRDemo Database Project properties, 515
      CREATE ASSEMBLY statement, 513, 517
      database project properties menu, 515
      FROM clause, 518
      .NET namespaces and classes, 517
      project, 516–517
      T-SQL database object-creation
         statements, 518
      Visual Studio 2013, 514
      WITH PERMISSION_SET clause, 518
   guidelines, 512
   ODS, 511
   stored procedures (*see* Stored procedures)
   triggers (*see* Triggers)
   UDAs (*see* User-defined aggregates (UDAs))
   UDFs (*see* User-defined functions (UDFs))
   UDTs (*see* User-defined data types (UDTs))
Clustered indexes, 9, 631, 670
COALESCE() function, 190
Code snippets
   category, 21
   create function, 21
   create stored procedure, 21
   CREATE TABLE, 22
   Insert Snippet command, 22
   manager, 21
   T-SQL Editor, 22
Columnstore index, 9
Command-line options, 683, 685–688
Common Language Runtime (CLR), 117
Common Object Request Broker Architecture
      (CORBA), 573
Common table expressions (CTE)
   benefits, 233
   BomChildren, 287–288

definition, 234
DML statement, 233
exercises, 267–268
32-level recursion limit, 83–84
multiple, 235
overloading, 234
parent_path_locator and path_locator, 311
readablility benefits, 236–238
recursive. Recursive CTE
simple, 234
SP, 121
syntax, 233
Compiled stored procedures, 173, 175
Complex number, 543–545
Computed constructors, 671
CONTAINS predicate
compound CONTAINS search term, 331–332
custom search, 333–334
FORMSOF inflectional generation term, 331
FREETEXT predicate, 330
prefix search, 332
proximity search, 333
simple CONTAINS query, 330
Content expression, 671
Context item expression, 671
Context node, 671
Control-of-flow statements
BEGIN and END keywords, 49–50
GOTO Statement, 54
IF...ELSE statement, 50–52
RETURN Statement, 56
WAITFOR statement, 55
WHILE, BREAK and CONTINUE
statements, 52–53
Coordinated Universal Time (UTC)
date and time data, 277
and military time, 278
CUME_DIST and PERCENT_RANK
functions, 259–261
CURRENT_TIMESTAMP functions, 280
Cursors
administrative tasks, 69–71
AdventureWorks database, 72
ALTER INDEX statement, 73–74
comparisons, 76
DBCCs, 74
dbo.RebuildIndexes procedure, 72–73
description, 68
design patterns, 75
@IndexList table, 73
options, 75
RBAR, 75
SQL's set-based process, 74
T-SQL extended syntax, 76
WHILE loops, 75

■ **D**

Database console commands (DBCCs), 74
Database master and encryption key, 671
Database master keys (DMK), 210, 671
Data control language (DCL), 4
Data definition language (DDL)
audit logging results, 201
CREATE TABLE statement, 198–200
CREATE TRIGGER statement, 197
definition, 4
DROP TRIGGER statement, 201
EVENTDATA() function, 198, 200
event types and groups, 197
nodes() and value() methods, 200–201
Data domain and page, 671
Data() function, 391
DATALENGTH() function, 269–270
Data manipulation language (DML)
auditing, 182
CREATE TRIGGER statement, 177, 180
definition, 4
disabling and enabling triggers, 178
HumanResources.Employee
table, 179–180
INSERT and DELETE statement, 181–182
multiple triggers, 178
multistatement TVF, 94
@@ROWCOUNT system function, 180
SELECT and UPDATE, 181
SET NOCOUNT ON statement, 180
statement, 177
trigger, 657
UPDATE statement, 180
Data() node test, 392
Data services. *See also* Service Oriented
Architecture (SOA); SQL Server 2012
Express LocalDB
ISV, 559
JDBC (*see* Java Database Connectivity (JDBC))
ODBC (*see* Open DataBase Connectivity (ODBC))
REST-style services, 575
WCF (*see* Windows Communication
Foundation (WCF))
Data types
characters, 269–270
date and time
date comparison, 274–275
DATEDIFF() function, 275
datetimeoffset, 277
datetime2 variables, 276
example, 276
functions, 278–282
sample, 275
SQL Server 2012, 274

Data types (*cont.*)
    standard time zones, 277
    @start_time variable, 276
  LOB, 270
  numerics, 272, 274
  nvarchar data type, 314
  (n)varchar(max)/varbinary(max), 270
  time zones and offsets, 282
  transactional coherence, 314
  UTC and military time, 278
  WRITE clause and string append, 271–272
  XML
    description, 366
    exist method, 369
    modify method, 371–373
    nodes method, 370
    query method, 366–367
    value method, 368
Data warehousing (DW), 153
Datum, 672
Daylight Saving Time (DST), 282
DCL. *See* Data control language (DCL)
DDL. *See* Data definition language (DDL)
DDL triggers, 657
Debugging tools
  PRINT statement, 598
  SSMS integration, 599–600
  trace flags, 599
  Visual Studio T-SQL debugger (*see* Visual Studio
    T-SQL debugger)
Declarative referential integrity (DRI), 8
Directive value, XML
  cdata, 360
  element, 360
  elementxsinil, 360
  hide, 360
  id, idref and idrefs, 360
  xml, 360
  xmltext, 360
Distributed Component Object Model (DCOM), 573
DMFs. *See* Dynamic management functions (DMFs)
DML. *See* Data manipulation language (DML)
DMVs. *See* Dynamic management views (DMVs)
DRI. *See* Declarative referential integrity (DRI)
Dynamic management functions (DMFs), 139
Dynamic management views and functions
    (DMVs and DMFs)
  categories, 438
  connection information, 445
  expensive queries
    blocked queries, 449–450
    cached query plan, 448–449
  index metadata
    ALTER INDEX statements, 438–443
    fragmentation, 441

    stored procedure, 438–441
    temporary objects, 443
    triggers, 443
  memory-optimized system views, 447–448
  retrieve, 443–444
  server resources
    configuration details, 453
    dump files, 454
    instance keys and values, 455
    volume information, 454
  SQL execution
    OPTION (FORCE ORDER), 447
    statements, 446
    sys.dm_exec_requests, 445
    sys.dm_exec_sessions, 445
  summarization, 444
  tempdb space system
    object allocations, 451–453
    queries, 450
    session data, 452–453
  unused indexes, 455–456
  wait stats, 457
Dynamic pivot table query, 62
Dynamic SQL
  debugging and troubleshooting code, 609
  EXECUTE statement, 606
  injection, 606–609
  pivot table query, 64–65

■ E

EF. *See* Entity framework (EF)
EM. *See* Enterprise Manager (EM)
Empty sequence, 672
Encryption functionality
  asymmetric keys, 216–217, 219–220
  certificates, 211–216
  CREATE SYMMETRIC KEY statement, 220
  DecryptByKey functions, 222
  DecryptByPassPhrase, 228
  DES, 220
  DMK, 210–211
  DPAPI, 208
  DROP Key, 222
  EKM, 229–230
  EncryptByPassPhrase function, 228
  HashBytes function, 228–229
  Identityvalue clause, 221
  KeyGUID function, 225
  RC2, 221
  salt and authenticators, 227
  server certificate, 208
  SMK, 208–209
  SQL server, 207
  TDE, 230–231

TestSymmetricKey, 220
varbinary format, 225
ENCRYPTION option, 655
Enterprise Manager (EM), 19
Entity data model (EDM), 576–577, 672
Entity framework (EF)
    database objects, 500
    model, 500–501
    properties, 502
    structures, 503–504
Error handling
    legacy, 589–591
    RAISERROR statement, 591–592
    THROW statement, 597–598
    TRY_CAST function, 596–597
    TRY…CATCH model (*see* TRY…CATCH
        exception handling)
    TRY_CONVERT function, 595
    TRY_PARSE command, 594
ExecuteAndSend() method, 529
ExecuteReader() method, 466
EXECUTE statement, 606
Extended events (XEvents)
    configuration, 647
    filters, 646
    ODBC drivers, 649
    page splits/locking, 649–650
    performance-tuning session, 649
    session, 645
    SQL Servers, 39–41
    target type, 648
    templates, 645
    user interface, 40
Extensible key management (EKM), 229–230, 672
Extensible Markup Language (XML)
    AUTO mode, 357–358
    clause, 355
    data type, 362, 366, 384
    exist method, 369
    EXPLICIT clause, 358–360
    indexes, 373–377
    legacy, 347
    modify method, 371–373
    nodes method, 370
    OPENXML, 347–348, 350–354
    PATH clause, 360–362
    query method, 366–367
    RAW mode, 355–356
    schema, 680
    SGML, 680
    SQL CLR security settings, 382–383
    SQL Server 2014, 347
    SQL Server's primary and secondary XML
        indexes, 384
    typed, 364–365

untyped, 363
value method, 368
World Wide Web Consortium, 347
XSL transformations, 378–382
Extensible Stylesheet Language (XSL), 681.
        See also XSL transformations (XSLT)
Extensible Stylesheet Language
        Transformations (XSLT)
    definition, 378
    SQL CLR SP code, 381–382
    SQL Server, 378
    style sheet to convert data to HTML, 380–381
    XML document into XHTML document, 681
Extent, 672
Extract, transform and load (ETL), 672

■ **F**

Facet, 672
Filegroup addition, 156–157
file_stream column, 310
FILESTREAM support
    access levels, 301
    AdventureWorks 2014, 302
    configuration information, 301
    enabling tables, 303–305
    existing database, 302
    filetable (*see* Filetable support)
    LOB data, 300
    NTFS, 300
    SQL Server, 300
FileTableRootPath() function, 309
Filetable support
    database creation, 305–306
    directory, 308–309
    Explore FileTable Directory, 308
    functions, 309–313
    OpenSqlFilestream, 305
    SQL Server tables, 305
    SSMS, 308
    structure, 307
    subdirectory, 308
    triggers, 313–314
    T-SQL context, 309
    T-SQL statements, 308
Filtered indexes, 636
FIRST_VALUE and LAST_VALUE
        function, 265–266
FLWOR expressions
    and filter, 673
    for and return keywords, 422–424
    let keyword, 426
    order by keywords, 425
    UTF-16 support, 427, 429–430
    where keyword, 425

Foreign key constraint, 673
Forward reference, 234
FOR XML PATH clause, 659
FREETEXT predicate, 327–328
FTI. *See* Full-text index (FTI)
Full-text catalogs, 319–321, 673
Full-text index (FTI)
    assignation, 325
    change-tracking option, 324
    context menu, 321
    management purposes, 673
    Production.ProductModel table, 321
    review wizard selections, 326
    searches of data and documents, 9
    selectable columns, 323
    single-column unique index, 321–322
    SSMS, 321
    T-SQL statements, 326–327
    word-breaker language, 322
Full-text querying, 327
Full-text search (FTS)
    architecture
        AdventureWorksFTCat, 320
        beneficial features, 318
        CONTAINS predicate, 330–334
        fdhost process, 317
        FREETEXT predicate, 327–328
        FREETEXTTABLE and CONTAINSTABLE
            functions, 334–336
        FTI (*see* Full-text index (FTI))
        full-text querying, 327
        and indexes, 318
        menu option, 319
        perfomance optimization, 329
        procedures and dynamic management
            views and functions, 341
        simplified, 318
        SQL Server, 344
        sqlserver process, 317
        statistical semantics, 342–344
        stoplist and theasaures objects, 317
        thesauruses and stoplists, 337–338, 340
        T-SQL statements, 320
        Window, 320
    SQL Server 2012, 673
    T-SQL search, 317
Full-text stoplist, 340
Functions and Operators (F&O), 673

■ G

GAM. *See* Global allocation map (GAM)
Geography Markup Language (GML), 673
GETDATE() functions, 280
GetEnvironmentVars CLR procedure, 531

GetFileNamespacePath() function, 310
GetPathLocator() function, 312–313
GetYahooNews() function, 527
1 Gigabyte price, 154
Global allocation map (GAM), 614
Grouping set, 674

■ H

Hardware security module (HSM), 220
Hash and heap, 674
Hash indexes
    vs. clustered index IO statistics, 168
    vs. clustered index range, 170
    vs. disk-based clustered index, 167
    LIKE operations, 167
Heterogeneous sequence, 674
Hierarchyid data type
    AdventureWorks BOMs, 286–289
    bill of materials table, 285–286
    BomNode column, 290
    description, 284
    methods, 290–291
    partial results, 290
    Production.HierBillOfMaterials table, 286
    representation, 284–285
Homogenous sequence, 674
HumanResources.JobCandidate
        Resume XML, 367

■ I

IAM. *See* Index allocation map (IAM)
IBinarySerialize interface, 539
IIF statement, 66
Imperative *vs.* declarative languages, 1–2
Independent Software Vendor (ISV), 559
Index allocation map (IAM), 614
Indexes
    actual query plans, 638–639
    clustered indexes, 631
    computed column, 640
    execution plans, 638
    filtered indexes, 636–637
    graphical query plans, 639
    guaranteed order, 632–633
    heaps, 630–631
    methodology, 640–642
    nonclustered indexes, 633–636
    reading query plans, 637
    recompilations, 640
    waits, 642–644
    XEvents (*see* Extended Events (XEvents))
Indirect recursion, 674
Inflectional form, 674

INFORMATION_SCHEMA views
    column information, 459–460
    lists, 457–459
Initialization vector (IV), 674
Init() method, 531, 534
Inline TVFs
    CASE expressions, 106
    comma-delimited list to retrieve product
        information, 107
    control-of-flow statement, 105
    CREATE FUNCTION statement, 105
    FnCommaSplit function, 107
    Jackson, 106–107
    Num and Element, 105
    SELECT statement, 104
    string-splitting function, 105
    T-SQL, 104
In-Memory OLTP table indexes
    hash and range indexes, 166
    in-memory *vs.* disk-based indexes, 165
In-Memory programming
    drivers, 153
    hardware, 153–155
    OLTP workloads, 153
International Telecommunication
    Union (ITU), 277
IsDescendantOf() method, 290

J, K

Java Database Connectivity (JDBC)
    Class.forName(), 572
    classpath, 570, 572
    javac command line, 571–572
    sqljdbc4.jar file, 570

L

LAG and LEAD functions, 263–265
Language integrated query (LINQ), 674
    AdventureWorksDataContext
        class, 491–492
    INNER JOIN clause, 498
    join clause, 496–497
    Main() method, 492
    .NET languages, 674
    orderby clause, 495–496
    retrieving person names and related e-mail
        addresses, 497–498
    SQL database querying, 488
    standard query operators, 494
    where clause, 494–495
Large objects (LOB)
    FILESTREAM, 300, 302
    FILESTREAM filegroup, 304

SQL Server and NTFS, 300
    standard varchar, nvarchar and varbinary
        data types, 270
    TEXTPTR, READTEXT and WRITETEXT
        statements, 270
    varbinary(max), 300
LayoutKind.Sequential property, 539
ldd command, 569
Legacy, error handling
    @@error system function, 589
    OUTPUT parameter, 590
    PRINT statement, 590
    TestError procedure, 590
LEN() string function, 269–270
LINQ. *See* Language integrated query (LINQ)
Linux. *See* Open DataBase
    Connectivity (ODBC)
LocalDB client program execution, 563
Logograms, 269
Logon triggers
    CREATE TRIGGER statement, 203
    creation, 202
    EVENTDATA() function, 204
    login, 204
    ROLLBACK TRANSACTION statement, 203
    sample data table, 202
    server LOGON event, 675
    SQL server, 202

M

MARS. *See* Multiple active result sets (MARS)
Materialized path model, 675
MAXRECURSION option, 239
Memory-optimized container, 157–158
Memory-optimized filegroups, 156–157
Memory-optimized index, 10
Memory-optimized table
    AddressLine1 Column, 163–164
    creation, 159–161
    data insertion, 163
    index properties, 161
    limitations, 165
    Management Studio, 160, 162
    properties, 161–162
Merge() method, 532, 534, 540
Metadata, 660
Microsoft JDBC driver, 571
Microsoft.SqlServer.Server, 517
Moore's Law transistor, 154
Multiple active result sets (MARS)
    active result sets, 487
    single connection, 483–486, 675
    SqlDataReader objects, 487
Multiple CTEs, 235

Multistatement TVFs
    bin-packing problem, 97
    business rules, 95–96
    CREATE FUNCTION keyword and
        RETURNS clause, 100
    declaration, 94
    DML, 94
    fulfillment, 96
    GROUP BY, 103
    individual inventory and order-detail
        items, 102–103
    INSERT INTO and SELECT clauses, 100
    InventoryDetails subquery, 101
    inventory/order fill scenario, 95
    loop-based solution, 97
    numbers table, 96
    product pull list, 96–99
    @result table variable, 100–101
    SELECT query, 99, 101
    set-based problem, 97
    WHERE/JOIN clauses, 103–104

■ **N**

Nested sets model, 675
.NET assembly, 669
.NET client programming
    ADO.NET (see ADO.NET)
    connected data access
        catch block, 466
        database table and iterating, 467
        ExecuteReader() method, 466
        SqlConnection, 465–466
        SqlDataReader, 463–464
        System.Data.SqlClient, 464–465
    deferred query execution, 498–499
    designer, 489–491
    disconnected datasets, 467–469
    EF (see Entity Framework (EF))
    ExecuteXmlReader() method, 474–476
    LINQ (see Language Integrated
        Query (LINQ))
    LINQ to SQL, 488
    MARS (see Multiple active result sets (MARS))
    nonquery, 474
    parameterization
        declaration, 472
        ExecuteReader() method, 473
        injection, 470, 473
        SQL statements, 470
        string query, 469
    querying entities, 504–509
    SQL, 462–463
    SqlBulkCopy, 477–480, 482–483
    XML, 476

Newid() Function, 283
Node
    comparison, 676
    test, 676
    types, 675
Nonclustered index
    bookmark lookup, 634
    B-tree structures, 633
    clustered-index columns, 633
    covering index, 635
    description, 9, 676
    nonclustered hash index, 10
    queries types, 636
    RID-lookup and key-lookup
        operations, 633–634
Nonrecursive CTE, 235, 238, 267
NT File System (NTFS), 300, 305
NTILE function
    OVER clause, 252
    PARTITION BY and ORDER BY, 252
    and rank salespeople, 253
    SalesPersonID, 254
    SELECT query, 254

■ **O**

Object-relational mapping (O/RM), 676
OFFSET and FETCH clauses
    client-side paging, 246
    ORDER BY clause, 245
    pagination, 245
    query plan, 246
    restrictions, 246
    SQL Server, 244
    @StartPageNum and @RowsPerPage, 245
OpenClipartsLibrary table, 313
Open Database Connectivity (ODBC)
    Apt-cache command, 567
    build_dm.sh command, 568
    Linux, 566
    ln command, 569
    sqlcmd, 570
    tar.gz format, 566
    TDS, 566
    temporary SPs, 139
    unixodbc driver, 568
Open Data Services (ODS), 511
Open Geospatial Consortium (OGC), 291
Open-world assumption (OWA), 49, 676
OPENXML
    Document Object Model, 350
    edge table format, 352
    explicit schema declaration, 353
    fine-grained XML document structure, 351
    flags parameter options, 351

legacy XML function, 347
Microsoft XML Core Services Library, 347
rowset provider, 350
simple OPENXML query, 348
spxmlpreparedocument procedure, 349
WITH clause, 352–355
Optional occurrence indicator, 676
OVER clause
   frame sizes, 257
   framing clause, 256
   ORDER BY and PARTITION BY clauses, 254
   PurchaseOrderDetail table, 254
   running total, 258
   SUM, 255
   TotalSalesDefaultFraming, 257
   window functions, 254, 267
   windowing specifications, 257

■ P

Page compressions
   column-prefix compression, 622–623
   methods, 622
   page-dictionary compression, 623–625
   recommendations, 625
Page free space (PFS), 614
Parameterization, 676
Parameter sniffing
   overridden, 145
   Production.GetProductsByName, 143
   Production.Product table, 142
   query plan, 142–143, 146
Parent_path_locator Column, 311
Parse method, 547
Path expression, 676
PathName(), 305
PERCENTILE_CONT and PERCENTILE_DISC
   function, 262–263
Performance enhancement and tuning
   indexes (see Indexes)
   SQL server storage
      description, 613
      file and filegroups, 613
      page compression, 622–625
      partitions, 619–620
      row compression, 620–622
      space allocation, 614–619
      sparse columns, 625–630
PFS. See Page free space (PFS)
PIVOT operator pivot table, 61
Primary expressions, XQuery
   context item, 398
   data type constructor/function call, 677
   function calls, 398
   literals, 397
   parenthesized, 397
   variable, 397
PRINT statement, 598
Procedural code
   control-of-flow statements (see Control-of-flow
      statements)
   cursors (see Cursors)
   SQL 3VL, 77
   T-SQL control-of-flow constructs, 47
   3VL (see Three-valued logic (3VL))
Procedural code. See CASE expressions

■ Q

Query plan, 677
QUOTED_IDENTIFIER option, 685

■ R

RAISERROR statement, 591–592, 661
RAM's price, 155
Range indexes
   B-tree disk-based table, 170
   comparisons, 173
   memory-optimized nonclustered index, 170
   nonclustered index, 171–172
   single-point lookup, 171
RANK and DENSE_RANK functions
   AdventureWorks' daily sales totals, 247
   differences, 247
   OrderMonth column, 250
   OVER clause, 248
   PARTITION BY clause, 248–249
   ranking value, 250–252
   SELECT query, 250
   WHERE clause, 248
Read() and Write() methods, 539–540
Recompilation, SPs
   dbo.GetRecompiledProcs, 149
   Execute statement, 147
   plan_generation_num, 149
   query plans, 146
   SalesPersonId parameter, 147
   Sales.SalesOrderHeader, 147
   selectivity, 147
   SQL Server, 677
   statement-level, 148
   statistics, 149
Recursion, SPs
   dbo.SolveTowers, 132
   Hanoi puzzle, 126–127
   multiple times, 677
Recursive CTE
   AdventureWorks database, 239
   anchor query, 242

Recursive CTE (*cont.*)
  BOM, 240–241
  ComponentID and ProductAssemblyID, 239
  MAXRECURSION option, 239
  name and column list, 242
  restrictions, 243
  SELECT statement, 242
  simple, 238
  UNION ALL, 238
Representational State Transfer (REST), 573
RETURNS NULL ON NULL INPUT option, 655
Row compressions, 620–622
Row constructor, 677
ROW_NUMBER function, 243–244

S

Scalar functions
  CASE expression, 83
  CREATE FUNCTION statement, 79–81
  creation-time options, 81
  CTE, 83–84
  procedural code
    AdventureWorks database, 91–93
    CASE expressions, 86
    CREATE TABLE statement, 86
    dbo.EncodeNYSIIS function, 93
    encode strings, 87–90
    INSERT statement, 86–87
    name-based searching, 84
    numbers table, 91
    NYSIIS encoding rules, 85–86
    SOUNDEX algorithm, 85
    WHERE clause, 92–93
  recursion, 82–83
  RETURNS keyword, 80
  SELECT statements, 80
  single atomic value, 677
Semantickeyphrasetable function, 344
Semantics database, 342
SendResultsRow() method, 530
SendResultsStart() method, 530
Server certificate, 678
Service master keys (SMK)
  administrative tasks, 208
  Alter statement, 209
  Backup and Restore, 209
  Control Server, 209
  Force keyword, 209
  SQL Server encryption key hierarchy, 678
Service Oriented Architecture (SOA)
  DCOM and CORBA, 573
  HTTP requests, 575
  ODBC, 573
  RESTful, 573

WCF data service (*see* WCF data service)
  WCF layers stack, 574
  web services (WS), 573
SET NOCOUNT ON statement, 657
SetValue() method, 530
SGAM. *See* Shared global allocation map (SGAM)
Shared global allocation map (SGAM), 614
Shredding, 678
Simple Object Access Protocol (SOAP), 573–575, 678
Solid state drive (SSD, 156
SOUNDEX algorithm, 85–86
Spatial data types
  coordinate pair, 295
  flat spatial representation, 292
  GML, 292
  Michigan and the Great Lakes, 297, 299–300
  MultiPolygon, 297
  OGC standard, 291
  polygon, 296
  spatial instance type (*see* Spatial instance type)
  SRID, 295
  the US Census Bureau's TIGER/Line data, 295
  WKT strings, 293
  Wyoming, 293–295
Spatial index, 9, 679
Spatial instance types
  GeometryCollection, 293
  hierarchy, 292
  LineString, 293
  MultiLineString, 293
  MultiPoint, 293
  MultiPolygon, 293
  Point, 293
  Polygon, 293
Spatial reference identifier (SRID), 295
sp_executesql stored procedure
  client-side parameterization, 611
  dynamic SQL executes, 610–611
  limitation, 610
  parameterization, 610
Splitter, 106
SP RETURN statement, 656
SPs. *See* Stored procedures (SPs)
SQL. *See* Language integrated query (LINQ);
        Structured Query Language (SQL)
SQL CASE expressions, 654
SQLCMD
  command-line options, 683, 685–688
  commands, 689, 691
  scripting variable, 654, 688–689
  utility
    interactive prompt, 35–36
    scripting variables, 34
SQLCMDDBNAME environment variable, 684
SQLCMDPASSWORD environment variable, 686

SQLCMDUSER environment variable, 687
SQL Distributed Management Objects
    (SQL-DMO), 433
SQL-DMO. *See* SQL Distributed Management
    Objects (SQL-DMO)
SQL injection
    EXECUTE method, 608
    queries, 606
    T-SQL string validation function, 608
SQLLocalDB.exe info SQLSrvWebApp1
    command, 561
SQL predicate, 677
SQL Server
    data tools, 679
    injection, 679
SQL Server 2012, 274
SQL Server 2012 Express LocalDB
    AttachDBFilename, 562–563
    automatic instances, 561
    create and start option, 560
    database names, 564
    localdb keyword, 561
    .mdf and .ldf file, 564
    MSI installations, 560
    named instance, 561
    security models, 562
    Serverless, 559
    sqlcmd command, 561
SQL Server 2012 Native Client (SNAC).
    See SQL Server 2012 Express LocalDB
SQL Server Data Tools (SSDT), 36–37, 513
SQL Server Integration Services
    (SSIS), 41–42, 434
SQL Server Management Studio (SSMS)
    code snippets, 21–22
    context-sensitive, 26–28
    editing options, 25
    EM, 19
    features, 19
    full-text index wizard, 326
    graphical query execution plans, 28–30
    IntelliSense, 20
    keyboard shortcut scheme, 23
    new full-text catalog, 319
    Object Explorer, 32–33
    project-management features, 30–31
    T-SQL debugging, 24–25
SQL server storage
    data, 662
    description, 613
    file and filegroups, 613–614
    page compression, 622–625
    partitions, 619–620
    row compression, 620–622

space allocation
    data allocations, 615–616
    dbo.SmallRows query, 618–619
    estimated I/O cost, 618–619
    GAM, 614
    IAM and PFS, 614
    I/O comparison, 617–618
    limitation, 614
    narrow rows, 615
    random-access file, 614
    SELECT query, 616–617
    SGAM, 614
sparse columns
    and nonsparse tables, 627
    NULL value, 625–626
    sets, 628–630
    space savings, columns, 628
SQL Server uses, 662
SQL server XQuery expressions, 659
SQL 2014 supported axis specifiers, 404
SqlTriggerContext class, 553
SqlUserDefinedAggregate attribute, 539
SSDT. *See* SQL Server Data Tools (SSDT)
SSIS. *See* SQL Server Integration Services (SSIS)
SSMS. *See* SQL Server Management Studio (SSMS)
SSMS integration, 599–600
STIntersection() method, 299
Stored procedures (SPs)
    AdventureWorks business, 122
    aggregate functions, 122
    ALTER PROCEDURE, 117
    best practices, 117–119
    business reporting task, 120
    CREATE PROCEDURE, 111
    CTE, 121, 124
    dbo.MyProc, 112
    description, 10
    DLL, 113
    DMFs, 139
    DMVs, 139
    Drop Procedure, 117
    Environment.GetEnvironmentVariables()
        functions, 530
    exception, 529
    execution, 530–531
    front-end applications, 125
    GetEnvironmentVars CLR procedure, 531
    GetProcStats procedure, 141
    int parameter, 121
    memory-optimization, 113
    metadata, 112–113
    namespaces, 528
    Native_Compilation, 115
    native machine code, 116

Stored procedures (SPs) (*cont.*)
- ODBC, 139
- OLTP database, 111
- parameters, 80, 111, 142–144, 146
- Person.GetEmployee_inmem, 114
- @ProductID, 124
- Production.Product table, 125
- product lists, 123
- query-plan recompilation, 139
- recompilation, 146–149
- recursion. Recursion, SPs
- return code, 116
- RETURN statement, 112, 122
- running sum, 122
- running total, sales, 120
- Sales.SalesOrderDetail, 124
- SampleProc class, 527–528
- Schemabinding, 115
- SendResultsStart() method, 530
- SqlProcedure(), 529
- statistics, 141
- subroutines, 111
- sys.dmexecsqltext, 141
- table-valued parameters, 136–138
- tempdb database, 139
- temporary tables, 112
- TVFs, 112
- UDFs, 111

String() function, 392

Structured Query Language (SQL)
- BOL, 43–44
- CLR assembly, 10
- databases, 5
- indexes, 9–10
- profiler, 37, 39
- schemas, 6
- SPs, 10
- statements
    - components, 3
    - order of execution, 3
    - relational model, 3
    - subsets, 4
    - three-valued logic, 4
- tables, 7–8
- transaction logs, 5–6
- UDFs, 10
- views, 8

SWITCHOFFSET() function, 281
SYSDATETIME() function, 280
SYSDATETIMEOFFSET() function, 280
Sys.dm_fts_parser, 341
System.Data.SqlClient, 517
System.Data.SqlClient namespace, 660
System.Data.SqlTypes, 517
SYSUTCDATETIME() function, 280

■ **T**

Table Production.HierBillOfMaterials, 285

Table-valued functions (TVFs)
- inline function. Inline TVFs
- multistatement. Multistatement TVFs

Table-valued parameters
- Create Type statement, 136
- HumanResources.GetEmployees, 137
- HumanResources.LastNameTableType, 136
- intermediate format, 136
- UDFs, 136
- variables, 138

Tabular Data Stream (TDS), 566
TCL. *See* Transactional Control Language (TCL)
Terminate() function, 535
Terminate() method, 532, 541

Three-valued logic (3VL)
- CWA, 49
- IS NULL and IS NOT NULL, 48
- NULL, 48
- propositions, 47
- quick reference chart, 48
- true, false, and unknown, 679

THROW statement, 597–598
TODATETIMEOFFSET() function, 281
ToString() method, 548
Transactional Control Language (TCL), 4

Transact-SQL (T-SQL)
- elements
    - defensive coding, 17
    - naming conventions, 12–13
    - one entry and one exit, 13–16
    - SELECT * statement, 17
    - variable initialization, 17
    - whitespace, 11–12
- history, 1
- imperative *vs.* declarative languages, 1–2
- SQL (*see* Structured Query Language (SQL))

Transistors, 153
Transparent data encryption (TDE), 230–231, 679

Triggers
- CDC (*see* Change data capture (CDC))
- DDL (*see* Data definition language (DDL))
- DML (*see* Data manipulation language (DML))
- E-mail address, validation, 554
- INSERT/UPDATE statement, 555
- invalid E-mail address, 555
- Logon, 202–204
- namespaces, 553
- Transaction.Current.Rollback() method, 553–554
- T-SQL trigger, 555
- UPDATE statement, 555
- validation, 552
- views, 194–197

TRY_CAST function, 596
TRY...CATCH exception handling
    CATCH block functions, 593
    limitations, 594
    sample code, 592
    XACT_STATE function, 594
TRY_CONVERT function, 595–596
TRY_PARSE command, 594
T-SQL. *See* Transact-SQL (T-SQL)
T-SQL UDFs types, 655
Typed XML variable, 364–365

■ U

UDFs. *See* User-defined functions (UDFs)
Union data types, 670
Uniqueidentifier data type
    GUIDs, 282
    Newid() function, 283
    NEWSEQUENTIALID() function, 283
    sequential GUIDs, 283
    usage of, 283
Untyped XML variable, 363, 679
UPDATE() and COLUMNS_UPDATED() functions
    COALESCE() function, 190
    COLUMNPROPERTY() function, 194
    description, 190
    NOCOUNT ON, 192
    @@ROWCOUNT, 191
    standard sizes, 190–191
    testing, 193–194
    trigger definition, 191
    unit-of-measure validation, 192
User-defined aggregates (UDAs)
    Accumulate() method, 534
    advances creation
        Merge() method, 540
        properties, 539
        Read() and Write() methods, 539–540
        statistical median, 536–537
        Terminate() method, 541
    Merge() method, 534
    methods, 531–532
    namespaces, 533
    results, 536
    SQL CLR routine, 679
    statistical range, 532–533
    struct declaration, 534
    Terminate() function, 535
User-defined data types (UDTs)
    advantages, 542
    attributes, 546
    declaration, 546
    description, 549
    IsNull and Null properties, 548

    NULL, 547
    Parse method, 547
    static properties, 549
    ToString() method, 548
User-defined functions (UDFs)
    CREATE ASSEMBLY with EXTERNAL_ACCESS
        permission set, 524–525
    CREATE FUNCTION statement, 522
    description, 10
    EmailMatch function, 521
    encryption, 82
    exercises, 110
    expression, 518–519
    fill-row method, 526
    GetYahooNews() Function, 527
    IsMatch function, 521–522
    parameters, 80–81
    project, 520
    restrictions
        database, 109
        deterministic function, 107
        nondeterministic functions, 107–108
        requirements, 108
    results, 522
    scalar functions. Scalar functions
    SqlFunction, 526
    TVFs (*see* Table-valued functions (TVFs))
    YahooRSS, 523
User-defined type (UDT), 680
UTF-16
    create record, 427
    and _SC collation, 429
    SQL Server, 428

■ V

Value comparison, 680
Visual Studio T-SQL debugger
    dbo.uspGetBillOfMaterials
        procedure, 600–601
    debug mode, 604–605
    output window, 605

■ W

WCF data service
    application project, 575
    consumer, 581–586
    creation, 577–581
    definition, 576
    entity access rules, 578
    entity data model, 576–577
    page calling, 580
    payload types, 580
    queries, 580–581

WCF data service (*cont.*)
    service entity/operation, 579
    string options, 581
Web services (WS), 573
Well-formed XML, 680
Well-known text (WKT) strings, 293, 295, 680
West coast customers with simple CASE
        expression, 57
Whitespace, 11–12
Window functions
    dataset partitions, 680
    exercises, 267–268
    NTILE function, 252, 254
    OFFSET/FETCH clauses, 244–247
    OVER clause, 243
    RANK and DENSE_RANK functions
        (*see* RANK and DENSE_RANK functions)
    ROW_NUMBER function, 243–244
Windows Communication Foundation (WCF)
    application project, 575
    consumer application
        aspx page, 581–586
        features, 586
        foreach, 585
        namespace, 585
        PageLoad event, 585
        PopulateDropDown()
            function, 585–586
        service reference, 582
        UpdateImage() function, 586
    creation, 577–581
    data services (*see* WCF data service)
    definition, 576
    entity data model, 576–577
WITH RECOMPILE option, 656
WITH SCHEMABINDING option, 655
Word-breaking and stemming, 342
World Wide Web Consortium (W3C), 680
WRITE Clause
    and string append, 271
    simple string concatenation, 272
    UPDATE statement, 270
Wyoming Polygon, 293–295, 298

■ X, Y, Z

XML clause, 355
XML data model, 387, 659
XML EXPLICIT clause, 358–360
XML index
    creation options, 378
    execution cost of the query, 375
    primary, 373
    query execution cost, 377
    reader with XPath filter, 376

resume column, 376
retrieving candidate names with FLWOR
        expression, 374
retrieving job candidates with bachelor's
        degrees, 374
secondary, 373
SQL Server, 9
XML PATH clause, 360–362
XML RAW mode, 355–356
XPath
    attributes, 389
    columns without names and
        wildcards, 389–390
    data function, 391–392
    element grouping, 390–391
    expressions, 388
    FOR XML PATH uses, 388
    names and e-mail addresses, 387–388
    node, 675
    node tests, 392, 395–396
    and NULL, 393
    sequence, 678
    SQL Server, 430
    WITH XMLNAMESPACES clause, 394
    XML path language, 680
    and XQuery XML trees, 675
XQuery
    arithmetic expressions, 416
    axis specifiers, 404–405
    comments, 409, 671
    comparison, 673, 676
    conditional expressions (if...then...else), 416
    constructors and casting, 420–421
    data types, 410
    date format, 413–414
    dynamic XML construction, 406–409
    expressions and sequences, 396–398
    FLWOR expressions (*see* FLWOR expressions)
    functions, 417–420
    general comparison operators, 412–413
    integer division, 417
    location paths, 399–400
    namespaces, 402–403
    node
        comparisons, 414–415
        DOM, 675
        tests, 400–401
    predicates, 410, 677
    primitive, 677
    query method, 398
    sequence, 678
    SQL Server, 430
    step, 679
    truth value, 677
    value comparison operators, 411–412

W3C XPath 2.0 standard, 396
XML integration, 387
XML query language, 681
XQuery Data Model (XDM)
    base types, 665
    binary types, 666

boolean types, 666
data types, 663–664
date/time types, 665
numeric types, 667
string types, 667–668
XSL transformations (XSLT), 681

Get the eBook for only $10!

Now you can take the weightless companion with you anywhere, anytime. Your purchase of this book entitles you to 3 electronic versions for only $10.

This Apress title will prove so indispensible that you'll want to carry it with you everywhere, which is why we are offering the eBook in 3 formats for only $10 if you have already purchased the print book.

Convenient and fully searchable, the PDF version enables you to easily find and copy code—or perform examples by quickly toggling between instructions and   applications. The MOBI format is ideal for your Kindle, while the ePUB can be utilized on a variety of mobile devices.

Go to www.apress.com/promo/tendollars to purchase your companion eBook.